PENGUIN REFE

A DICTIONARY

Florence Elliott read history at St Hilda's College, Oxford. She has spent her working life in adult education and is at present teaching for Oxford University Department for External Studies.

A DICTIONARY
OF POLITICS

Florence Elliott

7th Edition

PENGUIN BOOKS

Penguin Books Ltd, Harmondsworth, Middlesex, England
Penguin Books Inc., 7110 Ambassador Road, Baltimore, Maryland 21207, U.S.A.
Penguin Books Australia Ltd, Ringwood, Victoria, Australia
Penguin Books Canada Ltd, 41 Steelcase Road West, Markham, Ontario, Canada
Penguin Books (N.Z.) Ltd, 182–190 Wairau Road, Auckland 10, New Zealand

—

First published 1957
Second Edition 1959
Third Edition 1961
Fourth Edition 1964
Fifth Edition 1966
Sixth Edition 1970
Reprinted 1971
Seventh Edition 1973
Reprinted 1974

—

Copyright © Florence Elliott and
Michael Summerskill, 1957, 1959, 1961, 1964, 1966
Copyright © Florence Elliott, 1970, 1973

—

Made and printed in Great Britain
by Hazell Watson & Viney Ltd
Aylesbury, Bucks
Set in Monotype Times

AUTHOR'S NOTE

World affairs are so complex that the task of selection of entries for inclusion in this Dictionary has not been easy. I hope to be able to justify any particular entry either because there is frequent reference to it in political discussion or because it is important for a real understanding of international affairs. The Dictionary includes no political developments which have occurred after March 1973.

The letters *q.v.* are inserted after a term if a reference to that term might help the reader to understand better the subject under discussion. They are not inserted after every term elsewhere defined.

A

Absolutism. The principle of absolute government, the governed having no representation, vote, or other share in the administration.

Abu Dhabi. A member state of the United Arab Emirates, *q.v.*, on the Trucial Coast, *q.v.*, in the Persian Gulf; area approximately 25,000 sq. m.; population 16,000. It is the largest of the Trucial States, *q.v.*, and of particular importance because oil has been discovered in substantial quantities at Murban and under the coastal waters, and because the strategically significant oasis of Buraimi, *q.v.*, lies on the frontier between Abu Dhabi and Oman, *q.v.* The mainland oil concession is held by Abu Dhabi Petroleum Co., which has the same shareholders as the Iraq Petroleum Company, *q.v.* The sea-bed concession is held by Abu Dhabi Marine Areas Ltd, a subsidiary of the British Petroleum Co. Sheikh Shakhbut bin Sultan, who ruled Abu Dhabi from 1928 to 1966 when he was deposed by his younger brother, Sheikh Zaid, gave this concession to its predecessors in title, the D'Arcy Exploration Co.; his right to do so was contested by the I.P.C. interests, but upheld in arbitration.

From 1892 the British government was responsible for the external affairs of the state. The decision, announced in January 1968, to withdraw British military forces from the Persian Gulf by 1971, precipitated negotiations among the sheikhdoms. Abu Dhabi first agreed to a federation with Dubai, *q.v.*; then in March 1968 it entered into a Federation of Arab Emirates, *q.v.*, with Bahrain, *q.v.*, Qatar, *q.v.*, and the other Trucial States. In 1971 when Bahrain and Qatar declared their independence of the Federation the remaining members formed the United Arab Emirates with Sheikh Zaid as its first President.

Abyssinia. Strictly a specific ethnic unit, approximately covering the old kingdom of Aksum in north Ethiopia; in practice the word is used as a synonym for Ethiopia, *q.v.*

Activists. Those in a political group who want to take active steps towards the objectives of the group rather than merely to proclaim a programme.

Aden Protectorate. A former British protected territory in southern Arabia consisting of 2 states, 11 sultanates, 2 emirates and 9 sheikhdoms, all of which had entered into treaty relations with the U.K. between 1882 and 1914. They were known collectively as the Eastern and Western Aden Protectorates until 1959 when they formed the Federation of Arab Emirates of the South, retitled South Arabian Federation, *q.v.*, in 1962. By 1963 this comprised Aden State, *q.v.*, and all the territories of the former Protectorates, except for three which retained, collectively, the title of Eastern Aden Protectorate, *q.v.* When the South Arabian Federation achieved independence in November 1967 the Eastern Aden Protectorate was merged with it to form the People's Republic of Southern Yemen, *q.v.*

Aden State. A former British possession and, since 30 November 1967, part of the People's Republic of Southern Yemen, *q.v.* It consisted of the city and harbour of Aden which was, until the closure of the Suez Canal, *q.v.*, in 1967, an important port of call on the shipping routes to and from the east, and which has an oil and bunkering station and an oil refinery, and its immediate hinterland. It was first occupied by the British in 1839 and was for many years administered as part of India. Colonial status was granted in 1937; in January 1963 it became a member state of the former South Arabian Federation, *q.v.*, which achieved independence, as Southern Yemen, in 1967.

Adenauer, Dr Konrad. West German Christian Democratic leader and Chancellor from 1949 to 1963; a Roman Catholic; born 5 January 1876. He studied law and economics at Freiburg, Munich and Bonn Universities and after holding a succession of local government posts in Cologne he became Lord Mayor in 1917. He was a member of the Provincial Diet of the Rhine Province from 1917 to 1933, and in 1919 supported the French attempt to detach the Rhineland from Germany. In 1933 he ordered the Nazi flags to be taken down on Hitler's visit to Cologne, and was removed by Hitler's supporter, Hermann Göring, from his post as Lord Mayor. Between 1933 and 1945 he was twice arrested by the Nazis but later released. After the Second World War he became Mayor again, but was removed by the British occupation authorities for 'inefficiency'. He took part in the founding of the Christian Democratic Party in 1945 and was the President of the Bonn Parliamentary Council from 1948 to 1949. He first became a Bundestag member in 1949, when he was appointed Chancellor. He resigned from this post on 15 October 1963, and died on 19 April 1967.

Afghanistan. An independent Central Asiatic state on the northern frontier of Western Pakistan; area 250,000 sq. m.; population (1969 estimate) 15,944,275, of which nomadic tribes constitute 2,000,000; the majority belong to the Sunni sect of the Islamic religion; capital Kabul. In the eighteenth century Afghanistan conquered northern India but later declined in importance, and in the nineteenth century Russia and the U.K. decided that it should be a buffer state, *q.v.* In 1919 the U.K. agreed to recognize its independence, and this agreement binds Pakistan as the successor of the U.K. in that area.

In 1927 and 1928 King Amanullah toured Europe and the Near East and on returning ordered the modernization of Afghanistan along Turkish Kemalist lines, including monogamy, European clothing, and abolition of women's veils. Accordingly the Mullahs, the powerful Moslem clergy, revolted in 1929 and expelled the King. After some internal disorder the head of the anti-Amanullah revolt, an Afghan chief, seized power, but was later defeated by other Afghans (with British backing) under General Nadir Shah. The General became King and introduced gradual reforms; he was assassinated in 1933. His son Mohammed Zahir (born 1914) is the present King. The King (with his cousin, Daoud Khan, who was Prime Minister until March 1963) has repeatedly demanded the establishment of 'Pakhtunistan', *q.v.*, an enlarged Afghanistan which would rule the Pathans (Pakhtuns) in Western Pakistan, and incorporate all the territory west of the river Indus, down to the Arabian Sea. This plan is strongly opposed by Pakistan, and Afghan opinion is divided as to its merits. The resignation of Daoud was followed by the introduction of the 1964 Constitution. This established an elected Lower House and a partly elected Upper House. No member of the royal family may be a member of the government. However, the absence of political parties has prevented the efficient functioning of Parliament which passed only one measure (a bill signifying acceptance of an interest-free loan of $500,000 from the International Development Association, *q.v.*) during the 1969–70 session. Essential legislation to create an Industrial Bank was approved only because King Mohammed Zahir threatened to dissolve the assembly.

Scarcely 5 per cent of the land is cultivated, and most of the population is engaged in agriculture and sheep-raising; there is a flourishing export trade in Persian lamb skins. Both the U.S.A. and the U.S.S.R. have given financial aid, and U.S. and German engineers have assisted in the construction of dams in the southern desert. Oil and natural gas have been discovered near the Russian border and hydro-electric schemes are being developed. Afghanistan has one of the largest U.N. Technical Assistance missions.

A.F. of L. American Federation of Labor, *q.v.*

A.F. of L. – C.I.O. American Federation of Labor and Congress of Industrial Organizations, *q.v.*

African and Malagasy Union (Union Africaine et Malgache, or U.A.M.). An association of independent, largely French-speaking, African states, established in September 1961 and revived in February 1965 as the Organisation Commune Africaine et Malgache (O.C.A.M.), *q.v.*

African National Congress (A.N.C.). Originated in 1882 as the Native Education Association in the Cape, protecting Africans against pass laws. The Native National Congress, which later changed its name to African National Congress (now illegal), was formed at Bloemfontein in 1912. One aim is 'the creation of a united democratic South Africa'. *See also:* Luthuli *and* Pan Africanist Congress.

Afro-Asian Conference. Held at Bandung, Indonesia, in April 1955, it was the first inter-continental conference of African and Asian peoples. The states represented were: Afghanistan, Cambodia, Ceylon, China, Egypt, Ethiopia, Gold Coast (now known as Ghana), India, Indonesia, Iraq, Japan, Jordan, Laos, Lebanon, Liberia, Libya, Nepal, Pakistan, Persia, Philippines, Saudi Arabia, Sudan, Syria, Thailand, Turkey, North Viet-Nam, South Viet-Nam, and Yemen. Observers included representatives from Cyprus (Archbishop Makarios, then leader of the Enosis movement), the U.S.A. (a Negro Congressman), and the African National Congress. There were differences between the pro-western, pro-Communist, and neutralist blocs, but the Conference passed resolutions supporting economic and cultural cooperation and self-determination, and opposing colonialism. The Conference upheld the U.N. Declaration on Human Rights, in spite of Chinese objections.

Agency for International Development (A.I.D.). The U.S. government agency responsible, under the Act for International Development, 1961, for administering U.S. economic aid schemes. Formed in November 1961, it superseded the Development Loan Fund, *q v.*, and the International Co-operation Administration, *q.v.*

Agent Provocateur. A French term meaning 'provoking agent'; a person sent, during political or social conflicts, into the adversary's ranks, in the disguise of an adherent, to provoke compromising actions. *Agents provocateurs* have been used in struggles between governments and revolutionary movements. In international politics *agents provocateurs* have been used to provide pretexts for interventions and wars by stirring up disorder and bringing about 'incidents'.

Aggression. An attack; but aggressors often deny any aggressive intention and claim to be acting merely in self-defence against an actual or anticipated attack, or more generally on behalf of law, order, and civilization. It was easy to name the aggressor in the cases of the Italian invasion of Ethiopia in 1935, the German invasions of Poland in 1939 and of the Low Countries and Norway and Denmark in 1940, and the Japanese onslaught on the U.S.A. in 1941. In other cases it is arguable whether or not there is aggression, particularly where there is a *coup d'état* with external aid.

Aggression was defined in the Convention for the Definition of Aggression of 3 July 1933 between Afghanistan, Estonia, Latvia, Persia, Poland, Romania, Turkey, and the U.S.S.R. as existing wherever any of the following took place: (1) a declaration of war against another state; (2) an invasion by armed forces, without a declaration of war, of the territory of another state; (3) an attack by armed forces, without a declaration of war, on the territory, naval vessels, or aircraft of another state; (4) a naval blockade of the coasts or ports of another state; (5) aid to armed bands formed on the territory of another state and invading the other state, or refusal, despite the demands on the part of the state subjected to attack, to take all possible measures on its own territory to deprive those bands of any aid and protection. This definition was similar to one put forward in May 1933 by the Committee on Security Questions of the Disarmament Conference. The term is not defined in the United Nations Charter.

Agnew, Spiro. U.S. Republican Party politician; born 1918, the son of a Baltimore restaurant owner who had changed his name from Anagnostopoulos after emigrating from Athens to the U.S.A. in 1897. He served in Europe in the Second World War, returning to the University of Baltimore where he graduated in law in 1947. Originally a Democrat, he joined the Republican Party in 1946 and was elected to the county executive of Baltimore County where, in 1963, he was responsible for the first fair housing enactment south of the Mason-Dixon line. In 1966 he was elected Governor of Maryland, defeating an opponent (George Mahoney) who campaigned against the enforced desegregation of housing. As Governor he initiated Maryland's first legislation to outlaw racial discrimination in employment. He is not sympathetic to public demonstrations. During the 1968 Presidential election campaign he first supported Nelson Rockefeller, *q.v.*, for the Republican nomination, but later switched to Richard Nixon, *q.v.*, who selected him to be his Vice-President in 1968 and again in 1972.

A.I.D. Agency for International Development, *q.v.*

Al Fatah. *See* Fatah.

Åland Islands. A group of several hundred islands and islets in the northern Baltic Sea, half-way between Sweden and Finland, autonomous and administered with Finland since the Middle Ages; area 572 sq. m.; population (1969) 21,600, 97 per cent Swedish-speaking. Mariehamn is the principal town. The islands could be used as a base for an attack on Finland, Sweden, or the U.S.S.R. Their holder could control the shipping route of Swedish iron ore to Germany.

The Baltic powers therefore oppose their fortification. With Finland, they passed to Russia in 1809. Under an 1856 Convention between France, the U.K., and Russia, they were given a special international status and Russia, at Sweden's request, was forbidden to fortify them. After the Russian Revolution in 1917, the islanders by a plebiscite demanded annexation by Sweden. Swedish troops and later German troops occupied the islands until November 1918. Sweden and Finland disputed sovereignty over them and a treaty between ten states (excluding Russia) decided in 1921 that the islands belonged to Finland but should be granted self-government and demilitarized.

Alaska. A large peninsula on the north-western border of Canada and a member state of the U.S.A.; area 586,400 sq. m.; population (1970) 297,000; capital Juneau. Alaska was purchased from Russia by the U.S.A. in 1867 for $7,200,000 at the instigation of W. H. Seward, the U.S. Secretary of State. 'Seward's Folly', as Alaska then became known, produced sufficient gold in the subsequent 25 years to pay for itself 44 times over. The question of the grant of statehood was hotly disputed for years but in July 1958 Congress finally agreed to admit Alaska to the Union as the 49th state; formal entry took place on 4 July 1959. There are large forests, and minerals already identified include gold, silver, iron, coal, tin, and oil which has been commercially produced since 1959. An oil strike, of sufficient importance to make the U.S. independent of imports from the eastern hemisphere, was made in Prudhoe Bay in 1969; this oil is to be carried 800 miles south by a pipeline (the Trans-Alaska Pipeline) to the ice-free port of Valdez. In 1971 Congress approved a settlement of claims by some 50,000 Eskimos, Indians and Aleuts to their ancestral lands, by which they were awarded the freehold of, and mineral rights over, 40 million acres of land and $962,500,000 over a period of ten years in compensation.

Albania. An independent Balkan state on the Adriatic coast north of Greece; area 11,101 sq. m.; population (1969) 2,108,000, of whom more than half are Moslems; capital Tirana. The country was ruled by Turkey from 1467 to 1912, when it became an independent monarchy with a King, Prince Wilhelm of Wied, appointed by other European powers. From 1914 anarchy prevailed until a republic was proclaimed under President Zogu who, as King Zog, ruled over the kingdom of Albania from 1928 until the Italian invasion of 1939. The King of Italy then assumed the Albanian crown. After the defeat of Italy in the Second World War King Zog was deposed, and in 1946 a republic was again declared. The government is Communist, and since 1961 anti-revisionist, supporting China against the U.S.S.R. Enver Hoxha has led the Communist Party since 1945 and Haxhi Lleshi was appointed Head of State in 1953.

Albania was a founder member of the Council for Mutual Economic Assistance, q.v., and the Warsaw Pact, q.v., but was excluded from both in 1961 when diplomatic relations with the U.S.S.R. were severed following a Russian denunciation of Albania's deviationist policy at the 22nd Congress of the Communist Party of the U.S.S.R. In September 1968 Albania withdrew officially from the Warsaw Pact, thereby becoming wholly dependent upon China for economic and technical aid.

The country is economically backward, but with aid initially from eastern Europe has developed oil refineries (it has its own oilfields), large textile factories and a sugar refinery. Agricultural output is more than twice the pre-war level and by 1970 schemes for the electrification of all rural areas were completed. The government is probably the first in Albania to establish its supremacy over every village.

Algeria. An independent state in North Africa; area 855,900 sq. m., most of it mountain and desert; population (1966) 12,101,994, mostly Arab and Berber Moslems; capital Algiers. The population is increasing at the rate of 200,000 per year. The territory was annexed by Napoleon III in 1865 and became part of France; it achieved independence in 1962. The territory comprises 13 Algerian and 2 Saharan departments.

The early French policy of confiscating land and settling French citizens (*politique de peuplement*), to provide French leaders and administrators for an Arab community, inspired hostility among the natives. Before independence Europeans farmed 5,000,000 acres (one third of all the cultivable land) in the fertile coastal strip and produced early vegetables, wine and wheat for export to France at guaranteed prices, and virtually nothing for home consumption. Subsidies on Algerian wine and wheat were provided by Metropolitan France. The introduction of mechanization and efficient farming methods aggravated unemployment among Arab farmworkers; out of a working population of 2,300,000, Algeria had 400,000 permanently unemployed and a further 450,000 in seasonal employment. Attempts by the French government to extend to its Arab subjects the social services enjoyed by French citizens in France were strongly resisted by the settlers. In 1947 an Algerian parliament was set up to deal with local affairs, French nationality was extended to all Algerians, and posts in the civil service were opened to Moslems. Since it was treason to advocate nationalism in Algeria (as it is treason to attempt to overthrow the Republic on French soil), all nationalist organizations were driven underground.

In 1954 the Front de Libération Nationale, *q.v.* (F.L.N.), the major nationalist movement, 'declared war' on France with substantial unofficial assistance from the neighbouring Arab states of Morocco and Tunisia. The civil administration of Algeria was then transferred to the army. In May 1958 the military authorities under General Salan, with the connivance of the former Resident-Minister, Jacques Soustelle, and with the full approval of the French settlers, refused to recognize the government of France, and demanded that General de Gaulle should assume full powers. In June 1958 de Gaulle was appointed Prime Minister of France, but the proposals which he made for solving the Algerian problem were not acceptable to the settlers who then founded their own secret organization (O.A.S.) to combat Algerian nationalism. However, by the Evian Agreements, signed in March 1962, Algeria was granted independence and the French promised to withdraw all forces by the end of 1964. These were approved by referendum in France on 8 April and in Algeria on 1 July 1962. On 4 July 1962 Algeria became a sovereign independent state.

Ben Bella, *q.v.*, who had ruled Algeria since 1962 as head of a provisional government, was on 26 September 1963 constitutionally elected President of the Republic. The appointment of Ben Bella terminated a period of bitter controversy between his followers, who included Mohammed Khidder and Colonel Hourai Boumédienne, *q.v.*, and the followers of Ben Khedda, who had acted as Prime Minister from 1961 until July 1962 when he was ousted by Boumédienne, among whom were Belkacem Krim, leader of the F.L.N., and Mohammed Boudiaf. Ferhat Abbas became President of the National Assembly, but he resigned in 1963 in protest against the dictatorial methods employed by the F.L.N., the sole legal party, from which he was then expelled. In June 1965 Ben Bella was deposed by a *coup d'état* led by Boumédienne who, as President of the Council of the Revolution, assumed full powers. He survived an attempt by the army to remove him in December 1967.

Exports include barley, corkwood, esparto grass, iron and zinc ore, oats, olives, phosphates, skins, tobacco, wheat and wine; the most fertile areas are the plains and valleys near the coast. There are substantial reserves of oil and natural gas in southern Algeria; France invested considerable sums in oil-development schemes, laying pipelines from Bougie and extending the railway south from

Touggourt. Wells at Hassi-Messaoud, near Ouargla, and at Edjele, near the Libyan border, first came into operation in 1957. In 1969 oil production was more than 46 millions tons, and since 1964 liquefied natural gas has been exported in quantity. The special relationship with France was terminated in February 1971 when the Algerian government seized a 51 per cent interest in the local operations of the two French oil companies Entreprise de Recherches et d'Activités Pétrolières and Compagnie Française des Pétroles, having in the previous year nationalized all other oil companies. The withdrawal of French private investment and the intractable nature of much of the soil are among the factors which have prevented the chronically insolvent administration from balancing the budget. There is 30 per cent permanent unemployment, and even more under-employment, and the economy is heavily bolstered by foreign aid, mainly from France (£240,000,000 between 1962 and 1969) and from the World Bank. In principle the Algerian administration (which has close ties with the U.S.S.R.) is socialist. It has nationalized the numerous estates which belonged to French landowners and has limited land-holdings to a maximum of 60 acres. However, despite the permanent presence of 12,000 French experts, lack of technical skill and widespread illiteracy have severely retarded the agricultural reorganization and improvements necessary to feed the rapidly expanding population.

Allende, Salvator Gossens. Chilean Marxist Socialist politician; born 26 July 1908 in Valparaiso. He graduated in medicine and practised in Valparaiso hospitals and in the public welfare services. In 1933 he helped to found the Chilean Socialist Party; he became its General Secretary in 1942. He took part in the successful 1938 electoral campaign of the Popular Front, led by the radical Pedro Cerda, having himself been elected to the Chamber of Deputies from Valparaiso the previous year. He was appointed Minister of Health in 1942. From 1945 to 1970 he was a member of the Senate in which he served terms of office as its Vice-President and President. He contested unsuccessfully the Presidential elections of 1952, 1958 and 1964, but in 1970, as the candidate of the Popular Unity Front, he narrowly defeated the right-wing Nationalist Party candidate, Jorge Allesandro, by a majority of 1·4 per cent of the votes cast. His election was eventually confirmed by the National Congress and on 4 November 1970 he took office as President, declaring that his government would not be socialist; all it would do would be to open the road to socialism.

Alliance for Progress (Alianza para el Progreso). A movement;

sponsored by the U.S.A., with the object of developing economically (partly with U.S. help) the countries of Latin America and, incidentally, preventing Communism from advancing further in those countries. The scheme was inaugurated at Punta del Este, Uruguay, in August 1961, when a charter was signed by representatives of 20 American countries; operations began in March 1962. It was hoped to coordinate the Latin American economies and to increase the Latin American income per head by at least 2½ per cent per year. Most of the funds are provided by the Agency for International Development, *q.v.*

Alternative Vote. An electoral system which gives a voter the right to state a second preference. If any candidate receives an absolute majority of votes at the first count, he is elected, and the second preferences are ignored. If no candidate gains an absolute majority at the first count, the second preferences of those who voted for anyone other than the first two candidates are added to the votes of those two candidates. The system was recommended for use in British elections by the 1911 Royal Commission on electoral reform, but has never been adopted. It should not be confused with Proportional Representation, *q.v.*

Alto Adige. An alternative description of the Italian Province of Bolzano (known as Bozen when under Austro-Hungarian rule). The status of its German-speaking inhabitants was until 1971, when the problem was resolved, a matter of concern to the Austrian government, which describes the area as the South Tirol, *q.v.*

American Federation of Labor (A.F. of L.). A U.S. and Canadian labour movement with 9,605,840 members when it merged in December 1955 with the Congress of Industrial Organizations, *q.v.*, to form the American Federation of Labor and Congress of Industrial Organizations, *q.v.* The A.F. of L. was founded in 1881 by Samuel Gompers and Adolph Strasser, members of the cigar-makers' union; its strength lay in the craft unions of the carpenters, cigar-makers, printers, iron and steel workers, and iron-moulders. Their dislike of the emphasis on the importance of the craft unions caused certain union leaders to form the Committee for Industrial Organization, and eventually the Congress of Industrial Organizations, as a seceding body, in 1935 and 1936. Though politically less radical than the C.I.O., the A.F. of L. generally supported the policies of the Democratic Party. It was troubled, to a greater degree than the C.I.O., by inter-union raiding, racketeering (particularly in the longshoremen's union) and race discrimination. After the Second World War it refused to join the World Federation of Trade Unions, *q.v.*, on the ground that the Russian trade unions did not constitute a free and democratic movement. The President of the A.F. of L., George Meany, *q.v.*, signed the agreement for the merger of the A.F. of L. with the C.I.O. in February 1955.

American Federation of Labor and Congress of Industrial Organizations. A trade union movement established in December 1955 by the merger of the American Federation of Labor, *q.v.*, with the Congress of Industrial Organizations, *q.v.* The total membership is approximately 17 million. The merger marked the end of a split in the American labour movement which had lasted since 1936. George Meany, *q.v.*, became the President, and Walter Reuther, *q.v.*, became the leader of the Industrial Union Department, comprising most of the C.I.O. unions and some A.F. of L. unions.

American Samoa. A group of islands in the Pacific Ocean, which form constitutionally an unincorporated territory of the U.S.A.; area 76 sq. m.; population (1970) 27,769; seat of government Pago Pago. The legislature, comprising a Senate and a House of Representatives, has limited law-making authority. The territory, which has been under U.S. jurisdiction since 1899, must be distinguished from the independent country of Western Samoa, *q.v.*

Amnesty. From the Greek word meaning forgetfulness or oblivion; it is an act whereby the state pardons political or other offenders. Punishments threatened or imposed on them may be cancelled and those already in prison released. Amnesties are a frequent means of political reconciliation. They often occur after changes in the throne, presidency or regime. There are also amnesties for rebels and terrorists, and financial or tax amnesties, pardoning tax evaders on condition that they subsequently pay the taxes or subscribe to certain loans.

Anarchism. From the Greek word *anarchia* (non-rule), a political doctrine advocating the abolition of organized authority. Anarchists hold that every form of government is evil and a tyranny. They want a free association of individuals, without armed forces, courts, prisons, or written law. Their methods have varied greatly; some have advocated peaceful transition to anarchy and others have demanded revolution. Anarchists murdered Tsar Alexander of Russia, King Humbert of Italy, President Carnot of France, Empress Elizabeth of Austria, and President McKinley of the U.S.A. Leo Tolstoy (1828–1910) was a religious anarchist. He said that the state was inconsistent with Christianity and that love should rule; people should refuse to render military service, to pay taxes, or to recognize the courts, and the established order would collapse. His principles of non-violence and non-cooperation were adopted in India by Gandhi. International anarchist congresses were held in 1877 and 1907 but anarchism proper never succeeded in setting up a permanent organization. Syndicalism, q.v., a modified branch of anarchism, became an organized mass movement in a few, mostly Latin, countries.

A.N.C. African National Congress, q.v.

Andean Development Corporation. A privately financed organization with an initial capital of £50 million, set up in Bogota on 7 February 1968 by the South American states of Bolivia, Chile, Colombia, Ecuador, Peru and Venezuela. Its purpose is to accelerate regional economic integration and to speed measures that would facilitate the establishment of the Latin-American Free Trade Association, q.v., to which all six member states belong.

Andorra. A republic in the Pyrenees under the joint rule of France and Spain; area 175 sq. m.; population about 16,000, living in six villages, and speaking Catalan; capital Andorra. The Andorran valleys established their independence in the ninth century; in 1278 they were placed under the joint suzerainty of the Comte de Foix, whose rights passed to France on the accession of Henri IV in 1589, and of the Spanish Bishop of Seo de Urgel.

There is a General Council of the Valleys, of 24 members elected by some of the inhabitants, which can submit motions and proposals to the Permanent Delegations established by the co-suzerains. The franchise was extended by a bloodless revolution in April 1933 but restricted again in 1940. A French law nationalizing all French radio stations was ignored by the General Council of the Valleys, which continued to permit Radio Andorra to broadcast advertisements and uncensored programmes to Andorra and to a large area of south-west France. France claimed in 1953 that the General Council was unrepresentative and for some time jammed Radio Andorra and closed the frontier.

A.N.F. Atlantic Nuclear Force, q.v.

Angola. A Portuguese territory, also known as Portuguese West Africa, on the west coast of southern Africa, to the south of Zaïre (the former Congo (Kinshasa)) and north of South-West Africa; area 481,351 sq. m.; population (1969 estimate) 5,430,000, of whom 170,000 are white; capital St Paulo de Luanda, also known as Luanda. Angola was a colony until 1951, when it became technically an overseas territory; it was incorporated as a province of metropolitan Portugal in 1955. In July 1971 the Portuguese Constitution was amended to permit overseas territories a limited autonomy, including the right to levy taxes. There are considerable resources of iron ore, and valuable diamond deposits.

The region was discovered by the Portuguese in 1482 and, except for the years 1641 to 1648 when it was held by the Dutch, has been occupied by them since then. For 200 years it was exploited as a source of slaves, of whom several millions were exported to the Americas; now the main products are coffee, diamonds, maize, and fishmeal, and forced labour is forbidden by law except for public service, punishment, or non-payment of taxes. The laws as to forced labour are, however, evaded with official sanction. A commission appointed by the governing body of the International Labour Organization reported in 1962 that the publicly owned railways and ports had been recruiting labour 'in a manner inconsistent with the requirements of the Abolition of Forced Labour Convention'. Since 1960 nationalist movements have been in continuous conflict with Portuguese armed forces and the Union of the Peoples of Angola (U.P.A.) established a government in exile in Kinshasa. The Popular Movement for the Liberation of Angola (M.P.L.A.), the National Union for Complete Independence (U.N.I.T.A.) and the Revolutionary Government of Angola in Exile (G.R.A.E.) control considerable areas of Angola (all three together claim more than one third of the country); these are supported unofficially by neighbouring African states and officially by charitable organizations abroad, such as the Netherlands Angola Committee and the World Council of Churches.

Annexation. The act whereby a state takes possession of a territory formerly belonging to another state, or to no state at all. It is a unilateral action without the consent, or at least the voluntary consent, of the former possessor. It confers full rights of sovereignty, and thus differs from other actions which practically or temporarily confer similar rights but are not annexations proper, such as military occupation, a United Nations trusteeship, or the establishment of a protectorate. The annexed population become subjects of the annexing state. Acquisition of territory by purchase or lease, as a bilateral action, is not spoken of as annexation.

Antarctic Continent. An area of approximately five million sq. m. around the South Pole. Most of its coastline has been charted but little is known of large portions of the interior. The claimants to various parts include: Argentina, Australia, Chile, France, New Zealand, Norway, the U.K., and the U.S.S.R.

The U.K., with 16 bases in the Antarctic, claims the Falkland

Islands Dependencies (South Georgia and South Sandwich Islands), north of the 60th parallel, and British Antarctic Territory, *q.v.* (including Graham Land peninsula, the South Shetland Islands, and other islands) south of the 60th parallel. British claims are based on a number of acts of sovereignty between 1678 and 1843. Argentina, with eight bases in this area, claims sovereignty over most of the Dependencies and the Territory. Chile, with three bases in the area, claims sovereignty over the western part of the Dependencies and the Territory (including some of the land claimed by Argentina) and over a sector farther to the west. It claims that it is the rightful successor of Spain, and that Charles V in the sixteenth century regarded the area as Spanish and as coming within the jurisdiction of the Governors of Chile from 1555 onwards. British offers, in December 1954, to refer the matter to the International Court of Justice were not accepted by Argentina and Chile. In March 1956 the Court rejected a British request for the recognition of British sovereignty and for a declaration against Argentinian and Chilean 'pretensions and encroachment', on the ground that it had no powers in the matter since Argentina and Chile would not accept the Court's jurisdiction.

Norway claims Queen Maud Land, a sector east of the 20th meridian of west longitude up to the 45th meridian of east longitude. Farther east lies the Australian Antarctic Territory of about 2,742,000 sq. m., said to be rich with mineral deposits including coal, and a valuable source of food supplies (whale, fish, seals, plankton, etc.). It was established by an Order in Council dated 7 February 1933, and comprises all Antarctic territories (except Adélie Land, claimed by France) south of the 60th parallel and lying between the 45th and 160th meridians of east longitude. From the 160th meridian of east longitude to the 150th meridian of west longitude lies the Ross Dependency, established under the jurisdiction of New Zealand by an Order in Council dated 30 July 1923. The U.S.S.R., whose ships have whaled in and charted parts of the Antarctic, stated in 1950 that it would regard no boundary decisions as valid unless it participated in them.

In December 1959 the representatives of Argentina, Australia, Belgium, Chile, France, Japan, New Zealand, Norway, South Africa, the U.K., the U.S.A., and the U.S.S.R. concluded the Antarctic Treaty, the main effects of which were to suspend all territorial claims and disputes in the area, to establish free use of the Continent for scientific work, and to set up a mutual inspection system to prevent any military activities, including nuclear explosions.

The Treaty, which came into force in June 1961, applies to all land south of the 60th parallel and is subject to review after 30 years.

Anti-Clericalism. Opposition to organized religion and, in particular, to the influence of the Roman Catholic Church in politics. It is not a coherent political doctrine, but anti-clericalists of different parties tend to unite in their opposition to the Roman Catholics on specific issues, such as the provision of state grants for Roman Catholic schools, and facilities for divorce.

Anti-Semitism. Hostility towards the Jews. In the twentieth century religious anti-semitism has been replaced by racial anti-semitism; Germany under the Nazi regime (1933–45) was a centre of this doctrine. Racial anti-semitism emerged in the middle of the nineteenth century simultaneously with theories about the Aryan or Nordic race, which provided for it a pseudo-scientific basis. It arises partly from economic jealousy, the Jews having achieved important positions in many trades and liberal professions, and partly from a feeling of inferiority on the part of those who consider themselves to be failures and wish to blame some easily identifiable group.

In Nazi Germany Hitler adopted the distinction between Aryans and non-Aryans, and made laws along those lines. The Jews were declared to be a foreign and inferior race, with a poisoned blood which made them criminals by nature; marriage and love-making between Jews and Aryans were forbidden. Jewish scientists were driven into exile, and music by Mendelssohn and Offenbach was banned. The Jews were deprived of civic rights, banned from trades and professions, and sent to concentration camps where millions of them were murdered.

Eastern Europe was also a centre of anti-semitism in the early twentieth century. The post-1945 constitutions guaranteed racial tolerance, but there has been anti-semitism under the Communist regimes, though on a smaller scale. In Poland and Romania broadcasts and newspaper articles have attacked the Jews in general and Israel in particular. The high percentage of Jews who were in cabinet posts immediately after 1945 has diminished. In the U.S.S.R., where there are approximately 2,200,000 Jews, and where after the 1917 Revolution Jews were treated well and promised a Jewish autonomous state, Yiddish theatres, books, newspapers, and journals have largely disappeared. A new spate of anti-Jewish propaganda since 1970 has encouraged migration to Israel for those permitted to leave.

A.N.Z.U.S. (Australia, New Zealand, and the United States). The tripartite security treaty concluded between the three countries at San Francisco on 1 September 1951. Under the treaty, which remains in force indefinitely, 'each party recognizes that an armed attack in the Pacific area on any of the other parties would be dangerous to its own peace and safety, and declares that it would act to meet the common danger in accordance with its constitutional processes'. An armed attack is deemed to include 'an armed attack on the metropolitan territory of any of the parties, or on the island territories under its jurisdiction in the Pacific, or on its armed forces, vessels or aircraft in the Pacific'. The parties agree to maintain their capacity to resist attack 'by means of continuous self-help and mutual aid'. The pact symbolized a re-orientation by Australia and New Zealand towards the U.S.A. and away from the U.K., which, according to a British Ministerial statement made in April 1951, wanted to be a party to the treaty.

Apartheid. Afrikaans word (literally 'apart-hood') meaning racial segregation as practised by the National Party which came to power in South Africa in 1948. There had been racial segregation in South Africa from the mid-seventeenth century when European colonization began, but the National Party introduced measures affecting nearly all aspects of the life of the non-whites, who form over 80 per cent of the population. The policy involves racial purity and segregation, and white paramountcy (*baaskap*). Ideally it means that the races should be given separate and equal opportunities, but supporters and opponents alike agree that this is almost impossible. The laws introduced by the National Party have affected the political rights of non-whites, and their rights of movement, choice of residence, property, worship, choice of occupation, and marriage. Other laws have established separate non-white territorial units, known as Bantustans, *q.v.* In 1953 it was made a crime for a native worker to participate in, or to instigate, a strike; regulations as to the mixing of races were altered after a court decision that facilities must be equal, so that segregation became valid whether the facilities were equal or not; and responsibility for native education was transferred from the Provinces to the Minister for Native Affairs, who in introducing the law stated that teachers who believed in equality were not desirable teachers for the natives. *Apartheid* was debated by the General Assembly of the United Nations in 1952, it being suggested that the policy constituted a threat to peace and a violation of human rights. A commission investigated the problem, and, though refused permission to enter South Africa, condemned the policy of *apartheid* and hoped that the government would change its views. The United Party, the main opposition party in South Africa, approves of the principle of *apartheid*, though disagreeing with some of the methods used to carry it out.

Arab Federation. A federation of Iraq and Jordan, proclaimed on 14 February 1958 by the late King Faisal of Iraq and King Hussein of Jordan. There were to be an army and defence ministry, a diplomatic service and a foreign ministry, a currency and customs system, an educational structure and a legislature in common. The head of state was to be King Faisal, with King Hussein as his deputy. Membership was to be open to any Arab state. The federation was widely interpreted as a reaction to the establishment of the United Arab Republic by Egypt and Syria. It became effective on 13 May 1958, when it became known as the Arab Union, *q.v.*

Arab League. A loose confederation of Arab states (Egypt, Iraq, Jordan, Lebanon, Saudi Arabia, Syria, and Yemen) established on 10 May 1945 as a result of the Arab Unity Preparatory Conference held at Alexandria in the autumn of 1944. The League reflects Arab nationalist sentiments. It has been especially concerned with: (1) the crisis in the Levant in 1945, when it supported Syrian and Lebanese independence rather than continued French occupation; (2) opposition to the establishment and the continued existence of the state of Israel; (3) the French occupation of Algeria, where it believed that France was wrongly withholding self-government from the native population; (4) the economic unity of the Arab states; (5) since 1967 the expulsion of Israeli troops from Jordanian, Syrian and Egyptian territories occupied during the six-day war.

On achieving independence Libya and Sudan joined the Arab League. The significance of the League increased with the creation in February 1958 of the United Arab Republic, *q.v.* The League has also been joined by Morocco and Tunisia (1958), Kuwait (1961), Algeria (1962), South Yemen (1967), Bahrain, Oman, Qatar and the United Arab Emirates in 1971.

Arab South. A term formerly used by Arabs to describe the South Arabian Federation, *q.v.*, the Eastern Aden Protectorate, *q.v.*, and Yemen, *q.v.*, with the addition sometimes of the Sultanate of Muscat and Oman, *q.v.*

Arab Union. The name given to the Arab Federation, *q.v.*, uniting Iraq and Jordan when the Federation became effective on 13 May 1958. A Union cabinet was established under the premiership of the late General Nuri es-Said, who had resigned as Prime Minister of Iraq to take up the post. In addition to a Jordanian deputy-premier, there were ministers with responsibility for foreign affairs, defence, and finance (which were federal matters). After the *coup d'état* in Iraq on 14 July 1958, involving the murder of King Faisal and General Nuri es-Said, King Hussein claimed to have succeeded King Faisal as head of state; Iraq thereupon formally announced its withdrawal from the Union. The Jordan government then issued a decree acknowledging that, as from 1 August, the Union had ceased to exist.

Arabia. The Arab peninsula, also described as Arabia proper as distinct from other Arab-inhabited countries. It comprises the independent states of Bahrain, Kuwait, Oman, Qatar, Saudi Arabia, Yemen (the former People's Republic of Southern Yemen), Yemen Arab Republic and the United Arab Emirates.

Argentina. An independent federal republic and the second largest country in South America; area 1,079,965 sq. m.; population (1970 census) 23,375,705, mainly of Spanish and Italian descent and ninety per cent Roman Catholic; capital Buenos Aires. It was ruled by Spain for three centuries until it achieved independence in 1816; its government is based on the Constitution of 1853, revised in 1860, 1866, 1898 and 1957, and modelled on that of the U.S.A. The republic comprises 22 provinces, the National Territory of Tierra del Fuego, Antarctica (see Antarctic Continent) and the South Atlantic Islands, and the federal district of Buenos Aires. The British colony of the Falkland Islands, *q.v.*, is claimed by Argentina. A long-standing border dispute with Chile was settled in 1966. A President, who must be Roman Catholic and of Argentine birth, elected for six years, controls the executive and selects the cabinet; the National Congress, which was suspended in 1966, had a Senate representing the capital and the provinces and a House of Deputies elected for four years, on a population basis, with half the members retiring every two years.

The republic produces large cereal crops and is the world's leading exporter of raw meat (if Danish bacon exports are ignored), but its economic situation is unhealthy. There have been serious balance of payments deficits caused by falling exports and an emphasis on industrialization at the expense of agriculture, which lacked both manpower and technique. For many years the government failed to make the investment in fuel and power supplies necessary for the country's economic growth, or to create conditions that would encourage private enterprise to do so; but in 1967 eight hundred new oil wells were drilled and several irrigation and hydro-electric schemes initiated, the most important being the Chocón-Cerros Colorados project in northern Patagonia due to be completed in 1978.

In 1946, after three years of political upheaval, General Juan Domingo Perón came to power and established a totalitarian regime based on the support of the industrial workers, whose real income he increased by 47 per cent during his nine years of office as President at the expense of the agricultural workers and the professional and middle classes. The whole population benefited by some of his social measures, which included pensions, a contributory medical scheme and an enormous beneficent organization, the Eva Perón Foundation, established by his wife, to which everyone was obliged to contribute two days' pay yearly. From 1954 his policy of secularization, by which religious instruction in state schools and tax exemption for religious institutions, churches and schools were terminated, and divorce (for the first time in the country's history) and prostitution (banned since 1936) were legalized, alienated Roman Catholic support. In September 1955 his regime was overthrown by a military coup inspired by General Eduardo Lonardi, who became Provisional President. He dissolved the Perónista Party, reversed the policies of his predecessor, but roused suspicions that he intended to govern in Perón fashion, although with a pro-Catholic programme. In November 1955 he was deposed by General Pedro Eugenio Aramburu, Chief of the General Staff, who confirmed the measures introduced by Lonardi, abolished brothels and made divorce illegal.

The economic policy of the Aramburu government, which included devaluation of the peso and stringent foreign exchange regulations, was politically unpopular and the presidential election in February 1958 produced a substantial majority for a lawyer, Dr Arturo Frondizi of the Intransigent Radicals, who received considerable support from the working masses who had once favoured Perón. He reduced imports, developed industry and invited foreign companies to help in the exploitation of oil resources. When Perónistas won more than half the available seats in the House of Deputies at the elections in March 1962, Army leaders interned Frondizi, and the Chairman of the Senate, Dr José Maria Guido, was sworn in as President. The first presidential elections to be held on the basis of proportional representation in August 1963 were won on a minority vote by Dr Arturo Umberto Illia, of the Union Civical Radical del Pueblo. He annulled many of the contracts with foreign oil companies signed by Frondizi in 1958 and tried to reduce expenditure on armaments, diverting the country's resources to internal industrial development and educational and social reform. Elections to the House of Deputies in March 1965 produced further success for the neo-Perónista party, Partido Justicialista, which remained the largest political group, and on 29 June 1966 President Illia's government was overthrown by a military junta. Lieutenant-General Juan Carlos Ongania, the former Commander in Chief of the Army, who had resigned in November 1965 in protest against Illia's refusal to send an Argentine contingent to help suppress a left-wing revolt in the Dominican Republic, *q.v.*, assumed full powers. Congress was dissolved and political parties suppressed, but labour unrest continued and protests by university students increased. A further military coup deposed President Ongania on 8 June 1970. He was replaced by Brigadier General Roberto Marcelo Levingston who declared that there would be no return to 'outdated forms of democracy'. His government was unable to repress guerilla activity on the part of the Trotskyite E.R.P. and on 22 March 1971 he was ousted by a junta of General Alejandro Lanusse, Brigadier Carlos Alberto Rey and Admiral Gnavi. General Lanusse was appointed President for one year, to be succeeded in turn by the other two members of the junta, but he remained in office for a further year.

In July 1971 political parties which could command 0·4 per cent of votes in any one constituency were legalized and elections were promised for March 1973. These resulted in victory for Dr Héctor Cámpora, the Perónista presidential candidate, who won 49 per cent of the popular vote, and for Frejuli, the Péronist alliance, which gained control of Congress. Despite severe deflationary measures introduced since 1967, and a reorganization of the nationalized industries and public services, production has risen only slowly and has been accompanied by an annual inflation of some 30 per cent and continual budget deficits. The consequent reduction in living standards of the industrial workers has brought about direct confrontation between the army and the trade unions which have been profoundly influenced by the socialist policies introduced in neighbouring Chile.

A.S.E.A.N. Association of South East Asian Nations, *q.v*

Asian and Pacific Council. Was set up by Australia, Japan, South Korea, Malaysia, New Zealand, Philippines, Taiwan, Thailand and South Viet-Nam in 1966 to encourage solidarity and regional cooperation among Asian and Pacific countries. It is a purely consultative organization, but unity has been achieved over environmental issues, and especially over opposition to the atmospheric testing of nuclear weapons in the Asian and Pacific region.

Associate Status. A non-colonial relationship between the United Kingdom and a former colony. The arrangement is free and voluntary and may be terminated unilaterally by either party. The former colony exercises full internal self-government but recognizes the British sovereign as head of state. The status was devised in 1967 to cater for those of the former Leeward and Windward Islands (the Little Seven, *q.v.*) which desired a limited independence of the U.K. but which were economically incapable of existing as an independent federation when Barbados, *q.v.*, became self-governing. Antigua, Dominica, Grenada, St Kitts–Nevis–Anguilla, St Lucia and St Vincent are the West Indies Associated States, *q.v.*, which each have an individual associate status with the U.K.

Association of South East Asian Nations (A.S.E.A.N.). Was established in 1967 in Bangkok by Indonesia, Malaysia, Philippines, Singapore and Thailand to accelerate economic progress and increase the stability of the South East Asian region. It replaced the former Association of South East Asia to which Malaysia, Philippines and Thailand had belonged.

Aswan Dam. A dam on the river Nile in southern Egypt, completed in 1899 by British engineers. Its name is often used to describe a new and larger dam farther south, which is known as the High Dam, *q.v.*

Atlantic Nuclear Force (A.N.F.). A proposal by the British government to revise the U.S. plan for a Multilateral Nuclear Force (M.L.F.), *q.v.*, by combining mixed-manned and nationally-manned nuclear delivery systems under a comprehensive allied nuclear command. The U.K. had rejected the idea of a European deterrent which was independent of N.A.T.O., *q.v.*, and was already committed to the principle of mixed-manning, but was reluctant to accept M.L.F. largely because of the expense of maintaining a new weapon system (using Polaris missiles) which would make obsolete its existing land and air-based systems. As soon as the German Federal Republic, which had no independent nuclear deterrent, agreed to support M.L.F. the U.K. negotiated for an equal voice within M.L.F., and suggested an Atlantic Nuclear Force in the hope of combining its own nuclear deterrent (consisting of V-bombers and the three Polaris submarines under construction) with the proposed multilateral force. By this means the U.K. expected to save money, satisfy the powerful anti-nuclear left wing of the Labour Party, *q.v.*, and retain the traditional British balance of power in European affairs.

Atomic Energy Acts, 1946 and 1954. U.S. laws providing for the development of atomic energy. The 1946 Act authorized programmes: (1) to foster research and development in order to encourage scientific and industrial progress; (2) to disseminate as much information as was consistent with security requirements; (3) to make the benefits of the peaceful application of atomic energy available internationally; and (4) to ensure that the government should control the possession and production of fissionable material so as to make the maximum contribution to defence and security. The Act established an Atomic Energy Commission to supervise these programmes. The 1954 Act allowed private enterprises to participate in the development of peacetime uses of atomic energy, and permitted international agreements to be made for the exchange of secret information.

Atomic Energy Commission. A term used to describe: (1) the body set up by the United Nations in 1946 in its attempt to obtain international agreement on disarmament, *q.v.*, and merged in 1951 with the Conventional Armaments Commission to form the Disarmament Commission; and (2) the body established in the U.S.A. to supervise the atomic energy programme authorized by the Atomic Energy Acts, 1946 and 1954, *q.v.*

Attlee, 1st Earl, Clement Richard Attlee, Leader of the British Parliamentary Labour Party from 1935 to 1955; born 3 January 1883; educated at Haileybury College and University College, Oxford. After practising as a lawyer for three years he moved to the East End of London, where he worked in settlements, including Toynbee Hall, and became a Socialist. From 1913 to 1923 he was a lecturer at the London School of Economics. After serving in the First World War he was active in local government and entered the House of Commons in 1922 as the member for Limehouse. He was Parliamentary Private Secretary to Ramsay MacDonald, 1922–4, Under-Secretary of State for War in 1924, Chancellor of the Duchy of Lancaster, 1930–31 and Postmaster-General in 1931. He was then deputy leader of the Parliamentary Labour Party for four years and succeeded George Lansbury as leader in 1935, in an election in which he defeated Arthur Greenwood and Herbert Morrison. During the Second World War he was successively Lord Privy Seal, Dominions Secretary, and Lord President of the Council. He was Prime Minister from 1945 to 1951. After 1951 he led the Labour Party in opposition in the House of Commons, and retired in 1955, when he accepted an earldom. He rarely committed himself publicly on the supposed policy differences between the right and left wings of his party, but contrived to remain undisputed leader as a result of his political shrewdness and a refusal to identify himself with any faction. He died on 8 October 1967.

Australia. An independent state and member of the British Commonwealth; area 2,967,909 sq. m.; population (June 1970) 12,551,300; federal capital Canberra. It comprises the six former colonies of New South Wales, Victoria, South Australia, Queensland (which has the largest concentration of Aborigines – 24,000 out of 116,000), Western Australia and Tasmania which were federated as states, under the name of the 'Commonwealth of Australia', on 1 January 1901. The Northern Territory was transferred from South Australia to the Commonwealth in 1911. Each state retained the constitution, subject to changes in the Commonwealth constitution and subsequent alterations, by which it had been governed before federation, and the powers of the Federal Parliament, although they now embrace defence, foreign affairs, finance and social services, are strictly limited. Each state legislature consists of a Governor, representing the Queen, an upper and lower house of parliament (except in Queensland where the upper house was abolished in 1922), a cabinet led by a premier, and an executive council. The states have equal representation in the Senate, the upper house of the Federal Parliament, which comprises 60 senators, chosen for six years with half the members retiring every three years. In 1972 there were 125 members in the lower chamber, the House of Representatives, but as they are elected in proportion to the population the number may increase or decrease; no state may send fewer than five. Since 1922 the Northern Territory, and since 1948 the Australian Capital Territory (area 939 sq. m.) which includes Canberra, have each had one representative in the lower house who was not entitled to vote except on matters which directly concerned his Territory. Full voting powers were accorded these representatives in 1968 and 1966 respectively. Both chambers are elected by universal adult suffrage and voting has been compulsory since 1925. The House of Representatives is elected for three years.

The right-wing, conservative Liberal Party, led by William McMahon, *q.v.*,, until December 1972 when he was succeeded by Billie Mackie Snedden, was formerly in coalition with the Country Party, led by Douglas Anthony, which represents Australian farming interests. The coalition won only 58 seats (66 in 1969) at the General Election held in December 1972 and ceased to be the governing party for the first time in 23 years. The Australian Labour Party (67 seats as against 59 in 1969) has since the 1960s succeeded in reconciling the sectional interests of its Socialist, intellectual and trade union supporters. The Democratic Labour Party, a Catholic, anti-Communist break-away group which first ran its own candidates in the 1963 election, increased its representation in the Senate in 1971 from 4 seats to 5. Approximately three quarters of Australia's Catholic population of 3,000,000 vote labour, and Catholic Action organizations have tried to use the party as an instrument of Catholic social policy (e.g. on the subjects of birth control and religious education) and as a method of influencing the trade unions. The Labour Party was last united under the late Joseph Benedict Chifley who, while married to a Protestant, was a Catholic progressive; his successor, Arthur Calwell, held similar views; the present leader, and Prime Minister, Edgar Gough Whitlam, *q.v.*, is a Protestant and further to the right. The Communist Party has no representation in either house. A Bill which dissolved the Communist Party was ruled as unconstitutional in the High Court and abandoned in 1951 after it had been submitted to a referendum.

Although the Australian economy was until recently dependent on the export of wool, the country has been self-sufficient in iron and steel since 1958, and manufacturing industries have undergone rapid expansion since 1945. There are valuable uranium deposits, and since 1969 natural gas has been produced from off-shore fields. Not enough capital is attracted to keep pace with the demands of a growing population for an increasing standard of living, but there has been considerable U.S. investment and substantial borrowing by the state governments from private American investors. Trade with Japan and the U.S.A. is far greater in total than that with the U.K. which, however, remains an important trading partner and source of new immigrants, of whom 140,000 were admitted in 1970–71. The complete exclusion of non-European immigrants (the 'White Australia policy') has been relaxed in recent years and in 1972 there were 54,000 non-Europeans living permanently in the country. The issue of the Aborigines' claim to the freehold of their tribal lands in the Northern Territory (which is Crown Land) is still in dispute. On 26 January (Australia Day) 1972 the McMahon government upheld a Supreme Court ruling of April 1971 that the Yirrkala Aborigines had no legal title to their ancient lands in the face of an agreement, opposed by the tribe, between the government and Nabalco, a Swiss-Australian consortium, to mine alumina-bauxite in Arnhem Land. The Labour government is committed to vesting all Aboriginal lands in public trusts and to conferring freehold title on a tribe where this can be proved.

Australian New Guinea. Name by which Papua-New Guinea, *q.v.*, was known prior to 1968. It consists of New Guinea Territory, a trusteeship territory entrusted to Australia, and Papua, which is also administered by Australia; together the territories comprise the eastern half of the island of New Guinea, *q.v.* The western half is West Irian, *q.v.* an Indonesian territory,

Austria. A Central European state between Italy and the German Federal Republic, created after the First World War from the German-speaking Alpine provinces of the former Austro-Hungarian Empire; area 32,366 sq. m.; population (1971) 7,443,809, of whom over 90 per cent are Roman Catholics; capital Vienna. In 1934 a clerico-Fascist group seized power under Dollfuss and suppressed both a popular rising in defence of the republican constitution and a Nazi rising in which Dollfuss was killed. In 1938 German troops marched in and the German dictator Adolf Hitler annexed Austria. A majority of Austrians may have been ready to accept a federal relationship with Germany, but many Socialists, Catholics and Monarchists resented the compulsory union. In 1945 the victorious allied powers occupied Austria and divided it into four zones which were controlled by France, the U.K., the U.S.A. and the U.S.S.R., and a provisional Austrian government restored the republic as it had existed before 1938.

In July 1955 Austria became a free and independent state for the first time since 1938, upon the ratification of the Austrian State Treaty which was concluded in May 1955 by the four occupying powers. All occupation forces were withdrawn by 25 October 1955. A constitutional law was then passed by which Austria is pledged to remain permanently a neutral country.

A General Election was held in October 1971 under a new electoral law introduced in November 1970 which reduced the number of constituencies from 25 to 9 while increasing the number of deputies in the National Assembly from 165 to 183. The moderate left-wing Socialist Party, which had formed a minority government since the General Election of March 1970, won an absolute majority in the National Assembly, the lower house of the Federal Parliament, with 50·04 per cent of the total votes cast and 93 seats (81 in 1970). The Roman Catholic and conservative Austrian People's Party, led by Dr Karl Scheinzer, won 80 seats (79 in 1970), and the right-wing Austrian Freedom Party 10 seats (5). The Socialist Party therefore continued in office under Dr Bruno Kreisky, who remained as Chancellor.

The proportion of the population engaged in agriculture has fallen considerably in recent years, and there has been rapid progress in the industries concerned with hydro-electric power (which is exported to neighbouring countries), oil and steel. Between 1970 and 1972

Austria achieved the highest rate of economic growth in the world after Japan. In 1946 many commercial undertakings, including the three largest banks, every oil-producing and refining company, and most coal-mining, steel-producing and iron and steel manufacturing firms, were nationalized.

The status of the German-speaking inhabitants of the South Tirol, *q.v.* (alternatively known as the Alto Adige, *q.v.*) in Italy, which had been a source of friction between Austria and Italy since 1919, was resolved in 1971 by the Italian parliament's conferring a substantial measure of autonomy on the region. In July 1971 the two countries further agreed to submit any differences arising from the settlement to the International Court of Justice, *q.v.*

Autarky. From the Greek word *autarkeia* (often spelt 'autarchy', self-rule, by mistaken analogy with 'diarchy', dual rule) meaning self-sufficiency. In the economic sense it conveys the idea that a country should produce at home everything it requires and should cease to depend on imports. The drive for autarky was particularly strong in Germany before the Second World War, being adopted with a view to making Germany blockade-proof.

Authoritarian. A term denoting a dictatorial system of government, as opposed to a democratic system based on popular sovereignty. Adherents of authoritarianism criticize the alleged delays and inefficiency of the democratic system, and praise the advantages of a strong state authority.

Autonomy. A word of Greek origin ('self-law') meaning self-government.

Avon, 1st Earl, Robert Anthony Eden. Prime Minister and leader of the British Conservative Party from April 1955 to January 1957; born 12 June 1897; educated at Eton and Christ Church, Oxford, where he studied Oriental languages. After serving in the First World War he entered the House of Commons as the member for Warwick and Leamington and was appointed Parliamentary Private Secretary to the Under-Secretary of State for Home Affairs, 1924–6, to the Foreign Secretary, 1926–9, and Parliamentary Under-Secretary of State for Foreign Affairs, 1931–4. In 1934 he became Lord Privy Seal. At the 'peace ballot' of 1935 11 million persons had professed their loyalty to the League of Nations, and it was decided to set up a Ministry for League Affairs; Eden was appointed to this post. He urged League of Nations action when Italy attacked Ethiopia, opposed the Anglo-French 'Hoare-Laval plan' to give Italy wide powers in Ethiopia, and at the age of 38 replaced Sir Samuel Hoare (later Lord Templewood) as Foreign Secretary. In February 1938 he resigned in protest against the actions of the Prime Minister, Neville Chamberlain, whom he considered to have negotiated behind his back with the Italian Ambassador. In 1939 he was recalled as Secretary of State for Dominion Affairs; he became Secretary of State for War in 1940, and again Foreign Secretary from 1940 to 1945. He was Deputy Leader of the Opposition, 1945–51, and Foreign Secretary, 1951–5. In 1952 he married Clarissa Spencer Churchill. On the retirement from ministerial office of Sir Winston Churchill in April 1955 he became Prime Minister. He was, however, troubled increasingly by ill-health, and in January 1957 (three weeks after the British forces, which had attacked Egypt in October 1956, had been withdrawn and replaced by U.N. troops) he resigned from government office and from the House of Commons. He accepted an earldom in July 1961.

Awolowo, Chief Obafemi. Nigerian politician; born in 1910 and educated at London University where he graduated in law and commerce. He qualified as a barrister and on returning to Nigeria founded the *Nigerian Tribune* in Ibadan. He became Prime Minister of the Western Region of Nigeria and remained in power from 1952 to 1962. As the founder and leader of the Action Group, representing the interests of the Yoruba tribe and the businessmen and chiefs of the Western Region, he led the opposition in the Nigerian Federal Parliament from 1960 until November 1962 when he was arrested on charges of treasonable felony and sentenced to ten years' imprisonment. In August 1966, following the coup by which Major-General Gowon, *q.v.*, took control of the government, Awolowo was released from prison in order to secure the support of the Western Region for the new administration. He was appointed Vice-Chairman of the Federal Executive Council and Federal Commissioner for Finance in June 1967, and in September 1967 became one of the four civilian members of the war cabinet presided over by General Gowon. He resigned from government office in July 1971 for health reasons, and retired into private life.

Azerbaijan. Eastern Azerbaijan (population 2,600,000; capital Tabriz) and Western Azerbaijan (population 1,000,000; capital Rezayeh) are two of the ten *ustan* or administrative provinces of Persia, *q.v.* They were the subject of international tension when the U.S.S.R. attempted to establish a sphere of influence there after the Second World War.

Azikiwe, Dr Nnamdi. Nigerian statesman; born 16 November 1904 and educated at Lincoln and Pennsylvania Universities in the U.S.A. At Lincoln University he became an instructor in history and political science. He has been Governing Director of the African Continental Bank, Ltd, and Chairman of Associated Newspapers of Nigeria, Ltd, and of the African Book Company, Ltd, a member of the Nigerian Legislative Council and of the Eastern Region House of Assembly, and Prime Minister and Minister of Local Government in the Eastern Region. He led a political party, the National Council of Nigeria and the Cameroons. In January 1957 a tribunal reported the results of an inquiry into allegations of improper conduct arising from his government's acquisition of the African Continental Bank which he controlled. The tribunal found that although Azikiwe's primary motive was to liberalize credit, his conduct had 'fallen short of the expectations of honest, reasonable people'; it added that he should have relinquished his interest in the Bank when the proposal to inject public moneys into it was first made, and that 'he was guilty of misconduct as a minister in failing to do so'. He became Governor-General on 16 November 1960, after independence, and President on 1 October 1963, when Nigeria became a republic. The Presidency was suspended and he was deposed in January 1966 by a military *coup d'état*. In 1969, as the leading Ibo, he appealed to his fellow tribesmen to end the civil war over Biafra, *q.v.*, and to restore unity to Nigeria.

B

Baath. Arab word meaning 'renaissance' or 'revival'; it is also the name of a political party (founded by a Christian Syrian, Michel Aflaq) with considerable influence in Iraq and Syria. It has strong sympathies with the radical approach and Pan Arabism of the leaders of the Egyptian revolution of 1952; its insistence on free elections, a free press, and freedom of speech and assembly, has been described as being one of many factors dividing it (especially in its Syrian branch) from the Egyptians. In Iraq, however, the conduct of the Baathists towards the Kurds (after the revolution of 8 February 1963) could not be reconciled with democratic standards. The desire of Iraq and Syria to be independent of Egypt also plays a substantial part in the attitude of the party to that country. The party has branches in Jordan, Lebanon, and other Middle Eastern states.

Baghdad Pact. A treaty concluded between Iraq and Turkey in February 1955 and open, for accession, to any member-state of the Arab League or any state concerned with security and peace in the Middle East and 'which is fully recognized by both of the parties'. Israel, which is not recognized by Iraq, was therefore prohibited from joining the Pact. The U.K., Pakistan, and Persia acceded in 1955. Article One of the Pact stated: 'The parties will cooperate for their security and defence. Such measures as they agree to take to give effect to this cooperation may form the subject of special agreements with each other.' There was no provision that each member should regard an attack on another as an attack on itself, or that a member which was attacked must be helped. Iraq and the U.K. entered into one of the special agreements envisaged on 4 April 1955, when they renewed the Anglo-Iraqi treaty of alliance of 1930, which was due to expire in 1957. Under Article Six a permanent ministerial council was to be set up when at least four powers had acceded to the Pact. The council held its first meeting at Baghdad in November 1955. A military committee, and an economic committee to plan regional developments, were set up.

The Pact had been described in the U.K. and the U.S.A. as a 'northern tier' of defence for the Middle East against the U.S.S.R. The Russian government stated in October 1955 that the Pact involved the formation of a group which was an instrument of aggressive circles who were not interested in peace and international security. In 1957 U.S. representatives became members of the economic and military committees although the U.S.A. did not accede to the Pact.

Iraq ceased to take part in arrangements relating to the Pact after its revolution in July 1958, and withdrew in March 1959. On 21 August 1959 the organization was renamed the Central Treaty Organization. Its headquarters had already been transferred, in October 1958, from Baghdad to Ankara.

Bahamas. A British colony comprising some seven hundred islands, of which thirty are inhabited, in the Caribbean Sea, lying between Florida and Cuba; the principal islands are New Providence, Grand Bahama, Abaco, Long Island and San Salvador; area 5,386 sq. m.; population (1971 estimate) 174,365, more than half of whom live on New Providence: capital Nassau. The islands were first settled by the British in the seventeenth century, but were subject to continual raids by the French and Spaniards and used as a rendezvous for pirates until 1717 when a British Governor was appointed. British possession was eventually confirmed in 1783. Slavery was permitted until 1838 and accounts for the presence of an 80 per cent negro population. Internal self-government was introduced in 1964 and extended in 1969. The legislature consists of a Senate, and a House of Assembly of 38 members elected by universal adult suffrage every five years. At elections held in January 1967 the Progressive Liberal Party (P.L.P.), representing the negro community and led by Lynden Pindling, *q.v.*, won 18 seats and formed the first government with an all-negro cabinet, with the support of 1 Labour representative (a negro) and the 1 (white) Independent who agreed to serve as a non-party Speaker in the Assembly. The United Bahamian Party (U.B.P.), known as 'The Bay Street Boys' and representing mainly the white, business population, led by the former Prime Minister, Sir Roland Symonette, won 18 seats (a loss of 6) and went into opposition. The death of one Member of Parliament in April 1968 necessitated another General Election in which the P.L.P. won 29 seats and the U.B.P. only 7. During 1970 the P.L.P. split over the issues of policy towards the U.S.A. and Cuba and Bahamian independence, which Pindling promised for 1973; eight of its supporters created a new party which then became the main opposition in place of the U.B.P. At further elections held on 19 September 1972 the results were: P.L.P. 29 seats; Free National Movement (of the combined opposition parties) 8 seats. P.L.P. won the remaining seat at a by-election in October 1972 and Lynden Pindling continued to lead the government.

The principal exports are pulpwood, crawfish, rum and salt; there is a flourishing tourist industry and the absence of direct taxation, other than a small property tax, has encouraged a high level of foreign investment and settlement but has made the islands vulnerable to any recession in the U.S.A.

Bahrain. An independent state on the west coast of the Persian Gulf, comprising a group of islands, area 231 sq. m., of which the largest is Bahrain; population (1970 estimate) 215,000, mostly Moslems of the Shia and Sunni sects; capital Manama. It was ruled by Persia until 1782 and thereafter by a family originating in Kuwait. It was under British protection from 1861 until 15 August 1971 when its ruler, Sheikh Isa, declared independence, thereby dissociating Bahrain from the Federation of Arab Emirates, *q.v.*, which it had joined in 1968. Following a U.N. investigation in May 1970 into the wishes of the population regarding the reunification of Persia and Bahrain, Persian claims to sovereignty were not upheld and the Shah relinquished the claim.

In 1932 oil was discovered by the Bahrain Petroleum Co., of which Standard Oil of California and Texaco each own fifty per cent. In 1965 a sea-bed concession was granted to the Continental Oil Co. of America; Bahrain also receives, by an agreement signed with Saudi Arabia in 1958, 25 per cent of the profits of the oil produced by Aramco from the Abu Saafa sea-bed. Profits have been divided between the sheikhdom and the oil companies on a fifty-fifty basis; of the sheikhdom's share, the family of the ruler (Sheikh Isa bin Sulman al Khalifah, born 1933 and Sheikh since 1961) receives one third and the government two-thirds. Although the oil revenue accounts for three-quarters of its income, Bahrain is not wholly dependent on oil, reserves of which are expected to have been exhausted by 1990. It has long been a centre of Persian Gulf trade and the development of the new modern harbour of Mina Sulman with important storage facilities has attracted international shipping and created a considerable trade in re-exports. A new aluminium smelter was opened in 1971. The once-famous pearling industry is now in decline. The government provides comprehensive, but not compulsory, education and a free medical service for all residents of Bahrain.

Balance of Payments. The balance between the cost of a country's imports and the receipts for its exports. The chief items will usually be visible imports and exports, but there will also be invisible imports (such as tourist expenditure in foreign countries and the interest paid on loans from foreign countries) and invisible exports (such as the expenditure of foreign tourists, the interest paid by foreign countries on loans made to them and payments for banking, shipping, and insurance services performed for foreigners).

Balance of Power. The theory that the strength of one group of powers on the European continent should be equal to the strength of the other group, thus preventing any hegemony and ensuring peace. The maintenance of this balance was for many years the traditional object of British foreign policy, and the long period of peace from 1871 to 1914 was achieved by the balance between the German-Austrian-Italian group (the Triple Alliance) and the Anglo-French-Russian group (the Triple Entente). After the First World War the theory of the balance of power passed into diplomatic history; the U.K. appeased but did not oppose the most powerful continental state, Germany, until 1939. Since 1945 there has been no attempt by the U.K. to maintain a balance of power; its influence has been used in an effort to create a preponderance of power in favour of the western against the eastern nations.

Balfour Declaration. A letter from A. J. Balfour, then Foreign Secretary, to Lord Rothschild, Chairman of the British Zionist Federation, in which the founding of a Jewish national home in Palestine, *q.v.*, was promised. The letter, dated 2 November 1917, read as follows: 'His Majesty's Government view with favour the establishment in Palestine of a national home for the Jewish people, and will use their best endeavours to facilitate the achievement of this object, it being clearly understood that nothing shall be done which may prejudice the civil and religious rights of the existing non-Jewish communities in Palestine or the rights and political status enjoyed by Jews in any other country.' There was considerable dispute as to whether this Declaration contradicted the undertaking given to the Arabs in the McMahon Correspondence, *q.v.*, but Jews were admitted to Palestine, although only on limited annual quotas, between the First and Second World Wars. The independent state of Israel, *q.v.*, was established on 14 May 1948.

Balkan Pact. A military treaty of alliance between Greece, Turkey, and Yugoslavia, signed in Bled on 9 August 1954 and intended to last for 20 years. It is a development of a treaty of friendship and collaboration, signed in Ankara in February 1953.

A Yugoslavian alliance has been a basic principle of Greek foreign policy since before 1914, in view of Greek fears of Italy and Bulgaria. Since the fourteenth century there has been no serious conflict between Serbs and Greeks. The only exception has been the period 1944–8, when a pro-Russian Yugoslavia supported Bulgaria and Romania, old enemies of Greece. Friction between Italy and Yugoslavia has made Italy oppose this friendship between Greece and Yugoslavia. In 1934, during the negotiations with Yugoslavia for the first Balkan Pact, the Greeks had to insist on 'the Italian clause', which automatically prevented Greece from going to war if Italy were involved in any conflict with Yugoslavia. The Pact marked an improvement in Greco-Turkish relations but these deteriorated as a result of the Cyprus dispute. Yugoslavia and Turkey were estranged in the period 1944–8 when the U.S.S.R., in alliance with Yugoslavia, appeared to be threatening Turkey; nevertheless both countries have much to gain from mutual trade.

Banda, Dr Hastings Kamuzu. Malawi politician; born in 1905 and educated, after running away from home at the age of 13 to work in the gold mines of South Africa, at the Wilberforce University High School, Ohio, the University of Chicago, the Meharry Medical College in Nashville, Tennessee, and Edinburgh University, where he qualified as a doctor of medicine. He practised medicine for many years in London but his concern for the future of Malawi (then known as Nyasaland, *q.v.*) caused him to return in July 1958. There followed a series of meetings and riots which culminated in the declaration of a state of emergency on 3 March 1959, a declaration that the African National (later the Malawi) Congress was illegal, and the arrest of Banda, its President General, with 166 of its members. He was released in April 1960 and became the first Prime Minister of his country when Nyasaland was granted self-government on 1 February 1963. He has been President of Malawi since the republic was declared on 6 July 1966.

Bandaranaike, Sirimavo. Ceylonese politician; born 17 April 1916, the daughter of the Ratemahatmaya of Ratnapura, she was educated at Ratnapura High School and St Bridget's Convent, Colombo. She married, in 1940, Solomon Bandaranaike who founded the socialist Sri Lanka Freedom Party (S.L.F.P.) in 1951 and became Prime Minister of Ceylon in 1956. After his assassination by a Buddhist monk in 1959, she succeeded him as President of the S.L.F.P. and became a member of the Senate. Following the elections of July 1960, in which the ruling United National Party, under Dudley Senanayake, lost its parliamentary majority, she formed an S.L.F.P. government, becoming the world's first woman Prime Minister. She was elected to the House of Representatives in 1965 as the member for her husband's constituency, and led the opposition until May 1970 when, as a result of the electoral success of the S.L.F.P., she took office once more as Prime Minister at the head of a left-wing coalition government. She was responsible for the introduction of the Constitution of May 1972 by which Ceylon, under the new name of Sri Lanka, *q.v.*, became a republic.

Bandung Conference. *See* Afro-Asian Conference.

Bangladesh. An independent republic in south-east Asia, bordered by India to the west and north and Burma to the east; area 52,126 sq. m.; population estimated at 70,000,000, of whom at least 80 per cent are Bengalis, speaking the Bengali language, and 15 per cent are Biharis or members of the Scheduled Castes and Urdu-speaking; capital Dacca. It comprises the former East Bengal province of British India and the Sylhet district of Assam which together became part of Pakistan, *q.v.*, in 1947, and were known as East Pakistan.

The separation of East from West Pakistan by a distance of more than 1,000 miles created grave difficulties in communication which were exacerbated by political repression and by far-reaching economic, linguistic and political disputes. In 1952 the government, from Karachi, declared Urdu to be the national language; this decision was revoked, and Bengali given an equal status, only after rioting in East Pakistan. A further problem was the preoccupation of West Pakistan with Middle East affairs to which the Bengalis were indifferent, and the adoption of a policy of foreign alliances (the mutual defence agreement with the U.S.A. in 1954, S.E.A.T.O., *q.v.*, Cento, *q.v.*, and latterly the rapprochement, *q.v.*, with China) which the Bengalis regarded as a threat to their satisfactory relations with neighbouring India. But the greatest source of friction was the disproportionate share of the country's total investment received by East Pakistan, which produced and exported the jute and cotton which earned the foreign exchange by which the Federal budget was kept in balance. From 1956 to 1960 East Pakistan was accorded only 26 per cent of the national development expenditure; this rose to 32 per cent between 1960 and 1965, and to 36 per cent from 1965 to 1970. The larger population of the East (73 million as opposed to 60 million in the West) was retarded industrially in order to provide West Pakistan with a market for its exports.

The elections held in December 1970 resulted in an overwhelming victory in East Pakistan for the Awami League, led by Sheikh Mujibur Rahman, *q.v.*, on a programme of autonomy for the region within a new Federal Constitution. Since the Awami League would have exercised an absolute majority in the National Assembly its opening was postponed indefinitely. In January 1971 negotiations over a possible constitutional compromise broke down and on 26 March 1971 Sheikh Mujibur Rahman proclaimed East Pakistan an independent republic under the name of Bangladesh, or Bengal nation. Civil war then broke out; President Khan of Pakistan outlawed the Awami League and arrested its leaders. By mid-April the Pakistan Army had dominated the entire eastern province and more than 250,000 refugees had fled across the Indian border. The occasion of the trial of Sheikh Mujibur Rahman, which was held in secret, in August intensified the civil war. On 21 November 1971 the Liberation Army of East Bengal, the Mukti Bahini, launched an offensive against Pakistan Army troops, many of whom deserted to Bangladesh. On 4 December the Indian government, embarrassed by more than 9,500,000 refugees from East Bengal, declared war, which was brought to an end by the unconditional surrender of the Pakistan Army in East Bengal on 16 December. Sheikh Mujibur Rahman, who was released from prison on 8 January 1972, rejected the offer, by President Zulfiqar Ali Bhutto, *q.v.*, of the Presidency of a united Pakistan, and returned to Bangladesh to form a government. The Indian government, which agreed to withdraw all its forces by 25 March 1972, was the first to recognize the new republic on 6 December 1971; it was followed by the U.S.S.R. in January, the U.K. in February and the U.S.A. in April 1972. On 18 April 1972 Bangladesh was admitted to membership of the British Commonwealth. Its application for membership of the United Nations in August 1972 was vetoed by China.

A provisional Constitution, issued by Sheikh Mujibur Rahman, who had been acclaimed as President, declared Bangladesh to be a secular state and a parliamentary democracy. He then resigned the Presidency to Abu Sayeed Chowdhury, a judge and former Vice-Chancellor of Dacca University, and took office as Prime Minister, stating that socialism would be introduced by democratic means. All businesses which had been abandoned by Pakistanis were to be expropriated by the government, and banking, insurance, foreign trade and basic industries, with the exception of British interests in jute and tea, would be nationalized. The promised punishment of all war criminals was interpreted by the Bangladesh Army as licence to harass the non-Bengali minorities, especially the Biharis, of whom some 260,000 were disenfranchised in elections held in March 1973 which resulted in an overwhelming victory for the Awami League. The land is fertile and 85 per cent of the population is engaged in agriculture, but the area of cultivable land is inadequate to make the country self-sufficient in rice (the staple diet) and the population density is the highest in the world, and increasing at a rate of 3 per cent per year.

Bantustans. Lands in South Africa set aside for use and occupation by Africans under the Promotion of Bantu Self-Government Act, 1959. There are eight Bantu national units, each with limited powers of self-government, a white resident, and envoys to the white-occupied part of South Africa, where most of the Africans work. The units (of which the best known is the Transkei) occupy approximately 14 per cent of the total area of South Africa, and represent one aspect of the application of the policy of apartheid, *q.v.*

Barbados. An independent state and member of the British Commonwealth, it is the most easterly of the islands of the West Indies; area 166 sq. m.; population (1970 estimate) 238,100; capital Bridgetown. Barbados was occupied by the British in 1627 and has never changed hands. It has one of the oldest legislatures in the Commonwealth; its House of Assembly dates from 1639. A ministerial system of government was introduced in 1954, internal self-government in 1961, and the colony became fully independent on 30 November 1966. The legislature consists of a Governor-General, a Senate and a House of Assembly of 24 members elected every five years by universal suffrage. At elections held in September 1971 the Democratic Labour Party, led by the Prime Minister, Errol Walton Barrow, won 18 seats (14 in 1966); the Barbados Labour Party, led by Bernard St John, 6 seats (8); the Barbados National Party which had 2 seats in 1966 lost its representation.

The economy of the island is based on sugar; three-quarters of the cultivable land is planted to sugar cane. Tourism is an important source of revenue but much capital investment is needed to introduce light industry and provide for the rapidly increasing population.

Barber, Anthony Perrinot Lysberg. British Conservative Party politician; born 4 July 1920; educated at Oriel College, Oxford, where his legal studies were interrupted by the outbreak of war. He took his degree from a prisoner-of-war camp in Germany. He was called to the English Bar in 1948 and practised as a barrister until 1958 when he became financial director of a Barnsley glass-container manufacturing firm. He entered the House of Commons as the member for Doncaster in 1951 and was appointed Parliamentary Private Secretary to the Minister for Air in 1952, and a Government Whip, under Edward Heath, *q.v.*, in 1955. From 1957 to 1958 he was a Lord Commissioner of the Treasury, taking up the post of Parliamentary Private Secretary to the Prime Minister, Harold Macmillan, *q.v.*, in 1958. He held the offices of Economic Secretary to the Treasury from 1959 to 1962, Financial Secretary to the Treasury from 1962 to 1963, and Minister of Health from October 1963 until October 1964 when he lost his parliamentary seat at the General Election. He returned to the House of Commons as the result of a by-election in the constituency of Altrincham and Sale, and became the Opposition's principal spokesman on trade and steel. In 1967 he was appointed coordinator of the activities of the Conservative Party in parliament, at Conservative Central Office, and in the Party policy groups.

In June 1970 he became, briefly, as Chancellor of the Duchy of Lancaster, the Minister responsible for negotiating British entry into E.E.C., *q.v.*; on the sudden death of Iain Macleod in July 1970, he was appointed Chancellor of the Exchequer.

Barotseland, now Western Province. One of the eight provinces of Zambia, bounded by Angola to the west and Botswana to the south; area 44,920 sq. m.; population (1966 census) 399,000, mostly cattle-owners and fishermen; administrative centre Mongu Lealui.

Barotseland became a protectorate in 1891 on the application of its Paramount Chief, who on 17 October 1900 granted mineral and trading rights to the British South Africa Company in return for a subsidy and an assurance as to his control of tribal affairs. The concession was confirmed by the British government. In 1960 the Monckton Report, *q.v.*, stated: 'For the past sixty years the desire of the Barotse people to remain securely under the direct protection of the British Crown without the interpolation of any intermediaries has been clear and consistent.' In 1961 the Paramount Chief secured British agreement that he should be addressed as the Litunga of Barotseland, by which title his people know him.

Concerned at the possibility that Barotseland might come under the control of a Northern Rhodesian African nationalist government, the Litunga (Sir Mwanawina Lewanika III) and his followers tried to ensure that no constitutional change would be made without their consent. An undertaking to this effect was given by the British government in April 1961, but in March 1962 it felt unable to agree to Barotseland becoming separate within the Federation of Rhodesia and Nyasaland. At elections held in August 1963 the United National Independence Party (U.N.I.P.), which favoured central control, won all the 25 elective seats on the Barotseland National Council. Barotseland became a province of Zambia when the latter became independent, on 24 October 1964. It was renamed Western Province, and the existing Western Province became Copperbelt Province.

Agricultural expansion is largely dependent upon flood control and canals are being cleared to achieve this control. There are plentiful supplies of citrus, mangoes and other fruits, but inadequacy of transport hinders marketing.

Barzel, Dr Rainer Candidus. West German Christian Democratic politician; a Roman Catholic; born 20 June 1924 in Braunsberg, East Prussia, the son of a teacher, he was educated at the Jesuit College in Berlin. After serving as a naval fighter pilot during the war he studied law and economics at the University of Cologne. His political career began in the Centre Party, the remnant of the pre-war Catholic Party, which he left to join the staff of Karl Arnold, the Christian Democratic Prime Minister of North Rhine–Westphalia. He became a protégé of Konrad Adenauer, *q.v.*, entering the Bundestag in 1957 and in 1962 becoming, as Minister for All-German Affairs, the youngest member of the Adenauer Cabinet. He led the parliamentary group of the Christian Democratic Union and Christian Social Union (C.D.U.–C.S.U.) for seven years until he was elected in October 1971 to succeed Kurt Kiesinger, *q.v.*, as chairman of the C.D.U.

Basutoland. Name by which Lesotho, *q.v.*, was known before it became an independent state within the British Commonwealth on 3 August 1966.

Bay of Pigs (Cochinos Bay). About 100 miles west of Trinidad, in southern Cuba; Cuban exiles under U.S. control were landed there on 17 April 1961 in an attempt to overthrow the Castro regime. The project was conceived by the Republican Eisenhower administration and adopted and carried out by the Democratic Kennedy administration. The operation probably rested on two premises: that if only Cubans appeared to take part the U.S. government could dissociate itself from any consequences; and that the landings would be followed by defections from the Cuban armed forces. In the event the responsibility of the U.S. government was widely recognized. This occurred despite the attempts of the Central Intelligence Agency to provide cover stories, such as a flight by a B-26 from Nicaragua to Miami, where a Cuban exile announced himself as a Castro defector who had just bombed Cuban airfields. The attempted invasion was completely thwarted by the Cuban government by 20 April 1961, approximately 80 men being killed and 1,200 captured.

Bechuanaland. Name by which Botswana, *q.v.*, was known before it became an independent republic within the British Commonwealth on 30 September 1966.

Belgian Congo. The name by which Zaïre was known when it was Belgium's only African colony. It was created a state in 1885 under Léopold II as a result of a decision of the great powers at the Conference of Berlin; it became a Belgian colony in 1908. The Belgian government tried to develop the economy and to improve standards of education while blocking political progress. This policy of *paternalisme*, in which the state was absolute, was modified and some literate Africans were enfranchised for the 1957 local elections. A legislative Council was established in 1959, and the country became completely independent on 30 June 1960. (*See* Zaïre.)

Belgium. An independent state and the most densely populated country in Europe; area 11,799 sq. m.; population (1971) 9,730,000, consisting of Flemings, *q.v.*, in increasing numbers, and Walloons, *q.v.*, in decreasing numbers; the majority are Roman Catholics; capital Brussels. Belgium became an independent constitutional monarchy in 1831. It tried to preserve its independence (as guaranteed in the Treaty of London 1839) but was invaded by Germany in the First and Second World Wars, its strategic position on the northern flank of France inviting German attacks in 1914 and 1940. King Leopold III, who ascended the throne in 1934, abdicated in 1951 in favour of his son (born 1930) who became King Baudouin.

Since 1918 Belgium has been ruled by coalition governments, with the exception of the Social Christian administration of 1950–54. The issues of whether the Flemish or French language should predominate or co-exist in the economic and educational life of the country, and the role of the Roman Catholic church in the education system have blurred orthodox party divisions and dominated domestic politics since 1958 when Catholic resentment of increases in grants to state secular schools brought down the coalition government of the Socialist, Achille von Acker, and produced an electoral majority for the Catholic Social Christian Party. The failure of successive governments, led by different members of the Social Christian Party, Gaston Eyskens, Théo LeFèvre, and Pierre Harmel, to solve the language problem was reflected in declining support for the Party at the 1961, 1965 and 1968 elections. The act, introduced by Eyskens in February 1962, providing for a fixed linguistic frontier between French- and Flemish-speaking areas, was unacceptable to the French-speaking minority (representing 33 per cent of the population), and the decision of the bi-lingual Catholic University of Louvain in 1967 to segregate French and Flemish teaching departments produced further unrest and precipitated the dissolution of the government of Paul Vanden-Boeynants (formed March 1966) and fresh elections. These confirmed the decline in Flemish support for the Social Christians (the Socialists depend largely upon the industrial French-speaking areas of the south), with a corresponding increase in the votes given to the linguistic parties, the Flemish Volksunie and the French-speaking Front, both of which favour separatism, *q.v.* To ease friction between the French and Flemish-speaking communities the Constitution was amended in December 1970 to permit parliamentary responsibility for certain aspects of cultural life, and especially education, to be transferred to Cultural Councils. The problem of the status and territorial limits of Brussels, a predominantly French-speaking community in the heart of Flemish Flanders, remained unresolved.

The result of elections to the Chamber of Deputies held on 7 November 1971 were: Social Christian Party (P.S.C.) 67 seats (69 in 1968 and 77 in 1965); Socialist Party (P.S.B.) 61 (59 in 1968 and 64 in 1965); Party of Liberty and Progress, a right-wing liberal group representing small businessmen and shopkeepers, 34 (47 and 48); Volksunie (Christian Flemish People's Union) 21 (20 and 12); French-speaking Front 24 (12 and 5); Communists 5 (5 and 6). After prolonged negotiations, Gaston Eyskens, who had headed a coalition of the Social Christian and Socialist Parties since June 1968, formed a new coalition government, consisting of 9 Flemish Social Christians, 6 Walloon Social Christians and 14 Socialists. The further progress made in the elections by the linguistic parties forced his government, which fell in November 1972 because of Flemish P.S.C. insistence on a two-thirds majority for the last of the proposed decentralization measures, to accept a division of posts by language, and to declare its dedication to the realization of complete regional autonomy.

A small country, and comparatively poor in natural resources, Belgium has been increasingly troubled by its failure to modernize and to re-equip its industries, and by a national tendency to indulge in increased consumption and higher living standards. Successive Belgian governments have made determined efforts to stimulate a higher rate of fixed productive investment and to facilitate exports. These efforts included substantial investments in the Belgian Congo, *q.v.*, which became independent as the republic of Congo (Kinshasa) (now Zaïre) in 1960. There has been a customs union with Luxemburg since 1921, and with the Netherlands and Luxemburg, known as Benelux, *q.v.*, since 1947; in 1957 Belgium signed the Rome Treaties, *q.v.*

Belice. The name given to the colony of British Honduras, *q.v.*, by Guatemala, *q.v.*, which claims the territory and regards it as a Guatemalan department.

Bella, Mohammed Ben. Algerian politician; born 1916 at Marnia, Algeria, near the Moroccan border, he served in the French Army during the Second World War. After demobilization he first joined the Movement for the Triumph of Democratic Liberties (M.T.L.D.), an Algerian nationalist movement led by Messali Hadj; but later left it to form the more violent Organisation Spéciale. In 1950 he was arrested and sentenced to seven years' imprisonment, but he escaped in March 1952 and went to Cairo. He there founded the Revolutionary Committee for Unity and Action which later became the Front de Libération Nationale, *q.v.* (F.L.N.). In 1956 he was flying in a Moroccan airliner to Tunis to meet emissaries of the French government, when the French persuaded the French pilot to land at Algiers; Ben Bella was arrested and taken to France. He was released in 1962; he became the first Prime Minister on 26 September 1962, and later added to that office the post of President; in June 1965 he was deposed in a *coup d'état* led by Houari Boumédienne, *q.v.*

Benelux. A Customs Union between Belgium, the Netherlands, and Luxemburg, it is the result of a convention concluded in London on 5 September 1944, and came into existence on 29 October 1947; a common customs tariff came into force on 1 January 1948. After unification of the tariffs an attempt was made to unify excise and indirect taxes, which varied greatly between the communities. It was realized that the success of such negotiations would depend upon a considerable degree of economic integration, the reconciliation of the controlled economy of the Netherlands and the liberal economy of Belgium, and greater specialization by each state.

Measures to free the movement of goods from restrictions were for some time not coupled with any similar liberation of capital and labour. The restrictions on capital movements and the immobility of workers, combined with the exclusion of agriculture from the free-trade principle, hindered development of the union, although there was a steady expansion of mutual trade. Difficulties were caused in particular by intensive Dutch competition in Belgian markets, and it was necessary to introduce concessions by which a state could impose quotas and import duties against foreign competition.

In 1954 the members agreed to establish a common trade and payments policy for Benelux in relation to other countries. This meant that treaties with other countries concerning quotas, financial arrangements, and other commercial details would be negotiated by Benelux on behalf of all three members. No separate treaties were to be concluded.

A treaty establishing an Economic Union between the three countries was concluded at The Hague on 3 February 1958. It provided for a free flow of capital, goods, services, and traffic, and free movement of people; these aims were largely achieved before the Treaty came into force on 1 November 1960. It also envisaged a common commercial policy in relations with other countries, and coordination of policy on investments, agriculture, and social matters.

Benn, Anthony Wedgwood, British Labour Party politician; born 3 April 1925, the eldest surviving son of the late Viscount Stansgate whose title he disclaimed in 1963; educated at Westminster and Oxford University. After war service in the R.N.V.R., he went into journalism. In 1950 he entered the House of Commons as the member for Bristol South-East, and was returned again in 1951, 1955 and 1959. He was re-elected in May 1961 after his candidature had been questioned on the grounds that, having succeeded to his father's title, he was now a peer of the realm and eligible only for membership of the House of Lords, and he was unseated by the Election Court in July 1961. As soon as enabling legislation had been passed (the Peerage Act 1963 for which he was largely responsible) he officially relinquished his title and was reinstated as the member for his former constituency from August 1963. He was first elected to the National Executive of the Labour Party in 1959 and became the Party Chairman for the year 1971-2. He held office as Postmaster-General from 1964 to 1966, as Minister of Technology 1966 to 1970, and also as Minister of Power from 1969 to 1970, in the Wilson administration. He was a main spokesman of the opposition within the Labour Party to the terms of British entry into the E.E.C., *q.v.*, negotiated by the Conservative government in 1971.

Berlin. A city in the German *Land* (province) of Brandenburg, and until 1945 the capital of Germany. Under the Protocol of 5 September 1944 and the Berlin Declaration of 5 June 1945, it was agreed that whereas the rest of Germany was to be divided into four Zones of Occupation, Greater Berlin should be governed as a single entity by France, the U.K., the U.S.A., and the U.S.S.R. Though Berlin was within the Russian Zone, it would thus be impossible for any one power to claim that it occupied the former capital. Within Berlin itself the pattern of the quadripartite administration of Germany was reproduced, the city being split up into four areas. The position of the area occupied by France, the U.K., and the U.S.A. made it easy for the U.S.S.R. to cause difficulties for the western powers when international relations were bad, as it is dependent for its supplies on the main road through Eastern Germany to Western Germany. After the failure of the Foreign Ministers' Conference in Moscow, the declaration of the Truman Doctrine, *q.v.*, and the announcement of the Marshall Plan, *q.v.*, all of which events took place in 1947, the Russian authorities introduced new traffic regulations in March 1948 which threatened to force the western powers to abandon the Western Sector. The Berlin airlift, by which supplies were flown into Berlin by day and night for several months, defeated this manoeuvre. When the German Federal Republic, *q.v.*, became independent and sovereign on 5 May 1955, the new regime did not apply to the Western Sector, but instead the western powers declared that they would normally exercise powers only in matters relating to: (1) the interests of their forces in Berlin; (2) disarmament and demilitarization; (3) occupation costs; (4) Berlin's relations with foreign authorities; (5) authority over the Berlin police in connection with security matters. The treaty by which the U.S.S.R. gave independence and sovereignty to the German Democratic Republic on 6 October 1955 provided that the Republic should have control over traffic, except military vehicles, passing between Berlin and the German Federal Republic. The German Democratic Republic levies dues on western traffic and thus adds to the considerable expense of maintaining the Western Sector. This expense is borne partly by the German Federal Republic and partly by the U.S.A., which invested large sums in Berlin industries. There are an estimated 2,141,400 people in the Western Sector (1968) and 1,085,441 (1970) in the Eastern Sector. In August 1961 the German Democratic Republic effectively stopped all westward migration of refugees by erecting the Berlin Wall; illegal migration has continued, but there have been many deaths at the frontier.

In March 1970 talks were opened between the four powers concerned on the future status of Berlin. Agreement was to be a pre-condition of a European Security Conference. A final settlement was reached between competent German authorities, as defined by the quadripartite agreement, on 3 September 1971. This covered transit traffic, travelling and visiting facilities, and posts and telecommunications (including colour television transmission) between East and West Berlin. The agreement was to come into force when the treaties with Poland and the U.S.S.R. concerning the future of the Oder-Neisse Line, *q.v.*, which implied recognition of the German Democratic Republic, were ratified by the West German Parliament. This occurred on 17 May 1972.

Bermuda. A British colony comprising some three hundred small islands, of which twenty are inhabited, in the west Atlantic, 677 miles from New York; area 20·5 sq. m., of which a tenth was leased in 1941 for 99 years to the U.S. government for naval and air bases; population (1970) 53,000, mainly coloured; capital Hamilton. The islands were discovered in 1503 by Juan Bermudez, after whom they were named, but remained uninhabited until 1609 when they were settled by the British Somers' Islands Company. In 1684 they became a Crown colony.

Until 1963 the franchise was based on property. The introduction of universal suffrage in 1966 quadrupled the electorate, and a new Constitution of June 1967 abolished all electoral privileges attached to ownership of property. Government is by a Legislative Council, or Upper House, nominated by the Governor, and a House of Assembly of 40 members elected in two-member constituencies, a concession to the former custom of electing four members for each of the nine ancient parishes of Bermuda. At elections held in May 1968 the United Bermuda Party, a moderate right-wing party, largely representing the white population but with many negro members and led by Sir Henry Tucker, won 30 seats. The left-wing Progressive Labour Party, a predominantly negro party led by Lowis Browne-Evans, which had been formed in 1963 and which had campaigned for independence and the termination of British rule, won 10 seats; its electoral defeat was regarded as a demonstration of support for the British connection. Sir Henry Tucker then became Prime Minister at the head of the colony's first cabinet.

The tourist industry was developed during the nineteenth century and still provides the major source of revenue. Eighty-five per cent of tourists come from the U.S.A. The climate permits double cropping for most vegetables, some of which are exported together with concentrated essences and drugs. However the area of cultivable land is diminishing rapidly owing to building development which is encouraged by the low level of taxation.

Bessarabia. An area between the rivers Dniester and Prut in the extreme south-west of the European part of the U.S.S.R. It was part of the Turkish Empire until 1812, when it was ceded to Russia; after being defeated in war Russia was forced to yield most of the coastal area of Bessarabia to the principality of Moldavia (which was later united with Wallachia to form Romania) under the Treaty of Paris in 1856, but recovered this part in 1878. When Russia collapsed as a military power at the end of the First World War, Romania seized Bessarabia and incorporated it as a province. In June 1940 the U.S.S.R. forced Romania to return Northern Bukovina and Bessarabia. The greater part of the territory was then incorporated in the Moldavian Soviet Socialist Republic. The rest, with Northern Bukovina, was added to the Ukraine, q.v. Bessarabia and Northern Bukovina have the densest populations in the U.S.S.R. (approximately four million in 20,000 sq. m.).

Betancourt, Rómulo. Venezuelan politician; born 1908 in Miranda State, the son of a wholesale grocer, he studied law at Caracas but was imprisoned and forced to go into exile in Colombia following student demonstrations against the dictatorship of President Vicente Gómez. He moved to Costa Rica where he joined a pro-Communist group, but in 1936 he discarded his Communist affiliations and, after the death of Gómez, returned to Venezuela. He was again exiled in 1938 for leading an anti-Communist but left-wing underground movement; he returned to Venezuela three years later to organize the clandestine National Democratic Party, later renamed Acción Democrática en el Gobierno (A.D.). His support came mainly from the oil-workers, trade unions, and the peasants. In 1945 he helped to overthrow President Medina Angarita, and was elected provisional President, holding the office until the election of the A.D. candidate, Dr Gallegos, in 1947 at the first free elections in Venezuelan history. When the Gallegos government was overthrown by a military *coup* in 1948 and the A.D. declared illegal, he again left the country to live in Cuba and the U.S.A. for a period of ten years. A popular rising in January 1958, backed by a section of the army, deposed the dictator, Marcos Pérez Jiménez, and made possible the return to free elections which Betancourt contested. He was elected President in December 1958, winning 49 per cent of the total vote and defeating the out-going President, Rear-Admiral Wolfgang Larrazábal Ugueto. During his presidential term he survived an attempted assassination, plotted by the Dominican Republic which was later censured by the Organization of American States, *q.v.* He was succeeded in 1963 by his nominee, Dr Raúl Leoni, but continued to lead the A.D. and to contribute to published discussion on political philosophy. He remains one of the few effective democratic leaders in Latin America.

Bhutan. An Indian protectorate situated between India and Tibet, with the North-East Frontier Agency to the east and Nepal and Sikkim to the west; area 18,147 sq. m.; population approximately 810,000; capital Thimphu. The territory was annexed by the U.K. in 1865, but in 1910 the British government agreed not to interfere in the internal administration, while the Bhutan government agreed to be 'guided by the advice' of the British government in regard to its external relations. The old arrangements were superseded when India, which had become independent in 1947, concluded a fresh treaty with Bhutan in 1949, but the relationship with India is similar to the previous relationship with the U.K. India pays an annual subsidy to Bhutan. China claims part of the country, and

Chinese maps have shown approximately 300 sq. m. of eastern Bhutan as part of China.

Bhutan is ruled by a hereditary monarchy, with the assistance of the Tsongdu (Assembly). King Jigme Dorji Wangchuk (born 1929), was installed in 1952. In 1968 he introduced a constitutional amendment making continuity of any monarch's rule dependent on popular approval. Rice, timber, and wheat are exported, and there are valuable forests.

Bhutto, Zulfiqar Ali. Pakistini politician; born 1928 into a wealthy Moslem family of former Rajputs (a Hindu warrior caste) who had been converted in the sixteenth century; educated at the University of California and at Christ Church, Oxford. He lectured on International Law at the University of Southampton and then qualified as a barrister practising, on his return to Pakistan, in the West Pakistan High Court. He was appointed Minister of Commerce in President Ayub Khan's Cabinet in 1958, Minister for Information in 1960, Minister for Industry and Natural Resources in 1962 and Foreign Minister in 1963, in which post he was responsible for cultivating the new policy of close alliance with China. He resigned in 1966 because of his disapproval of the Tashkent Agreement, *q.v.*, with India, and went into open opposition the following year when he formed the Pakistan People's Party with a programme of 'Islamic socialism', a combination of economic radicalism and anti-Indian nationalism. In the elections held in December 1970 his party won 81 of the 138 West Pakistani seats in the National Assembly. When President Yahya Khan, following the secession of East Pakistan and the defeat of Pakistan in the war with India, resigned on 20 December 1971, he was appointed President of Pakistan (the fourth President and the first civilian to hold the post). He has described himself as 'a democratic socialist who believes in socialism on the Willy Brandt or British pattern'.

Biafra. The Eastern Region of Nigeria, *q.v.*, which unilaterally declared itself an independent republic on 30 May 1967. It was not recognized by the Federal Government of Nigeria, which declared the secession to be an act of rebellion and attempted to reassert its authority by force. After prolonged civil war in which the rebels were supplied with arms by France and Portugal, the Biafran army surrendered on 13 January 1970 and accepted the restoration of Federal authority.

Bilateral Agreements. Agreements between two parties, as opposed to multilateral agreements which are concluded by more than two parties.

Bipartisan Foreign Policy. A foreign policy on which both government and opposition parties agree. The expression is used with special reference to the U.S.A. A noted advocate of such a foreign policy, after he had abandoned isolationism, was the late Senator Vandenberg, who stated on 5 January 1950: 'To me "bipartisan foreign policy" means a mutual effort under our indispensable two-party system to unite our official voice at the water's edge so that America speaks with maximum authority against those who would divide and conquer us and the free world. It does not involve the remotest surrender of free debate in determining our position. On the contrary, frank cooperation and free debate are indispensable to ultimate unity. In a word, it simply seeks national security as a partisan advantage. Every foreign policy must be totally debated (and I think the record proves it has been) and the "loyal Opposition" is under special obligation to see that this occurs.' A bipartisan foreign policy poses a dilemma for an administration because in theory both administration and opposition are entitled to credit for any successes that the policy may have had. Critics say (a) that any fundamental differences of principle between parties should be reflected in foreign as well as in home affairs, and (b) that the Vandenberg statement shows how difficult it is to define bipartisan foreign policy; if argument is permitted while the policy is formulated, it is difficult to say when it should stop, for a nation should always be ready to discuss the bases of its foreign policy in order to adapt itself to an ever-changing world.

Black Power. The declared aim of the militant wing of the movement for Civil Rights, q.v., in the United States of America. The expression was first used on 17 June 1967 by Stokely Carmichael, chairman of the Student Non-Violent Co-ordinating Committee, in a speech during a march from Memphis, Tennessee, to Jackson, Mississippi, to encourage negroes to register as voters. The use of the slogan 'black power' led to serious divisions of opinion between the more moderate organizations engaged in the campaign for Civil Rights, such as the Southern Christian Leadership Conference (led by the late Martin Luther King, q.v.), the National Association for the Advancement of Colored People and the National Urban League, and the groups, the Congress on Racial Equality (C.O.R.E.) and the Student Non-Violent Co-ordinating Committee (S.N.C.C.) which regard the acquisition and exploitation of power by the negro as the most effective way of redressing the disabilities of Segregation, q.v.

Blockade. The prevention of supplies from reaching an enemy by sea, either by placing ships outside an enemy port or by an attempt to cut off an entire country. In international law neutral merchant ships which attempt to break a blockade can be confiscated. In the First and Second World Wars the U.K. attempted to blockade Germany. A pacific blockade may take place where there is no state of war; it consists of a temporary suspension of the commerce of an offending state, by the prevention of access to its shores, but without recourse to other hostile measures. In 1862 the U.K. instituted a peaceful blockade of Rio de Janeiro to exact redress for the plunder of a British ship wrecked on the Brazilian coast, but the blockade was confined to Brazilian ships.

Bogota Conference. April to May 1948; the Ninth International Conference of American States, held at Bogota, Colombia, which set up the Organization of American States, *q.v.*, a stronger version of the Pan American Union, *q.v.*

Bolivia. An independent South American state; area 424,160 sq. m.; population (1971 estimate) 5,062,500, of whom two thirds are Indians, the rest mixed races or white; capital Sucre; Government centre La Paz; the Catholic Church was disestablished in 1961 but is still subsidized by the state. The country's liberator was Simon Bolivar (1783–1830). Since the Pacific War (1879–82), Bolivia has had no sea outlet; it is barred from the Pacific by Chile and from the Atlantic by Paraguay, a situation which has caused wars with Paraguay. In 1952 the National Revolutionary Movement (M.N.R.) seized power after heavy fighting, and suspended the Senate and the Chamber of Deputies. Supported by most peasants and the Indian tin-miners, the M.N.R. won the elections held in June 1956 and in June 1960. On 6 August 1960 Dr Victor Paz Estenssoro (President from 1952 to 1956) again became President, but on 4 November 1964 he was deposed by a junta led by Vice-President René Barrientos Ortuño, an air force general disliked by the miners and those on the left. He shared the Presidency with General Alfredo Ovando Candia until January 1966, was elected President in July 1966 and was succeeded, on his death in April 1969, by his Vice-President, Luis Adolfas Siles Salinas. His party, the Bolivian Revolutionary Front, a coalition of five centre and right-wing parties, won 18 of the 27 seats in the Senate and 82 of the 102 seats in the lower house. On 26 September 1969 General Ovando ousted President Siles and assumed the presidency but was himself forced to resign from office on 6 October 1970 after a power struggle between right and left-wing army officers. The left wing installed General Juan José Torres as President; he agreed to implement a policy of nationalization, offering to pay full compensation for the assets of the U.S. Gulf Oil Corporation providing that the U.S.A. reopened world markets to Bolivian oil. Torres also released from prison Jules Régis Debray, a French journalist and intellectual, who had been sentenced in November 1967 to a term of thirty years for his participation in the guerilla rebellion led by Ernesto (Che) Guevara, *q.v.* Increasing left-wing activity, and the creation in April 1971 of a new Socialist Party comprising the National Union of the Revolutionary Left (U.N.I.R.), the Workers' Front of Revolutionary Action (F.A.R.O.) and the National Liberation Front (F.L.N.), produced a right-wing coup on 22 August 1971, the 193rd political coup since Bolivia achieved independence in 1825. Colonel Hugo Banzer Suarez assumed the presidency and appointed a cabinet consisting of members of the M.N.R., the Army, and the F.S.B., the extreme right-wing Bolivian Socialist Falange. He announced that there would be no reversal of the nationalization of the Gulf Oil Corporation and that Bolivia would continue the relationship with the U.S.S.R. which had been renewed in 1969. However there was to be no rapprochement with Cuba or the O.A.S., *q.v.*, and no elections would be held in the foreseeable future. He aimed to restore the confidence of foreign investors and raise Bolivia's declining level of production.

Bolivia is, after Malaya, the world's largest producer of tin, and also has oil, antimony and silver deposits. One of the most influential tin-mine owners was the Bolivian millionaire Patino; American companies also had extensive interests in the mines. The tin companies are said to have been able to bring down any government that was hostile to them but in 1952 their mines were nationalized by President Paz Estenssoro. This was the most important act of nationalization in Latin America since Mexico nationalized oil in 1938. The M.N.R. government tried to assert Bolivian economic nationalism, to utilize its mineral resources and to integrate the Indians, who had been virtually slaves, into the life of the country; they were given the vote in 1952. Land reform and improvements in agricultural techniques remain urgent necessities. There is acute poverty among the Indians and 70 per cent of the country's food has to be imported. To assist Bolivia, and protect the government from further revolt, the U.S.A. has bought much of the tin surplus for its strategic stockpile, and provided wheat and economic aid to a greater degree than to any other country in the world except Viet-Nam.

Bolshevism. An alternative name for Communism. When the Russian Social-Democratic Party split over the issue of radicalism or moderation in 1903, the radical faction, headed by Lenin (1870–1924, leader of the 1917 Revolution and first Head of State of the Soviet Union), polled a majority of votes at the Party congress. The Russian for majority is *bolshinstvo*, and hence the radicals were called Bolsheviki, meaning members of the majority. The moderate Socialists were called Mensheviki, derived from *menshinstvo*, meaning minority. In western countries the word Bolshevik is generally used in a derogatory sense, and sometimes to describe any radical.

Borneo. An island between the South China Sea and the Java Sea, belonging for the most part, under the name of Kalimantan, to Indonesia (which claims to be entitled to all of Borneo) but containing also, along its northern coast, Brunei, *q.v.*, and the Malaysian territories of Sabah, *q.v.*, and Sarawak, *q.v.*

Bosphorus. The northern part of the straits which connect the Mediterranean and the Black Seas, the southern part being the Dardanelles, *q.v.*

Botswana. An independent republic within the British Commonwealth, it lies between the Zambesi river on the north and the Molopo river on the south, with South-West Africa (Namibia) to the west and Rhodesia and Transvaal (part of South Africa) to the east; estimated area 220,000 sq. m.; population (1970 estimate) 648,000, of whom only 8,000 were of non-African stock; capital Gaberones. The leading tribes are the Bamangwato, whose capital is Serowe, the Bakwena, the Bangwakatse and the Batawana. As Bechuanaland, *q.v.*, it became a British protectorate in 1885 when the U.K., concerned to prevent the extension of German territory eastward from South-West Africa, eventually yielded to appeals from the chiefs of the Batawana tribes to defend their interests against the Boers from the Transvaal. When South Africa achieved independence in 1909, guarantees were given by the British government that the territory would not be transferred to South African rule without the consent of the inhabitants, and it became one of the High Commission Territories, *q.v.*, administered from Mafeking by the High Commissioner for South Africa. In 1963 Bechuanaland was made independent of High Commission rule and, under its own resident Governor, became internally self-governing on 1 March 1965. At the first election ever held, and on a basis of universal suffrage, the multi-racial Bechuanaland Democratic Party (B.D.P. or Domkrag), a moderate party with strong support from the tribal areas, led by Seretse Khama (hereditary paramount chief of the Bamangwato tribe, who has an English wife), won 28 seats in the Legislative Assembly. The remaining 3 seats went to the left-wing Bechuanaland People's Party, led by Philip Matante, which attracted support mainly from the towns. Seretse Khama then became Prime Minister; on 30 September 1966, when full independence was achieved, he became the first President of the Republic of Botswana He was reappointed for a second term after the elections of 1969 in which the B.D.P. won 24 seats, the B.P.P. 3 seats, the Bechuanaland National Front 3 seats and the Bechuanaland Independence Party 1 seat.

Government is by the President and an Assembly of 31 elected members and 4 specially elected members. A House of Chiefs acts in an advisory capacity and consists of the chiefs of the eight principal Batswana tribes, four members elected from among their own number by the sub-chiefs residing in the State Land Areas and three specially elected members. The economy of Botswana is based on cattle. In 1965 and 1966 severe drought killed off many herds and weakened the rest; total disaster was averted by assistance from U.N. agencies and from the British government. However, recent discoveries of copper-ore and copper-nickel at Matsitama and Pelikwe of medium grade coal (suitable for generating electricity), and the possibilities of exploiting salt and soda ash pans at Makari-kari have attracted U.S., Canadian and South African investment which could transform the economy. Meanwhile there is considerable dependence upon South Africa (the currency is the South African Rand), both economically and for technical and scientific services, although this has not prevented Botswana from giving asylum to South Africa's political refugees.

Boumédienne, Colonel Houari. Algerian politician; born Mohammed Boukharouba in 1925 at Guelmain Oran, the son of a farm labourer. He studied Arab literature at the University of Tunis and at the El-Azhar University in Cairo where he took up teaching. It was there in 1954 that he met Ben Bella, *q.v.*, and joined the insurrection against French rule. In 1955 he landed secretly on an Oran beach with nine men; the following year he was in command of the whole rebel movement in western Algeria. By 1960 he had taken command of the exiled army of the F.L.N., *q.v.*, in Tunis, where he built up a highly-trained fighting force of 60,000 men equipped with weapons from Egypt and the U.S.S.R. When Algeria became independent in 1963 he tried to exert political influence by military threats. In July 1962 the President, Ben Khedda, dismissed Boumédienne from command of the army; he reacted by marching on Algiers one month later and installing Ben Bella as head of the government. He was immediately appointed Minister of Defence. For three years he cooperated with Ben Bella and employed the army to crush opposition movements. But in June 1965, three weeks before a conference of Afro-Asian states, including China and possibly the U.S.S.R., was due to take place in Algiers, he deposed Ben Bella and as President of the Council of Revolution took control of the government. He is an advocate of international socialism; in 1963 he said: 'The Algerian revolution can no more be contained within its borders than was Colonel Nasser's by the Nile valley. The socialist revolution can triumph only if it spreads to Morocco and Tunisia.'

Bourbons. Once the French royal dynasty, but banned from France upon the establishment of the Third Republic in 1871. After the extinction of the direct Bourbon line in the last decade of the nineteenth century, the Bourbon-Orléans branch was recognized by French royalists as the legitimate pretender to the throne. Its head is the Comte de Paris. The Spanish line of the Bourbons, represented by Alfonso XIII, was dethroned in 1931; however, Spain was declared to be a monarchy in 1947 and the Spanish government indicated that Prince Juan Carlos de Bourbon (born 1938) might become King on the death or retirement of the head of state, General Franco.

Bourgeoisie. French for 'citizen class'; a term used by Marxist Socialists to denote the class of proprietors (other than agricultural), capitalists, manufacturers, merchants, persons with a business of their own, and members of liberal professions, as opposed to the 'proletariat', *q.v.*, who live only by selling their labour. Under this classification the bourgeoisie are subdivided into the industrialists and financiers on the one hand and the petty bourgeoisie on the other, comprising small artisans, shopkeepers, and others who are not far above the proletariat in their standard of living. According to this analysis the bourgeoisie became the ruling class with the rise of modern factory production, overthrowing the feudal class or aristocracy and its obsolete economic system. The rise of the bourgeoisie was accompanied by the spread of liberal ideas necessary to break the feudal bondage. According to the Marxist theory the bourgeois class is doomed to be succeeded by the proletariat, and turns to dictatorial systems to defend itself against this inevitable successor. At this stage the petty bourgeoisie is gradually proletarianized while the other section of the bourgeoisie is reduced to a small number of capitalists who control the nation's resources.

Bourguiba, Habib. Tunisian nationalist leader; born 1904. Educated in France, a moderate Moslem, he is the leader of the Destourian Socialist Party, *q.v.*, and for many years advocated the departure of the French and complete sovereignty for Tunisia. He was permitted by the French authorities to return to Tunis in June 1955, after ten years spent partly in exile and partly in French prisons. He became Prime

Minister on 8 April 1956, five days before Tunisian independence was declared. He was elected President and Head of Government on 25 July 1957, and re-elected to these posts, under the 1959 Constitution, on 8 November 1959.

Brainwashing. A treatment of persons designed to change their outlook. The expression was once limited to, and probably originated in, Communist treatment of prisoners aimed at altering their political and moral outlook on the western world. It is now often used loosely to describe any change in attitude on the part of a prisoner resulting in sympathy with his captors' views or a readiness to confess to crimes. There may be an apparent alteration in personality or a revision of opinions on certain topics. These changes may have been brought about by torture (mental, or physical, or both), rewards of preferential treatment instead of degrading circumstances, or propaganda and argument. Though there is no doubt that all these methods have been applied, there is little reliable information as to the effectiveness of each method or the extent to which each has been responsible for prisoners' altered outlooks. A U.S. governmental committee, which laid down a new code of conduct for prisoners, reported in 1955 that the failure of American officers to assume responsibility caused a decay of morale among U.S. troops in some Korean prisoner-of-war camps during the Korean War (1950–53), and that the average American prisoner was under a serious handicap when faced with attempts to indoctrinate him. He was unable, the report said, to answer pro-Communist arguments with democratic arguments, and the committee attributed to this fact the readiness of some prisoners to accept Communist teachings.

Brandt, Willy. West German Social Democratic politician; born in 1914 in Lubeck as Herbert Karl Frahm. His writings in Socialist newspapers made him unpopular with the Nazis, and in 1933 he fled to Norway, using the pseudonym which he has retained. He studied at the University of Oslo and later worked as a journalist in Sweden. In 1945 he returned to Berlin as a Norwegian citizen with the rank of Major, and in 1948 had his German citizenship restored. He was elected in 1950 to the Berlin House of Representatives of which he later became President, and in 1957 he became Burgomaster of Berlin. In 1964 he succeeded Erich Ollenhauer as leader of the Social Democratic Party (S.D.P.) and in 1966, when Kurt Kiesinger, *q.v.*, formed a coalition government of the Christian Democratic Union and the S.D.P., he was appointed Federal Vice-Chancellor and Minister of Foreign Affairs. After the Federal elections of September 1969 he formed a government in coalition with the Free Democratic

Party. He was elected Chancellor on 22 October 1969 by 251 to 235 votes, two more than the required constitutional minimum of 249, and became the first S.D.P. Chancellor of Germany for 39 years. He was re-elected Chancellor by 269 to 223 votes following the S.D.P. victory in the Federal elections in November 1972 which had been precipitated by the parliamentary opposition to his *Ostpolitik, q.v.*

Brazil, United States of. The largest and most populous South American republic; area 3,286,000 sq. m.; population (1970) 93,200,000; capital Brasilia; language Portuguese. Eleven per cent of the population is negro, 27 per cent brown, and 62 per cent white or of white descent. Brazil was a Portuguese colony until it achieved independence in 1822. It is the world's largest producer of coffee. Potentially a rich country, it is over-dependent on its vital coffee exports, in spite of the efforts to stabilize coffee prices which have been made by the group set up by 12 South American states. There are believed to be large reserves of oil, but the only important wells are at Bahia; the country produces less than one half of the oil that it consumes. The government oil monopoly, Petrobras, enforces a rule by which no oil interests can be acquired by foreigners, but it has insufficient resources to develop the reserves fully. The hydro-electric potential is nearly as great as that of the U.S.A., and is the fourth largest in the world; the country contains about one quarter of the world's known iron-ore deposits. There has been investment by Japanese interests in Brazilian cotton mills, by American business in the automobile and rubber industries and by the Schneider-Creusot group in heavy industry. Inflation, which in 1971 was curbed to 20 per cent, has consistently overtaken growth, despite a healthy annual expansion rate of some 9 per cent.

The Brazilian political scene was dominated for 30 years by President Getúlio Vargas who for much of that time ruled as a dictator. He committed suicide in August 1954. His proclaimed preoccupation was with the hardships of the underprivileged. Under the 1946 Constitution the President was elected directly by the people for five years and could not succeed himself. From 1956 to 1961 Juscelino Kubitschek held the office of President. He was supported by the Partido Trabalhista Brasiliero or P.T.B. (the Brazilian Labour Party created by Vargas) and the Partido Social Democratica (the Social Democratic Party, at that time the largest group in the Chamber of Deputies). In 1961 the candidate of Kubitschek was defeated in the presidential elections by Jânio Quadros, a P.T.B. member who was regarded as a reformist. He resigned the same year and was succeeded by the Vice-President, João Belchior

Marques Goulart, leader of the P.T.B. His inability to control a price inflation then running at 100 per cent gave the army, which was opposed to the proposed P.T.B. social reforms, the excuse to remove Goulart from office. He was succeeded in April 1964 by Marshal Humberto Castelo Branco who assumed dictatorial powers in October 1965. He nominated as his successor Marshal Artur da Costa e Silva, the Minister for War who had assisted in the overthrow of Goulart and was known to hold strong anti-Communist views, who was elected indirectly by Congress in October 1966 and installed in March 1967 for a four-year term.

In July 1967 an attempt, supported by former Presidents Kubitschek and Goulart, was made to restore direct elections through a Frente Ampla (Broad Front) by Carlos Lacerda, a former State Governor of Guanabara, who attacked the government as 'a marriage between the military and a decadent oligarchy'. The Front was banned in April 1968 and Lacerda imprisoned, as were several deputies of A.R.E.N.A. (Alliance for National Renewal), the pro-government party formed by presidential decree in 1965, who caused the suspension of Congress in December 1968 when they refused the army's request that they lift the parliamentary immunity on Moreira Alves, the deputy for Guanabara. In August 1969 da Costa e Silva was replaced by a triumvirate of the armed services, and his period of office was terminated. He was then formally succeeded by General Garrastazú Medici who assumed office on 30 October 1969 for a term to expire in March 1974, by which time he pledged the restoration of democracy and a return to indirect presidential elections. His Vice-President was Admiral Augusto Rademaker Grunewald, one of the triumvirate who had deposed President da Costa.

In the first Congressional elections held since 1966, on 15 November 1970, A.R.E.N.A. won 223 of the contested seats in the Chamber of Deputies and 59 in the Senate; the Movement for Democratic Brazil (M.D.B.), the sole opposition group, won 87 and 7 seats. Voting is compulsory but the number of spoiled ballot papers varied from 30 to 50 per cent of the total; in Sao Paulo some 2,500,000 invalid votes were cast. The government claimed that the result 'legalized' the appointment of General Medici as President in 1969; it was also regarded as reflecting public support for a determined campaign by the army during 1969 and 1970 against urban guerillas, whose activities had included the kidnapping of the U.S. Ambassador.

Brazzaville Group. Members of the African and Malagasy Union, *q.v.*

Bretton Woods. A town in New Hampshire, U.S.A., where the United Nations Monetary and Financial Conference set up the World Bank (International Bank for Reconstruction and Development, *q.v.*) and the International Monetary Fund, *q.v.*, in July 1944.

Brezhnev, Leonid Ilyich. President of the Presidium of the Supreme Soviet of the U.S.S.R.; the son of a steel-worker, he was born at Kamenskoye (now Dneprodzerzhinsk) in the Ukraine, 19 December 1906; educated at the Institute of Metallurgy, Dneprodzerzhinsk. After specializing in land utilization in the Urals from 1927 to 1931, he became a member of the Communist Party in 1931 and was an engineer at the Dzerzhinsky metallurgical plant from 1935 to 1937. During the war against Germany he was head of the political section of the Soviet 18th Army, with the rank of colonel. He became First Secretary of the Central Committee of the Moldavian Communist Party in 1950, in which year he was elected to the Supreme Soviet to represent the Lenin District of Dnepropetrovsk. He was then appointed to the Central Committee of the Communist Party of the U.S.S.R. in 1952, to the Presidium of the Central Committee in 1957, and to the Presidency of the Presidium of the Supreme Soviet (resigning his party offices) on 7 May 1960. Although the latter post is equivalent to that of head of state, he added to his duties on 22 June 1963 by becoming also one of the Secretaries of the Central Committee of the Communist Party of the U.S.S.R. He became First Secretary of the Communist Party of the U.S.S.R. in October 1964 upon the resignation of Nikita Khrushchev, *q.v.*

British Antarctic Territory. A British colony in the Antarctic Continent, *q.v.*, including the Graham Land peninsula, the South Shetland Islands, the South Orkney Islands and other islands. It is the British sector of the Antarctic, consisting (under an Order in Council which came into force on 3 March 1962) of all land south of the 60th parallel and lying between the 20th and 80th meridians of west longitude. The sector was formerly part of the Falkland Islands Dependencies (*see* Falkland Islands); the division took place as a result of the Antarctic Treaty, which came into force in June 1961, freezing territorial claims for 30 years.

British Cameroons. *See* Cameroons, British.

British Commonwealth. Formerly called the British Empire, it is an association of 31 independent states: Australia, Bangladesh, Barbados, Botswana, Canada, Cyprus, Fiji, Gambia, Ghana, Guyana, India, Jamaica, Kenya, Lesotho, Malawi, Malaysia, Malta, Mauritius, New Zealand, Nigeria, Sierra Leone, Singapore, Sri Lanka, Swaziland, Tanzania, Tonga, Trinidad and Tobago, Uganda, United

Kingdom, Western Samoa, Zambia and their dependencies. Its total population is about 800 million. The Commonwealth is neither a state nor a federation; it has no single parliament or government, and no central defence force or executive power. The states were formerly integral parts of the United Kingdom's imperial territories. Until 1925 the Colonial Office was responsible for all the territories except India, which was entrusted to a separate department. In that year there was created the post of Secretary of State for Dominion Affairs, with responsibility for the self-governing Dominions (which then comprised Australia, Canada, Newfoundland, New Zealand and South Africa), for the self-governing territory of Southern Rhodesia, and for the South African High Commission Territories, *q.v.*, of Basutoland, Bechuanaland and Swaziland. The 1926 Imperial Conference described the Dominions as 'autonomous communities within the British Empire, equal in status, in no way subordinate one to another in any aspect of their domestic or foreign affairs, though united by a common allegiance to the Crown, and freely associated as members of the British Commonwealth of Nations'. In 1931 the Statute of Westminster, *q.v.*, gave statutory force to the description of the Dominions as autonomous and equal in status. Newfoundland lost its Dominion status in 1933 and became part of Canada 16 years later. After the Second World War, India and Pakistan (in 1947) and Ceylon (now renamed Sri Lanka) in 1948 became Dominions. In the following years, however, the expression 'Dominion' began to fall into disuse. The title of Secretary of State for Dominion Affairs was altered to Secretary of State for Commonwealth Relations in 1947, with the additional responsibility of handling the affairs of India, Pakistan, and later Ceylon. In 1968 the Commonwealth Office was merged with the Foreign Office.

The concept of allegiance to the Crown has also fallen into disuse. Bangladesh, Botswana, Cyprus, Gambia, Ghana, Guyana, India, Kenya, Malawi, Nigeria, Sierra Leone, Singapore, Sri Lanka, Tanzania, Uganda and Zambia are republics and owe no allegiance to the Queen, recognizing her only as Head of the Commonwealth, while Lesotho, Malaysia, Swaziland and Tonga are themselves independent monarchies. Burma, Ireland and Sudan elected to remain outside the Commonwealth when they became independent states, and rejected offers of Dominion status. From 1953 to 1963 Northern Rhodesia (now Zambia), Southern Rhodesia (now known as Rhodesia) and Nyasaland (now Malawi) comprised the Federation of Rhodesia and Nyasaland, but the Federation was not wholly independent, the U.K. being responsible for its foreign relations, and it did not qualify for Dominion status. Since Sri Lanka became independent in 1948 there has been a net addition of 21 states to the Commonwealth, including Ghana and Malaya which joined in 1957 (Malaya joined Sabah, Sarawak and Singapore to form Malaysia in 1963); Nigeria in 1960; Uganda in 1962; Cyprus, Sierra Leone and Tanganyika (which joined Zanzibar to form Tanzania in 1964) in 1963; Zambia in 1964; Gambia and Singapore (which seceded from Malaysia to become an independent state) in 1965; Botswana (formerly Bechuanaland), Barbados, Guyana and Lesotho (formerly Basutoland) in 1966; Mauritius and Swaziland in 1968; Fiji and Tonga in 1970. Western Samoa and Malta became independent in 1962 and 1964 respectively and were thenceforth treated as members of the British Commonwealth. In 1972 the newly-formed republic of Bangladesh applied for membership at the same time as Pakistan withdrew. A special membership was devised on 29 November 1968 for the former Australian Trusteeship territory of Nauru, *q.v.*

The dependencies of the independent member states are part of the British Commonwealth, and may be divided into Colonies, *q.v.*, Protected States, *q.v.*, Protectorates, *q.v.*, Trusteeship Territories, *q.v.*, and territories with Associate Status, *q.v.* In June 1965 there was established a British Commonwealth secretariat, based in London, with a Canadian, Arnold Smith, as Secretary-General. Technical aid experts have been employed by the secretariat to advise member states on resources, concessions and taxation. In 1971 a multilateral fund for technical cooperation was set up; Canada agreed to provide 40 per cent of the finance required, and the U.K. 30 per cent.

British Guiana. The former British colony, on the north-eastern seaboard of South America. It was seized from the Dutch in 1796, and finally ceded to Britain in 1814 as the three separate colonies of Essequibo, Demerara and Berbice; in 1831 the three colonies merged to become British Guiana. On 26 May 1966 the country achieved independence as Guyana, *q.v.*

British Honduras. A British colony on the east coast of Central America to the south and east of Mexico and to the east of Guatemala; area 8,867 sq. m.; population (1970) 120,000; capital Belmopan. The population is predominantly Negro, but fewer than two fifths is of pure African descent; the rest comprises Europeans (especially Spaniards), Amerindians, Asians and Caribs. The first English settlers came to cut log wood in 1638 and in 1670, by the Treaty of Madrid, Spain granted settlement rights to British colonists on the shores of the Belize river estuary. The area became a British colony under Jamaica in 1862 and independently in 1884. Until the risings against the Spaniards in 1821 Spain claimed the area; Guatemala, which achieved independence in 1839 on seceding from the United States of Central America, has also claimed the colony, with increasing insistence since 1945. There is no access to the sea, other than through British Honduras, from El Petén, the northern province of Guatemala. In 1946 the U.K. invited Guatemala to submit the dispute to the International Court of Justice, but the offer was not accepted. In 1960 the Guatemalan government established a new department of Belice which incorporated British Honduras. The dispute was referred in 1965 to President Johnson of the U.S.A., who appointed a mediator; his proposals, which provide for close cooperation between the two countries in foreign affairs, communications and economic development, were rejected by the government of British Honduras in May 1968. Claims have also been made by the Mexican government which alleges that Britain, by a treaty of 1783, conceded part of the territory to Spain, and that Mexico (as successor of the Spanish Captain-General of Yucatan) has inherited Spanish rights in the area.

Internal politics in the colony are affected by the territorial dispute. At elections held in December 1969, the second to be held under the Constitution which came into force on 6 January 1964, the People's United Party (P.U.P.), led by George Price, won 17 of the 18 seats in the House of Representatives (16 in 1965); the National Independence Party, led by Philip Goldson, won the remaining seat (2 in 1965). Both parties are reluctant to accept independence, which was offered in 1971, unless it is accompanied by a defence treaty. Price, who became Prime Minister after the 1965 elections, opposed the idea of Caribbean Federation, *q.v.*, and has rejected any economic link with the West Indies; his views were acceptable both to those who disliked the prospect of distant rule from the West Indies and to the many Catholics who are in sympathy with Latin American aspirations.

The colony produces cedar, mahogany, pine, rosewood and many hardwoods and woods suitable for pulp. Over 90 per cent of the area is forest. Citrus fruits, especially grapefruit, and chicle (the basis of chewing-gum) are exported, but there is considerable seasonal unemployment, and attempts by the Commonwealth Development Corporation to diversify the economy by encouraging cattle breeding, banana-growing and tourism have met with little success. The colony cannot support itself, and sufficient investment from the U.K. and the U.S.A. has not been forthcoming.

British North Borneo. Area in the northern part of the island of

Borneo, *q.v.*, which was administered on behalf of, and later by, the British government from 1878 to 1963 when it joined the Federation of Malaysia and became the State of Sabah, *q.v.*

British Somaliland. From 1886 to 1960 this was a British protectorate on the Gulf of Aden, between French Somaliland and the former trusteeship territory of Somalia, area 68,000 sq. m.; population 600,000; capital Hargeisa. The population, which is almost entirely nomadic, consists of Somali tribes who are Sunni Moslems and who raise camels, goats and sheep. In 1884 the Egyptians withdrew from the Somali coast and in 1886 the tribes placed themselves under British protection, undertaking never to cede their lands to another government. In 1897 the British agreed with Emperor Menelik, the predecessor of the Emperor of Ethiopia after he defeated the Italians at Adowa, that Ethiopian territory was to include some traditional tribal grazing grounds and wells; the Somalis, however, who were not consulted, were given the right to enter Ethiopia to use the grounds and wells. Ethiopia never administered this area. After the liberation of Ethiopia and Italian Somaliland (which later became part of Somalia) from Italy, the British continued to manage this area of approximately 25,000 sq. m. with its population of some 300,000. In November 1954 an Anglo-Ethiopian agreement provided for the return of the area to Ethiopia, but preserved the grazing rights of the tribes from British Somaliland. Ethiopia had refused an alternative offer of access to a port (Zeila) in British Somaliland in return for continued British administration of the area. After the 1954 agreement Ethiopia opened negotiations with a U.S. firm which wanted an oil-prospecting concession in the grazing grounds. Somali representatives, regarding French Somaliland, British Somaliland, and Somalia as a national territory which might one day, as Greater Somalia, be self-governing, objected strongly to the 1954 agreement. The disputed area comprises the Haud and the Reserved Area.

The British protectorate ended on 26 June 1960, when there was created the independent state of Somaliland, whose newly-established national assembly met the next day to pass an act of union with the Italian trusteeship territory of Somalia, *q.v.*, which itself became independent on 1 July 1960.

British West Indies. The British and former British colonies in the West Indies. They comprised Jamaica, *q.v.* (since 1962 a Dominion), in the Great Antilles, and Barbados, *q.v.* (since 1966 a Dominion), the Leeward Islands, Trinidad and Tobago, *q.v.* (since 1962 a Dominion), and the Windward Islands in the Lesser Antilles. In 1947 proposals were made for a close association between most of these colonies, with British Honduras, *q.v.*, in Central America and British Guiana (now Guyana, *q.v.*), in South America. The proposed union was often described as the Caribbean Federation, *q.v.* It existed, as the West Indies Federation, *q.v.*, from 3 January 1958 to 31 May 1962. A further attempt to form an Eastern Caribbean Federation (*see* Little Seven) failed when Barbados declared its independence in November 1966. The remaining colonies, with the exception of Montserrat and St Vincent, then accepted associate status, *q.v.*, with the United Kingdom and became the West Indies Associated States, *q.v.*

Brunei. A British protected state on the north coast of Borneo which, except for its coastal strip, is surrounded by the Malaysian state of Sarawak; area 2,226 sq. m.; population (1971) 135,000; capital Brunei. The state established relations with the U.K. in 1847 when the Sultan concluded a commercial treaty with the British government; it came under British protection in 1888, and the British government thus became responsible for defence and external affairs. The 1959 Constitution, Brunei's first written Constitution, established a Privy Council, an Executive Council and a Legislative Council. In 1964 the Sultan yielded to British pressure to introduce an elected legislature and a ministerial system of government, and in 1965 the Executive Council was replaced by a Council of Ministers under his presidency. The Sultan, Sir Omar Ali Saifuddin Wasa'dul Khairi Waddin, who had succeeded his brother in 1950, abdicated in favour of his son, Crown Prince Hassanal Bolkiah, on 4 October 1967. In 1971 Brunei became internally self-governing and the British High Commissioner ceased to have the right to advise the Sultan. After strenuous efforts on the part of the new Sultan to prevent the withdrawal of British military forces according to the decision taken in 1967, the British government agreed temporarily to retain responsibility for external defence. In 1972 the Brunei People's Independence Front, in a memorandum to the United Nations, attacked the continued British presence in Brunei.

Under the Constitution the Sultan cannot, without the consent of the Council of Ministers, surrender or cede any part of Brunei, or amalgamate, federate or unite any part with another territory. This was an issue in 1962 when the Party Ra'ayat, or People's Party, led by the Indonesian-educated Sardar Asahari, which won all the elective seats on the Legislative Council, advocated the creation of an independent northern Borneo state comprising Brunei, Sarawak and Sabah (then British North Borneo). In 1963 Sarawak and Sabah became member states of the Federation of Malaysia; Brunei thus retained its character as a Malay-Islamic sultanate. It is wealthier than its neighbours as a result of its oil industry, which employs three-quarters of the working population, and which enables its exports to yield more than five times the cost of its imports. The oilfield, which is based on Seria but extends offshore, is controlled by the Brunei Shell Petroleum Company.

Brussels Treaty Organization. Renamed Western European Union, *q.v.*, in 1955, it was created by the Brussels Treaty in March 1948, when Belgium, France, Luxemburg, the Netherlands, and the U.K., promised 'all the military and other aid and assistance in their power' if one of them was the object of an armed attack in Europe. This is a stricter obligation than that laid down for members of the North Atlantic Treaty Organization, *q.v.*, who must take 'such action as they deem necessary' if one of them is attacked. The Brussels Treaty also provided for quarterly meetings of Foreign Ministers to coordinate foreign policies, a group of sub-committees on economic, social, and cultural matters, a Permanent Commission comprising the four ambassadors in London and a British Foreign Office representative, a Permanent Military Committee, and a secretariat. The parties agreed to the abolition of visas and the mutual recognition of social insurance benefits. On 5 May 1955 Italy and the German Federal Republic entered the Organization, which then became the Western European Union.

Buffer State. A small state established or preserved between two greater states to prevent direct clashes between them.

Buganda. A kingdom and one of the four regions of Uganda, *q.v.*; capital Kampala. The Kabaka of Buganda, Sir Edward Frederick Mutesa II, was deported in November 1953 as a result of an alleged breach by him of the Uganda Agreement of 1900 which governed relations between Buganda and the British government. The latter said that he had not fulfilled his obligation to cooperate loyally in matters of day-to-day administration. The cause of the disagreement was the Kabaka's demand for the separation of Buganda, as an independent state, from the rest of Uganda. The Uganda High Court held in November 1954 that the 1900 Agreement did not bind the U.K., which could withdraw recognition at any time as an act of state. It stated that if it were mistaken, and the agreement were binding, it was incorrect to say that the Kabaka had not cooperated loyally, although the government could have relied on a breach of another term in the agreement, for he had certainly failed to abide by a policy decision.

The 1954 Namirembe Conference recommended that Buganda

should continue to be an integral part of Uganda, and that, while all the traditional dignities of the Kabaka should be fully safeguarded, Kabakas should, in future, be constitutional rulers bound not to prejudice the security and welfare of the Buganda people (the Baganda) and Uganda. The new constitution came into force in 1955.

The Kabaka returned in October 1955. In February 1962 there were elections to the Lukiko (the assembly) on a basis of universal suffrage. Kabaka Yekka ('the Kabaka only') won 65 seats and the Catholic-orientated Democratic Party won 3 seats in the area inhabited by the Banyoro. In October 1963 the Kabaka was elected President of Uganda; he was deposed in February 1966 and exiled to Britain where he died of alcoholic poisoning on 21 November 1969. The office of Kabaka remains vacant.

Bulganin, Nikolai Alexandrovich. Former Russian leader; born 1895. He joined the Communist Party in 1917 and served in the Cheka from 1918 to 1922. He held various industrial posts from 1922 onwards and in 1931 became Chairman of the Moscow Soviet, in which capacity he visited London. He became a member of the Central Committee of the Communist Party in 1935 and in 1937 represented the Moscow district in the Supreme Soviet. After the German invasion in 1941 he organized defence as a Lieutenant-General, becoming a Marshal of the U.S.S.R. in 1945. He was appointed a Deputy Chairman of the Council of Ministers in 1949, a First Deputy Chairman in 1953 upon the death of Stalin, and Chairman (a post roughly equivalent to that of Prime Minister) upon the resignation of Malenkov in February 1955. He was replaced as Chairman in April 1958 by Khrushchev, and in the same year became chairman of the State Bank.

Bulgaria. Independent state on the western coast of the Black Sea between Romania and Greece; area 42,818 sq. m.; population (1971) 8,524,000, of whom over 80 per cent belong to the Eastern Orthodox Church, which receives a state subsidy, and 14 per cent are Moslems; capital Sofia. Already part of the Turkish Empire, it achieved more freedom by becoming a principality under Turkish sovereignty by the Treaty of Berlin, 1878; in 1908 it became an independent kingdom. Though successful in the first Balkan war against Turkey in 1912, Bulgaria was defeated in the second Balkan war in 1913 when its former allies, Greece and Serbia, turned against it, with Romania. In the First World War Bulgaria supported Germany and collapsed in 1918. It lost the fertile Dobrudja (to Romania; it was returned after the Second World War); Thrace (to Turkey and

Greece); and Macedonia (to Greece and Yugoslavia). A radical peasant party came to power, only to be overthrown in 1923 by a *coup d'état* led by the army and four parties which merged to remove the agrarian reformers.

There was considerable social and political unrest between the two world wars, when Bulgaria, a very poor country, suffered severely from the economic depression, and support for the Communists gradually increased. The German army occupied Bulgaria in the Second World War, and when it withdrew in 1944 there was another *coup d'état* which put into power the Fatherland Front, a coalition of the Communists, the Agrarian Party and the Social Democratic Party. In 1945 the Agrarians and Social Democrats left the government; in 1946 a referendum demanded and secured the abolition of the monarchy (as the result of which Simeon II lost his throne) and the proclamation of a republic, and elections were held to the Grand National Assembly. With one deputy to every 30,000 electors, the Fatherland Front won 364 seats (277 for Communists) and the opposition 101 seats. In 1947 the Agrarian Party was suppressed, its leader, Nikola Petkov, being arrested (with 23 other Agrarian leaders) by order of the Communist Georgi Dimitrov, charged with conspiracy, and hanged. In 1948 some Social Democrats joined forces with the Communists, while others were arrested. No opposition Social Democrats were allowed to sit in the National Assembly after July 1948. At the elections held in December 1949, 97·66 per cent of the votes were cast in favour of the Fatherland Front; the Front still contained two political parties, the Communists and the remnants of the Agrarians. Elections held in 1953, 1962, 1966 and 1971 produced similar majorities (99·9 per cent in 1971) in favour of the Fatherland Front.

By 1949 the economic structure had been radically altered and the Communists were in complete control. The private sector of industry dropped from 83·6 per cent to 5 per cent of the total number of enterprises. Land was taken from the monasteries and private owners and divided among landless peasants and cooperative farms. In spite of increasing industrialization the country is still essentially agricultural with 99 per cent of the land in collective ownership. The disappointing economic situation (economically the country is probably the most backward in eastern Europe, with the exception of Albania) remains a preoccupation of Bulgarian politicians, led by Todor Zhivkov, First Secretary of the Communist Party and, since the introduction of a new Constitution in May 1971, Chairman of the State Council. Vigorous attempts are being made to increase trade with western European countries, especially Italy and West Germany, and to encourage tourism; however almost 90 per cent of total foreign trade is with Comecon, *q.v.*

The pre-war border disputes with Greece over Macedonia, *q.v.*, continued after 1945 and Bulgaria supplied arms to the Communist forces in Greece until 1948, but an agreement concluded in August 1955 provided for the avoidance, and settlement, of frontier disputes. In 1971, following the enlargement of the European Economic Community, *q.v.*, to include the U.K., which is an importer of Bulgarian foodstuffs, overtures were made to Greece on possible economic cooperation between the two countries.

Buraimi. An inland oasis comprising nine villages on the frontiers of the Sheikhdom of Abu Dhabi, *q.v.*, and the Sultanate of Oman, *q.v.*, it was the subject of a protracted dispute between Saudi Arabia and the two states of Abu Dhabi and Oman, most of whose territory lies in the concession area of the Iraq Petroleum Company, *q.v.* The oasis was thought to be situated near rich oilfields and was therefore of great interest to the Arabian American Oil Company (Aramco), which holds the Saudi Arabian concession. In August 1952 a Saudi Arabian armed force passed through Abu Dhabi, occupied part of the Muscat portion and distributed money. Skirmishing and accusations of bribery continued for two years until the British and Saudi Arabian governments in July 1954 agreed to arbitrate on the correct frontier between Saudi Arabia and Abu Dhabi and the sovereignty of Buraimi. Proceedings in the court of arbitration broke down in October 1955 when the British arbitrator, Sir Reader Bullard, resigned when it transpired that the Saudi Arabian arbitrator had been in touch with his government during the hearing. The forces of the Sheikh of Abu Dhabi and the Sultan of Muscat and Oman, supported by the levies of the Trucial Coast, *q.v.*, then resumed their previous control of the oasis, and areas to the west of it, returning the Saudi Arabian troops, via Aden, to their bases. The large oil strikes made inland and offshore after 1963 have reduced the importance of the oasis to Abu Dhabi and Oman.

Bureaucracy. A hybrid word, originally a satirical combination of French *bureau* and Greek *kratein*, to rule, on the analogy of 'democracy' and 'aristocracy'. Now used as a serious term for (*a*) the rule of a caste of high officials, (*b*) this caste itself, hence the word bureaucrat.

Burma. An independent Asian state to the east of India and Bangladesh; area 261,789 sq. m.; population (1969) 26,980,000, of whom 85 per cent are Buddhists and the rest Animists, Moslems, Hindus and Christians; two-thirds of the population are Burmans, but there are also some two million Karens, 800,000 Indians and Pakistanis, 400,000 Chinese and Kachins, Chins, Shans, Mons and Arakanese; capital Rangoon. In the eleventh and twelfth centuries Burma was a great empire but its power was destroyed by the armies of Kublai Khan. It later became part of British India, some self-government being allowed in 1937. In 1941 it was occupied by the Japanese who were regarded as liberators by the Burmans. An all-Burmese government was set up; however, there was no real independence until the withdrawal of the Japanese and the creation, in 1948, of the independent Union of Burma. The Union, which comprises Burma proper, the Shan States and the Karenni States in the northeast, chose not to remain in the British Commonwealth. From 1948 to 1958 Burma was a parliamentary democracy with a Chamber of Deputies (250 members) and a Chamber of Nationalities (125 members). From 1951 the government was dominated by the Anti-Fascist People's Freedom League, which comprised the left-wing Socialist Party, the Trades Union Congress and a number of communal organizations representing the different ethnic groups. In April 1958 General Ne Win took over as Prime Minister, claiming that the army could run the country more efficiently than the politicians. At elections held in February 1960 for the Chamber of Deputies, the Union (Pyidaungsu) Party, the successor to the A.F.P.F.L. and led by U Nu, won, with its supporters, over 170 seats. In March 1962 army officers under General Ne Win seized power from U Nu, partly in order to defeat separatist and federalist moves by minorities such as the Shans. The government was replaced by a Revolutionary Council which then invested all powers in General Ne Win. U Nu fled to Thailand from where, in 1969, he formed the United National Liberation Front, consisting of the Burmese Parliamentary Democracy Party, the Karen National Union, the New Mon State Party, the Shan State Army and the Chin National Democratic Party. The Front has attempted to bring various tribal revolts in the country under a unified command in its campaign of guerilla warfare against the Burmese army and government.

Under the Constitution the state is the ultimate owner of all land. The government, which has encouraged the establishment of the Burma Socialist Programme Party, pursues a policy of land reform, industrialization, and social welfare. For some time there was serious trouble from rebellious Communists, Trotskyites, army deserters and Karens, and from supporters of Chiang Kai-shek who used the Shan states as a refuge. These have been suppressed by government military action, but the insurgent Communists and ethnic minority groups continue to threaten internal security in the rural areas. Burma has resources of teak, tungsten, tin, lead, petroleum, and precious stones. The biggest source of income is rice, exports of which provide the country with about 75 per cent of its earnings of foreign currencies. The market has declined owing to increased production in countries like India, which once imported Burmese rice in substantial quantities. Burma is therefore looking for new markets, such as the U.S.S.R., and turning to other forms of production.

Burnham, Lindon Forbes Sampson. Guianese politician; born 1923 in Georgetown, of African extraction; educated in Guyana (then a British colony) and London University, where he graduated in law. He was called to the English Bar in 1947. He returned to Guyana to help Cheddi Jagan, *q.v.*, form the People's Progressive Party (P.P.P.) which won the first general election under the Constitution of 1952. Until the Constitution was suspended, in October 1953, he was Minister of Education. In 1955, following his expulsion from the P.P.P., he founded the People's National Congress (P.N.C.) which advocated equal opportunity for the African Guianese as opposed to those of Indian extraction who supported Jagan. When the P.P.P. failed to win an absolute majority of seats at the election held in 1964 he became Prime Minister of a coalition dominated by the P.N.C. He continued in office when his party achieved an absolute majority at the election held in December 1968.

Burundi. An independent state in central Africa, bounded by Rwanda to the north, Tanzania to the east and south, and Zaïre to the west; area 10,747 sq. m.; population (1970 estimate) 3,340,000, of whom 85 per cent are Hutu or Bahutu (Bantu) and 15 per cent Tutsi or Batutsi (Nilotic); capital Usumbura (Bujumbura). Burundi was part of the trustee territory of Ruanda-Urundi, *q.v.* At elections held in 1961 under U.N. supervision the nationalist anti-Belgian Uprona Party obtained a large majority and the country achieved complete independence under King Mwambutsa IV Mwami of Urundi on 1 July 1952. On 8 July 1966, following tribal disturbances between Hutus and Tutsis, the assassination of Prime Minister Ngendandumwe and the subsequent execution of virtually all the leading Hutu politicians, the Crown Prince (a Tutsi) deposed his father, suspended the Constitution and appointed Captain Michel Micombero (born 1940) Prime Minister. On 1 September 1966 he was enthroned as King Ntare IV; on 28 November 1966 Micombero declared Burundi a republic with himself as President, and the King went into exile in

West Germany. On assurances of safe conduct given by President Micombero to President Amin of Uganda, the former King returned to Burundi from Uganda in April 1972. He was immediately arrested and was killed on 29 April during an attempt by his supporters to release him. This attempted *coup* gave rise to widespread fighting between Tutsi and Hutu in which an estimated 100,000 were massacred, the majority of them Hutus. In June 1972 the government announced the end of military operations. Burundi is still dependent on Belgium for economic and technical aid; the main economic activity is subsistence agriculture and cattle rearing, and the only cash crop of importance is coffee.

Byelorussia, *or* White Russia. One of the fifteen constituent Republics of the U.S.S.R.; area 80,134 sq. m.; population (1967 estimate) 8,744,000; capital Minsk. It is situated in the western part of the European section of the U.S.S.R. and was set up on 1 January 1919. An area inhabited by approximately two million Byelorussians was kept by Poland after its war with the U.S.S.R. in 1920 and re-occupied by the U.S.S.R. after the partition of Poland in September 1939. The Byelorussians or White Russians are a nation (speaking a language distinct from but akin to Russian and Ukrainian), not a political group; they should not be confused with the 'White' Russians of the civil war period who opposed the revolution. Byelorussia, like the Ukraine, *q.v.*, is a member of the United Nations Organization.

C

C.A.C.M. Central American Common Market, *q.v.*

Caetano, Dr Marcelo José das Neves. Portuguese politician and lawyer; born 1904, the son of a primary school teacher, educated at the University of Lisbon where he graduated in law. In 1929 he became the Judicial Auditor to the Ministry of Finance which had been taken over by Dr Antonio de Oliveira Salazar, *q.v.*, in the previous year. He was appointed to the chair of Constitutional and Administrative Law at the University of Lisbon in 1933, from which time he devoted himself to the interests of students and young people, becoming in 1940 leader of Mocidade, the state youth organization. In 1944 he was made Minister for the Colonies, in which office he drafted the Organic Law which determined that Portuguese territories overseas had the same constitutional basis as the provinces of metropolitan Portugal. Three years later, in 1947, he left the cabinet to become President of the Uniãs Nacional, the only legal political party, which was in urgent need of reform. Until 1955, when he was appointed Deputy Prime Minister, he acted as President of the Corporative Chamber, to which all bills introduced into the National Assembly must be submitted for review. He again left the government in 1958 to take up the appointment of Rector of the University of Lisbon, a post from which he resigned in April 1962 in protest at the un-authorized entry of police into the University grounds during a period of student unrest. He remained a Professor of Law however, continuing to teach while establishing a reputation as a successful company lawyer. He was also a member of the Council of State. On 26 September 1968 he was invited by President Tomas to succeed Dr Salazar, who had been released from his post on the prerogative of the President, as Prime Minister of Portugal.

Cairo Declaration. A statement of policy on 1 December 1943 by China, the U.K., and the U.S.A. after a meeting at Cairo between Chiang Kai-shek, Winston Churchill, and Franklin D. Roosevelt, from 22 to 26 November. The three governments said that they wanted the unconditional surrender of the enemy and that they did not seek territorial aggrandizement. They sought to relegate Japan to the status that it had occupied in 1895 and said that it was their purpose that Japan should be stripped of all the Pacific islands which it had seized since the beginning of the First World War, and that the territories that Japan had 'stolen from the Chinese', such as Manchuria, Formosa, and the Pescadores, should be restored to China. Japan was also to be expelled from the other territories that it had 'taken by violence and greed'; Korea was to become independent.

Callaghan, Leonard James. British Labour Party politician; son of a Chief Petty Officer in the Royal Navy, born 27 March 1912; educated at Portsmouth Northern Grammar School. He entered the civil service as a tax collector in 1929 and became Assistant Secretary of the Inland Revenue Staff Federation in 1936, a post which he held until 1947 except during the Second World War, when he served in the Royal Navy. In July 1945 he was elected to the House of Commons as the member for South Cardiff, and was Parliamentary Secretary to the Ministry of Transport from 1947 to 1950 and Parliamentary and Financial Secretary to the Admiralty from 1950 (in which year his constituency changed to South-East Cardiff) until the Labour Party defeat at the 1951 General Election. From 1955 until 1964 he was consultant to the Police Federation of England and Wales. He became Chancellor of the Exchequer in October 1964, resigning on 18 November 1967 after he had failed to prevent the devaluation of the £. Eleven days later he was appointed Home Secretary, which post he retained until 1970.

Cambodia. A former Associate State of the French Union, *q.v.*, and the name by which the Khmer Republic, *q.v.*, was known before October 1970.

Cameroons, British. Until 1961 a trusteeship territory lying (with one short break) along the eastern frontier of Nigeria; area 34,081 sq. m.; population (1961) approximately 1,430,000; capital Buea. The territory was part of the former German protectorate of Kamerun, *q.v.* In 1922 it was placed by the League of Nations under a British mandate, which in 1946 became a trusteeship territory under the United Nations.

The northern area, the Northern Cameroons (area 17,500 sq. m., population 700,000), was for many years attached to and administered with three provinces in the Northern Region of Nigeria. A plebiscite on 7 November 1959 showed that a majority wished to delay a decision on their future and not to join Nigeria. On 1 July 1960 it became the Trusteeship Province of the Northern Region; when Nigeria became independent on 1 October 1960 it was taken over by the U.K., but a second plebiscite on 11 February 1961 resulted in a majority for union with Nigeria, which took place later that year.

The southern area, the Southern Cameroons (area 16,581 sq. m., population 830,000), had also for many years been treated as part of Nigeria, but as a Region. A general election in January 1959 resulted in a narrow victory for the Kamerun National Democratic Party, favouring union with Cameroun, *q.v.* It won 14 out of 26 seats and its leader, John N. Foncha, became Prime Minister, succeeding Dr Emanuel M. L. Endeley, whose Kamerun National Congress favoured the retention of the association with Nigeria. In May 1960 the Congress merged with the Kamerun People's Party forming the Cameroons People's National Confederation. A second plebiscite, on 11 February 1961, resulted in a majority for union with Cameroun, which took place on 1 October 1961. The Southern Cameroons are now the Western Province of Cameroun.

Cameroons, French. The name by which the area to the east of Nigeria and the British Cameroons was known during its life as a French mandate (from 1922 to 1946) and a French trusteeship territory (from 1946 to 1960). It achieved independence on 1 January 1960, since when it has been known as Cameroun, *q.v*

Cameroun, United Republic of. An independent state on the Gulf of Guinea and to the south-east of Nigeria, with Nigeria to the north-west and Spanish Guinea, Gabon and Congo (Brazzaville) (formerly French) to the south; area 185,547 sq. m.; population (1972 estimate) 6,700,000; capital Yaoundé. The province of East Cameroun is part of the former German protectorate of Kamerun, *q.v.*, and from 1922 until it became independent on 1 January 1960 was administered by France, first as a mandate under the League of Nations (from 1922 to 1946) and then as a trusteeship territory (from 1946 to 1960). It was then known as the French Cameroons. The other province, of West Cameroun, was under British administration until 1 October 1961, and known as the Southern Cameroons (*see* Cameroons, British).

The extreme northern part of the country, which is thinly populated, is Moslem, relatively undeveloped, and largely controlled by its cattle-raising chieftains. Its savannah and steppe yield cotton, groundnuts, rice, yams, and other local foods. The southern part of the country is a region of tropical rain forest, producing mainly rice, bananas, cocoa, and coffee, with additional crops of cotton, palm oil, and rubber. Bauxite is mined in East Cameroun and in 1963 uranium was discovered in economic quantities. Since December 1964 Cameroun has been a member of an economic and customs union (U.D.E.A.C.) with Chad, Central African Republic, Congo (Brazzaville) and Gabon.

In the area bordering Nigeria the substantial and industrious Bamiléké tribe, which makes up one sixth of the total population, has, with the Bassa and Baoum, been dissatisfied with the government. Its discontent results from the shortage of land and the intense overpopulation; the Bamiléké tend to support the extreme left-wing Union des Populations Camérounaises (U.P.C.) – which was banned from 1955 to 1960 – led by Ernest Ouandié who was executed in 1970 for organizing a rebellion in which the Roman Catholic Bishop of Nkongsamba was also implicated.

Under the 1961 Constitution the country was governed by a President, directly elected for five years, a Vice-President, and nine Federal Ministers who could not be members of the Federal Assembly, comprising 40 members from East Cameroun and 10 from West Cameroun. Admadu Ahidjo, a northerner and leader of the Union Camérounaise, which obtained a majority in the elections of 1960 and 1964, became President on 5 May 1960, and was re-elected in May 1965 and March 1970. In the 1964 elections the Union Camérounaise secured all 40 East Cameroun seats; the 10 West Cameroun seats were won by the Kamerun National Democratic Party (K.N.D.P.), supporting the central government and led by John Ngu Foncha, the Vice-President. In 1966 the two parties merged with the Kamerun People's National Convention and the Kamerun United Congress to form the Union Nationale Camérounaise, which then became the sole legal political party. In May 1972 President Ahidjo announced the creation of a unitary state with a single National Assembly of 120 members which would replace the three existing governments (the Federal one and the two Federate administrations).

Canada. A Dominion and member of the British Commonwealth; area 3,851,809 sq. m.; population (1971) 21,568,311, of whom more than 40 per cent are Roman Catholic; capital Ottawa. The French took possession of the country in the sixteenth century but by the nineteenth century they had ceded all their conquests, except St Pierre and Miquelon, to the U.K. The British North America Act, 1867, united into a Federation the Canadian Provinces of New Brunswick, Nova Scotia, Ontario (formerly Upper Canada), and Quebec (formerly Lower Canada); provided that the Constitution should be 'similar in principle to that of the United Kingdom'; that the executive authority should be vested in the Sovereign and carried on in the Sovereign's name by a Governor-General and Privy Council; and that the legislative power should be exercised by a Parliament comprising a Senate and a House of Commons. Later, the provinces or territories of Alberta, British Columbia, Manitoba, Newfoundland, *q.v.*, Prince Edward Island, Saskatchewan, the Yukon Territory, and the North-West Territories were added to the Federation.

There are 102 Senators, appointed on a regional basis until the age of 75; the House of Commons is elected by the people for five years.

The Federal Parliament has exclusive power to legislate in certain specified fields which include defence, foreign affairs, finance and trade, and some social services (a national pension plan was introduced in 1966 and a federal health programme, known as Medicare, in 1968); it has a general authority in all matters not specifically assigned by the Constitution to the Provincial Legislatures. In this respect the Canadian Constitution is the reverse of that of the U.S.A. Each of the ten Provinces is headed by a Lieutenant-Governor with a single legislative assembly (except in Quebec where there are two chambers) and a cabinet led by a premier. Two Territories, Yukon and the North-West, are represented in the Federal House of Commons and locally by a Commissioner. Education and civil law are provincial matters.

Almost half the population is of British origin, and ten per cent are first-generation immigrants; 3,000,000 have been absorbed since 1945. There are two official languages, English and French, the French Canadians representing 30 per cent of the total. They live mostly in Quebec Province where there are two separate educational systems, one Roman Catholic, and of French tradition, and one Protestant, which is the English tradition of the other nine Provinces. Between 1967 and 1970 a separatist movement, encouraged by General de Gaulle, q.v., who visited the Province in 1967, gained ground among the French-speaking inhabitants of Quebec. The murder of the Quebec Minister of Labour, Pierre Laporte, and the kidnapping of a British diplomat, James Cross, in October 1970 by members of the Quebec Liberation Front (F.L.Q.), an extremist separatist organization, led to the assumption of emergency powers by the Canadian government under the War Measures Act, 1914. Since 1971 the economic problems caused by an annual inflation of 5 per cent and an unemployment rate of 6 per cent have overshadowed the separatist issue.

In 1968 Lester Pearson, who had held office as Prime Minister of a Liberal government since 1963, resigned as leader of the Liberal Party. He was succeeded by Pierre Elliott Trudeau, q.v., a French Canadian who strongly opposed the demand for Quebec separatism. At elections held on 30 October 1972 the results were: Liberal Party (advocating Canadian autonomy and independence of the U.S.A., comprehensive social security and more centralization) 109 seats (154 in 1965); Progressive Conservative Party (in power under John Diefenbaker from 1957 to 1963, now led by Robert Stanfield, q.v.) 107

(72 in 1965); New Democratic Party (founded in 1961 when the Cooperative Commonwealth Federation merged with organized labour and advocating extensive economic planning and a non-nuclear role for Canada; leader David Lewis) 31 (23); Ralliement des Créditistes (a breakaway movement from the Social Credit Party (*see* Social Credit) led by a Quebec member of the House of Commons, Real Caouette, 15 (14); Independents 2 (1). The Social Credit Party itself, which has provided the Provincial governments of Alberta since 1935 and British Columbia since 1952, was not represented in the Federal Parliament. The election results revealed that Liberal support was concentrated in Ontario and Quebec; the Anglo-Saxon, anti-Catholic, vote went largely to the Progressive Conservatives. Despite the failure of his party to obtain an absolute majority of seats Pierre Trudeau continued to lead a Liberal government, rejecting an offer by the New Democratic Party to join a coalition.

Canada exports newsprint, paper, wood pulp and wood, furs, petroleum, fish and fishery products, wheat, aluminium and copper. It is also the world's largest producer of nickel, platinum and zinc; it ranks second in asbestos, uranium, cobalt, elemental sulphur, gypsum and gold, and third in silver. Oil wells are being developed especially in Alberta, and oil and natural gas have been discovered in the North-West Territories and the Canadian Arctic islands. The government has raised ecological objections to the construction of the Trans-Alaska Pipeline, *q.v.*, and would prefer the pipeline to be routed through the Mackenzie River valley, which would stimulate the Canadian economy. More than $300 million is invested each year in the form of new capital, mostly from the U.S.A.

Capitalism. The economic system under which the ownership of the means of production is concentrated in the hands of a class, consisting of only a minor section of society, and under which there is a property-less class for whom the sale of their labour-power, as a commodity, is the only source of livelihood. It is not necessarily coincidental with free enterprise; in the nineteenth century, especially in England, the new factory industries repeatedly demanded free access to markets and to labour supplies, but by the beginning of the twentieth century there was a tendency towards monopolies in different industries and a growing demand for state protection against foreign competition. Under capitalism, as above defined, the means of production and the apparatus of distribution are controlled by private owners who run them at their discretion, driven by an urge for profit. Such a system has often been attacked by Socialists, who aim to nationalize the economic apparatus and to plan its development under central management, the driving principle being not individual profit but public welfare. They criticize capitalism as planless anarchy, leading to recurrent crises because of its lack of coordination. Defenders of the capitalist system point to its great achievements. They claim that private initiative cannot be replaced by state control and that the interests of capitalism are necessarily identical with public welfare. According to Socialist theories there is an inward tendency in capitalism which leads to ever larger concentrations of capital, the stronger enterprises ousting or absorbing the weaker ones, until a limited number of trusts, combines, and banks virtually controls a nation's economic life. Thus the liberal free-competition capitalism of former times passes into modern monopolist capitalism. The latter foreshadows the state administration desired by Socialists, the enormous combines and groups being necessarily run along bureaucratic lines. They are controlled by their senior executives rather than by their owners, the shareholders, who may have no interest in the businesses other than as reliable sources of dividends. This development is sometimes called the managerial revolution, *q.v.* Free competition, say such critics, is in any case being gradually replaced by large combines and groups, which do a great deal of planning.

Capitol. A building in Washington, D.C., U.S.A., where the Senate, *q.v.*, and the House of Representatives, *q.v.*, meet. Its cornerstone was laid by President Washington on 18 September 1793. The Capitol is on Capitol Hill, where the Senate Office Buildings, the House of Representatives Office Buildings, the Supreme Court, *q.v.*, and the Library of Congress are also to be found. It is one mile from the White House, *q.v.*, because Washington felt that the executive and legislative branches of the government should be separated.

Capitulations. Treaties by which the subjects of one state when entering another state remained under the jurisdiction of their own government, which was exercised by local consuls. The treaties were often made by European states with Asian and African states whose institutions were regarded as incapable of giving proper protection. Capitulations have been gradually discontinued; they ended in Japan in 1899, in Turkey in 1923, in Thailand in 1927, in Persia in 1928, in Egypt in 1937, in China in 1943, and apart from some minor exceptions, such as Muscat and Oman, had ceased to exist by 1970.

Caribbean Federation. An association of British colonies in the Caribbean Sea. In 1945 the U.K. proposed a federation which could eventually be granted full self-government. The Standing Committee for the Closer Association of the British West Indian

Colonies, set up at Montego Bay, Jamaica, in 1947, recommended the unification of public services, a single currency, planned inter-island migration and the establishment of a customs union; in 1950 a draft federal constitution was published. Conferences in 1953 and 1956 resulted in agreement by Barbados, Jamaica, Trinidad, the Leeward Islands (except the Virgin Islands), and the Windward Islands to set up a federation. The West Indies Federation, *q.v.*, was in existence from 3 January 1958 to 31 May 1962.

Caribbean Free Trade Area (Carifta). An agreement signed on 1 May 1968 by Antigua, Barbados, Guyana, Trinidad and Tobago, joined by Dominica, Grenada, St Kitts–Nevis–Anguilla, St Lucia and St Vincent on 1 July 1968, and by Jamaica and Montserrat on 1 August 1968, to establish free trade among the signatories in all but certain reserved commodities. The tariffs and quotas on these are to be eliminated over a five-year period for the more developed, and a ten-year period for the less developed, countries. British Honduras (Belize) acceded to the agreement in 1970. In October 1972 the 12 signatories, together with Bahamas, *q.v.*, decided to establish a Caribbean Common Market to come into force in May 1973.

Carifta. Caribbean Free Trade Area, *q.v.*

Carr, Robert Leonard. British Conservative Party politician; born 11 November 1916 and educated at Westminster School and Caius College, Cambridge. He was trained as a scientist and his extensive business interests have included Securicor Ltd, of which he was a director from 1961 to 1963 and from 1965 to 1970, and the Norwich Union Insurance Group, 1965 to 1970. He entered the House of Commons in 1950 as the member for Mitcham, becoming Parliamentary Private Secretary to Sir Anthony Eden, *q.v.*, in 1951. He was appointed Parliamentary Secretary to the Minister of Labour from 1955 to 1958, and Secretary for Technical Co-operation from 1963 to 1964. In 1970 he became Secretary of State for Employment and in April 1972 Lord President of the Council and Leader of the House of Commons in succession to William Whitelaw, *q.v.* He was appointed Secretary of State for the Home Department on the resignation of Reginald Maudling, *q.v.*, in July 1972.

Casablanca Powers (*or* Casablanca States). Title often given to a loose association of African states comprising Algeria, Ghana, Guinea, Mali, Morocco, and the United Arab Republic. In January 1961 at Casablanca it was decided to set up an African Military Command, and agreed that an African Common Market should be established. The grouping may be contrasted with that of the so-called Monrovia Powers, *q.v.* The secretariat is at Bamako, Mali.

Castle, Barbara Anne. British Labour Party politician; born 6 October 1911, the daughter of Frank Betts, she was educated at Bradford Girls' Grammar School and St Hugh's College, Oxford. A career in journalism was interrupted by the Second World War when she became, from 1941 to 1944, an Administrative Officer in the Ministry of Food. She was a member of the St Pancras Borough Council from 1937 until 1945, and a member of the Metropolitan Water Board from 1940 to 1945, in which year she was elected to the House of Commons as member for Blackburn (East Blackburn from 1950 to 1955), a seat which she has retained ever since. She was appointed Parliamentary Private Secretary to Sir Stafford Cripps in 1945, and to Harold Wilson, *q.v.*, at the Board of Trade in 1947. In 1944 she married a journalist, Edward Castle. She has been a member of the National Executive of the Labour Party since 1950, on three occasions, in 1965, 1966 and 1968, receiving the highest number of votes in the election for the seven constituency members. She was chairman of the Party in 1958. From October 1964, when she first entered the Cabinet, until December 1965 she held the office of Minister for Overseas Development. In January 1966 she was appointed Minister of Transport and in April 1968 First Secretary of State for Employment and Productivity, a post which incorporated the duties of the former Minister of Labour and which she retained until June 1970.

Castro, Dr Fidel Ruz. Cuban politician; born in 1926 in Cuba, the son of a Spanish immigrant who had been a successful Galician farmer, and educated at a Roman Catholic boarding school in Santiago, the Jesuit Belén College, and from 1945 to 1950, the University of Havana. In 1947 he took part in an unofficial raid on the Dominican Republic; on 26 July 1953 he organized an attack on an army barracks in Santiago and was subsequently sentenced to fifteen years' imprisonment, his brother Raúl being sentenced to thirteen years' imprisonment. When President Batistá granted an amnesty to political prisoners in 1955 he was released. In 1956 he went to Mexico to organize a Cuban revolutionary movement, and on 2 December 1956 he landed in Oriente province with a small group, who included Ernesto Guevara, *q.v.*, which then found refuge in the Sierra Maestra. In 1958 the rebels, led by Castro, had many successes, and on 1 January 1959 they occupied Havana. He became Prime Minister and Minister of the Armed Forces on 16 February 1959.

Cento. Central Treaty Organization, *q.v.*

Centrafrican Republic. *See* Central African Republic, of which the official title is La République Centrafricaine.

Central African Federation. A Federation, from 1953 to 1963, of the protectorates of Nyasaland (now Malawi) and Northern Rhodesia (now Zambia), and the self-governing colony of Southern Rhodesia (now known merely as Rhodesia). In 1938 a commission was appointed under the chairmanship of Lord Bledisloe as a result of which the Central African Council was established in 1945 as a consultative body. With the support of the British Labour government, the possibility of a federation of the three territories was studied; the final proposals for a self-governing federation were accepted by referendum in Southern Rhodesia in 1953 and approved by the governments of the U.K. and of the three territories. The federation was known as the Federation of Rhodesia and Nyasaland, *q.v.*

Central African Republic, also known as Centrafrican Republic (the official title is La République Centrafricaine). An independent republic; area 234,000 sq. m.; population (1968 census) 2,255,236 (mostly in the west and south), comprising Bayas, Manjas, Badas, Saras and some 5,000 non-Africans; capital Bangui. The country is land-locked with Cameroun, Chad and Soudan to the west, north and east respectively, and Zaïre and Congo (Brazzaville), the border with which runs along the river Oubangui, a tributary of the river Congo, and the chief artery of transport to the south. The area was annexed by France in 1888 and became, as Ubangi Shari, one of the four territories of French Equatorial Africa, *q.v.*; it achieved self-government within the French Community, *q.v.*, on 1 December 1958, and complete independence, still within the Community, on 13 August 1960.

Executive power is exercised by the President, Colonel Jean-Bedel Bokassa, who deposed David Dacko by a military *coup* in January 1966. The Constitution, which had provided for a legislative assembly elected every five years, was suspended; meanwhile Bokassa assumed from his predecessor the leadership of the Movement for the Social Evolution of Africa, the sole legal political organization since November 1962 when all the opposition parties were dissolved. The economy is predominantly agricultural, although there are valuable deposits of iron and uranium. The principal product is cotton which is exported, together with coffee, tobacco, diamonds and lumber. Since December 1964 the Republic has been a member of an economic and customs union (U.D.E.A.C.) with Cameroun, Chad, Congo (Brazzaville) and Gabon. In December 1968 the Republic rejoined the French-orientated Union of Central African Republics.

Central American Common Market (C.A.C.M.). An organization which came into existence in 1960 when Costa Rica, Guatemala, Honduras,

Nicaragua and Salvador signed the General Treaty on Central American Economic Integration. It aimed to establish free trade, a common external tariff for all imports and joint consultation on monetary policy among member countries. It has been more successful than the Latin American Free Trade Association (L.A.F.T.A.), *q.v.*, largely owing to the economic disadvantages common to all five countries, none of which was sufficiently advanced industrially to pose any threat of domination over the others.

Central Treaty Organization (Cento). Was set up on 21 August 1959 by Pakistan, Persia, Turkey, and the U.K. to succeed the structure established by those countries, with Iraq, under the Baghdad Pact, *q.v.* Iraq ceased to take part in arrangements relating to the Pact after its revolution in July 1958, and formally withdrew in March 1959.

Centralism. A political system under which the whole country is controlled from a central point, as opposed to decentralized systems of administration such as federalism and regionalism, under which local units (states, provinces) enjoy a greater or lesser degree of autonomy.

C.E.R.N. European Organization for Nuclear Research, *q.v.*

Cession. The giving up of territory by one state to another state. It may be the result of war, as when Spain ceded the Philippines to the U.S.A. after the Spanish-American War in 1898, or of peaceful negotiations, as when Denmark sold the Danish West Indies to the U.S.A. for $25 million in 1916, or when Austria ceded Venice to France as a gift in 1866. The citizens of the ceding state living in the territory become citizens of the other state, unless some special arrangement is made by which they may keep their old nationality.

Ceylon. Name by which Sri Lanka, *q.v.*, was known before it became a republic on 22 May 1972.

Chaban-Delmas, Jacques Michel Pierre. French politician, born 3 March 1915 and educated at the Lycée Lakanal, Sceaux and the École Libre des Sciences Politiques in Paris. He achieved the rank of Brigadier-General in the French Army in 1940 and became Inspector-General of the Army in 1944, having acted as co-ordinator of military planning during the later stages of the resistance. He entered government service in 1945 as Secretary-General to the Ministry of Information and became politically active in 1946, when he was elected Radical Deputy for the Gironde, and Mayor of Bordeaux the following year. From 1953 to 1956 he led the Gaullist group (Républicains Sociaux) in the National Assembly. He was appointed an Inspector of Finance in 1956 and in May 1957 joined the Gaillard cabinet as Minister of

National Defence. He was President of the National Assembly from 1958 until 1969 when President Pompidou invited him to form a government. He was relieved of office in July 1972, and succeeded as Prime Minister by Pierre Messmer, *q.v.*

Chad. An independent republic; area 487,920 sq. m.; population (1968 estimate) 3,500,000, comprising Arabs, Saras and Peuls, and 3,750 non-Africans; capital Fort Lamy. The country is landlocked, with Niger, Nigeria and Cameroun to the west and sharing Lake Chad, Libya to the north, Sudan to the east, and the Central African Republic to the south. The territory was annexed by France in 1913 and later became one of the four territories comprising French Equatorial Africa, *q.v.*; it achieved self-government within the French Community, *q.v.*, on 28 November 1958 and complete independence, still within the Community, on 11 August 1960.

Legislative powers are vested in an assembly of 85 members normally elected every five years by universal suffrage. The last contested elections were held in 1959 when the Chad Progressive Party (P.P.T., the local section of the Rassemblement Démocratique Africain) led by François Tombalbaye, won a majority of the seats. Since 1962 Chad has been a one-party state, and the Chad Progressive Party the sole permitted political party. Executive power is exercised by the President (François Tombalbaye) who assumed the title on 23 April 1962 for an initial term of seven years under the constitution adopted on 14 April 1962. There have been continual disturbances since 1965, especially in the Wadai region, a province near the Sudan border which was once an independent sultanate; these reflect the differences between the pastoral, and Moslem, north, and the wealthier, Christian, south. More recently these have been exploited to create a Chad National Liberation Front (Frolina) with headquarters in Algiers. This guerilla force, which once controlled most of the countryside north of Fort Lamy, has been driven back to the frontiers with Libya and Sudan by French troops. In August 1971 President Tombalbaye survived an unsuccessful *coup*; as a result Chad broke off diplomatic relations with Egypt and Libya.

The most important cash crop is cotton, which accounts for 90 per cent of all exports; fish, livestock and groundnuts are also exported. Rice and millet are grown for home consumption and there are, as yet undeveloped, deposits of tin and tungsten. Chad was in an economic union from April to December 1968 with Zaïre (the former Congo Kinshasa) and the Central African Republic, until the latter rejoined the French-orientated Union of Central African Republics. Since 1964 it has been a member of an economic and customs union

(U.D.E.A.C.) with Cameroun, Central African Republic, Congo (Brazzaville) and Gabon.

Channel Islands. A part of the United Kingdom of Great Britain and Northern Ireland, *q.v.*, comprising a group of islands off the northwest coast of France; area 75 sq. m. They consist of the islands of Jersey (population (1970) 65,000; administrative headquarters St Helier), and of Guernsey and its dependencies – Alderney, Great and Little Sark, Herm, Jethou, Brechou, Lithou and some uninhabited islets – (population (1971) 51,351; administrative headquarters St Peter Port). They are the only portion of the Duchy of Normandy still retained as a dependency of the English crown. From July 1940 until May 1945 they were under German occupation. Both islands have their own legislatures, or Assemblies of the States, and Royal Court, and, until the entry of the U.K. to the European Economic Community, *q.v.*, in January 1973, exercised autonomy in income tax and purchase tax while enjoying the protection of British tariffs. Guernsey has adopted English as its official language; Jersey retains Norman French. The islands are economically dependent upon potato and tomato growing, dairy and cattle farming, and tourism.

Chapultepec, Act of. A declaration made on 3 March 1945 by the Inter-American Conference on War and Peace. It asserted, in terms similar to those of the Declaration of Panama made in 1939 by the Pan American Union, *q.v.*, the determination of American states to assist each other and to prevent any non-American state from violating their political independence. In anticipation of the Charter of the United Nations, the Act stated that the agreement between the American states was a regional arrangement not inconsistent with the principles of the United Nations. The Act was reaffirmed and its provisions extended by the Rio Treaty, *q.v.*, of 2 September 1947.

Chiang Kai-shek. President of Nationalist China; born 31 October 1886. He was sent from China to Japan in 1907 to complete his military training but deserted from the Japanese army in 1911 to take part in the Chinese revolution. As chief of staff to the revolutionary leader Sun Yat-sen, whose sister-in-law he later married, Chiang studied Russian military methods in Moscow in 1923. He opposed the Chinese Communists and in 1928 became the head of the government established at Nanking, the new capital. His forces then fought local war-lords, Japanese invaders, and the Communists (who captured Chiang in 1936 but released him so that he could continue to fight the Japanese). He led the Chinese government and the Kuomintang, *q.v.*, during the Second World War, but in 1948 his forces were defeated by the Communists and he retired to Formosa (now

Taiwan, *q.v.*). He has repeatedly asserted that his forces will one day invade the Chinese mainland and overthrow the government.

Chile. An independent state on the west coast of South America; area 286,397 sq. m.; population (1970 census) 8,834,820, comprising descendants of Spanish settlers, Spanish Indians, natives and Europeans; capital Santiago. Chile was ruled by Spain from the sixteenth century until it achieved independence in 1818. Under the 1925 Constitution laws are passed by a National Congress consisting of a Senate of 50 members elected for eight years and a Chamber of Deputies with 150 members elected for four years. The President is elected for six years by direct popular vote. Since the fall in world copper prices at the end of the Korean War in 1953 the economy has experienced severe inflation; production, especially in agriculture, has lagged behind the annual population increase of 2·3 per cent, and food accounts for more than a quarter of the total imports. Sectional interests predominate in politics largely because the army has traditionally refrained from intervening.

The Presidential elections in September 1964 were won by a Christian Democrat, Eduardo Montalva Frei, *q.v.* His programme included the expropriation of land from big landowners and its re-allocation to peasants' cooperatives, investment in education and the reduction of interest rates. However his policy did not progress far enough along 'a non-capitalist road of development for Chile' to satisfy the left-wing of his party which seceded to form the Action Movement for Popular Unity (M.A.P.U.) and gave its support to the Popular Unity Front, led by Dr Salvador Allende, *q.v.*, at the Presidential elections held in September 1970. These were won by Allende who, as the Marxist candidate, had a majority of only 1·4 per cent over his nearest opponent, the right-wing candidate and son of a former President, Jorge Alessandri. President Allende assumed office on 4 November 1970 after endorsement by Congress in which he depended for his majority on the former governing party, the Christian Democrats, whose presidential candidate, Radomiri Tomic, had already announced his personal support for Dr Allende on condition that he would maintain a democratic regime and respect the electoral system. He formed a government of Popular Unity consisting of his own party, the Chilean Socialist Party (which is pro-Castro), the Communist Party (which follows the Moscow line and is the third largest, after the Communist parties of France and Italy, outside Communist countries), the left-wing of the Radical Party, the Independent Popular Action (A.P.I.), and M.A.P.U. His programme included a redistribution of wealth in favour of Chile's depressed peasantry, a stimulus to the production of goods for popular consumption, especially housing, to exploit under-used industrial capacity and increase employment, and the nationalization of foreign-owned assets. In July 1971 the country's five largest copper mines, worked and partly owned by subsidiaries of U.S. companies (Kennecott, Anaconda and Cerro de Pasco), were nationalized. A protracted dispute followed with the U.S. State Department over the compensation payable, the U.S. threatening to withdraw all economic aid (amounting to some £416,000,000 over the previous ten years) unless adequate compensation was rendered.

During 1972 Dr Allende faced mounting hostility from Congress, in which his Popular Unity Front was in a minority, to the nationalization of cement and textile plants and plans to take over more than 90 large private businesses and private banks. He also had difficulty in controlling his supporters on the extreme left who had urged the dissolution of Congress, the abandonment of parliamentary democracy and rule by plebiscite. Their strength was reflected in the high abstention rate, in spite of the fact that voting is mandatory, at elections. In November 1972 one high-ranking officer from each of the three armed services was brought into the government, the Army Commander-in-Chief, General Carlos Prats, becoming Minister of the Interior, to deal with protracted strikes which were disrupting the economy. The composition of the Chamber of Deputies after elections held on 4 March 1973 was:— Government Parties: Communist Party 25 (22 in 1969); Socialists 28 (15); Radicals 5 (24); M.A.P.U. 2 (0); A.P.I. 2 (0); Christian Left 1 (1).

Opposition Parties: Christian Democrats 50 (55); National Front (a right-wing coalition of Liberals, Conservatives and National Democrats) 34 (34); Dissident Radicals 3.

Chile is potentially a rich country. It has considerable reserves of nitrates and coal, and produces 12 per cent of the world's copper (from the world's third largest copper reserve), and 20 per cent of the copper available to the non-Communist world. In 1971 a Russian technical aid mission advised Chile on extraction of raw materials.

China. Officially the People's Republic of China; area 4,300,000 sq. m.; population (1970 estimate) 697,260,000, including 12,040,000 in Taiwan, *q.v.*; capital Peking. The Imperial Manchu dynasty was overthrown by the 1911 revolution organized by the Kuomintang, *q.v.*, under Sun Yat-sen, who was proclaimed President of the Republic in 1912. When Sun Yat-sen died in 1925 Chiang Kai-shek, *q.v.*, carried on his work and undertook the task of establishing a Republic throughout China. The Kuomintang government became and remained a military dictatorship, opposed to political democracy, with little concern for the welfare of the people and indifferent to the popular rights which Sun Yat-sen expounded. Meanwhile the Chinese Communist Party had been founded in 1921 in the north and had developed independently of the Kuomintang, which regarded it as a rebel force. In 1928 Chiang marched north to Peking, defeated the war-lord Chang Tso-lin, and massacred the Communists in Shanghai. He then concentrated on restoring peace in the Yangtse valley, driving out Communists who had sovietized two provinces and introduced land reforms. In 1934, led by Mao Tse-tung, *q.v.*, they made their historic 3,000-mile trek to the northern province of Shensi.

Japan had taken advantage of the confusion to invade Manchuria in 1931, and a series of clashes took place culminating in a full-scale invasion of China by Japanese forces in 1937. The Communists cooperated with the Kuomintang in resisting Japanese aggression; in return Chiang agreed to reorganize his government at Nanking so as to include all parties. The Japanese succeeded in conquering large areas of China and in driving Chiang's government westwards out of Nanking to a new capital at Chungking. When the war with Japan ended in 1945 the struggle between the Communists and the Kuomintang continued. In 1946 President Truman's envoy, General Marshall, persuaded the two sides to sign an armistice, but fighting continued; he concluded that the proper solution was for the Kuomintang to permit elections and to enforce its plan for constitutional government, which it had postponed seven times since 1936. In 1947 Chiang declared that the one-party rule of the Kuomintang was at an end and a National Assembly was elected to serve a term of six years. After a number of successes the Communists obtained full control in 1949 and the Kuomintang forces retreated to Formosa. A 1949 U.S. State Department White Paper stated that the U.S.A. had given to the Kuomintang government large quantities of military equipment and arms, most of which was captured by the Communists or handed to them by Kuomintang deserters; it said that there was no evidence of Russian help to the Communists between 1946 and 1948. The Chinese government was recognized by the U.K. and by most other countries, but not by the U.S.A. until 1971. On 25 October 1971, after the U.S. government had indicated its readiness to recognize the People's Republic of China, the United Nations General Assembly voted to admit China to membership and to a seat on the Security Council, *q.v.*, and to expel Taiwan (Formosa).

The constitutional laws of China, as finally approved on 20 September 1954, consist of: (1) a 'Common Programme' of 60 articles chosen by the People's Consultative Conference of 636 delegates in 1949; (2) an 'Organic Law' of 31 articles; and (3) the Constitution of 106 articles. The basic aim of government is the replacement of capitalist by popular ownership. The National People's Congress is the legislature, and by a two-thirds majority can amend the Constitution. When the Congress is not in session its powers are delegated to a Standing Committee (corresponding to the Presidium of the Supreme Soviet in the U.S.S.R.), a permanent body which has power to interpret the laws passed by Congress, to supervise government departments, to issue decrees and to supervise the courts. The Chairman of the Standing Committee of the National People's Congress is Chu Teh, *q.v.*, and the Chairman of the Central Committee of the Communist Party is Mao Tse-tung, *q.v.*; in practice the Central Committee nominates the members of the State Council, or cabinet, of 46 headed by the Premier, Chou En-lai, *q.v.* Marshal Lin Piao, *q.v.*, who was the Vice-Premier and Vice-Chairman of the Central Committee, and Mao Tse-tung's nominated successor, was reported in 1972 to have been killed in an air accident the previous year while attempting to flee the country after an unsuccessful *coup*. The office of Chairman of the Republic, which is similar to that of President of the U.S.A., although China, unlike the U.S.A., also has a Prime Minister, has been vacant since 1969 when Liu Shao-chi, *q.v.*, who had held the post since 1959, was constitutionally deposed. Tung Pi-wu was appointed Acting Chairman.

From 1965 to 1969 a cultural revolution, designed to enforce the ideology of Mao Tse-tung against the more orthodox Communism of Liu Shao-chi (known as China's Khrushchev), gained momentum. New organs of administration were established within the Party, and in February 1967 revolutionary committees were appointed to take over Peking and Shanghai, assisted by 'Red Guards' of the People's Liberation Army. By October 1968 revolutionary committees had been set up in all 26 provincial regions including Tibet, *q.v.*, Wuhan, and Sinkiang which had offered violent resistance. Mao Tse-tung then denounced Liu Shao-chi, depriving him of all his offices except that of Chairman of the Republic which he lost the following year when the National People's Congress deposed him.

A period of land redistribution from 1949 to 1952 was followed by intensive collectivization. By 1958 almost all the peasants, who represent 80 per cent of the population, were organized in agricultural cooperatives, or communes. The country is not self-supporting, and large quantities of wheat are imported from Canada, Australia and South America. There are abundant resources of coal, antimony, manganese, tungsten, timber, tin and iron-ore, and a sufficiency of oil is produced from fields in Kansu, Sinkiang and Sining. To increase literacy, and to enable all Chinese to speak the official national language instead of the numerous dialects, the State Council in 1957 approved the use of a Latin alphabet of 25 letters which could eventually supplant the existing script of 30,000 characters. In 1971 the introduction of a Roman script was made a matter of urgency.

Since 1949 China has pursued a foreign policy aimed at the re-acquisition of those areas which, at the height of its Imperial power, were integral parts or vassals of China. The government has accordingly reasserted its authority over Inner Mongolia, *q.v.*, Manchuria, *q.v.* and Tibet; it has given support to Chinese and Viet-Minh in Viet-Nam, *q.v.*, Malaysia, *q.v.*, and Hong Kong, *q.v.*, and has sent military forces to Korea, *q.v.* In 1962 there was a brief frontier war with India over disputed territory in Ladakh. There has been a prolonged dispute with the U.S.S.R. over shipping rights along the Amur river which forms the border between Siberia and China.

The close relationship between China and the U.S.S.R., cemented in 1950 by the Sino-Soviet treaty of friendship, alliance and mutual assistance, ended in 1960 with the withdrawal of Soviet economic aid. The ideological conflict between Soviet and Chinese Communism has been aggravated by lack of capital and technical expertise which is needed to speed the industrial revolution and sustain the re-organization and mechanization of agriculture. Increasing emphasis has been placed on the Maoist theory that the rural proletariat will encircle the cities from revolutionary bases in the countryside; Communist success in Viet-Nam is cited as evidence of its validity.

Chou En-lai. Chief of the State Council (Premier) of the Chinese People's Republic; born 1898 in Central Kiangsu into a Mandarin family. He graduated at Nankai University and went to Paris to continue his studies, where he organized a Communist cell among Chinese expatriates. He returned to China in 1923, became Communist Party Secretary for the Kuangtung Region and then Chief of the Political Section of the Whampoa Military Academy. In 1936 he advocated the unification of the Communist Party and the Kuomintang, *q.v.*, against the Japanese invaders. He became Chief of the State Council in 1949. In the cultural revolution of 1965–8 he retained his authority in the Central Committee of the Communist Party. He became a member of the 'Red Guards' in 1967 thus indicating his support for Mao Tse-tung, *q.v.*

Chu Teh. Chinese Communist and military leader, born 1886 in Szechuan; son of a prosperous farmer. He graduated from Yunnan Military Academy and took part in revolutionary activities against the Manchu dynasty, which was overthrown in 1911 in what has been called the Old Revolution. He joined the Communist Party while in Berlin in 1922. After the 1927 split between the Communists and the Kuomintang, *q.v.*, he led the Nanchang revolt and later helped Mao Tse-tung, *q.v.*, to organize the Red Army. He took part with Mao in the Long March (3,000 miles) from Kiangsi to Shensi. After the Japanese invasion he held a number of high military posts and his soldiers played a very large part in the defeat of the Kuomintang. He is Commander-in-Chief of the Armies of the Chinese People's Republic and Chairman of the Standing Committee of the National People's Congress.

Churchill, Sir Winston Leonard Spencer. British statesman; born 30 November 1874, son of Lord Randolph Churchill (third son of the seventh Duke of Marlborough) and an American mother; educated at Harrow and Sandhurst. He entered the army in 1895, served with the Spanish forces in Cuba, 1895, and in two colonial campaigns (Malakand 1897, Tirah 1899), and contested the Oldham Parliamentary Division as a Conservative in 1899. He was war correspondent of the *Morning Post* in the South African War, 1899–1900, and taken prisoner by the Boers. On his return to England in 1900 he was elected Conservative M.P. for Oldham; however he opposed Joseph Chamberlain's high tariff plans, and as a free-trader felt compelled to join the Liberals. He became Under-Secretary of State for the Colonies in 1905 and furthered a federation policy in South Africa. He served as Liberal M.P. for North-West Manchester, 1906–8, and for Dundee in 1908, and was President of the Board of Trade, 1908–10, when he carried through important social legislation. In 1910 he became Home Secretary, and in 1911 First Lord of the Admiralty, where he brought about extensive naval reforms, increasing the pay of ratings and raising the educational standard of naval cadets. His preparations for the creation of a naval war staff were cut short by the outbreak of the First World War in which he developed the strategic thesis of the 'Eastern Front', including the Dardanelles expedition, but was not given sufficient forces for its successful realization. In 1915 he resigned from the cabinet, went on active service in France and became Lieutenant-Colonel of the 6th Royal Scots Fusiliers. Recalled by the Prime Minister, Lloyd George, in 1917, he became Minister of Munitions and was then Secretary of State for Air and for War, and later Colonial Secretary from 1921 to 1923. At that time he strongly opposed the Russian Revolution. His views aroused Liberal dislike, and in 1922 he was rejected by his Dundee constituency. He was out of Parliament for two years and began his work on pre-war and war policies, *The World Crisis*. In 1924 he returned to the Conservative Party, was elected M.P. for Epping, and made Chancellor of the Exchequer by Baldwin, a post that he held until 1929. The return to the gold standard in 1925 took place while he was in office.

From 1930 to 1939 Churchill was given no office. He turned his attention to foreign affairs and until 1933 he opposed French disarmament but favoured redress of Germany's grievances. On the advent to power of the Nazis in Germany in 1933 he urged early British rearmament, especially in the air, but he supported a non-intervention policy in Spain. He strongly opposed German Nazism, partly because it offended his deeply-rooted liberalism and partly because of the growing menace to the U.K. He predicted German expansion in Central Europe, exposed Hitler's intent to dominate the world, attacked the appeasement policy, supported the Eden resignation, rejected the Munich Agreement, *q.v.*, and saw his policies being adopted in 1939 when the U.K. opposed German aggression in Poland. On the outbreak of war he became First Lord of the Admiralty and was later Prime Minister of the coalition government from 1940 to 1945, and of the 'caretaker' Conservative government in 1945. His leadership during the darkest hours of the war, and during the years of preparation for the ultimate victory, earned him the lasting gratitude of the British people and of many millions of people throughout the world.

When the Conservative Party was defeated in the 1945 General Election he became Leader of the Opposition. From 1945 he was M.P. for Woodford. While out of office he repeatedly championed a close link between the U.K. and western Europe on the one side and the U.S.A. on the other. He was Minister of Defence, 1951–2, and Prime Minister and First Lord of the Treasury from 1951 until 1955 when he relinquished all ministerial offices. Before he retired he became a Knight of the Garter, refusing the offer of a peerage, and he remained in the House of Commons as the Member for Woodford until his death on 24 January 1965. He was given a state funeral.

C.I.O. Congress of Industrial Organizations, *q.v.*

Civil Rights. The name given to a bill, submitted to the U.S. Congress by President Kennedy in June 1963, and eventually passed by the Senate on 19 June 1964, to end segregation, *q.v.* It was carried by 73 votes (46 Democrats, 27 Republicans) to 27 (21 Democrats, 6

Republicans) after the longest debate in the history of the Senate. A filibuster, *q.v.*, was organized by the Democratic Senators representing all the Southern States except Texas and Tennessee, and continued for 83 days. The terms of the bill were: that voting qualifications, especially literacy tests, were to be identical for whites and negroes; there was to be equal opportunity of employment between whites and negroes and no discrimination in pay or promotion prospects; discrimination in public places, restaurants, shops and public transport was to be illegal. This clause, known as the public accommodation clause, was immediately tested by negroes individually and through the National Association for the Advancement of Colored People, *q.v.* The powers of the Civil Rights Commission were extended to 1967 to ensure enforcement of the bill.

In 1966 the House of Representatives accepted a bill submitted by President Johnson to end racial discrimination in the sale and leasing of houses; this was rejected by the Senate. On 11 March 1968, after a prolonged attempt by Senator Everett Dirksen (Republican) of Illinois to obstruct its passage, the Senate passed a further bill covering the protection of civil rights in housing, riot control, civil order and the rights of American Indians. This was carried by 71 votes (42 Democrats, 29 Republicans) to 20 (17 Democrats, 3 Republicans). The House of Representatives then endorsed the bill by 249 votes to 171, narrowly defeating a motion to refer the measure to a Conference Committee of both Houses.

Coexistence. Existing together, or with each other. The term is used with special reference to the ability or desire of the western powers, led by the U.S.A., and the eastern powers, led by the U.S.S.R., to exist without going to war with each other, though not necessarily in harmony. Nikita Khrushchev said in June 1963 that those who rejected the principle 'show that they do not have faith in the revolutionary strength of the working class'. He added (according to *Pravda* on 29 June 1963) 'peaceful coexistence in the sphere of ideology is impossible', and said that those who said that there could be peaceful coexistence of ideologies were betraying the cause of Communism.

Cold War. A state of tension between countries in which each side adopts policies designed to strengthen itself and weaken the other, but falling short of actual or 'hot' war. The term is frequently used to describe the relationship which has existed between the western powers and the U.S.S.R. since 1947.

Collective Security. A system by which the security and territorial integrity of each country are guaranteed by all countries. The principle was embodied in the Covenant of the League of Nations, *q.v.*, and in the Charter of the United Nations, *q.v.* A system of collective security requires the acceptance by individual countries of collective decisions, and their willingness to carry out those decisions, if necessary by military action. Under the United Nations Charter, power to deal with threats to peace is vested in the Security Council, *q.v.*, which cannot act if one of the five major powers (China, France, the U.K., the U.S.A., and the U.S.S.R.) dissents. The principle of collective security has thus not been fully established.

Collectivism. A term covering all economic and political systems based on cooperation and central planning, including not only socialism proper but also looser systems such as cooperativism, corporatism, state control, and the general coordination of economic life.

Colombia. An independent state in South America; area 439,737 sq. m. population (1970) 21,156,300, of whom about 68 per cent are mestizo, 20 per cent European, 7 per cent Indian and 5 per cent Negro; Spanish-speaking; capital Bogota. Roman Catholicism is the official religion. It was a Spanish colony from 1536 until it achieved independence as part of Greater Colombia (which included Panama, Venezuela and Ecuador) in 1819, and as a separate republic in 1830. From 1922 to 1953 every President except one completed his four-year term, ruling with a Senate and a House of Representatives. There was civil war from 1949 to 1953 when the army displaced a dictatorship established by President Gómez. The presidency was then seized by the right-wing General Gustavo Rojas Pinilla who was overthrown by a military junta in May 1957. Supported by the first vote ever held on a basis of universal adult suffrage, the junta amended the Constitution in December 1957 so that Congress would consist of equal numbers of Liberals and Conservatives and the presidency would alternate between them. The parties agreed that this 'National Front' should continue until 1974. Congress then elected as President a Liberal, Alberto Lleras Camargo, who took office in August 1958; he was succeeded in 1962 by a Conservative, Dr Guillermo Léon Valencia, and in August 1966 by the Liberal, Dr Carlos Lleras Restrepo. The small majority by which the National Front won the 1958 Congressional elections did not prevent President Lleras from pursuing a vigorous economic policy; by allowing the peso to float against the dollar he kept inflation down to an annual eight per cent (acceptable in Latin American terms), but he was frustrated by the big landowners in his attempts to redistribute land among the peasants. During his presidency several left-wing guerilla movements established themselves, of which the two most important were the Ejercito de Liberación Nacional (E.L.N.), operating in Santander in north-east Colombia, and the Fuerzas Armadas Revolucionarias Colombianas (F.A.R.C.), active mainly in Huila, Tolima, Quindio and Valle. The E.L.N. was supported by the pro-Peking Communists, the official Communist Party having condemned guerilla warfare as 'an erroneous form of revolution'; the guerillas were also aided by a number of left-wing priests of whom Camilio Torres, who was killed in February 1966, had become a legendary figure.

In the presidential elections held on 19 April 1970 the candidate of the National Front, Dr Misael Pastrana Borrero, narrowly defeated General Pinilla whose party, A.N.A.P.O., challenged the result, which was upheld by the National Election Registry after four recounts. Congressional elections, which were held simultaneously, resulted in the National Front losing its majority in both chambers. Results of elections to the House of Representatives were: National Front 89 (Liberals 58, Conservatives 31 – 94 and 48 in 1968); National Popular Front (A.N.A.P.O.) the party of General Pinilla and his daughter, Maria Eugenia Moreno, who announced that she would contest the presidential elections in 1974, 72 (Liberals 28, Conservatives 44); Belisaristas, a moderate conservative party which supported the presidential candidacy of the defeated Dr Belisario Betancur, 24 (Liberals 6, Conservatives 18); Sourdiastas, supporters of the fourth presidential candidate, Dr Evaristo Sourdis, a conservative in the Gómez tradition, 21 (Liberals 9, Conservatives 12). Since the elections the army has maintained presidential authority, and was employed in March 1971 to break a general strike called by the unions in protest against rising unemployment of nearly 1 million.

There is recurrent difficulty in keeping a stable price level owing to fluctuations in the world price of coffee, of which Colombia is the second largest producer, and which provides 70 per cent of the country's exports. Cotton, tobacco, rice, bananas and wood (mainly cedar and mahogany) are exported, and copper, steel, gold, emeralds, platinum and, since 1966, petroleum, are produced. Successive foreign exchange crises have encouraged the rapid development of new industries, including the assembly and partial manufacture of motor vehicles, radio sets and office machinery. However, the exceptionally high birth-rate threatens any possibility of an increased standard of living.

Colombo Plan. A plan devised at Colombo, Ceylon, in January 1950, by British Commonwealth Foreign Ministers, for the cooperative development of the countries of south and south-east Asia. The member countries are Afghanistan, Australia, Bhutan, Burma, Canada, India, Indonesia, Japan, Khmer Republic, Laos, Maldives,

Malaysia, Nepal, New Zealand, Pakistan, Persia, Philippines, Singapore, South Korea, Sri Lanka, Thailand, U.K., U.S.A., and Viet-Nam. The Asian member countries produce almost all the world's jute and natural rubber, more than three-quarters of its tea, two-thirds of its tin, and one-third of its oils and fats. The Commonwealth governments (including Australia, Canada, New Zealand and the U.K.) set up a Council for Technical Co-operation with headquarters in Colombo and agreed to help in planning public administration, health services, scientific research, agricultural and industrial activities, and the training and equipment of personnel. The United Nations provides expert advisers but not supplies. Funds come from the assisted areas themselves, other Commonwealth countries, the International Bank and Japan, but mostly from the U.S.A. which, before 1970, had contributed nearly £10,500,000 out of a total aid programme of £12,000,000.

Colonial Development Corporation. *See* Commonwealth Development Corporation.

Colony. An area of land which, with its inhabitants, is entirely subject to the rule of an independent state, of which it does not form an integral part. It is not itself an independent state, though it may, according to its degree of political maturity, be given some self-government. A grant of self-government and of a representative legislature does not prevent the ruling state from disallowing any legislation of which it may disapprove. Colonies have usually originated in settlements by traders or explorers of territories unoccupied by any other independent states, or in conquests of territories already occupied by other states.

In British colonies the Sovereign is represented by a Governor, who is in most cases assisted by an executive council which he must consult although he is not bound to follow its advice. In many British colonies there is also a legislative council, usually with a minority of elected members, the majority consisting of the chief officials of the colony and a number of unofficial members appointed by the Governor. There is said to be a representative legislative council when at least one half of its members is elected by the inhabitants of the colony. When the Governor is ordered by the British government to select his executive council from members of the legislative council who can command a majority in that body, the colony is said to have attained self-government, although it is still subject to the Acts passed by the British Parliament in London.

Comecon. Council for Mutual Economic Assistance, *q.v.*

Cominform. The Communist Information Bureau, set up in Belgrade on the initiative of the Communist Party of the U.S.S.R. in October 1947 to coordinate the activities of the Communist Parties of Bulgaria, Czechoslovakia, France, Hungary, Italy, Poland, Romania, the U.S.S.R., and Yugoslavia. Its headquarters were moved to Bucharest in 1948 after the expulsion of Yugoslavia from the Cominform, and it was used as an instrument in the Stalinist domination of eastern Europe. In April 1956, after the *rapprochement* of Yugoslavia and the U.S.S.R., the Cominform was dissolved; its winding-up was interpreted as a gesture to disarm western suspicions of Russian intentions.

Comintern. The Communist International, also known as the Third International in contrast to the First International (the International Working Men's Association), founded by Karl Marx in London in 1864, and the Second International, established in 1889. The Comintern was founded in Moscow on the initiative of the Russian Communist Party in March 1919 in order to rally all extreme left-wing Socialists and Communists who disliked the moderating influence of the Second International. For many years the Comintern encouraged revolution against capitalist governments, but it was dissolved in May 1943, largely as a gesture of goodwill by the U.S.S.R. towards its western allies in the Second World War. The Cominform, *q.v.*, 1947–56, took over some of the functions of the Comintern but operated over a smaller area.

Common Market. The scheme for a progressive reduction of tariffs established by the European Economic Community, *q.v.*

Commonwealth Development Corporation. Was established, as the Colonial Development Corporation, by the British government under the Overseas Resources Development Act, 1948. Its name was changed to its present one by the Commonwealth Development Act, 1963. Its duties were to develop both British colonial territories and countries which had achieved independence within the British Commonwealth since 1948, with a view to increasing their general protective capacity and trade. In 1965 the Act was extended for a final five years and loans towards the cost of approved development programmes amounting to £125 million were authorized. The development needs of the remaining dependencies were provided for under the Overseas Aid Act, 1966.

Communism. May mean either the type of society in which property is vested in the community, every individual receiving what he needs and working according to his capacity, or the revolutionary movement which seeks to achieve that type of society by overthrowing the capitalist system and establishing a dictatorship of the proletariat. Modern Communism has its basis in Marxism, *q.v.*, as developed by the

Russian revolutionary leader Vladimir Ilyich Lenin (1870–1924), who applied the Marxian analysis to the new forms of capitalism which had developed since the days of Marx. Lenin studied the trusts and combines which, with the inevitable concentration of capital, had superseded the small producers who characterized the earlier stages of capitalism. He concluded that the state and large capital interests were collaborating in imperialist policies leading to recurrent wars, that capitalists would pay higher wages to skilled workers who would then betray the proletariat by adopting moderate policies, and that the poorer classes of workers would continue to adhere to revolutionary Socialism as expounded by Marx. Like Marx, he regarded the state as the instrument of the ruling class and believed that the proletariat must destroy it and replace it by a new state machinery of its own. Communists believe that their first task is the establishment of Socialism, and that the next stage is true Communism. They say that under Socialism they give effect to the principle 'From each according to his ability, to each according to his work', and that there are still distinctions between classes, between mental and manual labour and between state property and cooperative property. Under Communism social life would be guided by the principle 'From each according to his ability, to each according to his needs', and class, labour, and property distinctions would disappear. Eventually the machinery of government would no longer be needed and the state would wither away.

Concentration, Theory of. The Marxian theory that the larger and stronger capitalists gradually oust or absorb the smaller and weaker ones, until all the capital is concentrated in the hands of a few powerful combines, trusts or banks.

Conclave. A secluded assembly of the Cardinals of the Roman Catholic Church for the election of a new Pope. Conclaves are always held in Rome. They must be convoked within three weeks after the death of a Pope. All the Cardinals in the world are summoned to Rome to take part in the Conclave; they are then cut off from communication with the outside world. Each Cardinal may bring into the Conclave a secretary and an attendant. There are, as a rule, about 300 persons in the Conclave, which must not end until it has elected a Pope.

The Conclave can act if at least half the number of Cardinals is present. The Cardinals are pledged to lifelong secrecy as to the proceedings of the Conclave. The Pope must be elected by a two-thirds majority. If the ballot does not produce this majority the voting papers are wrapped in wet straw and burnt. This produces black smoke which escapes through the chimney and indicates to the crowd waiting outside that no Pope has yet been elected. Ballots are repeated until the prescribed majority is obtained. The voting papers are then burnt without straw so as to produce white smoke. This is the traditional sign for the election of a Pope. The oldest Cardinal-Deacon steps out on the balcony and tells the crowd: 'Habemus papam' (We have a Pope).

Concordat (from the Latin *pactum concordatum*, agreed pact). An agreement between the Pope and a government, providing for mutual rights and duties, the status of the Catholic clergy and religious orders, state subsidies for the Church, the position of Catholic schools, protection of Church property, state influence on the appointments of bishops, etc. It is tantamount to an international convention. Where a Concordat cannot be reached, there is sometimes a *modus vivendi, q.v.*, an informal agreement with similar purposes.

Condominium. The common rule of a territory by two or more countries. There is an Anglo-French condominium in the New Hebrides, in the South Pacific Ocean, and there was an Anglo-Egyptian condominium over Sudan, *q.v.*, until it became independent in 1956.

Confederation. An association of several states which unite for the purpose of mutual cooperation and defence, but which does not have a direct power over the citizens of the associated states, and is not usually entrusted with the conduct of their foreign affairs. It differs from a federation, *q.v.*, which is a much closer association acquiring direct power over its states or provinces and their citizens. From 1778 until 1787, when a federation was created, the U.S.A. was a confederation. There was a Germanic Confederation from 1815 to 1866, and a Confederation of the Netherlands from 1580 to 1795. Switzerland, though in name a confederation, is a federation. The members of a confederation remain separate international persons (while members of a federation usually lose their international personality) but prohibit war between themselves.

Confrontation. A threat initiated by the former President Sukarno, *q.v.*, to confront the Federation of Malaysia, *q.v.*, with opposition from Indonesia on the grounds that it was 'neo-colonialist'. It took the form of ceasing trade with Singapore, expropriating British businesses in Indonesia and breaking off all diplomatic relations. Raids were made into Sarawak and Sabah by Indonesian guerillas, and landings and air-drops across the Straits of Malacca. In September 1964 Malaysia took the issue to the United Nations Security Council which voted 9:2 for a Norwegian resolution deploring Indonesian landings and calling for respect for territorial integrity.

Congo (Brazzaville), or People's Republic of the Congo. An independent

African state (formerly French Congo, or Middle Congo); area 129,960 sq. m.; population (1966) 826,210, comprising Bavilis, Balalis, Bakétés, M'Bochis, and 10,000 non-Africans; capital Brazzaville, the former capital of French Equatorial Africa, *q.v.* It has approximately 65 miles of coastline on the Atlantic Ocean between Gabon to the north and part of Portuguese Angola to the south, and borders with Cameroun and the Central African Republic in the north and Zaïre (the former Belgian Congo), from which it is divided by the river Oubangui, to the east. The territory was annexed by France in 1888 and later became one of the four territories comprising French Equatorial Africa; it achieved self-government within the French Community, *q.v.*, on 28 November 1958, and complete independence, still within the Community, on 17 August 1960.

The first President of the Republic, Abbé Fulbert Youlou, was forced to resign in August 1963. He was replaced by Alphonse Massamba-Débat of the Bakongo, the dominant southern tribe, and a left-wing member of the majority party, the Democratic Union for the Defence of African Interests (the local section of the Rassemblement Démocratique Africain) to which both men belonged. The government then assumed full powers. At elections held in December 1963, under a new constitution, the newly-created Mouvement National de la Révolution (M.N.R.), an organization similar to that of the Soviet Communist Party with a Central Committee and a Politburo, led by Massamba-Débat, won all 55 seats in the legislative assembly; in 1965 all other parties were banned. In August 1968 a military *coup*, organized by the army chief of staff, Captain Marien Ngouabi, who was a northerner, removed Massamba-Débat from the Presidency, but he was re-installed, with reduced powers, when no national figure could be found to replace him. Following an attempt to use the youth movement of the M.N.R. to restore his former authority by force, Massamba-Débat was again ousted by Captain Ngouabi who banned both the M.N.R. and its youth wing. The new ruler, attempting to keep an acceptable ethnic balance in the government, appointed a southerner, Captain Raoul, as Prime Minister. Disturbances continued during 1969 and after two further attempted *coups*, in November 1969 and March 1970, for which the neighbouring state of Zaïre was blamed, Ngouabi dissolved the M.N.R. It was replaced by the Congolese Workers' Party, which was to be the ultimate source of political authority in the state, of which Ngouabi was President. In November 1970 he became Chairman of the Council of State.

The principal exports are lumber, palm oil, sugar, peanuts, lead ore and tobacco. The country is not rich in mineral resources except for iron ore and potash, the extraction of which is partly financed by the World Bank and the European Investment Bank in a project designed to double exports. Although nominally a member of the French Community and receiving technical aid and loans from France, it has since 1964 sought increased political and economic ties with Communist countries. The presence of Cuban military instructors was thought to have incited an attempted army *coup*, which was suppressed in June 1966. In that year several French industrialists were expelled from the country and relations with France deteriorated rapidly until the change of government in 1968. In 1972 it relinquished membership of O.C.A.M., *q.v.* It remains a member of the economic and customs union (U.D.E.A.C.) which was established with Cameroun, Chad, Central African Republic and Gabon in December 1964.

Congo (Kinshasa). The former Belgian Congo, *q.v.*, and the name by which the republic of Zaïre, *q.v.*, was known before 27 October 1971.

Congress. The bicameral federal legislature of the U.S.A., comprising the Senate, *q.v.*, and the House of Representatives, *q.v.* Article One of the U.S. Constitution begins: 'All legislative powers herein granted shall be vested in a Congress of the United States, which shall consist of a Senate and House of Representatives.' Elections take place by popular vote on the Tuesday after the first Monday in November in the even-numbered years, except in Maine where they are held in September. The Congressional term begins on the following 3 January and continues for two years. A member of the Senate is usually referred to as a senator and a member of the House of Representatives as a congressman.

Congress of Industrial Organizations (C.I.O.). A U.S. and Canadian labour movement with six million members when it merged in December 1955 with the American Federation of Labor, *q.v.*, to form the American Federation of Labor and Congress of Industrial Organizations, *q.v.* The C.I.O. arose after the formation of a Committee for Industrial Organization within the A.F. of L. in 1935. This Committee and its affiliated unions favoured industrial unions comprising all the workers, skilled as well as unskilled, in an industry, in contrast to the craft unions of the A.F. of L. which were limited to skilled workers. They said that the A.F. of L. was out of date and that the mass-production industries, such as the automobile, radio, tyre, steel, and aluminium industries, had produced a new type of worker. After vain demands for a modification of the A.F. of L. structure, eight large unions formed the C.I.O. in November

1935, led by the miners' leader, John L. Lewis, who later left the C.I.O. These unions represented mine, textile, clothing, oil, smelting, typographic and millinery workers; they were later joined by steel, glass, automobile, radio and rubber workers. The C.I.O. started to recruit the unorganized workers, and its affiliated unions were expelled by the A.F. of L. in 1936. During the Democratic administrations of President Roosevelt and President Truman the C.I.O. was, through its political action committee, more willing than the A.F. of L. to declare its support for Democratic candidates. In 1945 it joined the World Federation of Trade Unions, *q.v.*, from which it withdrew in 1949. The President of the C.I.O., Walter Reuther, *q.v.*, signed the agreement for the merger of the C.I.O. with the A.F. of L. in February 1955.

Congress Party (Indian National Congress). The largest political party in India. It was founded in the late nineteenth century at the instigation of an Englishman, Allan Octavian Hume, who urged Calcutta University graduates to form a party which would encourage national trades, bridge religious differences, and have as its principal aim the improvement of relations between the U.K. and India. Originally the party included Moslems, Hindus, and Untouchables; it emerged as a Hindu nationalist movement pledged to expel the British, under the domination first of Bal Gengadhar Tilak, who fomented anti-British riots in Bombay in 1903, and then of Mahatma Gandhi, the advocate of Civil Disobedience. British policy in India between 1919 and 1947 consisted largely of attempts to conciliate the Congress Party. In 1935 it obtained control of 8 of the 11 state legislatures; it refused to cooperate in the war against Germany in 1939, and in the war against Japan in 1941, and its leaders were imprisoned. Since independence was achieved in 1947 it has been the governing party but after the death of Jawaharlal Nehru, *q.v.*, in 1964 its popularity waned. It received a setback in the 1967 elections, winning 280 out of the 521 seats in the House of the People as compared with 356 out of 500 seats in the elections of 1962, and retaining control of only nine of the seventeen State governments. In November 1969, 96 members of the parliamentary Party, led by Morarji Desai, *q.v.*, formed an Opposition Congress. The Ruling Congress, led by Indira Gandhi, *q.v.*, won an overwhelming victory in the 1971 elections with 350 seats in the House of the People, regaining control of all except five of the State governments.

Conseil de L'Entente. *See* Entente, Council of the.

Conservative Party. A British political party, also known as the Conservative and Unionist Party; it obtained 13,106,965 out of the

28,258,332 votes cast at the 1970 General Election and 330 out of 630 seats in the House of Commons. It is traditionally the right-wing party in Parliament and successor to the Tory Party of the eighteenth and nineteenth centuries, but very different from Conservative parties in continental countries. Such parties are often reactionary, indifferent or hostile to democracy, and opposed to social progress. The Conservative Party, particularly after its defeat in 1945 (when it won 213 out of 640 seats in the House of Commons), adopted a moderately progressive policy and accepted the principles of the welfare state. It is by no means a liberal party in the economic sense, since it believes in social measures which involve heavy direct and indirect taxation. The influence of the extreme right wing of the party has diminished as the Conservative leaders have realized the importance of obtaining a substantial following in the lower income groups; however, this influence is often felt in the constituency organizations.

The Conservative Party today has strong support both from the aristocracy and large business interests and from the lower-income groups in the population. It remains to be seen whether a Conservative economic policy can, over a long period, reconcile the interests of these groups, or whether it would be forced to abandon the support of one group to retain the confidence of the other.

The leader of the Conservative Party is Edward Heath, *q.v.* Other leading figures are Anthony Barber, *q.v.*, Robert Carr, *q.v.*, Sir Alec Douglas-Home, *q.v.*, Quintin Hogg (Lord Hailsham), *q.v.*, Reginald Maudling, *q.v.*, Enoch Powell, *q.v.*, Geoffrey Rippon, *q.v.*, and William Whitelaw, *q.v.*

Contraband (from Latin *contra bandum*, against the ban). Goods forbidden to be supplied by neutrals to belligerents. The Declaration of London, agreed by the International Naval Conference in 1909, distinguished between absolute contraband (arms and ammunition) and conditional contraband (goods normally destined for peaceful purposes but also useful in war). A list of conditional contraband, including certain raw materials, was compiled, but did not come into effect as the Declaration was not ratified. In the First and Second World Wars the contraband list was extended to almost every article of importance to an enemy, including foodstuffs. Neutral merchant ships in wartime can, by international law, be visited and searched, and any contraband may be seized.

Corporate State. A system of government in which trade and professional corporations are the basis of society. The corporations represent the employers and the employed in the various branches of the economic life of a country; parliament is elected not by territorial constituencies but by the corporations. They are supposed to make regulations for industrial production and working conditions. The advocates of the system say that it excludes party politics and makes people conduct public affairs in a realistic manner. The system has attracted those who wish to end the struggle between workers and employers and to concentrate on increasing national production. The corporate states set up hitherto (notably in Portugal and in Fascist Italy) have been in fact dictatorships with a partly corporate structure, so that there has been little opportunity to assess the true value of the system.

Cosgrave, Liam. Irish politician; born 1920 in Dublin; son of a former President of the Executive Council of the Irish Free State; educated at Castleknock College, Dublin. He served in the National Army and was called to the Irish Bar in 1943, when he joined the Fine Gael group in the Dáil as the member, first, for Dublin County, and, from 1948, for Dun Laoghaire. He was chairman of the Committee of Public Accounts in 1945, and Parliamentary Secretary to his party leader, John Costello (who was then Prime Minister), from 1948 to 1951 and Minister of Industry and Commerce from 1951 to 1954. In Costello's second administration, 1954–7, Cosgrave held the Ministry of External Affairs, leading the Irish delegation to the United Nations in 1956. He succeeded Costello as leader of Fine Gael in April 1965, becoming Prime Minister in March 1973.

Costa Rica. An independent republic in the southern part of Central America between Nicaragua and Panama; area 19,653 sq. m.; population (1969 estimate) 1,680,000 and Spanish-speaking, with a high rate of literacy; capital San José. Roman Catholicism is the official and subsidized religion. Spain ruled the area from 1530 until the revolt of 1821; Costa Rica then became part of the United States of Central America until it achieved independence in 1839. In 1948 the army was abolished, the President declaring that a peace-loving country needed no army. In that year the stability of the democratic regime was seriously threatened by a revolt; in 1954 the same revolutionaries, with support from Nicaragua, attempted an unsuccessful invasion. At the request of the Organization of American States, q.v., the U.S.A. provided aircraft to repel the invaders. Costa Rica and Nicaragua signed a treaty of friendship in 1956. The government of President José Figueres Ferrer, leader of the National Liberation Party (P.L.N.) in power from 1953 to 1958, carried out a policy of nationalization and rigorous taxation, including a capital levy of 10 per cent, in an unsuccessful attempt to improve the country's financial position. In 1958 the opposition leader, Mario Echandi Jiménez, a

Conservative lawyer, was elected President. He reversed Figueres' policy of nationalizing banks and insurance companies and encouraged private enterprise. His successor, Francisco Orlich Bolmarich (President from 1962 to 1966), who was supported in his election campaign by ex-President Figueres and the National Liberation Party, continued this policy, and achieved considerable social progress while preserving economic stability. The presidential elections held in February 1966 were won narrowly by a moderate Conservative, José Joaquin Trejos Fernandez, the candidate of the Party of National Unification (U.N.), a coalition of the two main parties in opposition to the P.L.N., the Republican Party (P.R.) and the Party of National Unity (P.U.N.). However at the elections held in February 1970 Figueres defeated his former Presidential rival, Echandi, by 294,266 votes to 221,152.

Under the 1949 Constitution executive authority rests with the President, directly elected for a four-year term providing that he receives 40 per cent of the votes, two Vice-Presidents (also elected), and a Cabinet. The legislative organ is one chamber of 57 deputies, the Constitutional Congress. Voting is compulsory to the age of 70. At elections held in February 1970 the results were: P.L.N. 32 seats (29 in 1966); U.N. 22 (26); others 3. President Figueres assumed office in May 1970 following riots in protest against the signing of a contract between the government and the Aluminium Company of America (A.L.C.O.A.) granting the right to prospect for bauxite.

The economy is mainly agricultural, exporting coffee, which represents approximately half the foreign exchange earnings, sugar and bananas. The United Fruit Company handles most of the banana crop and ships it through the Company's two Pacific Ocean ports. Sulphur was discovered in 1966. Costa Rica enjoys the highest per capita income of Latin America.

Council for African and Malagasy Affairs. Created by the French government in May 1961, the Council was the successor to the principal organs of the French Community, *q.v.*, and was responsible for French policy towards the members of the African and Malagasy Union, *q.v.* The members of the Council include the French President, Prime Minister, Foreign Minister, and Minister for Cooperation.

Council for Mutual Economic Assistance (Comecon). Was established in January 1949 by a number of eastern European countries to provide an economic structure similar to that set up by the countries of western Europe in 1948, when the Organization for European Economic Co-operation, *q.v.*, was born. Its members are Bulgaria, Czechoslovakia, the German Democratic Republic, Hungary, the Mongolian People's Republic, Poland, Romania, the U.S.S.R., and Cuba. Albania ceased to be a member in October 1961. The Council has drawn up plans for the development and coordination of the various national economies with a view to specialization in production, adequate provision of raw materials, and cooperation in scientific research and technology.

Council of Europe. Set up on 5 May 1949 by Belgium, Denmark, France, Ireland, Italy, Luxemburg, the Netherlands, Norway, Sweden, and the U.K. It comprises: (1) a Committee of Foreign Ministers or their deputies and (2) a Consultative Assembly composed of representatives chosen by the governments, meeting at Strasbourg and empowered to discuss all matters of common concern with the exception of national defence. The Assembly can offer recommendations to the Ministers but has no other powers. Any European state accepting the principles of freedom, political liberty, and the rule of law is eligible for admission and since 1949 Austria, Cyprus, the German Federal Republic, Greece, Iceland, Malta, Switzerland, and Turkey have become members, although Greece withdrew in December 1969.

Coup d'État. A sudden change of government by force, brought about by those who already hold some governmental or military power. It differs from a revolution in that it is effected from above, while a revolution involves the participation of the masses. Examples of *coups d'état* are the seizures of power by Napoleon III in 1851, by Mussolini in 1922, by Pilsudski (in Poland) in 1928, by the Czechoslovak Communists in 1948, by the anti-Perón movement in Argentina in 1955 and by military factions in Iraq in July 1958 and February 1963. The usual method employed by organizers of a *coup* is to seize government buildings, railways, radio and television stations, power plants, and waterworks, in order to gain control.

Couve de Murville, Maurice. French politician, born 14 January 1907 into an upper-class French Protestant family, and educated at the École des Sciences Politiques in Paris where he obtained his doctorate. He entered the French Civil Service, rising from the rank of tax inspector in 1930 to become, eight years later, Deputy Director of a department of the Bank of France (le Mouvement Général des Fonds). He escaped to Algiers during the German occupation of France to join General Giraud and in 1943 was appointed his administrative secretary. He was also a member of the National Liberation Committee and of the Committee of Finance. In 1944 he embarked on a diplomatic career as Ambassador-Extraordinary to Italy, and the following year became Director General of Political Affairs at the French Foreign Ministry. He was Ambassador to

Egypt from 1950 to 1954, to the U.S.A. in 1955 and to the German Federal Republic from 1956 to 1958 when he was recalled to Paris and appointed Minister of Foreign Affairs in de Gaulle's government. He held this office for ten years, longer than any previous occupant with the exception of Vergennes, the first Foreign Minister of Louis XIV. He failed to secure election to the French Assembly in 1967 when he stood, for the first time, as a candidate in the seventh arrondissement of Paris; he was subsequently elected for another Paris constituency but did not contest the 1968 elections. For a short period from June 1968 he was Minister of Finance, changing office with Michel Debré. In July 1968, following the massive Gaullist electoral victory, he was appointed to succeed Georges Pompidou, *q.v.*, as Prime Minister. He resigned in June 1969, on Pompidou's election as President of France, and was succeeded by Jacques Chaban-Delmas, *q.v.*

Crosland, Charles Anthony Raven. British Labour Party politician; born 29 August 1918; educated at Highgate School and Trinity College, Oxford. After war service from 1940 to 1945, he returned to Oxford and became a Fellow and Tutor in Economics at Trinity College. He first entered Parliament in 1950 as the member for South Gloucester, a constituency which disappeared in the boundary re-organization of 1955. In 1959 he was re-elected as the member for Grimsby. From 1956 to 1958 he acted as secretary of an independent commission of inquiry into the British Co-operative Movement. He was appointed Economic Secretary to the Treasury in October 1964, entering the Cabinet in January 1965 as Secretary of State for Education and Science. He became President of the Board of Trade in August 1967 and was Secretary of State for Local Government and Regional Planning from October 1969 until June 1970.

Crypto-Communist. A secret sympathizer with, or member of, a Communist movement.

Cuba. An independent Central American state which occupies the largest island in the Caribbean Sea, ninety miles south-east of the coast of the U.S.A.; area 44,206 sq. m.; population (1970 census) 8,553,395; Spanish-speaking; capital Havana. It was governed by Spain from the sixteenth to the nineteenth centuries; as the Spanish hold weakened there were many revolts and in 1898 the U.S.A. defeated Spain in war and occupied Cuba. Under the 1901 Constitution a republic was proclaimed, but there was a U.S. military occupation until 1902 and again from 1906 to 1909. Until 1959 Cuba was ruled as a dictatorship by General Fulgencio Batistá y Zaldivar, who had seized power, as an army sergeant, in 1933. He introduced in 1940 a Constitution modelled on that of the U.S.A. and was President from 1940 to 1944, and again from 1952 until November 1958 when he nominated Andres Rivero Aguero as his successor. In January 1959 the military success of the rebel bands of Fidel Castro, *q.v.*, forced Batistá to flee from Cuba, and his regime collapsed.

From January to July 1959 Dr Manuel Urrutia held office as President; he was succeeded by Dr Osvaldo Dorticos Torrado. Castro became Prime Minister and Minister of the Armed Forces, with his brother Raúl as his deputy. The Constitution was suspended in January 1959 and government is by decree. Elections were promised within eighteen months of the revolution but have not yet taken place.

On 17 April 1961 President Kennedy launched a short-lived invasion, by Cuban émigrés under U.S. control, at the Bay of Pigs, *q.v.* On 22 October 1962 he revealed that the U.S.A. had discovered Soviet offensive missile sites in Cuba; he announced that ships carrying offensive weapons to Cuba would be blockaded. On 27 October Nikita Khrushchev agreed to withdraw from Cuba weapons 'regarded as offensive' if U.S. missiles were removed from Turkey. On the same day the U.S.A. insisted that, as a preliminary to consideration of any proposals, work on the bases must stop, offensive weapons must be rendered inoperable, and further shipments of such weapons to Cuba must cease. On 28 October Khrushchev replied that he had ordered that 'offensive weapons' in Cuba should be dismantled, crated, and returned to the U.S.S.R. On 2 November Kennedy announced that the weapons were being dismantled and crated. The crisis itself thus lasted 11 days.

The radical and nationalist policies of the Castro government have included a comprehensive, but unrealistic, education programme (by 1972 only 21 per cent of Cuban children who started primary schooling completed it, and there was a shortage of 18,000 teachers), and sweeping land reforms. The maximum holding is limited to approximately 166 acres for each person or company, except for sugar, rice and cattle farms, for which the maximum is 3,300 acres. The government also set up the National Institute for Agrarian Reform (I.N.R.A.) which administers the 1,400 cooperative holdings established since the revolution and controls some 70 per cent of the cultivable land. Previously 1 per cent of the population had owned more than one-third of the land. Sugar is grown on 56 per cent of the cultivated area and production is the highest in the world, amounting to one-tenth of the world total. The surplus, most of which, since 1960, has been bought by the U.S.S.R., constitutes 85 per cent of Cuba's exports. Tobacco is another important export, and the island produces one-tenth of the world supply of nickel. Before 1958 70 per cent of Cuban trade was with the U.S.A. In 1962, following the seizure of a large number of American-owned firms and the abortive invasion in 1961, the U.S.A. imposed an economic blockade which cut off the customary supplies of oil from the American continent and caused food and clothes to be rationed. Since 1964 more than 80 per cent of Cuba's trade has been with the Communist bloc, and especially the U.S.S.R. which provides oil from Baltic and Black Sea ports and which has sustained the Cuban economy at an estimated daily cost of $1 million.

In 1962 the Organization of American States, *q.v.*, expelled Cuba because of her alignment with the Sino-Soviet bloc. The support given by the Castro government to the guerilla activities of Ernesto 'Che' Guevara, *q.v.*, in Bolivia, and to similar revolutionary groups operating in Guatemala, Peru, Uruguay, Colombia, Argentina, and especially in Venezuela, have further isolated Cuba from South and Central American economic activity and excluded it from participation in the Central American Common Market, *q.v.* The official ideology of the Cuban revolution is Marxism-Leninism, *q.v.*, although its principal advocate, Anibal Escalante, was purged by Castro in 1962 and subsequently imprisoned. In 1965 the Cuban Communist Party was reconstituted with a central committee of 100, an eight-man politbureau and a six-man secretariat, but Castro's version of Communism rates the activities of the guerilla of greater importance in the revolutionary struggle than the role of the party. This conflicts with Russian policy of penetrating Latin America by supporting existing left-wing political organizations, while maintaining correct diplomatic relations with the individual governments.

Curzon Line. An eastern boundary for Poland, with a racial basis, excluding White Russians and Ukrainians, proposed by Lord Curzon, British Foreign Secretary, after the First World War. After the Russian Revolution Poland had taken the western Ukraine and western White Russia from the U.S.S.R., but lost some of these territories as the result of a Russian counter-attack. Poland would have had to withdraw further if it had accepted the Curzon Line. When Germany invaded Poland from the west in 1939, the U.S.S.R. occupied eastern Poland roughly up to the Curzon Line, and it remained the eastern frontier after the end of the war. Poland was compensated by being awarded German territory as far as the Oder-Neisse Line, *q.v.*

Customs Union. An arrangement whereby two or more states, while retaining their independence and sovereignty, are united into a common tariff area, lifting the tariff frontier between themselves and establishing a common tariff frontier with other countries, as in the case of Belgium, the Netherlands, and Luxemburg, which formed Benelux, *q.v.*

Cyprus. An island in the eastern Mediterranean (about 40 miles south of Turkey and 60 miles west of Syria) which is an independent state and member of the British Commonwealth; area 3,572 sq. m.; population (1970 estimate) 633,000, of whom four fifths are Greek-speaking or belong to the Cypriot branch of the Greek Orthodox Church, and the rest are Moslems of Turkish origin; capital Nicosia. The island was part of the Byzantine Empire until it was captured in 1191 by King Richard I. It was subsequently ruled by the Templars, by the French Lusignan family, by Venice, and from 1571 to 1878 by the Turks. Except for a short time during the fourth century it never belonged to Greece. In 1878 the British acquired rights in Cyprus, annexing it in 1914 and in 1915 offering it to Greece in return for Greek support in Serbia; the offer was rejected. Turkey recognized British sovereignty in 1924; in 1925 Cyprus became a colony. It became independent on 16 August 1960 and joined the British Commonwealth in March 1961.

Under the Turks the Ethnarchy, or Church leadership, first became politically active. It headed the anti-Moslem movement which, in the nineteenth century, became linked with the idea of union with an independent Greece. Enosis (union with Greece) was for years a rallying-cry for Cypriots opposed to foreign rule. An Enosis uprising in 1931 reached such serious proportions that the legislative council was suspended and two bishops were exiled. Later the movement, led by the Ethnarch, Archbishop Makarios, *q.v.*, united two parties: the right wing, pledged to support the Greek monarchy; and the Communist Reform Party of Working People, known as A.K.E.L. From 1944 to 1948, while the Communists were engaged in civil war in Greece, A.K.E.L. advocated independence for Cyprus. In 1948, the parties rejected British proposals for a new constitution, demanded a plebiscite, and, in the absence of any constitutional channel through which to register their opposition, turned to strike action and rioting, which were intensified in 1954 when the British transferred the headquarters of their Middle East Land Forces from Egypt to Cyprus.

Civil war eventually broke out between the Greek and Turkish communities in 1955. The following year Archbishop Makarios was deported to the Seychelles on the ground that he had been implicated in the terrorist activities of E.O.K.A., the militant right-wing of the Enosis movement. The conflict was ended in February 1959 by an agreement, concluded by Greece, Turkey, Cyprus and the U.K., by which Cyprus became independent, although the U.K. was to retain sovereignty over the areas containing its military bases. On 14 December 1959 Archbishop Makarios was proclaimed President, having received 144,501 votes, against 17,753 votes for his opponent, John Clerides, who was supported by the left wing. Under a further agreement of July 1960 Cyprus undertook 'not to participate, in whole or in part, in any political or economic union with any state whatsoever'. After three years of disagreement over the working of the 1960 Constitution civil war again broke out and in 1964 a United Nations Peace-Keeping Force (U.N.P.F.C.Y.P.) was established in Cyprus, and a mediator appointed. His proposals, recommending continued independence, majority rule with safeguards for minorities, and rejecting Turkish Cypriot suggestions for a federation of two separate regions, were unacceptable to the Turkish community who then appealed to Turkey for support. War between Greece and Turkey was narrowly averted in 1967 by their mutual acceptance of a peace plan under which Greece agreed to withdraw its troops from Cyprus, and Turkey to disband the forces, particularly the naval forces, which had been mobilized.

In July 1970, at the first elections for the House of Representatives to be held since 1960, the results were: Unified Party (moderate right-wing, supporting President Makarios and a feasible solution to the deadlock between the Greek and Turkish communities) 15 seats; A.K.E.L. 9; Progressive Front (right-wing and favouring Enosis but within the context of self-determination for Cyprus) 7; Democratic Centre Union or E.D.E.K. (moderate left-wing and advocating the political independence of Cyprus, the nationalization of the mainly American-owned mining enterprises, and the abolition of the British military bases) 2; Independents 2. The extreme right-wing Democratic National Party, which had campaigned for Enosis, was unrepresented. The Turkish community held separate elections for the 15 seats allocated to them in the House of Representatives, which they have declined to attend since 1964 when the Turkish Vice-President, Dr Fazil Kutchuk, resigned. In 1967 they set up a Transitional Turkish Cypriot Administration, attended by the 15 elected representatives, which is not recognized by the Cyprus government. Since 1968 talks between the representatives of the two communities have continued, but have foundered on the Turkish demand for regional autonomy for the 20 per cent of the island occupied by their people. In 1970 there was a recrudescence of Enosis and an attempt was made on the President's life. The clandestine return to Cyprus in the autumn of

1971 by General Grivas, the former E.O.K.A. resistance leader, an unsuccessful, but well-publicized, campaign by the Bishops of Kitium, Paphos and Kyrenia to persuade President Makarios to resign on the grounds that he was prevented by the rules of the Church from exercising temporal power and that he had abandoned the ideal of Enosis, and the importation of large quantities of arms into Cyprus in 1972, prompted the Greek government to press for a peace settlement which would be acceptable to Turkey.

The island produces wine, cereals, locust beans, tobacco, citrus and other fruits and various vegetables. The most valuable industry is mining, which involves the export of asbestos, pyrites and other minerals. In 1966 an oil refinery was opened at Larnaca by a consortium of Shell, B.P. and Mobil oil companies and the government of Cyprus. The potentially flourishing tourist industry has been adversely affected by the political situation. Cyprus is not self-supporting; the reduction in British military expenditure since 1960 has created unemployment, and substantial grants have been made by the U.K. and the U.S.A. to help development plans. In 1971 approximately one-third of the imports came from, and over 70 per cent of the exports went to, the U.K.

Czechoslovakia. An independent federal republic in Central Europe; area 49,381 sq. m.; population (1970 census) 14,362,000, including 9 million Czechs and 5 million Slovaks; capital Prague. The republic was created in 1918 from the former Austrian provinces of Bohemia, Moravia, and Silesia, and the former Hungarian provinces of Slovakia and Sub-Carpathian Russia. It brought under one government 7,500,000 Czechs, 2,300,000 Slovaks, 3,250,000 Germans, and 690,000 Magyars. The Slovak minority opposed Bohemian centralism and the severance of commercial connections with Budapest, while the German inhabitants of the Bohemian and Moravian border districts formed the Sudeten-German Party under Henlein in 1933 and demanded autonomy within Czechoslovakia. When this had been granted in 1938 Hitler announced his intention of incorporating the Sudetenland in Germany. By the Munich Agreement, *q.v.*, the Sudetenland was ceded to Germany, which guaranteed the new frontier; other parts of Czechoslovakia were ceded to Hungary and Poland. When Germany invaded Czechoslovakia in March 1939 Slovakia was separated from the new 'Protectorate of Bohemia and Moravia', which became part of Germany, and was made an 'independent' state under German protection and occupation.

In 1945 the Sudeten-Germans were expelled and, with the exception of the cession of Ruthenia to the U.S.S.R., the pre-1938 frontiers were re-established. The presence of the Germans from 1939 to 1945 caused a resurgence of nationalism and the first post-war government was a coalition of Socialists, Social Democrats, Communists, and Agrarians, and of Slovak Democrats and Communists; its immediate policy was large-scale nationalization, particularly of former German assets. At the 1946 elections the Communists emerged as the leading party, obtaining 38 per cent of the votes. They formed a National Front government, under Klement Gottwald, with 13 Social Democrat members (who had polled 13 per cent of the total vote) and 4 representatives from each of the other three major parties. Drought and a bad harvest in 1947 were responsible for a shortage of food which, combined with Gottwald's rejection of aid under the Marshall Plan, *q.v.*, made the government, especially the Communists since they were the controlling party, unpopular. The 12 moderates in the government had declared their intention to ask for Marshall Aid if the Communists should ever cease to be the dominant party. Fearing that he would lose ground in the elections which were to be held in June 1948 (and foreseeing a repetition in Czechoslovakia of the manoeuvres in the French Assembly which had resulted in 1947 in the exclusion from the French government of the Communists, although they had obtained the highest percentage of votes), Gottwald forced a crisis by 'packing' the police. On 20 February 1948 the 12 moderates resigned in protest, hoping for a dissolution of parliament before the Communists should have time to prevent free elections from being held, but the Social Democrats supported the government and it remained in office. Five days later President Beneš had to accept a new cabinet from which the 12 were excluded, drawn from all parties which, under Communist instructions, had now purged themselves of 'hostile elements'. The Social Democrats' acceptance of the Communist *coup* is explicable only in terms of foreign policy. The West had failed the Czechs at Munich; they still feared Germany and were convinced that only by a military alliance with the U.S.S.R. would they be guaranteed the necessary protection.

At the 1948 elections to the National Assembly the electorate was presented with a single list of National Front candidates. The Front, which now incorporated the Communist Party, the Social Democrats (Socialist), the Popular Party (Roman Catholic), and the Slovak National Reconstruction Party, secured 89 per cent of the total vote and obtained similar majorities in 1954, 1960 and 1964. The highest executive organ is the Communist Party Politburo; in 1954 Antonin Novotný (born 1904) became First Secretary of the Communist Party, and in 1957 he was also elected President of the Republic for a seven-year term, and re-elected for a further five years in November 1964.

The country was highly industrialized before 1939 and a succession of post-war Five-Year Plans brought about substantial increases in production of machinery, hydro-electric power, steel, and minerals which include iron, coal, silver, lead, copper and graphite. The third Five-Year Plan however was abandoned in 1962 because agriculture and fuel and power developments did not reach their targets. A major economic reorganization was introduced in 1965 to stimulate agricultural production and those manufactures which could be exported to Western Europe; increasing emphasis was to be placed on profitability and competition, and a reduction in central planning was to be accompanied by greater devolution of responsibility to individual factories. A very high rate of increase in industrial production (56·5 per cent in the 1966–70 plan) was demanded of Slovakia under this scheme without comparable investment, and Alexander Dubček, q.v., First Secretary of the Slovak Communist Party, accused Novotný, who is a Czech, of favouring the more backward areas in Bohemia. Slovak unrest combined with general economic discontent brought about Novotný's resignation as First Secretary of the Communist Party in January 1968. He was succeeded by Alexander Dubček. On 22 March 1968 he resigned as President and was replaced by General Ludvik Svoboda, Commander of the Czech forces in the U.S.S.R. during the Second World War and a former Minister of Defence.

A programme of democratic reforms, which included the abolition of press censorship, was initiated by the Prime Minister, Oldřich Černík, and accompanied by economic decentralization under the supervision of Dr Ota Šik. Czechoslovakia agreed to negotiate with other signatories of the Warsaw Pact, q.v., on the possible military implications of the new policy. On 21 August 1968 Soviet troops, accompanied by forces from four Warsaw Pact countries (Bulgaria, the German Democratic Republic, Hungary and Poland), invaded Czechoslovakia. Romania and Yugoslavia dissociated themselves from the invasion. A U.N. resolution condemning the action as a violation of the Charter was carried by 10 votes to 2, with three abstentions, but was vetoed by the U.S.S.R. A phased withdrawal of the troops was then negotiated in Moscow in September 1968 by the Czech leaders who were forced to accept a protocol which specified: the strengthening of the Ministry of the Interior and the reimposition of censorship; direction of the State and the economy by the Communist Party; adherence to all existing treaties and agreements and rejection of neutrality; closer economic cooperation with the U.S.S.R.

Since the major part of Czechoslovakia's trade (68 per cent in 1966) is with Communist countries, this last condition would effectively prevent the expansion of foreign trade envisaged by the Černik government.

On 28 October 1968, the fiftieth anniversary of the founding of the state, Czechoslovakia became a federal republic comprising the Czech Socialist Republic and the Slovak National Republic. Each nation has autonomy in education, justice, agriculture and housing; defence, foreign affairs, economic affairs and police security are reserved to the federal government. Parliament consists of two houses, one elected on a population basis, and one with equal representation for both nations; each house can veto the resolutions of the other, thus ensuring Slovak equality with the more numerous Czechs. Alexander Dubček was elected first President of the Federal Assembly following his replacement as First Secretary of the Communist Party by Dr Gustav Husák on 17 April 1969, but he was soon demoted, and most of his supporters were removed from the government by 1970; Husák temporarily resisted pressure from the Russians for political trials but these occurred on a large scale during 1972. In November 1971, at the first elections to be held since 1964, 99·81 per cent of the electorate voted for the candidates of the National Front.

D

Dahomey. An independent republic; area 47,000 sq. m.; population (1969 estimate) 2,645,000 comprising Fons and Adjus, Boribas, Yorubas, Mahis, and 3,000 Europeans; capital Porto Novo. It occupies 70 miles of the Western African coast, between Togo and Nigeria, with the republics of Upper Volta and Niger to the north, and was an independent African kingdom until in 1851 a coastal strip was taken by the French, who annexed the whole territory in 1893. It later became one of the eight territories comprising French West Africa, *q.v.*, and achieved self-government within the French Community, *q.v.*, on 4 December 1958, and complete independence, after breaking with the Community in June 1960, on 1 August 1960. With Ivory Coast, Niger and Upper Volta, Dahomey is a member of the Conseil de l'Entente (*see* Entente, Council of the). It is one of the most densely populated areas of West Africa, with a high level of education; but the economy is dependent upon agriculture, producing maize, manioc and yams, and the extensive forests of oil palms providing palm kernels and palm oil, which constitute 80 per cent of the country's exports. French aid helps to balance the budget.

At elections for an assembly of 70 members held in December 1960 the Parti Dahoméen de l'Unité (P.D.U.), led by Hubert Maga (the outgoing Head of State) and Sourou Migan Apithy, defeated the Union Démocratique Dahoméenne (U.D.D.) led by Justin Ahomadegbe. Maga and Apithy became President and Vice-President on 31 December 1960. In October 1963 Maga was deposed by the army, the assembly was dissolved and a new constitution promulgated. Apithy and Ahomadegbe then became President and Chief of Government but they, in turn, were ousted in November 1965 by an army *coup* inspired by General Christophe Soglo who became Head of State, suspending the Constitution, banning all political parties and dissolving the municipal councils. All trade union activity was forbidden in December 1967 owing to the workers' refusal to accept a continuation of the wage reduction of 25 per cent which had been introduced in 1965. Strikes followed, and army units, under Major Maurice Kouandeté, brought into Porto Novo to control industrial unrest, deposed General Soglo. On 21 December 1967 Lt-Colonel Alphone Alley (formerly Chief of Staff to Soglo, but known to have been in conflict with him) became Head of State and Major Kouandeté Prime Minister.

A return to civilian rule was promised in May 1968 and presidential elections were held from which former Presidents were excluded as candidates. Maga and Apithy appealed successfully to the Supreme Court against the ruling, but the military government confirmed its original decree. In response to Maga's call for a boycott 74 per cent of the electorate abstained, and in northern areas, where support for Maga was strong, only 1 per cent polled. The election was declared void and Dr Emile Derlin Zinzou, Minister of Foreign Affairs in the Soglo administration, was appointed President. He was confirmed in office by a referendum, held on 28 July 1968, in which he obtained 76 per cent of the total votes in a heavy poll, but on 10 December 1969 he was deposed by Kouandeté, now Commander in Chief of the Army. His policy of allowing the airlift of supplies from Dahomey to Biafra, *q.v.*, had brought a cessation of trade with Nigeria and economic distress in the eastern border areas. A Military Directorate then ruled the country until May 1970 when it handed over authority to a Presidential Council, consisting of the three veteran politicians, Maga, Apithy and Ahomadegbe, all of whom had been candidates in the presidential elections arranged for March 1970 but cancelled by the Army. It was agreed that each should be Head of State in rotation for a two-year period. Maga was appointed Head of State in May 1970 and was succeeded by Ahomadegbe in March 1972.

Dáil Eireann. The lower house of the Parliament of Ireland, *q.v.*

Danzig (known as Gdansk). A Polish port on the Baltic Sea and at the mouth of the river Vistula; population (1967) 299,000. The city was a Slav foundation, but was conquered in 1310 by the Teutonic Knights who massacred the Slav population. It became a German town but the Poles continually demanded it as their only outlet to the sea. It was a Free City under Polish suzerainty from 1450 until 1793 when it was annexed by Prussia. Apart from 1807 to 1815, when it was restored to Poland by Napoleon, it was in German hands until the Versailles Treaty, *q.v.*, which created a Polish corridor separating East Prussia from Germany and ending at Danzig. The major powers took into account the German character of the population and did not award Danzig to Poland, but established it as a Free City within the Polish customs area, entrusting to Poland the conduct of its foreign relations. Its constitution was guaranteed by the League of Nations, which was represented there by a High Commissioner who arbitrated on disputes between Danzig and Poland. In March 1939, after entering Czechoslovakia and demanding the Lithuanian port of Memel, Germany asked Poland for Danzig and the strip of territory connecting East Prussia with the rest of Germany. Disguised German troops occupied the city in August 1939, and on 1 September the local Nazi leader proclaimed the reunion of Danzig with Germany; this was at once confirmed by the German government. Germany invaded Poland on the same day, and the U.K. and France declared war on Germany on 3 September in accordance with their previous undertakings to protect Poland. Danzig became part of Poland after the Second World War as a result of the Potsdam Agreement, *q.v.*, of 2 August 1945.

Dardanelles. The southern part of the straits which connect the Mediterranean and the Black Seas. The Bosphorus (the northern part of the straits), the Sea of Marmara (between the two parts) and the Dardanelles belong to Turkey and are of strategic importance. In the eighteenth and nineteenth centuries Russia pushed towards the straits to find an outlet to the Mediterranean Sea. The straits were under the sovereignty of Turkey until 1841 when the major powers and the Sultan pledged themselves not to permit 'vessels of war belonging to foreign powers' to enter the Dardanelles. After the Crimean War France and the U.K. forced the defeated Russia, by the Treaty of Paris, 1856, to declare the Black Sea neutral, and thus to abandon the right to maintain there any military or naval establishment. Russia denounced this provision in 1870. After the First World War the straits were occupied by British, French, and Italian forces, and the peninsula of Gallipoli, forming the European shore of the Dardanelles, was given to Greece. The straits were demilitarized, opened to navigation of every kind, and placed under an international commission. After Turkey had defeated a Greek invasion, Gallipoli was given back to Turkey, and the Treaty of Lausanne, concluded in July 1923, largely restored Turkish sovereignty over the straits whilst still providing for their demilitarization. The Treaty was modified by the Montreux Convention, 1936, *q.v.* Since the Second World War Turkey has rejected several Russian suggestions that a joint Russo-Turkish naval base should be established in the Dardanelles.

D.C. District of Columbia, *q.v.*

De Facto Recognition. An act whereby a new government or state is recognized as being actually independent and wielding effective power in the territory under its control, although not yet willing nor fully able to carry out international obligations. According to British practice, *de facto* recognition does not involve full diplomatic relations or the right of the representatives of the government to diplomatic immunity. The U.S.A. grants diplomatic immunity to such representatives. Strictly speaking, it is not the act of recognition that is *de facto*, but the government or state.

De Gaulle, General Charles André Joseph Marie. French political and military figure, born 22 November 1890 in Lille into a bourgeois

Catholic family. He entered the Military Academy of Saint Cyr in 1911, campaigned in the First World War and in 1920 fought against the Russians in Poland under General Weygand. Between the wars he gained a reputation as a military theorist, and when the German threat to France became apparent he recommended the creation of a highly mechanized core of professional troops to be used in attack. In 1940 he became France's youngest general and was made Under-Secretary at the Ministry of Defence in the Reynaud cabinet. Ten days later France surrendered and de Gaulle flew to London from where he called on French troops to reject the armistice and continue the resistance. He commanded the Fighting French forces until 1944, when he became Head of the Provisional Government of liberated France, and Chief of the Armed Forces. For 18 months in 1945 and 1946 he was President of France, during which period more than one quarter of the national revenue was spent on the armed forces and inflation was allowed to ride unchecked. In response to demands for a reduction in the army estimates he resigned and went into retirement, but re-emerged in 1947 at the head of a right-wing political organization, the Rally of the French People (Rassemblement du Peuple Français) which called for a revision of the Constitution and a stronger executive. It had enormous initial success, but it never secured control of the National Assembly. De Gaulle opposed the formation of any western defence community in which France might play a subordinate role, and was believed to favour a Latin bloc of Spain, Italy, and a predominant France, which would serve as adequate protection for France against Germany. He retired a second time in 1951, and formally dissolved the R.P.F., the members of which formed the Gaullist Social Republican Party (U.A.R.S.). After French army officers seized power in Algeria on 13 May 1958, de Gaulle stated, on 15 May: 'I hold myself in readiness to assume the powers of the Republic.' President Coty then invited him to form a government and he was invested as Prime Minister by the National Assembly on 1 June with a majority of 329 to 224. He was elected President on 21 December 1958 and re-elected on 19 December 1965 after a second ballot in which he secured 55·2 per cent of the total votes. He resigned on 28 April 1969 following his defeat in a constitutional referendum by 52·4 to 47·6 per cent, and retired to write his memoirs, of which he completed the first volume, *Le Renouveau 1958–62*, before he died on 9 November 1970.

De Jure Recognition. Unconditional acknowledgement that a new government or state is independent, wields effective power in the territory under its control, and is willing and able to carry out its international obligations. Recognition of a regime as a *de facto* government is provisional, but recognition as a *de jure* government entitles it to full diplomatic relations and its representatives to diplomatic immunity.

De Valera, Eamonn (Edward). Irish politician, born 14 October 1882 in New York, U.S.A., the son of a Spanish musician and his Irish wife. At the age of two he was sent to Ireland to be brought up by relations at Bruree, County Limerick. After graduating in mathematics at Dublin University in 1904 he became a teacher. He joined the Irish Nationalist movement and, as a member of the Gaelic League, learned, and taught, the Irish language. He took part in the Dublin Easter Rising in 1916 and commanded a battalion of the Irish Volunteers. The British captured him and sentenced him to death but he had his sentence commuted and was released from Dartmoor under the general amnesty of June 1917. He was President of the Sinn Fein movement from 1917 to 1926 and was elected Member for County Clare in the British Parliament but, as a Sinn Feiner, refused to take his seat. In May 1918 he was arrested and imprisoned for a further year after which he went to the U.S.A. to raise a loan of six million dollars for the Irish Republican government. On his return he became the Member for County Clare in the Dáil Éireann and President of the Dáil, a post which he resigned in 1922 when the Assembly accepted the treaty by which the six northern counties were excluded from the Irish Free State. He fought with the Irish Republican Army, *q.v.*, against the Free State government in the second Irish civil war and spent another year in gaol from 1923 to 1924, continuing to lead the republicans who would not accept partition. In 1926 he founded a new party, Fianna Fáil (Soldiers of Ireland), with the declared aims of complete independence, union with Northern Ireland, and revival of the Irish language and culture. These were to be achieved through parliamentary action and participation in the Free State Parliament. The irreconcilable republicans withdrew their support but Fianna Fáil, in an electoral coalition with the Labour Party, won a majority in the Dáil in 1932 and De Valera became Prime Minister. While he was in office Ireland became a sovereign independent state (Eire) and all ties with the British Commonwealth were dissolved. In 1948, the year in which Ireland became a republic, Fianna Fáil was defeated by the Fine Gael (United Ireland) party. De Valera was Prime Minister (Taoiseach) again in 1951, when his party secured 70 out of the 147 seats in the Dáil, by a coalition of Fianna Fáil members and Independents, but resigned after the elections of May 1954 in which Fianna Fáil lost 5 seats. He continued to lead the party in opposition until the elections of 6 March 1957, when he again became Prime Minister after Fianna Fáil increased its membership in the Dáil to 78. He resigned from the post of Prime Minister in June 1959 on being elected President. He was re-elected for a second term on 25 June 1966.

Defferre, Gaston. French politician, lawyer and journalist; born 1910; educated at the Collège de Nîmes and Aix-en-Provence University. He took an active part in the French Resistance and in 1944 became the manager of the newspaper *Le Provençal*. In 1945 he entered the Constituent Assembly as a Socialist deputy for Bouches-du-Rhône, and continued to represent this region in the National Assembly from 1948 to 1958. During this period he held a number of minor government offices, including those of Minister of the Merchant Marine (1950–51) and Minister for Overseas France (1956–7). He was elected to the Senate in 1959 but he returned to the National Assembly in 1962 when he won the election in Marseilles, of which he had been Mayor in 1945 and continuously since May 1953, after the Communist candidate had withdrawn in his favour before the second ballot. He opposed ratification of the Franco-German treaty in June 1963. In 1964 he was nominated as Socialist candidate for the Presidency of the Republic and he tried to create a democratic federation of the non-Communist left-wing and centre parties. His failure to accomplish this in June 1965 caused him to withdraw his candidacy. He contested the Presidential elections held in June 1969, on the resignation of de Gaulle, but obtained only 5 per cent of the votes cast.

Deflation. A reduction in money circulation, the opposite of inflation, resulting in lower prices and shortage of credit. This usually follows if interest rates are raised; the rate of addition to real capital slows down, the income and purchasing power of the community are restricted, and purchases of foreign goods and securities are reduced. The balance-of-payments problem is eased, but mere deflation without other measures may involve lower output and more unemployment.

Demagogy. Appeals to the prejudice of the masses, usually by means of lies and half-truths. It is derived from the Greek *demagogoi*, a word used to describe popular leaders who appeared in Athens and other cities of ancient Greece during their period of decay.

Démarche. A diplomatic or political development, proceeding, or step, not to be confused with a *détente*, *q.v.*

Democracy. From the Greek *demos*, people, and *kratos*, power, meaning government by the people. Democracy may be either direct, and exerted by popular assemblies or by plebiscites on all legislation, or indirect, and exerted by representative institutions. Direct democracy was practised in some of the city states of Ancient Greece; indirect democracy, which is better suited to modern nation states with large populations, was developed in England in the seventeenth century and imposed on France and North America, as a result of revolution, in the eighteenth century. By 1850 the majority of civilized nations had adopted democratic institutions.

Democracy, in the sense of the word generally accepted in western Europe, the British Commonwealth, and the U.S.A., is based on the theory of the separation of powers, *q.v.*, legislation being carried out by a freely elected parliament and executive power being vested either in a government responsible to the legislature (as in the U.K.) or in a president responsible to the people (as in the U.S.A.). This implies free choice at regular intervals between two or more parties; an election in which the electorate can only choose or reject a single list of candidates is not democratic in this sense of the word.

In addition to a separation of powers and free elections, other characteristics of western democracy are the rule of law, by which is meant a certainty that one is free from arrest unless charged with some recognized crime and that one will be given a fair trial before an impartial tribunal; freedom of opinion and speech; freedom of association; and protection from arbitrary interference on the part of the authorities.

The expression 'rule of the people' is interpreted in a very different sense in the U.S.S.R., and in parts of Asia and eastern Europe, though the title 'People's Republic' is used of Bulgaria, China, and Outer Mongolia. The principles of the separation of powers, free elections, rule of law, freedom of opinion, speech, and association are not generally accepted. However, the supporters of these systems regard them as democratic. There is state ownership and central planning to increase the national wealth. The private ownership of the means of production is regarded as undemocratic. In the U.S.S.R. no class differences prevent people from securing a good education. The governments of these Communist countries believe that the subordination of every interest and activity to the state ensures that the common good takes precedence over all private interests. This belief that Communism represents the true interests of the common man underlies their claim to be democracies.

Democratic Party. One of the two great political parties in the U.S.A.; the other is the Republican Party, *q.v.* It emerged about 1787 in opposition to the federalists, and advocated restrictions on the powers of the federal government. It was then also known as the Republican Party. Its leader Thomas Jefferson became President in 1801, and during the so-called 'era of good feeling', from 1817 to 1825, it was the only political party. A group which favoured high tariffs then seceded and became known as the Republican Party, while the remainder, led by Andrew Jackson, was known as the Democratic Party. The Democratic Party split again before the civil war, 1861 to 1865, over the question of slavery, the northern Democrats uniting with the National Republicans to form the Republican Party. In the twentieth century the southern states have for the most part continued to support the Democratic Party, though the Party has gained adherents in the northern industrial states of New York, Michigan, and Illinois. There have been Democratic Presidents from 1933 to 1968, with the exception of the Eisenhower presidency from 1953 to 1961.

Among the most important members of the Party are: Hubert Humphrey, q.v., Edward Kennedy, q.v., George McGovern, q.v., Michael Mansfield, q.v., Edmund Muskie, q.v., and Sargent Shriver, q.v. Former Presidents Lyndon Johnson, q.v., John Kennedy, q.v., and Harry Truman, q.v., were all Democrats. The party emblem is a donkey.

Denmark. An independent state in the Baltic and North Seas; area 16,608 sq. m.; population (1971 estimate) 4,950,598; capital Copenhagen. It has been a separate monarchy since the fifteenth century; Denmark and Norway were one kingdom until, after an unsuccessful war with Sweden, Denmark retained the Faroes, Greenland and Iceland but was forced to relinquish Norway in 1814 under the Treaty of Kiel. Holstein and Schleswig were lost to Prussia in 1864 but North Schleswig was recovered after the First World War. In 1940 Denmark was attacked and occupied by Germany, which wanted control of the rich Danish agricultural resources and needed a base from which to secure Norway and dominate access to the Baltic. Independence was regained after the war. Iceland, q.v., became an independent state in 1944.

Under the 1953 Constitution, by which the law of succession was amended to permit the present Queen Margrethe to ascend the throne, legislative power is vested in the monarch (who acts through the cabinet) and Parliament jointly. Since 1953 there has been only one chamber, the Folketing, with 179 members, elected for four years by proportional representation. Except for the three years 1950–53 the Social Democrats were the dominant group in the Folketing from 1945 until 1967, governing in coalition with the Radical Liberals and the Single-Tax Party (eliminated from Parliament in 1960), or as a minority administration. From 1962, when he succeeded Viggo Kampmann as leader of the Social Democratic Party, Jens Otto Krag led a minority government, reinforcing left-wing (although not Social Democrat) representation in the Folketing by calling mid-term elections in November 1966 at which the Socialist People's Party (a national Communist Party, independent of the U.S.S.R., formed in 1958 by Aksel Larsen and advocating total unilateral disarmament) gained 24 seats. Although there was no coalition between the two parties Krag's government was dependent on the support of the Socialist People's Party for his majority in the legislature. When this was partially withheld in December 1967 from government-sponsored legislation to control inflation and restrict wage-increases, the administration was defeated and Krag resigned.

At the subsequent general election held in January 1968 the Radical Liberals (representing mainly small landowners, professional townspeople and intellectuals) made spectacular gains, and their leader, Hilmas Baunsgaard, formed a government in pre-arranged coalition with the Liberal Democrats and Conservatives. However, at elections held in September 1971, following widespread criticism of Denmark's application for entry to the European Economic Community, q.v., the results were: Social Democratic Party 72 (62 seats in 1968); Liberal Democrats (or Farmers, led by Poul Hartling) 30 (34); Conservatives (led by Poul Möller) 31 (37); Radical Liberals 27 (27); Socialist People's Party (opposing entry to E.E.C. on any terms) 17 (11); Faroes Representatives 2 (2); Greenland Representatives 2 (2). The Left Wing Socialists and the Communist Party, both of which had in the past been represented in the Folketing, failed to win the 2 per cent of votes necessary to secure a seat. Of the representatives from the Faroes and Greenland, who were normally of no party affiliation, one from each area affirmed his support for the Social Democrats which gave the Party an effective strength of 74. The Social Democrats refused to enter a national coalition proposed by the former Prime Minister, Hilmar Baunsgaard, and formed another minority government, with the parliamentary support of the Socialist People's Party, under the leadership of Jens Otto Krag. After a national referendum in October 1972 had approved Danish entry to E.E.C. Krag resigned from political life. Anker Jørgensen, a former trade union leader, succeeded him as Prime Minister.

Denmark has a high standard of living, a comprehensive education system which has developed from the introduction of compulsory schooling in 1814, and extensive social services (including a social security scheme instituted before those of Norway and Sweden). The chief exports are dairy produce, bacon, eggs, livestock, machinery, meat, seeds and ships. The most important trading partners are the

U.K. and the German Federal Republic. Denmark is a member of N.A.T.O., and was a signatory of the 1955 London and Paris Agreements by which the German Federal Republic was re-armed within the Western European Union and admitted to N.A.T.O. Denmark was a member of the European Free Trade Association, *q.v.*, until it signed the Treaty of Accession to the European Economic Community in January 1972. The Faroes, *q.v.*, Greenland, *q.v.*, and Schleswig-Holstein, *q.v.*, are considered separately.

Desai, Shri Morarji Ranchhodji. Indian politician; the son of a schoolteacher, born 29 February 1896 at Bhadeli, near Bulsar, he is a Gujerati; educated at Wilson College, Bombay. In 1918 he entered the Provincial Civil Service of the Bombay government; he resigned from his post in the Civil Service as a District Deputy Collector in 1930 to join the civil disobedience campaign organized by Mahatma Gandhi, and was later convicted and imprisoned three times. He was Secretary of the Gujerat Pradesh Congress Committee from 1931 to 1937 and 1939 to 1946, spending the two intervening years as Minister for Revenue, Cooperation, Agriculture, and Forests in the Bombay government. He was imprisoned twice during the Second World War, from 1940 to 1941 and 1942 to 1945. He then served again in the Bombay government, from 1946 to 1952 as Minister for Home Affairs and Revenue, and from 1952 to 1956 as Chief Minister. He was then appointed to the Indian central government, as Minister for Commerce and Industry, from 1956 to 1958, and Minister of Finance from 1958 to 1963, when he resigned with other Ministers to reorganize the Congress Party, *q.v.* He has been described as pragmatic and un-ideological (by his supporters) and alternatively as right-wing (by his opponents). He unsuccessfully challenged Shastri, in 1964, and Indira Gandhi, in 1966, for the Premiership. In 1969 he formed an Opposition Congress which unsuccessfully challenged the Ruling Congress of Mrs Gandhi at the 1971 elections.

Desegregation. The process of ending segregation, *q.v.*

Détente. A diplomatic term meaning the cession of strained relations between states. It represents an earlier stage in the development of good relations than a *rapprochement*, *q.v.* An alternative word, the Italian *distensione*, is sometimes used.

Devaluation. A reduction of the value of the currency.

Development Loan Fund. A U.S. organization established by the Mutual Security Act of 1958 'to assist, on a basis of self-help and mutual cooperation, the efforts of free people abroad to develop their economic resources and to increase their productive capacities'. The Fund granted loans for specific projects, if financially sound, whether organized by private or government organizations, which, subject to the consent of the Fund, were repayable in local currency or U.S. dollars. It was superseded in November 1961 by the Agency for International Development, *q.v.*

Dewline. Distant Early Warning Line, *q.v.*

Dialectical Materialism. The combination of the dialectical method with a materialistic philosophy. It is politically important because it is the philosophical basis of Marxism, *q.v.* Dialectic, as developed by Greek philosophers, was the art of argument, or the technique of persuasion. It became the name of a method of thinking by the resolution of successive contradictions, as in the philosophical 'dialogue'. Later it was claimed that not only the development of thought, but also actual developments in nature and history, take the course of a dialectical process in which, as in a philosophical discussion, 'thesis' and 'antithesis' follow each other until a solution is found in the form of 'synthesis'. This teaching was particularly developed in the first half of the nineteenth century by Hegel, the German idealistic philosopher, who saw history as the reflection of a dialectical process in the development of certain ideas. Marx and Feuerbach 'reversed' the dialectical principle, denying the dominant role of ideas in history claimed by Hegel, and declaring that material things, while actually developing as dialectical processes, do so in their own right, as it were, and not as reflections of the development of independently existing ideas. On the contrary, it was the ideas which were the reflections of material reality. Marx used dialectical materialism as a method of social criticism and analysis, setting up the theory of 'historical materialism'. Thus every phase of human society, while moved by material forces, develops as a dialectical process, producing within itself its own opposite. Capitalist society creates the proletarian class which is of necessity opposed to it and bound eventually to overthrow it. Marx defined the dialectical method as that of 'including in the positive understanding of existing things also the understanding of the negative implications of their necessary termination'.

Dictatorship. From the Latin *dictator*; the absolute rule of a person or group without the necessity of the consent of the governed. The term dates from Roman republican times; during an emergency, a man could be appointed dictator by the Senate for seven years, and held absolute power for this period. He then had to retire, and constitutional rule was re-established. Modern dictatorship is either personal or that of a group or class (party, army, proletariat), but even in the latter case it is usually embodied in the person of a leader.

Disarmament. Reduction of armaments. Many attempts were made between 1918 and 1939 to reach international agreement on the limitation of armaments. In 1941 the Atlantic Charter, *q.v.*, envisaged 'measures which will lighten for peace-loving peoples the crushing burden of armaments'. The Moscow Declaration of October 1943, by the American, British, Chinese, and Russian governments, advocated 'a practical general agreement with respect to the regulation of armaments'. Article 26 of the United Nations Charter provides for the Security Council to draw up plans for the regulation of armaments. The United Nations set up in 1946 the Atomic Energy Commission to eliminate the use of atomic energy for destructive purposes and in 1947 the Commission for Conventional Armaments, 'for the general regulation and reduction of armaments and armed forces'. These Commissions were separately established as it was thought that the chances of agreement would be lessened if they depended on agreement on general disarmament.

In the Conventional Armaments Commission the U.S.S.R. argued that nations must first disarm and then evolve a system of control and inspection; the west wanted reduction of armaments accompanied by control and inspection. In 1948 the U.S.S.R. proposed a reduction of armed forces by one third but this was rejected by the west on the ground that it would continue the Russian preponderance in the field of conventional armaments.

In the Atomic Energy Commission the west advocated international management and control of atomic energy plants, believing that inspection alone could not determine whether nuclear material was applied to dangerous uses. The U.S.S.R. proposed a convention for the prohibition of atomic weapons and the destruction of existing stocks.

In 1952, in view of the limited progress made, the two Commissions were merged into the United Nations Disarmament Commission. The U.S.S.R. continued to demand reduction of armed forces by one third, prohibition of atomic weapons followed by exchange of information, and creation of a control organization. The west regarded disclosure and verification of information as a first and indispensable step.

The U.S.A. and the U.S.S.R. exploded their first hydrogen bombs in 1952 and 1953 respectively. The U.S.S.R. repeated its demand for unconditional prohibition of atomic weapons and a one-third reduction in armed forces. The U.S.A. proposed an atomic pool in which all could develop nuclear energy for peaceful purposes – 'Atoms for Peace'. In May 1954 abortive disarmament talks were held in London by Canada, France, the U.K., the U.S.A., and the U.S.S.R.

In May 1955 the U.S.S.R. altered its approach. It agreed that elimination of nuclear arms should not begin until cuts in other arms had ,been made, and that there should be a reduction of forces to absolute levels rather than proportional cuts. Its agreement was subject to the abolition of 'foreign bases', which would have involved the withdrawal of U.S. ground and air units from Europe and the Far East. The U.K. demanded further concessions in August 1955, insisting on unlimited rights of inspection. The U.S.A. suggested aerial supervision supplemented by ground inspectors. In London in April and May 1956, the U.S.S.R. continued to demand reductions in conventional armaments, but was criticized by the west for refusing to give the controlling organization power to act against violations of the proposed agreements.

The problem was referred to the sub-committee of the Disarmament Commission, which met in London from March to September 1957. The U.S.A. proposed information exchanges on nuclear tests, reductions in armed forces, and international inspection of the use of fissionable materials. The U.S.S.R. for the first time suggested reciprocal aerial inspection, though not of the same areas as those suggested by the U.S.A. earlier. The U.K. proposed advance registration and eventual cessation of nuclear tests. The talks were then abandoned.

The U.S.S.R. withdrew from the Disarmament Commission in November 1957, alleging that it, and the U.N. Political Committee, had 'lost prestige in the eyes of the peoples by the fruitless nature of their work'. The Russians said that this need not prevent exchanges on disarmament, and in January 1958 they proposed a conference in Geneva to discuss (1) the ending of nuclear and thermo-nuclear tests for two or three years; (2) the renunciation of the use and manufacture of atomic and hydrogen weapons; (3) a non-aggression pact between N.A.T.O. and the members of the Warsaw Pact, *q.v.*; and (4) the creation of an atomic-free zone in Central Europe, comprising Eastern and Western Germany, Poland and Czechoslovakia, in which atomic and hydrogen weapons would be neither stock-piled nor manufactured. The last proposal was based on the Rapacki Plan, *q.v.* The State Department, commenting on the proposals in March 1958, said: 'The United States is not prepared to disregard the United Nations in its efforts to resume disarmament talks.'

There were no significant developments in disarmament negotiations until March 1960, when the governments of Canada, France, Italy, the U.K., and the U.S.A. proposed the creation of an international disarmament organization to supervise disarmament, and a separate peace-keeping organization, to be an organ of, or linked to, the United Nations, to prevent aggression and to preserve world peace and security. They also proposed a three-stage programme for nuclear and conventional disarmament. Counter-proposals by the U.S.S.R. in June 1960 proved to be unacceptable to the western powers, who said that they involved too early an abandonment of the nuclear deterrent and western bases in Europe.

In August 1960 the U.S.S.R. proposed that there should be 3 sites in each country from which inspectors should operate, whereas the U.S.A. proposed that there should be 20 sites in each country. By February 1963 the figures suggested had become 2 or 3 (according to the U.S.S.R.) and 7 (according to the U.S.A.). In August 1963 a Test Ban Treaty, q.v., was signed in Moscow. In October 1963 the U.N. General Assembly adopted unanimously a resolution giving effect to an agreement, between the U.S.A. and the U.S.S.R., not to put nuclear weapons into outer space.

From 1965 to 1967 the Disarmament Commission concentrated its attention on extending the 1963 partial Test Ban Treaty to cover underground nuclear tests, but the difficulty of providing on-site inspections proved insurmountable. However, discussion on nuclear non-proliferation resulted in agreement between the U.S.A. and the U.S.S.R. on a Non-Proliferation Treaty, q.v., which introduced a comprehensive system of safeguards to be operated by an international inspectorate. The Treaty was signed on 1 July 1968, and came into force on 5 March 1970.

In October 1971 the Commission submitted to the U.N. General Assembly a draft convention on the prohibition of the development, production and stockpiling of bacteriological and toxin weapons and on their destruction. This was intended to strengthen the Geneva Protocol of 1925 against chemical and biological warfare. Failure to make progress on the banning of chemical weapons entailed limiting the convention to biological weapons control, and this was eventually agreed by the U.S.S.R., the U.S.A. and the U.K., who signed the agreement on 10 April 1972. The convention, which would eliminate germ warfare, q.v., was to be effective as soon as 19 signatories, other than the three principals, had ratified the treaty. It was the first arms control agreement to require the destruction of existing stocks and to outlaw an entire class of weapons.

An important development in the proposals for nuclear disarmament occurred in May 1972 when the U.S.A. and the U.S.S.R. signed a Treaty on the Limitation of Anti-Ballistic Missile Systems, and an interim agreement on the limitation of strategic offensive arms. (*See* S.A.L.T.)

Displaced Persons. *See* Refugees and Displaced Persons.

Distant Early Warning Line (Dewline). Part of the comprehensive radar system established in 1957 by the North American Air Defence Command ('NORAD') to detect the approach of missiles, satellites, and aircraft. The line stretches along the Aleutian Islands, the north coast of Alaska, and then through the northern islands of Canada and across southern Greenland to Iceland. The Russian equivalent is known as the Tallinn Line.

District of Columbia (D.C.). The U.S. capital and seat of government, until 1790 part of the state of Maryland; area (co-extensive with the City of Washington) 69 sq. m.; population (1970 census) 756,510.

Dollar Gap. An adverse balance between a country's receipts from, and its payments to, the group of countries which pay, and can demand settlement of, debts in dollars.

Dominican Republic. An independent Central American state, sharing the Caribbean island of Hispaniola with Haiti; area 19,322 sq. m.; population (1970 estimate) 4,324,760, Spanish-speaking and mainly of mixed European, African and Indian descent; capital Santo Domingo (formerly Ciudad Trujillo). Roman Catholicism is the state religion; three-fifths of the population is Catholic. The country was discovered by Columbus in 1492, ruled by Spain until 1795, by France 1795–1808, by Spain 1808–21, by Haitian Negroes 1822–44, and became an independent republic in 1844. The Constitution of 1961, amended in 1962, provides for government by a Council of State (of seven members) headed by the President who is elected by direct vote for five years.

Rafael Leonidas Trujillo Molina, called 'el Benefactor', was dictator from 1930 until his assassination in May 1961. His brother, Hector Bienvenido Trujillo, was President from May 1952 to August 1960 when he was replaced by the Vice-President, Dr Joaquin Balaguer; by the end of 1961, largely as the result of economic pressure from the United States, the supporters of Trujillo had been removed from power. In December 1962 free elections were held for the first time in many years. Juan Bosch, leader of the Partido Revolucionario Dominicano (P.R.D.), who favoured land reform and had been in exile for almost thirty-two years, was elected President with 62 per cent of the vote; he was ousted by the army in September 1963. Six right-wing parties endorsed the appointment of a civilian triumvirate, led by Emilio de los Santos, which antagonized sections of the army by forcibly retiring officers of high rank and preventing illegal army transactions in duty-free goods. In April 1965 a pro-Bosch revolt, led by Colonel Francisco Caamaño Deño, was followed by U.S.

intervention, justified by fears that the country might fall under the control of a Communist regime. By 23 May 1965 the U S forces had been incorporated in an Inter-American Peace Force, established by the Organization of American States (O.A.S.), *q.v.*; collaborating with a junta led by General Antonio Imbert Barrera (who took part in the plot to assassinate Trujillo) the Peace Force suppressed the revolt, and withdrew in September 1965 when Imbert appointed Dr Hector Garcia-Goday provisional President. At Presidential elections held in June 1966, under the scrutiny of observers from member countries of the O.A.S., the former President, Joaquin Balaguer, was elected with 57 per cent of the votes cast; his nearest rival, ex-President Bosch, had 39 per cent. He was re-elected in May 1970 for a further four-year term, with a 54 per cent majority, following demonstrations against his decision to stand in which the U.S. Air Attaché was kidnapped and exchanged for 20 political prisoners.

Sugar is produced and exported by sixteen main companies, of which two (one controlled by U.S. interests) produce 80 per cent of the total; there are exports of cocoa beans, coffee and tobacco. The country is largely agricultural, with 70 per cent of the population living and working on the land, but only two-thirds of the cultivable land is in use. In 1967, to halt the waste of forest, all saw-mills were closed for ten years and the destruction of trees was made a criminal offence. There are bauxite deposits and capital investment in industry, half of it by U.S. firms, is increasing.

Dominion. A self-governing member state of the British Commonwealth, *q.v.* In recent years the term has fallen into disuse. Although there are, apart from the U.K., 31 such states, most of them have never claimed Dominion status.

Douglas-Home, Sir Alexander (Alec) Frederick. British Conservative Party politician; born 2 July 1903 and educated at Eton (with Cyril Connolly, the critic and essayist, who in 1938 described him in *Enemies of Promise* as 'a votary of the esoteric Eton religion, the kind of graceful, tolerant, sleepy boy who is showered with favours and crowned with all the laurels, who is liked by the masters and admired by the boys without any apparent exertion on his part') and Christ Church, Oxford. After unsuccessfully contesting Coatbridge, Lanarkshire, in 1929, he was elected to the House of Commons in 1931 for South Lanark; he was then Lord Dunglass, having not yet succeeded to his father's title. From 1937 to 1939 he was Parliamentary Private Secretary to the Prime Minister, Neville Chamberlain, whom he accompanied in September 1938 for the conclusion of the Munich Agreement, *q.v.* He joined the army in

1939, and was invalided out in 1943, and was Joint Parliamentary Under-Secretary at the Foreign Office from May to July 1945. He lost his seat at the 1945 General Election, but represented Lanark from 1950 to 1951, when his father died and he entered the House of Lords, becoming Scottish Minister of State until April 1955. He was Secretary of State for Commonwealth Relations from then until July 1960, when he became Foreign Secretary. He succeeded Harold Macmillan as Prime Minister in October 1963, renounced his peerage, and was elected to the House of Commons as member for Kinross and West Perthshire. He resigned the Premiership and became Leader of the Opposition in October 1964, when the Conservative Party was defeated at the General Election. He gave up the post of Leader of the Opposition in July 1965 and was succeeded by Edward Heath, *q.v.*, who appointed him Foreign Secretary in 1970.

Doves. Name used to describe those Americans who advocated negotiation, or a reduction of the U.S. military commitment in Viet-Nam, in order to terminate the war. It is employed to contrast with the Hawks, *q.v.*, a term originally applied to those who supported an intensification of the war. Examples of Doves are: Senator William Fulbright, Senator Eugene McCarthy, Senator George McGovern, *q.v.*, and the late Senator Robert Kennedy, *q.v.*

Downing Street. In Westminster, London; it contains the residences of the Prime Minister (at No. 10) and the Chancellor of the Exchequer (at No. 11), and the Foreign Office.

Doyen. A French word meaning dean, or senior member of a body, and used to describe the senior member of the diplomatic corps.

Dubai. A member state of the United Arab Emirates, *q.v.*, on the Trucial Coast, *q.v.*, in the Persian Gulf. Though the country itself is not as large as Abu Dhabi, *q.v.*, Dubai is the biggest town on the Trucial Coast, has a population of 70,000, and is the port for the other Trucial States, *q.v.* Most of its present revenues are derived from the customs dues paid in respect of its entrepot trade; but oil in considerable quantity was struck off-shore in 1966. The mainland oil concession is held by Dubai Petroleum Co., and the sea-bed concession by Dubai Marine Areas. Dubai was formerly under British protection and in February 1968, following the announcement of the British government's decision to withdraw military forces from the Persian Gulf by 1971, the ruler, Sheikh Rashid bin Said al Naktum, agreed firstly to federate with Abu Dhabi, then to join the Federation of Arab Emirates, *q.v.* In 1971 it became a member of the United Arab Emirates and Sheikh Rashid assumed office as Vice-President.

Dubček, Alexander. Czechoslovak politician; born 1921 in the Slovak town of Uhrovec, he was brought up in the U.S.S.R. where his father was a member of a group of Czechoslovak Communists who established an industrial cooperative in 1925. He became an engine-fitter, returning with his family to Czechoslovakia in 1938. The following year he joined the Czechoslovak Communist Party and, in 1944, the guerilla forces of the Slovak National Uprising against the Germans. He was wounded twice in skirmishes with them; his brother was killed. From 1945 he rose steadily in the Communist Party, becoming secretary of the regional Party Committee in Banská Bystrica, and in 1962, a member of the Presidium of the Czechoslovak Communist Party and secretary of the Party's Slovak Branch. In January 1968 he became the first Slovak to be elected First Secretary of the Czechoslovak Communist Party. After the Russian invasion of Czechoslovakia he was replaced, in April 1969, by Dr Gustav Husak, and elected President of the new Federal Assembly. In September 1969 he was dismissed from this office and from the Party Presidium, and in January 1970 he ceased to be a member of the Central Committee. He was appointed Ambassador to Turkey in December 1969, but lost this post in June 1970 and was subsequently expelled from the Communist Party. In a denunciation aimed at destroying the 'Dubček legend' the Communist newspaper, *Rude Pravo*, condemned him as egotistic and weak, and declared him to have been an 'unprincipled, compromising and cowardly member of the Party'.

Dumbarton Oaks Conference. A meeting held from August to October 1944 at a mansion called Dumbarton Oaks in Washington, D.C., U.S.A., at which representatives of China, the U.K., the U.S.A., and the U.S.S.R. discussed the structure of the proposed United Nations, *q.v.* The proposals, which resembled the Covenant of the League of Nations, *q.v.*, provided that the key body in the United Nations for preserving world peace was to be the Security Council, *q.v.*, on which China, France, the U.K., the U.S.A., and the U.S.S.R. were to be permanently represented, and which was to have more power than the League Council. The question of how the Security Council was to vote was left unsettled until February 1945 when the Yalta Conference, *q.v.*, between the U.K., the U.S.A., and the U.S.S.R., established the principle of the veto, *q.v.*

Dunkirk Treaty. Concluded in March 1947 by France and the U.K.; the two countries agreed that they would consult and act together against any aggression or threat of aggression by Germany, and that they would be in constant consultation about their economic relations. It symbolized the re-emergence of France as a major European power after its wartime occupation and its non-participation in the Potsdam Agreement, *q.v.*, of 1945.

Durand Line. The border agreed between Afghanistan and British India in 1892, and now affirmed by Pakistan, as the successor to the U.K., to constitute the correct boundary between Afghanistan and Pakistan. Afghanistan claims an area to the south of the Line which it describes as Pakhtunistan, *q.v.*

Dutch New Guinea. *See* Netherlands New Guinea.

Dutch West Indies. *See* Netherlands West Indies.

E

East African Economic Community. A trade agreement, signed on 6 June 1967 and operative from 1 December 1967, between Kenya, Tanzania and Uganda to achieve common tariffs and mutual economic aid. Its terms meant that Kenya, as the most industrially advanced partner, agreed to provide a form of development assistance to Tanzania and Uganda.

Eastern Aden Protectorate. Three former territories of the Eastern and Western Aden Protectorates (known as the Aden Protectorate, *q.v.*) which did not join the South Arabian Federation, *q.v.* They are the Quaiti state of Shihr Mukalla, the Kathiri state of Sai'un and the Mahri sultanate of Qishn and Socotra. When the Federation achieved independence in November 1967 they were incorporated in the People's Republic of Southern Yemen, *q.v.*

Eastern European Mutual Assistance Treaty. A 20-year treaty of friendship, cooperation, and mutual assistance, signed by the representatives of Albania, Bulgaria, Czechoslovakia, the German Democratic Republic, Hungary, Poland, Romania, and the U.S.S.R. in Warsaw in May 1955. Albania, *q.v.*, was excluded from the treaty in 1961 and resigned in 1968. It established a unified military command for the armed forces of all those countries. Each contracting party undertook to refrain in its international relations from the threat or use of force and to give immediate assistance to any party which was attacked in Europe, by all the means it might consider necessary. The conference at which the Treaty was concluded met five days after the date on which the Western European Union, *q.v.*, came into force and the German Federal Republic, *q.v.*, attained full sovereignty.

Eastern Germany. The part of Germany that, under the Berlin Declaration of June 1945 and the Potsdam Agreement, *q.v.*, of August 1945, became the Russian occupation zone at the end of the Second World War. It comprises the former Prussian province of Saxony, the former *Länder* of Saxony, Thuringia, Mecklenburg, and Anhalt, and such parts of the former Prussian provinces of Brandenburg, Pomerania, and Silesia as were situated on the west banks of the rivers Oder and Western Neisse. The U.S.S.R. tried to eradicate Nazi influence and to reorganize the social and economic structure of Eastern Germany to an extent not attempted in Western Germany, *q.v.* East German industrial equipment was largely dismantled and removed to the U.S.S.R., while, until 1956, a substantial proportion of the industrial output was taken by the U.S.S.R. as reparations.

Many large estates were broken up and redistributed, and other agricultural properties were run directly by the Russian administration. The quadripartite control of Germany which had been planned in 1945 was the subject of many disputes, particularly over the Russian demands for reparations. The failure of the Foreign Ministers' Conference in Moscow in May 1947, the clarification during that conference of the Truman Doctrine, *q.v.*, and the announcement in the following month of the Marshall Plan, *q.v.*, were followed by measures on both sides which made the division between Eastern and Western Germany more pronounced. Under Russian supervision a People's Congress of 1,629 delegates, set up in 1947 and claiming to represent both Eastern Germany and Western Germany, elected in 1948 a People's Council of 400 members; a Presidium of 29 members was then elected, and began to prepare a constitution for a united Germany. The individuals most concerned in these developments were all members of the Communist-controlled Socialist Unity Party. After the establishment in May 1949 of the German Federal Republic, *q.v.*, the People's Council was converted into a provincial People's Chamber; elections were held at which voters could accept or reject a single list of candidates, and although the official list was accepted by a majority, 33·9 per cent of voters rejected it. On 7 October 1949 the People's Chamber enacted the constitution of the German Democratic Republic, *q.v.*

E.C.E. Economic Commission for Europe, *q.v.*

Economic and Social Council. One of the six principal organs of the United Nations, *q.v.*, responsible under the authority of the General Assembly for carrying out the functions of the United Nations in economic, social, cultural, educational, health, and related matters, and for promoting the observance of human rights and fundamental freedoms. It comprises 27 members elected by the General Assembly, 9 of whom are elected each year for a three-year term.

The United Nations Charter provides for the relating of the various inter-governmental agencies, which have wide responsibilities in economic, social, cultural, educational, health, and other fields, to the United Nations as 'Specialized Agencies'. This is done through the Economic and Social Council, which negotiates with the Agencies subject to approval by the General Assembly. The Council is responsible for coordinating the activities of the Specialized Agencies, which are: the Food and Agriculture Organization, *q.v.*, the Inter-Governmental Maritime Consultative Organization, the International Bank for Reconstruction and Development, *q.v.*, the International Labour Organization, *q.v.*, the International Monetary Fund, *q.v.*, the International Telecommunication Union, the United Nations Educational, Scientific, and Cultural Organization, *q.v.*, the Universal Postal Union, the World Health Organization, *q.v.*, the World Meteorological Organization, the International Civil Aviation Organization, the International Atomic Energy Agency, *q.v.*, and the International Finance Corporation, *q.v.*

The Council has established the following Commissions to review international problems: Trade, Human Rights, Narcotic Drugs, Population, Social Development, Statistical, and Status of Women. It has set up regional Economic Commissions for Asia and the Far East, Africa, Europe, and Latin America, each consisting of United Nations members in the areas concerned and other United Nations members having special interests there.

Economic Commission for Europe (E.C.E.). Was set up on 28 March 1947 by the Economic and Social Council, *q.v.*, of the United Nations to plan concerted action to raise the level of European economic activity, and to strengthen the economic relations of European countries, both among themselves and with other countries. The members include the European members of the United Nations, and the U.S.A. It has subsidiary committees on coal, electric power, industry and materials, inland transport, manpower, steel, timber, the development of trade, and agricultural problems. The other regional commissions are the Economic Commission for Asia and the Far East (E.C.A.F.E.), set up in 1947, the Economic Commission for Latin America (E.C.L.A.), set up in 1948, and the Economic Commission for Africa (E.C.A.), set up in 1958.

Economic Co-operation Administration. A U.S. organization established by the Economic Co-operation Act, 1948, as a government agency to administer the European Recovery Programme, *q.v.* It was abolished and its functions were transferred to the Mutual Security Agency, *q.v.*, on 30 December 1951.

Ecosoc. Economic and Social Council of the United Nations, *q.v.*

E.C.S.C. European Coal and Steel Community, *q.v.*

Ecuador. An independent state on the north-west coast of South America; area (approximately) 116,270 sq. m. (the area exempt from dispute is 104,505 sq. m., and excludes the Oriental Region and the Galapagos Islands); population (1969 estimate) 5,973,300, mainly Roman Catholic and comprising descendants of Spanish settlers, aboriginal Indians and mestizos; capital Quito. Ten per cent of the population is white, 30 per cent Indian, 40 per cent of mixed blood, and the rest is mulatto or negro. The country was conquered by Peru in the fifteenth and by Spain in the sixteenth century; complete

ECUADOR

independence was achieved in 1830. It has a long tradition, broken only in recent years, of political peace, and the currency is relatively stable. Ecuador exports more bananas than any other country and also exports cocoa, coffee and rice. The U.S.A. has been the most important trading partner, but on a decreasing scale, buying 55 per cent of all exports and providing 40 per cent of the imports. However, the discovery of oilfields in the eastern jungles (the Oriente) in 1967, in which the Anglo-Ecuadorian Oil Company, Texaco-Gulf and Cayman Oil of California have substantial interests, has transformed the economic outlook. World Bank estimates for oil production in 1976 exceed in value the 1972 total annual exports of all other commodities. After prolonged disputes with Peru the vexed question of the ownership of the upper banks of the Amazon was ostensibly settled at Rio de Janeiro in 1942 by Argentina, Brazil, Chile and the U.S.A., which awarded the territory to Peru. Minor frontier clashes continued and in 1961 Ecuador unilaterally repudiated the decision.

Government is by an Assembly consisting of a Senate, elected every four years, a Chamber of Deputies elected every two years on a population basis, and a President who is elected for a four-year term by direct popular vote. A 61-year-old tradition of Liberal presidents was broken in June 1956 when a Conservative lawyer, Dr Camilo Ponce Enriquez was returned on a minority vote. He was succeeded in September 1960 by a former President, the populist, non-party Dr José Maria Velasco Ibarra, q.v., who was deposed in November 1961 and succeeded by his Vice-President, Dr Carlos Julio Arosemena Monroy. The latter was in his turn deposed in July 1963 by a junta of the armed forces, the leader of whom, Rear-Admiral Ramón Castro Jijón, assumed the office of President. During its three years of administration the junta introduced economic planning (abhorred by President Velasco), but retained martial law, and was unable to restrain prices even by the imposition of unpopular import duties. On 29 March 1966 the Air Force dismissed the junta and invited the major political parties to appoint an interim civilian President until elections could take place and a new Constitution be introduced. Clemente Yerovi Indaburu was chosen but was forced to resign when the Assembly (elected in October 1966) proposed a new Constitution which prohibited the intervention of the armed forces in politics. He was replaced as provisional President by Dr Otto Arosemena Gómez until the elections of June 1968 when Dr Velasco Ibarra returned from exile in Argentina to win the presidency for a fifth time. In June 1970, with the aid of the army, he suspended the Constitution and dissolved the Assembly, but having survived an unsuccessful attempt to depose

140

him in April 1971 when he appointed his nephew as Minister of Defence, he was himself ousted by the army on 15 February 1972. The presidency was then assumed by General Rodriguez Lara, who had supported Dr Velasco in 1971, forestalling the predicted victory at presidential elections planned for June 1972 of Assad Bucaram, leader of the left-wing Concentration Fuerzas Populares and former mayor of Guayaquil, the traditional stronghold of opposition to the government in Quito, who had declared that he would 'break the power of the forty families who exploit the workers'. The new regime immediately published a five-year plan which included proposals for land redistribution, incentives for foreign investors and tax reform. It reintroduced the Constitution which ex-President Velasco had abolished in 1946 as 'bolshevistic', and opened negotiations to improve the royalties payable on oil exports and to increase state participation in the industry.

E.D.C. European Defence Community, *q.v.*

Eden, Sir Robert Anthony. *See* Avon, 1st Earl.

E.E.C. European Economic Community, *q.v.*

E.F.T.A. European Free Trade Association, *q.v.*

Egghead. A derisive term used to describe the more intelligent and thoughtful members of the population.

Egypt. An independent state in North Africa on the eastern Mediterranean; area 386,110 sq. m.; population (1971 estimate) 34,000,000 of Egyptians (*fellahin* or soil-workers), Bedouin nomads, and Nubians of mixed Arab and Negro blood; capital Cairo. The great majority of the population is Moslem.

Egypt was a semi-independent state with a hereditary viceroy or Khedive, and under Turkish sovereignty, from 1841 to 1916. From 1882 it was occupied by British troops and under British administration. In 1914 a British protectorate was declared and the pro-German Khedive was deposed; in 1922 the pro-British Sultan Fuad was proclaimed King. The Anglo-Egyptian Treaty of 1936 recognized Egyptian sovereignty but gave to the U.K. the right to maintain a garrison on the Suez Canal, *q.v.*, to use Alexandria and Port Said as naval bases, and to move troops across Egypt in case of war or the threat of war; Sudan, *q.v.*, was to remain an Anglo-Egyptian condominium under joint administration. The 1936 Treaty did not satisfy the growing numbers of Egyptians who resented the presence of foreign troops, and who had since 1918 demanded their departure.

The protests against foreign influence were accompanied after the Second World War by discontent with the economic structure, which permitted a small number of individuals to hold large areas of the fertile land, and with the Egyptian government itself, which failed to develop the industries and natural resources of the country as fully as possible. A *coup d'état* by a group of officers on 23 July 1952 led to the abdication of King Farouk and the eleven-month reign of his infant son, Ahmed Fuad II. Civilian titles such as Pasha were abolished on the grounds that they were undemocratic; taxes were increased to abolish the budget deficit; an agrarian reform was introduced, limiting the area of land which any one person could hold; a Council for the Promotion of National Production was established to develop systematically the production of cotton of a longer staple, more rice, sugar, sugar cane, and maize, and to establish more industries; severe penalties were introduced for corrupt practices; plans were made to build the High Dam, *q.v.*; social welfare services were extended; and the Moslem Brotherhood, *q.v.*, was dissolved. Negotiations began with the U.K. on the question of the Suez Canal Zone and in 1954 the 1936 Treaty was terminated, it being agreed that all British forces were to leave the zone by June 1956. General Mohammed Neguib declared a republic in June 1953 and was President until 1954, when he was accused of trying to concentrate all power in his own hands and relieved of all his posts. Presidential powers were then vested in the Council of Ministers; Colonel Gamal Abdel Nasser, *q.v.*, became Prime Minister, and in June 1956 became President when the Council was dissolved. After his death in September 1970 he was succeeded by his Vice-President, Anwar Sadat, *q.v.*, who took office on 17 October 1970 and immediately embarked on a ruthless purge of colleagues who could have challenged his political supremacy. He appointed as Prime Minister Dr Mahmoud Fawzi.

In 1955 and 1956 relations between Egypt and the western powers deteriorated. Foreign capital was needed for the High Dam; the country had difficulty in selling its cotton and was attracted by Russian offers to buy part of the crop; and, after unsuccessful attempts to purchase arms from the west, the government concluded an arms deal with Czechoslovakia. On 19 July 1956 Egypt was informed that it was not 'feasible in present circumstances' for American aid to be given for the construction of the High Dam. The U.K. made a similar decision and the World Bank's offer lapsed as it had been contingent on American and British assistance. On 26 July President Nasser announced that Egypt would take over the Suez Canal forthwith, and would use the revenue to build the High Dam. Suez Canal Company shareholders were to be paid the Paris Stock Exchange closing prices of their shares as on that day. On 2 August the British government declared its intention of taking 'precautionary measures of a military nature' to strengthen the British position in the eastern Mediterranean. It then requisitioned merchant ships and called up reservists.

On 19 October 1956 Israel attacked Egypt and on the following day the U.K. informed Egypt and Israel that British and French forces would occupy the Canal Zone unless both sides immediately ceased hostilities and withdrew their forces to a distance of ten miles from the Canal. Egypt rejected the ultimatum, as compliance would have involved abandonment of Egyptian control of the Canal. On 31 October Franco-British forces attacked Egypt. In response to appeals from the United Nations the French and British ceased fire on 6 November when they had occupied only the northern part of the Suez Canal Zone. By 22 December a United Nations Emergency Force had replaced the Franco-British armies, and the Israelis yielded their last foothold in Egypt, the Gaza Strip, *q.v.*, in March 1957.

Since 1 February 1958, when Egypt entered into a union with Syria (which terminated on 28 September 1961), the country was known as the United Arab Republic. The name was changed following a referendum to approve a new Constitution and the proposed accession of Egypt to the Federation of Arab Republics, *q.v.* During 1964 a joint Presidential Council was established with Iraq, but unified political leadership between the two countries rapidly proved to be unworkable. Egypt has contested the leadership of the Arab League, *q.v.*, since its formation in 1945, with Saudi Arabia. Both countries strongly opposed the conclusion in 1955 of the Baghdad Pact, *q.v.*, which weakened the League by attracting the temporary support of Iraq. But the differences were reinforced when Nasser introduced a policy of socialism into Egypt, and in 1962 intervened in Yemen to assist the republicans in the war against the Imam; an army of some 70,000 Egyptians was maintained in Yemen until it was withdrawn, by agreement with Saudi Arabia, in December 1967.

Resentment at the existence of the neighbouring state of Israel, which Egypt failed to defeat in 1948, which defeated the Egyptian army in 1956, and which occupied a larger area of Palestine, *q.v.*, than was originally allotted to it by the United Nations, has been a predominant factor in foreign policy. The Tripartite Declaration of 1950, *q.v.*, by France, the U.K. and the U.S.A., was made partly with a view to deterring Egypt from aggression against Israel. On 18 May 1967, taunted by other Arab states (especially Jordan and Saudi Arabia) that Egypt needed U.N. troops to defend its own frontiers, President Nasser ordered the U.N. Emergency Force to leave Sinai, and moved his own troops into battle positions. On 22 May the Egyptians blocked the Gulf of Aqaba, thereby cutting off the Israeli port of Eilat. On 28 May Iraqi forces moved into Jordan, and on 30 May a defence pact was concluded between Jordan and Egypt, emphasising their mutual dependence in the event of war with Israel. But the simultaneous Israeli assault on 5 June 1967 on Syria, Jordan and Egypt, which drove Egyptian forces back to the Suez Canal in five days, reopened the Gulf of Aqaba, and resulted in the permanent Israeli occupation of Sinai, the Golan Heights and the west bank of the Jordan, inflicted another humiliating defeat on Nasser. The loss of oil from Sinai and of the revenues from the Suez Canal, which has remained blocked since June 1967, has been redeemed by an annual subsidy of £75 million provided by the Arab Economic Development Fund, which was set up in September 1967 by Libya, Kuwait and Saudi Arabia, to sustain Jordan and Egypt until they had recovered the occupied territories. Military and technical aid was supplied by the U.S.S.R. until 1972 when President Sadat expelled all Russian personnel from Egypt. The U.N. mediator, Gunnar Jarring, who was appointed in November 1967 to negotiate a peace settlement between Israel and the Arab states involved in the six-day war, found the continuing Arab refusal to recognize the state of Israel an insurmountable obstacle to settlement. Subsequent peace moves have been thwarted by Israeli insistence on open negotiation, which implies recognition of Israeli sovereignty by Egypt, and Egyptian reluctance to enter into an agreement which does not include Syria and Jordan.

Eire. Name by which southern Ireland, now the Republic of Ireland, *q.v.*, was known from 1937 to 1948, during which time it was a Dominion within the British Commonwealth.

Eisenhower, Dwight David. President of the U.S.A. from 1953 to 1961; born 14 October 1890 in Denison, Texas. He graduated from West Point Military Academy in 1915, and in 1926 passed out of the General Staff School at Fort Leavenworth, Kansas. For some years afterwards he held Army office and staff appointments. He was with the Battle Monuments Commission in Paris in 1927, was an Assistant Executive in the office of the Assistant Secretary of War from 1929 to 1933, served in the office of the Chief of Staff from 1933 to 1935, and was Assistant Military Adviser in the Philippines from 1935 to 1940. When Japan attacked Pearl Harbour on 7 December 1941 he was a divisional chief of staff, and became assistant chief of staff in charge of the Operations Division in Washington. He was in command of the European theatre of operations in 1942, and was then successively Commander-in-Chief of the Allied Forces in North Africa from 1942 to 1944, Supreme Commander of the Allied Expeditionary Force in

Western Europe from 1944 to 1945, Commander of the U.S. Occupation Zone in Germany in 1945, Chief of Staff of the U.S. Army from 1945 to 1948, and Supreme Commander of the North Atlantic Treaty Forces in Europe from 1950 to 1952. In 1952 he retired from the Army, won the Republican Party Presidential nomination against strong opposition from the supporters of Senator Taft, and was elected President of the U.S.A., defeating the Democratic candidate, Adlai Stevenson. He is believed to have been a moderating influence on the right wing of the Republican Party, but his personal political position was obscure. He was baptized as a National Presbyterian after his election; he had formerly been a non-sectarian Christian, having been brought up in a Nonconformist sect, the Brethren of Christ. In September 1955 he suffered a heart attack; in June 1956 he underwent an operation for the relief of an intestinal obstruction caused by ileitis, but nevertheless stood again as Presidential candidate in November 1956 and defeated Adlai Stevenson again. In a message to Congress in January 1957 he expounded what has become known as the Eisenhower Doctrine, *q.v.* His second term of office ended in January 1961, when he was succeeded by John Kennedy, *q.v.* He died on 28 March 1969.

Eisenhower Doctrine. Proposals for a new Middle East policy made by President Eisenhower to Congress on 5 January 1957. He proposed that (1) U.S. armed forces should be used to secure and protect the independence of nations requesting such aid against overt armed aggression from any nation controlled by international Communism; (2) the U.S.A. should help nations to develop their economic strength; and (3) the U.S.A. should give military aid to those who desired it. The area to which the Doctrine was to apply lay between (and included) Libya in the west, Pakistan in the east, Turkey in the north, and the Arabian peninsula (with Ethiopia and Sudan) in the south.

E.L.D.O. European Space Vehicle Launcher Development Organization, *q.v.*

El Salvador. *See* Salvador.

Embargo. An order preventing or impeding the movement of ships of a foreign power, either by detaining them in a port or by forbidding them access to a port. Ships are sometimes obstructed in this way in anticipation of a state of war, but this procedure is rare today, and they are usually given liberty to complete their journeys. The term is also used to describe any suspension of trading with a particular state or in particular commodities.

Encirclement. In German *Einkreisung*, a description used by Germans to describe the formation of an alliance between western and eastern powers to prevent German expansion. The term was first used by Reich Chancellor von Bülow in 1906 to recruit popular support for expenditure on the German navy, and it was revived when the U.K. in 1939 (after the annexation of Czechoslovakia by Germany) gave guarantees to Greece, Poland, Romania, and Turkey, and made a half-hearted attempt to conclude an alliance with the U.S.S.R. The object of encirclement, according to German propaganda at various times, was to deny to Germany its necessary *Lebensraum*, *q.v.*

Encyclical. From the Latin *bulla encyclica*, a circular letter by the Pope on religious and political questions. The opinions and directions contained in an encyclical have not the power of a dogma but are almost as powerful. Issued only on important occasions and defining papal policies over a length of time, they are significant documents. Famous political encyclicals include Leo XIII's *Rerum Novarum* (against a socialist state); Pius XI's *Quadragesimo Anno* (for a Christian corporate state), *Mit Brennender Sorge* (in German, attacking the extravagancies of Nazi doctrines in a way that did not condemn political and social totalitarianism), and on Atheistic Communism (describing Communism as intrinsically wrong); and John XXIII's *Mater et Magistra* (revising *Rerum Novarum* and stating that in certain cases socialization could be for the common good) and *Pacem in Terris* (dealing with nuclear weapons and the need for peace).

Enosis. *See* Cyprus.

Entente, Council of the (Conseil de l'Entente). Supreme organ of an association set up by the independent states of Dahomey, Ivory Coast, Niger, and Upper Volta. Before independence these countries were, with four other territories which are now independent, part of French West Africa, *q.v.* The association, which is also known as the Sahel-Bénin Union, was set up in 1959. It was joined by Togo in 1965. This loose grouping may be compared with the Union of Central African Republics (an economic union of the four states which once formed part of French Equatorial Africa, *q.v.*), the Casablanca Powers, *q.v.*, and the Monrovia Powers, *q.v.*

Entente Cordiale. From the French, 'cordial understanding'; the understanding reached in 1904 between the U.K. and France. The friendship between the two countries has continued ever since, but there has not always been agreement on foreign policy. Between the two World Wars and after 1945 there was much greater opposition in France than in the U.K. to the resurgence of Germany and a correspondingly greater reluctance on the part of France to join an anti-Soviet coalition. The friendship was reaffirmed in 1947 by the Dunkirk Treaty, *q.v.*

Entrenched Provisions. Those sections of the South Africa Act, 1909, which can be altered or repealed only by a Bill passed by both South African Houses of Parliament sitting together, and agreed to at the third reading by not less than two-thirds of the total number of members of both Houses. The 1909 Act gave to South Africa full powers of constitutional amendment, but stated, in Section 152, that Sections 33 and 34 (regulating the proportionate representation of the original four colonies), Section 35 (safeguarding the Coloured franchise in Cape Province), and Section 137 (guaranteeing the equality of the English and Dutch languages), could only be altered or repealed in the way described. Section 152 was also made subject to this rule, so that it should itself be safeguarded from a mere majority vote in separate sessions. Nationalists in South Africa considered that the Statute of Westminster, *q.v.*, passed in the U.K. in 1931, gave their Parliament power to repeal the entrenchment provisions, because it empowered it to repeal any Act which was part of the law of South Africa. In 1951 Cape Coloured voters were removed from the common roll; Section 35, an entrenched provision, was thus altered. The law was passed by the two Houses sitting separately. The Appellate Division of the South African Supreme Court, in a decision of great constitutional importance, decided that, although South Africa was a sovereign independent state, its Parliament must pass, repeal, and alter laws, including the entrenched provisions, in the manner laid down by Section 152 of the 1909 Act; if it wanted to alter Section 152, it must do so in the prescribed manner. The Nationalist Party administration then introduced laws to increase the membership of the Senate from 48 to 89 (the number was later reduced to 54), and to change the method of electing Senators, so that it could obtain the two-thirds majority in a joint session necessary to alter an entrenched provision and place the Cape Coloured voters on a separate electoral roll. The 1951 law was then reintroduced, and passed in the prescribed manner in 1956.

E.P.U. European Payments Union, *q.v.*

Equatorial Guinea. An independent state in West Africa known until 1963 as Spanish Guinea or the Spanish Equatorial Region; population (1968 estimate) 250,000. It consists of the two provinces of Rio Muni, *q.v.*, and Fernando Póo, *q.v.*, and the small island of Annobon (population 1,410) in the Gulf of Guinea lying to the south of Fernando Póo; total area 10,966 sq. m.; capital Santa Isabel, which is also the capital of Fernando Póo. From 1960 the two provinces had representation in the Cortes at Madrid, but as a result of a plebiscite held in December 1963 a measure of self-government was introduced. A

147

further plebiscite held in August 1968 favoured independence of Spain; this was achieved on 12 October 1968. Cocoa is exported from Fernando Póo and timber from Rio Muni, and offshore oil exploration began in 1970, but the country is not self-supporting and until 1968 Spain provided three-quarters of the revenues. After an unsuccessful attempt to depose President Francisco Macías Nguema and a series of anti-European demonstrations in 1969, Spain withdrew all her forces.

Eritrea. An area of 45,000 sq. m. on the Red Sea, formerly an Italian colony and since November 1962 a provincial unit of Ethiopia; population (1970 estimate) 1,800,000, of whom some 55 per cent are Moslems speaking the Tigrinya language as opposed to the Ethiopian Amharic tongue; capital Asmara. Eritrea was occupied by British forces in the spring of 1941 and from then on was administered by the U.K. On 2 December 1950 the U.N. General Assembly adopted a resolution whereby Eritrea was to constitute an autonomous unit federated with Ethiopia under the sovereignty of the Ethiopian crown. An Eritrean government was organized under the supervision of a U.N. Commissioner, and the British administration ended on 15 September 1952. In May 1960 the central government at Addis Ababa announced that the Eritrean government would henceforth be known as the Eritrean administration. In November 1962 the Eritrean parliament ended its federal status and Eritrea became an integral part of Ethiopia. A National Liberation Movement (E.L.F.), founded in 1963 and actively supported by Libya, Iraq and Syria, has engaged the major part of the Ethiopian army in guerilla warfare, including the hijacking of aircraft and the sabotaging of trains, for the past ten years. It has demanded a U.N. referendum with the object of establishing an independent, Arab-orientated, Eritrea. In December 1970 a state of emergency was declared and a six-mile strip of territory bordering the Sudan was designated a prohibited area.

E.R.P. European Recovery Programme, *q.v.*

Escalation. Process in which each supposedly limited and controlled military measure by one country is met by a supposedly equally limited and controlled counter-measure; each country hopes that its own measure, or 'controlled response', will not result immediately in the other replying with an extreme measure, such as a nuclear weapon. In practice each measure tends to be more violent than its predecessor. U.S. experts on the subject of so-called 'war games' try to distinguish between degrees of escalation even after nuclear weapons have been used; thus, they argue, a U.S. government might protect New York, at the cost of Los Angeles, by destroying Odessa rather than Leningrad, so checking the process of escalation.

Eshkol, Levi. Israeli politician; born 25 October 1895 near Kiev. He settled in Palestine in 1913 and, after the 1914–18 war in which he served with the Jewish battalion of the Royal Fusiliers, he founded a number of agricultural colonies including the Degania Kibbutz. He became secretary of Histraduth (the Jewish Federation of Labour) and of Mapai (Labour Party) and was active in the Jewish Agency as its treasurer and head of its colonization department. He entered the government of Ben Gurion in 1951 as Minister of Agriculture and Development and transferred to the Ministry of Finance in 1952 where he remained for eleven years. He was responsible for devaluing the Israeli pound in 1962 and for the economic and financial reforms and economic stabilization programmes which accompanied this measure. He became Israel's third Prime Minister on 16 June 1963 when Ben Gurion resigned. He died on 26 February 1969 and was succeeded by Golda Meir, *q.v.*

E.S.R.O. European Space Research Organization, *q.v.*

Estonia. Since 1940 one of the fifteen constituent Republics of the Union of Soviet Socialist Republics; area 17,413 sq. m.; population (1969) 1,374,000; capital Tallinn. The language is related to Finnish, having nothing in common with that of the Latvians to the south. The Republic, which is on the Baltic Sea, was ruled by foreigners (including Danes, Swedes, Germans, and Russians) for 700 years and was a Russian province when it achieved independence, with Finnish and British assistance, at the end of the First World War as a result of the simultaneous collapse of Russia and Germany. The people are mostly Lutherans, the Tsarist Russians having failed in their efforts to convert the country to the Russian Orthodox faith. The existence of a literate peasantry and of a substantial class of bourgeois and intelligentsia facilitated the establishment of a peaceful and democratic society in the 1920s. An Agrarian Law transformed a semi-feudal system of land-holding, in which nearly half of Estonia had belonged to 600 families of the Germanic Balt nobility, into a society in which the redistributed land was owned by individuals (each allowed as much as could be worked by his family and two horses), educational, cooperative, and industrial institutions, and workers' collective associations. The world-wide economic crisis of 1929 was largely responsible for the emergence of an authoritarian regime under Konstantin Päts, under whose leadership the land was more intensively cultivated and the valuable oil shale deposits were more efficiently exploited. By 1939 there had been a material improvement in the economic position, there was no unemployment, and the Constitution of 1938 had marked the beginning of a return to normal parliamentary government. The government found itself unable to reject a Russian demand for the use of Estonian naval bases, and concluded a treaty with the U.S.S.R. on 28 September 1939, which was followed by the Russian occupation of the country with German consent in June 1940, and the establishment of Estonia as a constituent Republic on 6 August 1940. Approximately 60,000 Estonians, or 5 per cent of the population, including many of the country's leading figures, were deported to the U.S.S.R. within a year of the occupation. From 1941 to 1944 Estonia was occupied by German troops; after their withdrawal an unsuccessful attempt was made to re-establish an independent government. The U.K. and the U.S.A. do not recognize Estonia as being in law a constituent Republic of the U.S.S.R. Agriculture, dairy farming, and cattle breeding are the mainstays of the economy. Mining of shale has been developed to supply Leningrad with gas. There are highly developed engineering and textile industries, valuable peat deposits, and good timber supplies from the forests which cover 22 per cent of the total area.

Ethiopia. Also known as Abyssinia, q.v.; an independent empire in north-east Africa; area 400,000 sq. m.; population (1969 estimate) 24,700,000, comprising Amharas, the ruling race, and the Tigréans, both of Semitic and Hamitic origin, Gallas, Guraghi, and Negro tribes, in the west and south, Danakil and Somalis in the east; Coptic Christianity is the religion of the majority and some 35 per cent are Moslem; capital Addis Ababa. It was originally a group of kingdoms and later 12 land-locked provinces; as a result of a United Nations resolution in 1950, the provinces were federated in 1952 with the former Italian colony of Eritrea, q.v., on the Red Sea, but the federation ended in November 1962 when Eritrea became an integral part of Ethiopia. Since 1930 it has been ruled by Emperor Haile Selassie I, q.v., who exercises almost absolute power in spite of the limitations imposed on him by the 1955 Constitution, which provides for universal suffrage and a two-chamber assembly, comprising an upper chamber of nobles (partly elected and partly nominated by the Emperor) and a lower chamber (nominated by the nobles and local chiefs). Ethiopia was invaded by Italy in 1935 and, with Eritrea and Somalia, q.v., became part of the Italian East African Empire until the Italian forces were defeated in 1941.

The economy is largely dependent on agriculture and stock breeding. The exports of coffee make up 50 per cent of the value of exports. The fertile central province of Shoa, in which a subsistence agriculture is still practised, remains undeveloped owing to insufficient investment and failure to attract foreign capital into

Ethiopia. Gold is mined in the south. There is nearly 85 per cent illiteracy. In 1970 a state of emergency was declared owing to the activities of two clandestine opposition groups with separatist aims; the Eritrean Liberation Front (E.L.F.), founded in 1963 and led by Osman Salah Sebbe, which has conducted a guerilla war on behalf of independence for the northern province of Eritrea, *q.v.*, and the West Somalia Front, founded in 1970, and based in the east of Ethiopia and allied with the E.L.F., which represents the Somali of Ogaden, *q.v.*

Ethnographical Principle. The principle that all persons of the same race or language should be united in a common state.

Euratom. European Atomic Energy Community, *q.v.*

European Atomic Energy Community (Euratom). An organization established with effect from 1 January 1958 by Belgium, France, the German Federal Republic, Italy, Luxemburg and the Netherlands, and enlarged from 1 January 1973 by the accession of Denmark, Ireland and the U.K. to create the technical and industrial conditions necessary to utilize nuclear discoveries and to produce nuclear energy for peaceful purposes on a large scale. On the same day the European Economic Community, *q.v.*, also known as the Common Market, with the same member countries, came into existence. Both Communities were established as a result of the Rome Treaties, *q.v.*, which were concluded on 25 March 1957.

Executive powers were originally vested in a Council of Ministers and a Commission of six members appointed for four years, which reached decisions unanimously or by a weighted or non-weighted majority, depending upon the issue. (In the case of a weighted vote France, Germany and Italy each had 4 votes, Belgium and the Netherlands 2 each, and Luxemburg 1.) On 1 July 1967 the Councils of the three European Communities (the European Coal and Steel Community, *q.v.*, the European Economic Community and Euratom) were merged into a single Council of Ministers, and the High Authority of the Coal and Steel Community, and the Commissions of the other two into a single Commission. This was a first step towards the fusion of the three Treaties to establish a single European Community, *q.v.* An Assembly of 198 members (*see* European Parliament) exercises a general control over the Communities. Legal problems concerning the interpretation of the Treaty and the legality of decisions of the Commission and the Council of Ministers are submitted to the Court of Justice of seven judges nominated by agreement; the Court performs a similar function for the other two Communities.

The Community established on 1 January 1959 a common market for nuclear products. It has also undertaken a comprehensive research programme which is carried out mainly through the Euratom Joint Nuclear Research Centre.

European Coal and Steel Community. An organization established with effect from 10 August 1952 by Belgium, France, the German Federal Republic, Italy, Luxemburg and the Netherlands, to control the production and marketing of coal and steel in those countries. Membership was extended in 1972 to Denmark, Ireland and the U.K. Executive powers were originally vested in the High Authority, comprising the President and eight others, and a Council of Ministers which acted mainly in a consultative capacity. The Community set up its own Common Assembly which was replaced on 1 January 1958 by the European Assembly, known since 1962 as the European Parliament, *q.v.*, which also supervises the work of the European Atomic Energy Community and the European Economic Community. The Community established its own Court of Justice to test the legal validity of actions of the High Authority; this was superseded in 1958 by a Court which serves all three Communities. On 1 July 1967 the High Authority of the Coal and Steel Community and the Commissions of the other two Communities were merged into a single Commission and the Councils of all three Communities were merged into a single Council of Ministers. This was a first step towards the fusion of the three Treaties to establish a single European Community, *q.v.*

The treaty by which the Coal and Steel Community was set up authorizes the High Authority to limit prices for coal and steel in certain carefully defined situations in the different coal- and steel-producing regions. It also forbids certain trade activities, such as 'double-pricing', and all private agreements, the effect of which is to restrict or control production, such as cartels. Decisions of the European Commission in E.C.S.C. affairs are now directly binding on the industries concerned.

In the period 1952 to 1966 the High Authority achieved notable success in encouraging Community production of steel, which rose from 41·9 to 85 million tons, and in effecting a painless reduction in the output of coal, when it became uncompetitive in relation to oil, and its sale at a price which would avoid social or economic dislocation. Grants were allocated for industrial adaptation and redevelopment, and for the housing of coal and steel workers. The merger of the High Authority into the European Commission in 1967 has permitted the coordination of energy policy, a field in which responsibility had previously been divided among the E.C.S.C. (coal), E.E.C. (oil and natural gas) and Euratom (nuclear energy).

European Community. The institutional framework shared by the European Coal and Steel Community, *q.v.*, the European Economic Community, *q.v.*, and the European Atomic Energy Community, *q.v.* It consists of a Commission of 13 members (originally 3 each from France, Germany and Italy, 2 each from Belgium and the Netherlands, and 1 from Luxemburg, and after the enlargement of the Communities 2 each from France, Germany, Italy and the U.K., and 1 from each of the other states) appointed for a four-year renewable term. Decisions are reached by majority vote. This is the High Authority of the three Communities, and was created on 1 July 1967 by the merger of their former executive authorities, each of which had nine members. Its role is to initiate proposals for implementing the Treaties, of which it is the guardian, and to mediate between the member governments in Community affairs. It shares executive power and responsibility with the Council of Ministers, which represents the national interests of the member governments and comprises one minister from each country selected according to the matter under discussion. The Council's decisions may be reached unanimously, or by a weighted or non-weighted majority, depending on the issue. (In the case of a weighted vote France, Germany, Italy and the U.K. each have 10 votes, Belgium and the Netherlands, 5 each, Denmark and Ireland 3 each, and Luxemburg 2.) In practice the unanimity rule is usually observed but where a qualified majority is required it must consist of 43 votes cast by at least six members.

Some democratic control is exercised by the European Parliament, *q.v.*, which has a consultative role in the decision-making process of the Communities and can, by a two-thirds majority vote of censure, dismiss the Commission *en bloc*. A Court of Justice, which superseded that of the European Coal and Steel Community, consisting of seven judges appointed by the agreement of the member governments for a six-year term, is the final arbiter in all matters arising from the interpretation and application of the Treaties.

European Defence Community (E.D.C.). A supra-national community with common institutions, common armed forces, and a common budget, which was to assure the security of its members against aggression; an attack on one member was to be considered as an attack against all. The aim was to produce a more coherent group than the North Atlantic Treaty Organization and a counterpart to, but embracing more member countries than, the European Coal and Steel Community, *q.v.*, with an international army. The participants were to be the members of the Coal and Steel Community, with the addition of any other Western European countries, including the

U.K., prepared to join. The E.D.C. never came into existence. Negotiations began in Paris in February 1951 and on 8 May 1952 a draft treaty was initialled on behalf of Belgium, France, the German Federal Republic, Italy, Luxemburg and the Netherlands. The treaty was signed by the six foreign ministers on 27 May 1952, the day after the signature in Bonn of the new contractual agreements between the German Federal Republic and the Western Powers, which restored West German sovereignty and formally terminated the occupation of the Republic.

The E.D.C. treaty could not come into force until ratified by the parliaments of the six parties; only the French parliament refused ratification, although the ratification vote was never taken in the Italian parliament since the treaty had already been vetoed. The project was abandoned and there was instituted instead the Western European Union, *q.v.*, with effect from 5 May 1955. The six parties to the proposed European Defence Community, with the addition of the U.K., all became members of the W.E.U.

European Economic Community (Common Market). An organization which came into existence on 1 January 1958, with Belgium, France, the German Federal Republic, Italy, Luxemburg, and the Netherlands as member countries, to establish a common market and a common external tariff or customs union for all their goods, to devise common policies for agriculture, the movement of capital, labour and transport, and to coordinate the general economic policies of member governments. On the same day the European Atomic Energy Community, *q.v.*, also known as Euratom, with the same member countries, came into existence. Both Communities were established as a result of the Rome Treaties, *q.v.*, which were concluded on 25 March 1957.

Executive powers were originally vested in a Council of Ministers and a Commission of six members appointed for four years, which reached decisions unanimously or by a weighted or non-weighted majority, depending on the issue. (In the case of a weighted vote France, Germany and Italy each had 4 votes, Belgium and the Netherlands 2 each, and Luxemburg 1.) On 1 July 1967 the Councils of the three European Communities (the European Coal and Steel Community, *q.v.*, the European Atomic Energy Community and the European Economic Community) were merged into a single Council of Ministers, and the High Authority of the Coal and Steel Community and the Commissions of the other two into a single Commission. This was a first step towards the fusion of the three Treaties to establish a single European Community, *q.v.* An

Assembly originally of 142 members, but after 1 January 1973 of 198, (*see* European Parliament) exercises a general control over the Communities. Legal problems concerning the interpretation of the Treaty and the legality of decisions of the Commission and the Council of Ministers are submitted to the Court of Justice of seven judges nominated by agreement; the Court performs a similar function for the other two Communities.

The U.K., which did not want to bind itself to discriminate against imports from the British Commonwealth, refused to join the Community but entered the European Free Trade Association, *q.v.*, in November 1959. Nevertheless, in July 1961 the U.K. applied for membership of the Community. Negotiations were broken off in January 1963, largely as a result of French objections to the British application. On 11 May 1967 the U.K., together with Ireland and Denmark, and later Norway, made a further application for membership; this was again obstructed by France until the retirement of de Gaulle in 1969 allowed negotiations to proceed. The Treaty of Accession was signed by the four new applicants on 22 January 1972 and was to come into effect on 1 January 1973 providing that the four respective parliaments had ratified the terms agreed. Norway, however, withdrew its application following a national referendum in September 1972 in which 53 per cent voted against entry. Special trading arrangements with the non-applicant members of the European Free Trade Association (E.F.T.A.), *q.v.*, were to become effective simultaneously.

European Free Trade Association (E.F.T.A.). An association of seven west European states (Austria, Denmark, Norway, Portugal, Sweden, Switzerland, and the U.K.) which agreed to eliminate, over a period, tariffs and restrictions on trade with each other without the necessity of bringing into alignment their individual tariff and trade policies with countries outside the area. Proposals for such an area were made in July 1956 at the Council of Ministers of the Organization for European Economic Co-operation, *q.v.*, and an O.E.E.C. committee reported in January 1957 that such an Association was technically feasible. Meanwhile six members of O.E.E.C. (Belgium, France, the German Federal Republic, Italy, Luxemburg and the Netherlands) were themselves conducting negotiations which led in March 1957 to the Rome Treaties, *q.v.*, and to the establishment on 1 January 1958 of the European Atomic Energy Community, *q.v.*, and the European Economic Community, *q.v.*

The U.K., itself a member of O.E.E.C., supported the proposals for this Association, with the proviso that foodstuffs should be excluded from their scope; the reasons given for this exception were that many areas in the British Commonwealth relied on the preferential treatment which their exports of foodstuffs received in the U.K., and that several European countries, including the U.K. and Denmark, protected their home agriculture and wished to continue to do so. The Stockholm Convention establishing the Association was initialled on 20 November 1959, and the first tariff cut, of 20 per cent on industrial goods, was made on 1 July 1960. The agreed programme was then accelerated; by 1 January 1966 duties had been cut by 80 per cent, and by 1 January 1967 all import duties and quantitative restrictions were officially eliminated. The U.K., however, broke the agreement in 1966 by introducing an import surcharge to help correct a balance-of-payments deficit. Agricultural products were not affected by the removal of tariffs, but members could negotiate agreements relating to such products. Finland was linked with E.F.T.A. in associate membership by an agreement signed on 27 March 1961, and on 1 January 1968 the Faroes (as a dependency of Denmark) entered the Association. Iceland became a member in March 1970.

The accession of Denmark and the U.K. to the European Communities in January 1973 brought the association to an end. Bilateral agreements were negotiated between individual E.F.T.A. members which had not applied for membership of the E.E.C. and the Community, which were to come into force at the same time as the accession treaties and would be binding on the enlarged Community.

European Monetary Agreement. Was concluded on 5 August 1955 by the members of the Organization for European Economic Co-operation to provide for a return to convertibility of their currencies. The Agreement provided facilities for monthly dollar settlements and established a European Fund of $600 million to assist in these settlements between the various central banks and to grant short-term credits (up to two years) to members. The machinery envisaged by the Agreement came into operation on 27 December 1958, upon the termination of the European Payments Union, *q.v.*

European Organization for Nuclear Research (C.E.R.N.). Was established in 1954 on the initiative of U.N.E.S.C.O., *q.v.*, to encourage collaboration in nuclear research of a pure scientific kind, and exclusive of military research, among European states. The member countries are: Austria, Belgium, Denmark, France, German Federal Republic, Greece, Italy, Netherlands, Norway, Spain, Sweden, Switzerland and the U.K. Yugoslavia was originally a member, but withdrew on financial grounds and was accorded observer status. In 1963 Poland and Turkey were also given observer status. France, West

Germany and the U.K. contribute 64·8 per cent of the total budget.

European Parliament. The parliamentary body of the European Community, *q.v.*, which comprises the European Atomic Energy Community, *q.v.*, the European Coal and Steel Community, *q.v.*, and the European Economic Community, *q.v.* It was inaugurated on 19 March 1958 at Strasbourg where it holds its plenary sessions; there is a permanent secretariat at Luxemburg. It consists of 198 members (originally 142) nominated by the national parliaments of the participating countries. France, Italy, the German Federal Republic and the U.K. have 36 members each, Belgium and the Netherlands 14 each, Denmark and Ireland 10, and Luxemburg 6. It must be consulted on all major issues, has the right to address questions to the Commission and the Council of Ministers, and can force the dismissal of the Commission *en bloc* by a two-thirds majority vote of censure.

European Payments Union. Set up as from 1 July 1950 by the Organization for European Economic Co-operation to encourage European trade by removing impediments preventing payments from one European country to another. European currencies were to be freely convertible into each other but not into dollars. With the movement towards the re-introduction of convertibility of sterling and of the other main European currencies, it was agreed that E.P.U. should be continued temporarily and that a European Fund and Multilateral Clearing System should provide short-term credits for any member adversely affected by the convertibility of the currency of one or more of its neighbours. On 27 December 1958 a majority of the voting strength notified the Secretary-General of O.E.E.C. of its wish to terminate E.P.U. and bring into force the European Monetary Agreement, *q.v.* The Union accordingly came to an end.

European Recovery Programme. Proposals for economic cooperation presented to the U.S.A. on 22 September 1947 by 16 European states (Austria, Belgium, Denmark, France, Greece, Iceland, Ireland, Italy, Luxemburg, the Netherlands, Norway, Portugal, Sweden, Switzerland, Turkey, and the U.K.) which founded the Organization for European Economic Co-operation, *q.v.*, in response to the Marshall Plan, *q.v.* The Programme covered the four years 1948–51 and was based on (1) a strong production effort by each country, (2) internal financial stability, (3) economic cooperation, and (4) a solution of the problem of the deficit with the American continent, particularly by increased exports.

President Truman proposed that U.S. aid (often called Marshall Aid) should be given over the period 1948–51, and the U.S. Congress appropriated $522 million of interim aid to Austria, France, and Italy in 1947, and by the Economic Co-operation Act in April 1948 authorized expenditure on the Programme. It set up the Economic Co-operation Administration, *q.v.*, to supervise the Programme. The following annual amounts were appropriated by Congress under the Programme: 1948–9 $5,000 million; 1949–50 $5,430 million; 1950–51 $2,850 million.

European Space Research Organization (E.S.R.O.). Was established in 1964 to promote cooperation among European states in space research and technology for peaceful purposes. Member countries are: Belgium, Denmark, France, German Federal Republic, Italy, Netherlands, Spain, Switzerland and the U.K. Austria and Norway have observer status; Spain has notified her intention to withdraw. France, West Germany and the U.K. contribute 67·61 per cent of the total budget.

European Space Vehicle Launcher Development Organization (E.L.D.O.). Was founded in 1962 and formally established in 1964 to provide Europe with an independent satellite launching capability for peaceful applications. Member countries are: Australia, Belgium, France, German Federal Republic, Italy, Netherlands and the U.K. Denmark and Switzerland have observer status. The initial programme involved the development and construction of the Europa I satellite launching vehicle at the Woomera Test Range in Australia, and the Europa II at Kouron in French Guiana; the project has been financed by Belgium, France and the German Federal Republic.

Exchange Control. A system under which the government or the central bank controls all transactions in foreign exchange in order to conserve the country's supply of foreign currency. The government or central bank buys all foreign currency accruing to exporters and others with credit abroad, and then allocates it, usually on special application, to importers and others owing foreign debts. In the U.K. the Exchange Control Act, 1947, contains the fundamental provisions of the British exchange control system.

Extradition. The removal of a person, by the state where he happens to be, to the state on the territory of which he is alleged to have committed or been convicted of a crime. As there is no rule of international law by which states must hand over people in this way, many extradition treaties have been concluded specifying the cases in which extradition shall take place. The treaties generally provide that individuals charged or convicted of the more important crimes, with the exception of political crimes, shall be surrendered.

F

Fair Deal. A policy proclaimed by President Truman in January 1949, and designed, like President Roosevelt's New Deal, *q.v.*, to improve the U.S. standard of living, especially among lower-income groups, and to extend social justice by fair labour legislation and civil rights measures. It denied the need for a planned economy but looked to Presidential influence to prevent undue inflation or deflation so that programmes for housing, health, education, and the development of national resources could be undertaken. It also involved programmes of foreign economic and military aid.

Falangists. Spanish Fascists. The Spanish falange, or falangists, were created on 29 October 1933 by José Antonio Primo de Rivera, son of Primo de Rivera, the dictator of Spain from 1923 to 1931. Their founder was shot by the Republicans. On 19 April 1937 the right-wing political groups, including the falange española (which had shown unwelcome signs of social radicalism), were merged to form the Falange Española Tradicionalista y de las Juntas de Ofensiva Nacional Sindicalistas. This body replaced the Cortes (Assembly) from June 1939 until the Cortes was reinstituted in July 1942. It is the only political organization allowed in Spain.

Falkland Islands. A British colony in the South Atlantic, 300 miles east of the Magellan Straits; the island group has a total area of 4,618 sq. m.; population (1969) 2,107; capital Port Stanley. The colony, which has been occupied continuously by the U.K. since 1833, is claimed by Argentina, which includes the population of the islands in its official census where they are described as the Islas Malvinas. Economic pressure has been exerted by Argentina on the islanders who, in 1964, expressed their wish to retain the British connection. In 1965 the United Nations General Assembly recommended that Argentina and the U.K. should find a peaceful solution to the dispute; in 1971 agreement was reached between the two governments on the establishment of regular air and sea communications between Argentina and the Falklands and for improving postal, cable and telephone connections, as measures which might contribute to the 'process of a definitive solution' to the dispute. The Falkland Islands Dependencies and British Antarctic Territory, *q.v.*, in the Antarctic Continent, *q.v.*, have been the subject of both Argentinean and Chilean claims.

F.A.O. Food and Agriculture Organization, *q.v.*

Faroes (Faerøerne, or Sheep Islands). A group of islands under Danish sovereignty, in the Atlantic Ocean, north of U.K.; area 540 sq. m.; population (1970) 38,681, descended from Norsemen; capital

Thorshavn. More than half the population is engaged in fishing activities or agriculture. There are 18 inhabited islands, 12 uninhabited islands on which sheep graze, and other almost inaccessible small islands and rocks. The islands were Norwegian from 1030 to 1814, when they passed to Denmark. The Danes suspended the ancient Lagting (parliament) for many years and forbade teaching and preaching in Faroese, a mixture of Icelandic and Norwegian. In 1816 the islands became a Danish county. They were occupied by British forces in the Second World War, and in 1946 the Lagting held a plebiscite by which a narrow majority favoured separation from Denmark and the creation of an independent state. In 1948 a Danish law, supported by four out of the five parties in the Lagting, made the islands self-governing, but without conceding independence. The Faroes return two members to the Danish Parliament (Folketing) in Copenhagen.

The Landsstyre (provincial government), representing the Danish government in Copenhagen, found itself in conflict with the islanders from 1953 onwards. The arrival of a new doctor, appointed by Copenhagen, to take charge of a hospital at Klasvig was the occasion of rioting. Further differences arose in 1958 when the Lagting passed a Bill to abrogate the Anglo-Danish Fishery Convention of 1901. The Convention, as modified in April 1955, provided for a 4-mile limit for territorial waters as far as fishing rights were concerned. The Bill followed a decision of the government of Iceland, q.v., to extend its fishing limits to 6 miles from 1 September 1958. The Danish government rejected the Bill on the ground that it related to foreign affairs which were outside the competence of the Lagting. In April 1959 a temporary Anglo-Danish agreement was signed permitting British vessels to fish up to 6 miles within the 12-mile limit, as they were regarded as having historic rights in these waters. After the expiry of the agreement in April 1963, the Landsstyre insisted that the 12-mile limit should apply to British as well as other fishermen.

Fascism. A nationalist, anti-Communist, and authoritarian political creed followed by Benito Mussolini in Italy in 1919. The Italian Fascist movement adopted as its emblem the fasces, a bundle of rods with an axe in the middle, which was the symbol of state power carried in front of the consuls by the lictors in ancient Rome. The movement claimed to be neither capitalistic nor socialistic, and advocated the founding of a corporate state, q.v. After Mussolini came to power in 1922 the Fascist Party became the only authorized political organization in Italy; its members wore black shirts, used the Roman greeting of the outstretched arm, were organized as a military formation, and adopted the slogan *Mussolini ha sempre ragione* (Mussolini is always right). Italian Fascism served as a model to a number of similar movements in other countries, and in particular to National Socialism in Germany. In the U.K. a Fascist movement called the British Union, which was active between 1931 and 1939, advocated the abolition of free speech and greater interest in the British Commonwealth, and preached anti-semitic propaganda. It was proscribed in 1940, but revived again in 1948 as the Union Movement, *q.v.*, under the leadership of Sir Oswald Mosley.

Fatah, *or* **al Fatah.** A Palestine nationalist organization which originated in 1956 in the Gaza Strip, *q.v.*, where many Palestinian refugees had sought shelter after the victorious Israeli campaign in Sinai. It is the largest of the Palestine guerilla movements and its leader, Yassir Arafat, is chairman of the Palestine Liberation Organization, *q.v.* The word Fatah, which means conquest, was formed by the Arabic initials in reverse order of 'Harakat al Tharir al Falastin', or Palestine Liberation Movement. In 1959 Fatah created the military commando organization of Al Assifa which, in 1964, developed into an operational force trained chiefly on Syrian territory. From 17 January 1965 until the Israeli victory in the Six Day War of June 1967 Fatah made continuous raids along the shores of Lake Tiberias and across the Jordan river. After the Israeli occupation of the west bank, Fatah retreated into Jordanian territory, renewing operations against Israel in September 1969. It was prominent in the unsuccessful attempt in 1970 to oust King Hussein (*see* Jordan). Although it is dedicated to the destruction of Israel Fatah is opposed to indiscriminate terrorism and particularly to the activities of the left-wing revolutionary Popular Front for the Liberation of Palestine, *q.v.*; it is recognized as representative of the more moderate centre of the Palestine movement.

F.B.I. Federal Bureau of Investigation, *q.v.*

Federal Bureau of Investigation. A branch of the U.S. Department of Justice. Its Director has responsibility for investigating all alleged violations of federal laws except those which, by federal enactment or otherwise, have been assigned to some other body. It is especially concerned with internal security, espionage, and sabotage.

Federal Reserve System. The U.S. central bank system, organized in 1915 under the Federal Reserve Act, 1913. There are twelve Federal Reserve Banks located in the most important regions of the U.S., and the member banks of the Federal Reserve System are normally indebted to the Federal Reserve Banks, which re-discount trade bills on their behalf. The Federal Reserve Banks jointly constitute the central banking system and correspond to the Bank of England. The system is controlled by the Federal Reserve Board, a Board consisting of government nominees, created in 1936 under the Banking Act, 1935. The Reserve Banks have the power to influence the member banks in the matter of loans to customers.

Federation. A political unit on which a number of smaller political units devolve certain power over themselves and their citizens, and to which they usually entrust the conduct of their foreign affairs. The individual provinces or states, as they are often called, retain some control over their internal affairs, and in order that their rights should be clearly defined there is usually a federal constitution which allocates powers between them and the federal government. As disputes often arise as to the constitutional legality of executive decisions or laws made by the federal government, a supreme court is generally created to interpret the constitution. It is frequently provided that amendments to the constitution can be made only with the consent of a fixed number of the provinces or states.

Examples of federations, or federal unions, may be found in the United States of America, the United States of Argentina, the United States of Brazil, the United States of Mexico, the Union of Soviet Socialist Republics, Canada, Malaysia, Australia, and Venezuela. The U.S. Constitution forbids the individual states to make treaties with foreign governments, but the Russian Constitution permits such treaties and even allows the constituent Republics of the U.S.S.R. to have separate military forces, though this right is not exercised. The Ukraine and Byelorussia, however, which are constituent Republics, have separate representation at the United Nations Assembly.

A federal constitution can be contrasted with a unitary constitution where a supreme legislature may enact any law, and with the constitution of a confederation, *q.v.*, which is a looser association than a federation. The essential difference between a federation and a confederation is that the organs of a federation have a direct power over the citizens of its component provinces or states. Thus Switzerland is officially called a confederation but is really a federation.

Federation of Arab Emirates. An association of the seven Trucial States, *q.v.*, of the Persian Gulf, and of Bahrain, *q.v.*, and Qatar, *q.v.*, which became effective on 30 March 1968. The agreement, which was signed at Dubai on 27 February 1968, provided for a Supreme Council consisting of the nine rulers who would hold the Presidency in rotation for one-year terms. The Council, whose decisions were to be unanimous, was responsible for foreign affairs, defence and economic policy, and for preparing a federal budget. In practice the interests of Bahrain and Qatar proved incompatible with those of the smaller Trucial States, and both countries seceded from the Federation in 1971 and declared their own independence. Six of the remaining states had, in the meantime, agreed on a Constitution for a proposed United Arab Emirates, *q.v.* This came into existence on 18 July 1971.

Federation of Arab Republics. An association of Egypt, Libya and Syria, the establishment of which was approved by the respective electorates of the three countries by referenda held on 1 September 1971. There is a Presidential Council, of which President Anwar Sadat, *q.v.*, of Egypt became the first chairman, and a Federal Council of Ministers headed by the Prime Minister of Syria. The Federation was to provide a nucleus of total Arab unity and an example of a unified Arab socialist society. It declared its objectives as: the liberation of the Occupied Arab Territories, *q.v.*; no compromise over Palestine, *q.v.*; no reconciliation with, or recognition of, the state of Israel. Close links were to be maintained with Sudan in anticipation of its future accession to the Federation.

Federation of Rhodesia and Nyasaland. A largely self-governing British territory in Central Africa, created as a Federation on 1 August 1953, and dissolved in December 1963; area 486,109 sq. m.; population (1961 estimate) 8,630,000, including 308,000 Europeans; capital Salisbury. It comprised the self-governing territory of Southern Rhodesia, known, since Northern Rhodesia became independent on 24 October 1964, as Rhodesia, *q.v.*, and the protectorates, as they were then, of Northern Rhodesia, *q.v.*, and Nyasaland, *q.v.*; the union was often called the Central African Federation, *q.v.* The economic argument for federation was strong: Nyasaland (now known as Malawi, *q.v.*) was almost entirely agricultural, with insufficient work for its inhabitants; Northern Rhodesia (now known as Zambia, *q.v.*) was almost wholly dependent on the wealth to be derived from its copper belt, and would benefit from the development of secondary industries; while Southern Rhodesia had the most balanced economy of the three units but a shortage of labour. In spite of this, many Africans in the two protectorates regarded federation, and the end of Colonial Office supervision, as a setback to their hopes for self-government. Under the 1953 Constitution an African Affairs Board could draw attention to any Bill disadvantageous to Africans by asking that it should be reserved for the approval of the British government. The Board comprised the three European members appointed to the federal legislature to represent African interests, and one of the elected African members from each territory.

The objections of the Board, in 1957, to the Federal Franchise Bill and the bill to amend the composition of the federal legislature, were overruled by the U.K. The possibility of introducing amendments to the 1953 Constitution was considered by a British government advisory commission under the chairmanship of Viscount Monckton which in 1960 issued its report known as the Monckton Report.

The Federal Assembly elected on 12 November 1958 consisted of 59 members. Of these, 12 were Africans and 3 Europeans specially elected to represent African interests. The United Federal Party (U.F.P.), led by Sir Roy Welensky, won 46 seats; it favoured the elevation of the Federation to full membership of the British Commonwealth as soon as possible and opposed any rapid transfer of power to Africans. The Federal Dominion Party, led by Winston Field, won 8 seats; it sympathized with some of the South African Nationalist Party views on apartheid.

In 1962 Sir Roy Welensky, dissatisfied with the concessions given to the Africans in Northern Rhodesia, dissolved the Federal Assembly and held an election on 27 April. Of the 55 elective seats, 40 were uncontested, the U.F.P. candidates being returned unopposed. The U.F.P. also won all but one of the 15 contested seats. The Rhodesian Front, comprising the Federal and Southern Rhodesian Dominion Parties, the Southern Rhodesia Association, and the Rhodesia Reform Party, and led by Winston Field, did not fight the election; it wanted to concentrate on winning the next Southern Rhodesian election.

The African leaders in Nyasaland and Northern Rhodesia insisted on those territories being granted the right to secede from the Federation. This right was recognized by the U.K. in December 1962 in the case of Nyasaland which became independent, as Malawi, on 6 July 1964, and in March 1963 in the case of Northern Rhodesia which became independent, as Zambia, on 24 October 1964. The Central African Office in London, setting out the views of the British government, said on 29 March 1963: '. . . they accept that none of the territories can be kept in the Federation against its will and they therefore accept the principle that any territory which so wishes must be allowed to secede'.

Federation of South Arabia. *See* South Arabian Federation.

Federation of the West Indies. *See* West Indies Federation.

Fellow Traveller. One who accepts most Communist conclusions but is not, or denies that he is, a Communist. The term usually has a derogatory meaning. It is a useful expression when applied to people who, favouring a particular Communist policy, falsely claim that they, as independents, have come to the same conclusion. It is a malicious and unilluminating expression when used by politicians of persons whose honest left-wing deviations from their own views they wish to attack.

Fernando Póo. An island off the coast of West Africa; area 776 sq. m.; population (1966) 62,612, including some 40,000 Nigerian contract labourers 75 per cent of whom are Ibo; the largest indigenous ethnic group is Bubi; capital Santa Isabel. It is one of the two provinces (the other is Rio Muni, *q.v.*), which form Equatorial Guinea, *q.v.*

Fertile Crescent. The area between the Mediterranean Sea and the Persian Gulf, now occupied by Jordan, Syria, and Iraq, which was once a fertile region, particularly in the valleys of the Euphrates and the Tigris, but which is now largely an arid desert region.

Fifth Amendment Communist. A term of abuse or reproach, used in the U.S.A. It has been employed to describe witnesses, suspected of being Communists or Communist sympathizers, who plead the Fifth Amendment to the Constitution of the United States to justify their refusal to answer questions before a civil court or Congressional committee.

The Amendment says: 'No person . . . shall be compelled in any criminal case to be a witness against himself.' The classic interpretation of the Amendment was given by Chief Justice Marshall (1755–1835) in the treason trial of Aaron Burr. He said that two principles, that the United States was entitled to the testimony of every citizen, and that every witness was entitled not to accuse himself, had to be reconciled. It would be virtually a perjury, he said, to use the Fifth Amendment to protect oneself against social disgrace or other embarrassments, for it should only be used where one might be accused of a crime. In law, therefore, his disapproval of the activities of a court or committee would not entitle a man to plead the Fifth Amendment in order to avoid answering questions. The Amendment was criticized on the ground that it enabled Communist sympathizers to conceal information. It was similarly attacked in the early years of the twentieth century by American liberal writers on the ground that it was being improperly pleaded by politicians and businessmen in anti-trust cases.

Fifth Column. A term originating from the Spanish Civil War, 1936–9, when the rebels under Franco attacked Madrid in four columns, while their adherents organized uprisings, espionage, and sabotage within the government ranks. These secret fighters behind the front were called the 'fifth column'.

Fifth Republic. The system of government established in France in 1958. The First Republic lasted from 1793 until 1804 when Napoleon

Bonaparte set up the First Empire. The Second Republic, which was created in 1848, became the Second Empire in 1852, and the Third Republic was set up in 1870 following the deposition of the Emperor Napoleon III. France was governed by the Constitution of the Third Republic until the German occupation of 1940. After the liberation of Paris in 1944 a provisional government under General de Gaulle, *q.v.*, was set up with a single-chamber legislature (the National Constituent Assembly). By a referendum held in October 1945 the Constitution of the Third Republic was abandoned. In May 1946 a draft constitution was rejected by the Assembly: a second draft constitution was eventually accepted by the Assembly on 29 September 1946, and adopted by a referendum, held on 13 October, in which 9,297,470 voted in favour, 8,165,459 against, and 8,519,635 abstained. The Fourth Republic lasted from 24 December 1946 to 5 October 1958, when it was replaced by the Fifth Republic. The Constitution of the Fifth Republic was approved by a referendum, held in France and the overseas departments and territories on 28 September 1958, in which 31,066,502 voted in favour and 5,419,749 against.

Fiji. An independent state and member of the British Commonwealth comprising some 844 islands, of which about 100 are inhabited, in the Pacific Ocean 1,200 miles south of the equator; the largest island is Viti Levu; area 7,055 sq. m.; population (1970 estimate) 524,457, mainly Fijians and Indians; capital Suva. The islands, which were discovered by Tasman in 1643, were first charted by Captain Bligh after the mutiny on the *Bounty* in 1789. They were visited extensively by European traders in the search for sandalwood during the nineteenth century and ceded to the British by Chief Catabau in 1874; the dependency of Rotuma was formally annexed in 1881. Indentured Indian labour, which was abolished in 1917, was used to work the cotton plantations and later to produce sugar, which replaced cotton as the main crop in the 1880s. A form of local government was introduced in 1945 and independence was eventually achieved on 10 October 1970. The legislature consists of a Governor-General, a Senate of 22 nominated members, and a House of Representatives of 52 members elected for five years, of whom 12 Fijian, 12 Indian and 5 general (European) members are elected on communal rolls, and 10 Fijian, 10 Indian and 5 general members are elected on a national roll on which all races vote together. The main exports are sugar, bananas, coconut-oil, copra and gold; there is a flourishing tourist industry.

Filibustering (U.S.A.). Holding up Bills in the Senate by organizing a continuous succession of interminable opposition speeches. If more than one third of the Senators present and voting are opposed to a closure, it is impossible to end a filibuster.

Finland. An independent state on the Baltic Sea; area 130,127 sq. m.; population (1970) 4,679,000; capital Helsinki. It was part of Sweden from 1154 to 1809 when it became an autonomous Grand Duchy of Russia. After the Russian Revolution its independence was declared (1919); the new Russian government tried to retain it, but with the help of German troops the Finns were victorious. Defeated in 1939–40 by the Russians, who forced them to cede 16,170 sq. m. (including the Karelian Isthmus and the west shore of Lake Ladoga), the Finns allied with Germany to invade the U.S.S.R. in 1941 but concluded a separate armistice in 1944.

The President is appointed for six years by an electoral college elected by popular vote. The legislature is a single chamber of 200 members elected for four years by universal suffrage and proportional representation. At elections held in January 1972 the results were: Social Democrats, a left-wing but strong anti-Communist group representing the poorer townspeople, 55 seats (52 in 1970); Centre Party, until 1965 the Agrarian Party, 35 (36); Popular Democrats, an extreme left-wing group which includes both Stalinist and Revisionist wings of the Communist Party, 37 (36): National Coalition Party (Conservative) 34 (37); Rural Party 18 (18); Swedish People's Party, representing the Swedish-speaking Finns, 10 (12); Liberal People's Party, an organization based on the amalgamation in 1965 of the former Liberal Party and the right-wing Finnish People's Party, 7 (8); Christian League 4 (1).

Since 1951 there has been a series of cabinet crises with no government remaining in office for more than two years. This has been due to the even distribution of electoral support among political groups with strong sectional interests. The Centre Party, for instance, favours agricultural subsidies to an extent disputed by all the other parties; it brought down a popular coalition government led by Dr Karl-August Fagerholm in 1957 on the issue of butter and milk prices and more recently the government of Dr Ahti Karjalainen in October 1971. The Social Democrats have obligations to their trade union supporters, and the left-wing groups tend to oppose all wage restraint. Until Rafael Paasio (Social Democrat Party) formed a coalition government of the Centre Party and the three left-wing groups in May 1966 (the fiftieth since 1919) the Communists had never participated in the administration. Their inclusion followed the elections of March 1966 when the three parties of the left obtained for the first time a majority of 51 per cent of the total vote. The draft programme presented to the 1969 Party Congress urged Communists to try to obtain power by democratic means instead of by force. In 1967 the Centre Party and the Social Democrats formed an electoral alliance to insure the re-election of President Urho Kekkonen (a former Centre Party Premier first elected President in 1956 and re-elected in 1962). Following President Kekkonen's re-election in February 1968 for a third six-year term (extended in October 1972 to 1978), Paasio resigned as Prime Minister and was succeeded by his former Minister of Finance, and Governor of the Bank of Finland, Dr Manuel Koivosto (Centre Party). He formed a coalition of the three left-wing parties, the Centre Party and the Swedish People's Party.

The 1970 elections showed a marked swing to the right and the five parties of the government coalition commanded only 136, as opposed to 165 in 1966, of the 200 parliamentary seats. The Centre Party resolved to go into opposition and stalemate ensued; but less than one month after President Kekkonen had appointed a Cabinet of experts, containing no members of Parliament, with Teuvo Aura, the Lord Mayor of Helsinki, as Prime Minister, Dr Ahti Karjalainen, the Centre Party leader, agreed to enter the government. In June 1970 he was appointed Prime Minister of another five-party coalition. After five years in government the Popular Democrats resigned in March 1971 over a relaxation of price controls, and in October 1971 the government fell when the Social Democrats rejected increased agricultural subsidies. Another caretaker government of experts, led by Teuvo Aura, held office until new elections were arranged for January 1972. The refusal of the Popular Democrats to contemplate any form of cooperation with the European Economic Community, *q.v.*, and their insistence on the recognition by Finland of East Germany, made another centre-left coalition impossible. Rafael Paasio then formed a Social Democrat minority government which resigned in July 1972 because it did not want the responsibility for negotiating the terms of Finland's special trade agreement with the European Economic Community, *q.v.* A new coalition of the Centre Party, the Liberals, the Swedish People's Party and the Social Democrats took office under Kalevi Sarsa.

Finland has an important strategic position between east and west as one of the two democracies (the other is Turkey) which share major land frontiers with Russia. It concluded a Treaty of Friendship and Mutual Assistance with the U.S.S.R. in April 1948, and in 1959 renewed the long-term agreement between the two states. Finland, however, resisted pressure to be the first non-Communist state to join the Eastern European Mutual Assistance Treaty, *q.v.* A military alliance with Finland would give the U.S.S.R. the use of radar bases and air-strips on Finland's north-western coast. After the Second World War the U.S.S.R. occupied the important coastal base of Porkkala, west of Helsinki, but gave it up in 1955 in return for a twenty-year prolongation of the 1948 Russo-Finnish Treaty. The Åland Islands, *q.v.*, are under Finnish sovereignty and have potential strategic importance. The U.K. and the U.S.S.R. are Finland's most valuable trading partners; two-thirds of all foreign trade, mainly timber, pulp and paper, is with Western Europe. Finland was an associate member of the European Free Trade Association (E.F.T.A.), *q.v.* A trading arrangement with the enlarged European Economic Community is essential to the country's economy, but full membership would jeopardize Finland's neutrality.

Flemings. Predominantly Flemish-speaking inhabitants of northern Belgium (including Flanders) with whom may be contrasted the predominantly French-speaking Walloons, *q.v.*, of southern Belgium. They tend to be Catholic, right-wing, and pro-royalist, and to live in farming areas, though these areas are now rapidly being developed industrially. The Catholic Church has encouraged the Flemings to take a pride in their own language, which has gradually become accepted as the alternative official language. In the Flemish areas, which have many Dutch connections, education is conducted in Flemish, and Ghent University is entirely Flemish. By a law of 1932, certain facilities, including a French-speaking teacher or post-office clerk, must be provided where the decennial census shows that one third or more of the residents speak the other language. Their increased strength and coherence in recent years (more than half the population are now Flemings), which have resulted in political recognition of their cultural autonomy, have disturbed the Walloons, who in the past have been the dominant influence in Belgium, *q.v.*

F.L.N. Front de la Libération Nationale, *q.v.*

F.L.O.S.Y. Front for the Liberation of Occupied South Yemen, *q.v.*

Food and Agriculture Organization (F.A.O.). Came into being on 16 October 1945 as a result of the United Nations Conference on Food and Agriculture at Hot Springs, Virginia, in May 1943. It has numerous functions: (1) it continually reviews world food and agricultural conditions, and supplies member governments with facts and figures relating to nutrition, agriculture, forestry, and fisheries, and appraisals and forecasts of the production, distribution, and consumption of agricultural products; (2) it promotes and recommends national and international action to improve processing, marketing, and distribution, to conserve resources and to provide agricultural credit; (3) it gives technical assistance to enable members to cultivate new land, to improve yields, to reduce production costs, to improve the efficiency of distribution, to raise levels of consumption, and to improve rural living conditions. The Conference, on which each member has a representative, and which meets every two years, is the policy-making body. A Council of 25 members elected by the Conference supervises the work of the F.A.O. between sessions of the Conference, reviews the world food and agricultural situation, and makes recommendations to members and other international bodies on measures to improve the situation. There is a Director-General and a permanent staff at the headquarters in Rome. F.A.O. is one of the specialized agencies of the United Nations.

Foreign Operations Administration. A U.S. organization set up on 1 August 1953 to coordinate programmes of non-military assistance to foreign countries. All the functions of the Mutual Security Agency, *q.v.*, the Technical Co-operation Administration, the Institute of Inter-American Affairs, and of several other foreign assistance organizations were transferred to the F.O.A. The F.O.A. was replaced on 30 June 1955 by the International Co-operation Administration, *q.v.*

Formosa. The name by which the island of Taiwan, *q.v.*, was known until 1945.

France. An independent republic; area (including the island of Corsica) 212,895 sq. m.; population (1971 estimate) 51,030,000; capital Paris. Under the Constitution of the Fifth Republic, *q.v.*, which came into force on 5 October 1958, the President is elected for seven years. Article 5 provides that: 'The President of the Republic ensures that the Constitution is observed. He intervenes in order to ensure the proper working of the public authorities and the continuity of the State. He is the guardian of national independence, territorial integrity, and respect for Community [the French Community, *q.v.*] agreements and for treaties.' Under Article 16 he may assume emergency powers 'if there is a serious and immediate threat to the institutions of the Republic, the Nation's independence, its territorial integrity, or fulfilment of its international undertakings, and the constitutional machinery breaks down'. He nominates the Prime Minister and appoints Ministers on his recommendation; he is empowered to dissolve parliament, but not more than once a year, after consulting the Prime Minister and the presidents of the two houses of parliament. He negotiates and ratifies international treaties, and if called on to do so by the government or by both houses jointly, he can submit certain legislation to a referendum. On 21 December 1958 General de Gaulle, *q.v.*, was elected President, re-elected on 19 December 1965, and succeeded by Georges Pompidou, *q.v.*, on 15 June 1969. Parliament consists of an upper house, the Senate, and a lower house, the National Assembly, which is elected by universal suffrage and proportional representation for five years.

From the liberation of France in 1944 until May 1958 there were 25 cabinets, and more than one-quarter of the non-Communist deputies in the National Assembly held cabinet office. The *immobilisme* of French governments, and their apparent inability to enact legislation, were largely due to the constitution of the Fourth Republic, which had been framed in fear of a Communist-dominated administration. It specified two-thirds and three-fifths, rather than simple, majorities on most legislation, thereby weakening the executive and creating a powerful legislature. The absence of party discipline in the Assembly and the vulnerability of ministers to lobbying also contributed to political instability.

The *coup* by French army officers in Algeria, *q.v.*, on 13 May 1958, precipitated a crisis in France; it was thought that the army would seize control. On 15 May General de Gaulle announced his readiness to assume power. On 1 June, by 329 votes to 224 (147 Communists and Progressistes, 49 Socialists, 18 Radicals including Mendès-France and Daladier, 4 U.D.S.R., 3 M.R.P. and 3 others) de Gaulle was invested as Premier by the Assembly, giving up this post for the Presidency in January 1959. The new Constitution was adopted by a referendum held on 28 September 1958. Michel Debré, *q.v.*, was appointed Prime Minister in January 1959, and was succeeded in April 1962 by Georges Pompidou.

Gaullist policy since 1959 has been to reassert French hegemony in Europe. Support has been given to European military or economic organizations only so long as France could dominate them. U.K. applications for entry to the European Economic Community, *q.v.*, in 1961 and 1967 were blocked by France, which withdrew from its military commitment to the North Atlantic Treaty Organization, *q.v.*, in March 1966. Declared opposition to U.S. involvement in South Viet-Nam, in the Middle East, as well as in the defence of Europe, was accompanied by a *détente* with China and the U.S.S.R. Former French connections with Romania and Persia were revived and active encouragement given to Quebec separatists in defiance of the Federal Government of Canada, *q.v.*, and to the rebels in Biafra, *q.v.* A favourable balance of payments and substantial gold reserves enabled France to pursue an independent economic policy and to invest heavily in nuclear weapons and research; but no comparable social investment was made in education or housing. The presidential elections of 1965, when François Mitterrand, *q.v.*, leader of the newly created Federation of the Democratic Left which embraced Socialists and Radicals and had an electoral agreement with the Communist Party, won 44·8 per cent of the votes cast in a second ballot against de Gaulle, indicated electoral dissatisfaction; this was reinforced at the elections to the National Assembly in March 1967 after which the Gaullists, although still the largest single party, were in a minority. In May 1968 a demonstration by Paris University students for higher investment in education and curricular reform turned into a revolt against the government which precipitated the biggest general strike in French history. After three weeks of economic paralysis the government increased the minimum wage by one third and other earnings by some 13 per cent; the students were promised a reform of the educational system.

De Gaulle then called fresh elections in June 1968. The support given to the Gaullists, who won 44 per cent of the votes cast on the first ballot, and the defeat of the popular front candidates reaffirmed traditional French fears of Communist-dominated government and restored de Gaulle's personal authority. This did not survive a referendum on the Constitution in April 1969 which was defeated by a 52·4 per cent vote. De Gaulle resigned and the new President, Georges Pompidou, appointed Jacques Chaban-Delmas, *q.v.*, as Prime Minister, which post he held until July 1972 when he was succeeded by Pierre Messmer, *q.v.* Under Pompidou's presidency the Gaullist Union des Démocrates pour la République (U.D.R.) was broadened to include the Independent Republicans of Giscard d'Estaing, the Fédération Nationale des Républicains, and the Progrès et Démocratie Moderne group (P.D.M.), which had broken away from the Europe-orientated Centre Démocrate of Jean Lecanuet in 1967. The government survived a challenge by Jean-Jacques Servan Schreiber, *q.v.*, and his Reformist movement for greater regional investment which was made in by-elections during 1970; in 1971 the administrative reform, envisaged by de Gaulle, was cautiously introduced and public investment increased. Elections held on 4 and 11 March 1973 produced a marked swing to the left, but the Gaullist and Centre Parties retained a majority in the Assembly. Results were:— U.D.R. 185 (299 in 1968); Independent Republicans 54 (58); Centre Démocratie et Progrès 23 (29); Socialists, led by François Mitterrand, 89 (60); Communists, led by George Marchais

73 (34); Reformists 32; Left Wing Radicals 13; Extreme Left 3; others (including 14 pro-Gaullists) 19 (24).

France remains the leading agricultural country of western Europe, with three-quarters of its total area under cultivation, and 14 per cent of its population still working on the land, despite the scale of industrial activity which includes motor vehicle and aircraft production, engineering, textiles and chemicals. The political power exerted by the peasant farmers and the vulnerability of a relatively inefficient agriculture to competition from Denmark, Ireland and the U.K. within an enlarged European Economic Community, have made France reluctant to accept an extension of the original six signatories to the Rome Treaties, *q.v.*, except on the basis of political union, which would ensure permanent protection against a potentially assertive Germany. In the referendum on the enlargement of the Community called by President Pompidou in April 1972, only 68 per cent of the 54 per cent of the electorate who voted registered approval.

Franchise. The right to vote, especially at parliamentary elections.

Franco, Francisco Bahamonde. Prime Minister, Chief of State and Generalissimo of the armed forces of Spain; born 4 December 1892 in Galicia. He was commissioned in the army in 1910 after three years at the Toledo Infantry Academy, and served in Spanish Morocco before and after the First World War. He commanded the Spanish Foreign Legion from 1923 to 1927, and while in Morocco helped to defeat the Rif chieftan, Abd-el-Krim. From 1927 to 1931 he directed the Saragossa Military Academy, which was dissolved by the new Republican government in 1931 as a result of its monarchist tendencies. In 1935 he became Chief of the Army General Staff, and in 1936 led a Fascist revolt and formed a government which was at once recognized and supplied with arms by Germany and Italy. In 1937 Franco proclaimed himself El Caudillo (the leader); in 1939 his government was recognized by France and the U.K., his forces took Madrid, and he became Prime Minister. At the outset of the Second World War he declared his sympathy for Germany and Italy and made plans to enter Gibraltar and French Morocco. He later professed neutrality and in 1943 urged Anglo-German unity against the U.S.S.R. In 1947 he was declared Chief of State for life, with the right to choose his successor.

Free Economy. A school of economists wishing to cure economic evils by a new monetary system. The basic idea is that the value of money should be automatically reduced every month by a certain percentage, and replaced by new money. This would enforce steady circulation of money, as people would try to pass it on by buying goods before its value went down. A steady flow of money would ensure steady employment, and there would be no economic crises. Free economists wish to maintain freedom of enterprise and to avoid socialism. Silvio Gesell (1862–1930) developed the theory in Germany, and its English and Commonwealth variant is Social Credit, *q.v.*

Free Port. *Also* Free Harbour; a port in one state which other states are allowed to use freely, loading and unloading goods and conveying them to and from the harbour without interference and without customs duties.

Free Trade. An economic policy which does not discriminate between foreign goods and goods produced at home and thus gives no protection against foreign competitors. It may involve a complete absence of tariffs in respect of all goods or of a class of goods; alternatively, any tariffs are matched by an excise duty on goods produced at home. The doctrine of free trade arose in the seventeenth and eighteenth centuries as a reaction to mercantilism (a policy involving the closing of frontiers to foreign goods and producing everything at home). The U.K. became the leading exponent of free trade after the repeal of the Corn Laws in 1846 and Peel's low tariff Acts. (Towards the end of the nineteenth century industrialization in many countries, especially Germany and the U.S.A., was followed by the erection of high tariff barriers.) A high tariff movement in the U.K., which was concerned to protect Empire industry and trade, was defeated in the 1906 General Election by the Liberals, who professed free trade. After the First World War protection policies prevailed nearly everywhere, and with the passing of the Import Duties Act in 1932 the U.K. adopted a protective tariff as a permanent institution. Adherents to the doctrine of free trade claim that free international exchange of goods is most economical and encourages specialization and international collaboration. Advocates of high tariffs claim that their system protects domestic industries and the workers employed in them from foreign competition.

Free Trade Area. *See* European Free Trade Association.

Freedom Ferry. The name given to the ferry across the river Zambesi from Kazungula, *q.v.*, in Botswana to Zambia by political refugees from South Africa, South West Africa, Rhodesia and Angola.

Frei, Eduardo Montalva. Chilean politician; born January 1911, the son of a Swiss immigrant, and educated at the Catholic University of Chile where he later became a Professor of Law. He travelled to Europe in 1933, acting as Secretary General of the Ibero-American Congress in Rome. He entered politics through the executive committee of Conservative Youth and in 1935 helped to establish the National Falange (a political organization, totally unconnected with the Spanish Falangists, *q.v.*, which supported the Allied cause in the Second World War and sympathized with left-wing solutions to domestic problems). He made economic planning his special interest and in 1945 held government office as Minister of Public Works, and subsequently as Minister of Transport and Communications. He was elected Senator for Atacoma and Coquimbo in 1949, and for Santiago in 1957 in which year the National Falange merged with the Social Christian Conservatives to form the new Christian Democratic Party, with the express intention of elevating Dr Frei to the presidency. He contested the elections of 1958 without success, but was elected President of Chile in 1964. His nominee came third in the presidential elections of 1970 which were won by the Marxist, Dr Salvador Allende, *q.v.*

French Cameroons. *See* Cameroons, French.

French Community. Established by the Constitution of the Fifth Republic, *q.v.*, which came into force on 5 October 1958. As a result of voting against the proposed Constitution, the territory of Guinea had become independent on 2 October 1958, but the remaining departments and territories were then offered a choice between (*a*) retaining their respective statuses (Article 76 of the Constitution) and (*b*) becoming member states of the Community with full internal autonomy (Article 77) but leaving the control of many matters, including currency, defence, foreign affairs, and higher education, with the Community (Article 78). The 4 existing overseas departments (Martinique, Guadeloupe, Réunion, and Guiana) chose to retain their status, but 12 of the 19 overseas territories (Central African Republic, Chad, Congo, Dahomey, Gabon, Ivory Coast, Madagascar, Mauritania, Niger, Senegal, Soudan, and Upper Volta) agreed, in October and November 1958, to become members.

The restrictions on sovereignty became irksome, and although the Constitution (Article 86) specifically prohibited complete independence within the Community (by stating that upon achieving independence a member state 'then ceases to belong to the Community'), it proved impossible to resist the demand for greater liberty of action. On 3 June 1960 the Community Senate amended the Constitution to allow member states to remain in the Community after attaining full independence. Between April and November 1960 all the members made declarations by which they attained complete independence but the so-called Entente states (Dahomey, Ivory Coast, Niger, and Upper Volta) left the Community in June 1960. Those states, with Cameroun (which had been a trusteeship territory and not an overseas territory) and Mauritania, established a special relationship with the Community, while the others, with a closer relationship, concluded 'Community participation agreements'.

The organs of the Community, which now has no practical functions, are (or have been): (1) the President, who is the President of France; (2) the Executive Council, consisting of the Prime Minister of France, the heads of government of the member states, and the Ministers responsible to the Community for common affairs; (3) the Senate, comprising delegates from the parliaments of France and the member states (abolished in March 1961 as all the member states had chosen independent sovereignty and only France remained constitutionally linked with the Senate); (4) the Court of Arbitration (abolished in July 1961).

French Congo. *See* Congo (Brazzaville).

French Equatorial Africa. The name formerly given to the group of four French overseas territories which are now independent states under the names of the Central African Republic, *q.v.*, Chad, *q.v.*, Congo (Brazzaville), *q.v.*, and Gabon, *q.v.* In January 1959 the four states established an economic and technical union.

French Morocco. The name formerly given to the southern portion of Morocco, *q.v.*, which from 1912 to 1956 was recognized as a French sphere of influence; area approximately 164,065 sq. m.; population eight million, of whom all but 560,000 are Sunni Moslems of Arab or Berber stock; capital Rabat. France acquired the areas as a result of the Treaty of Fez with the Sultan of Morocco signed on 30 March 1912, and by agreement with Italy, Spain and the U.K. The first Resident-General, Hubert Lyautey, created favourable conditions for French settlement, and immigration and investment gave France a valuable stake in the country's mineral wealth – manganese, cobalt, oil, and one-sixth of the world's supply of phosphates – and in its agriculture.

In principle Morocco continued throughout the protectorate to be an Empire ruled by a Sultan, reigning through a government consisting of a Grand Vizier and his deputies. Effective authority, until October 1955, was exercised by the French Resident-General, who acted as the Sultan's Minister of Foreign Affairs. The French encouraged Arab–Berber hostility, which had its origins in the opposing interests of town-dwellers (Arabs) and nomad tribesmen (mainly Berbers), and used the Pasha of Marrakesh, El Glaoui (1874–1956), to maintain their authority against the Nationalists. An Arab rising was imminent in 1953 when they enrolled El Glaoui's support to depose the Sultan, Sidi Mohammed Ben Youssef, the eighteenth of his dynasty, who was exiled to Madagascar, and to enthrone his uncle, Sidi Mohammed Ben Arafa, whom the Istiqlal, *q.v.*, denounced as a usurper.

In August 1955 the French sanctioned the creation of a Regency Council and the recall of the former Sultan from exile. Attempts were made by the Présence Française, the settlers' organization with a powerful lobby in the National Assembly, to obstruct reform, but in October 1955 the government agreed to the return of Sidi Mohammed Ben Youssef, to arrange the abdication of Sidi Mohammed Ben Arafa, and to permit the formation of a government representing all parties, including the outlawed Istiqlal. The French capitulation was confirmed when El Glaoui announced his support for Ben Youssef; practically all the former opponents of Ben Youssef made similar declarations.

Following the return of Ben Youssef to Rabat in November 1955, the Moroccan and French governments announced, on 2 March 1956, the abrogation of the Treaty of Fez and the emergence of Morocco as an independent sovereign state.

French Somaliland. The name by which the French Territory of the Afars and Issas, *q.v.*, was known before 5 July 1967.

French Territory of the Afars and Issas. A French overseas territory in the Gulf of Aden between Eritrea and that part of Somalia which was until 1960 British Somaliland; area 9,000 sq. m.; population (1969 estimate) 125,000, including 7,000 Europeans; capital Djibouti, through which Addis Ababa, the capital of Ethiopia, maintains its principal rail connection to the sea. Formerly French Somaliland, *q.v.* the Territory was renamed on 5 July 1967 to emphasize the existence of the two main ethnic groups in the population; a referendum held in March 1967 confirmed that the Territory wished to remain part of France. Administrative powers are vested in a governing council responsible to a Chamber of Deputies of 32 members elected by universal suffrage. The French High Commissioner retains responsibility for external affairs, currency and credit, and defence. The economy has to be subsidized by France, and also relies considerably on the transit trade with Ethiopia. The port of Djibouti is used principally by French vessels trading to the East.

French Togoland. A former trusteeship territory which became independent on 27 April 1960 under the name of Togo, *q.v.*

French Union. An association of French overseas possessions and Metropolitan France, established under the Commission of the Fourth Republic in 1946. It had as President the President of the Republic, a High Council and a representative Assembly. The High Council was to advise the French government in the management of the Union; its powers were negligible. In 1954 the Associate States (Viet-Nam, Laos, and Cambodia) withdrew from the Union. The overseas departments and territories which remained as members were: Algeria, Martinique, Guadeloupe, Réunion, Guiana, French Equatorial Africa, French West Africa, Madagascar, Comoro Archipelago, French Somaliland, New Caledonia, French settlements in Oceania, Saint-Pierre and Miquelon, the trusteeship territories of Togoland and the Cameroons, and the Anglo-French condominium of the New Hebrides. The French settlements in India were members until they acceded to India in 1954. On the inception of the Fifth Republic, *q.v.*, in 1958, the Union was succeeded by the French Community, *q.v.*

French West Africa. The name formerly given to the group of eight French overseas territories which are now independent states under the names of Dahomey, *q.v.*, Guinea, *q.v.*, Ivory Coast, *q.v.*, Mali, *q.v.*, Mauritania, *q.v.*, Niger, *q.v.*, Senegal, *q.v.*, and Upper Volta, *q.v.*

Front de la Libération Nationale (F.L.N.). The National Liberation Front, the only political party in Algeria, *q.v.* The Nationalist movement developed through two main groups; the moderate Democratic Union of the Algerian Manifesto (U.D.M.A.), which originally supported federation within the French Union, *q.v.*, and the Movement for the Triumph of Democratic Liberties (M.T.L.D.), which demanded complete independence. Leaders of the M.T.L.D. and other nationalist organizations, including Mohammed Ben Bella, *q.v.*, a former French army sergeant-major, fled to Cairo where they founded a military organization (C.R.U.A.) to foment rebellion against the French in 1954. Ben Bella then launched the F.L.N. with the aim of expelling the French from North Africa. It was supported by the majority of members of the M.T.L.D., but the leader of U.D.M.A., Messali Hadj, formed a rival Algerian National Movement (M.N.A.) because he disagreed with the ultimate objectives of the F.L.N. and was prepared to cooperate with the French.

On 1 November 1954 the F.L.N. declared war on France, and fighting began in earnest. Bitterness between the two factions was dividing the rebels to such an extent that efforts were made during 1956 to fuse the movement into one fighting force. Negotiations between the leaders broke down because the F.L.N. demanded the dissolution of the M.N.A., but there was subsequent cooperation between the guerillas of the M.N.A. and the National Liberation Army, the fighting wing of the F.L.N., and the two parties restricted their rivalry to France itself where some 600 Algerians were murdered in 1956–7.

The F.L.N., which after the capture of Ben Bella by the French in 1956 was led by Ferhat Abbas and Krim Belkacem, was determined not to negotiate except on the basis of Algerian independence. After this was achieved on 4 July 1962 the movement was transformed into the only Algerian political party.

Front for the Liberation of Occupied South Yemen (F.L.O.S.Y.). A South Yemeni nationalist organization formed in January 1966 with the aim of expelling the British from the South Arabian Federation, *q.v.*, of which Aden State, *q.v.*, and South Yemen were a part, and achieving immediate independence. Its leader, Abdulla al-Asnag, a former airline booking clerk, commanded support among Aden trade unionists. The movement, which was assisted by the Egyptian government, had its headquarters in Cairo; it recruited and trained an army in Ta'iz, Yemen, which has been involved in civil war in the area since mid-1966. F.L.O.S.Y. refused to negotiate with the British High Commissioner in Aden, and when the British troops withdrew in November 1967 and an independent People's Republic of South Yemen, *q.v.*, was established, its major rival nationalist party, the National Liberation Front, took over the government and declared F.L.O.S.Y. to be an illegal organization.

Führer. A German word meaning 'leader'. This was the title assumed by the German dictator and Nazi leader, Adolf Hitler (born 1889), who came to power in 1933 and is presumed to have committed suicide in Berlin in 1945.

Full Employment. Defined by Lord Beveridge, in his *Full Employment in a Free Society*, as a state of affairs in which there are 'more vacant jobs than unemployed men'. There can therefore be unemployment and full employment at the same time, but Beveridge further defined the expression by saying that in the U.K. an unemployment rate of over 3 per cent would be incompatible with full employment. This rate was to be taken as a percentage of those who were capable of work and willing to work. The incapable and the unwilling were not, in his definition, to be included among the unemployed.

G

Gabon. An independent republic; area 101,400 sq. m.; population (1970 estimate) 475,000, comprising Pahouins, Pongwés, Adounas, Chiras, Punu, and Lumbu, and 4,000 non-Africans; capital Libreville. Sixty-five per cent of the population is Christian. The country is on the west coast of Africa, between Equatorial Guinea (Rio Muni) to the north and Congo (Brazzaville) to the south and east. The territory was annexed by France in 1888 and later became one of the four territories which formed French Equatorial Africa, *q.v.* It achieved self-government within the French Community, *q.v.*, on 28 November 1958, and complete independence, still within the Community, on 17 August 1960.

Legislative powers are vested in an assembly of 47 members elected every five years by universal suffrage. As a result of the elections held in 1969 the Gabon Democratic Bloc, led by President Bernard-Alberto Bongo, controls the assembly; it became the sole legal political party on Bongo's assurance that it was pledged to national unity and the abolition of ethnic discrimination. Executive power is exercised by the President, who is elected by the assembly.

The principal exports are lumber, petroleum, cocoa and gold. There are deposits of iron and manganese, and crude oil production is the fifth highest in Africa. Gabon is a member of an economic and customs union (U.D.E.A.C.), established in December 1964, with Cameroun, Central African Republic, Chad and Congo (Brazzaville); an oil refinery for these five states, of which Gabon is the wealthiest, was completed in 1967 at Port-Gentil.

Gallup Poll. A method devised by an American, Dr Gallup, of assessing public opinion. Questions are asked of a representative cross-section of the population. The method has been used in the U.S.A. and by the British Institute of Public Opinion in the U.K. to forecast election results, which it has done with only a narrow margin of error.

Gambia. An independent state and member of the British Commonwealth, in West Africa, bounded by Senegal to the north, east and south, and consisting of a narrow strip of land on each side of the Gambia river extending some 150 miles inland; area 3,976 sq. m.; population (1971 estimate) 378,730; capital Bathurst.

The area became British by the Treaty of Versailles, 1783, and was governed with Sierra Leone from 1807 to 1843. Full internal self-government was achieved on 4 October 1963; Gambia became independent on 18 February 1965 and declared itself a republic under a new Constitution on 24 April 1970. At elections held in March 1972 the People's Progressive Party (P.P.P.), led by the Prime Minister, Sir Dawda Kairaba Jawara, won 28 out of the 32 seats in the legislative assembly (24 in the 1966 elections), the United Party, which had been in office until 1962 under its leader, Pierre N'Jie, won 3 seats (8 in 1966); Independent 1. Sir Dawda Kairaba Jawara was appointed the first President of Gambia.

Decorticated ground-nuts constitute over 90 per cent of the exports, and are sold mostly to Italy and the U.K.; the rest comprises palm-kernels, dried fish and hides. There are many close links with Senegal with whom a Treaty of Association was signed in April 1967.

Gandhi, Indira. Indian politician; born 19 November 1917, the daughter of Jawaharlal Nehru, *q.v.* She was educated in Switzerland and in England, at Badminton School and Somerville College, Oxford, and at the Santiniketan University of Bengal. She joined the Congress Party, *q.v.*, at the age of 21, spending thirteen months in prison for her political activities. She was active in the Party for many years, as chairman of the Women's Department and as a member of the Congress Working Committee, and was elected President of the Indian National Congress in 1959. Her husband, Feroze Gandhi, whom she married in 1942 and who died in 1960, was a Congress Party member of the Lok Sabha. After her father's death in 1964 she was appointed Minister of Information and Broadcasting in the cabinet of Lal Bahadur Shastri, *q.v.*, in which she was the fourth-ranking member in order of seniority. She became leader of the Congress Parliamentary Party, in succession to Shastri, on 19 January 1966, receiving 355 votes against 169 for Morarji Desai, *q.v.*, in the first contested election for the leadership. She took office as Prime Minister of India on 24 January 1966 retaining, as had the two previous Premiers, personal responsibility for Atomic Energy. In November 1969 she survived a temporary expulsion from the Party leadership by a group, organized by Desai, which seceded to form an Opposition Congress, and was reinstated by the Ruling Congress. Her position as Party leader and as Prime Minister was confirmed in the elections of March 1971 in which the Ruling Congress won an overwhelming victory.

G.A.T.T. General Agreement on Tariffs and Trade, *q.v.*

Gaza Strip. An area of approximately 100 sq. m. in south-western Palestine on the Mediterranean Sea and adjacent to the Egyptian border. The United Nations, proposing the partition of Palestine in 1947, decided that the Strip should be part of a new Arab state. It includes the town of Gaza, six miles from the Israeli border, and the railway junction of Rafa. Armed forces from Egypt, Iraq, Jordan,

Lebanon, and Syria invaded Palestine when the British mandate ended in May 1948, and hostilities ceased in January 1949. Egyptian forces then occupied the Gaza Strip, and remained there after the armistice on 24 February 1949. Thereafter there were frequent raids by Israelis on the Egyptian forces (whose headquarters were at Khan Yunis, between Gaza and Rafa) and by Egyptian-led forces on Israeli villages. The Egyptian raiders have often been recruited from the 200,000 Arab refugees from other parts of Palestine who live in the Gaza Strip. The Israeli government does not accept the line held by the Egyptians as a permanent frontier, and maintains that the frontiers of Israel in this area should be those of the old mandated territory of Palestine. A United Nations Truce Supervisory Organization was made responsible for supervising this and other areas on the borders of Israel, and for preventing, as far as possible, breaches of the armistice agreement. In the Gaza Strip it collaborated with the Egyptian-Israeli Mixed Armistice Commission. The Tripartite Declaration of 1950, q.v., made it unlikely that the Egyptian or the Israeli government would launch a full-scale attack unless it was confident of a speedy victory. In October 1956 Israeli forces, hopeful of such a victory, overran the Strip in their successful attempt to defeat the Egyptian army and reach the Suez Canal, q.v. While British and French troops withdrew from Egypt by 22 December 1956, and were replaced by the United Nations Emergency Force (U.N.E.F.), Israeli troops remained in the Strip until 7 March 1957. The border between the Strip and Israel was then taken over by U.N.E.F. and an Egyptian civil governor was reappointed. In May 1967, following the departure from Sinai and Gaza of U.N.E.F. forces, at the request of President Nasser, Egyptian troops, supported by detachments from Iraq and Kuwait, moved into battle position. When the Six-Day War broke out in June, Israeli forces once more overran the Strip, driving the Egyptians back to the Suez Canal. Gaza was then given the status of Israeli 'occupied territory' and became known throughout the Arab world as one of the Arab Occupied Territories, q.v.

Gdansk. See Danzig.

General Agreement on Tariffs and Trade (G.A.T.T.). An international trade agreement on tariffs, which resulted from negotiations at Geneva between 10 April and 30 October 1947, arranged by the Preparatory Committee of the International Trade Organization, q.v., while the Havana Charter, q.v., was in the course of preparation. The Agreement came into force on 1 January 1948. The countries adhering to G.A.T.T. account for over four-fifths of world trade.

Many individual tariff bargains between pairs of countries have been concluded and the reductions in tariffs have been extended to all through the operation of the principle of the most favoured nation. The sixth negotiating conference, the Kennedy Round, q.v., begun in 1964 and completed in 1967, resulted in unprecedented tariff reductions, an agreement on cereals, and the adoption of an anti-dumping code. The accession of East European countries (of which Poland was the first) to G.A.T.T. raised problems of how to determine internal prices in economies where a cost–price relationship is virtually non-existent. Since 1968 G.A.T.T. allowed western countries to measure Soviet-bloc export prices against the general level of western prices in order to determine anti-dumping regulations.

The Agreement contains provisions which protect the tariff concessions from being nullified by other methods of protection, e.g. by quantitative import and export restrictions, internal taxes, customs administration, as well as arrangements for consultation and for settlement of differences arising out of the administration of the Agreement. The introduction by the U.S.A. in 1971 of a 10 per cent import surcharge marked a decisive retreat from the principles of G.A.T.T.

General Assembly of the United Nations. Comprises all the members of the U.N., of whom there were 132 in 1972: Afghanistan, Albania, Algeria, Argentina, Australia, Austria, Bahrain, Barbados, Belgium, Bhutan, Bolivia, Botswana, Brazil, Bulgaria, Burma, Burundi, Byelorussia, Cameroun, Canada, Central African Republic, Chad, Chile, China, Colombia, Congo (Brazzaville), Costa Rica, Cuba, Cyprus, Czechoslovakia, Dahomey, Denmark, Dominican Republic, Ecuador, Egypt, Equatorial Guinea, Ethiopia, Fiji, Finland, France, Gabon, Gambia, Ghana, Greece, Guatemala, Guinea, Guyana, Haiti, Honduras, Hungary, Iceland, India, Indonesia, Iraq, Ireland, Israel, Italy, Ivory Coast, Jamaica, Japan, Jordan, Kenya, Khmer Republic, Kuwait, Laos, Lebanon, Lesotho, Liberia, Libya, Luxemburg, Malagasy, Malawi, Malaysia, Maldive Islands, Mali, Malta, Mauritania, Mauritius, Mexico, Mongolia, Morocco, Nepal, Netherlands, New Zealand, Nicaragua, Niger, Nigeria, Norway, Oman, Pakistan, Panama, Paraguay, Persia, Peru, Philippines, Poland, Portugal, Qatar, Romania, Rwanda, Salvador, Saudi Arabia, Senegal, Sierra Leone, Singapore, Somalia, South Africa, Spain, Sri Lanka, Sudan, Swaziland, Sweden, Syria, Tanzania, Thailand, Togo, Trinidad and Tobago, Tunisia, Turkey, Uganda, U.K., Ukraine, United Arab Emirates, U.S.A., Upper Volta, Uruguay, U.S.S.R., Venezuela, Yemen (formerly South Yemen), Yemen Arab Republic, Yugoslavia, Zaïre and Zambia.

It is one of the principal organs of the United Nations; each member can be represented at its annual meetings by five delegates and five alternate delegates, but has only one vote. Its meetings begin on the third Tuesday in September, but special sessions can be convoked by the Secretary-General if so requested by the Security Council, *q.v.*, by a majority of members of the United Nations, or by one member with the concurrence of the majority of members. Decisions on 'important questions' (defined in the Charter as including recommendations concerning international peace and security; election of members of the Councils; admission, expulsion, and suspension of members; questions relating to the trusteeship system; and budgetary matters) are made by a two-thirds majority of members present and voting.

The General Assembly is the only organ of the United Nations in which all members are represented. It elects by itself, or with the Security Council, some or all members of the other organs, and it has the right to discuss all matters within the scope of the Charter. The Security Council, the Economic and Social Council, *q.v.*, the Trusteeship Council, and the Secretary-General submit annual and special reports to the Assembly, which discusses them and makes recommendations thereon, thus reviewing and guiding the work of the entire organization. It also controls the budget of the organization and the contributions of members. It elects its President for each session.

The General Assembly does most of its work in committees, of which there are four types: main committees, procedural committees, standing committees, and *ad hoc* committees. Main committees consider agenda items referred to them by the Assembly and prepare recommendations for submission to the plenary meetings; they are the Political and Security; Economic and Financial; Social, Humanitarian and Cultural; Trusteeship; Administrative and Budgetary; Special Political; and Legal Committees. Procedural committees deal with the organization and conduct of the Assembly's business; they are the General and the Credentials Committees. Standing committees deal with continuing problems; an example is the Advisory Committee on Administrative and Budgetary Questions. *Ad hoc* committees are committees appointed by the Assembly or any of its committees for a special purpose; examples are the United Nations Relief and Works Agency and the Collective Measures Committee.

Geneva Agreements, 1954. The terms by which the war between France and the three Associated States of Laos, Cambodia and Viet-Nam was brought to an end. They were agreed at a conference held in

Geneva in May 1954 and attended by China, the U.K., the U.S.A., the U.S.S.R., France and representatives of Laos, Cambodia and North and South Viet-Nam. The conference sessions were presided over alternately by the foreign ministers of the U.K. and the U.S.S.R. A cease-fire line between North and South Viet-Nam was approved, and an International Supervisory Commission, consisting of Canada, India, and Poland, established to enforce peace. The members of the conference agreed to consult one another on any questions which might be referred to them by the Commission concerning the maintenance of a cease-fire.

In June 1961 the Commission, by a two to one majority vote against Poland, decided that it had authority to investigate complaints, made by the government of South Viet-Nam, of 'subversion', 'terrorism' and 'sabotage' against the North Viet-Namese government. Since these words were nowhere mentioned in the Agreements the articles which required North and South Viet-Nam not to follow aggressive policies and which prohibited both from committing any act or undertaking any aggression against the other had to be reinterpreted. On 10 January 1962 the Russian government in protest against this sent an *aide-mémoire* to the British government accusing the U.S.A. of 'open violations of international agreements on Indo-China'. This was rejected by the U.K. and on 24 February 1962 China protested against 'United States imperialist aggression in South Viet-Nam' and called on the co-chairman of the Geneva conference and the countries concerned to take 'appropriate measures to eliminate the serious danger of war in Viet-Nam'.

Gentlemen's Agreement. An informal agreement based on verbal assurances or the exchange of mere letters without a formal treaty being signed.

German Democratic Republic. A state not recognized by the western powers; area 41,380 sq. m.; population (1970) 17,056,983 including Berlin, *q.v.* It is sometimes known as Eastern Germany; its constitution was enacted on 7 October 1949 by a provisional People's Chamber which had been set up in the Russian Zone of Germany under the supervision of the U.S.S.R. In July 1950 the Republic defined its eastern boundary by an agreement with Poland by which the Oder-Neisse Line, *q.v.*, was declared to be a permanent frontier. Under the constitution there is a more centralized form of government than in the German Federal Republic, *q.v.*; the abolition in July 1952 of the *Land* governments and diets of Brandenburg, Mecklenburg, Saxony, Saxony-Anhalt, and Thuringia, and their replacement by 14 regions (*Bezirke*) increased the degree of centralization. In 1953 the Russian Commander-in-Chief was replaced by a High Commissioner who also held the post of Ambassador. At elections in July 1967 the Communist-controlled National Front, which comprises the Socialist Unity, the Liberal Democratic, the Christian Democratic, the Democratic Peasant, and the National Democratic Parties, obtained 99·93 per cent of the votes. Electors voted publicly for the single list of candidates by placing it, unmarked, in a ballot box. Otto Grotewohl (1894–1964, Socialist Unity Party) became Prime Minister in 1952; Walter Ulbricht, *q.v.*, First Secretary of the Socialist Unity Party, became Chairman of the Council of State in September 1960; he retained the latter office when he resigned as First Secretary of the Socialist Unity Party in favour of Erich Honecker in May 1971. Willi Stoph became Prime Minister in September 1964 upon the death of Grotewohl, and Deputy Chairman of the Council in 1968.

Under a treaty between the German Democratic Republic and the U.S.S.R., which came into force on 6 October 1955, the Republic became a sovereign state with freedom to decide all questions concerning its internal and foreign policy, including its relations with the German Federal Republic. Russian forces stationed there under Four-Power agreements continued to be stationed there with the approval of the government. As a member of the Warsaw Pact, *q.v.*, the Republic participated in the invasion of Czechoslovakia in August 1968. The conclusion on 21 December 1972 of a treaty of friendship with the German Federal Republic enabled negotiations for formal recognition, and for the future representation of both German Republics at the United Nations, to begin.

The First and Second Seven Year Plans (1958–64 and 1964–70) provided for substantial increases in production, but the Third Plan (1971–5) envisaged a reduction in capital investment to allow for greater expenditure on transport and housing. The Republic contains in its area a large part of the mechanical engineering, chemical, optical, and electrical industries of pre-war Germany, and their products have found ready buyers in eastern Europe. The area yielded only a small proportion of pre-war Germany's iron and steel, but these are now manufactured by a process which dispenses with hard coal, which is scarce in the east, and employs brown coal, of which the Republic is the world's largest producer.

German Federal Republic. A federation which was established by France, the U.K., and the U.S.A. in May 1949, and which became completely independent on 5 May 1955; area 95,737 sq. m.; population (1969) 61,194,600, including that of Berlin, over 25 per cent higher than that of the same area before 1939, largely owing to immigration from the East; capital Bonn. Approximately 45 per cent of the population are Roman Catholics. It is sometimes known as Western Germany; a constitution (known as the Basic Law), enacted by a Constituent Assembly, came into force on 23 May 1949. The Republic was given full legislative, executive, and judicial powers, except in respect of armaments, reparations, decartelization, foreign affairs, the admission of refugees, and other matters mentioned in the Occupation Statute, a proclamation by France, the U.K. and the U.S.A. which became effective on 21 September 1949. On that day the authority of the three commanders-in-chief was transferred to three High Commissioners.

The Occupation Statute was superseded by the London and Paris Agreements of October 1954, which came into force on 5 May 1955 after they had been ratified by the three occupying powers and the Republic. The Republic then attained full sovereign independence and American, British, and French forces were given permission to remain on German territory. The High Commission ended and the Republic became a member of the North Atlantic Treaty Organization, *q.v.*, and the Western European Union, *q.v.*

Under the Basic Law, a Federal Diet (Bundestag) is elected by universal suffrage for a term of four years and a Federal Council (Bundesrat), consisting of members of the governments of the *Länder*, is elected by the ten *Länder* of Baden-Württemberg, Bavaria, Bremen, Hamburg, Hessen, Lower Saxony, North Rhine-Westphalia, Rhineland-Palatinate, Saarland, *q.v.*, and Schleswig-Holstein. Berlin, *q.v.*, is accorded the right of election to the Diet but its representatives may not vote. Federal laws are passed by the Diet, and, after their adoption, submitted to the Council which has a limited veto. The 1965 elections gave a majority, but not an absolute majority, of seats to the conservative Christian Democratic Union (C.D.U.), led by Ludwig Erhard, and acting in Bavaria through the Christian Social Union (C.S.U.), led by Franz-Josef Strauss, *q.v.* Erhard formed a government in coalition with the Free Democratic Party (F.D.P.), a right-wing anti-Catholic party led by Erich Mende and Walter Scheel. In October 1966 the four F.D.P. ministers brought down the government by resigning over proposals for the 1967 budget. Erhard then resigned as leader of the C.D.U. and was replaced by Kurt Kiesinger, *q.v.*, who formed a new government coalition with the main opposition group, the Social Democratic Party (S.D.P.). Its leader, Willy Brandt, *q.v.* was appointed Vice-Chancellor to Kiesinger and Minister of Foreign

Affairs. The F.D.P. then went into opposition. This was the first occasion in the history of the Federal Republic that the S.D.P. had been in power; it had last been in office from 1928 to 1930 during the Weimar Republic. At the Diet elections held on 28 September 1969 the S.D.P., supported by the German Trade Union Congress (D.G.B.), won 224 seats (202 in 1965); the C.D.U. and the C.S.U. together won 242 seats (245 in 1965); the F.D.P. won 30 (49). The F.D.P. joined a coalition with the S.D.P., with whom it was in substantial agreement over domestic issues, and Willy Brandt was elected Chancellor by 251 to 235 votes, a margin of two votes over the necessary constitutional minimum. Walter Scheel, who had succeeded Mende as leader of the F.D.P., became Vice-Chancellor and Minister of Foreign Affairs.

From 1967, interrupted only by the Russian invasion of Czechoslovakia in August 1968, a policy of *détente* with Eastern Europe was pursued, the Hallstein Doctrine, *q.v.*, was abandoned, and attempts were made to improve trade and cultural relations with the German Democratic Republic, *q.v.*, without committing the Federal Republic to recognition of the sovereignty of East Germany. Under the Chancellorship of Willy Brandt this policy, or Ostpolitik, *q.v.*, brought about the signing in December 1970 of a peace treaty with Poland which recognized the Oder-Neisse Line, *q.v.*, as constituting Poland's western frontier, and a pact of non-aggression with the U.S.S.R. In September 1971 agreement was reached among the four powers occupying Berlin as to the future status of the city; the terms were to become operative when the treaties with Poland and the U.S.S.R. had been ratified by the Federal Diet. After narrowly surviving a vote of confidence in the Bundestag, a situation created by the defection of three F.D.P. representatives, Brandt secured the ratification on 17 May 1972 of the treaties with Poland (by 248 votes to 17) and with the U.S.S.R. (by 248 votes to 10). The abstention of the opposition, which had originally supported the treaties, on such an important issue, and the tenuous nature of the government's majority in the Bundestag (it was in a minority of one in the Bundesrat) made imperative the calling of fresh elections. Brandt then allowed himself to be defeated on a constructive vote of no-confidence and at elections which took place on 19 November 1972 the results were: S.D.P. 230 seats; C.D.U./C.S.U. 224 seats; F.D.P. 42. Willy Brandt who was re-elected Chancellor then formed another S.D.P. government in coalition with the F.D.P., with Walter Scheel continuing to hold office as Vice-Chancellor. On 21 December 1972 a treaty of friendship was signed with the German Democratic Republic, *q.v.*

The Federal Republic is the second largest trading nation in the world, and belongs to the European Economic Community, *q.v.*, of which it is the most powerful member economically. The principal products are iron and steel, electric power, agricultural and industrial chemicals, textiles, passenger cars and commercial vehicles. Sweden, Switzerland and the U.S.A. are the main trading partners outside the Common Market countries.

Germany. An area in central and northern Europe which consists of the German Federal Republic, *q.v.*, and the German Democratic Republic, *q.v.* Modern Germany was created in 1871 by Bismarck, who established the Germanic Federation, consisting of the North Germanic Confederation, led by Prussia, and Bavaria, Württemberg, and Baden. The King of Prussia took the title of German Emperor. The Federation was thought by Germans to be the lawful successor of the Holy Roman Empire, which was created by Otto the Great of Saxony in 962 and came to an end in 1806. When Germany was defeated in the First World War the emperor, Wilhelm II, abdicated, and the Weimar Republic, *q.v.*, was established. At the elections held in 1933 the Nazis (the National Socialist German Workers' Party) won a majority in the legislature (the Reichstag) and their leader, Adolf Hitler, became Chancellor, or Prime Minister. On the death in 1934 of President von Hindenburg the offices of President and Chancellor were fused and Hitler became a dictator. Between 1934 and 1939 the Germans rearmed in defiance of the Versailles Treaty, *q.v.*, built many roads for the speedy carriage of troops and supplies, persecuted Jews and liberals, and tortured them in concentration camps, won the sympathy of British and French right-wing politicians by denouncing the U.S.S.R., and occupied Saarland, *q.v.*, the Rhineland, Austria, and Czechoslovakia. In 1939 Germany concluded a non-aggression treaty with the U.S.S.R. and invaded Poland on 1 September, thus precipitating a war with France and the U.K., which had promised to defend Poland. During the subsequent war Germany occupied most of the European continent west of the U.S.S.R., and joined forces with Italy in 1940, and Japan in 1941, against the U.K., the U.S.A., the U.S.S.R., China, and many other countries. Germany was defeated and occupied by British, French, Russian, and U.S. forces in 1945, and the unconditional surrender of all German forces was accepted on 8 May 1945. Under the Berlin Declaration of June 1945 and the Potsdam Agreement, *q.v.*, of August 1945, the country was divided into four Zones and occupied by the forces of France, the U.K., the U.S.A., and the U.S.S.R., respectively. Special arrangements were made for Berlin, *q.v.* The four powers were unable to agree upon common policies for Germany as a whole, and there were differing political and economic developments in the Russian Zone, or Eastern Germany, *q.v.*, on the one hand, and in the British, French, and U.S. Zones, or Western Germany, *q.v.*, on the other hand. As power was gradually transferred to the Germans by the occupying forces, two rival governments emerged. In 1949 the German Democratic Republic in the east and the German Federal Republic in the west were established. In 1955 the two Republics became sovereign and independent.

Gerrymandering. A reorganization of electoral districts to gain some advantage in a forthcoming election. When Elbridge Gerry was Governor of Massachusetts in 1812, the state legislature divided Essex County into two districts with borders so drawn as to give the maximum advantage to the Republican Party. On a map one of the districts, with pencilled additions, looked like a salamander, and the expression 'to gerrymander' was coined. It should be distinguished from the reorganization of electoral districts which is sometimes essential to ensure that every parliamentary representative speaks for approximately the same number of voters, and which is known as redistribution, *q.v.*

Gestapo. The Geheime Staatspolizei, or German secret police, which became an official body immediately after Adolf Hitler and the Nazis came to power in 1933. Its task was to discover and punish the opponents of Nazism; its agents became members of many illegal anti-Nazi organizations which were subsequently dissolved. Although the Gestapo came to an end with the collapse of the Nazi regime in 1945, the term is often used to describe secret police forces or methods characteristic of the Gestapo.

Ghana. A republic and member of the British Commonwealth; area 92,100 sq. m.; population (1970) 8,545,561, living in the Central Region, the Eastern and Western Regions (formerly the Gold Coast Colony), the Northern Region (formerly the Northern Territories), the Ashanti Region (formerly Ashanti), the Volta Region, the former British-administered Trusteeship Territory of Togoland, *q.v.*, the Upper and Brong-Ahafo Regions and the Greater Accra District; capital Accra.

Ghana was a West African empire which existed from the third to the thirteenth century, though it never included the area now known by that name. The U.K. eventually assumed control of the trading settlement in the region from the Danes and the Dutch in 1820, and the coastal strip was constituted as a colony in 1874. Ashanti and the Northern Territories were brought into the administrative area of the Governor of the Colony in 1901. As a result of a plebiscite in May 1956 authorized by the United Nations, the British-administered part of the Trusteeship Territory of Togoland was integrated into the Gold Coast Colony which became an independent state on 6 March 1957. A republic was declared on 1 July 1960. For a few months in 1961 Ghana was party to a Union of African States with Guinea and Mali.

The Constitution of 1960 provided for an elected legislative assembly of 104 members, chosen for five years, and 10 specially elected women members. The Regions each had a House of Chiefs which selected its own President, except in Ashanti where the Asantahene was to be the Head. Executive authority was vested in the President of the Republic. Kwame Nkrumah, *q.v.*, leader of the Convention People's Party (C.P.P.) which came to power as a non-Communist left-wing group in 1950, retaining its political dominance at the elections in 1956 in which it won 71 seats, became first President of Ghana. A referendum in January 1964 approved the creation of a one-party state, the C.P.P. being the one party, and authorized Dr Nkrumah to dismiss Supreme Court and High Court judges at his discretion.

During 1965 a serious economic crisis developed. The former favourable dollar and sterling balances, built up from the export of cocoa, gold, manganese, timber and diamonds, had been absorbed by uncompleted capital projects and heavy investment in schools, hospitals and public services. Nearly £250 million was owed to overseas creditors, including the World Bank, the U.K. and the U.S.A. which had financed development schemes such as the Volta river aluminium and power project. There was a large budget deficit and the world price of cocoa, which is Ghana's most important export, fell, and did not begin to recover until 1967. Dr Nkrumah abandoned his previous policy of non-alignment, established close associations with the Communist powers, and accepted substantial economic and financial aid from the U.S.S.R. in particular. He meanwhile consolidated his personal position by appointing C.P.P. members to high office in the army and police force.

On 24 February 1966 a *coup d'état* by disaffected elements in the army and police overthrew the government of Nkrumah while he was on a state visit to Peking. A National Liberation Council, consisting of four representatives each from the army and police was set up under the chairmanship of Major-General Ankrah, who had been forcibly retired in 1965, with the Commissioner of Police, J. W. K. Harlley, as vice-chairman. It dissolved the National Assembly, proscribed the C.P.P., and repealed the 1960 Constitution. The

Apaloo Commission was then appointed to inquire into the mal-practices and property-holdings of the C.P.P. and the former President with the aim of discrediting the Nkrumah administration.

Rigorous measures were taken in 1967 to balance the budget; these included devaluation, higher internal taxation, import restriction and reduced capital expenditure. An unsuccessful *coup* by three young army officers in April 1967 was followed by the establishment, in July, of a Committee of 31, under Dr Kofi Busia, to advise the National Liberation Council on civil matters and to speed the transition to civilian rule. Major-General Ankrah resigned as Chairman of the National Liberation Council after admitting to charges of corruption. Following the introduction of a new Constitution in 1969 elections were held in which Dr Busia's Progress Party won 105 out of the 140 seats in the Assembly. He formed a government and a civilian President, Edward Akufo-Addo, was appointed in August 1970 for a four-year term. By December 1971, when the currency suffered a 44 per cent devaluation, the economy had run into another serious recession, and on 13 January 1972 the Army seized power once more. Colonel Ignatius Kutu Acheampong, commander of the 1st Army Brigade, abrogated the Constitution, dissolved parliament and banned all political parties. He then formed a National Redemption Council to govern Ghana with himself as chairman.

Gibraltar, City of. A former British colony on the southern tip of the Iberian peninsula at the entrance to the Mediterranean Sea; area 2 sq. m.; population (1970) 26,833, of whom 77 per cent are Roman Catholic. Its usefulness as a port of call for the British Levant Company, and those doing business with the Company, was one of the motives for its capture by British troops in 1704 during the war of the Spanish Succession. Spain formally ceded Gibraltar to Britain under the Treaty of Utrecht in 1713; by the Treaty of Versailles in 1783 Spain renounced all claims to the area, receiving as compensation Florida and Minorca. From 1939 the government of Spain has reclaimed Gibraltar, and since 1963 has intensified its campaign through the United Nations for the end of British colonial rule and the cession of Gibraltar to Spain. While negotiations, initiated at the request of the U.N., were being conducted between the two governments, Spain imposed restrictions on the use of airspace, thereby limiting access to Gibraltar airport, and on traffic coming from the colony into Spanish territory. In accordance with a U.N. request that the interests of the people of Gibraltar should be taken into account, the British held a referendum in September 1967. This produced an overwhelming majority of 12,138 to 44 in favour of retaining the link with the U.K. rather than passing under Spanish sovereignty. A further U.N. resolution, in December 1967, condemned the referendum as against the best interests of the people of Gibraltar.

A measure of self-government was introduced by the British in 1964 and in May 1969 a new Constitution came into effect by which the colony became the City of Gibraltar and 'part of Her Majesty's dominions unless and until an Act of Parliament provides otherwise'. The British government undertook never to enter into arrangements by which Gibraltar would come under the sovereignty of another state against the freely and democratically expressed wishes of the inhabitants. At the first elections to be held under the new Constitution in July 1969 the Gibraltar Labour Party (previously known as the Association for the Advancement of Civil Rights), led by Sir Joshua Hassan, the Chief Minister, won 7 of the 15 seats in the House of Assembly. The Integration with Britain Party, led by Major Robert Peliza, won 5 seats, and the remaining 3 seats went to a group of Independents led by Peter Isola, the former Deputy Chief Minister. A government was eventually formed by the Integrationist Party and the Isola group and Major Peliza became Chief Minister.

The colony is without natural resources; its chief assets are the tourist industry, the Admiralty Dockyard, and the re-export of manufactured goods. Until 1969 when Spain closed the frontier, it provided daily employment for some 12,000 Spanish workers.

Goa. Until 1961 a Portuguese settlement on the west coast of India; area 1,619 sq. m.; population (1971 estimate) 860,000, of whom all but 2,000 are of Hindu origin. Thirty-seven per cent are Roman Catholic converts; the rest are Hindu. The enclave, with a coastline 62 miles long, included the deep-water harbour of Mormugao. It was administered by Portugal with the two smaller enclaves of Damão and Diu. Goa was economically dependent upon India, from which it imported most of its rice. More than 40 per cent of the total export trade was with India and 0·5 per cent with Portugal. Its iron and manganese mines are largely run by Indian industrialists and worked by Indian labour. The trade deficit was met by income from shipping, tourists, and emigrants' remittances. After 1953, encouraged by the support of 200,000 Goans who work in Bombay, the Indian government accelerated its attempts to exclude Portuguese sovereignty from the Indian mainland and to bring Goa into the Indian Union. Congress declared its policy to be one of non-violence and relied on an economic blockade. Air and rail communications were severed, money-order services were suspended and the Bombay Transport and Dock Workers' Union boycotted foreign ships bound for Goa.

Tacit approval was given to the Goa Liberation Aid Committee, which organized strikes in Bombay, and to the Satyagrahis (exponents of 'soul-force', or non-violent resisters) who attempted several 'invasions' of Goa without using arms.

New Portuguese legislation, permitting the inclusion of elected members in the Legislative Council and extending the electoral roll to 50,000, was introduced on 1 August 1955. However, in the first elections, held on 22 August, all but one of the candidates were returned unopposed. It was illegal to criticize the legislature or the Portuguese government: Portuguese threats to invoke the Anglo-Portuguese Treaty of 1642 or Article IV of the North Atlantic Treaty, which guarantees the territorial integrity of the signatories, were ignored in India, as were the protests of various European and South American Roman Catholic states. In 1951 Portugal altered its status from 'colony' to 'overseas territory'. On 18 December 1961 the Indian army moved into Goa, Dámão, and Diu, which surrendered on the next day; they were formally incorporated in the Indian Union on 14 March 1962; subsequently there was disagreement between the states of Maharashtra and Mysore as to which should incorporate Goa, and the area was put temporarily under the control of Delhi. A referendum held on 16 January 1967 produced a large majority in favour of its remaining a Union Territory.

Gold Coast. The name given to the British territory in West Africa, comprising the Gold Coast colony, Ashanti, and the Northern Territories, until it became, on 6 March 1947, together with the British-administered Trusteeship Territory of Togoland, *q.v.*, a Dominion within the British Commonwealth. It then took the name of Ghana, *q.v.*

Gold Standard. A currency system under which money is either unconditionally, or subject to certain conditions, exchangeable for a fixed weight of gold. To say that a country is on the gold standard may mean one of three things: (1) that its central bank is in a position to redeem its currency in gold and is bound by law to buy and sell gold at a fixed price (this is the full gold standard, as it existed in the U.K. before 1914); (2) that the central bank is merely bound to buy and sell gold at a fixed price (the gold bullion standard, as it existed in the U.K. from 1925 to 1931); (3) that the central bank is bound to buy and sell at a fixed price, not gold, but merely the currencies of countries that are on the full gold or the gold bullion standard (the gold exchange standard).

The system was practised in Europe and America from the middle of the nineteenth century until 1914. It was an internationally convenient system, for each country valued its own currency in terms of gold and arranged for its central bank to convert gold into currency and currency into gold whenever it was asked to do so. A debtor could therefore settle a debt abroad almost as easily as in his own country. As all debts could be taken as representing a definite amount of gold, gold did not often have to be sent from place to place, and debts could be set off against each other in a free market. Difficulties arose whenever it was not possible simply to balance debts against each other, and where a country had actually to pay in gold. As its currency was based on gold, internal restriction of credit and falling prices would follow.

If many countries are on the gold standard international trade is facilitated because the rates of exchange between their different currencies are fixed and certain and because, as a result, their price levels tend to become equal. However, since the effect of a country being on the gold standard is that its internal purchasing power and price level are dependent upon its balance of payments, *q.v.*, the gold standard has now been generally abandoned in favour of the greater degree of autonomy given by fluctuating exchange rates.

Gowon, Major-General Yakubu. Nigerian army officer and politician; born 19 October 1934 in Gram, a village of the Angas tribe in the Plateau Province of Northern Nigeria, the son of the first convert to Christianity among the Angas who moved his family to a Christian settlement near Zaria and became an evangelist. He was educated at Government College, Zaria, the Regular Officers' Special Training School at Teshie, in Ghana, and at Eaton Hall and Sandhurst Military Academy, England. He was commissioned in the Nigerian Army in 1957 and appointed a Platoon Commander in the Southern Cameroons in 1960. He served with the U.N. forces in the Congo (*see* Zaïre) from 1960 to 1961; his experiences there made him a firm opponent of secession. In 1961 he was promoted to the Staff Office at Nigerian Army Headquarters, and Adjutant-General to the Army in 1963. He was the senior Northern officer to survive the mutiny of January 1966, and in his appointment as Chief-of-Staff to General Aguyi-Ironsi, the head of the new military government, he played a major role in restoring discipline. When the army mutinied again in July 1966, and Brigadier Ogundipe fled the country, he was left as the senior officer. He accepted the invitation of the largely Northern mutineers to take control, becoming Head of the Federal Military Government and Supreme Commander of the Armed Forces. When the army, as a result of the outbreak of civil war, had been increased in number to 80,000 men, he took the rank of Major-General. He has frequently stated that he opposes the use of the army for political purposes and has declared his conviction that no soldier should seek political power.

Great Britain and Northern Ireland. The Kingdoms of England and Scotland, the Principality of Wales, and Northern Ireland, which with the dependencies of the Channel Islands, *q.v.*, and the Isle of Man, *q.v.*, are officially called the United Kingdom of Great Britain and Northern Ireland, *q.v.*

Great Society. On 22 May 1964 President Lyndon Johnson, in a speech to the university's graduating class at Ann Arbor, Michigan, said: 'In your time we have the opportunity to move not only toward the rich society and the powerful society, but upward to the Great Society.' The phrase (which was also the title of a book by Graham Wallas, published in New York in 1914) has been taken to epitomize the desire of the Johnson administration to use the wealth of the U.S.A. to enrich the quality of American civilization. It may be compared with the New Deal, *q.v.*, and the New Frontier, *q.v.*

Greece. An independent south European state; area (including the island of Crete and the Dodecanese Islands) 51,182 sq. m.; population (1961) 8,745,084, of whom more than seven million belong to the established Greek Orthodox Church; capital Athens. After gaining independence from Turkey, Greece was declared a kingdom in 1830 and Prince Otto of Bavaria was offered the crown. Since 1862, when Otto was expelled, Greek kings have all been members of the Glucksburg branch of the Danish royal family: George I of Greece was assassinated, his second son, Constantine, was twice deposed, in 1917 and in 1921, and his eldest son, George II, was exiled between 1923 and 1935, during which time a republic was declared, and again from 1941 to 1946. Paul I (born 1901), reigned from 1947 until his death on 6 March 1964. He was succeeded by his son, who is King Constantine XIII (born 1940 and married in 1964 to Princess Anne-Marie of Denmark). Although the Constitution of 1911 allowed for parliamentary government most administrations have been authoritarian. There was a dictatorship before 1935, and from 1936 to 1941 General Metaxas introduced a 'Third Civilization', a semi-Fascist regime, to which no opposition was permitted. The Communist Party went underground.

In 1940 the Italians invaded Greece from Albania. They met with unexpected resistance and were decisively defeated until Germany entered the war in April 1941, overran Greece, and forced the evacuation of British troops by way of Crete. King George and the Greek government went into exile. Early in 1942 a central committee of the Greek Resistance (E.A.M.) was formed. It was built on the Communist underground network but it embraced all parties of the left. Its guerilla army, E.L.A.S., achieved such success that by the summer of 1943 one third of the mainland had been liberated. The U.K., however, supported a second partisan movement, the 'X-Bands' of the pro-monarchist General Zervas. There were clashes between the two resistance groups which led to the expulsion of Zervas in 1943, and the landing of fresh British troops in Greece in 1944 to prevent civil war. A truce was declared and the Patriarch of Athens, Archbishop Damaskinos, was appointed Regent until the burning question of the monarchy could be settled by a plebiscite. In 1946 King George II returned, and the United Nations Security Council rejected a complaint by the U.S.S.R. that British troops in Greece were endangering the peace of the world. At the request of the U.S.A. they remained in Greece until 1950. The militant remnants of E.L.A.S., under the command of General Markos Vafiades, began a new offensive in the autumn of 1946. They received arms and supplies from Yugoslavia, Bulgaria, and Albania, and in 1948 had 25,000 men and women under arms. Vafiades was murdered by his own Communist supporters on instructions from Moscow. Yugoslavia's expulsion from the Cominform, q.v., in 1948 closed the supply lines, and the war ended in 1949.

From 1946, when a Liberal-Social Democratic coalition replaced the right-wing government of Giorgios Papandreou, Greece was governed by parties of the centre. Between 1947 and 1951 thirteen cabinets held office and repeated government changes hindered the country's economic recovery. In July 1951 Field-Marshal Papagos launched his right-wing Greek Rally 'to rescue Greece from political bankruptcy and give her the strong government she needs'; it secured a majority in the General Election in 1952 and became the governing party. The Constitution of 1911 was amended in 1951–2 to include provision for land expropriation and redistribution, and for the dismissal of civil servants and public employees suspected of Communist sympathies. In May 1952, women over 21 were given the vote, and those over 25 allowed to stand for parliament. On the death of Papagos in October 1955, Constantine Karamanlis, previously Minister of Works, became Prime Minister. A new electoral law substituted the simple majority system for proportional representation; it was introduced in order to exclude Communists from the legislature. In the elections of 1956 held under the new system the National Radical Union, a new party founded by Karamanlis as the successor to the Greek Rally, became the largest single party.

After four consecutive terms in office Karamanlis resigned in June 1963 in protest at the Greek Royal visit to the U.K. while civil war continued in Cyprus, *q.v.* He was succeeded as Prime Minister by Papandreou, leader of the new Centre Union Party formed in 1961 from the Liberal splinter groups which oppose the National Radical Union. Papandreou headed a minority government until elections in February 1964 produced a comfortable majority for the Centre Union which obtained 174 seats (138 in November 1963), as against 104 for the National Radical Union and Progressive Party (134 in 1963), and 22 for the extreme left-wing United Democratic Left (E.D.A.), which had 28 seats in 1963. In July 1965 Papandreou was dismissed from office by King Constantine, an action which raised publicly the issue of whether the King was entitled to dismiss a Prime Minister who commanded a majority in Parliament. There followed two short-lived administrations which could not summon majorities in the Chamber until Stefanos Stefanopoulos, of the Centre Union, succeeded in holding together a government from September 1965 to December 1966. A non-party administration was then appointed to arrange fresh elections in 1967. These were expected to produce a further substantial majority for the Centre Union, but an army *coup* on 21 April 1967, in which Colonel George Papadopoulos was instrumental, prevented them from taking place.

A military junta (the Colonels) was established, with Papadopoulos as Prime Minister, which suspended the Constitution, dissolved the Chamber of Deputies and banned all political parties. There ensued a period of political repression and rigorous censorship of press, theatre and music. Political figures of both left and right, including Papandreou (who died on 1 November 1968), were imprisoned and the Universities of Athens and Salonika were purged. In December 1967 the King, in an attempt to dissociate the monarchy from the unpopularity of the junta, failed to raise the armed forces against the regime, and went into exile in Rome. The Colonels then named General George Zoitakis as Regent and exercised full executive powers. A new Constitution became effective on 10 November 1968. It had been approved by 92 per cent of the electorate in a referendum held under martial law on 29 September 1968, in which voting was compulsory for all between the ages of 21 and 70. To enable the junta to continue to rule by decree, ten provisions of the new Constitution concerning individual rights, reduced to eight by 1971, remained indefinitely suspended. These included: protection against arbitrary arrest, the inviolability of the home, freedom of expression, safeguards against emergency powers adopted by governments, freedom to create political parties, and a ban on special courts. Papadopoulos' position was sufficiently strengthened by cabinet reshuffles in November 1970 and December 1971 that he was able to depose Zoitakis and declare himself Regent on 21 March 1972.

The country, which is predominantly agricultural, is not economically viable. Half the population is engaged in agriculture but only fifteen per cent of the land is productive and soil erosion and the depredations of goats are diminishing the area. Tobacco accounts for one third of the total visible exports which also include olives, currants, fresh fruit and vegetables, and there is an expanding tourist trade. Minerals such as bauxite, iron ore and pyrites, manganese, chrome, lead, zinc and emery are mined, but shortage of capital has restricted processing and industrial development. Aid is received from the United States mainly in the form of military equipment and foodstuffs.

Greece was admitted to the Council of Europe in 1949, to N.A.T.O. in 1951, to the European Economic Community as an Associate Member in 1962, and is a party to the Balkan Pact, *q.v.*, with Turkey and Yugoslavia. During 1968 the Council of Europe debated the expulsion of Greece since the junta, by repressing political liberty, no longer observed the prior conditions of membership; in December 1969 Greece withdrew.

Greenland. A strategically important island in the Atlantic Ocean, most of which lies north of the Arctic Circle; it has been an integral part of Denmark since 1953; area 840,000 sq. m., of which 85 per cent is under an ice-cap; population (1970) 46,331; administrative centre Godthaab. It began to be colonized by the Danes in 1721; since 1953 it has returned two members to the Danish parliament.

The people, who are mostly of mixed Eskimo and Scandinavian blood, live in some 185 settlements, mainly on the south-western coastal fringe. Meteorological stations and air bases were established in the Second World War, and in 1951 the U.S.A. was permitted by Denmark to use, rent-free, bases at Narssarsuak, Søndre Strømfjord, and Thule. A radar network was established (*see also* Distant Early Warning Line) and supply depots and runways were built. Greenland is also an important air base for civil flights between Europe and the Pacific Ocean.

The economy was once dependent on the hunting of seal, but now relies on the fishing and processing of cod, shrimps, and prawns; there are deposits of coal, copper, graphite, lead, wolframite, uranium, zinc, and cryolite, which is essential in the manufacture of aluminium. Oil has been discovered in the west. The ice-cap, which is two miles deep in places, is retreating and this will make development of these resources less difficult.

Gromyko, Andrey Andreyevich. Russian politician; born 6 July 1909 in the Gomel region of Byelorussia and educated at the Minsk agricultural institute and at the Lenin Institute of Economics in Moscow, where he took a degree in economics. From 1936 to 1939 he was the senior scientific worker at the institute of economics of the Academy of Science, and simultaneously edited *Problems of Economics*, an official economic review. In 1939 he became head of the American section in the Foreign Ministry, and soon afterwards was appointed Counsellor at the Russian Embassy in Washington, becoming Ambassador there in 1943. He was the Russian representative to the United Nations from 1946 to 1949, when he became deputy Foreign Minister, and Ambassador to the U.K. from 1952 to 1953; in February 1957 he succeeded Dimitri Shepilov as Foreign Minister.

Guatemala. An independent Central American state, area 42,042 sq. m.; population (1970) 5,400,000, of whom over half are illiterate and poor Indians, about 38 per cent are of mixed Indian and white ancestry (*ladinos*), and the rest white; capital Guatemala City. Guatemala was conquered by Spain in 1536, became independent in 1823 and has at most times been a dictatorship. Its most important products are coffee (the world's fourth largest crop and representing over 70 per cent of its exports) and bananas. More than 70 per cent of its exports go to the U.S.A. After a revolution in 1944 Jacob Arbenz became President and during his rule enacted social health schemes in the cities, schemes to protect many coffee and banana workers, and, in 1952, a measure of land redistribution. He prohibited the entry of foreign oil prospectors and expropriated about 408,000 acres of land owned by the U.S.-controlled United Fruit Company on the Pacific and Atlantic coasts for redistribution among the peasants. The Arbenz government offered compensation which was rejected as inadequate by the United Fruit Company; this bitter dispute was resolved in July 1954 by a revolt by the exiled right-wing opposition under Colonel Carlos Castillo Armas, who became President, repealed the land confiscation laws, and admitted U.S. oil companies. In the overthrow of the Arbenz government he was aided by Honduras and Nicaragua, and advised by the U.S. Ambassador to Guatemala. He restored all the expropriated estates and in return the Company undertook to pay income and profits taxes in conformity with Guatemalan legislation, with an upper limit of 30 per cent of any profits made.

Following the assassination of Armas in July 1957, General Miguel Ydigoras Fuentes was elected President for a six-year term which began in March 1958, but he was deposed in March 1963 by army officers who claimed that pro-Communist groups were plotting revolution. The Minister of Defence, Colonel Enrique Peralta Azurdia, assumed full powers, dissolving parliament, suspending the Constitution and prohibiting all political activity. A new Constitution was introduced in September 1965 which reduced the presidential term to four years, and in elections held in March 1966 Dr Julio César Méndez Montenegro, a non-Communist left-wing professor of law and the candidate of the Revolutionary Party (P.R.) which gained 30 out of the 55 seats in the National Congress, defeated two army opponents. During his presidential term there was an upsurge of terrorist activity, the worst outrages being the assassination of the U.S. and German ambassadors in 1968 and 1970 respectively. At elections held in March 1970 General Carlos Araña Osorio, the candidate of the right-wing National Liberation Movement (M.L.N.) had a majority over his P.R. and Christian Democrat (D.C.G.) opponents, and was declared President by Congress in which the seats were distributed as follows: M.L.N. 34; P.R. 17; D.C.G. 4.

Only 10 per cent of Guatemala's land is cultivated; 70 per cent of the cultivated land is held by 2 per cent of the population. Guatemala has repeatedly claimed the adjacent territory of British Honduras, *q.v.*, with its Caribbean port of Belize which would be a convenient outlet for Guatemalan oil.

Guevara, Ernesto 'Che'. Latin-American Communist revolutionary who adopted Cuban citizenship; born 14 June 1928 in Rosario, Argentina, the eldest of five children of an architect and builder. His maternal grandmother had been a U.S. citizen. He left Argentina in 1953 immediately after qualifying as a doctor because of his opposition to Perón, and became involved with left-wing movements in Bolivia, Costa Rica, Ecuador, Panama and Peru before joining Fidel Castro, *q.v.*, and his brother Raúl in Mexico in 1956. In Guatemala he held a minor post in the Arbenz government; its overthrow by the U.S.A. in 1954 is said to have increased his antipathy to all things American. He was one of the twelve survivors of Castro's abortive invasion of Cuba in 1956 and helped to organize, from the mountains of the Sierra Maestra, the successful *coup* by which Batistá was driven from Cuba in 1959.

He became a leading figure in the new Cuban regime, taking Cuban citizenship, and working first on agrarian reform, then travelling as a trade envoy and acting as President of the National Bank. He helped to train the civilian militia to meet invasion (*see* Bay of Pigs) and published a treatise on guerilla warfare. In February 1961 he took office as Minister for Industries. In October 1965 Castro announced that Guevara had resigned his ministerial post on 1 April that year and had renounced Cuban nationality to undertake revolutionary tasks elsewhere. He was later identified in Bolivia where, after being ambushed and captured in the Eastern Andes by Bolivian Army forces, he was executed on 9 October 1967.

The guerilla activities which he initiated and encouraged throughout Latin America fostered a novel theory of revolutionary Communism propagated by Fidel Castro through the Latin American Solidarity Organization, *q.v.*, that the party is subordinate to the guerilla revolutionary who alone can inspire the rural peasant to overthrow the existing capitalist social and political structure. He was himself highly critical of Russian Communism, publicly aligning himself with Chinese Maoists and believing that the peasants of Latin America would 'provide the great liberating army of the future as it has already done in Cuba'.

Guild Socialism. A British variant of syndicalism, *q.v.* The movement emerged in 1906 and advocated a restoration of the medieval guild system along modern lines. Guild Socialists believed that value was created corporately by society rather than by individuals singly, and that capitalist economists had defended the acquisition of wealth without reference to the responsibilities and the opportunities for rendering service to the community which it entailed. The trade unions were to be organized as guilds to take over and run their respective industries after nationalization. This policy was also opposed to that of state Socialism, which provided that the state should assume control of industry. No Guild Socialist movement has existed in the U.K. since the dissolution of the National Guilds League (founded in 1915) in 1925, but the theories of Guild Socialism are frequently referred to by British Labour Party theorists.

Guilt by Association. The responsibility of a person for the alleged faults of those with whom he associates or has associated in the past. In the U.S.A. persons testifying before Congressional committees, or being considered for employment, have often been blamed in this way for present or past association with Communists or Communist sympathizers. This does not mean that they have been regarded as guilty of a legal offence, but their evidence has been regarded as unreliable, and they have sometimes been considered unfit for particular posts.

Guinea. An independent state on the west coast of Africa with Portuguese Guinea to the north and Sierra Leone to the south; area

96,865 sq. m.; population (1970 estimate) 4,000,000, mostly Moslem, of whom some ten per cent speak French and among whom the leading tribes are the Fullah (1,020,000), the Malinké (600,000) and the Soussou (325,000); capital Conakry. The country was formerly one of the eight territories comprising French West Africa, *q.v.*, but at the referendum held on 29 September 1958 Guinea, by an over-whelming vote, rejected the proposed constitution of the Fifth Republic, *q.v.*, and thus chose immediate independence which was proclaimed on 2 October 1958. Following severance of the ties with France there was a brief period of union with Ghana, which provided financial assistance; in May 1966 Guinea gave refuge to the deposed President of Ghana, Kwame Nkrumah, *q.v.*

The country is controlled by its only effective political party, the Democratic Party or Parti Démocratique de Guinée (P.D.G.), which is left-wing and inclined to Marxism, *q.v.*; there is no articulate opposition. Since independence a policy of nationalization and state control of industry and trade has been carried out. The government is appointed by the President, Ahmed Sekou Touré, *q.v.*, in his capacity as head of the P.D.G., and party policy is decided by a bureau of 17 members elected every five years by delegates from regional committees. The efficiency of the party organization did much to overcome the problems which arose after independence, when French subsidies were withdrawn and the public services were left without their French administrators.

Bauxite deposits in the Los Islands are exploited by an international consortium, and the revenue from them provides nearly a quarter of the annual budget. Other minerals found include diamonds (of which many are smuggled across the border with Senegal and Sierra Leone) and iron ore There are also exports of citrus fruits, palm kernels, millet, rice, bananas and coffee; trade is mainly with the French Community and East European countries. Guinea belongs to the West African Free Trade Area with the Ivory Coast, Liberia and Sierra Leone.

Guyana. An independent state within the British Commonwealth on the north-east coast of South America; area 83,000 sq. m.; population (1970 estimate) 721,089, of whom more than half are of East Indian descent and one third are African; capital Georgetown. The territory, which comprised the Dutch colonies of Essequibo, Demerara and Berbice, was seized by the British in 1796 and finally ceded to them in 1814. The three colonies merged in 1831 to become British Guiana. An extensive area in the west of the country is claimed by Venezuela.

The Constitution of 1953, which introduced a two-chamber

legislature and a ministerial system, was suspended after six months on the ground that there was Communist infiltration into the government, which comprised a partly-elective Executive Council. The elective places had been taken up by members of the People's Progressive Party (P.P.P.), an extreme left-wing party led by Dr Cheddi Jagan, q.v. (of Indian origin), and Forbes Burnham, q.v., an African Guianese, which had won 18 out of the 23 seats in the National Assembly. The P.P.P. demanded immediate self-government and encouraged industrial unrest, especially on the sugar estates, to support their policy. British armed forces were landed to prevent public disorder. A new Constitution, giving the colony internal self-government, was introduced in 1961, and in elections held in August that year the P.P.P. won 20 out of the 35 seats in the new Legislative Assembly and Dr Jagan became Prime Minister. Further elections, on a basis of proportional representation, were held in December 1964 when the P.P.P. won 24 seats, the People's National Congress (P.N.C.), a predominantly African offshoot of the P.P.P. founded in 1955 by Forbes Burnham and supported by the Creoles, 22 seats, and the right-wing United Force, led by Peter d'Aguiar and supported by the Amerindians in the north-west and southern Savannah country, 7 seats. Forbes Burnham then became Prime Minister of a coalition government which included members of the P.N.C. and the United Force. Independence was achieved on 26 May 1966 and the country was renamed Guyana (an Amerindian word meaning Land of Waters); a republic was declared in February 1970 and Arthur Chung was elected the first President. Under the 1966 Constitution Parliament consists of one Assembly of 53 members elected every five years by universal suffrage and the single list system of proportional representation. At elections held in December 1968 the P.N.C. secured an absolute majority, winning 30 seats; P.P.P. won 19 seats and the United Force 4. Forbes Burnham continued in office as Prime Minister.

The population, which is increasing rapidly, is in the main dependent on part-time employment on the estates which grow sugar, the country's largest source of income. Bauxite, rice and rum are the other chief products. The government reversed the foreign policy of the Jagan administration which had cultivated friendship with Cuba and Eastern Europe at the expense of its relations with the Commonwealth, and has advocated regionalism and cooperation with other Commonwealth Caribbean countries, thus attracting capital from the U.S.A. to improve communications, organize land settlements and electrify rural areas. In 1972, however, a trade and technical assistance agreement was concluded with China. Despite greater economic stability racial divisions and discontent persist between the Africans, who dominate the urban and industrial communities, and the Indians, who provide most of the labour force for the rice and sugar plantations.

H

Haile Selassie I, Emperor of Ethiopia. Born 24 July 1892. His dynasty claims descent from Menelik I, the son of King Solomon and the Queen of Sheba; he is the son of Ras Makonnen, cousin of Menelik II and one of his generals. Menelik's daughter became Empress, and he became heir, in 1916 when the British organized a revolt which deposed the Emperor Lidj Yassu, his cousin, who had shown sympathy towards Germany and Turkey. He became King or Negus in October 1928 and was proclaimed Emperor after the death of Empress Zauditu in April 1930. He introduced a new constitution in July 1931, and was forced to flee from Ethiopia after the Italian invaders had captured Addis Ababa in May 1936. He went to the Anglo-Egyptian Sudan in July 1940, where he organized the Ethiopian forces which marched from Khartoum into Ethiopia and defeated the Italians. He was reinstated in Addis Ababa in June 1941.

Hailsham, 2nd Viscount. Title renounced in November 1963 by Quintin McGarel Hogg, *q.v.*, and re-adopted when, on his appointment as Lord Chancellor in 1970, he accepted a life peerage.

Haiti. Independent state sharing the Caribbean Island of Hispaniola with the Dominican Republic; area 10,700 sq. m., largely mountainous; population (1970 estimate) 4,870,000, of whom the majority are negro, speaking a French dialect, and 85 per cent illiterate; capital Port-au-Prince. Haiti was once ruled by France and provided one half of the revenues of Louis XIV; it became independent in 1804. It is now one of the world's poorest and most primitive countries, virtually without industry; coffee and sugar exports to the U.S.A. are the mainstay of the economy. There are U.N. plans to provide hydro-electric power, to irrigate the land, to develop the tourist industry, to spread literacy and to improve agricultural techniques, but progress has been slow and is hindered by a traditional rivalry between the aristocracy of mulattoes (of mixed European and negro blood) and the negro masses. Paul Eugène Magloire was the first popularly elected President of Haiti, being returned in 1950 with 99 per cent of the votes cast. Under army pressure, and after a general strike he resigned in 1956. There followed four Presidents in rapid succession until, in September 1957, Dr François Duvalier was elected by a substantial majority. As a result of the adoption, by the National Assembly, of a new Constitution in 1964 the President was granted absolute power and Duvalier was re-elected President for life. On his death on 21 April 1971 he was succeeded by his son, Jean Claude Duvalier. The government maintains its authority by using a private army, known as the Tonton Macoute (Creole for 'bogeyman') which extorts money, intimidates the people by voodoo practices and eliminates opposition. It has thwarted several attempts by Haitian exiles, under the former President Magloire, to start a revolution. The government printing office has circulated a 'Catechism of the Revolution' which contains a prayer: 'Our Doc who art in the National Palace of Life, hallowed be thy name by present and future generations, thy will be done at Port-au-Prince and in the provinces. . . .'.

Hallstein Doctrine. The doctrine that the German Federal Republic would break off diplomatic relations with any country which recognized the German Democratic Republic and would refuse to enter into diplomatic relations with any Communist country except the Soviet Union. It was first defined by Konrad Adenauer, *q.v.*, on 22 September 1955 in a speech to the Bundestag following West Germany's establishment of diplomatic relations with the U.S.S.R. in order to secure the return of German prisoners of war, and it was named after Dr Walter Hallstein, State Secretary in the German Foreign Office from 1951 to 1958. It was enforced twice: in 1957 against Yugoslavia and in 1963 against Cuba. It was eroded in January 1967 when the coalition government of Dr Kurt Kiesinger, *q.v.*, established diplomatic relations with Romania, and abandoned in January 1968 with the restoration of diplomatic relations with Yugoslavia.

Haud. A disputed territory on the borders of Ethiopia, *q.v.*, and the former British Somaliland, *q.v.*

Havana Charter. A document summarizing the agreements reached at the United Nations Conference on Trade and Employment, held at Havana, Cuba, from 21 November 1947 to 24 March 1948. The Charter provided for an International Trade Organization, *q.v.*, which would expand world trade and remove trade barriers. Though 54 states agreed to the Charter at Havana, the U.S. Congress did not ratify it and the I.T.O. never came into existence. Before the meeting at Havana the General Agreement on Tariffs and Trade, *q.v.*, had been concluded at Geneva between April and October 1947, and the Havana Charter stated that if the Charter had not come into force by 30 September 1949, the contracting parties should meet before 31 December 1949 to decide whether G.A.T.T. should be amended, supplemented, or maintained. It was thus recognized that the rules of the Charter were stiffer and more comprehensive than the terms of G.A.T.T.

Hawks. Name given to those Americans who favoured an intensification, or even escalation, *q.v.*, of the war in Viet-Nam as the most effective way of bringing about its termination. Those who opposed this policy are known as Doves, *q.v.* The expression came into use in 1964 and is thought to have originated inside the State Department. Examples of Hawks are: Governor George Wallace, *q.v.*, and President Nixon, *q.v.*

Healey, Denis Winston. British Labour Party politician; born 30 August 1917; educated at Bradford Grammar School and Balliol College, Oxford. After war service in the Army he took up a post at Labour Party headquarters in 1946, and remained secretary of the Party's International Department until 1952 when he entered Parliament as the member for South-East Leeds (a constituency which was re-organized in 1955 and renamed Leeds, East). In 1959 he became the Labour Party's chief spokesman on foreign affairs; in 1963, on defence matters. He was Secretary of State for Defence from October 1964 until June 1970 in which office he was responsible for the policy of withdrawing British military and naval forces from the Persian Gulf and the Far East.

Heath, Edward Richard George. British Conservative Party politician; born 9 July 1916; educated at Chatham House School, Ramsgate, and Balliol College, Oxford, where he was President of the Oxford Union in 1939. After serving in the army in the Second World War, and becoming a Lieutenant-Colonel, he entered the civil service in 1946 but left in 1947 to become the Conservative candidate for Bexley, a seat which he won in 1950. From 1948 to 1949 he was News Editor of the *Church Times*. He became a Lord Commissioner of the Treasury and an Assistant Whip in 1951, Joint Deputy Government Chief Whip in 1952, Deputy Government Chief Whip in 1953, Chief Whip in December 1955, and Minister of Labour immediately after the General Election of October 1959. In July 1960 he became Lord Privy Seal, with special responsibility for foreign affairs; from October 1963 until the Conservative Party was defeated in the General Election of October 1964, he was President of the Board of Trade and Secretary of State for Industry, Trade, and Regional Development. He became leader of the Conservative Party, and Leader of the Opposition, in July 1965; he then received 150 votes on the first ballot for the leadership, against 133 votes cast for Reginald Maudling, *q.v.*, who conceded defeat without insisting on the second ballot permitted by the election rules. He became Prime Minister in June 1970.

Hegemony. Leadership; the word is often used to describe the powerful influence exercised by one state over other states.

High Commission Territories. The former British colony of Basutoland, *q.v.*, and the two former British protectorates of Bechuanaland, *q.v.*, and Swaziland, *q.v.*, all of which have boundaries within, or adjacent to, South Africa, *q.v.* The Act of Union of 1909 provided for the possible inclusion into South Africa of the three Territories which were then administered by a High Commission in Mafeking, Cape Province. From 1909 until 1960 successive South African governments asked for the transfer to be implemented. However the Chiefs in the Territories objected to any scheme which would bring them under South African rule and the U.K. government refused their transfer on the ground that the wishes of the inhabitants of the Territories should be paramount. In 1965 the headquarters of the administration was moved to Gaberones in Bechuanaland. The Territories were gradually made independent of the Commission, Bechuanaland and Basutoland becoming the independent republics of Botswana, *q.v.*, and Lesotho, *q.v.*, respectively in 1966 and Swaziland an independent monarchy in 1968.

High Dam. A dam built by the Egyptian government, with Russian aid and technical assistance, on the river Nile and completed in 1970. It is intended to provide for Egypt: (1) a steady supply of water, so that there need be no shortage in a dry year; (2) electric power of 2 million kilowatts potential; (3) irrigation of approximately 2 million acres of land, as a result of which Egypt's cultivated area would be increased by one third. The High Dam is 300 miles farther upstream than the Aswan Dam, *q.v.*, and can hold more than twenty times as much water. The population of Egypt increased from 20 million in 1952 to nearly 35 million in 1972; the High Dam was planned by President Nasser, *q.v.*, as a partial answer to the problem of feeding a fast-expanding population.

Hispaniola. The island in the Caribbean Sea occupied by the Dominican Republic, *q.v.* (in the east), and Haiti, *q.v.* (in the west). It was discovered by Christopher Columbus in 1492 and then named La Isla Española.

Ho Chi-Minh (The Seeker of Enlightenment). Founder of the Viet-Minh, *q.v.*, in Indo-China and effectively in control of the Democratic Republic of Viet-Nam, or North Viet-Nam. He was probably born on 19 May 1890, the son of a local official who lost his job for opposing the French; self-educated and multi-lingual, he went to sea from 1911 to 1914, then worked in London, cleaning silver at the Carlton Hotel Restaurant, and (in 1918) in Paris, where he preached revolution to the Viet-Namese community. He attended the 1922 Congress of the French Communist Party, spent the next three years in Moscow, then worked under Borodin in Canton (in 1925) from where he organized the South-East Asia Comintern and encouraged nationalist revolts in Indo-China. In 1941, when Vichy France agreed to co-operate with the Japanese, he formed a resistance movement of Communists and Nationalists called the Viet-Minh. Four years later its guerilla army received the Japanese surrender in Tonkin and Annam and defied British, French, and Nationalist-Chinese Liberation forces while Ho declared a Democratic Republic of Viet-Nam. In the negotiations of 1945–6 to determine the future status of Indo-China, the French recognized him as the effective political leader of the Viet-Namese but denounced him as a rebel when the negotiations broke down and Viet-Minh troops launched an attack on Hanoi in December 1946. The U.S.S.R. and China formally recognized him as Head of State of the Democratic Republic of Viet-Nam in 1950, while the western powers acknowledged the French-sponsored Bao Dai; after the Geneva Agreement (q.v.) of 1954, however, he was universally recognized as the leader of North Viet-Nam. He assumed office as President in 1945 and was re-elected in July 1960. He died in Hanoi on 3 September 1969.

Hogg, Quintin McGarel (Lord Hailsham). British Conservative Party politician; born 9 October 1907 and educated at Eton and Christ Church, Oxford; after being elected to a Fellowship at All Souls College, Oxford, he practised at the Bar. He entered the House of Commons in 1938 as the member for Oxford, having fought a by-election as an ardent supporter of the Munich Agreement, q.v. After serving in the army in the Second World War, he was Parliamentary Under-Secretary of State for Air in the Conservative 'caretaker' government from April to July 1945. He entered the House of Lords reluctantly on the death of his father in 1950, and returned to office as First Lord of the Admiralty in 1956. He became Minister of Education in 1957, but in September of the same year gave up that post to become Lord President of the Council and Chairman of the Conservative Party. After the General Election of October 1959 he was replaced as Lord President by Lord Home and as Chairman by R. A. Butler, and became instead Lord Privy Seal and Minister of Science. In a further reshuffle in July 1960 he was restored to the office of Lord President, while remaining Minister of Science, and became Leader of the House of Lords. From January 1963 until the Conservative defeat in October 1964 he was responsible for reviving industrial activity in north-east England. In 1970 he was appointed Lord Chancellor, an office held by his father, Viscount Hailsham, in 1928–9 and from 1935 to 1938. He is the first person to have renounced a hereditary peerage (in 1963) and to have returned to the House of Lords as a life peer.

Holland. Comprises two of the provinces of the Netherlands, *q.v.*, and is an alternative name for that country.

Home, 14th Earl of. Title renounced in October 1963 by Sir Alexander (Alec) Frederick Douglas-Home, *q.v.*

Home Rule. The aim of those who sought self-government for Ireland when that country was still part of the U.K., and who expressed their goal in the words 'Home Rule for Ireland'. The term is used to describe the aims of many movements towards autonomy by national or minority groups.

Honduras. An independent Central American state on the isthmus between the Caribbean Sea and the Pacific Ocean; area 43,227 sq. m.; population (1969) 2,490,000, of whom nine-tenths are of mixed Spanish and Indian descent and the majority Roman Catholic; capital Tegucigalpa. Honduras was ruled by Spain from the sixteenth century until independence was proclaimed in 1821; the federation of Central America was then formed, Honduras emerging from that federation as an independent state in 1838.

Although silver is mined in quantity, and there are deposits of gold, copper, antimony and iron, the chief commercial activity is the cultivation of bananas and coconuts along the Atlantic coast. Bananas account for nearly half of the exports; the banana industry is dominated by the United and Standard Fruit Companies. In 1954 the banana workers struck for higher wages and confiscation of the estates owned by the United Fruit Company. They also demanded an improvement in working conditions similar to those granted to the Guatemalan banana workers. The strike was settled by the intervention of the President on terms which for the first time gave the country a functioning trade union movement.

Under the 1965 Constitution government is by a legislative assembly, the National Congress, elected for six years by universal suffrage and proportional representation. Executive authority lies with the President, elected by popular vote for a six-year term. At elections held in February 1965 the seats in Congress were divided between the two traditional political parties, the right-wing National Party (35 seats) and the Liberal Party (29); the left-wing Popular Progressive Party and the Orthodox Republican Party were not given official recognition and could not propose candidates. At elections held in March 1971, which were boycotted in response to appeals from the left-wing parties by more than 40 per cent of the electorate, the two main parties concluded a Pact of National Union. 32 seats were to be allotted to each party, out of the total of 64, and the party winning the elections would elect the President who would give his additional vote to the victorious party. The National Party defeated the Liberal Party by approximately 256,000 to 240,000 votes.

Honduras was ruled as a dictatorship from 1939 to 1949 by General Tiburcio Carías Andino, leader of the National Party; he was succeeded by Juan Manuel Galvez, a lawyer and former employee of the United Fruit Company, who, in his five years of office, granted considerable civil freedom, re-establishing a free press and permitting criticism of his government by the Liberal Party. When the Liberal leader, Dr José Ramón Villeda Morales, won the presidential election of October 1954 he was immediately deposed by Julio Lozando Diaz who had been Vice-President under Galvez. He was, in turn, removed by a military junta in 1956 which organized popular elections in September 1957; these resulted in another victory for Dr Villeda's party which had campaigned for improved social conditions. Villeda became President for a six-year term in December 1957, but was overthrown in October 1963 by Colonel Osualdo López Arellano, Commander-in-Chief of the Army, who had been unsuccessful in his attempt to secure the National Party nomination for the December presidential elections. Arellano suspended the 1957 Constitution and assumed direct powers. He authorized the 1965 elections, on the basis of a new constitution; the resulting victory for the National Party confirmed his tenure of power and he was appointed Constitutional President on 6 June 1965. He was succeeded in June 1971 by Dr Ramón Ernesto Cruz, leader of the National Party and a former judge, whose electoral victory was ascribed to his doubts about the value to Honduras of continued participation in the Central American Common Market, *q.v.* In December 1972 the army again seized power.

Hong Kong. A British colony claimed by China and comprising part of the Chinese mainland and some islands; total area 398 sq. m.; population (1971 estimate) 4,045,300, including more than a million refugees from China; capital Victoria, on Hong Kong Island. The island was seized by British forces in 1841 after the Chinese government had prohibited the import of opium, which was a valuable source of income for British businessmen exporting to China. Kowloon was acquired in 1860; in 1898 the U.K. was granted a lease of the New Territories, comprising a peninsula in the mainland province of Kuangtung and some adjacent islands, which expires in 1997. Hong Kong declined in importance as an entrepôt port during and after the Korean War, when it was prevented by the United Nations resolution of 18 May 1951 from re-exporting tin, rubber, and other strategic materials to China. It has since concentrated on developing its manufacturing industries, which provided 10 per cent of the value of its exports in 1947 and over 90 per cent by 1967. Two thirds of the manufactured exports are cotton goods, and the main export markets are the U.S.A. followed by the U.K. and other E.E.C. countries.

House of Commons. The lower house of the United Kingdom Houses of Parliament, and virtually the ruling one since the reduction of the powers of the House of Lords by the Parliament Acts, 1911 and 1949, *q.v.* The House of Commons has 630 members elected by adult male and female suffrage. England has 511 members, Wales 36, Scotland 71, and Northern Ireland 12. These members were returned at the General Election of June 1970 by 28,258,332 votes, representing 72 per cent of the electorate, as against 27,263,606 (75·9 per cent) in 1966. Lunatics, felons, traitors, members of the House of Lords, clergymen of the Church of England, and ministers of the Church of Scotland and the Roman Catholic Church are ineligible as candidates, as are certain government officials, Sheriffs, government contractors, and others regarded in law as holding an 'office of profit under the Crown'. The House of Commons is elected for a maximum period of five years but earlier dissolution is possible. Members of the House (who can add the initials M.P. to their names) receive a salary of £4,500 a year, all of which is taxable, allowance being made for proved parliamentary expenses. The Speaker, who is elected by the members from among their number at the beginning of each parliament, presides over the House, which usually sits for not less than 150 days each year. The Leader of the Opposition receives an annual salary of £9,500 from the government.

House of Lords. The upper house of the United Kingdom Houses of Parliament, comprising the Lords Spiritual and the Lords Temporal. The 2 Archbishops and 24 Church of England bishops constitute the Lords Spiritual, while the majority of the Lords Temporal (there were approximately 830 hereditary peers in January 1972) consist of the Royal Dukes, other Dukes, all Lords (whether Earl, Marquis, Viscount or Baron) who are peers of the United Kingdom, and the hereditary peeresses. The other Lords Temporal are the Scottish peers, all of whom may attend – the electoral system was abolished in 1963 – 9 Lords of Appeal (who hold life peerages), and life peers and peeresses (204 in January 1972) under the Life Peerages Act, 1958. Members are unpaid but may draw a daily expense allowance of not more than £8·50. An ordinary meeting of the House of Lords is seldom attended by more than 50 members, although the full membership is over 1,000. In earlier days the House had the right to veto Bills passed by the House of Commons. This right has been greatly restricted by the Parliament Acts of 1911 and 1949, *q.v.* The Lord Chancellor presides over the House of Lords and is also a member of the government. The 9 Lords of Appeal and certain other peers sit as the highest court of appeal in the United Kingdom. Under the Peerage Act, 1963, hereditary peers can surrender their peerages during their own lifetime.

House of Representatives. The lower house of the U.S. Congress, *q.v.* Under the Constitution each state is entitled to at least one representative, but beyond that minimum number representatives are apportioned among states according to population as shown by the decennial census. Under the law now in force the membership is fixed at 435 indefinitely. A new House is elected every two years, towards the end of the Congressional term. A member must reside within the state, but not necessarily within the district, for which he is elected; he must be at least 25 years of age and must have been a U.S. citizen for at least seven years. The House appoints one of its members as Speaker, to preside over its meetings and to appoint chairmen of committees, and to appoint special committees. The Constitution (Article One) provides, as an adaptation of British practice, that all Bills for raising revenue shall originate in the House, although the Senate has power to amend revenue legislation. The origin of this rule lies in an old practice by which members of the Senate were chosen by the state legislature, and were thus not directly responsible to the people. Although Senators are now chosen by direct vote, this rule remains. To some extent the House is the more representative of popular opinion, as its members submit to election every two rather than every six years, and representation depends upon the size of the population, whereas in the Senate an under-populated state has the same representation as a densely populated state. A representative is paid $42,500 per annum.

Humphrey, Hubert Horatio. U.S. Democratic Party politician; born 27 May 1911 at Wallace, South Dakota, the son of a pharmacist. His university education was interrupted by lack of funds and he worked for six years in his father's pharmacy before returning in 1937 to the University of Minnesota and then to the University of Louisiana for his master's degree. He subsequently taught political science at Minnesota University, but relinquished an academic career for politics in 1945 when he became Mayor of Minneapolis. His four-year term as Mayor was noteworthy for the establishment of the first U.S. Fair Employment Practices' Commission to eliminate discrimination of race, colour and creed in employment. In 1949 he was elected Senator for Minnesota. He has been prominently identified with the liberal wing of the Democratic Party and was a strong protagonist of civil rights, *q.v.*; he has advocated the suspension of nuclear tests and has twice sponsored bills in the Senate on this issue. He became Senate Majority Whip in 1961 and in 1964 was selected by Lyndon Johnson to be his Vice-President. He contested the 1968 Presidential election as the Democratic candidate but narrowly lost to the Republican Richard Nixon, *q.v.* He was defeated in his attempt to secure the Presidential nomination in 1972 by George McGovern, *q.v.*

Hungary. An independent eastern European state; area 35,912 sq. m.; population (1971) 10,347,000; capital Budapest. The country was declared an independent republic upon the collapse of the Empire of Austria-Hungary in 1918, but was reconstituted as a kingdom in 1920. Admiral Nicholas Horthy de Nagybana, who had served in the Austro-Hungarian navy, against the U.K., in the First World War, became Regent and left the throne vacant, refusing to allow the Habsburg claimants to return.

Between the two World Wars Hungary pursued a policy of recovering the areas which had been incorporated in other nation states when the Austro-Hungarian Empire was dissolved. These included Slovakia, which was taken by Czechoslovakia, Transylvania (by Romania), Croatia and other areas (by Yugoslavia), and Burgenland (by Austria). Hungary allied itself with Germany and obtained a large part of Slovakia at the first partition of Czechoslovakia in September 1938, and the province of Sub-Carpathian Ruthenia at the second partition in March 1939. Hungary joined the Anti-Comintern Pact on 24 February 1939 and from 1941 supported Germany in the Second World War. An armistice concluded with the Allied Powers on 20 January 1945 restored the frontiers of 1 January 1938.

Before 1945 some 2,000 Hungarians owned one half of the arable land; under the Land Reform Act of that year 5,599,645 acres of large estates were confiscated and partitioned among the peasants. Heavy industries and the mines were nationalized in 1946 and the banks were taken over in 1947. In the 1947 elections the Communists became the largest single party with 22·7 per cent of the vote, the Smallholders' proportion falling from 57 per cent in the 1945 elections to 15·4 per cent; by skilful political manoeuvring they obtained the most important government posts and under the leadership of Matyas Rákosi (1892–1971) secured absolute power. A People's Independent Front, comprising the Communists, the Smallholders, the National Peasant Party, the Trade Union Federation, the

Association of Working Peasants, the Democratic Women's Association and the Federation of Working Youth, was established in February 1949. At elections in May the Front, with no opposition, obtained 95·6 per cent of the votes, and a predominantly Communist government was then appointed. The monasteries were dissolved and a campaign to collectivize agriculture was opened and by 1952 practically the entire economy had been brought under the control of the state. Elections held in May 1953 produced a result similar to that of 1949.

In July 1953 the government admitted the failure of its agricultural policy (the grain yield barely exceeded the average for 1940–46), and confessed to serious economic and political errors. Rákosi, while retaining his post as First Secretary of the Party, was replaced as Prime Minister by Imre Nagy. A more liberal policy, based on increased investment in agriculture rather than heavy industry, was then introduced and the supply of consumer goods was increased. When the economic situation showed no improvement Nagy was accused of impeding industrial development and cooperative farming. He was dismissed and subsequently expelled from the Party. He was succeeded by Andras Hegedüs who re-introduced the Rákosi policy, accompanied by considerable political repression. Opposition within the Party to Rákosi mounted, and on 18 July 1956 he was removed from his post as First Secretary and succeeded by Ernö Gerö, a Deputy Premier who had been one of his closest associates. In the course of an anti-Russian revolution, provoked by the presence of foreign troops as well as by discontent with the Party leadership, Nagy replaced Hegedüs as Prime Minister on 23 October 1956. On 1 November it was announced that Hungary had withdrawn from the Warsaw Pact, *q.v.* Russian forces in Hungary and from outside attacked Budapest on 4 November and set up a new government under János Kádár, who had succeeded Gerö as First Secretary of the Party in October. This government gave Nagy a guarantee of safety, as a result of which he left the sanctuary of the Yugoslav Embassy in Budapest on 22 November; it announced on 17 June 1958 that he had been executed for treason.

In January 1958 Kádár resigned the premiership in order to concentrate on his duties as First Secretary of the Hungarian Socialist Workers' Party, as the Communist Party had been renamed, but he returned to the office from September 1961 to July 1965. He was succeeded first by Gyula Kállai, and from April 1967 by Jenö Fock. His administration gradually modified the totalitarianism associated with former governments, and the country became more prosperous.

Ninety-seven per cent of the land has been collectivized and half the exports to western Europe still consist of agricultural produce, but industry is now responsible for half the total economic resources. There are exports of engineering products and machine tools, electrical equipment and shipping mostly to other Comecon countries. Since 1967 there has been an attempt to reduce the gap between the living standards of the peasants and the rest of the population and to halt the drift to the towns. In 1968 a New Economic Mechanism was introduced by which manufacturing industries were given greater freedom to deal directly with foreign firms; by 1970 imports from western Europe had doubled.

Under the 1949 Constitution supreme power is vested in a National Assembly of 340 deputies elected for four years. At elections held in 1958, 1963 and 1967, the Patriotic People's Front had no opponents, but in 1971 independently nominated candidates were allowed to stand for election, and 49 seats were contested. A Presidium of 21 members exercises the functions of parliament between parliamentary sessions. On 21 August 1968 Hungary took part in an invasion of Czecho-slovakia by the U.S.S.R. and three other members (Bulgaria, the German Democratic Republic and Poland) of the Warsaw Pact.

I

Iceland. An independent island state in the North Atlantic Ocean, near
the Arctic Circle; area 40,500 sq. m.; population (1970) 204,344;
capital Reykjavik. An independent republic was set up in 930, but
Iceland came under the rule of Norway from 1263 to 1381 and of
Denmark from 1381 to 1918. It then recovered its independence,
acknowledging, with Denmark, the Danish king as a common
sovereign; on 24 May 1944 the people of Iceland decided, by an
overwhelming majority in a referendum, to establish a republic, and
this was done on 17 June 1944 when the present Constitution came
into force.

Iceland is a member of the North Atlantic Treaty Organization,
q.v., but possesses no armed forces except for her fishery protection
vessels. Under the Treaty and a 1951 agreement the U.S.A. has
maintained at the Keflavik base army, navy, and air forces, known as
the Iceland Defence Force. In 1971 negotiations were begun for their
withdrawal by 1975.

The Icelandic parliament (the Althing, founded in 930) elects one
third of its 60 members to form an upper house. The remaining two
thirds of the members form the lower house. Executive power is
vested in the cabinet, under the President (Dr Kristjan Eldjarn,
elected 30 June 1968) who is elected by popular vote for a four-year
term. At the elections held on 13 June 1971 the results were: Independence Party 22 (23 in 1967); Progressive Party 17 (18); People's
Union (Communist) 10 (9); Social Democrats 6 (9); Liberal Left, a
new party formed in 1970 by dissident members of the People's
Union, 5. The government is a left-wing coalition of the Progressive
Party, the People's Union and the Liberal Left under the premiership
of Olafur Johannesson, chairman of the Progressive Party and
Professor of Law at Reykjavik University. It is governmental policy
to diversify the economy, which has hitherto been based on the
fishing industry, and aluminium smelting accounts for 13 per cent of
total exports; only one per cent of the land is cultivated.

Iceland exports fish, fish meal, herring oil, and sheepskins. There
have been serious disputes as a result of heavy fishing by British
trawlers off the coast. In 1952 the International Court of Justice
found in favour of Norway's claim to extend the limits of its territorial waters to 4 miles, and to measure them from headland to
headland instead of following the coastline, and Iceland accordingly
made a similar claim. The British trawler owners retaliated by refusing
the use of their landing gear for Icelandic fish. This put a total

stop to imports of Icelandic fish into the U.K. The Icelanders tried to circumvent this by using their own gear, but as British trawler skippers and mates then threatened to refuse to go to sea if English distributors handled Icelandic fish, the trade would not distribute such fish, and the attempt was abandoned. In 1956 the British trawler owners accepted the 4-mile limit, and in June 1958 the territorial waters were, for the purpose of fishery limits only, extended to 12 miles with effect from 1 September 1958. The U.K. accepted this in February 1961 and Iceland granted British trawlers a three-year period of grace to fish at certain times and places between the 6- and 12-mile lines. The 12-mile limit was imposed in March 1964. In September 1972 Iceland extended its territorial waters to 50 miles; this decision was unacceptable to West Germany and the U.K. especially since it would thereby lose some 25 per cent of its total catch. The U.K. placed the dispute before the International Court of Justice which had ruled against the 50-mile limit in August 1972, but the Iceland government refused to acknowledge its jurisdiction. Subsequent attempts by the U.K. during 1972 to negotiate a settlement were unsuccessful.

Iceland joined E.F.T.A., *q.v.*, in March 1970 and applied for a special trade agreement with E.E.C., *q.v.*, in 1971. Its principal trading partners are Denmark, the U.K. and West Germany.

I.C.F.T.U. International Confederation of Free Trade Unions, *q.v.*

I.F.C. International Finance Corporation, *q.v.*

Ifní. A former Spanish province on the Atlantic coast of Africa, surrounded on the north, east, and south by the independent state of Morocco, *q.v.*; area 950 sq. m.; population (1960) 49,889, the majority being of Moorish origin; capital Sidi Ifní. It was ceded to Morocco on 30 June 1969. In the late fifteenth century there was, in the area of Ifní, a Spanish settlement known as Santa Cruz di Mar Pequeña. Its exact site became a matter of dispute in succeeding centuries, but it was named in the Treaty of Tetuan in 1860 between the Queen of Spain and the Sultan of Morocco, who admitted Spanish sovereignty over it. Under the Madrid Convention of 1912 it was agreed that the term 'Santa Cruz di Mar Pequeña' referred to Ifní, over which the Spanish flag was eventually hoisted in 1934. After Morocco became independent in 1956, sporadic raids were made from Moroccan territory on Ifní, which was elevated to the status of a Spanish province in January 1958; the Moroccan government disclaimed responsibility for the raids. The port of Ifní is used by Spanish fishing vessels but the area has no known economic resources. The refusal of Spain to yield the province to Morocco until 1969 was determined largely by Spanish fears for the province of Spanish Sahara, *q.v.*

I.L.O. International Labour Organization, *q v.*

Imperial Preference. The system of preferential arrangements by which the U.K. accords duty-free entry to most imports from the British Commonwealth. The General Agreement on Tariffs and Trade, *q.v.*, concluded in 1947, recognized existing preferential arrangements in respect of import duties but did not permit the 'margin of preference' (the difference between the most favoured nation rate and the preferential rate) to be increased. A waiver was granted which enabled the U.K. to increase the protective tariff on goods not bound under the Agreement, while maintaining duty-free entry for these same goods when imported from the Commonwealth, if they were traditionally imported duty-free, and thereby allowing the margin of preference to be increased. The existence of imperial preference made it difficult for the U.K. to devise a satisfactory method of joining the European Free Trade Association, *q.v.*, or the European Economic Community, *q.v.*

Imperialism. The practice, by a country, of acquiring and administering colonies and dependencies after it has achieved national unity and embarked upon commercial or industrial expansion. Belgium, the Netherlands, France, Spain, Portugal, and the U.K. acquired overseas territories before and during the nineteenth century, whereas Germany, Italy, and Japan, which did not achieve unity and industrial and military power until the late nineteenth century, made their efforts to acquire such territories, usually by war, during the twentieth century. The U.S.S.R. has also been described as an imperialist power, since it has continued the Tsarist policy of trying to dominate the countries (such as Finland, Poland, Hungary, Romania, Czechoslovakia, Bulgaria, Persia, Afghanistan, and China) which are on, or near, its borders, and has actually absorbed three formerly independent countries (Estonia, Latvia, and Lithuania). The economic dependence of many states (particularly in Latin America) upon the U.S.A. is often regarded as yet another expression of imperialism.

India. An Asian republic and member of the British Commonwealth; area 1,262,275 sq. m.; seat of government New Delhi; population (1971) 547,367,926. According to the 1961 census returns the religious affiliations of the population were as follows: Hindu 366,502,000, Moslem 46,939,000, Christian 8,000,000, and Sikh 7,845,000. By the terms of the India Independence Act, 1947, India comprises the former provinces of British India which had Hindu majorities, and those among the 507 States which chose to join India rather than Pakistan.

q.v. Under the Constitution, which came into force on 26 January 1950, India is a Union of States, each with its own Governor and legislative assembly. As a result of the States Reorganization Act, 1956, and legislation passed in 1960 and 1966, India comprised 17 States (including Jammu and Kashmir, *q.v.*, and Nagaland, *q.v.*), and 6 centrally administered Territories. In 1967 it was decided to reorganize the State of Assam on a federal basis to allow the Hill people greater autonomy; they were eventually accorded full statehood as Meghalya. By 1972 new states had also been created in Punjab, Haryana, Himachal Pradesh, Manipur and Tripura, while Mizoram and the former North-West Frontier Agency had become Union Territories. The State legislatures are subordinate to the President of the Union, who appoints the Governors and is himself elected by an electoral college consisting of all the elected members of Parliament and of the various State legislative assemblies, and to the Parliament of the Union; the division of authority between Union and State is carefully defined in the Constitution. Parliament consists of the President of the Republic (elected for a five-year term and then eligible for re-election), in whom all executive power is vested; the Council of States ('Rajya Sabha') of not more than 250 representatives of the States elected, indirectly, through the State legislatures; and the House of the People ('Lok Sabha') of 500 or more members, directly elected by the voters of the States on the basis of adult suffrage. The Council of States is a permanent assembly, but one third of its members retire every second year; the House of the People is dissolved after five years. An Election Commission supervises all elections.

The Congress Party, *q.v.*, which retains much of the prestige it acquired before 1947 as the principal nationalist movement opposing the British, and as the chosen political instrument of Mahatma Gandhi, dominates Indian politics. In the biggest democratic elections ever organized, from February to March 1962, in which 126 million votes were cast, the Congress Party won 361 seats out of 500 in the House of the People. In elections held in February 1967 it experienced a severe setback, winning only 280 out of 521 seats. However under the leadership of Indira Gandhi, *q.v.*, daughter of Jawaharlal Nehru, *q.v.*, who succeeded Lal Bahadur Shastri, *q.v.*, as Prime Minister on his death in 1966, the Party achieved an absolute majority in the elections held in March 1971. The results were as follows: Ruling Congress Party 350 seats; Opposition Congress, a break-away right-wing group under Morarji Desai, *q.v.*, who had contested the leadership of Congress with Indira Gandhi, 16 seats;

Jan Sangh, a Hindu right-wing movement which is anti-Moslem and anti-Sikh, 22 (35 in 1967); Swatranta Party, which advocates free competition and is sympathetic to the western powers in foreign policy, 8 (42); Communist Party 23 (23); Marxist Communist (pro-Peking) 25 (19); Samyukta Socialists, founded in 1964 to unite the former Socialist Party and the Praja Socialists, 2 (23); Praja Socialists, a left-wing party with a trade union base, which united temporarily in 1964, and again in 1971, with the Samyukta Socialists, 2 (13); Dravida Munnetra Kazhagan (Madras Party) 22; Moslem League 3; regional parties 27; others 20. There is no unified opposition, although in 1967 nine of the seventeen States of the Union elected non-Congress governments. In five of these, notably West Bengal which had been terrorized by the Naxalites, *q.v.*, it became necessary for the President (since August 1969 Varahgiri Venkata Giri, the former Vice-President who defeated the official Congress candidate) to use his emergency powers to impose direct rule in 1968, 1970 and again in 1971. The strongest political organization is that of the Communist Party, led by C. Rajeswara Rao, with its own 'All India' Trades Union Congress (one of four major union groupings) and a membership in 1971 of 230,000. Many industrialists prefer to deal with Communist unions because of the reputation of their leaders for keeping agreements with management; but the split in the Party, and the support given by the Marxist (pro-Peking) Communists to Naxalite activities, have diminished their political and industrial authority.

India is almost entirely agricultural; 70 per cent of the population depend on the land for their livelihood. The *ryotwari* system of landholding, by which each peasant becomes a freeholder, is fast superseding the *zamindari* system of tenant-farming and absentee landlords. Although socially desirable, the *ryotwari* system is un-economic since the peasant farmer employs primitive methods and is too poor to buy equipment and fertilizers so that the food supply for the family is inadequate. To remedy this situation the government has introduced the *mahalwari* system by which the village commun-ities hold, and work, an estate in common. Irrigation projects on the upper Ganges and in the East Punjab have reduced flooding and have increased rice and maize yields. Tea provides 25 per cent of the total exports. The country is being gradually industrialized. Iron and steel, coal-mining, cotton textiles, sugar, cement and matches, give employ-ment to 10 per cent of the working population, and small-scale industries to another 10 per cent. But the population (increasing by 2·2 per cent a year) continues to grow at a greater rate than India's capacity to produce food and work. Nehru's first Five Year Plan

(1951–6) to increase food production and simultaneously decrease births by government instruction in contraception and the opening of sterilization clinics was hindered by religious opposition and illiteracy (assessed as 70 per cent in 1971). During the first and second (1956–61) Five-Year Plans national income rose by 38 per cent but, as a result of the rise in population and the need for investment, income for consumption rose by only 16 per cent. The principal aims of the third Plan (1961–6) of a 30 per cent increase in the national income, self-sufficiency in food, and a rapid expansion of basic industry, were not realized; the population estimate for 1966 of 478 million was exceeded by 20 million. A fourth Five-Year Plan was introduced in 1970, but although there has been substantial progress towards self-sufficiency as a result of the 'Green Revolution', mounting inflation and unemployment are endangering its success.

India, which has frontiers with China, Nepal, Pakistan and Bangladesh, q.v., has tried to maintain an independent neutralist foreign policy and has frequently acted as arbiter between east and west in the United Nations. It has withheld support from any Asian military alliance involving non-Asian powers, for example the South-East Asia Collective Defence Treaty, q.v., and has refused U.S. military aid. In December 1961 India assumed control of the Portuguese possessions of Goa, q.v., Diu, and Damão (renamed Daman). It had previously incorporated in the Union the former French settlements of Chandernagore, Pondicherry, Karikal, Mahé and Yanaon. There is an unresolved dispute with China over the delimitation of the frontier in Ladakh, q.v. Relations with Pakistan, which had been strained since the partition of the continent in 1947, degenerated into war over Kashmir in 1965; through the mediation of the U.S.S.R. a ceasefire was arranged by the Tashkent Agreement, q.v., in January 1966. When the separatist movement in East Bengal, under Sheikh Mujibur Rahman, q.v., who had declared that he wanted peaceful relations with India, was frustrated by the Pakistan army during 1971, and more than nine million refugees had crossed from East Pakistan into India, the Indian government, already provoked by Pakistani air attacks, sent troops into East and West Pakistan on 4 December 1971. On 16 December the Pakistan army in East Bengal surrendered; the new state of Bangladesh was recognized by India, and in March 1972 a twenty-five year treaty of friendship was signed between the two countries. By an agreement concluded with Pakistan at Simla in July 1972 India withdrew from over 5,000 sq. m. of Pakistan territory occupied during the war, and Pakistan accepted that the continuing dispute over Kashmir should be removed from the

U.N. agenda, and settled bilaterally; but the question of the repatriation of 91,000 Pakistan prisoners-of-war was deferred.

Indo-China. A former French dependency in South-East Asia created in 1887 and comprising the colony of Cochin China, and the four protectorates of Annam, Tonkin, Laos, *q.v.*, and Cambodia (now Khmer Republic, *q.v.*). In 1949 Annam, Tonkin, and Cochin China were merged into the single independent state of Viet-Nam, *q.v.*, which, with Cambodia and Laos, became an Associate State of the French Union until all three achieved independent status under the Geneva Agreements of 1954.

Indonesia. Formerly the Netherlands East Indies, now an independent republic comprising the 4 large islands of Java, Sumatra, most of Borneo and Celebes, West Irian, Madura, the Moluccas, and Bali, and thousands of small islands; area 896,865 sq. m.; population (1971) 122,864,000, of whom 90 per cent are Moslems; capital Djakarta in Java. The islands were controlled by the Dutch from the seventeenth century until 1941 when they were occupied by the Japanese who encouraged a nationalist movement and set up a nationalist Indonesian government. Two days after the surrender of the Japanese in 1945 Dr Sukarno and Dr Hatta declared an independent republic and formed a government the authority of which was recognized by the British and U.S. liberation forces. However, the Dutch attempted to oust the new administration and in some instances employed surrendered Japanese forces against the Indonesians. In 1948 troops landed in Java to suppress a Communist rising in Madium, and civil war broke out. The U.N. intervened; two Good Offices Missions were sent to Indonesia, and on 28 December 1949 power was officially transferred to the Indonesian government. Excluded from this agreement was West Irian, *q.v.* (Netherlands New Guinea), which became part of Indonesia on 1 May 1963.

Under the provisional Constitution adopted in August 1950 the legislature consisted of a President (Dr Ahmed Sukarno, *q.v.*), a Vice-President (Dr Hatta until 1956), a Senate, and a House of Representatives. The original plan for a federation of the United States of Indonesia was abandoned in favour of a centralized state administered from Djakarta, a decision which produced innumerable difficulties. Lack of experience in administration and illiteracy (18 per cent of the population in 1963) have impeded cooperation between the scattered islands with their different peoples and traditions. The Dutch discouraged higher education among the natives, and the Indonesians have had to struggle to set up both educational institutions and a system of government.

Communist risings, led by the Tan Malaka, and guerilla activity on the part of Dar-ul-Islam, a militant and fanatical sect which opposes the religious toleration extended to three million Christians and one million Buddhists and aims to establish a Moslem theocracy, weakened the authority of the central government. There was continual unrest in west Java, north-eastern Sumatra, Borneo and in the Moluccas. The army became an essential instrument of government policy, forcing in August 1955 the resignation of Dr Sastroamidjojo, whose Minister of Defence, it claimed, had promoted only Communist officers. Sastroamidjojo, who had pursued a foreign policy sympathetic to China, was replaced by Dr Burhanuddin Harahap, a member of the Masjumi (Moslem) Party executive. He formed an administration of 12 parties which excluded the Nationalists (P.N.I.), the party of Sastroamidjojo, and the Communists (P.K.I.), and promised to re-establish the confidence of the army in particular, and the people in general, in the government. In his first three months in office he secured the appointment of an anti-Communist, General Abdul Haris Nasution, as commander-in-chief, acted ruthlessly against corruption in the civil service, reduced the budget deficit, and checked inflation by an intelligent use of import controls.

Following the first national elections to the House of Representatives, in which the P.K.I. and the P.N.I. obtained the largest number of seats, Harahap resigned; it was found impossible to govern without the P.K.I., but too dangerous to include them in the administration. From July 1959 Sukarno acted as his own Prime Minister, and in 1960 he dismissed the House of Representatives after it had criticized his budget proposals. His policy inclined more and more towards that of China, and in 1963 Indonesia opposed the establishment of Malaysia, *q.v.*, and initiated a confrontation, *q.v.*, which was designed to harass the Federation and give support to the Communists in Malaya. On 30 September 1965 an attempted Communist *coup d'état* assisted by the Palace Guard, which resulted in the murder of six generals, was crushed by the army. The P.K.I. was charged with attempting to set up a Peking-oriented regime nominally under President Sukarno. He remained in office but his foreign minister, Dr Subandrio was sentenced to death. In March 1966 the military commanders, under General Suharto, *q.v.*, took over executive powers, dissolving both the P.K.I. and the P.N.I., which was regarded as corrupt and politically unreliable. An agreement was concluded with Malaysia on 11 August 1966 ending confrontation, and Indonesia resumed membership of the United Nations which it had left in 1965 in protest against Malaysia becoming a member of the Security

Council. In 1967 it actively promoted the formation of A.S.E.A.N., *q.v.*

Mounting pressure from the army, combined with a motion passed unanimously in the House of Representatives on 9 February 1967 that he should stand trial for corruption and for his own part in the 1965 *coup*, forced Sukarno on 27 February to resign all his powers to Suharto, who immediately cautioned parliament against humiliating a former President. A full-scale persecution of Communists was then launched in which an estimated 80,000 were killed, the P.K.I. was proscribed in March 1967, and in March 1968 Suharto was sworn in as President for five years by the Provisional People's Consultative Congress. A Communist resurgence in 1968 led to further mass arrests; some 100,000 of Indonesia's 3·5 million Chinese were held without trial in concentration camps. In an effort to halt the galloping inflation which had by 1966 exhausted the foreign exchange reserves, Suharto increased the number of those paying taxes (hitherto 0·25 per cent). Official salaries were raised to levels which make possible the extermination or control of corruption, and the subsidies on petrol and fuel, transport, posts and telegraphs which had distorted the economy were withdrawn. In July 1971, at the first elections to be held since 1955, the government-sponsored Sekber Golkar, a federation of trade, regional and professional organizations founded by President Suharto to counterbalance growing Communist influence especially among civil servants, won 227 of the 360 seats in the House of Representatives. Nine other parties contested the elections, compared with 28 in 1955, and criticism of the government, or reference to the ideas of the former President Sukarno (who had died in 1970), was forbidden during the election campaign.

Given stable and honest government Indonesia could prosper. Its mineral resources are among the most valuable in the world; it is the principal producer of petroleum in the Far East and rivals Malaysia in its output of rubber and tin. It also exports coffee, tea, sugar and copra, but is not self-sufficient in rice. It lacks capital for investment, and until 1967 pursued a policy of discrimination against foreign, and particularly Dutch, firms, that forced many of them out of business. Nevertheless the Netherlands and the U.S.A. remain Indonesia's foremost trading partners, although an export trade to China and Viet-Nam through Singapore has been developed. The Indonesian government's repayment in 1968 of a $70 million debt, outstanding since 1963, to Stanvac, a subsidiary of Mobil and Esso, has encouraged foreign oil companies, including Continental Oil of America and E.N.I. of Italy, to negotiate inland and off-shore concessions from Pertamina, the Indonesian State oil company which owns the land. Seventy per cent of the existing production of crude oil is from the Caltex (U.S. owned) fields in North Sumatra.

Indus Waters Treaty. An agreement signed in September 1960 and negotiated over a period of nine years by the International Bank for Reconstruction and Development (World Bank) with the governments of India and Pakistan, to share the waters of the rivers and canals flowing from Kashmir and the East Punjab into West Pakistan and used for irrigation purposes by both countries. It decided that India was to have full use of the waters of the three eastern rivers, the Sutlej, Beas, and Ravi, while the Pakistan areas affected would receive water brought from the western rivers, the Indus, Jhelum and Chenab, by a new canal system. The completion of the Mangla Dam, *q.v.*, on the river Jhelum in 1967, was the first stage of a vast irrigation project; the second stage involves the construction of the much larger Tarbela Dam over the Indus in Abbottabad district. It is expected to be in use by 1974.

Inflation. A rise in the level of prices due not to a rise in import or production costs but to a relative increase in purchasing power as compared with the volume of goods available for purchase. A rise in the level of prices means a fall in the value of money. If the value of money falls greatly people try to exchange it for goods, and so increase still further the rise in the level of prices. A moderate inflation appears in practice to be necessary for full employment, since this depends on purchasing power being always maintained at a high level.

Initiative. An instruction by the electorate to parliament to proceed with a measure. In Switzerland, for example, any of 50,000 citizens may propose a total or a partial revision of the federal Constitution. The device is usually found as a supplement to the referendum, *q.v.* It is not used in the U.K.

Inner Mongolia. *See* Mongolia, Inner.

Insurgent (derived from the Latin *surgere*, to arise). One who rises in revolt. This is one of several terms, such as bandit, loyalist, partisan, resistance-worker, revolutionary, and terrorist, *q.v.*, which may be used to describe a person who employs force to attack the established order. Unlike these other terms, however, it does not in itself suggest either praise or blame.

International Atomic Energy Agency. Came into existence on 29 July 1957 and is one of the United Nations specialized agencies, although also an independent international organization. Its aims are to ensure that atomic energy contributes to world peace, health, and prosperity, and to prevent its own activities from contributing in any way to military purposes. There is an annual general conference, and the board of governors (of 23 members) and staff have their headquarters in Vienna, where the Agency has a research laboratory. Requests for technical assistance, which the Agency has tried to meet, have concerned such activities as agricultural research, uranium mining, and prospecting for and analysing nuclear material.

International Bank for Reconstruction and Development. Often known as the World Bank, it was set up, with the International Monetary Fund, *q.v.*, by the United Nations Monetary and Financial Conference of 44 nations which met at Bretton Woods, New Hampshire, U.S.A., in July 1944. The Articles of Agreement of the Bank came into force in December 1945. It is a specialized agency of the United Nations, but is also an independent international organization.

The aims of the Bank are to help to develop member countries by facilitating the investment of capital for productive purposes, to promote the long-range growth of international trade, to encourage private foreign investment by guaranteeing and participating in such investment, and to arrange loans for productive purposes where private capital is not available on reasonable terms. Lord Keynes, on behalf of the U.K., and Harry Dexter White, on behalf of the U.S.A., had once hoped to persuade the Bretton Woods Conference to accept far-reaching proposals for a central bank which would be able to eliminate world-wide financial crises.

From 1946 to 1965 the Bank made 424 loans amounting to $8·9 billion. These loans were for such purposes as flood control, communications, mining, irrigation, transport, agriculture, forestry, electric power, and industrial development generally. Political conditions in a member country are considered only in so far as they are likely to affect economic conditions and the prospects of repayment. Loans are usually made only to a member country, or to a private enterprise within a member country, if the loan is guaranteed by the country's government or central bank. The Bank also gives technical assistance, where required, by sending missions to survey the economies of member countries which can then be helped to draw up investment programmes and to improve their productive efficiency. It also advises on particular development programmes or recommends outside consultants for this purpose.

Each member has a right to appoint persons to the Board of Governors, which meets annually. Most of the Board's powers are delegated to 18 Executive Directors, who meet monthly in Washington, D.C., U.S.A. Five Directors are appointed by the 5 members having the largest share of capital stock. The other Directors are elected by the Governors representing the remaining members. In board meetings each Director can cast as a unit the number of votes of the member or members by which he was appointed or elected. A President is appointed by the Directors. The Bank had a subscribed capital, in December 1971, of $24,046,300,000 from its 117 members. Ten per cent of this subscribed capital is paid up and is used for loans. The remaining 90 per cent constitutes a reserve fund which can be called upon only to meet the obligations of the Bank. In 1956 the Bank set up the International Finance Corporation, *q.v.*, to supervise private investment in underdeveloped countries. The International Development Association, *q.v.*, was established as an affiliate of the Bank in 1960.

International Confederation of Free Trade Unions. An international organization established in 1949 by the American Federation of Labor, *q.v.*, the Congress of Industrial Organizations, *q.v.*, the Trades Union Congress, *q.v.*, and other national unions, to represent those labour movements which wished to have no connection with the World Federation of Trade Unions, *q.v.* In February 1969 the A.F. of L.-C.I.O. withdrew from the Confederation because the United Automobile Workers' Union, which had seceded from the U.S. organization in 1968, had applied for admission. The I.C.F.T.U. suffered a reduction of one fifth of its revenue, but still represents more than 47 million workers in 93 countries.

International Co-operation Administration. A semi-autonomous organization within the U.S. State Department, set up on 30 June 1955 to supersede the Foreign Operations Administration, *q.v.* It supervised all U.S. foreign aid programmes, including economic and military assistance, and technical aid. It was superseded in November 1961 by the Agency for International Development, *q.v.*

International Court of Justice. The principal judicial organ of the United Nations; it held its inaugural meeting at The Hague on 18 April 1946; its Statute is an integral part of the U.N. Charter. Its predecessor, in the days of the League of Nations, *q.v.*, was the Permanent Court of International Justice, established in 1921. States had in previous centuries arranged arbitral tribunals, with chosen arbitrators, to settle their disputes, but the principles of a standing court and compulsory jurisdiction were only generally accepted in 1921, although the Central American Court of Justice, 1908–18, had introduced compulsory jurisdiction on a regional scale.

The 15 judges of the Court are, indirectly, elected jointly by the General Assembly and the Security Council, 5 places falling vacant every three years. The Statute of the Court states that it shall be comprised of 'a body of independent Judges, elected regardless of their nationality'. This clause was intended to ensure that it was understood that the major powers had no special right to be represented. In practice there has always been a judge corresponding to the nationality of each permanent member of the Security Council, and a judge retiring or dying is usually replaced by one of the same nationality. Where there is not a judge who is a national of one party to a dispute, an *ad hoc* appointment is made of such a national for the duration of the hearing.

By accepting the 'optional clause' of the Statute of the Court a state agrees that the jurisdiction of the Court is compulsory in all legal disputes concerning: (1) the interpretation of a treaty; (2) any question of international law; (3) the existence of any fact which, if established, would constitute a breach of an international obligation; and (4) the nature or extent of the reparation to be made for the breach of an international obligation. About 40 states have accepted the optional clause, though in some cases for limited periods and with reservations. The U.K., for example, excludes disputes with members of the Commonwealth from the compulsory jurisdiction of the International Court. The U.S.A. excludes 'disputes which are essentially within the jurisdiction of the U.S.A., as determined by the U.S.A.' This reservation conflicts with the clause in the Court's Statute that entitles the Court itself to decide whether a dispute is within a state's own jurisdiction; serious disputes could arise over problems such as tariffs if the U.S.A. and another country quarrelled over a tariff treaty.

International Development Agency. *See* Agency for International Development.

International Development Association. An affiliate of the International Bank for Reconstruction and Development, *q.v.*, used to finance economic growth in less developed countries by low-interest loans, it came into being on 26 September 1960 and began operations on 8 November 1960. Membership is open to all members of the International Bank. The aims of the Association are stated to be: 'to promote economic development, increase productivity, and thus raise standards of living in the less developed areas of the world included within the Association membership, in particular by providing finance to meet their important developmental requirements on terms which are more flexible and bear less heavily on the balance of payments than those of conventional loans, thereby furthering the developmental objectives of the International Bank for Reconstruction and Development and supplementing its activities.'

The Association has considerable latitude as to the manner in which loans are repaid. The President of the International Bank is, ex-officio, President of the Association.

International Finance Corporation (I.F.C.). Set up by the International Bank for Reconstruction and Development, *q.v.*, to encourage the growth of productive private enterprise, particularly in the less developed areas of the world, by investing in undertakings where sufficient private capital is not available on reasonable terms; by seeking to recruit private capital and to find experienced management; and by generally creating conditions which will stimulate the flow of investment. There is an authorized capital of $100 million, paid in gold or U.S. dollars and subscribed by members in amounts proportionate to their capital in the International Bank. The I.F.C. came into existence in July 1956. It is a specialized agency of the United Nations, and has its headquarters in Washington, D.C.

International Labour Organization (I.L.O.). Came into being in 1919 as an autonomous institution, associated with the League of Nations, seeking to improve labour conditions, raise living standards, and promote economic and social stability. In 1946 the United Nations recognized the responsibility of I.L.O. in these fields, and established I.L.O. as one of the United Nations' specialized agencies. Its tripartite structure, representing governments, employers, and workers, is unique. It is especially concerned with: the regulation of hours of work; the regulation of the supply of labour and the prevention of unemployment; the provision of an adequate living wage; the protection of the worker against sickness and injury arising out of his employment; the protection of children, young persons, and women; provision for old age and injury; protection of the interests of workers when employed in countries other than their own; recognition of the principles of equal pay for equal work and of freedom of association; the organization of vocational and technical education.

Policy is decided by the annual International Labour Conference, at which each state is represented by two governing delegates, one employer and one employee. A Governing Body, comprising 24 government delegates, 12 employers and 12 employees, appoints the Director-General and supervises the work of the International Labour Office (the permanent secretariat of I.L.O.) at the I.L.O. headquarters at Geneva. Ten governments (Canada, China, France, German Federal Republic, India, Italy, Japan, U.K., U.S.A., U.S.S.R.) are allocated seats on the Governing Body because of their industrial importance. Each of the three groups represented at the Conference elects its own representatives to the remaining 38 places on the

Governing Body. Western employer delegates have in the past tried to exclude employer delegates from Communist countries on the ground that they merely echo their governments' policies and represent no separate interest. This issue came to a head in May 1970 when the U.S. Director-General, David Morse, who had held office since 1948, resigned. He was replaced by the British Wilfrid Jenks who appointed a Russian, Pavel Astapenko, as an assistant Director-General. At the instigation of George Meany, *q.v.*, President of the American Federation of Labor and Congress of Industrial Organizations, *q.v.*, the U.S. House of Representatives Appropriations Committee ceased payment of contributions (which constitute 25 per cent of the total budget) to the I.L.O., and the U.S.A. may withdraw from the organization.

International Monetary Fund. Was set up, with the International Bank for Reconstruction and Development, *q.v.*, by the United Nations Monetary and Financial Conference of 44 nations which met at Bretton Woods, New Hampshire, U.S.A., in July 1944. The Articles of Agreement of the Fund came into force on 27 December 1945. It is a specialized agency of the United Nations, but it is also an independent international organization.

The aims of the Fund are to expand international trade, and thus to establish a high level of employment, real income, and production, to make exchange rates stable, and to make its own funds available to members. To achieve its aims it discusses with member countries their balance-of-payments problems, currency par values, exchange restrictions, and the use of their resources. It arranges with members a pattern of exchange rates fixed in proportion to the value of gold and the U.S. dollar. A member is not allowed to alter this rate by more than 10 per cent without obtaining the approval of the Fund's Board of Executive Directors. In May 1971 the German Federal Republic and the Netherlands both informed the Fund that they could not maintain their exchange rates within the established margin; in August 1971 the U.S.A. suspended the gold convertibility of the dollar and a float of all the major currencies followed. This threat to the purpose of the Fund was averted in December 1971 when the financial representatives of ten member countries reached a settlement whereby a major realignment of currencies was agreed, the U.S. dollar was devalued and the import surcharge, imposed at the height of the crisis, removed.

The Fund has a Board of Governors, a Board of Executive Directors a Managing Director and a staff. Each member government is represented on the Board of Governors, which meets annually and delegates most of its powers to the Directors. The Board of Executive

Directors conducts the general operation of the Fund. Each of the five nations which subscribe the largest quotas appoints a Director; there must be at least seven other Directors, who are elected by the Governors representing the remaining members. Voting in this election and by the appointed Directors is in proportion to each member's quota. Voting by the elected Directors is in proportion to the votes they received.

Quotas are fixed on joining; a member must pay either 25 per cent of its quota in gold or, as part of its quota, 10 per cent of its net official gold and dollar holdings, whichever is the less. The balance of the quota is payable in the member's national currency. In December 1971 the total quotas in gold and national currencies from the 120 member nations amounted to $28,807·8 million.

International Refugee Organization (I.R.O.). Was responsible from 20 August 1948 to 31 December 1951, when it was brought to an end, for the care and repatriation of refugees and displaced persons, for their identification and classification, and for their settlement in countries able and willing to receive them. Its constitution was approved by the United Nations General Assembly on 15 December 1946; its Preparatory Commission took over many functions of the United Nations Relief and Rehabilitation Administration, q.v., on 30 June 1947, including the direct care of 719,600 refugees and displaced persons throughout the world, and responsibility for the protection of the interests of 900,000 other refugees and displaced persons eligible for I.R.O. assistance. Between 1947 and 1951 the Preparatory Commission and I.R.O. resettled more than one million persons in new homes, repatriated approximately 73,000 to their former homelands, and gave some form of assistance to more than 1,600,000. I.R.O. became a migration organization because only a small minority of refugees was willing to be repatriated. It was a temporary organization, designed to deal with the problems raised by the cessation of U.N.R.R.A.; when it was abolished at the end of 1951 its responsibilities passed to the United Nations High Commissioner for Refugees, q.v.

International Trade Organization (I.T.O.). Was to have come into existence when the Havana Charter, q.v., was ratified by the 54 states which met at Havana in 1947–8 to make plans for the removal of trade barriers. An interim commission (I.C.I.T.O.) was created to prepare for the first conference of I.T.O., but the organization was never set up as the result of the U.S. refusal to ratify the Charter. I.C.I.T.O. concerned itself instead with liaison duties for the contracting parties to the General Agreement on Tariffs and Trade, *q.v.*, which was concluded in 1947 as an interim measure. In 1955 the parties to G.A.T.T. agreed to set up the Organization for Trade Co-operation, *q.v.*, to administer the Agreement.

Inter-state Commerce Commission. Established in 1887, it is responsible for federal, as opposed to state, transport in the U.S.A. It has jurisdiction over passenger and cargo rates and facilities for passengers. In 1955 it ruled that there should be no segregation of Negro inter-state railway and bus passengers; Negroes were to be allowed to use the same accommodation and railway waiting-rooms as whites. The decision accorded with the views of the Supreme Court, which has condemned the belief that it is possible to give Negroes facilities that are separate but equal. (*See* Segregation.)

Intervention. Interference in the domestic or external affairs of another state which violates the state's independence. A state may justify an act of intervention where it has a treaty right to interfere in the external affairs of one of its protected states; where it interferes to protect one of its citizens; where it invades in self-defence; where it joins with other members of the United Nations to restrain a state which disturbs world peace by resorting to war; and in certain other cases. Unless there is some such justification any intervention is a breach of international law.

Invisible Exports. That part of a country's income from overseas which is derived otherwise than by exports of goods which are visible exports. They include insurance premiums, tourist expenditure, interest on debts and on capital invested abroad, and payments for banking and shipping services.

I.R.A. Irish Republican Army, *q.v.*

Iran. *See* Persia.

Iraq. An independent state between the rivers Tigris and Euphrates, covering the territory once known as Mesopotamia; area 172,000 sq. m.; population (1970 estimate) 9,465,800, nearly all Moslems, mostly of Shiite but some of Sunni sects; capital Baghdad. The language is Arabic. Formerly a Turkish province, Iraq was prepared for independence under a British Mandate after the First World War and Emir Faisal (son of King Hussein of Mecca), who had just been driven out of Syria by the French, was made King in 1921. Under the Treaty of Lausanne, 1923, Turkey gave up its claim to rule the area. In accordance with the terms of the Mandate, the U.K. recognized Iraq's independence in 1927, and in 1932 the Mandate was terminated and Iraq became a sovereign state with a seat in the League of Nations.

From 1932 until 1958 Iraq was a constitutional monarchy with a two-chamber legislature. On 14 February 1958 King Faisal II (who was born in 1935 and became King in 1939) proclaimed the establishment of the Arab Federation, q.v., with Jordan. On 13 May he became head of state of the Arab Union, q.v., as the two countries then were known. In the course of a *coup d'état* on 14 July King Faisal, the Prime Minister of the Arab Union, General Nuri-es-Said, and Faisal's uncle, Crown Prince Abdul Illah, were murdered. The new government, led by Brigadier Abdul Karim Kassem, dissolved the Arab Union and declared a republic, but he was unable to reconcile the demands of the Pan-Arabists for greater involvement in Arab affairs with the demands made internally for the autonomy of Kurdistan, q.v.; he was assassinated in February 1963. Field-Marshal Abdul Salem Muhammad Aref, who favoured closer relations with the U.A.R., became head of state. Initially he enjoyed the support of the Baath Party, q.v., but when Lt-General Tahir Yahya became Prime Minister in November 1963 the Baathists were ousted from the government. Civilian rule was restored in September 1965 when Dr Abdul Rahman Bazzaz was appointed Prime Minister.

In March 1966 Field-Marshal Aref was killed in an air accident and was succeeded by his brother, Major-General Abdul Rahman Muhammad Aref, who in July 1968 was deposed and exiled as a result of a conspiracy between right-wing Baathists and a group of young army officers. They formed a revolutionary council which appointed General Ahmed Hassan al Bakr, who had been Prime Minister in 1963, as President of the Republic. The declared policy of the new government, the composition of which was Baathist, nationalist, but not pro-Nasser, was a settlement of the Kurdish problem, which was resolved by the grant of autonomy to Kurdistan in March 1970, support for the Arab commando groups in Palestine (*see* Jordan), and a development programme which would end Iraq's dependence on its oil revenues.

Oil exports, the revenue from which represents nearly half the national income, increased by more than 20 per cent between 1963 and 1966 but dropped by 14 per cent in 1967 owing to the interruption in supply from December 1966 to March 1967 when the Syrian government, as a result of a disagreement with the Iraq Petroleum Company, q.v., over royalties, cut the pipelines from the Kirkuk oilfield to Banias on the Mediterranean. The Kirkuk oilfield had been established in 1927 by Iraq Petroleum; other firms with concessions included Mosul Petroleum Co. and Basra Petroleum Co., both with the same ownership as I.P.C. In August 1967 a state oil company, I.N.O.C., was awarded the sole exploitation rights to concessions taken over from foreign companies in 1961; these included the North Rumailah oilfield, compensation for which has never been agreed between the Iraq government and I.P.C. Early in 1972 a 40 per cent reduction in output from the North Iraq oilfields brought a corresponding reduction in oil revenues which the Iraq government interpreted as punitive. According to the I.P.C. the fall in production was the result of three factors; the higher prices negotiated for crude oil by members of the Organization of Petroleum Exporting Countries (O.P.E.C.), *q.v.*, to which Iraq belonged; the high comparative cost of transporting oil by pipeline and through the Mediterranean as against the sea route from the Persian Gulf and round the Cape; and a glut in world oil supplies. In June 1972 the Iraq government nationalized the assets of all foreign oil companies but made a special arrangement with E.R.A.P., the French State oil company, which had been appointed contractor to I.N.O.C. for exploration and marketing purposes in 1968. O.P.E.C. then undertook to mediate between the parties, since without legal agreement Iraq would have difficulty in marketing the nationalized oil. The only other products are wheat, barley, beans, rice and 80 per cent of the world's dates. Extensive irrigation is badly needed in this area which was once able to support 30 million people.

In foreign policy the 1955 mutual assistance treaty with Turkey, later joined by Pakistan, Persia and the U.K., known as the Baghdad Pact, *q.v.*, which became the basis of the Central Treaty Organization, *q.v.*, was a significant development for Iraq. By supporting the Pact, Iraq was the first Arab state to join the western chain of alliances. This weakened the Arab League, *q.v.*, which Iraq helped to found in 1945, but the country withdrew from the Pact in March 1959 and has since aligned with the Arab group in international policy. In 1967 it gave assistance to Syria and Jordan in the war against Israel, and has made the issue of Arab refugees in Palestine, *q.v.*, paramount in relations with foreign states. Relations with Persia deteriorated in April 1969 following a dispute over the Shatt el Arab waterway which forms the frontier, and the seizure by Persia of the Trucial Coast islands of Greater and Lesser Tumbs in November 1971 (*see* United Arab Emirates) resulted in the expulsion of 60,000 Iranians from Iraq.

Iraq Petroleum Company. An oil company holding concessions in many states throughout the Middle East. It has interests, directly or indirectly, in Abu Dhabi, Lebanon, the Trucial Coast, Qatar, Syria, and elsewhere. In 1972 the government of Iraq, *q.v.*, expropriated all I.P.C. holdings and installations in that country. The controlling interests in the Company are: British Petroleum 23·75 per cent; the Shell Group 23·75 per cent; Compagnie Francaise des Pétroles 23·75 per cent; Standard Oil of New Jersey 11·875 per cent; Socony Mobil Oil 11·875 per cent; and the Gulbenkian group (Participations and Explorations Corporation) 5 per cent.

Ireland. An independent state, area 26,600 sq. m.; population (1971) 2,971,230, of whom more than 90 per cent are Roman Catholic; capital Dublin. Ireland was divided into a number of Celtic kingdoms until 1152, when one king invoked the aid of the Anglo-Normans. This led to the first English landings; the Irish, however, constantly opposed English rule, especially after the reformation of the English Church, when Ireland remained Roman Catholic. Cromwell ordered the evacuation of the northern counties, now known as Northern Ireland, *q.v.*, and settled Protestant Englishmen and Scots there. An Irish Parliament existed till 1800 when the United Kingdom of Great Britain and Ireland was created. In the nineteenth century there was mass emigration to the U.S.A. by peasants who could not obtain a living from the land or had been driven from their tenancies by English landowners to whom they owed rent. One half of Ireland's total income went to absentee English landlords.

The Liberal Gladstone government increased the security of tenure of the Irish peasant and in 1886 and 1893 made unsuccessful attempts to introduce Home Rule. A Home Rule Act was eventually passed against Conservative opposition, in 1914, but its operation was delayed until after the war. A group of Southern Irish Nationalists (Sinn Feiners) cooperated with Germany in organizing the Easter Rising in Dublin in 1916. The executions and repressions which followed hardened the division between loyal Irishmen (mainly in Ulster) and the nationalists, who dominated the south. After the First World War the Government of Ireland Act provided for a Northern Irish Parliament at Belfast and a Southern Irish one at Dublin. This was resisted forcibly by the Sinn Feiners, who were opposed by a special British police force known as the Black-and-Tans. Outrages were committed on both sides, the Irish nationalists attacking not only the British but that section of the Irish population which did not sympathize with them. The Irish Free State Act, 1922, repealed the Government of Ireland Act of 1920 and set up the Dominion of the Irish Free State.

In 1937 a new constitution, adopted by plebiscite, renamed the country Eire and declared the national territory to be the whole of Ireland, although the laws of the Irish Parliament were to apply only to Eire. The country was neutral in the Second World War, and in 1948 the Republic of Ireland Act removed the last constitutional link with the U.K. The official name is now the Republic of Ireland.

Since 1970, when British politicians made new proposals for the re-unification of Ireland, there has been an increasing demand for constitutional and legal change to remove those features of Irish law which seemed to reflect the undue influence of the Roman Catholic Church, and which might impede eventual political union. In January 1972 Ireland signed the treaties of accession to the European Economic Community, *q.v.*; this was subsequently approved by referendum.

Ireland comprises the provinces of Leinster, Munster, Connacht, and part of Ulster, *q.v.*, or 26 of the 32 Irish counties. The President (Éamonn de Valéra, *q.v.*, first elected June 1959 and re-elected June 1966) is appointed for seven years by direct popular vote. The Prime Minister, or Taoiseach, is appointed by the President on the nomination of the House of Representatives. Legislation is by the President and Parliament, or Oireachtas, which consists of a Senate (Seanad Éireann) of 60 who represent the universities, labour, the public services and the arts, and a House of Representatives (Dáil Éireann) of 144 elected for five years by adult suffrage and propor-tional representation. An attempt by the government to change the electoral system from proportional representation to direct voting in single-member constituencies was heavily defeated in a referen-dum held on 16 October 1968.

In the elections to the Dáil in June 1969, Fianna Fáil (which main-tains the Sinn Fein tradition, has been the largest single party for over 20 years, and is led by John Lynch, *q.v.*) won an absolute majority over the two other major parties, Fine Gael, the moderate nationalist party led by Liam Cosgrave, *q.v.*, and the Labour Party led by Brendon Corish; however, this was gradually eroded. As a result of the civil disturbances in Northern Ireland the government, which advocated a political solution and denounced the use of force, introduced drastic measures against the illegal Irish Republican Army, *q.v.*, which was using the Republic as a base for its terrorist activities in Ulster. Five Fianna Fáil dissidents then went into opposi-tion, and although he survived a motion of censure in the Dáil over his Northern policy, by November 1971 John Lynch was heading a minority government. Fine Gael and the Labour Party formed a coalition to contest elections called in March 1973. The results were:—Fianna Fáil 69 (75 in 1969); Fine Gael 54 (50); Labour Party 19 (18); others 2. Liam Cosgrave then formed a government with Brendan Corish as his deputy Prime Minister.

Irish Republican Army. An association of radical Irish nationalists claiming to be a continuation of the Irish Republican Volunteers (Sinn Feiners) who seceded from the Southern Irish Volunteers in

1914 over the question of participation in the First World War, received German cooperation in their Easter Rising at Dublin in 1916, proclaimed an Irish Republic, and fought the Irish Free State government in the Civil War of 1922. They regard themselves as the Army of an Irish Republic which includes the six northern counties ruled by the U.K. They were outlawed in 1931 by President Cosgrave, and in 1939 conducted a series of attacks in London and Manchester by means of bomb explosions. Several hundred members were imprisoned in the U.K. and in Ireland. In 1954 and 1955 the I.R.A. carried out raids on barracks in Northern Ireland and the U.K. to obtain arms. At the 1955 General Election to the British Parliament two members of the I.R.A., standing as Anti-Partitionists, obtained a majority of votes in two Northern Ireland constituencies although they were at the time serving jail sentences; they were eventually held to be ineligible as convicted felons. At the 1959 and 1964 General Elections none of the Anti-Partitionists secured a majority, but in 1966 and 1970 one Republican Labour candidate was returned, to be joined in 1970 by one Unity and one Independent Unity candidate (Bernadette Devlin). The campaign gained ground with the formation of the Civil Rights Association in Northern Ireland, and they were instrumental in organizing the armed insurrection in Belfast and Derry. The movement split in December 1969 when the Provisional wing embraced Eire Noa, a plan for a decentralized socialist republic for Ireland to be achieved by military means. The Official wing of the I.R.A., while participating in military retaliation for specific incidents, particularly against the British Army, retains its long-term political programme which is anti-sectarian, unconcerned with the issue of the border, and foresees the unity of the working class throughout Ireland.

I.R.O. International Refugee Organization, *q.v.*

Iron Curtain. The frontiers dividing the U.S.S.R. and the pro-Chinese (Albania) and the pro-Russian (Bulgaria, Czechoslovakia, Hungary, Poland, and Romania) Communist states of eastern Europe from the rest of Europe. The term is used to indicate the lack of freedom of ideas and movement into and out of these seven countries. At Fulton, Missouri, in March 1946, Winston Churchill said: 'From Stettin in the Baltic to Trieste in the Adriatic an Iron Curtain has descended upon the Continent.'

Irredentism. From the Italian word *irredentista,* meaning unredeemed. The advocacy of the recovery by one's country of its lost territories.

Isle of Man. An island in the Irish Sea, off the Cumberland coast, which is part of the United Kingdom of Great Britain and Northern

Ireland, *q.v.*, but which is, for legal purposes, an independent sovereign state under the British crown, with its own judiciary, administering its own common and statute law; area 227 sq. m.; population (1969) 48,000; capital Douglas. The island, which was sold to Alexander III of Scotland by a Norse chieftain in 1266 and was later captured by Edward III of England, was owned from 1609 until 1828 by the Derby family from whom the British parliament purchased the manorial rights. A form of Home Rule was restored in 1866. Government is exercised by the Tynwald, which comprises a House of Keys of 24 members, elected by adult suffrage for five years, and a Legislative Council consisting of the Lieutenant-Governor, the Lord Bishop of Sodor and Man, the First Deemster, the Clerk of the Rolls, the Attorney-General and 7 members elected by the House of Keys. The 1958 Isle of Man Act gave greater fiscal control to the Tynwald which, until the entry of the U.K. into the E.E.C., *q.v.*, in January 1973, determined income tax and customs dues. Since 1961 an Executive Council of 5 members of the House of Keys and 2 members of the Legislative Council has acted with the Lieutenant-Governor.

Isolationists. A group in the U.S.A., particularly active before the Second World War, which opposed any involvement of the U.S.A. in European affairs. The result of the Japanese attack on the U.S. base at Pearl Harbour on 7 December 1941 was a state of war between the U.S.A. and the Japanese-Italian-German alliance. This entry by the U.S.A. into a war with European powers, combined with a close post-war economic relationship between the U.S.A. and Europe, brought about a decline in the number of isolationists. They were succeeded by those who felt that the prime object of American economic and military commitments should be Asia, but admitted the necessity for European commitments.

Israel. An independent state at the eastern end of the Mediterranean Sea; area 7,993 sq. m.; population (1971) 2,999,000, of whom 2,560,000 are Jews; capital Jerusalem. The state was established by proclamation on 14 May 1948 when the British Mandate in Palestine, *q.v.*, came to an end. According to a recommendation by the United Nations General Assembly, a Jewish state and an Arab state were to be set up in Palestine and their boundaries were defined. On the day after the establishment of Israel as the Jewish state its territory was invaded by Egypt, Iraq, Jordan, Lebanon, and Syria; during the fighting (known to Israelis as the 'War of Independence') Israel acquired some of the land allotted to the Arab state but lost an area west of the river Jordan to Jordan, and the Gaza Strip, *q.v.*, to Egypt.

Hostilities ceased in January 1949 and the Tripartite Declaration of 1950, *q.v.*, helped to stabilize the situation although raids by both Israelis and Arabs continued to take place. On 29 October 1956 Israeli forces, probably acting in accordance with an agreement made with France and the U.K., invaded Egypt and soon occupied most of the Sinai peninsula to the east of the Suez Canal. On the next day the U.K. demanded that Egypt and Israel should each withdraw to a distance of ten miles from the Canal. At the United Nations Security Council, however, the U.S.A. asked that Israel should withdraw to its own borders, and did not suggest that Egypt should give up its own territory. The U.S.A. also moved a resolution urging United Nations members to withhold help from Israel until Israeli forces had left Egypt. This resolution, which was supported by the U.S.S.R., was vetoed by the U.K. and France. On 31 October Franco-British forces attacked Egypt, but, after the arrival of a United Nations Emergency force, both they and the Israeli forces withdrew from Egypt, the last Israelis leaving the Gaza Strip in March 1957.

Owing to the Arab refusal to recognize the State of Israel no peace settlement could be negotiated, and for ten years the United Nations Emergency force maintained a cease-fire by policing a demilitarized zone along all Israel's frontiers. On 18 May 1967 President Nasser ordered U.N. forces to leave Sinai and Egyptian troops moved into battle positions. On 22 May the Egyptians blocked the Gulf of Aqaba thereby cutting off the Israeli port of Eilat; on 28 May Iraqi troops entered Jordan as reinforcements and a three-year defence pact was concluded between Jordan and Egypt. On 5 June Israel attacked Egyptian, Jordanian and Syrian-held territory, and in a six-day war drove the Egyptians out of the Sinai peninsula to the west bank of the Suez Canal, captured the Golan Heights from Syria and the West Bank of the river Jordan from Jordan. The old city of Jerusalem was immediately integrated with the State of Israel; the other territories were given the status of 'occupied areas'.

In the U.N. General Assembly, on this occasion, the U.S.A. defended Israel's action as one of self-defence, but owing to Russian support for the Arab position no decision could be agreed and the question was referred back to the Security Council. On 22 November 1967 the Security Council unanimously adopted a resolution, drafted by the U.K., which demanded: (1) that Israel withdraw all troops to her former boundaries; (2) that there should be freedom of navigation and a settlement of the refugee problem; (3) that the political independence of every state in the area be guaranteed; (4) that a special representative be appointed to try to achieve a peace settlement on these terms with the governments concerned. The following day Gunnar Jarring, Swedish Ambassador to Moscow and a former U.N. Mediator in Kashmir, was appointed to head the U.N. Mission to the Middle East. Its failure in 1967–8 and again in 1970 has been due to three factors: the refusal of the Arab states to recognize Israeli sovereignty; continuing guerilla activity, supported by Iraq, Syria and Libya, of the members of the Palestine Liberation Organization, *q.v.*, in defiance of any peace initiatives taken by the principals involved; the increasing reluctance of Israel, in view of the Arab attitude, to withdraw from the strategically important Occupied Arab Territories, *q.v.*, and to negotiate over the future of Jerusalem.

By the Law of Return, enacted on 5 July 1950, every Jew has the right to immigrate to Israel. 1,316,327 had immigrated in the twenty years prior to 1968, when, it was estimated by the Jewish Agency, *q.v.*, that, apart from Russian Jewry, there remained fewer than 250,000 prospective Jewish immigrants from the 'lands of distress'. While the working population increased so rapidly, the government attempted to expand production so that the state could be self-supporting. An adverse trade balance has been partly bridged by German reparations, which ceased in 1965, of about £14 million each year, U.S. aid of a gradually decreasing amount, and gifts and loans from Jews in other parts of the world. In spite of increased agricultural and industrial production the sum earned from exports (which include citrus fruits, textiles, wine and polished diamonds) is less than half the sum required to pay for Israel's essential imports of foodstuffs, crude oil, machinery, iron and steel, chemicals and armaments. In 1970–71 one half of all government expenditure was allocated to defence. The discovery of oil in the Negev has lessened the dependence of the country on imported petroleum, and the completion of an oil pipeline from Eilat to Ashqelon in February 1970 has partly compensated for the interruption in supplies occasioned by the closure of the Suez Canal in 1967. Approximately one half of the total area of Israel is taken up by the Negev, an infertile desert region with an increasing number of farms. A pipeline 66 inches in diameter, which was completed in 1955, carries water from the river Yarkon by Tel Aviv to irrigate 50,000 acres of the western plateau of the Negev. Extensive irrigation of the Negev would necessitate the diversion of the waters of the river Jordan (*see* Jordan Waters).

A coalition government was formed after the 1961 election of Mapai, Mapam, the National Religious Party and A'hdut Avoda with David Ben-Gurion as Prime Minister. He resigned in June 1963 and was succeeded by Levi Eshkol, *q.v.*, then Minister of Finance, a member of Mapai. Personal and political differences (Ben-Gurion was considered to be slightly to the right of Eshkol) led to a split in Mapai, which expelled Ben-Gurion in July 1965. He then founded a new party, the Israel Workers' Party (Rafi) which attracted several former Mapai supporters, including Moshe Dayan, who had been Minister of Agriculture in the Ben-Gurion government. On 4 June 1967 a national government was formed by co-opting to the Cabinet Manahem Beigin (Herut), Joseph Saphir (Liberal), and Dayan (Rafi) who became Minister of Defence. In December 1967, in defiance of Ben-Gurion, Rafi merged with Mapai and A'hdut Avoda thus creating a Labour front controlling 59 of the 120 seats in the Assembly. On the death of Eshkol in February 1969 Golda Meir, *q.v.*, became Prime Minister, retaining Yigal Allon as her Deputy.

At elections to the seventh Knesset, the legislative assembly which consists of a single chamber of 120 members elected for four years by universal suffrage and proportional representation, held on 28 October 1969, the results were: Alignment, a coalition of the Labour Front and Mapam (United Workers' Party), a radical party which believes in a planned economy, and, until the Russians supplied arms to the Arab states, wanted closer ties with the U.S.S.R., 56 seats (63 in the 1965 elections); the Herut-Liberals or Gahal, a right-wing alliance (the nucleus of Herut was the Irgun Zvai Leumi) 26 (22 in 1965); National Religious Party (Hapoel Hamizrachi and Mizrahi, an orthodox religious group which wants to ban public transport on the Sabbath and the sale of pork) 12 (11); National List, led by Ben Gurion, 4 (1); Independent Liberals 4 (4); the ultra-orthodox Agudat Israel 4 (4); Communists 4 (4), three being returned, as in 1965, for the pro-Peking New Communist Party and one for the pro-Moscow Israel Communist Party; Arab lists Co-operative and Fraternity Party 2 (2) and Party of Progress and Development 2 (2), both affiliated to Mapai; Poalei Agudat Israel, the labour wing of Agudat Israel, 2 (2); Ha'olam Hazah (One World), a party founded in 1965 to advocate Israeli-Arab federation 2 (1); Free Centre, formed in the sixth Knesset by a group of defectors from Gahal, 2 (previous strength 4). The result of the election made inevitable the formation of a coalition government since no party had an absolute majority in the Knesset. Golda Meir became Prime Minister of a government which included the Labour Front, Mapam, Gahal, the National Religious Party and the Independent Liberals. In July 1970, following the Israeli government's decision to accept the U.S. peace initiative (the Rogers Plan) which proposed a ninety-day cease-fire between Egypt and

Israel on the Suez Canal front and between Jordan and Israel on the eastern front so that Dr Jarring could continue mediation, the Gahal members withdrew; the government remained in command of a comfortable parliamentary majority.

Istiqlal. The Moroccan Independence Party, founded in 1943. For most of its existence until Morocco became independent in 1956 it was banned by the French; it held its first National Congress in Rabat in November 1955. It defied the French administration by acknowledging only Sidi Mohammed Ben Youssef, the Sultan of Morocco, as head of state and in 1955 it combined with the Algerian National Liberation Front (F.L.N., *q.v.*) to form the Liberation Army of North Africa, pledged to expel the French by military action if necessary. The Party, which contains both conservative and radical elements, draws its support from the townspeople, intellectuals, and parts of the trade union movement. It held a majority of seats in the governments of Si Bekkai (November 1955 to April 1958) and of Ahmed Balafrej (May to November 1958), but in January 1960 the Party split. The political crisis which resulted was one of the factors affecting the decision in May 1960 of King Mohammed V (who died in February 1961) to become Premier. The emergence of a party organized by King Hassan II weakened the Istiqlal, which, in 1970, joined with the Union Nationale des Forces Populaires (U.N.F.P.) to form a National Front opposing the Constitution of 1970 and the amendments of 1972. The merger was to some extent a reversal of the split in 1960.

Italian Somaliland. The name of an area in East Africa which was an Italian colony from 1925 to 1947, when it became the trusteeship territory (now independent) of Somalia, *q.v.*

Italy. An independent European state; area (including the islands of Sicily and Sardinia) 131,000 sq. m.; population (1970) 54,683,000; capital Rome. After years of struggle in which Mazzini, Cavour and Garibaldi played important roles, Italy achieved unity in 1870 under the House of Savoy. From 1925 to 1943 the country was effectively ruled by the dictator Benito Mussolini. A former Socialist, he became Prime Minister in 1922 after entering Rome at the head of 40,000 Fascists: he secured a Fascist majority in the legislature by introducing a law allotting two thirds of the seats to any party which obtained one quarter of the votes at an election. In 1935, prompted by the rapid increase in population and a lack of raw materials, Italy conquered Ethiopia; it then gave assistance to Franco with his Fascist revolution in Spain, and from 1940 supported Germany in the Second World War. As the allied powers invaded Italy the Fascist regime crumbled; Mussolini was killed by partisans in 1945 and King Victor Emmanuel III abdicated in 1946 in favour of his son, Umberto II, who was rejected by a popular referendum which, by a narrow majority, established a republic.

Under the 1947 Constitution there is a bicameral legislature with a Senate of 315 members elected for six years on a regional basis, and a Chamber of Deputies of 630 members elected for five years by universal suffrage. The President is elected for a seven-year term by a two-thirds majority of a joint session of the legislature, sitting with delegates from each of the nineteen Regions of Italy. Giovanni Leone, *q.v.*, a former Christian Democrat Prime Minister and a life Senator, was elected President on 24 December 1971 after 23 ballots. At elections for the Chamber of Deputies held on 7 May 1972 the results were: Christian Democrats, a Roman Catholic party including both right-wing and land-reforming members, led by Giulio Andreotti, the out-going coalition Prime Minister, Mariano Rumor, Emilio Colombo (both former Premiers), and Amintore Fanfani, leader of Democratic Initiative, a militant Christian land-reforming group, 267 seats (266 in May 1968); Communists (the largest Communist Party in Western Europe, with two million members, led by Enrico Berlinguer) 179 (177 in 1968); Socialist Party (left-wing and led by Pietro Nenni, *q.v.*) 61 seats; Social Democratic Party of former President Giuseppe Saragat, *q.v.*, which is comparatively right-wing and anti-Communist and supported by the British Labour Party, 29 seats. In 1968 the combined total of seats for the two Socialist parties, which were then united, was 91. Liberals (fundamentally opposed to land reform) 21 (31 in 1968); Italian Social Movement, which is neo-Fascist, 56 (30); Republican Party, led by Ugo La Malfa, 14 (9). The Socialist Party of Proletarian Unity (a left-wing offshoot of the Nenni Socialists), which had 23 seats in 1968, united with the Communist Party at the 1972 elections; similarly the Monarchists, who had 6 seats in 1968, combined with the Italian Social Movement. Representatives of the German-speaking minority of the South Tirol, *q.v.*, won 3 seats.

From 1948 to 1962 there were nine governments, mainly coalitions between the Christian Democrats and other centre and right-wing parties. In February 1962 Amintore Fanfani formed a government, supported by the Social Democrat and Socialist Parties, which included members of the Social Democrat and Republican Parties as well as Christian Democrats. It was an experiment in the 'opening to the left' or *apertura alla sinistra*. In November 1963 Aldo Moro formed a coalition of the three centre parties and the Socialist Party, with Nenni as Deputy Prime Minister. This participation in a non-

Socialist administration caused the left wing of the Socialist Party to secede in December 1963 and to form the Independent Socialist Party of Proletarian Unity (P.S.I.U.P.); however in October 1966 the remaining Nenni Socialists merged with the Social Democratic Party to form a unified Socialist Party with Nenni as its President. Communist gains in the 1968 elections made the Socialists hesitate to commit themselves to a further coalition with the Christian Democrats, and from June to November 1968 the administration was drawn entirely from Christian Democrats, but dependent for its parliamentary majority on the support, or abstention, of the left. Another coalition government, led by Mariano Rumor (C.D.), with Nenni as Foreign Minister, remained in office until the Socialist Party again divided in July 1969. The success of the Italian Social Movement in local elections dissuaded the Christian Democrats from seeking alliances on the right, but the divisions in the Socialist ranks made the centre-left coalitions of Emilio Colombo and Giulio Andreotti ineffective. The issue of the Divorce Law, approved by the legislature but vigorously opposed by the Vatican, *q.v.*, produced a new crisis in 1971. The Christian Democrats, fearful of losing their Roman Catholic supporters over legalization of divorce, indicated their willingness to join with the extreme right in calling for a general referendum to have the law repealed. This has threatened the traditional cooperation between the Christian Democrats and the secular democratic parties, which has been responsible for keeping the politically powerful Communist Party in opposition.

Nearly half of the working population of Italy is employed on the land, but the number is decreasing rapidly. Olives and olive oil, grapes, wheat, potatoes, cheese, maize and sugar beet are produced. The country is poor in mineral resources, although there are valuable deposits of iron pyrites, mercury and sulphur, and supplies of natural methane. There are large oil reserves in Sicily. Exports, the bulk of which are to other member countries of the European Economic Community, include fruit and citrus fruit, vegetables and tomato preserves, wine, textiles and machinery, but are normally exceeded in value by imports; this adverse balance, which in the past has been offset by foreign aid, tourist traffic, shipping and remittances from Italians overseas, was in 1967 converted into a surplus largely owing to an increase in tourism. There are many depressed agricultural areas, particularly in southern Italy which is at a disadvantage compared with the industrialized north and its excellent road and rail communications with the rest of Europe. Extensive unemployment and under-employment, although relieved in recent years by mobility of labour within the Common Market, have strengthened the Communist Party, and there has not been sufficient investment to solve these problems, and the related problem of under-development in southern Italy.

I.T.O. International Trade Organization, *q.v.*

Ivory Coast. An independent republic; area 124,504 sq. m.; population (1969 estimate) 4,200,000, comprising Agnis-Ashantis, Baoulés, Senoufos, Kroumen, Mandés, Dan-gouros, Kouas and 15,000 Europeans; capital Abidjan. It occupies some 330 miles of the West African coast, between Liberia and Ghana, with the republics of Guinea, Mali and Upper Volta to the north-west and north. The French took a coastal strip in 1842 and annexed the territory in 1893. It later became one of the eight territories comprising French West Africa, *q.v.*, and achieved self-government within the French Community, *q.v.*, on 4 December 1958 and complete independence, after seceding from the Community in June 1960, on 7 August 1960.

Legislative powers are vested in an assembly of 70 members elected every five years by universal suffrage. At elections held on 29 November 1970 every seat was won by the Democratic Party of the Ivory Coast, the only legal political party which replaced the former Union for the Economic and Social Development of the Ivory Coast (the local section of the Rassemblement Démocratique Africain). Both parties were the creation of the President, Félix Houphoüet-Boigny (re-elected in 1970 for a third five-year term) who represented Ivory Coast in the French National Assembly and who supports a close relationship with France.

Agriculture occupies 95 per cent of the population, who produce groundnuts, manioc, yams, rice and rubber for home consumption, and export coffee (which earns nearly half the national income), cocoa, bananas and timber. There are forests of mahogany and palm-oil trees, and deposits of manganese, gold and diamonds. Abidjan is the port not only for Ivory Coast, but also for Upper Volta which is connected by railway to the coast.

Izvestia. A newspaper which is the official organ of the Supreme Soviet, *q.v.*, the legislature of the U.S.S.R. It devotes much of its space to the laws passed by the Supreme Soviet and to the administrative orders of the Russian government, on which it also comments. However, it is not so reliable an exponent of the Communist Party line as *Pravda*, *q.v.* The word *izvestia* means news; the newspaper was founded in 1916.

J

Jagan, Cheddi. Guianese politician; born 1918; educated at Queen's College, British Guiana, Howard University, Washington and the North West University Dental School, Chicago. From 1947 to 1953 he was a member of the Legislative Council; he founded, with Forbes Burnham, *q.v.*, the People's Progressive Party (P.P.P.) of which he has always been the leader. In the short-lived administration of April–October 1953 he was Minister of Agriculture, Lands and Mines and leader of the House of Assembly. He spent six months during 1964 in political detention following riots and demonstrations among the sugar workers for independence. From 1957 to 1961 he was Minister of Trade and Industry and when, in 1961, the P.P.P. won a parliamentary majority with 42·6 per cent of the total vote he was appointed the first Prime Minister of British Guiana. In the 1964 elections, which were held on a basis of proportional representation, *q.v.*, his party failed to win an absolute majority and he was unable, because of his identification with the East Indian section of the population, to form a coalition government with either the People's National Congress or the United Force Party. He refused to resign as Prime Minister; the Governor obtained an order in council to force him to vacate the post and appointed Forbes Burnham to succeed him. He boycotted the Constitutional Conference at which the terms for the independence of British Guiana (now Guyana) were discussed, but remained constitutional leader of the opposition after 1966.

Jamaica. An independent state and member of the British Commonwealth; it comprises the West Indian islands of Jamaica, with an area of 4,411 sq. m., and other islands, including the Turks and Caicos Islands, with an area of 202 sq. m.; population (1970 estimate) 1,861,300, of whom 40 per cent are illiterate; capital Kingston. The main island was seized from the Spaniards by the British in 1655. Of its exports, the majority of which go to the U.S.A., the U.K. and Canada, the most valuable are sugar, bananas, bauxite (the largest in the world) and rum. The tourist trade and remittances from emigrants overseas are important sources of foreign exchange.

In 1944, when the islands were still a British colony, self-government was introduced and extended in November 1957 to include a cabinet system. Jamaica joined the West Indies Federation, *q.v.*, in January 1958, and on 4 July 1959 was granted full self-government. By a referendum held on 19 September 1961 Jamaica voted by 251,935 (53·8 per cent) to 216,400 (46·2 per cent) to leave the Federation, which was dissolved on 31 May 1962. Jamaica became an independent state on 6 August 1962, and has since become a member of the Caribbean Free Trade Area, *q.v.*, and the Organization of American States, *q.v.*

At elections to the House of Representatives held on 29 February 1972 the People's National Party (P.N.P.) won 37 seats (20 at elections held on 21 February 1967), the Jamaica Labour Party 15 seats (33 in 1967) and Independents 1 seat. The P.N.P., led by Michael Manley, *q.v.*, whose father Norman, a former Prime Minister (1955–62), had founded the party in 1938 with the support of the National Workers' Union, to which it is affiliated, on the model of the British Labour Party, advocates moderate socialism and represents the middle class as well as the organized urban workers. The Jamaica Labour Party, founded in 1943, which was in power from 1945 to 1955 under the leadership of Alexander Bustamante, again formed the government after the 1962 elections. Hugh Shearer succeeded to the leadership in April 1967 and became Prime Minister until 1972 when, following the electoral victory of the P.N.P., Michael Manley was appointed in his place. The party is anti-socialist and is supported by most of the business community and many of the illiterate poor. The standard of living is low and unemployment seldom falls below 15 per cent. Both parties agree on the need for increased agricultural and industrial investment.

The sugar and banana industries have suffered in recent years by the British abandonment of colonial preference in favour of buying in the cheapest possible markets, although the U.K. made its accession to the E.E.C., *q.v.*, in 1971 conditional upon a sugar agreement to protect Jamaican exports. The citrus fruit industry has been seriously threatened by Israeli competition and by subsidized U.S. exports to the U.K. Foreign investors have been encouraged to establish new industries by tax concessions and the free import of plant and equipment. An oil refinery was opened in 1964 (by the Esso Standard Oil Co.) and there has been a vast expansion of bauxite and aluminium production since 1967.

Jammu and Kashmir. The name by which the state of Kashmir, *q.v.*, is known in India, and under which it was integrated with the Republic of India on 26 January 1957.

Japan. An independent empire in the Pacific Ocean; area 142,727 sq. m., comprising the four large islands of Honshu, Kyushyu, Hokkaido, and Shikoku, and many smaller islands; population (1971) 104,649,017, including the Ryuku Islands, *q.v.*, most of whom profess Buddhism or Shintoism; capital Tokyo. The Emperors are said to be descended from a dynasty founded in 660 B.C., but from 1186 until 1867 their powers were largely ceremonial. Japan resisted contact with the west until 1853 when Commodore Perry from a gun-boat in Tokyo Bay forced an exchange of goods with U.S. merchants. In 1859 a commercial treaty was signed with the U.S.A. and a rapid process of westernization was begun, during which Japan became a dominant power in Asia. Its first war with China in 1894, in which it acquired Formosa, was followed by war with Russia in 1905, and the acquisition of Karafuto, Korea, and leased territory, including the port of Dairen, in the Kuangtung peninsula; by participation in the First World War on the allied side, which resulted in a Japanese Mandate over the former German South Sea Islands – Bismarck, Marshall, and the Carolines; by intervention in the U.S.S.R. in 1918; by seizure of Manchuria in 1931; by a second war with China in 1937; and by its attack on the U.S.A. in 1941. When U.S. aircraft dropped the first atomic bomb upon Hiroshima on 6 August 1945, and a second atomic bomb upon Nagasaki on 9 August 1945, the Emperor broadcast an appeal for terms of surrender and the war ended. The large population of Japan and the shortage of raw materials were partly responsible for its expansionist policies and the accession to power of a military caste, the Gunbatsu, supported by the leading industrial combines, known as the Zaibatsu.

After the 1945 surrender Japan was occupied by the allied forces under General Douglas MacArthur. A new Constitution came into force in 1947; it established a Supreme Court, renounced war, and abandoned the doctrine of the divinity of the Emperor. Legislative authority is vested in a Diet comprising a House of Representatives of 486 members elected for four years and a House of Councillors for which elections are held every three years to elect half of the House's 250 members, whose terms run for six years. Executive authority is vested in a Cabinet responsible to the Diet. The functions of the Emperor are purely ceremonial. The Allied Supreme Command broke up the Zaibatsu and removed 1,200 firms from the control of 11 huge concerns, although by 1952 the pre-war position had been largely restored by Japanese business interests in defiance of allied policy. The 1947 Constitution provided that Japan should never have any land, sea or air forces, but at the request of General MacArthur a constabulary of 75,000 men was recruited in 1950. This National Police Reserve, equipped with tanks, later became the National Safety Force and then the Ground Self-Defence Force; the uniformed strength of the army was 250,000 in 1968. Japan regained independence by the San Francisco Peace Treaty of 1952; since 1960 her defence has been guaranteed by the U.S.–Japan Security Treaty, which may be reviewed at the request of either party any time after 1970.

The Liberals, who came to power in 1948, were often attacked for being too closely linked with the U.S.A. although the special trade arrangements made by the U.S.A. were largely responsible for Japan's swift economic recovery and highly favourable trade balance. In November 1954 dissident Liberals and the Progressives (the principal opposition party) merged to form the Democratic Party, which won the largest number of votes at the 1955 election. In November 1955 the Democrats and the Liberals merged themselves into the Liberal-Democratic Party. At elections on 22 May 1958 the ruling Liberal-Democrats were returned to power with 298 seats, the Socialists winning 167 seats. Both the major parties advocated the immediate ending of nuclear tests, but disagreed over the proposal that the Constitution should be revised, and the Liberal-Democrats did not obtain the two-thirds majority needed to make constitutional amendments. Nobusuke Kishi, a lawyer, who had become Premier in February 1956, continued in office until July 1960, when he was succeeded by Hayato Ikeda who resigned in November 1964 as the result of ill health, and was in turn succeeded by Eisaku Sato. Mounting criticism of the U.S. military presence, and the conditions under which Okinawa, q.v., was restored to Japanese sovereignty, was reflected in an increased Socialist vote at local elections. Japan's failure, and subsequent discrediture at the U.N., to save a seat in the General Assembly for Taiwan in October 1971, caused Sato to resign. He was succeeded in July 1972 by Kakuei Tanaka, q.v. At elections held on 10 December 1972 for the 491 seats in the House of Representatives the results were: Liberal-Democrats 271 (297 in the previous parliament); Socialists 118 (87); Democratic Socialists 19 (29); Communists 38 (14); Independents 16 (3); Komeito, or Clean Government Party, the secular arm of the Buddhist Soka Gakkai movement, 29 (47).

Japan is the most highly industrialized power in Asia, with a wide range of heavy and light industries and important exports of cotton and rayon fabrics, cotton yarn, raw silk, iron and steel and knitted goods; it is one of the world's largest shipbuilders. Although there is still a strong antipathy towards China, the success of Japan's export drive before the Second World War was largely due to the China trade, and in June 1972 the Japanese Foreign Minister offered to apologize to China for Japan's wartime actions in order to normalize relations between the two countries. Many of Japan's pre-war economic problems remain unsolved; the population is still increasing at the rate of 1 per cent each year, and there is a dearth of natural resources. Some right-wing elements have demanded the return of southern Sakhalin and some of the Kurile Islands, which became part of the U.S.S.R. after the Second World War. Others seek to reach agreement with the Asian Communist powers and so improve the prospects for Japanese trade in China. Trade with China represents 4 per cent of Japan's total trade, whereas before the Second World War it represented 40 per cent. The chief exports to China are fertilizers, industrial plant, steel and textiles.

Jenkins, Roy. British Labour Party politician; born 11 November 1920; educated at Abersychan Grammar School and Balliol College, Oxford. After war service in the Army from 1942 to 1946 he went on to the staff of the Industrial and Commercial Finance Corporation. He entered Parliament in 1948 as the member for Southwark Central; since 1950 he has represented the Stechford division of Birmingham. From 1949 to 1950 he was Parliamentary Private Secretary to the Secretary of State for Commonwealth Relations. He is the author of several important political biographies of British Prime Ministers and parliamentarians. From 1962 to 1964 he undertook the direction of financial operations for the John Lewis Partnership. In October 1964 he became Minister of Aviation. In December 1965 he entered the Cabinet as Home Secretary, and in November 1967 was appointed to succeed James Callaghan, *q.v.*, as Chancellor of the Exchequer until 1970. In July 1970 he was elected Deputy Leader of the Parliamentary Labour Party with an absolute majority in the first ballot over his two opponents, Michael Foot and Frederick Peart. In November 1971, following the decision of the House of Commons to enter the European Economic Community which he had supported, he was re-elected Deputy Leader for the year 1971-2, but on a second ballot, polling 140 votes to 126 for Michael Foot. He resigned from the Shadow Cabinet, *q.v.*, and from the Deputy Leadership in April 1972 in protest against the decision of the Parliamentary Labour Party to press for the holding of a consultative referendum on the Common Market issue. He regarded the referendum as a 'dangerous innovation in British politics' and a 'splendid weapon for demagogues and dictators'.

Jewish Agency. An organization which links the state of Israel with Jews in the rest of the world. It was established under the terms of the Mandate for Palestine, *q.v.*, given by the League of Nations to the U.K., which said that 'an appropriate Jewish Agency shall be recognized as a public body for the purpose of advising and cooperating with the administration of Palestine in such economic, social, and other matters as may affect the establishment of the Jewish national home' The Jewish Agency today is, for all practical purposes, a world organization, with headquarters divided between Jerusalem and New York. A law passed in the Israeli parliament gave the Agency extra-territorial rights and made it responsible for the absorption of immigrants, land development, and cooperation with Jewry outside Israel, including Jewish institutions and organizations willing to participate in the building up of the state. Its activities include all problems concerned with the cultural and economic progress of Israel as far as they interest or affect Jewry outside the state. It has, for example, received 18 per cent of the reparations paid by the German Federal Republic to Jews between 1952 and 1966, and it records all the statistical information relating to immigration into Israel.

John XXIII. Angelo Giuseppe Roncalli, 263rd Pope; born 25 November 1881 at Sotto il Monte, near Bergamo, Lombardy, the son of a peasant; educated at the episcopal seminary in Bergamo and at the pontifical seminary in Rome, where he was ordained on 10 August 1904, thereupon becoming private secretary to the Bishop of Bergamo, a leading figure in the Catholic Social Movement. He served in the army in the First World War, returning to Bergamo until 1921, when he was called to Rome by Benedict XV to reorganize the missionary work of the Sacred Congregation for the Propagation of the Faith. In 1935 Pius XI made him Titular Archbishop of Areopoli and Apostolic Visitor to Bulgaria; he later became Nuncio to Bulgaria and (in 1925) Apostolic Delegate to Greece and then to Turkey where he stayed until the end of the Second World War. In January 1945 he was appointed Papal Nuncio to France, where he carried out successfully the difficult task of resisting French requests for the withdrawal of a large number of Bishops who were alleged to have collaborated with the Germans; he also concerned himself with the activities of worker priests. He was created a Cardinal and Patriarch of Venice in January 1953, and was elected by conclave to succeed Pius XII as Pope on 28 October 1958. His tenure of office was remarkable for the liberalizing influence he exerted on the Church's attitude to social questions; his encyclical, *q.v.*, *Mater et Magistra*, revising the earlier *Rerum Novarum* of Leo XII which denounced the socialist state, accepted that socialization could, in certain cases, be for the common good. He died on 3 June 1963, and was succeeded by Paul VI, *q.v.*

Johnson, Lyndon Baines. Sworn in as President of the U.S.A. on 22 November 1963 upon the assassination of President Kennedy; born 27 August 1908 in Gillespie County, Texas, the son of a member of the Texas legislature. His first appearance in Washington, D.C., was in 1931 as assistant to a Texas member of the House of Representatives, and in 1935 he became Texas director of the National Youth Administration. He was elected to the House of Representatives in 1938 and to the Senate in 1948, becoming Democratic leader of the Senate in 1953. He held that post, despite a severe heart attack in 1955, until, after the elections of November 1960, he became Vice-President in January 1961. Having served for nearly a year as President after the assassination of Kennedy he was chosen as Democratic Presidential candidate and defeated the Republican candidate, Barry Goldwater, in the elections of November 1964. He did not contest the elections of November 1968. He died on 22 January 1973.

Jordan. An independent kingdom bounded on the north by Syria, on the east by Iraq, on the south by Saudi Arabia and on the west by Israel; area 37,700 sq. m.; population (1971 estimate) 2,418,000, of whom 1,600,000 live in East Jordan; capital Amman. The language is Arabic and Islam is the state religion. Formerly an Emirate under Turkish rule, the area was put under British Mandate after the First World War and became independent as the Hashemite Kingdom of Jordan in 1946, although the name of Transjordan was in general use until 1949. Jordan originally consisted of territory to the east of the river Jordan but, on the establishment of Israel, it extended its frontiers to include part of Palestine, *q.v.*, west of the river, which it formally incorporated on 24 April 1950.

Under the 1951 Constitution the country is governed by an Executive Council of 12 Ministers which is responsible to the legislature of a Senate (30 nominated by the King) and a House of Representatives (60 members, 30 from each side of the river Jordan, elected by manhood suffrage). King Hussein (born 1935) ascended the throne in 1952 on the deposition, by the legislature, of his father, King Tala, who was mentally ill. In April 1965, the King nominated his brother, Crown Prince Hassan, as his successor, passing over his own son whose mother, the English-born Princess Muna and Hussein's second wife, was never accorded the title of Queen.

In 1958 Jordan joined Iraq in the Arab Federation, *q.v.*, which became known as the Arab Union, *q.v.* After the overthrow of the monarchy in Iraq King Hussein claimed to have succeeded King Faisal as head of the Union, but he soon accepted that the Union had ceased to exist. During 1958, despite the termination the previous year of the Anglo-Jordanian Treaty of 1948, King Hussein was given the support of British forces to maintain his regime against an attempted *coup d'état* instigated by Egypt. From 1960 Jordan became increasingly committed to Arab League policies. At the League summit conference in 1964 King Hussein pledged support for a joint Arab force against Israel, which implied his acceptance of Russian arms with which all other League members were equipped. He also agreed to exploit the Jordan Waters, q.v., for the sole benefit of the Arab states.

In May 1967, in anticipation of a military conflict with Israel, Iraqi troops entered Jordan and a defence agreement was concluded with Egypt. However the Six-Day War of June 1967 between Israel and the bordering Arab states of Jordan, Syria and Egypt resulted in the recapture by Israel of all Jordanian territory on the west bank of the river Jordan. The old city of Jerusalem was incorporated into the state of Israel and the rest of the area (approximately 2,165 sq. m.) was accorded the status of 'occupied territory'. From 1967 to 1970 militant guerilla organizations, determined to prevent Jordan and Egypt from concluding any political settlement with Israel which would recognize as permanent the loss of Palestine, q.v., threatened the authority of King Hussein within Jordan and nullified the cease-fire arrangements made with Israel. These groups of Fedayeen (commandos), of which the two most prominent are Fatah, q.v., and the Popular Front for the Liberation of Palestine, q.v., were largely recruited from the refugees, estimated at 730,000 in number, who had fled from the west bank since 1956. In 1970 their activities, together with the multiple hijacking of aircraft all over Europe and the destruction of three western aircraft on an airstrip in Jordan, brought about a civil war. Between January and July 1971 government troops effectively re-established their authority over the country, and the Fedayeen were thereafter confined to certain border areas and to exclusively anti-Israel activity. By July the Prime Minister of Jordan, Wasfi Tal, had announced the extermination of the guerillas; he was assassinated in Cairo in November 1971 by exiled Fedayeen. In March 1972 King Hussein made new proposals for an Israeli-Jordan settlement: the east and west banks of the Jordan were to be linked in a federation to be called the United Arab Kingdom; the west bank would be known as Palestine and the two regions would have their separate governments and judiciaries; their capitals would be respectively Amman and Jerusalem. Israel rejected the plan as unacceptable although it resembled in many respects a plan for the west bank produced by Yigal Allon, Israel's Deputy Prime Minister, shortly before the 1967 war. Egypt broke off diplomatic relations with Jordan.

The loss of the west bank, which contains Jordan's most fertile land (25 per cent of the total cultivable area) supporting some half of the population, and which includes all the historical and biblical places of interest to the tourist, has had serious economic consequences. Jordan now depends on its main resource, the extraction of phosphate rock from the Dead Sea and its export through the country's only port, Aqaba, on the Gulf of Aqaba. Plans for road development, the restoration of the Hejaz railway, the canalization of the Yarmuk river, a Jordan tributary on the Syria–Jordan frontier, and a hydro-electric power station at Zarqa, which were dependent upon overseas, and especially U.S., aid, have been interrupted by the war. There is a major unemployment problem; more than one-third of the population are refugees from Palestine. Through the Arab Economic Development Fund, established in September 1967, Jordan receives £40 million annually from Kuwait, Libya and Saudi-Arabia to help sustain the economic losses that were suffered in the war; since 1970 Libya has withheld its contribution. British and U.S. aid continues on a reduced scale, and payments are received from the Trans-Arabian Pipeline Company, *q.v.* (Tapline), whose oil pipeline runs across Jordan.

Jordan Waters. The name by which the river Jordan and its main tributaries, the Hasbani which rises in Lebanon, the Dan, rising in Israel, the Banias, rising in Syria, and the Yarmuk rising in Syria and flowing through Jordan, are known. Only Israel and Jordan depend on these waters for irrigation purposes and neither country can afford the necessary investment without foreign aid. A plan for the unified development of the Jordan Waters by which Jordan was allocated 60 per cent and Israel 40 per cent of the total flow, was proposed in 1953 by the U.S.A., but political differences between Israel and the Arab states prevented its implementation and foreign countries became resigned to assisting individual national schemes. The first of these was the construction by the Israelis in 1960 of a canal south from Lake Tiberias; in 1961 Jordan diverted nearly half the annual flow of the Yarmuk river through a tunnel into the East Ghor canal which runs from north to south along the east bank of the Jordan. But when in 1964 the Israelis used pumps to raise the water from Lake Tiberias to the level of the coastal plain, in the hope of irrigating the desert region of the Negev, the Arab states threatened to divert the waters of the Hasbani and the Banias and thus restrict the flow of the river Jordan. The harm which this would inflict on Israel is questionable. The river Dan provides a constant flow of 45 per cent of the total volume of water into the north of Lake Tiberias; Israel is embarking on extensive sea-water distillation projects; and U.S. and other Western governments have made their investment contingent upon both Israel and the Arab states observing the share of the Jordan Waters allocated in the original plan of 1953.

Junta. From the Latin word *juncta* meaning joined. An administrative council, especially in Italy or Spain. This word and the word *junto* are also used to describe a political faction or group in power, especially where such power has been secured by force or by political manoeuvring as opposed to a democratic process.

K

Kamerun. The name of a German protectorate on the Gulf of Guinea south-east of Nigeria, which was conquered by British and French forces during the First World War and divided, by the Milner-Simon Agreement of 1919, into a British sphere (*see* Cameroons, British), and a French sphere (*see* Cameroons, French) which in 1960 became the independent republic of Cameroun, *q.v.*

Kardelj, Edward. Yugoslav Communist politician; President of the Federal Assembly of Yugoslavia from 1963 to 1967; Secretary of the Central Committee of the League of Communists of Yugoslavia since 1966; member of the Council of the Federation since 1967, and of its Executive Bureau since 1969; born in Ljubljana, Slovenia, on 27 January 1910. After qualifying as a teacher in 1928 at the Ljubljana Teachers' College, he studied economics and political science and worked in the then illegal Yugoslav Communist Party, being imprisoned from 1930 to 1932 for his political activities. He was the author of many hundreds of Communist pamphlets. From 1934 to 1937 he lived abroad and visited among other places Moscow and Odessa, where he underwent a training course in the organization of underground movements; on his return to Yugoslavia he spent several years in prison.

After the German invasion in 1941 he helped to organize the Partisan movement in Yugoslavia, and became a member of the headquarters staff of the National Army of Liberation. In November 1943 Kardelj, representing Slovenia, was elected as the first Vice-President of the new National Liberation Committee, and on 2 March 1945 became Vice-President of Yugoslavia, Minister for the Constitution (which he largely drafted), and President of the Control Commission, holding the two latter posts till 31 August 1948, when he became Foreign Minister. He had already represented his country many times at United Nations and other international conferences. He is a leading Communist theorist, having written a number of books on Yugoslav international and domestic policy, and has been described as the chief political architect of the new Yugoslavia. He was in frequent touch with Russian Communist leaders until Yugoslavia's secession from the Cominform, *q.v.*, in 1948, and is one of the few non-Russians ever to be honoured with the Order of Lenin.

Kashmir. The most northerly state of British India, area 86,024 sq. m.; population (1941 census), 4,021,616, of whom all except 880,000 were Moslems; capital Srinagar. Most of the 807,000 Hindus live in the Jammu district, and in deference to them the state is known throughout India as Jammu and Kashmir. After the partition of India in 1947, the Maharajah, Sir Hari Singh, who was himself a Hindu, announced the accession of Kashmir to the Republic of India, a decision unacceptable to Pakistan in view of the large numbers of Moslems in the state. Fighting broke out between Hindus and Moslem tribesmen, and both India and Pakistan moved in troops. In December 1947 the Indian government, alleging armed intervention in the state by Pakistan, referred the dispute to the Security Council. A Peace Commission was set up and on 26 July 1949 a cease-fire line was agreed, but the Indian government rejected the Commission's suggestion to appoint an arbitrator whose decision would be binding on both sides, lest this should involve a plebiscite, the result of which would undoubtedly favour Pakistan. On five occasions between 1948 and 1957 the Security Council passed resolutions urging that a plebiscite should be held in Kashmir to determine its future status; India's refusal to agree has so far rendered them unenforceable.

The government of Kashmir, headed by Sheikh Abdullah, the leader of the National Conference from 1947 until 1953 when he was imprisoned and replaced by Bakshi Ghulam Mohammed, resisted integration with the Indian Union until 26 January 1957 when the state was incorporated, in spite of U.N. protests, into the Republic of India. In 1951 the Maharajah left Kashmir, a republic was proclaimed and the Maharajah's son, Karan Singh, was elected as Sadar-i-Ryasat, or head of state. The Bakshi was removed from office, and subsequently imprisoned, and the National Conference replaced by the Congress Party, q.v., in 1964 when Ghulam Mohammed Sadig became Chief Minister. Open war broke out between India and Pakistan in Kashmir in August 1965; by the Tashkent Agreement, q.v., a truce was arranged in January 1966. In December 1971 Indian forces invaded Azad Kashmir after repeated breaches of the 1966 cease-fire line had been reported. A truce was agreed on 17 December but neither side withdrew immediately, and the issue of Kashmir was deferred, the Indian government indicating that a peace settlement with Pakistan would be contingent upon recognition of Indian sovereignty.

India has spent considerable sums on the development of its communications with the south-east part of the state. Roads and schools have been built, hydro-electric projects initiated, land redistribution carried out, and jobs have been found elsewhere in India for Kashmir's educated urban unemployed. This is in sharp contrast to the policy pursued in Azad ('Free') Kashmir, the north-west area held by Pakistan, in which there was increasing poverty and economic stagnation, as well as political repression, until a new Constitution in September 1970 provided for a legislative assembly of 25 members and an elected President.

The allocation of water to Pakistan from the rivers which flow through, or rise in, Kashmir, was settled in 1960 by the Indus Waters Treaty, *q.v.*; this disposed of Pakistan's claim to Kashmir on the ground that its water supply was endangered.

In January 1968 Sheikh Abdullah, who remains Kashmir's most influential politician, was freed after nearly fourteen years in detention. His release coincided with the passing, in the Indian Parliament, of the Unlawful Activities Bill, which prohibits the preaching of secession. His party, the Kashmiri Plebiscite Front, which, although not represented in the National Assembly, is the most popular political organization, has kept alive the issue of the future status of Kashmir within the Indian Union. The decision of the Front to contest local elections in 1969 and five of the six Lok Sabha seats for the State in 1971 led to its prohibition by the Indian government, and the serving of externment orders on Sheikh Abdullah and two other Front leaders. Following the Simla agreement between India and Pakistan in March 1972 that the Kashmir question should be settled bilaterally, Sheikh Abdullah continued to press for a U.N. plebiscite. The Indian government's attitude, that Kashmir is not in dispute and remains irrevocably part of India, reflects parliamentary pressure from Jan Sangh and other Hindu opposition groups, and Congress Party fears that any move to give Kashmir more autonomy might encourage separatism throughout India.

Katanga (Shaba). One of the 6 provinces (there are now 8) of Zaïre, *q.v.*, the former Belgian Congo, it purported to secede from the rest of the country on 11 July 1960, eleven days after independence had been declared. The revenues (and therefore the foreign exchange) obtained from the rich cobalt, copper, and other mines in Katanga would have been lost by the central government at Léopoldville if the secession had been successful. Katanga, in the south-east of Zaïre, is bounded to the east, south-east, and south by Tanzania, Zambia, and Angola, respectively. It had a population in 1967 of 1,853,089.

On 8 August 1960 Moïse Tshombe, *q.v.*, of the Conakat Party, helped by Belgian interests (including especially the Union Minière de Haut Katanga) was declared head of state. For the next 12 months there were inconclusive negotiations between the central government, Tshombe, the United Nations, South Kasai, and others, often interrupted by fighting; on 13 September 1961 United Nations forces entered Katanga and declared that secession had ended, but in fact fighting continued. Five days later the United Nations Secretary-General, Dag Hammarskjöld, was killed in an air crash while visiting the country.

In December 1961 Tshombe agreed at Kitona to end the secession on condition that Katanga should retain control of its own taxation within any Congolese federation. In September 1962 he agreed that half of the mining revenues should go to the central government and that the Katangese forces were to be merged with those of the central government within two months. In December 1962 United Nations forces, with active support from the U.S. government, broke the Katangese resistance and established control of the principal towns. They remained in Katanga until June 1964.

As a province, Katanga was divided first into two (North and South) and then into three (North, South, and Lualaba) in 1962; further boundary alterations took place in 1963, and the provinces became known as North Katanga, East Katanga, and Lualaba provinces. The latter alterations also had the effect of removing Tshombe from the presidency of the government of South Katanga. However, after July 1964, when Tshombe became Prime Minister of Zaïre, Katanga came more firmly under the control of the central government than any other province. In December 1966 the assets of the Union Minière were expropriated by the government and transferred to a new company, Société Générale Congolaise de Minerais, in which the government held 60 per cent of the shares. In the course of the policy of 'Africanization', launched by President Mobutu in January 1972, Katanga province was renamed Shaba, the Swahili word for copper.

Kaunda, Kenneth David. Zambian politician; born 1924 at Lubwa and educated at Lubwa Training School where he later, from 1944 to 1947, was headmaster. After working as a welfare officer in the Chingola copper mine he became active in African nationalist politics. From being secretary of the Lubwa branch in 1950, he quickly rose to be provincial organizer in 1952, and Secretary-General in 1953, of the North Rhodesian African National Congress (A.N.C.). Five years later he established the Zambia African National Congress as a breakaway group, and was imprisoned when the party was banned. In 1960 he was elected first president of the United National Independence Party (U.N.I.P.), and in 1963 president of the Pan-African Freedom Movement for East, Central and South Africa, q.v. As a result of the elections held in 1962 the U.N.I.P. and A.N.C. (led by Harry Nkumbula) obtained together a majority of 21 to 16 seats over the United Federal Party; a nationalist coalition was formed and Kaunda was appointed Minister of Local Government and Social Welfare. In January 1964 he was made Prime Minister of Northern Rhodesia and when independence was achieved on 24 October 1964 he became President of the Republic of Zambia.

Kazungula. A strip of land, 400 yards in extent, on the south bank of the Zambesi river which constitutes the border between Botswana and Zambia. South Africa has questioned the existence of such a border, claiming that the Kazungulan river frontage is part of the Caprivi strip which extends from South-West Africa. Botswana bases its claim on long-unchallenged usage as well as on law. The issue is of importance because of the plan to build a modern highway and commercial ferry to link Zambia with Botswana, which is otherwise completely surrounded by countries which practise some form of apartheid, *q.v.* South Africa wants to close this frontier because it is the escape route for political refugees from the Union and from South-West Africa, Rhodesia and Angola, who pass through Botswana and across the 'Freedom Ferry', *q.v.*, at Kazungula into Zambia.

Kellogg Pact. Officially called a General Pact for the Renunciation of War, it was a treaty concluded by nine powers on 27 August 1928 on the initiative of Frank B. Kellogg, then U.S. Secretary of State, and by 1930 adopted by nearly all the nations in the world, by which war was condemned as an instrument for settling international disputes. The nine original signatories were Belgium, Czechoslovakia, France, Germany, Italy, Japan, Poland, the U.K., and the U.S.A. Although the signatories agreed that settlement of disputes should be achieved only by pacific means, there was no provision for the enforcement of this obligation or for consultation among the signatories in the event of a breach of the pact.

Kennedy, Edward Moore. U.S. lawyer and Democratic politician; born 22 February 1932 at Boston, Massachusetts; a Roman Catholic, and, like his brother Robert Kennedy, *q.v.*, educated at Harvard University and the University of Virginia Law School. He served as a private in the U.S. army from 1951 to 1953, subsequently taking up a legal career and becoming Assistant District Attorney for Massachusetts. He acted as a campaign manager in the successful Presidential campaign of his brother, John Kennedy, *q.v.*, in 1960, and in 1962 and 1970 was elected Senator for Massachusetts. He was given a two-months suspended sentence for leaving the scene of an accident in the river at Chappaquidick Island on 18 July 1969 when he escaped from his submerged car but his passenger was drowned. In January 1969 he was elected Assistant Majority Leader in the Senate, but was defeated by Robert Byrd when he stood for re-election in January 1971. He was the first choice of George McGovern, *q.v.*, whom he had supported throughout the Democratic Primary election campaign in 1972, as his Vice-Presidential nomination, but he refused to stand.

Kennedy, John Fitzgerald. President of the U.S.A. from January 1961 to November 1963; born 29 May 1917 in Boston, Massachusetts, son of Joseph Kennedy, a former Ambassador to the U.K. and highly successful businessman of Irish extraction; he was a Roman Catholic. He graduated from Harvard University in 1940 and later served in the U.S. Navy, earning distinction in 1943 when he saved the lives of his crew members after his motor torpedo vessel had been run down and sunk by a Japanese destroyer. He was invalided out of the Navy, and after working as a journalist for the International News Service was elected as a Democrat to the House of Representatives in 1946. He defeated Cabot Lodge in 1952 in a contest for the Massachusetts seat in the Senate, and in November 1960 defeated Richard Nixon, *q.v.*, in the Presidential election by a narrow margin. His Presidency was remarkable for his handling of the discovery of Russian offensive missile sites in Cuba, *q.v.*; the encouragement he gave to U.S. participation in the economic development of Latin America through the Alliance for Progress, *q.v.*, and in the General Agreement on Tariffs and Trade, *q.v.*, by which the tariff cuts of the Kennedy Round, *q.v.*, were effected; and the legislation on Civil Rights, *q.v.*, which he and his successor, Lyndon Johnson, *q.v.*, forced through a hostile Congress. On 22 November 1963 he was shot dead in Dallas, Texas. A Commission, headed by Chief Justice Warren of the Supreme Court, issued a report stating that his assassin was one Lee Harvey Oswald.

Kennedy, Robert Francis. U.S. Democratic politician; born 20 November 1925 at Boston, Massachusetts, and educated at Milton Academy, Massachusetts, Harvard University, and the University of Virginia Law School. He served in the U.S. Naval Reserve as a Lieutenant from 1944 to 1946 and in 1948 was a war correspondent in Palestine. He was an attorney in the Criminal Division of the U.S. Department of Justice from 1951 to 1952; he was then successively manager of the successful election campaign of his brother John Kennedy, *q.v.*, for a Senatorship in 1952; Assistant Counsel of the Senate Permanent Sub-Committee on Investigations (the so-called McCarthy Committee) in 1953; and Chief Counsel to the Democratic Minority Party in 1954, to the Hoover Commission, 1953–4, and to the Senate Select Committee on Improper Activities in the Labor or Management Field, 1957–9. In 1960 he was manager of his brother's successful campaign for the Presidency, and in 1961 he was appointed Attorney-General. He retained this office in the administration of President Johnson until his resignation from the cabinet in September 1964 to contest the New York Senatorial Election. In November 1964 he defeated the incumbent Republican, and became Senator for New York State. He was a contender for the Democratic Presidential nomination in 1968, and in the course of the campaign, at the count of the Californian Primary elections, he was shot by a Jordanian Arab, Sirhan Bishara Sirhan, on 4 June 1968. He died of the wound two days later.

Kennedy Round. Name given to the meetings at Geneva of the sixth negotiating conference of the General Agreement on Tariffs and Trade (G.A.T.T.), *q.v.*, which began in 1964. Their completion in June 1967 coincided with the expiry (on 30 June) of the Trade Expansion Act, enabling the U.S.A. to make substantial tariff concessions, which was put through Congress by President Kennedy in 1962. The Kennedy Round resulted in unprecedented tariff reductions, a cereals agreement and the adoption of an anti-dumping code. The Act made possible tariff cuts of 100 per cent on manufactured goods in which the U.S.A. and the member countries of the European Economic Community (Common Market), *q.v.*, among them accounted for more than 80 per cent of the trade of the free world; this provision could have been applied over a wide range of products had the British application to join the Common Market in 1961 been successful. The Trade Expansion Act was used as a basis for proposals for a North Atlantic Free Trade Area, but these were abandoned in 1971 when the U.K. signed the treaties of accession to E.E.C.

Kenya. An East African republic and member of the British Commonwealth; area 224,960 sq. m.; population (1969) 10,942,705 including 10,733,202 Africans, 139,037 Asians, 40,593 Europeans and 27,886 Arabs; capital Nairobi. The Africans comprise four main ethnic groups: Bantu (Kikuyu, Kamba, Luyha and others), which is the largest, Nilotic (Luo), Nilo-Hamitic (Masai, Samburu, Nandi and Kipsigis), and Hamitic (Somali, Boran and others). The Kikuyu and Luo tribes provide most of the personnel for government administration and commerce, and there is considerable rivalry between them, and between both and other tribes as a result. Since 1966 a policy of Africanization has caused large numbers of Asians to leave the country; those who had not taken out Kenyan citizenship relied on their British passports to give them sanctuary in the U.K., but restrictions imposed on immigrants by the U.K. government rendered many of them stateless. Kenya is economically dependent on its agricultural products (especially coffee, tea, sisal, maize, hides and skins) which provide nearly 40 per cent of the annual income. The Royal Commission on East Africa reported in 1955 that increased agricultural productivity was essential and could be achieved by substituting private ownership for the customary African system of tribal ownership, by the use of fertilizers, crop specialization, and mechanization, and by the construction of more roads and railways. There are scarcely any minerals; wollastonite was discovered in 1965 and has encouraged hopes of a ceramic industry. The basic problem of government is the maintenance of the fertility of the land, and the attraction of capital, so as to create work for an expanding population in manufacturing industry, farming and forestry.

For some time before independence the structure of government was influenced by the need for strong measures against Mau Mau, q.v. The success of these measures was followed by pressure for reform from the African leaders. Elections to the Legislative Council in 1961 and to the House of Representatives in 1963, when Kenya became self-governing, were contested by two major parties: Kenya African National Union (K.A.N.U.), whose leaders included Jomo Kenyatta, q.v., Tom Mboya, who was assassinated in July 1969, Oginga Odinga, q.v., and James Gichuru, and Kenya African Democratic Union (K.A.D.U.) led by Ronald Ngala. The African People's Party, which drew most of its support from the Kamba tribe in the Eastern Region, united with K.A.N.U. in September 1963. At the 1963 elections K.A.N.U., which obtained 83 seats, favoured a policy of centralization, while K.A.D.U. (33 seats) inclined to federalism and regional autonomy for the one special area and seven Regions, Nairobi area, Coast Region, Eastern Region, North-Eastern Region, Central Region, Rift Valley Region, Nyanza Region, and Western Region, into which Kenya was divided.

Jomo Kenyatta, who took office as Prime Minister 1 June 1963, and as President when Kenya became a republic on 12 December 1964, introduced, in November 1964, a Constitution Amendment Bill to diminish the powers of the Regions and concentrate all legal authority in the central government. Changes in the 1963 Constitution required the endorsement of 75 per cent of the members of both Upper and Lower Houses. After initial protest, K.A.D.U. went into voluntary dissolution, Ngala gave his support to the Bill, becoming a member of the government until his death in 1972, and Kenya became temporarily a one-party state. A unicameral legislature with 170 members was introduced in December 1966. Following the resignation of the Vice-President, Oginga Odinga, in April 1966 and his formation of a new party, the Communist Kenya People's Union (K.P.U.), a further Constitutional Amendment Act was passed requiring those members who had changed their party allegiance to seek re-election. At the little election held in June 1966 K.A.N.U. gained a majority of the contested seats, but Oginga Odinga was returned to lead the K.P.U. which was recognized as the official parliamentary opposition until it was banned in October 1969 following Luo demonstrations at Kisumu against President Kenyatta. In 1971 Oginga Odinga rejoined K.A.N.U.

In 1967 Kenya entered an East African Economic Community, *q.v.*, with Uganda and Tanzania.

Kenyatta, Jomo. President of Kenya; born in 1893 near Nairobi into a Kikuyu family, and educated at a Scottish Presbyterian Mission School. He worked for some years as a clerk in Nairobi and later for the Kikuyu Independent Schools Association. In 1922 he became General Secretary of the Kenya Central Association, which wanted to recover the lands lost by Africans under a law, passed in 1921, which made them tenants-at-will and permitted only whites to hold leases. He represented the Kikuyu on several government committees and Royal Commissions and travelled widely, studying at the London School of Economics and at Moscow University. In 1938 his book, *Facing Mount Kenya*, one of the first reliable contributions to African ethnography by an African, was published. In 1945 he presided over the first Pan-African Congress which was held in Manchester, returning to Kenya the following year. In 1947 he became President of the Kenya African Union, which was banned during the emergency in Kenya when it was used as a screen for the activities of Mau Mau, *q.v.*; as President he demanded for Africans the removal of the colour bar, equal representation in government, higher wages and a re-distribution of land. He was arrested in 1952 and sentenced in 1953 to seven years' imprisonment for assisting in the management of Mau Mau and three years for being a member of a proscribed cult. He was released in August 1961 and elected to the Legislative Council in 1962. He took office as Prime Minister on 1 June 1963, when his party, the Kenya African National Union (K.A.N.U.), obtained a majority in the elections held immediately before Kenya became self-governing, and President of Kenya on 12 December 1964 when Kenya became an independent republic within the British Commonwealth.

Khan, Ayub, Field-Marshal. Pakistani politician; born 1908 in Abbottabad on the North-West Frontier, the son of a non-commissioned officer (a Bugler Major) in the British Indian Army; educated at

Aligarh Moslem University and Royal Military College, Sandhurst, he was commissioned in the army in 1928 and served in the Second World War on the Burma front. He was appointed to be the first commander of the East Pakistan Division, with the rank of Major-General, in December 1948; Adjutant-General in 1950; and the first Pakistani Commander-in-Chief of the Pakistani Army, with the rank of General, in January 1951, holding that post till 1958. From October 1954 (during a political crisis) to August 1955 he was Minister of Defence. In October 1958 he became the Chief Martial Law Administrator and succeeded Major-General Iskander Mirza as President. He was re-elected President for a further five-year term on 2 January 1965, but resigned on 24 March 1969 and was succeeded by General Yahya Khan.

Khmer Republic (Cambodia). An independent state, formerly of the French Union, *q.v.*, situated in south-west Indo-China; area 71,000 sq. m.; population (1969 estimate) 6,701,000, mostly Indians and Malays but including some 500,000 Viet-Namese and 400,000 Chinese; religion Hinayana Buddhism; capital Pnom Penh. In the ninth and tenth centuries Cambodia was the seat of the great Khmer Empire which ruled most of Indo-China; from the fourteenth century it was disputed territory between Thais and Annamites until the French established a protectorate in 1863. Although grateful for this protection the Cambodians resisted all French influences, religious and cultural. In 1930 the French modified their assimilation policy by founding the Buddhist Institute at Pnom Penh and the Institute of Cambodian Arts.

From 1949 to 1954 Cambodia was an Associate State of the French Union. Independence was proclaimed on 9 November 1953 and confirmed on 21 July 1954 at the Geneva Conference, where Cambodia's eleventh hour refusal to sign the Agreements because they neutralized the country secured, for Cambodia and Laos, the right to make treaties and enlist foreign aid (other than French) in their own defence.

Norodom Sihanouk (born 1922) succeeded to the throne on 26 April 1941. In 1947 he introduced a new Constitution with an elective assembly and manhood suffrage, except for Buddhist priests and soldiers who were disenfranchised. In March 1955 the King abdicated in favour of his parents, King Norodom Suramarit and Queen Kossamak, entered politics and founded the Sangkum (Popular Socialist Community) Party which supported a parliamentary monarchy, strong central government and provincial assemblies to administer local affairs. In elections held in 1955, 1958, 1962 and 1966 the Sangkum won all the seats (82 in 1966) in the assembly. King Norodom Suramarit died on 3 April 1960, and the royal powers were then vested in a Council of Regency until 20 June 1960 when Sihanouk became head of state without becoming king. Viet-Minh guerilla forces, which had officially been evacuated from Cambodia following the 1954 Geneva Agreements, *q.v.*, were allowed to establish bases in Cambodia for operations in South Viet-Nam, and in 1970 the country was invaded by North Viet-Nam forces. A right-wing *coup*, organized by Marshal Lon Nol, deposed Sihanouk on 18 March 1970. Cheng Hang was appointed head of state in his place, and in August 1970 Lon Nol took office as Prime Minister. A republic was declared in October 1970 and the name of the country changed to Khmer Republic. A new Constitution, which was to have introduced an elective Presidency, was suppressed on 10 March 1972 when Lon Nol assumed supreme power as head of state and proclaimed himself first President.

There are few industries and little commerce, although French aid has been used to build the new port of Sihanoukville, later re-named Kompong Som, on the Gulf of Siam, and Chinese aid to construct textile mills and cement and paper factories. In 1963 Sihanouk refused to accept further aid from the U.S.A., and diplomatic relations were severed in May 1965. The country is mainly agricultural and, owing to the preponderance of celibate priests (Bonzes) and the subsequent low birth-rate, self-supporting; the economy has been relatively unaffected by the fighting between North Viet-Nam forces and South Viet-Nam and U.S. troops in 1970 and 1971. Since 1970 there has been an increasing amount of U.S. military and economic aid to compensate for the country's former dependence on France and the Communist bloc.

Khrushchev, Nikita Sergeyevich. Former Chairman of the Council of Ministers of the U.S.S.R.; born 17 April 1894 in the Ukraine, the son of a mine-worker. He served with the Russian Army in the First World War, then joined the Communist Party and fought with the Red Army during the Russian civil war. After 1921 he worked in the Ukrainian mines and directed party work at Kiev and Stalino; after studying at the Moscow Industrial Academy from 1929 to 1931 he became a party secretary in Moscow. In 1935 he became first secretary of the Moscow Regional Committee with responsibility for industrialization which included the building of the Moscow underground railway, for which he received the Order of Lenin. In 1937 he became a member of the Supreme Soviet and in 1938 he was appointed First Secretary of the Communist Party in the Ukraine. From 1941 onwards he organized guerilla warfare in the Ukraine; after the war he supervised the execution of many Ukrainians who were believed to have assisted the Germans, and he helped in the reconstruction of the area. In 1949 he assumed responsibility for Russian agriculture. Upon the death of Stalin in 1953 he was appointed First Secretary of the Communist Party (a post held by Stalin for thirty years). At a secret session of the Russian Communist Party Congress in February 1956 he said that Stalin had abused his powers, had permitted loyal communists to be falsely accused and punished, had failed to prepare for the German invasion, had made blunders in strategy, and had been responsible for the rupture with Yugoslavia in 1948. In March 1958 he replaced Marshal Bulganin as Chairman of the Council of Ministers, while retaining his post as First Secretary of the Communist Party.

He was deprived of both these posts on 14 October 1964 and was succeeded in the first by Alexei Kosygin, *q.v.* His advanced age and poor health were the initial excuses for his dismissal, but charges against him were later stated in *Pravda, q.v.*: his revival of the Stalin personality cult, *q.v.*; nepotism; disorderly and authoritarian conduct of the business of the party and the state. These were amplified in a document issued by the new leaders to Russian Communist Party organizations and to foreign Communist delegations which had demanded explanations of Khrushchev's dismissal, in which he was accused of causing a Soviet defeat in the Cuban missile crisis, reducing the Sino-Soviet ideological conflict to the level of a personal feud between himself and Mao Tse-tung, underestimating the scientific progress of the Chinese Communists and disrupting the economy by emphasizing the development of consumer goods at the expense of heavy industry and by encouraging decentralization in agriculture. He died on 11 September 1971.

Kiesinger, Kurt Georg. West German Christian Democratic politician and lawyer, and Federal Chancellor from October 1966 until October 1969; born 6 April 1904 at Ebingen. He is a Roman Catholic. Throughout his political career he was a leading exponent in Germany of European unity and reconciliation with Eastern Europe. He joined the Nazi Party in 1933 but claims to have been disillusioned by its methods and to have refused to disseminate anti-Semitic or false propaganda even during the war. He was exonerated by an Allied de-nazification tribunal in 1946, and in 1948 by a West German de-nazification court. From 1949 to 1956 he was a member of the Bundestag and from 1958 to 1966 Minister-President (Premier) of Baden-Württemberg. He served as President of the Bundesrat from 1962 to

1963. He replaced Ludwig Erhard as chairman of the Christian Democratic Party (C.D.U.) in October 1966, automatically succeeding him as Federal Chancellor until the Federal elections of September 1969 in which the C.D.U. lost its commanding majority over the Social Democratic Party in the Bundestag. He retired from the leadership of the C.D.U. in October 1971; Dr Rainer Barzel, *q.v.*, was elected to succeed him.

King, Martin Luther. U.S. Negro leader; born 15 January 1929 in Atlanta, Georgia, the son of a pastor of the Ebenezer Baptist Church. He was educated at Boston University where he studied systematic theology. After entering the Church his first ministry was in Montgomery, Alabama, in 1955, where he immediately became involved in an organized boycott of buses by the negro community, an act of passive resistance which eventually produced a federal court desegregation order. The success of this campaign against segregation, *q.v.*, encouraged him to extend his operations, and he helped to organize most of the passive demonstrations in favour of civil rights, *q.v.*, including the assembly of 200,000 negroes at Washington in 1964, the march from Selma to Montgomery in 1965, and the march from Memphis to Jackson in 1967. As the head of the Southern Christian Leadership, which supports broadly the policies of the larger National Association for the Advancement of Colored People, *q.v.*, and which is now led by the Reverend Dr Ralph Abernathy, he emerged as the spokesman for the American negro. He was awarded the Nobel Peace Prize in 1964 for his efforts to solve peacefully, and without violence, the racial problems of the United States. He was shot dead in Memphis, Tennessee, on 4 April 1968.

Korea. A former kingdom in north-east Asia, for 500 years a vassal of China. In 1905 it was occupied, and in 1910 annexed, by the Japanese. It has always been of strategic importance to Russia, China, and Japan because its ports are never ice-bound, and coveted for its fertile soil and its mineral wealth – gold, copper, coal, iron, graphite, and tungsten are found in abundance in northern Korea. In 1896, in 1903, and in 1910 Russia entered into secret negotiations with Japan to divide Korea along the 38th parallel. Russian troops eventually entered Korea on 8 August 1945, immediately after the Russian declaration of war on Japan, and the country was temporarily partitioned, along the 38th parallel, between the U.S.S.R. and the U.S.A. who established zones of occupation. It remains divided into the two states of North Korea, *q.v.*, and South Korea, *q.v.* Negotiations on re-unification began in 1972.

Kosygin, Alexei Nikolayevich. Russian politician; born 1904 in Leningrad. He first joined the Communist Party in 1927 and began a special study of textile engineering. In this capacity he was largely responsible for the development of textile production and the growth of light industries in the Soviet Union. In 1946 he was made a deputy chairman of the Soviet Council of Ministers, and appointed Minister of Finance, and then of Light Industry, in 1948. In 1954 he returned to the Ministry of Finance and two years later became first vice-chairman of the State Economic Planning Commission. He was made first vice-chairman of the Council of Ministers in 1960 and succeeded Nikita Khrushchev as Chairman on 14 October 1964.

Kremlin. Russian term meaning 'citadel', but applied especially to the Moscow citadel occupied by the former Imperial Palace and now the administrative headquarters of the government of the U.S.S.R.

Kuomintang. A Chinese nationalist party founded in 1891 by Sun Yat-sen. It was active in the first Chinese revolution of 1911 and led the second revolution in 1912 against Marshal Yuan Shi-kai; it dominated south China by 1930 and conducted China's defence against the Japanese invasion from 1937 until 1945. Under the leadership of Chiang Kai-shek, *q.v.*, who succeeded Sun Yat-sen in 1925, the party subordinated its political and social ideals to the achievement of military victory. In 1946 Sun Fo, the son of Sun Yat-sen, deplored its departure from the principles of political democracy and the welfare of the people on which his father had founded the Kuomintang. In 1948 the Communist Party replaced the Kuomintang as the governing party of China. Chiang Kai-shek and his followers were driven from the mainland to Taiwan, *q.v.*

Kurdistan. The territory inhabited by the Kurds; it stretches for about 600 miles from Malatya in Turkey, along the northern frontiers of Iraq, to Luristan in Persia. Its maximum breadth is about 225 miles; there are Kurds in the U.S.S.R. and Syria. This mountainous region has been inhabited by Kurds, of whom there are about 5,000,000 (1,000,000 in Iraq, over 1,000,000 in Persia, over 250,000 in Syria, over 2,000,000 in Turkey, and 60,000 in the U.S.S.R.), since before 2,000 B.C. The Kurds, who speak an Indo-European language, have for centuries had a distinct national consciousness, and there were in the Middle Ages about thirty Kurdish principalities. The establishment of national frontiers (especially those of the Ottoman Empire and Persia) forced the Kurds to look towards different countries, while retaining a Kurdish culture.

Since the end of the First World War there have been repeated attempts by the Kurds to achieve regional autonomy in Iraq, Persia, and Turkey. In Iraq, where the Kurds (who have received encouragement from the U.S.S.R.) occupy the north-eastern province of Sulaimaniya and parts of the provinces of Arbil, Kirkuk and Mosul, the Barzani tribe, under Mullah Mustafa Barzani, have been particularly persistent in their demands. The Kurds have asked for a Kurdish police force; for Kurdish control of communications, education, health services, and of local affairs; for Kurdish to be the first language in the Kurdish areas; and for their autonomous region to be granted a share, based on population, of the country's oil and customs revenues. Since 1961 there has been continuous fighting between government forces and Kurdish guerillas punctuated by cease-fire agreements. In 1965 the Kurds set up their own parliament, courts and tax-offices; this was in reply to the Iraq government's decision in December 1964 to establish a unified political authority with Egypt, q.v., irrespective of the Kurdish demand for federal autonomy within Iraq. In June 1966 the Iraq government offered peace proposals, which were acceptable to Barzani, by which a semi-autonomous Kurd state would co-exist inside a unified and independent Iraq. However, these were not implemented and severe fighting broke out in 1968 and continued throughout 1969. In 1970 the new government of General al Bakr, who had promised to solve the Kurdish problem, reached a settlement which granted autonomy to the Kurds and gave them representation proportionate to their numbers in the legislature, the government, the army and the public service. Five Kurdish ministers were appointed to government posts in 1970, and by 1971 much of the agreement had been put into effect with the exception of the provision for a Kurdish Vice-President and Kurdish representation on the Revolutionary Council.

Kuwait. Emirate at the north-western end of the Persian Gulf; area 5,800 sq. m., mostly desert; population (1970) 733,000, of whom half are under twenty; capital Kuwait. It is an independent state; under a treaty of 1899 (concluded by the Emir to obtain protection from Turkey) the U.K. was responsible for foreign relations, but the treaty was terminated on 19 June 1961 when Kuwait established its own foreign service. British obligations to aid Kuwait militarily were observed until May 1968 when the U.K. gave notice that it would terminate the arrangement in 1971. The ruler is the Head of State and the Heir Apparent is the Prime Minister. Two other ministries are held by members of the Emir's family. There are no political parties, but a small group of deputies with a radical nationalist platform have challenged government candidates at elections which must take place every four years. At elections held in January 1971 the Arab Nationalist Movement won 10 of the 50 seats in the National Assembly.

Kuwait has the highest *per capita* income in the world. The source of four-fifths of its revenues is oil, found in southern Kuwait and also in the Neutral Zone farther south, an area delineated by treaty in 1922 and in which the Emir shares an undivided half-interest with Saudi Arabia both as to sovereignty and as to oil. In Kuwait, itself the largest oil producer in the Middle East, the oil concession (granted in 1934 for 75 years) is held by the Kuwait Oil Company, in which the British Petroleum and Gulf Exploration Companies hold equal shares. In 1962 the Company relinquished some half of its original concession area; this was subsequently awarded to the state-owned Kuwait National Petroleum Company (founded in 1960) in partnership with the Spanish Company Hispanoil on a 51–49 per cent basis. By an agreement concluded in 1951 the Emir receives personally one half of the profits; a large proportion of these have been used to provide social services, a development scheme, the world's largest sea-water distillation plant, roads in and around Kuwait town, free education and a number of excellently built schools, hospitals and sanatoria. In the Neutral Zone, where oil was discovered in 1953, the oil concession is held, as to the Kuwaiti share, by the American Independent Oil Company. The Saudi Arabian share was held by the Arabian American Oil Company till 1948 but was given up by them to the Saudi Arabian government in exchange for undersea rights. It is now held by the Getty Oil Company. The Kuwaiti concession to the American Independent Oil Co. does not include offshore rights in the Neutral Zone. These were the subject of an agreement in May 1958 with the Arabian Japanese Oil Company which promised to pay Kuwait 57 per cent of the profits. The increasing importance of the Neutral Zone could produce tension between Kuwait and Saudi Arabia on problems such as policing and taxing the area. Until October 1963 Iraq claimed Kuwait, alleging that it was once ruled by Iraq, and describing it as part of Basra province. The ruler from 1950 until his death in 1965 was Sheikh Abdullah al-Salin al-Sabah. He was succeeded by his brother, the former Prime Minister, Sheikh Sabah as-Salim as-Sabah. The new Prime Minister, designated Crown Prince in 1966, Sheikh Jabir al-Ahmed al-Jabir as Sabah, is also a member of the Sabah dynasty which has been in power since 1756.

L

Labor Management Relations Act, 1947. *See* Taft-Hartley Act.

Labour Party. A British political party; it obtained 12,141,676 out of 28,258,332 votes cast at the 1970 General Election and 287 out of 630 seats in the House of Commons. In 1892 the first Labour members, John Burns and Keir Hardie, were elected to the House of Commons, with 13 Liberal-Labour members. In 1900 the Trades Union Congress, *q.v.*, the Independent Labour Party, the Fabian Society and the Social Democratic Federation formed the Labour Representation Committee, comprising 7 trade unionists, 2 members of the I.L.P., 1 member of the Fabian Society, and 2 members of the S.D.F., to establish a Labour group in Parliament. In 1906 the L.R.C. became known as the Labour Party, and in 1922 it replaced the Liberal Party as one of the two major British parties. In 1924 and in 1929 it formed a government, but on each occasion it was in a minority in the House of Commons and was unable to introduce radical legislation. In 1945 it obtained an overwhelming majority; it nationalized the coal, electricity, gas, steel, and transport industries, introduced a national health service and a comprehensive scheme of national insurance and national industrial injuries insurance, and encouraged the emergence as independent countries of India, Pakistan, Ceylon, and Burma. After losing 81 seats but retaining its majority in 1950, the Labour Party was defeated at the General Elections of 1951, 1955, and 1959, but won the General Election of October 1964, securing an overall majority of 4 seats, and was again successful at the General Election of 31 March 1966, increasing its majority to 96. It was defeated in the General Election of 18 June 1970, losing 76 seats.

The administrative organ of the British Labour Party is the National Executive, which is elected annually by the annual conference. The conference is composed of delegates from the constituency parties, the trade unions, and Socialist, cooperative, and professional organizations. The National Executive consists of the leader and the deputy leader of the Parliamentary Labour Party, the party treasurer, 7 constituency members, 1 representative of the Socialist, cooperative and professional organizations, 5 women members, and 12 trade union representatives. The trade unions provide over 75 per cent of the Labour Party's income. The conference can decide the Labour Party's election policy. The leader of the Parliamentary Labour Party, who is the effective leader of the Labour Party as a whole, the Chairmanship of the National Executive being only a courtesy appointment for one year, is Harold Wilson, *q.v.*, who was elected in February 1963 after the death of the former leader, Hugh Gaitskell (born 1906), who had led the party since December 1955. Other leading figures in the Labour Party are Anthony Wedgwood Benn, *q.v.*, James Callaghan, *q.v.*, Barbara Castle, *q.v.*, Anthony Crosland, *q.v.*, Denis Healey, *q.v.*, Roy Jenkins, *q.v.*, Edward Short, *q.v.*, and Shirley Williams, *q.v.*

Ladakh. A district in eastern Kashmir adjacent to Tibet and inhabited by Buddhists. In 1962 the Chinese, who claim the area, the borders of which are ill-defined, occupied 12,000 square miles of it, having previously built a road across it. Chinese forces established a number of posts, some of which were in the Galwan Valley and on the Chip-chak river (an upper tributary of the Indus) south-east of the Kara-koram pass, and one of which (established in 1963) was on a traditional Indian caravan route to the Karakoram pass. India alleged that the Chinese action of 1962 was on territory admitted as Indian by China in 1960. China accused India of trying to assert its territorial claims on China by armed force, and of deliberately provoking a military clash on the border. A cease-fire along the entire Sino-Indian frontier was announced by the Chinese in November 1962; it has not yet been stabilized by any truce agreement.

L.A.F.T.A. Latin American Free Trade Association, *q.v.*

Land Reform. A redistribution of land among, or a reduction of the rent of land to, those who farm it. Since 1945 all the progressive parties of Asia have included land reform in their social policy and several Asian governments have undertaken programmes of land reform. In China it has taken the form of expropriation and free redistribution; in Kashmir all who farm more than $22\frac{1}{2}$ acres have had to yield the excess to the man who tills it; the Indian state governments have acquired land, compulsorily but with compensation, from the *zamin-dars* (landlords) and have rented out plots to peasants under a *ryotwari* system which enables the farmer to hold his land directly from the state. In South Korea the peasants have been encouraged to become freeholders and to purchase land previously owned by the Japanese in grain, the total price being three times the annual yield. In Persia large landowners are (in law) limited to one village each. Effective land reform has been possible only in countries from which foreign landowners have been recently expelled, as in Korea, or in which the landowning class has been, or is being, overthrown by the workers or by the army, as in China or North Viet-Nam. Where the landowner retains powerful domestic influence, as in the case of the Roman Catholic Church in Italy, land reform, in the sense here described, has not taken place. Latin American countries which have undertaken land reform include Mexico (1910), Bolivia (1952), Cuba (1959), and Chile (1971).

Laos. An independent state, formerly of the French Union, *q.v.*, predominantly Buddhist, situated in north-west Indo-China; area 90,000 sq. m.; royal capital Luang Prabang; old French administrative capital Vientiane; population (1970 estimate) 2,962,000, of whom more than two thirds are of Laotian origin. The country is unproductive and mountainous and has poor communications with the rest of Indo-China, and the peasantry are among the most primitive in Asia. The gold trade and the export of tin are the principal sources of income. It became a French protectorate in 1893 and an Associate State of the French Union in 1949. The Geneva Agreements, 1954, *q.v.*, recognized Laos' freedom to enlist foreign military aid (other than French) for its own protection.

From 1904 to 1954 the French governed through King Somdet Prachao Sisavong Vong (1885–1959) who maintained a strong private army of 10,000 men. A free Laotian movement, the Lao Issarak, was founded in 1940 to end French rule. Three of its members, the Princes Petsarath, Souvanna Phouma, and Souphanou Vong, formed a government early in 1945 under Japanese protection. When the French returned in 1946, Petsarath and Souvanna Phouma fled to Thailand while Souphanou Vong rejoined the underground Lao Issarak. With the declaration of independence in 1949 Souvanna Phouma returned to lead a new government. The Lao Issarak then split; several of its older members supported the government, and the rump, led by Souphanou Vong, was renamed Pathet Lao. In 1950 it established contact with the Viet-Minh, with whom it collaborated in the invasion of Laos in 1953. At Geneva the authority of the Pathet Lao over the northern provinces of Phong Saly and Sam Neua was recognized until such time as elections could be held for the whole country. After July 1954 these two permitted enclaves were extended by more than 13,000 sq. m. of territory seized in violation of the Agreements, but in 1956 they were yielded to the government. In 1957 Souvanna Phouma and Souphanou Vong (his half-brother) agreed that there should be: (1) immediate cessation of hostilities; (2) restoration of the government's authority over the two northern provinces; and (3) the granting of civil rights to Pathet Lao followers. Two Pathet Lao representatives joined the cabinet.

The situation deteriorated in 1959 as armed forces from North Viet-Nam gave their support to dissident elements in the frontier areas. In 1960 Souvanna Phouma formed a neutralist government and tried to come to terms with the Pathet Lao, which continued to be led by Souphanou Vong, but he was forced to take refuge in Cambodia in December 1960 and was succeeded as Prime Minister by the right-wing Prince Boun Oum, who, with General Phoumi Nosavan, received strong support from the U.S.A.

The King is the Head of State and the supreme religious authority. Tiao Savang Vatthana became King on 29 October 1959, upon the death of his father. The legislature is the National Assembly, elected every four years by indirect universal suffrage. Continued fighting during 1961 among the pro-Communist, neutralist (under the command of General Kong Lae) and right-wing forces caused the convening of a conference of the original parties to the Geneva Agreements by the British and Russian co-chairmen. On 23 July 1962 a new agreement was signed providing for the withdrawal of foreign troops and international guarantees of Laotian neutrality. A government of National Union under Souvanna Phouma which included General Phoumi, Boun Oum and Souvanna Vong was formed. However the intensification of Viet Cong activity in neighbouring South Viet-Nam gave encouragement to the Pathet Lao who achieved military successes in 1964 and in 1970 against the neutralist forces occupying the strategically important Plain of Jars. Since the escalation of military activity by the North Viet-Nam forces in 1969 and U.S. intervention in Cambodia in 1970, the Viet-Minh became active in the protection of their main supply route to the south, the Ho Chi Minh trail, which runs through Laos. This became of vital importance to them in March 1970 when the Americans closed the port of Kompong Som through which most of their supplies to troops in South Viet-Nam had infiltrated. When a cease-fire agreement was eventually signed on 21 February 1973 only one third of the country was under the control of the Vientiane government.

Latin American Free Trade Association (L.A.F.T.A.). An association of eleven Latin American states, requiring the elimination of virtually all tariffs on existing trade among themselves over a 12-year period, while leaving them free to control imports as they wish, and encouraging the coordination of their industrial development. The treaty was originally signed at Montevideo in 1960 by ten countries, Bolivia joining in 1967. At the same time Costa Rica, Guatemala, Honduras, Nicaragua and Salvador formed the Central American Common Market, *q.v.* Progress was made initially by granting tariff concessions on non-competitive agricultural products; it was found impossible to extend these to industrial goods owing to the disparity of industrial development of the eleven member countries. These were subsequently classified into three groups: Argentina, Brazil and Mexico (as the most industrially advanced); Colombia, Chile, Peru, Uruguay and Venezuela; and Bolivia, Ecuador and Paraguay. Similar problems and groupings have been experienced in the Alliance for Progress, *q.v.*

Latin American Solidarity Organization. Set up, at the instigation of Fidel Castro, *q.v.*, on 18 January 1966 by 27 delegates from Latin American and Caribbean countries attending the Three Continents Solidarity Organization of Communist Parties of Asia, Africa and Latin America in Havana in January 1966. It represented a victory for Castro's advocacy of guerilla warfare to overthrow capitalist regimes. Until 1964 most Latin American Communist Parties condemned insurgent movements led by pro-Castro revolutionaries, such as Ernesto Guevara, *q.v.*, and favoured the use of constitutional means to assume power. However U.S. intervention in the Dominican Republic, *q.v.*, in 1965 gave substance to Castro's argument that the U.S. would never accept the loss of Latin America and that sooner or later the people would have to take up arms to free themselves. By establishing his own organization, with headquarters in Cuba, Castro hoped to propagate his theories of peasant revolution throughout the continent.

Latvia. One of the 15 constituent Republics of the Union of Soviet Socialist Republics since 1940; area 25,590 sq. m.; population (1971) 2,400,000, of whom 30 per cent are Russians and 57 per cent Letts; capital Riga. The Republic, which is situated between Estonia and Lithuania on the Baltic Sea, was ruled by foreigners, including Germans, Poles, Danes, Swedes, and Russians, for hundreds of years, and was a province of the Russian Empire when it proclaimed independence in April 1918. The large estates of the German 'Baltic Barons' were broken up and redistributed to the peasants. As an independent state Latvia had highly developed chemical, engineering, shipbuilding, textile, and wood-working industries, but there were also many cattle-breeders and dairy-farmers. The democratic Constitution was suspended in May 1934 largely as a result of the world economic crisis which damaged the Latvian economy; all political parties were dissolved and government passed into the hands of a conservative, agrarian, and nationalist group. Under an agreement between the U.S.S.R. and Germany, made on 23 August 1939, Latvia was occupied by the U.S.S.R. in June 1940, and became a constituent Republic on 5 August 1940. Many Latvians were deported to camps east of the Ural Mountains. The U.S.S.R. ordered the redistribution of land to those with no land or only very small holdings, and nationalized most of the industrial enterprises. There are valuable deposits of gypsum, peat, and soft coal. Forests occupy 20 per cent of the whole area. There are two strategically important ice-free ports, Liepaja (Libau), which is used by the U.S.S.R. as a naval base and from which commercial shipping has been excluded, and Ventspils (Windau).

League of Nations. An international organization established in 1920 under a Covenant of 26 articles forming part of the Versailles Treaty, q.v., which was concluded after the First World War. It came to an end in 1945 when the United Nations, q.v., was founded. The formation of the League was Point 14 of President Wilson's Fourteen Points, but the U.S. Congress refused to ratify the Versailles Treaty and to join the League. The League Covenant bound the members to respect and to preserve against aggression their independence and territorial integrity and not to employ force for the settlement of a dispute until they had first submitted it to the League or to arbitrators; if the League or the arbitrators failed to reach a unanimous decision within six months, the disputing nations could go to war only after an additional delay of three months, Sanctions could be applied against any country committing aggression in breach of the Covenant. The League Assembly met annually and the League Council (of 15 members, including France, the U.K., and the U.S.S.R. as permanent members) three times a year. Decisions had to be by a unanimous vote.

The objects of the League of Nations were fundamentally the same as those expressed in the Covenant and Charter of the United Nations, although the Charter avoids the use of League of Nations terms which might have unfortunate associations. The expressions Security Council, General Assembly, and Trusteeship were all new. Under the League one power (the U.S.A.) refused to join, one (the U.S.S.R.) was ostracized by the others, two (France and the U.K.) gave half-hearted support, and three (Germany, Italy, and Japan) ignored their responsibilities. The United Nations has been considerably more successful in engaging the participation of the major powers, although the exclusion of Germany and, until 1971, the Chinese People's Republic clearly make it impossible to say whether they would discharge their duties as members.

A fundamental difference between the two organizations lies in the methods of dealing with threats to security. In spite of the unanimity rule in the Covenant, the effectiveness of the League depended not on the ability of its organs to reach decisions, but on the individual members' observance of their obligations under the Covenant. No decision or lack of a decision could alter these obligations. Under the United Nations Charter the Security Council has the primary responsibility of maintaining peace, and a decision is necessary if the machinery is to be put into operation at all. To enable the organization to reach decisions the principle of majority voting has been accepted, but the price of that advance, demanded by the major powers, has been the veto, q.v.

Lebanon. An independent state on the eastern Mediterranean; area 3,400 sq. m.; population (1970) 2,700,000, half of whom are Christians, the rest being Moslems and Druses. About ten per cent of the population are Arab refugees from Palestine. The capital is Beirut. Lebanon was part of the Ottoman Empire until its capture in 1918 by the U.K. with French and Arab help; France became the mandatory power in 1920 under the League of Nations. As the French in Syria favoured Vichy France, q.v., and could not be trusted to resist German penetration, British troops fought and removed the French garrison in 1941. The independence of Lebanon was declared on 26 November 1941, both the U.K. and the Free French forces agreeing to this step, and the first President of the independent republic was elected in 1943. All foreign troops departed by December 1946.

Fruit, tobacco, silk, cotton and cement are produced, and gold and precious metals are mined and worked. Only 26 per cent of the area is cultivated. The country is not wealthy, and about 500,000 have emigrated to the U.S.A., 250,000 to Brazil, and 150,000 to Argentina. There is a transit trade in crude oil, Lebanon being the terminal for the pipelines of the Iraq Petroleum Company which has a refinery at Tripoli, and the Trans-Arabian Pipeline Company, q.v., with a refinery at Sidon. In March 1973 all I.P.C. installations were nationalized. The financial stability of the country was jeopardized in October 1966 when its principal banking house, Intra, ceased trading; it was, however, reopened in January 1968.

The Constitution creates a delicate balance of power between the Christians and the Moslems, who may now comprise a majority of the population, but makes no provision for ideological differences. There is a President who appoints a Prime Minister and a Cabinet; there is also a unicameral legislature elected by universal adult suffrage for four years. Conventionally the President is a Maronite Christian, the Prime Minister a Sunni Moslem, and the Speaker a Shia Moslem. The electoral law is designed to produce a legislature representing the sects in proportion to their strengths. The 99 deputies elected in March and April 1968 consisted of: Maronite Christians (a sect in communion with Rome, and to which approximately 425,000 people belong) 30 seats, Sunni Moslems 20, Shia Moslems 19, Greek Orthodox 11, Uniate Greek 6, Druses 6, Armenian Orthodox 4, Uniate Armenian 1, others 2. Attempts to create national, rather than religious, parties were largely unsuccessful until 1966, although the Druse leader, Kemal Jumblatt, had formed the Progressive Socialist Party in 1947. By 1966 political as well as religious divisions were becoming identifiable; they include the moderate Moslem group led by Rashid Karami; the Christian, Pan-Arabic but anti-Nasser, Constitutional Party of Camille Chamoun, known as the Tripartite Alliance; the Ahmed El-Assaad group of southern Moslems; Falangists; a National Democratic Bloc (slightly to the left of the Tripartite Alliance); Progressive Socialists; and National Liberals. The Baath Party, *q.v.*, was banned in 1963.

The President, by the Constitution, is not eligible for immediate re-election. Moslem and Druse discontent, already considerable because of Christian political and economic dominance, and encouraged by Egypt, increased when it was understood that Camille Chamoun (elected President in September 1952 for a six-year term) wanted a second term as President. Not only Moslems and Druses, but also a number of Christians of various sects (including the Maronite Patriarch) had for some time been opposed to the pro-western orientation of the government's foreign policy.

Disturbances on the Syrian frontier led to an investigation by a United Nations observation group which was unable to determine in July 1958 the extent of Syrian infiltration into Lebanon because both countries had for many years ignored the frontier. Chamoun then appealed for military aid as a result of which U.S. forces were in the country from July to October 1958. With the active assistance of U.S. diplomats, who sought to bring the various sects together, Chamoun stepped down in favour of General Fuad Chehab, a Maronite Christian who had been educated at the French Military Academy of St Cyr; he was elected President by the legislature with the necessary two-thirds majority, and took office in September 1958. He was succeeded in August 1964 by Charles Helou (born 1913 and also a Maronite Christian) whose tenure of office was remarkable for the number of changes of government. He was, in turn, succeeded in August 1970 by Sulaiman Frangié, a nominee of Chamoun. After the success of the Tripartite Alliance in the 1968 elections pressure mounted for the party to be represented in the administration; this was opposed by the Karami Moslems and the Progressive Socialists. The issue was complicated by the custom of appointing a Moslem as

Prime Minister. Since an Israeli attack on Beirut airport in December 1968 the country has been increasingly divided between neutralists and supporters of the Palestine guerillas who use Lebanon as a base from which to conduct their operations against Israel.

Lebensraum. A German word meaning 'living-space', and a slogan adopted by German nationalists, particularly between 1933 and 1945. The word was used with reference to: (1) Germany's alleged over-population and its consequent need to acquire more territory, so that it could produce all its own food; (2) Germany's claim to bring certain neighbouring zones, particularly in eastern Europe, within its sphere of influence.

Legitimists. Monarchists who advocate the return of the head of a deposed dynasty whose claim is based on direct descent. The term is used especially with reference to the Habsburg followers of Arch-duke Otto, son of the last Emperor of Austria-Hungary.

Leone, Giovanni. President of Italy; born 3 November 1908 in Naples. He trained as a lawyer and practised in Naples where he subsequently taught at the university. In 1946 he was elected to the Constituent Assembly, in which as a member of the 'Commission of 75' he helped to draft the Constitution. In 1948 he was elected for the constituency of Naples-Caserta to the Chamber of Deputies, of which he became Vice-President from 1950 to 1955 and Presiding Officer from 1955 to 1963, continuing in the meantime to teach at the University of Rome as Professor of Criminal Law and Criminal Procedural Law. From June to November 1963 and again from June to December 1968 he was Prime Minister of Christian-Democratic minority governments. In August 1967 he was appointed a life senator in consideration of his academic achievements. On 24 December 1971 he was elected to succeed President Saragat on the twenty-third ballot, eventually defeating his nearest rival, Pietro Nenni, *q.v.*, by 518 votes to 408. He then became Italy's sixth post-war President and its third Christian Democrat Head of State.

Lesotho. An independent kingdom within the British Commonwealth; it consists mainly of high mountains and is entirely surrounded by the independent state of South Africa, being bounded to the north-west and west by the Orange Free State, to the north-east and east by Natal, to the south-east by Transkei (East Griqualand), and to the south by Cape Province; area 11,716 sq. m., population (1966 census) 976,000, of whom 115,380 were absent working in South Africa; capital Maseru. It came under the protection of the U.K. in 1868 as a result of appeals from the Basuto (or Basotho) who wanted to avoid annexation by the Boers. It was annexed to the Cape Colony in 1871 but restored to British control in 1884 through the administration of the High Commissioner in South Africa; in 1910 when the Union of South Africa came into existence the territory, by its own wish, remained a British colony. Government was formerly by the British Resident Commissioner and the Paramount Chief, Constantine Bereng Seeiso Moshoeshoe II, acting in conjunction with the National Council (the legislature) and the Executive Council (the cabinet), both of which came into existence in 1960. The territory became internally self-governing in 1965 and fully independent on 3 August 1966, as a monarchy under Moshoeshoe II. The legislature consists of a Senate, comprising the 22 principal chiefs and 11 members nominated by the King, and a National Assembly of 60 members elected every five years on the basis of universal adult suffrage. At the elections held in April 1965 the Basutoland National Party, a moderate conservative party led by Chief Leabua Jonathan, who entered the Assembly to become Prime Minister in July 1965, won 31 seats; the Congress Party, a left-wing party led by Ntsu Mokhehle, 25 seats; and the Marema Tlou Freedom Party, led by B. M. Khaketla, 4 seats. A serious crisis developed in December 1966 when the King attempted to obtain wider powers, and in January 1967 he signed an undertaking, under pain of compulsory abdication, to abide by the Constitution. After elections held in January 1970, which gave a majority of seats to the opposition Congress Party, Chief Jonathan declared a state of emergency, suspended the Constitution and arrested Mokhehle. King Moshoeshoe, who had been put under house arrest, was exiled, but allowed to return in December 1970 after accepting a government prohibitory order that the monarchy should stay out of public life.

Wheat, maize and sorghum are grown, but, apart from diamonds, there are no mineral resources; a hydro-electric project is planned for Oxbow. The country is over-populated with no possibility of increasing its food supply, and closely linked to South Africa (the currencies are the same) by its export of labour; about a quarter of the population work on South African farms and gold mines. In September 1966 South Africa turned down a request from Chief Jonathan for aid for his 'economically embarrassed country' and Lesotho is dependent on U.K. assistance.

Liberal Party. A British political party; it obtained 2,117,638 out of 28,258,332 votes cast at the 1970 General Election (7·4 per cent of the total poll) and 6 out of 630 seats in the House of Commons. It is the successor to the Whig Party of the eighteenth and nineteenth centuries and was one of the two major British political parties until it was supplanted by the Labour Party at the 1922 General Election. It is a moderately progressive party. It wants employees to be given a share in the decisions and profits of the companies in which they work, protection of individual liberties, decentralization of power towards the north and west of England, and Scotland and Wales, and strict measures to prevent the growth of monopolies. In 1967 Jeremy Thorpe, *q.v.*, succeeded Joseph Grimond as leader of the Parliamentary Liberal Party.

Liberia. An independent West African state between Sierra Leone and the Ivory Coast; area 43,000 sq. m.; population (1970 estimate) 1,523,050, of whom some 12,000 are Negroes of U.S. origin; capital Monrovia, a free port; official language English. Liberia was founded in 1820 by the philanthropic American Colonization Society as a country for freed slaves from the U.S.A., and became an independent republic in 1847. Executive power is vested in a President, elected for eight years and eligible for further periods of four years, and his cabinet. William Vacanarat Shadrach Tubman, first elected President in May 1943, was re-elected in 1951, 1955, 1959, 1963, 1967 and 1971. He died in July 1971 and was succeeded by his Vice-President, William Richard Tolbert. The Constitution, modelled on that of the U.S.A., provides for a legislature comprising a Senate of 18 elected for six years, and a House of Representatives of 52 elected for four years. The political parties are the Independent True Whigs and the True Whigs. Electors must be of Negro blood and landowners or hut tax-payers; women can also vote if so qualified. Liberia exports crude rubber, high-grade ores (especially iron), gold, palm kernels and palm oil, and obtains revenue from registration fees of the world's largest merchant fleet (more than 33 million gross tons in 1970). The country has received loans from the Export-Import Bank of America for road construction and the improvement of electricity supplies, assistance for education from the Agency of International Development, and U.S. government aid. A free trading zone embracing Liberia, Guinea, Ivory Coast and Sierra Leone came into existence in March 1965.

Libya. An independent state in North Africa; area 679,358 sq. m., mostly consisting of barren deserts; population (1969 estimate) 1,875,000, mostly Arabs, with some Berbers in the west and African Negros in the Fezzan; the Jewish population was expelled in 1967 and the Italian minority in Tripolitania in 1970; official religion Islam and official language Arabic; capital Tripoli; before 1969 Benghazi was a co-capital. From the sixteenth century the land was ruled by the Turks; in a secret agreement of 1900 the French, who controlled Tunisia, undertook not to oppose Italian claims in Libya, while

Italy promised France a free hand in Morocco. In 1912 France established its protectorate over Morocco, and Italy annexed Libya after the Turco-Italian War of 1911–12. Under Italian rule there was considerable migration from Italy to Libya, road construction and agricultural improvement, all of which met with strong local resistance, particularly among Senussi tribesmen of Cyrenaica.

In 1942 the U.K. gave a pledge that the Senussi would never again be subjected to Italian rule, but after the defeat of Italy in the Second World War there was considerable disagreement among the victorious powers as to the fate of Libya. France advocated Italian trusteeship, feeling the need of a companion in its own position. The U.S.S.R. also advocated Italian trusteeship, hoping in this way to win support for the Communists in the Italian elections. On 21 November 1949 the United Nations General Assembly resolved that Libya should become independent, and this was achieved on 24 December 1951. Mohammed Idris el Mahdi el Senussi, Emir of Cyrenaica, leader of the Senussi religious sect since 1916 and exiled since 1922, became King Idris I. From April 1963 until September 1969 Libya was a constitutional monarchy with a Council of Ministers and a bicameral legislature. On 1 September 1969 King Idris was deposed in a bloodless *coup* by army officers led by Colonel Muammer Qadhafi; they formed a Revolutionary Command Council and declared a republic. A new Constitution was proclaimed on 11 December 1969 and Colonel Qadhafi became Head of State. On 2 September 1971 Libya entered into a Federation of Arab Republics, *q.v.*, with Syria and Egypt, which thereupon renounced the name of United Arab Republic. In August 1972 plans were announced to merge Libya and Egypt into a single state by 1 September 1973.

Technical and financial help was essential prior to the discovery of oil in 1959 to prevent Libya from reverting to its former primitive pastoral economy. By a treaty of alliance and friendship signed on 29 July 1953 the U.K. promised financial aid for 20 years, including £5,000,000 for economic development and £13,750,000 for balancing the budget over the first five years of that period. The responsibility for assistance in economic development was taken over by the U.S.A., which agreed to pay $5,500,000 annually, quite apart from any other aid provided under special agreements. In return Libya permitted the U.K. and U.S.A. to maintain military bases; but in 1967, following the Arab-Israeli war, it began to negotiate their closure. By 31 March 1970 the British military establishment had been evacuated. Oil, which was first exported in 1962 when the pipeline from the Esso-Zelten field to the sea was opened, accounts for 99 per cent of Libya's export earnings, although providing employment for only 5 per cent of the total labour force. In 1971 Libya's output of crude oil, of 160 million tons, was equal to that of Persia and greater than Saudi Arabia's. On 7 December 1971 the Libyan government announced that, in retaliation for British failure to prevent the occupation by Persia on 30 November of the islands of Greater and Lesser Tumbs in the Persian Gulf (*see* Trucial States), it had nationalized the assets and operations of British Petroleum. A new company was formed, the Arabian Gulf Exploration Co., to take over the assets, worth about £75,000,000 and representing some 5 per cent of the total crude oil output of the Middle East.

Liechtenstein. An independent state on the Upper Rhine between Austria and Switzerland; area 62 sq. m.; population (1970) 21,350; language German; capital Vaduz. The principality, which has one town and ten villages, was formerly part of the Holy Roman Empire, achieving complete independence in 1806. It has a customs union with Switzerland, and the currency is Swiss. Under the 1921 Constitution the legislature is a Diet of 15 members elected for four years by universal suffrage and proportional representation. Prince Franz Josef II (born 1906) became Head of State in 1938. There is no army.

Lindsay, John Vliet. U.S. politician; born 1922, the son of an investment banker; educated at Yale University. He is a lawyer and a former assistant to the attorney-general during the presidency of Dwight D. Eisenhower, *q.v.* He belonged to the liberal wing of the Republican Party, *q.v.*, and campaigned vigorously on behalf of civil rights, *q.v.* As the Congressman for New York, Manhattan, he withstood the Democratic landslide in the City and retained his seat in November 1964. He was elected Mayor of New York in 1965 and re-elected in 1969 as an Independent, having lost the official Republican nomination. He had been extremely critical of Federal inaction over gun controls, and blamed the violence of New York city on the continuation of the war in Viet-Nam. In August 1971 he announced that he had left the Republican Party to join the Democratic Party, *q.v.*

Lin Piao. Chinese Communist politician and soldier; born 1910. He graduated with honours as an officer-cadet from the Whampao Military Academy in Canton in 1926, and in 1927 followed his former superior officer, Chou En-lai, *q.v.*, to defend the Communists in the Yangste valley against the Kuomintang, *q.v.* He became a member of the Communist Party in 1927, and in 1934 joined the march, led by Mao Tse-tung, *q.v.*, to Shensi. He fought the Japanese in Manchuria and in 1945 organized the Communist offensive which eventually drove Chiang Kai-shek, *q.v.*, from the Chinese mainland. He fought in Korea at the head of an army of Chinese volunteers; he subsequently contracted tuberculosis. In 1959 he was appointed Minister of Defence with the task of restoring discipline to an army discontented through a lack of efficient modern weapons. He transformed the army into an instrument of Mao's cultural revolution, designed to support the peasants of Asia in their liberation of the towns; emphasis was placed on training for guerilla warfare, rankings were abolished and every soldier took the title of comrade. In 1966 he took precedence over Chou En-lai, and was placed second only to Chairman Mao, in the Communist Party hierarchy. In 1972 it was confirmed that he had died in an air crash over Mongolia in September 1971, fleeing the country after an abortive attempt to seize power.

Liquidation. Literally the winding up of the affairs of a company and its termination as a legal entity. The term is used also to describe the removal of people for political reasons, usually by execution but sometimes by imprisonment in an unknown place. In recent years the Communists in China and the French authorities in North Africa (especially in Algeria before it became independent in 1962) have been euphemistically described as having 'liquidated' many who opposed their regimes.

Lithuania. One of the 15 constituent Republics of the Union of Soviet Socialist Republics since 1940; area about 25,170 sq. m.; population (1969) 3,160,000, of whom about 2,000,000 are Roman Catholics; 79·3 per cent of the population are Lithuanians, 8·5 per cent Poles, 8·5 per cent Russians and the rest Byelorussians; capital Vilnius (Vilna). The Republic, which is on the Baltic Sea, was a great power in the fourteenth and fifteenth centuries with territories stretching to the Black Sea, but was a province of the Russian Empire when it recovered its independence in 1918. Poland seized the capital, then called Vilna, in 1920. Quarrels with Poland over Vilna and with Germany over Memel (a seaport detached from Germany in 1919 and made a free city to give Lithuania a port on the Baltic Sea but seized by the Lithuanians in 1923) were the main preoccupation of Lithuanian foreign ministers between the two world wars. A benevolent dictatorship was overthrown in 1926 and the parliamentary Constitution ignored by the conservative and agrarian Nationalist Union Party which allowed no opposition at all. In March 1939 Germany re-annexed Memel after local elections in which the German Party had secured 87 per cent of the vote, but Lithuania was granted a free zone in the port. The U.S.S.R. restored Vilna to Lithuania in 1939 after it had invaded Poland, but manned the town with a

Russian garrison. Under an agreement between the U.S.S.R. and Germany made on 23 August 1939, Lithuania was occupied by the U.S.S.R. in June 1940, and became a constituent Republic on 3 August 1940. Large numbers of Lithuanians and Poles were deported to the east. The chief industries have always been agriculture and forestry (forests occupy 16·3 per cent of the whole area), but since 1945 intensive industrialization has taken place in heavy engineering, ship-building, electrical equipment, cement production and footwear.

Little Ruhr. A term used to describe an area in eastern Europe similar to the concentration of industry around the river Ruhr in western Europe. It is an area which produces coal and steel, comprising the Moravská Ostrava coalfield of Czechoslovakia, Upper Silesia (formerly part of Germany but awarded to Poland under the Potsdam and Yalta agreements) and the district between Kraków and Czestochowa, in Poland. It is exploited not by the two nations separately but as an economic unit, thus resembling the European Coal and Steel Community, *q.v.*, and its development is linked to the Russian industrial plan.

Little Seven. The seven British Caribbean islands of Barbados, *q.v.*, St Vincent, St Lucia, Dominica, Montserrat, St Kitts–Nevis–Anguilla and Antigua. Following the dissolution of the West Indies Federation, *q.v.*, and the withdrawal of Grenada which opted for unitary association with Trinidad, the Regional Council of Ministers for these seven islands prepared a draft scheme for a federal government. This proposed a two-chamber federal legislature with responsibility for customs, the judiciary, income tax, prisons, postal services and telecommunications, civil aviation, meteorology, currency, banking, university education and external affairs. Barbados was to have been the capital; no member would have been allowed to secede from the federation. When Barbados, the only one of the islands which was independent of British financial assistance, became self-governing on 30 November 1966, the remaining islands were offered Associate Status, *q.v.*, within the Commonwealth, and those which accepted formed the West Indies Associated States, *q.v.*

Liu Shao-chi. Chinese Communist leader, and Chairman from 1959 to 1969 of the People's Republic of China; born in 1905, the son of a Hunan peasant farmer. He attended the same school as Mao Tse-tung, *q.v.*, took up a scholarship in Moscow in 1920, and in 1921 joined the Socialist Youth Organization. The following year he became a member of the Secretariat of the China Labour Union; his assignment was the organization of Communist unions in the towns. From 1927, when he was elected to the Central Committee of the

Chinese Communist Party and leader of the Chinese Revolutionary Trade Union Movement, he worked underground until 1932 when he was appointed to organize the workers' movement in Kiangsi (where Mao had set up a soviet government). In 1935 he became active in the students' resistance movement against the Japanese invaders, and as Secretary of the North and Central China Bureaux of the Communist Party Central Committee he spent the years from 1936 to 1942 building up cells in the occupied cities of Peking, Tientsin and Shanghai. He then joined the Secretariat of the Central Committee and became Vice-Chairman of the People's Revolutionary Military Council in 1943. He was subsequently Chairman of the International Labour Federation and Vice-Chairman of the People's Political Consultative Council. He was considered to be one of the Chinese Communist Party's leading theorists and among its most influential members until 1966 when he was subjected to public criticism of his ideology by Mao, and his wife to a private vendetta on the part of Chiang Ching (Mao's wife). He was accused of Soviet Revisionism, *q.v.*, and of emphasizing the importance of the industrial worker in the revolution at the expense of the peasant, who, according to Mao, would liberate the cities from the countryside. In 1968 he was stripped of all his public offices, except that of Chairman of the Republic, from which he was constitutionally removed in 1969.

Lobbying (originally a U.S. expression). Persuading members of a legislature to support or oppose a Bill by means of personal contacts, especially in the 'lobbies' or parts of a legislative building to which the public has access. Reference is frequently made in the U.S.A. to the China Lobby (advocating support of Chiang Kai-shek), and to the Farmers' Lobby (advocating higher federal subsidies for agricultural interests).

Locarno Treaty. An agreement concluded between Belgium, France, Germany, Italy, and the U.K. on 16 November 1925, by which Belgium, France, and Germany undertook to maintain their frontiers as they then were and to abstain from the use of force against each other. Germany recognized the status of the Rhineland, which had been demilitarized in perpetuity by the peace treaties after the First World War. Italy and the U.K. guaranteed the Treaty, and there were provisions for mutual assistance in the event of its breach. The Treaty was brought to an end by Germany in 1936 when Adolf Hitler sent German troops into the Rhineland. In 1953 Sir Winston Churchill, then Prime Minister of the U.K., proposed a new agreement between the German Federal Republic, Poland, the U.K., the U.S.S.R., and others, by which the eastern European frontiers established after the Second World War could be guaranteed in a manner similar to that adopted in the Treaty of Locarno.

Low Countries. A collective name for Belgium, Luxemburg, and the Netherlands.

Luthuli, Chief Albert John. African nationalist; born about 1898 in Rhodesia; during his childhood his father was an interpreter at a Congregationalist mission in Natal; his uncle was chieftain of the Abasemakholweni Zulu tribe; he was educated at a mission school in Natal, the Ohlange Institute, and a Methodist institution near Pietermaritzburg. He was a teacher at Adams Mission Station College from 1921 to 1936, when he became chieftain of the Abasemakholweni tribe at Groutville. He was later a member of the Christian Council of South Africa, Chairman of the Congregational Churches of the American Board, and President of the Natal Mission Conference. In 1952 he took part in a passive resistance campaign organized by the African National Congress (of which he was the Natal leader). The South African government later deposed him as chief because he refused to abandon the campaign and resign from the African National Congress. The tribal elders refused to appoint a successor and he then became President of the African National Congress. In December 1956 he was arrested, with 156 other Africans, and charged with high treason, but the charges against him were withdrawn a year later. In May 1959 he was banished to his sugar-cane farm for five years under the Riotous Assemblies Act and the Suppression of Communism Act. In March 1960 72 Africans were shot dead at Sharpeville while making a peaceful demonstration; Luthuli burnt his pass in public. He was fined for doing so, and then arrested (and later released) when the government banned the African National Congress. In 1961 he was awarded the Nobel Peace Prize for 1960. The Prize Committee stated that the award was made because 'in his fight against racial discrimination he had always worked for non-violent methods'.

Luxemburg. An independent state, and a Grand Duchy, situated between Germany, Belgium, and France; area 999 sq. m.; population (1970 estimate) 339,848, nearly all Roman Catholics; capital Luxemburg. Most people speak German or Letzeburgesch but the official language is French; they are a Germanic people with a French outlook.

Luxemburg was given to the Orange family (rulers of the Netherlands) in 1815 in compensation for their estates in Nassau, which were handed over to Prussia. In 1890 the King of the Netherlands died and it passed to the Duke of Nassau. It was occupied by Germany in the First World War and in 1921 entered a customs union with Belgium. After being again occupied by Germany in the Second World War it was freed and, with Belgium, entered the customs union of Benelux, *q.v.*, on 29 October 1947. On 28 April 1948 Luxemburg amended its Constitution so as to abandon its former neutrality (which had prevailed since 1867) and then joined the Brussels Treaty Organization, *q.v.*, and the North Atlantic Treaty Organization, *q.v.*

The ruler since November 1964 has been Grand Duke Jean (born 5 January 1921) who succeeded his mother Grand Duchess Charlotte, when she abdicated. There is a Chamber of 56 Deputies, elected by universal suffrage, general elections for the whole Chamber being held once every five years. At elections held in November 1968 there were returned: Christian Socials 21 (22 in 1964); Socialists 18 (21); Liberals 11 (6); Communists 6 (5); the two Independents elected in 1964 lost their seats. After a three-month cabinet crisis Pierre Werner (Christian Social), who had been Prime Minister since 1959, agreed to form another coalition government of Christian Socials and Liberals.

There is an important steel industry with an annual productive capacity of 5 million tons, giving the country the world's highest output per head; the headquarters of the European Coal and Steel Community, *q.v.*, are in Luxemburg.

Lynch, John. Irish politician; born 1917 in Cork and educated at the North Monastery Christian Brothers' School, Cork. In 1936 he entered the Civil Service, as a clerk in the Department of Justice, studying law in his spare time at University College, Cork, and then at King's Inn, Dublin. He qualified as a barrister in 1945 and practised in Cork and Munster. In 1948 he was elected to the Dáil Éireann as a Fianna Fáil candidate and was appointed Parliamentary Secretary to the Government and to the Minister for Lands in 1951. He held successively the ministerial posts of the Gaeltacht, in 1957, Education, 1957 to 1959, Industry and Commerce, 1959 to 1965, and Finance, 1965 to November 1966 when he succeeded Sean Lemass as Prime Minister.

After the defeat of Fianna Fáil in the general election of March 1973 he resigned, and was succeeded as Prime Minister by Liam Cosgrave, *q.v.*

M

Macao. A Portuguese overseas territory comprising a peninsula, and two islands off the Chinese mainland, at the mouth of the Canton river, and to the west of Hong Kong; area 6 sq. m.; population (1960 census) 169,299. The land is held as the result of a treaty with China concluded on 1 December 1887.

McCarthyism. Intolerance of liberalism. Joseph McCarthy (1909–57), was elected to the U.S. Senate to represent Wisconsin in 1946; in February 1950 he said that there were 205 Communists in the State Department (a figure which he later reduced to 57 and then increased to 81) and subsequently made other attacks on the integrity of individual government employees. In a large majority of cases his accusations, often made at public sessions of Senate sub-committees, so that he was protected by Congressional privilege, were found to have no substance. In December 1954 his colleagues, by a majority of 67 to 22, censured him for bringing the Senate into dishonour and disrepute. His activities, which probably hampered the government in its task of seeking out Russian spies, won the approval of many Americans who suspected most liberals, and even those who tried to be impartial politically, of being sympathetic to the Communist cause.

Macedonia. A region in the centre of the Balkan peninsula which gives its name both to a Greek prefecture and to one of the Federal Republics of Yugoslavia; it has never been a racial, linguistic, or political unit. It was for many years under Turkish rule and, in the latter half of the nineteenth and the early years of the twentieth century, was coveted by Austria-Hungary, Bulgaria, Greece, Russia, and Serbia. The population is a mixture of Serbs, Bulgars, Greeks, Turks, Arnauts, Gipsies, Spanish Jews, and Kutso-Vlakhs.

After the Second Balkan War of 1912–13 Macedonia was partitioned, mainly between Serbia and Greece, although Bulgaria obtained a small area in the east near Strumitza. Thereafter the parts were called South Serbia and North Greece respectively. After the First World War Bulgaria retained a still smaller area, the Petritch district. Approximately 209,000 Macedonians fled to Bulgaria, where they formed an influential political group. A secret organization in Macedonia, the Internal Macedonian Revolutionary Organization (I.M.R.O.), which had been created to fight the Turks, carried on subversive activities against the Yugoslavian government in Macedonia, with support from Bulgaria and at times from Italy. In 1941 Bulgaria occupied Yugoslavian Macedonia and the eastern part of Greek Macedonia, but the Paris Peace Treaty of January 1947 restored the frontier to its pre-1941 limits. The Greek prefecture of Macedonia has a population of approximately 1,900,000, the Yugoslavian Republic of Macedonia has approximately 1,500,000 people, while there are also nearly 300,000 Macedonians across the border in Bulgarian Macedonia (Pirin). Occasional Bulgarian and Yugoslavian references to the Macedonian minority in northern Greece are resented by the Greek government.

McGovern, George. U.S. Democratic Party politician; born 19 July 1922 in Avon, South Dakota, and educated at Dakota Wesleyan University and at Northwestern University, where he later held a teaching post and fellowship. He served in the U.S. Air Force, earning distinction as a bomber pilot, during the Second World War, after which he returned to university life. From 1950 to 1953 he was a Professor of History and Government at Dakota Wesleyan University. In 1953 he became Executive Secretary of the South Dakota Democratic Party, entering the House of Representatives in 1956 where, as a member of the Agricultural Committee, he urged wider distribution of U.S. food surpluses. President Kennedy appointed him as director of the Food for Peace Programme in 1961; his published works, *War Against Want* and *Agricultural Thought in the Twentieth Century*, reflected his involvement in the problem of world hunger. In 1962 he won a seat in the Senate for South Dakota, in which the Democrats are in an electoral minority, and was re-elected by an even larger margin of votes in 1968. He presided over the Democratic Commission on Party Structure and Delegate Selection in 1971 which introduced reforms designed to broaden the social, ethnic, age and sex qualifications of delegates to the Party Convention. In 1972 he contested the Presidential election as the Democratic candidate, winning the nomination from Hubert Humphrey, *q.v.*, Edmund Muskie, *q.v.*, and George Wallace, *q.v.* He represents the radical and liberal wing of the Democratic Party, advocating a redistribution of income, an extension of welfare and drastic cuts in defence expenditure; as a 'Dove', *q.v.*, he campaigned on a policy of immediate peace in VietNam. He antagonized many traditional Democratic Party supporters; George Meany, *q.v.*, refused A.F. of L.–C.I.O. endorsement of his nomination because he had voted in the Senate to retain the Right to Work Laws which made the closed shop illegal. He was overwhelmingly defeated in the Presidential election, receiving 38 per cent of the total vote and winning only one State.

McMahon Correspondence. Eight letters, written between Emir Hussein, Sherif of Mecca, and Sir Henry McMahon, the High Commissioner for Egypt, in 1915 and 1916, which the Arabs regarded as involving a

British promise to include at least part of Palestine, *q.v.*, in an Arab state. In the correspondence McMahon agreed that an Arab state should be established as payment to the Arabs for their help to the allied powers in the war against the Turks. Hussein had in July 1915 demanded Arab independence in Arabia, Syria, and Mesopotamia, in an area bounded on the south and east by the Indian Ocean, the Persian Gulf, and the Persian frontier, on the west by the Red Sea and the Mediterranean, and on the north by latitude 37 from Messina to Persia. McMahon, realizing the urgent need for Arab help, wrote to Hussein on 24 October 1915, stating that the U.K. was prepared 'to recognize and uphold the independence of the Arabs in all the regions lying within the frontiers proposed by the Sherif of Mecca', with the exception of certain areas 'lying to the west of the districts of Damascus, Homs, Hama, and Aleppo', on the ground that they were not purely Arab. The U.K. later claimed that Palestine, which in 1919 was still almost entirely Arab, had been included in this exemption as lying west of Damascus. There was considerable argument as to whether the McMahon undertaking contradicted the Balfour Declaration, *q.v.* After the First World War only Saudi Arabia, in Arabia proper, became independent; farther north, Iraq, Palestine, and Transjordan were established as British Mandates, and Lebanon and Syria as French Mandates.

McMahon Line. The border between India and China as agreed at Simla in 1914 by China, Tibet, and the U.K. McMahon led the British delegation. The agreement has been repudiated by China, which claims 30,000 square miles of the North-East Frontier Tract, known also as the North-East Frontier Agency, *q.v.*, to the south of the Line and almost to the Brahmaputra valley. The Line was intended to run across the watersheds of the highest mountains. China claims that the border should run along the southern foothills of the mountains. The boundary between Burma and China, to the east, is in effect a continuation of the McMahon Line, but was recognized by China in 1960.

McMahon, William. Australian politician; born 23 February 1908 and educated at Sydney Grammar School and Sydney University where he graduated in law and economics. Until 1939, when he volunteered for war service in the Australian Army, he practised as a solicitor. He was first elected to the House of Representatives in 1949, becoming Deputy Leader of the Liberal Party in 1966 and Leader in 1971. Before he succeeded John Gorton, by Gorton's own casting vote against himself, as Leader of the Liberal Party on 10 March 1971 he had held government office continuously for twenty years. He was

Minister for Navy and Air from 1951–4, Minister for Social Services from 1954–6, Minister for Primary Industry 1956–8 and Minister of Labour and National Service from 1958 to 1966. He became Federal Treasurer in 1966, Minister for Foreign Affairs in 1969, and Prime Minister from 1971 to 1972 when the Liberal Party was defeated at the general election. In December 1972 he was succeeded as Leader of the Liberal Party by Billie Mackie Snedden.

Macmillan, Harold. Prime Minister (from 1957 to 1963) and Conservative Party politician; born 10 February 1894, educated at Eton. He served during the First World War in the Grenadier Guards, being wounded three times, and was at Balliol College, Oxford, from 1918 to 1919; when he left he became A.D.C. to the Governor-General of Canada, a post which he held until 1920. He contested unsuccessfully the Stockton-on-Tees Parliamentary Division in 1923, but later served as M.P. for the Division from 1924 to 1929 and from 1931 to 1945. He was for some time a Director in the family publishing firm of Macmillan and Co. In the years between his election as an M.P. and the outbreak of the Second World War, Macmillan repeatedly attacked the leaders and the doctrines of the Conservative Party. He criticized the party for its foreign as well as for its domestic policy, and temporarily withdrew from the Conservative Parliamentary Party in 1936 in protest against the government's acceptance of the Italian invasion of Ethiopia. He became Parliamentary Secretary to the Ministry of Supply, his first office, when the Churchill government was formed in 1940, and Parliamentary Under-Secretary of State for the Colonies in 1942. From 1942 to 1945 he was Minister Resident at Allied H.Q. in North-West Africa, and helped to negotiate the settlement between the French Generals de Gaulle and Giraud. He became Secretary of State for Air in 1945. At the General Election of that year he lost his parliamentary seat, but won a by-election at Bromley in November 1945. In opposition he did much, with R. A. Butler, to modernize Conservative policy. On the return to power of the Conservatives in 1951, he became Minister of Housing and Local Government. He was Minister of Defence from 1954 to 1955, and Foreign Secretary from May to December 1955 when he succeeded R. A. Butler as Chancellor of the Exchequer. He was Prime Minister from January 1957, after the resignation of Sir Anthony Eden, until October 1963.

Madagascar. An island, off the east coast of southern Africa, which in 1958 became an independent republic known as the Malagasy Republic, *q.v.*, and one of the member states of the French Community, *q.v.*

Maghreb. Arab name describing the area covered by the three independent states of Morocco, Algeria, and Tunisia. Attempts have been
made to establish policies common to all three states.

Makarios, Archbishop. Ethnarch (church leader) of the Orthodox
Church in Cyprus, *q.v.*; born 13 August 1913 at Panayia, Cyprus;
educated at a village school, at Kykko Monastery, at the Pan-
cyprian gymnasium, Nicosia, and the Athens School of Theology,
from which he graduated in 1943. He was ordained as a priest of
the Greek Orthodox Church in 1946; with a scholarship awarded
by the World Council of Churches he studied at Boston University.
He returned to Cyprus when he was elected Bishop of Kitiou and
after two years was elected Archbishop. He advocated Enosis
(Union with Greece) but opinions varied as to the extent of his
responsibility for the acts of violence that took place in Cyprus.
In March 1956 he was deported to the Seychelles Islands by order
of the Governor of Cyprus, who said that Makarios was 'deeply
implicated in the campaign of terrorism'. He was released in March
1957, and after the Cyprus settlement had been concluded was
elected President, being proclaimed on 14 December 1959. Cyprus
became independent on 16 August 1960.

Malacca Straits. *See* Straits of Malacca.

Malagasy Republic. An independent republic; area 229,975 sq. m.;
population (1968) 7,027,415, of whom 95 per cent are of Asian
origin and the rest are French, Comorian, Indian and Chinese;
capital Tananarive. The country is an island 240 miles off the east
coast of southern Africa and was originally called Madagascar after
being discovered by the Portuguese Diaz in 1500, owing to a confusion with the Kingdom of Mogadishu on the north-eastern coast of
Africa. France controlled the island from 1885 until it achieved self-
government within the French Community, *q.v.*, on 14 October 1958,
followed by complete independence, still within the Community, on
4 April 1960.

Legislative powers are vested in two bodies: the National Assembly
of 107 members elected by universal suffrage every five years, and the
Senate of 54 appointed members. The principal political parties are
the Social Democratic Party (P.S.D., which won an overwhelming
majority in 1965), led by Philibert Tsiranana (the President of the
Republic), and the Malagasy Democratic and Social Union. Executive
powers are exercised by the President, who is also leader of the government; he is elected for seven years by an electoral college consisting
of the National Assembly, the Senate, and representatives of local
authorities. In January 1972 President Tsiranana was re-elected for

a third term, despite widespread unrest among students and urban workers. An armed insurrection in the south was suppressed in April 1971 with the aid of the French who are universally disliked. A student revolt of May 1972 was directed both against the autocratic rule of the President and against his policy of cooperation with South Africa.

The principal exports are rice, coffee, sugar, groundnuts, sisal, raffia, cloves, vanilla, meat, graphite, tobacco and mica; there are also deposits of beryl, phosphates, columbium, and quartz. Most of the trade is with France.

Malawi. An independent state and member of the British Commonwealth. It is in central Africa, with Tanzania to the north and east (across Lake Nyasa), Zambia to the west, and Mozambique to the south and east; land area 36,686 sq. m.; population (1971 estimate) 4,039,583, of whom 20,000 are Asians and Europeans and the rest Africans; seat of government Zomba, but a new capital is to be built at Lilongwe.

The country became a British protectorate in 1891 and was known as British Central Africa until 1907, when it became known as Nyasaland. In 1953 it became part of the Federation of Rhodesia and Nyasaland, *q.v.* Demands by its African leaders for self-government and the right to secede were eventually met in 1961 by the introduction of a new Constitution and an extension of the franchise in 1962 by the granting of the right to secede; and in 1963 by the amendment of the Constitution and the introduction of self-government. On 31 December 1963 the Federation was dissolved.

The elections held on 15 August 1961 resulted in the Malawi Congress Party, led by Dr Hastings Banda, *q.v.*, and Y. K. Chisiza, winning 22 seats, the United Federal Party 5 seats, and an independent 1 seat. The right to secede from the Federation was recognized by the British government in December 1962. Nyasaland became self-governing on 1 February 1963, when Banda was sworn in as Prime Minister. It became an independent state, as Malawi, and within the British Commonwealth, on 6 July 1964. It was decided in 1965 that Malawi would become a republic and a one-party state with the introduction of the new Constitution on 6 July 1966. Dr Banda became the first President, and in 1971 was appointed President for life. The name of the country is derived from the African Maravi, the old name for the lake area now covered by the country.

Malawi, which is land-locked and largely agricultural, produces tea (the largest exported crop), cotton, groundnuts and tobacco; until November 1965 the U.K. encouraged economic collaboration with Zambia and Rhodesia, but the application of economic sanctions to Rhodesia, from which 36 per cent of all imports were obtained, caused a diversion of trade to South Africa. Malawi's recognition of the republic of South Africa in 1967 provoked strong criticism within the Organization of African Unity, *q.v.*, of which Malawi is a member. In August 1971 Dr Banda became the first African head of state to visit South Africa.

Malaya. One of the three constituent parts of the Federation of Malaysia, *q.v.*, area 50,700 sq. m.; population (1967 estimate) 8,655,299, including 4,351,021 Malays, 3,157,423 Chinese, and 957,944 Indians and Pakistanis; capital Kuala Lumpur. In 1948 it became a federation of the nine states of the Malay peninsula and the two straits settlements of Penang and Malacca. The first Prime Minister was Tunku Abdul Rahman, *q.v.*, who was the first Chief Minister to be appointed under the 1955 Constitution, when a ministerial system of government replaced the old wholly-nominated Executive Council. He led the Triple Alliance (formed by the United Malays' National Organization (U.M.N.O.), the Malayan Chinese Association (M.C.A.) and the Malayan Indian Congress) which in July 1955 won 51 out of the 52 elective seats on a programme of self-government by 1959. On 31 August 1957 Malaya became a sovereign and independent member of the British Commonwealth. Under the Constitution which then obtained, the nine rulers of the states elected a Paramount Ruler who took office as Head of State for five years. The Head of State elected in September 1970 was Sultan Abdul Halim Mu'azzam Shah ibni Al-Marhum Sultan Badlishah, ruler of Kedah; he was subsequently elected Head of State of Malaysia

The country was the centre of Communist guerilla warfare from 1948 to 1960. British armed forces were engaged in putting down a small jungle army, recruited from members of the Malayan Communist Party (banned since 1926) who had resisted the Japanese occupation, and supplied with arms smuggled across the Thai frontier from China. General Templer, the High Commissioner from 1953 to 1954, employed punitive measures against the Min Yuen, the civilian wing of the Communist army which provided it with information and equipment; at the same time he introduced social reforms and arranged the first municipal elections. On 31 July 1960 the state of emergency was terminated. In July 1963 the U.K., Malaya and Singapore agreed to establish Malaysia, and the Federation was inaugurated on 16 September 1963. Singapore has since seceded.

Politics are complicated by the country's economic dependence on rubber, of which Malaya is the world's largest producer, and tin (40 per cent of world output), the price of which fluctuates considerably.

By imposing tolls on shipping in the Straits of Malacca, *q.v.*, Malay politicians hope to compensate for the shortage of foreign currency occasioned by a fall in world prices. Differences between the races are reflected in their respective economic status; in 1971 the Chinese, who constitute 36 per cent of the population, owned 22·8 per cent of the share capital in limited companies whereas the Malays, comprising 50 per cent of the population, owned only 1·5 per cent of shares. The government has undertaken a programme of investment designed to achieve 30 per cent Malay ownership of the total commercial and industrial sector within 20 years. Serious disturbances occurred in May 1969 and rioting broke out in Kuala Lumpur between Malays and Chinese following Federal and State elections in which the Alliance Party lost its overwhelming majority; a state of emergency was declared which continued until February 1971 when the Legislature was reconvened. Tunku Abdul Rahman then resigned as Prime Minister of Malaysia and was succeeded by his Deputy, Tun Abdul Razak.

Malaysia. An independent member of the British Commonwealth, it is a Federation of Malaya, *q.v.*, Sabah, *q.v.* (formerly British North Borneo), and Sarawak, *q.v.*; area 128,703 sq. m.; population (1968 estimate) 10,455,119; federal capital Kuala Lumpur. The official religion is Islam. Agreement was reached by Malaya, Singapore, *q.v.*, and the U.K. in July 1963 that the Federation (which Brunei, *q.v.*, decided not to join) should be established, and it came into existence on 16 September 1963 under the premiership of Tunku Abdul Rahman, *q.v.* As a result Malaya and Singapore ceased to be separate Dominions; Singapore seceded from the Federation in August 1965 and became an independent republic. The Head of State and Prime Minister of Malaysia are the Head of State and Prime Minister of Malaya. The federal parliament comprises a House of Representatives of 144 members (104 from Malaya, 24 from Sarawak and 16 from Sabah), and a Senate of 58 members, 32 of whom are appointed by the Head of State, and the rest elected by the legislative assemblies of Sabah, Sarawak and the eleven States of Malaya.

Malaysia, divided by the South China Sea, consists of the Malayan peninsula and the north-western part (Sabah and Sarawak) of the island of Borneo, *q.v.* There was opposition to the creation of the Federation from Indonesia and the Philippines. Indonesia, which originally claimed the whole of the island of Borneo, proposed the adoption of Maphilindo, *q.v.*, and engaged in a policy of confrontation, *q.v.*, from 1963 to 1966. In September 1968 the Philippines claimed sovereignty over most of Sabah. In November 1971 the governments of Malaysia and Indonesia, who had concluded a boundary treaty the previous year based on mutual acknowledgement of a 12-mile territorial limit round their coasts, claimed sovereignty over the Straits of Malacca, *q.v.*, which for more than 200 miles of their length are less than 24 miles wide. About 75 per cent of the land area of Malaysia is forest; the major exports include tin and rubber, timber, sago, copra, iron ore, and pepper. Owing to its tin and rubber industries the country enjoys one of the highest standards of living in Asia.

Maldives, Republic of. An independent state south-west of Sri Lanka, known as the Maldive Islands until April 1969, comprising over 7,000 islands in 12 groups; area 115 sq. m.; population (living on approximately 220 of the islands) 114,469 in 1971; capital Malé, on King's Island. The people are of Sinhalese extraction and were once Buddhists, but they were converted to Islam in the twelfth century. In 1887 the Sultan recognized British suzerainty and agreed not to enter into treaty relations with other states, except through the U.K. in its capacity as ruler of Ceylon (now Sri Lanka). When Ceylon became independent in 1948 this obligation continued, but was transferred to the U.K. High Commissioner in Ceylon. During the Second World War there was a British air base on Gan Island in the Addu Atoll of the Maldive Islands. In January 1957 the Maldivian government agreed to the re-establishment of the base to compensate for the cession of the British bases of Trincomalee and Katunayake to Ceylon. In July 1965 Gan Island was leased to the U.K. for 21 years.

Until March 1968 the Maldives were ruled by a Sultan, Al Amir Mohamed Farid Didi. After a referendum had been held a republic was declared, and Amir Ibrahim Nasir, who had been Prime Minister under the Sultan, was elected President. There is a legislative assembly (Majlis) of 54 members; 8 are elected from Malé, 2 from every atoll, and there are 8 nominated members. The principal export is dried Maldive fish, made from bonito; the entire output is sold to the Sri Lanka government.

Malenkov, Georgy Maximilianovich. A former Chairman of the Council of Ministers of the U.S.S.R.; born 8 January 1902. He fought in the Red Army during the civil war which followed the 1917 Revolution, joined the Communist Party in 1920, and then attended a Moscow higher technical school, where he was secretary of the Communist students' group. From 1925 onwards he worked with the Central Committee of the Communist Party and on Stalin's personal staff. During the Second World War he was appointed to the war cabinet, the only other members of which were Stalin, Molotov, Beria, and Zhdanov, and took charge of aircraft and tank production. When Stalin died in 1953 Malenkov succeeded him as Chairman of the Council of Ministers, but resigned in February 1955, saying that he was not competent to hold the post; he was appointed Minister of Electric Power Stations and a Vice-Chairman of the Council of Ministers, and succeeded as Chairman by Bulganin. In July 1957 he was dismissed from these posts and expelled from the Presidium and the Central Committee of the Party, allegedly for assisting in the creation of an 'anti-party group'.

Mali. An independent republic; area 528,437 sq. m.; population (of whom 80 per cent are illiterate) 4,929,000 (1969), comprising Bambara, Peulh, Markas, Songhais, Malinkés, Touareg, Miniunkas, Senoufos, Dogons and 7,000 Europeans; capital Bamako. The country is land-locked, with Mauritania and the Sahara departments of Algeria to the north, Senegal to the west, Guinea, Ivory Coast and Upper Volta to the south, and Niger to the east. For twelve centuries it was ruled successively by the Ghana, Mali and Songhai empires and by local Bambara chiefs; the French took it over in 1904 and, as French Soudan, it later became one of the eight territories of French West Africa, q.v.; as the Soudanese Republic it achieved self-government within the French Community, q.v., on 24 November 1958. On 4 April 1959 it entered into a federal union with Senegal, known as the Mali Federation, which itself achieved complete independence, still within the Community, on 20 June 1960. Senegal seceded from the Federation in August 1960, and on 22 September 1960 the Soudanese Republic declared that it would thenceforth be known as the Republic of Mali.

Legislative powers were originally vested in an assembly of 80 members elected every five years by universal suffrage. At the elections held in March 1959 and April 1964 all the seats were won by the Soudanese Union, the sole permitted political party from 1959 until 1967, when it was dissolved and replaced by the National Committee for the Defence of the Revolution. Executive authority rested with the President of the Council. Modibo Kéita, who had been elected to the French Parliament in 1956, had become its Deputy Speaker, and had held office in two French governments in 1957 and 1958, was elected President in 1960 and re-elected in 1964. A Moslem of the Malinké tribe, he was the former leader of the African Federation Party and Secretary-General of the Soudanese Union; his socialist policy gained him enemies inside Mali, mainly from the Touareg tribe of Iforas in the mountainous region of the north-east. He dissolved the Assembly in January 1968 and assumed full powers, becoming his own Prime Minister in May 1968. On 19 November 1968 he was deposed by a group of army officers led by Lieutenant Moussa Traore, and a National Liberation Committee was established to govern the country.

The principal exports are groundnuts, cotton, kapok, rice, live-stock and dried fish. Millet, maize and sorghum are produced, but only 20 per cent of the land is suitable for cultivation, and the most favourable area for crops is in the south, along the Niger. Most of the country's trade has to pass through the port of Dakar, in Senegal. Economic aid and advice have been received at various times since independence from China, Czechoslovakia, France, the German Federal Republic, and the U.S.A., among others. In 1967 Mali, which had issued its own non-convertible money since 1962, devalued its currency by 50 per cent and was readmitted to the French financial community.

Mali Federation. Created on 4 April 1959 by Senegal and the Soudanese Republic, it came to an end in the autumn of 1960, with the secession of Senegal in August of that year and a proclamation by the Soudanese Republic on 22 September that it would thenceforth be known as the Republic of Mali. Political and personal differences between the Senegalese, who are more prosperous, and whose population is smaller, and the Soudanese, who were hoping for a federal policy of planning and controls, brought about the dissolution of the Federation.

Malta. An island in the Mediterranean, between Sicily and Africa, it became an independent state within the British Commonwealth on 21 September 1964; it was seized by the British from the French in 1800 and, with Maltese consent, made a British colony in 1814; area, with two adjacent islands, 121·8 sq. m.; population (1970) 322,187, mostly Roman Catholics; capital Valletta. It has one of the highest population densities in the world, and there has been large-scale emigration. During the Second World War Malta suffered severe air bombardment and was awarded the George Cross in 1942 by King George VI. Under the 1947 Constitution the colony became self-governing through an elective Legislative Assembly, except that powers relating to defence, immigration, currency and foreign policy were reserved to the Governor. In a referendum held in February 1956, 75 per cent of those voting demanded integration with the U.K. and a status for Malta similar to that of Northern Ireland, including seats for Malta in the British House of Commons and the extension of British social services to Malta in return for the payment of British taxes. The Maltese Labour Party, led by the Prime Minister, Dom Mintoff, supported integration; the Nationalist Party, led by Giorgio Borg Olivier, boycotted the referendum. Mintoff resigned in 1958 after rejecting a British proposal for a five-year trial period for integration, and as a result of the disturbances that followed, a state of emergency was declared and the Constitution suspended. By 1961 both major political parties desired independence; internal self-government was reintroduced and elections held in February 1962 at which the Nationalist Party won a majority of seats. Dr Borg Olivier became Prime Minister and, with British approval, prepared a new Constitution, by which Malta is governed by a House of Representatives of 50 members (increased to 55 in 1971), elected every five years by universal suffrage and proportional representation; executive authority is vested in a Governor. This was approved by referendum and introduced on 21 September 1964. At elections held in March 1966 the Nationalist Party won 28 out of the 50 seats and Dr Borg Olivier continued in office as Prime Minister. But in the elections of June 1971 the Labour Party won 28 seats (22 in 1966), the Nationalist Party 27. The minor parties, including the Progressive Constitutional Party led by Mabel Strickland, which together had won 8 seats in 1962, were not represented, and Mr Mintoff formed a government.

Under a Defence Agreement, concluded at independence, British forces were entitled to remain in Malta for ten years. Most of Malta's products are purchased by the U.K., by British forces on the island and by tourists. Between 1967, when troops began to be withdrawn from Malta, and 1970 there was a dispute over £23 million in U.K. aid to development which was still outstanding; it was eventually resolved by 75 per cent being paid as a grant and 25 per cent as a loan over a five-year period. Immediately after his electoral victory Mr Mintoff terminated the Defence Agreement and requested rent for the facilities enjoyed by N.A.T.O. vessels. He expelled the Italian commander of the N.A.T.O. Mediterranean fleet, forced the replacement of the British Governor by a Maltese (Sir Anthony Mamo) in July 1971, banned the visits of U.S. naval vessels to Malta and initiated talks with the Libyan government on the island's future. After prolonged negotiations British troops began a complete withdrawal, but a new agreement was eventually reached on 26 March 1972 which restricted the use of Malta as a base to British forces for seven years. The U.K. was to pay an annual rent to Malta of £14 million of which £8,750,000 would be provided by her allies of N.A.T.O., q.v., on condition that no member country of the Warsaw Pact, q.v., would be allowed to use the island's military and naval facilities. In addition another £7 million in bilateral aid from N.A.T.O. sources was to be made available over the seven-year period. Shortly after the conclusion of the new agreement Mr Mintoff announced that he had negotiated additional aid from China and Libya.

Managerial Revolution. The passing of control from capitalists into the hands of the administrators in business and government. James Burnham (a New York University lecturer) in his book, *The Managerial Revolution*, published 1941, said that the future governing class would be the possessors not of wealth but of technical or administrative skill. They would control the instruments of production and receive preferential treatment in the distribution of the product of those instruments. The capitalists once had the benefits because they held property rights in the instruments of production. The managers would gain these benefits indirectly by control of the state which in turn would own and control the instruments of production. The state would, in effect, be the 'property' of the managers, and that would be enough to place them in the position of a ruling class.

Manchukuo. The name given by Japan to Manchuria, *q.v.*, when, after expelling the Chinese, it proclaimed a new independent state on 18 February 1932. The last Chinese Emperor of the Manchu dynasty, Henry Pu Yi, deposed as a boy in 1911 and brought up in Japan, was made President of Manchukuo. On 1 March 1934 he took the title of Emperor under the name of Kang Teh. The Empire of Manchukuo was at all times a puppet state under Japanese control. The country was occupied by a large Japanese army and there were Japanese advisers at all government offices. Japan did much to develop the agriculture and the rich mineral resources of Manchuria, established a number of industries, and in March 1935 forced the government to buy the Russian share in the East Chinese Railway (running through Manchuria to Vladivostok) for £10 million. The state was not recognized by China, the U.S.S.R., or any other powers except Germany, Italy, and Japan. When the Japanese armies were defeated it reverted to China, to which it had never ceased, in law, to belong. Pu Yi was captured by the Russians in 1945 and later handed over to the Chinese government.

Manchuria. Part of north-east China, covering Heilungkiang, Liaoning, and Kirin provinces and the former Jehol province (which in 1955 was abolished and shared by the Liaoning and Hopei provinces and the Inner Mongolia Autonomous Region); area 825,700 sq. m.; population approximately 50 million; three main cities Shenyang (Mukden), Changchun, and Lü-ta (Port Arthur–Dairen). Japan tried to gain control of Manchuria's mineral resources. After defeating Russia, whose forces had occupied much of Manchuria, the Japanese were granted special privileges under the Treaty of Peking, 1905, including the right to maintain some 15,000 soldiers in Manchuria to protect the South Manchurian Railway, the line running south from the Trans-Siberian Railway to the naval base of Port Arthur. Russia continued to control the Trans-Siberian Railway through its own territory and the East Chinese Railway through Manchuria, both of which lines ran to Vladivostok. In September 1931 Japan accused the Chinese of having blown up part of the South Manchurian line at Mukden, north of Port Arthur, and at once took military action, occupying the whole of Manchuria by the end of 1932. The Japanese proclaimed a new state called Manchukuo, *q.v.*

In the Cairo Declaration, *q.v.*, in 1943, it was stated that Manchuria was part of China, and it was reincorporated in China on the withdrawal of the Japanese forces. The U.S.S.R. occupied Port Arthur towards the end of the Second World War, and after protracted negotiations finally withdrew its forces in May 1955.

Largely as a result of the exploitation of its fuel and mineral resources Manchuria has become China's most important area of industrial development. It provides approximately one half of the total Chinese output of coal, and one half of the oil and two thirds of the iron reserves.

Mangla Dam. A dam on the lower reaches of the river Jhelum in Mirpur district of Azad Kashmir, completed in 1967 and financed by a consortium of the governments of Australia, Canada, the German Federal Republic, New Zealand, the U.K. and the U.S.A. together with the World Bank. It represented the conclusion of the first phase of the Indus Waters Treaty, *q.v.*, signed in September 1960, which ensured a fair allocation of the waters of the river Indus and its five tributaries, the Sutlej, Beas, Ravi, Jehlum and Chenab, between India and Pakistan. The functions of the dam are: to increase flood water storage for the five rivers; to distribute their waters so that Pakistan's needs are met from the three western rivers, the Indus, Jhelum and Chenab, as provided in the Treaty; to generate 900,000 kilowatts of power.

Manila, Treaty of. Concluded in September 1954, and also known as the South-East Asia Collective Defence Treaty, *q.v.*

Manley, Michael Norman. Jamaican politician; born 10 December 1923 at Kingston, the son of Norman Manley who was Chief Minister of Jamaica from 1955 to 1962. He was educated at Jamaica College and the London School of Economics and went into journalism, working for the B.B.C. from 1950 to 1951 and as an associate editor of *Public Opinion* from 1952 to 1953, in which year he was appointed sugar supervisor of the National Workers' Union. In 1955 he became the island sugar supervisor and first Vice-President of the Union. He held various positions in other unions and sat on a number of labour committees until 1962 when he entered the Senate. In 1967 he was elected to the House of Representatives for Central Kingston and in February 1969 succeeded his father as leader of the People's National Party (P.N.P.), to which the N.W.U. is affiliated. When the P.N.P. won the elections held in February 1972 he became Prime Minister of Jamaica.

Mansfield, Michael Joseph (Mike). U.S. Democratic Party politician; born 16 March 1903 in New York. He served successively in the U.S. navy, army and marine corps until 1922 when he took up a career in mining. From 1927 to 1928 he was a student at the Montana School of Mines; he then went to Montana State University where he taught Latin American and Far East History from 1933 to 1942. He was a member of the House of Representatives from 1943 until 1953 when he was elected Senator for Montana. He was appointed Assistant Majority Leader in the Senate in 1957 and Majority Leader in 1961, undertaking various presidential assignments in different parts of the world on behalf of Lyndon Johnson, *q.v.* His political importance increased after 1968 when, despite the election of a Republican president, the Democratic Party retained a majority in the Senate.

Mansholt, Sicco Leendert. Dutch politician; born 13 September 1908 at Ulrum in Groningen, and educated at the School of Tropical Agriculture at Deventer. He worked on Dutch farms from 1924 to 1934 and in the soil-testing laboratory at Groningen, and was employed on a tea plantation in Java from 1934 to 1936. He returned to Holland to farm on the Wieringmeer Polder, where he remained throughout the German occupation, becoming Burgomaster of Wieringmeer in 1945. He was appointed Minister of Agriculture, Fisheries and Food in the Schermerhorn cabinet 1945–6, in the Beel cabinet 1946–8, and in the Drees cabinet in 1948, 1951, 1952 and 1956–8. He was involved in the negotiations which preceded the coming into force of Benelux, *q.v.*, and in 1953 prepared a plan for the integration of European agriculture which was to form the basis of the agricultural policy of the European Economic Community, *q.v.* He became Vice-President of the E.E.C. Committee in 1958, a Vice-President of the Commission of the combined Communities in 1967, and President from 1972 to 1973, when he was succeeded by Francois-Xavier Ortoli.

Mao Tse-tung. Chairman of Central Committee of Chinese Communist Party; born 26 December 1893 in Hunan. He took part in the assembly which founded the Chinese Communist Party in 1921, and in 1927 organized the Hunan Autumn Revolt. In the same year there was a split between the Communists and the Kuomintang, *q.v.*, and Mao thereupon organized the Kiangsi Red Army with Chu Teh, *q.v.*, set up a soviet government, and instituted land reforms in the province of Kiangsi. In 1934 he led the trek of 3,000 miles from Kiangsi to Shensi, during which his first wife died. For some years he advocated a common front with the Kuomintang against Japan, and reorganized the Red Army in 1937 so that it could fight as part of the Chinese national army. In 1945 he took part with the U.S. Ambassador to China in an unsuccessful attempt to reach agreement with the Kuomintang leader Chiang Kai-shek, *q.v.* In 1949 he left China for the first time to visit Moscow, where he signed a treaty of mutual alliance with the U.S.S.R. From 1949 to 1959 he was Chairman of the People's Republic. His *Thoughts of Mao Tse-tung*, which assert the right of Communist leaders to adapt Marxism-Leninism to the needs of their own countries, have been imposed on China as the sole true doctrine of revolutionaries since 1960. His second wife died at a Kuomintang strangling-post; he has been married since 1939 to his fourth wife, Chiang Ching, a Shanghai actress.

Maphilindo. The name proposed for a confederation between Malaysia, the Philippines, and Indonesia. Such a grouping has been advocated particularly by Indonesia, which was opposed to the establishment, on 16 September 1963, of the Federation of Malaysia, *q.v.*

Marshall Plan. A proposal outlined by George Marshall, U.S. Secretary of State, in a speech at Harvard on 5 June 1947: 'It is logical that the United States should do whatever it is able to do to assist in the return of normal economic health in the world without which there can be no political stability and no assured peace. Our policy is directed not against any country or doctrine but against hunger, poverty, desperation, and chaos. . . It would be neither fitting nor efficacious for this government to draw up unilaterally a program designed to place Europe on its feet economically. That is the business of the Europeans. The initiative, I think, must come from Europe. The role of this country should consist of friendly aid in the drafting of a European program and of later support of such a program so far as it may be practical for us to do so. The program should be a joint one, agreed to by a number of, if not all, European nations.'

The proposal was welcomed by the British Foreign Secretary,

Ernest Bevin, on 13 June 1947. The Foreign Ministers of France, the U.K., and the U.S.S.R. met on 27 June to discuss the offer, which the U.S.S.R. later rejected. No Communist countries accepted the offer; Czechoslovakia accepted and then withdrew its acceptance; Finland and Spain did not participate. Sixteen nations (Austria, Belgium, Denmark, France, Greece, Iceland, Ireland, Italy, Luxemburg, Netherlands, Norway, Portugal, Sweden, Switzerland, Turkey and the U.K.) met for a Conference on European Economic Co-operation in Paris on 12 July 1947.

These nations then outlined a plan for 1947–51 which came to be known as the European Recovery Programme, *q.v.* The report and plan were handed to Marshall on 22 September 1947. The Organization for European Economic Co-operation, *q.v.*, was set up to administer the European Recovery Programme.

Marxism. The philosophy of history and the programme of revolutionary reform expounded by Karl Marx (1818–83), a German Jew. The underlying basis of Marxism as a philosophy of history is dialectical materialism, *q.v.*, by which Marx sought to prove that capitalism, *q.v.*, carried within itself the seeds of its own decay and that revolution was inevitable. In the Communist Manifesto, published in London in February 1848, he advocated: (1) the expropriation of landed property and the use of rent from land to cover state expenditure; (2) a high and progressively graded income tax; (3) the abolition of the right of inheritance; (4) the centralization of credit by the establishment of a state bank; (5) the nationalization of transport; (6) an increase in the state ownership of factories and the redistribution of land; (7) the duty of all to work; (8) state education of all children and abolition of factory labour for children. The Manifesto stated that Communists believed that their aims could only by achieved by the violent overthrow of the whole contemporary social order, and concluded with the words: 'Let the governing classes tremble before the Communist revolution. The proletarians have nothing to lose in it but their chains. They have the whole world to gain. Proletarians of all countries, unite!' Marx and his colleague, Friedrich Engels, are today regarded as the first exponents of Communism as a coherent body of doctrine. Marxian Socialists are those who accept the Marxist analysis of history but do not wish to plan the violent overthrow of governments; Marxism-Leninism is a description of the interpretation and application of this doctrine in the U.S.S.R. since 1917.

Matsu. A group of five islands, with a combined area of less than 10 sq. m., approximately 10 miles from the Chinese mainland, and

130 miles north-west of Taiwan, *q.v.*, to the government of which the Chinese forces occupying Matsu are loyal.

Mau Mau. A militant African secret society, active among the Kikuyu, Meru, and Embu tribes in Kenya between 1952 and 1959. Its aim was to expel the white settlers, and to achieve this end it terrorized the Kikuyu in particular so that they became divided into loyalists, Mau Mau supporters, and others who gave passive support to the society. Members of Mau Mau were bound by secret oaths to mutilate and kill their enemies, African and European. Reluctant Africans were sometimes forced to take oaths, which involved rituals of a barbarous nature, and which they were then terrified to disobey. The Kenya government found it difficult to eradicate the influence of Mau Mau; the thick forests provided shelter for the gangs, while many Africans in the overcrowded Kikuyu reserves sympathized with the uncompromising opposition of Mau Mau to the white way of life. A proclamation was issued on 10 November 1959, announcing the end, after seven years, of the state of emergency resulting from the activities of Mau Mau.

Maudling, Reginald. British Conservative Party politician; born 7 March 1917 and educated at Merchant Taylors' School and Merton College, Oxford. After qualifying as a barrister in 1940 he served in the Royal Air Force until 1945, when he unsuccessfully contested a parliamentary seat. He then concerned himself with economic research in the Conservative parliamentary secretariat, and was elected to the House of Commons to represent Barnet in 1950. He became Parliamentary Secretary to the Minister of Civil Aviation in 1952, and then successively Economic Secretary to the Treasury, Minister of Supply, and Paymaster-General. In this last capacity he was entrusted with negotiations between the U.K. and the European Economic Community, and with the task of working out the place of the U.K. in the Free Trade Area. He became President of the Board of Trade in October 1959, Secretary of State for the Colonies in October 1961, and was Chancellor of the Exchequer from July 1962, until the Conservative Party was defeated in the General Election of October 1964. In the election for leadership of the Conservative Party in July 1965, he received 133 votes on the first ballot, against 150 cast for Edward Heath; he conceded defeat without insisting on the second ballot permitted by the election rules. In 1970 he was appointed Secretary of State for Home Affairs, a post which he resigned in July 1972 because of the possible implications of his name having been mentioned in the bankruptcy proceedings of one John Poulson.

Mauritania. An independent republic; area 322,340 sq. m.; population

(1969 estimate) 1,120,000, of whom more than half are nomad white Moors, and the rest Toucouleurs, Sarakollés, Peulhs, Bambaras, Ouolofs and 1,000 Europeans; capital Nouakchott. The country lies on the west coast of Africa, with Rio de Oro (part of Spanish Sahara) to the north, Senegal to the south, and Sahara and Mali to the east. It became a French protectorate in 1903 and later was one of the eight territories comprising French West Africa, q.v.; it achieved self-government within the French Community, q.v., on 28 November 1958, and complete independence on 28 November 1960. It is known officially as the Islamic Republic of Mauritania, since the state religion is Islam, the white Moors being descendants of an ancient Moslem civilization.

Under the 1961 Constitution legislative powers are vested in an assembly of 40 members elected by universal suffrage. At elections held in May 1965, the Party of the Mauritanian People, the only recognized party since 1961, won every seat. Executive power is exercised by a President and a Council of Ministers. Mocktar Ould Daddah was elected President in August 1961 and re-elected in 1966 and 1971.

Millet, dates, maize, cattle, dried and salted fish, gum and salt are the main products; there are deposits of copper, and the very considerable deposits of iron ore in the region of Fort Gouraud, in the hills 400 miles inland to the east of Spanish Sahara, are being exploited by an international company, the Société de Mines de Fer de Mauritanie, with the aid of a loan from the World Bank. Most of the trade is with Senegal, Mali and Gambia, but there are also links with the north; a Moroccan claim to sovereignty was allowed to lapse in 1969 and diplomatic relations were restored with Morocco in 1970.

Mauritius. An island in the Indian Ocean, 550 miles east of Madagascar; it became an independent state within the British Commonwealth on 12 March 1968; area (including the island dependency of Rodrigues) 805 sq. m.; population (1969) 798,684 (and Rodrigues 20,300), including 412,000 Hindus, 131,000 Moslems of Indian descent, 225,000 Creoles of mixed French and African descent, and mainly Roman Catholic, 25,000 Chinese and 14,000 French-speaking Europeans; capital Port Louis.

The island was discovered early in the sixteenth century by the Portuguese; it was settled by the Dutch in 1598 and given the name Mauritius, but abandoned by them in 1710 as economically unprofitable. In 1715 the French began to colonize the island which they renamed Île de France and, under the French governor, Mahé de Labourdonnai, encouraged sugar planting. It was captured in

1810 by the British who acquired permanent possession by the Treaty of Paris in 1814, with the proviso that the inhabitants would be allowed to retain their own laws, language, customs and religion. As a result, the island, although renamed Mauritius and administered by the British for 158 years, has retained the imprint of French colonization.

Government is by a Governor acting through a Council of Ministers and a Legislative Assembly, elected by adult suffrage with a residence qualification of two years. The island became internally self-governing in 1964. At elections held in that year neither of the two main political parties, the Labour Party, led by Sir Seewoosagur Ramgoolam, which is Hindu-dominated and supported largely by the unskilled workers, or the Parti-Mauricien, led by Gaston Duval, which represents the Creoles and the middle-class and skilled workers, won an absolute majority. The Parti-Mauricien opposed independence and wanted to continue in association with the U.K. for economic reasons. The Labour Party formed a government and Sir Seewoosagur Ramgoolam became Prime Minister, increasing his popular support at the elections held in August 1967, when the Labour Party obtained 43 seats and the Parti-Mauricien 27. He continued in office when Mauritius achieved full independence in 1968.

The island has no mineral resources and its future prosperity depends exclusively on sugar; ninety per cent of the cultivable area is planted to sugar cane and sugar constitutes some ninety-five per cent of all exports. So long as it is protected by the Commonwealth Sugar Agreement (due to expire in 1974) Mauritius is guaranteed a price of £45 per ton for two thirds of her total production, as opposed to the world price (in 1968) of £25. This is barely adequate to pay for the existing social services which include redundancy payments to workers in the sugar industry, and relief schemes for the unemployed. The eradication of malaria and the government's reluctance to introduce birth control have made inevitable an increase in population (half of whom at present are under eighteen) which the island has little prospect of being able to feed or employ.

Meany, William George. President of the American Federation of Labor and Congress of Industrial Organizations, *q.v.*, the combined trade union organization formed in 1955; born in 1894 in Harlem, the son of a plumber; he is a Roman Catholic. He became a journeyman plumber at the age of 16, and soon became active in trade-union affairs. In 1923 he became Secretary and Treasurer of the New York Building Trades Council, and from 1934 to 1939 was President of the New York branch of the American Federation of Labor, *q.v.* during which period he persuaded the State to pass many laws improving the status of organized labour. He became Secretary and Treasurer of the A.F. of L. headquarters in Washington and was a member of the government War Labor Board from 1941 to 1945. Unlike his colleague, Walter Reuther, *q.v.*, he has never taken part in a strike. He successfully opposed participation by the A.F. of L. in the World Federation of Trade Unions, *q.v.*, and in February 1961 withdrew the A.F. of L.–C.I.O. from the International Confederation of Free Trade Unions, *q.v.*, the anti-Communist federation, on the grounds that it was making undesirable contacts with unions in the U.S.S.R. In 1970 he persuaded the House of Representatives Appropriations Committee to withhold its contribution to the I.L.O., *q.v.* He refused the support of organized labour to the Democratic candidate for the presidency in 1972, George McGovern, *q.v.*, although he was unable to prevent individual unions from declaring their adherence.

Meir, Golda. Israeli politician; born 3 May 1898 in Kiev. She left Russia as a child of eight when her parents emigrated to the U.S.A., where she attended high school and the Teachers' Seminary in Milwaukee. She and her husband Morris Mayerson (she hebraicized the name to Meir) settled in Palestine in 1921 where they worked on the Merhavia kibbutz whose members drained the swamp land of Lower Galilee. She was a founder member of Mapai, the Zionist Socialist Party, and active in Histradut, the General Federation of Labour, becoming a member of the executive committee in 1929 and head of the Political Department of Histradut in 1936. In 1946 when Moshe Sharett was detained by the British authorities she took over the Jewish Agency's Political Department. In 1948, immediately prior to the outbreak of the Arab-Israeli war, she was sent in disguise into Transjordan to discuss a possible compromise settlement with King Abdullah, but her mission was unsuccessful. After independence had been declared she was appointed the first Israeli ambassador to the U.S.S.R., and was subsequently Minister of Labour for seven years from 1949 to 1956. During her term of office as Foreign Minister, from 1956 until January 1966 when she was succeeded by Abba Eban, she pursued a policy of cooperation with non-aligned nations, and was instrumental in regaining for Israel the friendship of the U.S.A. She left the government in 1966 to become General Secretary of Mapai, and in January 1968, when the party merged with Rafi to form the Labour Front, she retired under pressure from the right wing which was promoting younger candidates. In February 1969 she was the unanimous choice of the Cabinet (except for the abstention of the

Minister of Defence, General Moshe Dayan) to succeed Levi Eshkol as Prime Minister.

Mendès-France, Pierre. French politician; born 11 January 1907; educated at the law faculty and school of political science at Paris University. He joined the Radical Socialist Party when he was 16 and took his doctorate of laws in 1925, having won first place out of 800 students. He also obtained a diploma in political science and wrote a study of the financial policy of the government of Poincaré, who was then Prime Minister, and books on cartels and the function of an international bank. In 1932 he became the youngest member of the Chamber of Deputies, and in 1938 he was Under-Secretary of State to the Treasury in the Popular Front government of Léon Blum. In 1939 he joined the Air Force, and later served with the Free French forces in England, from where he took part in air raids over France and Germany. In 1943 he became Commissioner of Finance in the Committee of National Liberation at Algiers under General de Gaulle, and in 1944 represented France at Bretton Woods, *q.v.*, becoming a Governor of the International Monetary Fund and an Alternate Governor of the International Bank for Reconstruction and Development. He was Minister of National Economy under de Gaulle from 1944 to 1945 but resigned when his plans for wage and price limitations, levies on profits, rationing, abolition of the black market, and other anti-inflationary measures, were rejected by the cabinet. He managed to form a cabinet in June 1954 without the aid of Communist votes in the Chamber of Deputies. He brought new young men into his cabinet, stopped cabinet leakages to the press, advocated withdrawal from Indo-China, tried to renovate the economy, and strove for peace in French North Africa, setting up a Ministry for Moroccan and Tunisian Affairs. He suggested that France and the U.K. should together join the European Defence Community or create an alternative organization, but this plan was rejected by the U.K. In February 1955 his government was defeated on a vote of confidence in connection with his North African policy. He was Minister of State in the Mollet government from January to May 1956, resigning because he disagreed with the government's Algerian policy. He was one of the 77 non-Communist Deputies who voted against the investiture of de Gaulle as Prime Minister on 1 June 1958. He lost his seat in the Chamber of Deputies when he was defeated at Grenoble by the Gaullist candidate in the elections of June 1968.

Mensheviks. The moderate Russian Socialists who opposed Bolshevism, after the split in the Russian Socialist Party in 1903, and particularly in the Russian Revolution in 1917. They had been in a minority (Russian: *menshinstvo*) at the Party congress preceding the split; hence the name.

Messmer, Pierre. French politician; born 20 March 1916 at Vincennes and educated in law. He served in the Free French Forces in North Africa and in 1946 began a career in colonial administration as Secretary-General of an Inter-Ministerial Committee on Indo-China. After holding office as Governor of Mauritania in 1952, of the Ivory Coast in 1954 and as High Commissioner for Cameroun in 1956, he returned to France as *directeur du cabinet* under Gaston Defferre, *q.v.*, who was then Minister for Overseas Territories. He was High Commissioner General in French Equatorial Africa in 1958 and in French West Africa from July 1958 until 1960, when he was appointed Minister for the Armed Forces. He lost his parliamentary seat in the 1967 elections but remained in the government, and in June 1968 he was elected for the Moselle constituency which he still represents. He delegated the seat to his *suppléant* (substitute), but took it up again in October 1969 when he lost his ministerial post. In 1971 he became Mayor of Sarrebourg, and until February 1972 when he re-entered the government as Minister for Overseas Departments and Territories, he was concerned to publicize the 'Presence of Gaullism', an extension of the Gaullist parliamentary group, which he founded with Michel Debré and Louis Joxe. On the resignation of Jacques Chaban-Delmas in July 1972 he was appointed Prime Minister of France.

Mexico. An independent republic; area 761,375 sq. m.; population (1970) 48,381,547; capital Mexico City. It was ruled by Spain from the sixteenth century until the revolutionary war of 1810–21. A series of wars then occurred, involving at various times France, the U.S.A., and Austria, and the present republic was inaugurated after the execution of the Emperor Ferdinand Maximilian of Austria in 1867. Under the 1917 Constitution, amended frequently between 1929 and 1953, Mexico is a federative republic of 29 states, 2 territories and the federal district of Mexico City. Congress consists of a Senate of 60 members, elected for six years, and a Chamber of Deputies, at present numbering 210, elected for three years. The President is elected by direct popular vote in a general election, and holds office for six years. Luis Echevarría Alvarez became President in 1970. The Partido Revolucionario Institucional (P.R.I.) has been the dominant political party since 1929. At elections held in July 1967 all the seats in the Senate were won by the P.R.I.; in the lower house they were distributed as follows: P.R.I., which is nominally a party of the left, 175; Partido Accion Nacional (P.A.N.), a conservative Catholic group, 20; the left-wing Partido Popular Socialista 10; Autenticos, who are pledged to sustain the ideology of the Mexican social revolution, 5. Concern at the absence of a political opposition brought the introduction of new laws in 1966 which would provide five deputies for every 2·5 per cent of the recorded vote; this was to ensure the representation of minority groups, and it raised the number of P.A.N. representatives from 1 in 1964 to 20 in 1967.

Violent demonstrations, which seriously threatened the staging of the Olympic Games in Mexico City, occurred in the universities in 1968. Students protested against the inertia of the government, the laws of 'social dissolution' by which its critics were gaoled, and its abandonment of the revolutionary ideals to which it publicly subscribed. Except for the Presidency of Adolfo Lopez Mateos (1958 to 1964), who opposed the expulsion of Cuba from the Organization of American States, q.v., in 1962, the leadership of the P.R.I. has moved steadily to the right since 1942.

The country is fertile; agriculture represents 25 per cent of the national income, but more than 40 per cent of the agricultural land requires artificial irrigation, and food has to be imported. Mexico is the world's second largest exporter of cotton, and produces, from the Yucatan peninsula, half of the world's supply of sisal. Sulphur is mined by three large American firms, the Texas Gulf, Panamerican Sulphur and Mexican Gulf Sulphur Companies. There are substantial reserves of oil; most of the oil properties, which had belonged to U.K., U.S., and Dutch Companies, of which the most important was Mexican Eagle Oil of the Royal Dutch Shell group, were expropriated in March 1938, and placed under a government organization called Petroleos Mexicanos (Pemex) with a board of five government and four workers' representatives. Uranium ore is exported together with lead, silver, gold, copper, zinc, antimony and coffee. Rapid industrial expansion during the past ten years has quadrupled the output of electricity, and brought such progress in the manufacture of footwear, clothing and domestic appliances that these industries are now protected by high import duties and import licence restrictions. This has made full cooperation within the Latin American Free Trade Association, q.v., difficult for Mexico.

Mikoyan, Anastas Ivanovich. Russian politician; born at Sanain, Armenia, 25 November 1895; educated at the American Ecclesiastical Seminary, Tiflis. After joining the Communist Party in 1915 he fought at Baku during the revolution and its aftermath (1917–19). Since then he has been a member of various central committees of the Communist Party, i.e. the All-Russian Central Executive Committee (1919–23), the All-Union Central Executive Committee (1923–37), and (since 1937) the Central Committee itself. In 1926 he became People's Commissar of Trade, Member of the Council of Labour and Defence, and Candidate Member (until 1933, when he became a full Member) of the Political Bureau (Politburo) of the Central Committee. He was People's Commissar of Supply from 1930 to 1934, and of the Food Supply Industry from 1934 to 1938. In the latter year he became People's Commissar of Foreign Trade, a post which he held until 1949; he was then successively Vice-Chairman of the Council of Ministers, until 1955, Minister of Domestic and Foreign Trade, from March to September 1953, and Minister of Domestic Trade, from 1953 to 1955. In 1955 he became a First Vice-Chairman of the Council of Ministers, and from 1964 to December 1965 was President of the Presidium of the Supreme Soviet, of which he remains a member.

Mintoff, Dominic. Maltese Labour Party politician; born 1916 in Cospicua, Malta, and educated at Jesuit schools and at the University of Malta where he was awarded a Rhodes scholarship to Oxford. He graduated in engineering science and was employed as a civil engineer in the U.K. from 1941 to 1943. He returned to Malta in 1944 to practise as an architect. He helped to organize the Malta Labour Party of which he became successively general secretary, deputy-leader and in 1949 party leader. He was elected to the Council of Government and the Executive Council in 1945 and to the legislative assembly in 1947 in which year he was appointed Deputy Prime Minister and Minister of Public Works and Reconstruction, a post he resigned in 1949. In 1952 he became Leader of the Opposition, and Prime Minister and Minister of Finance in 1955, resigning in 1958 after protracted negotiations with the U.K. on the future constitutional status of the island. (*See* Malta.) After the Labour Party's narrow electoral victory in the general election of June 1971 he formed the first Labour government for thirteen years. He has advocated a more neutralist policy for Malta, with closer cultural and economic links with Arab countries and especially Libya. In his dramatic re-negotiation of the Defence and Aid Agreement with the U.K. in 1972 he emphasized that British aid to Malta was a commercial payment for facilities provided and not charity.

Mitterrand, François Maurice Marie. French Socialist politician; born 26 October 1916, and educated at the University of Paris. He was active in the French resistance movement, conducting missions to London and Algiers in 1943. Since 1946, when he first entered the

French Assembly, he has been a Deputy continuously, except for the four years 1958 to 1962 during which he was a member of the Senate. He has held several government posts: 1947–8 Minister for Ex-Servicemen; 1948–9 Secretary of State for Information; 1950–51 Minister for Overseas Territories. He was three times Minister of State, in 1952, from 1952 to 1953 and from 1956 to 1957; and in the 1954–5 government of Pierre Mendès-France, *q.v.*, he was Minister of the Interior. He was elected chairman of the Union of Democratic Socialist Republicans (U.D.S.R.) in 1951–2, and in 1965, as leader of the Federation of the Democratic and Socialist Left, he stood as candidate for the presidency against General de Gaulle, *q.v.*, obtaining 44·8 per cent of the total votes cast in the second ballot. He resigned from leadership of the Federation in November 1968 after the defeat of the left at elections held in June. In 1969 he formed a Convention for Republican Institutions which in June 1971 merged with the existing Socialist Party. He was elected to the post of General Secretary of the new Socialist Party, thereby consolidating his position as leader of the Democratic Left.

M.L.F. Multilateral Nuclear Force, *q.v.*

Modus Vivendi. Latin term meaning 'way of living'; used to describe provisional and informal arrangements in political affairs, whether international or internal. It is employed especially in relation to an agreement between the Pope and a government for the regulation of Roman Catholic affairs within a country, when it is a substitute for a Concordat, *q.v.*

Mollet, Guy. French Socialist politician; born 31 December 1905 in Normandy. He became a teacher at the age of 17, when he also joined the Socialist Party, and in 1932 he became secretary of the teachers' union. He was a prisoner of war from 1940 to 1942 and after repatriation to France worked for the resistance movement. After his election as a deputy from Pas-de-Calais to the Constituent Assembly in 1946, he became General Secretary of the Socialist Party. He was Minister of State in the all-Socialist cabinet of Léon Blum from 1946 to 1947, and Deputy Premier in the Pleven government in 1951. In January 1956 he became Prime Minister of a coalition government which did not fall until May 1957, and which thus had the longest life of any post-war French cabinet. He was one of the 44 (out of 93) Socialist Deputies who on 1 June 1958 voted for the investiture of de Gaulle as Prime Minister. He then took office as Minister of State under de Gaulle, but in December 1958 the Socialist Party decided not to serve in the government which was to be formed when de Gaulle became President, and Mollet was therefore not included in the Debré ministry chosen in January 1959. He remained Secretary of the French Socialist Party until 1969 when the party was reconstituted under the leadership of Alain Savary.

Molotov, Vyacheslav Mikhailovich. A former Vice-Chairman of the Council of Ministers of the U.S.S.R.; born 9 March 1890 with the surname of Scriabin and educated at a polytechnic in St Petersburg (now Leningrad). He became a Bolshevik when he was 16, took the name of Molotov ('the hammer'), helped Stalin to found *Pravda*, *q.v.*, and when the revolution broke out in 1917 he had been in jail six times and in exile twice. By 1921 he was the Second Secretary of the Communist Party, the First Secretary being Stalin. From 1930 to 1941 he was Chairman of the Council of People's Commissars, a post then roughly equivalent to that of Prime Minister, in which capacity he supervised the completion of the first two Five-Year Plans for agriculture and industry. In 1939 he succeeded Maxim Litvinov as Foreign Minister and negotiated the Russo-German Pact. He was active in international affairs until 1949, when Vyshinsky took over his post, but he was Foreign Minister again from 1953 until his resignation in June 1956 in favour of Shepilov. In July 1957 it was announced that Molotov, with Malenkov and Kaganovich, had been expelled from the Presidium and the Central Committee of the Communist Party for establishing an 'anti-party group'. He then became Russian Ambassador to the Mongolian People's Republic, until 1960 when he was appointed to be the Russian representative to the International Atomic Energy Agency.

Monaco, Principality of. An independent state on the French Riviera, ruled since 1949 by Prince Rainier III (Louis Henri Maxence Bertrand, born 1923), and by his family, the Genoese Grimaldi dynasty, since 1297; area (which includes Monte Carlo) about two miles by half a mile, or 368 acres; population (1970) 23,152, of whom 2,000 are citizens of Monaco (Monégasques). Under the 1962 Constitution legislative powers are vested in the Prince and a National Council of 18 members elected every four years. The Constitution, unlike its predecessor which could be abrogated, suspended, or modified at the ruler's will, can only be modified with the approval of the elected National Council. A Council of Government has executive powers. In January 1959 Prince Rainier suspended the 1911 Constitution after disputes with the National Council which, in his view, had been trying to extend its powers at his expense. Monaco has a customs union with France, but Monégasques do not pay French taxes. Under a 1918 treaty Monaco would have become a protectorate of France, although an autonomous state (and Monégasques would pay French taxes), if the Prince had died without an heir. A son, Prince Albert Alexander Louis Peter, was born in March 1958.

Mongolia, Inner. An autonomous region of north-western China which, like Tibet, is outside the Chinese system of provinces; population (1957) 9,200,000; capital Huhehot. For some years after 1932 it was under the influence of the Japanese, who set up an autonomous Mongol administration and tried to turn the Mongols against China. An Inner Mongolian autonomous government set up by the Chinese in 1947 was an amalgamation of Inner Mongolian with some Manchurian elements. The government, most of the members of which are Chinese and not Mongols, has launched a programme designed to remove the special privileges of the Mongol princes and aristocracy, and has redistributed land and animals.

Mongolian People's Republic. (Sometimes called Outer Mongolia.) An independent state to the north-west of China; area about 604,095 sq. m.; population (1970) 1,230,000; capital Ulan Bator, formerly known as Urga. The country was under Chinese suzerainty until 1911 when it declared its independence. A provisional People's Government was later established which appealed for help to Moscow. By the Russo-Chinese Treaty of 1924 the U.S.S.R. formally acknowledged Chinese authority, but the Mongolian People's Republic proclaimed in that year relied almost entirely on Soviet support. After 1930 several Japanese attacks were repulsed by joint forces of Mongolian and Soviet troops. By the second Russo-Chinese Treaty of 1945 China recognized the complete independence of Outer Mongolia. Under the 1960 Constitution there is a Great People's Khural (Parliament) elected for three years by universal suffrage, which elects seven of its number to a Presidium, which acts as a cabinet. The population is largely nomad and is dependent on cattle-breeding (sheep, goats, cattle, yaks, horses and camels); a self-sufficiency of wheat was achieved in 1961 by ploughing virgin lands, and a series of Five-Year Plans have encouraged the development of meat-packing and engineering industries, the establishment of tractor stations, and the building of a new industrial centre at Darkhan, where there are considerable deposits of iron ore. Oil has been discovered in the Gobi desert. Mongolia receives economic aid from the Council for Mutual Economic Assistance (Comecon), *q.v.*, of which it is a member. More than 60 per cent of trade is with the U.S.S.R., and the rest with the countries of Eastern Europe.

Monroe Doctrine. A principle of U.S. policy, opposing any European intervention in the political affairs of the American continent. In 1821 the Russian government, then still in possession of Alaska (which it later sold to the U.S.A.), attempted to exclude all but Russian ships from the north-western coast of America; in the next year the reactionary Holy Alliance of Prussia, Austria, and Russia, having just quelled the Spanish revolution, contemplated intervention to help Spain against the newly created South American republics. President Monroe declared in a message to Congress on 2 December 1823, 'that the American continents, by the free and independent condition which they have assumed and maintained, are henceforth not to be considered as subjects for future colonization by any European Powers. . . With the movements in this hemisphere we are of necessity more immediately concerned. The political system of the Allied Powers is essentially different from that of America. . . . We should consider any attempt on their part to extend their system to any part of this hemisphere as dangerous to our peace and safety.' The British Foreign Secretary, George Canning, had suggested, unsuccessfully, a joint Anglo-American declaration against intervention in South America. The Monroe Doctrine grew in popularity in the U.S.A. in the mid-nineteenth century, but the French intervention in Mexico in 1860 challenged it seriously. The American Civil War hampered the application of the Doctrine for some time, but in 1865 the U.S.A. insisted on it, and the French had to withdraw.

Once firmly established, the Doctrine was applied to the building of the Panama Canal, and the Clayton-Bulmer Treaty of 1850, which had provided for joint Anglo-American control of the Canal, was replaced by the Hay-Pauncefote Treaty of 1901, recognizing complete U.S. control. In 1896 President Cleveland said that it gave to the U.S.A. the right to decide the frontier dispute between British Guiana and Venezuela, and his Secretary of State declared that the U.S.A. was 'practically sovereign' and 'her *fiat* law'. In 1902 the Anglo-German-Italian blockade of Venezuela (to enforce payment of debts) angered Americans and President Theodore Roosevelt extended the theory (by the so-called 'Roosevelt Corollary') so that the U.S.A. could act preventively to forestall European intervention. U.S. control of customs in San Domingo was the first result, and the Doctrine has since been repeatedly invoked in connection with U.S. actions in the Caribbean Sea.

The Doctrine has become a common principle of all the American republics instead of a unilateral U.S. policy. By the Declaration of Lima, 1942, the members of the Pan American Union, *q.v.*, declared their determination to defend themselves against all foreign intervention. In the Rio Treaty, *q.v.*, in 1947, they reaffirmed this attitude and agreed that an attack against one of them should be considered to be an attack against them all.

John Foster Dulles, then U.S. Secretary of State, said in 1954, at the Inter-American Conference in Caracas, that among the most fundamental of U.S. foreign policies was an objection to the existence of Communist or pro-Communist governments in the American continent. If a pro-Communist government were freely elected in a Latin American state, the U.S. objection to it would in fact be inconsistent with that part of the Monroe Doctrine which encouraged Latin American self-determination; the U.S. attitude would presumably be that such a government must of its nature be subject to a foreign influence and that this was directly contrary to the Doctrine. President Eisenhower said in February 1960 that the U.S.A. would consider it an intervention in the internal affairs of an American state if any power, 'whether by invasion, coercion or subversion', succeeded in denying freedom of choice to the people of that state. The action taken by the U.S.A. against Cuba in April 1961, at the Bay of Pigs, *q.v.*; in October 1962, after Russian missile sites had been discovered in Cuba; and in April 1965, after an allegedly left-wing revolt in the Dominican Republic, could be taken as examples of the enforcement of the Doctrine.

Monrovia Powers (*or* Monrovia States). Title often given to a loose association of African states. The grouping may be contrasted with that of the so-called Casablanca Powers, *q.v.*

A meeting was held at Monrovia, Liberia, from 8 to 13 May 1961, attended by representatives of 19 states, i.e. the 4 countries of the Conseil de l'Entente (*see* Entente, Council of): Dahomey, Ivory Coast, Niger, and Upper Volta; the 4 countries which once formed French Equatorial Africa: Central African Republic, Chad, Congo (Brazzaville), and Gabon; 4 other countries formerly associated with France; Cameroun, the Malagasy Republic, Mauritania and Senegal: and 7 others: Ethiopia, Liberia, Nigeria, Sierra Leone, Somalia, Togo, and Tunisia. They met again (with the exception of Tunisia and the addition of Zaïre (the former Belgian Congo)) in January 1962 at Lagos, setting up a permanent secretariat and a standing committee of Finance Ministers, and accepting a draft charter for an Organization of Inter-African and Malagasy States. A revised version of the charter was signed at Addis Ababa in May 1963, and formed the basis of the Organization of African Unity, *q.v.*

Montreux Convention, 1936. An international agreement permitting Turkey to fortify the Dardanelles, *q.v.*, and laying down rules for the passage of warships between the Mediterranean and Black Seas in time of peace and war. It modified the Treaty of Lausanne, concluded in 1923, which had provided that Turkey, defeated in the First World War, should demilitarize the Dardanelles. In peacetime commercial shipping must be allowed to use the straits freely; warships of more than 10,000 tons, submarines, and aircraft carriers are excluded, and other naval vessels may pass only by day. In any war in which Turkey is neutral, warships of the belligerent powers are banned from the straits, except where they are proceeding by order of the United Nations, or in fulfilment of a pact of assistance to which Turkey is a party. If Turkey is a belligerent, commercial navigation is forbidden to countries at war with Turkey, and to neutral ships carrying men or materials to support the enemy. The passage of warships in such a case is left to the discretion of Turkey.

Morocco. An independent state in north-west Africa, bordering the Mediterranean Sea in the north and the Atlantic Ocean in the west; area approximately 171,305 sq. m.; population (1969) 15,030,000, of whom most are Sunni Moslems; main capital Rabat. Although it has in theory been an independent sultanate since the Middle Ages, the country was in effect partitioned and subject to foreign rule from 1912 to 1956. As a result of a treaty signed at Fez by the Sultan and by France, and a Convention at Madrid agreed between Spain and France, Morocco was, in 1912, divided into French and Spanish spheres of influence, known as French Morocco, q.v., and Spanish Morocco, q.v. In 1923 the city of Tangier, q.v., with a small enclave in Spanish Morocco, was neutralized and demilitarized.

After a lengthy period of unrest the French government was forced, on 2 March 1956, to recognize Morocco as an independent sovereign state; the Spanish government agreed on 7 April that Spanish Morocco was an integral part of Morocco; and on 18 May 1956 the Tangier International Control Committee agreed to the integration of Tangier with the rest of Morocco. Spanish Morocco was transferred to Moroccan jurisdiction on 10 April 1958. There remained a dispute as to the two Spanish provinces in Spanish Sahara, q.v. (Rio de Oro and Saguia el-Hamra), and Ifni, q.v. which was ceded to Morocco on 30 June 1969. Morocco still claims Spanish Sahara.

The Sultan of Morocco, Sidi Mohammed ben Youssef, took the title of King Mohammed V in August 1957, and ruled with governments formed from members of the Istiqlal, q.v., until May 1960 when he became Prime Minister himself. He was personally responsible for the administration until his death in February 1961. His son, Hassan II, formed a coalition in June 1961 of all parties, except the left-wing National Union of Popular Forces (U.N.F.P.), which had student and trade union connections. The Constitution, which was adopted in December 1962 and which provided for an elective legislature, was suspended in 1965 and the King declared a 'State of Exception' which lasted until July 1970. Following an attempted *coup* by senior military officers, including the commander of the Royal Household General Mohammed Medbouh, which was supported by the Libyan government, a programme of immediate reform was announced. A new Constitution provided for a unicameral legislative body with two-thirds of the deputies directly elected every four years. Despite a boycott by the opposition parties, Istiqlal and U.N.F.P., this was approved by referendum on 1 March 1972 and elections were promised for the summer of 1972 but postponed when the National Opposition Front refused to join the government. A further attempt on the King's life was made in August 1972 involving 220 officers and men of the Kenitra air base and the Minister of Defence, General Oufkir, who committed suicide. In November 1972 Ahmed Osman, the King's brother-in-law, was appointed Prime Minister in an effort to end the political impasse.

Seventy per cent of the population is dependent on agriculture; the most important crops are cereals, linseed, olives, almonds, and citrus fruits which are exported. Phosphates account for 25 per cent of the total exports which also include anthracite, manganese, iron ore, lead and zinc. In July 1966 King Hassan initiated a policy of agrarian reform by distributing some of the land appropriated from French settlers. However the unemployment level is still estimated to be between 25 and 30 per cent. France is the major trading partner and provides economic and financial aid which was doubled in 1971 to £39 million.

Moslem Brotherhood (Ikhwan al Muslimin). A movement, founded in Egypt in 1929 by Hasan al-Banna, favouring a return to strict Islamic faith, as practised in the eighth century. It attracted support among fervent Moslems of all classes and by the end of the Second World War had nearly two million members and considerable influence on Arab governments, particularly in Egypt. It arranged the murder of the Egyptian Premier who suppressed it in 1948; as a result Banna was killed, but the Wafd government allowed the Brotherhood to resume its activities. It at first supported the revolution of 1952, but it opposed Egyptian attempts to establish better relations with the west, and demanded that the government's policies be submitted to the Brotherhood for approval. In 1954 it made an attempt on the life of Nasser, who dissolved it and ordered the confiscation of its properties. Its headquarters were then moved from Cairo to Damascus.

Moslem League. The first political party of Pakistan. It was founded as an orthodox religious organization to protect the interests of Moslems in British India. Its members ceased to support the Congress Party in 1935 when Hindu aspirations predominated in that Party; they left it to mould the League into a political organization representative of Moslems of all classes. Under the leadership of Mohammed Ali Jinnah the League opposed the Congress Party and demanded partition and the creation of a Moslem state. It automatically secured control in 1947 of Pakistan's Constituent Assembly. Jinnah realized that the League needed to be reorganized to undertake its new role as a responsible political party, but after his death in 1948 it lapsed into complacency, losing its absolute majority at the 1955 elections and being forced into coalition first with the United Front and then with the Republican Party of Dr Khan Sahib. It left the government in December 1957. In 1962 the League split, the Convention Moslem League continuing to support the regime of President Ayub Khan, *q.v.*, which the Council Moslem League opposed. A third faction led by Khan Abdul Qayyum Khan, which won 7 seats in the North-West Frontier Province, emerged at the elections of December 1970, in which the total Moslem League representation was 18 out of the 138 seats in West Pakistan. The League continues to assert its two principal aims: the defence of the tenets of Islam, including the recognition of Urdu as the sole national language; and the development of a prosperous Pakistan.

Most Favoured Nation Clause. A common clause in trade treaties whereby each signatory undertakes to extend to the other signatory automatically any tariff reduction, or other favour, granted in the future to any third country. The aim is to exclude preferences for any particular country.

Mozambique. An overseas territory (known until 11 June 1951 as a colony) belonging to Portugal, it is also known as Portuguese East Africa, and is bounded by Tanzania to the north, Malawi and Rhodesia to the west, and Swaziland and the Union of South Africa to the south-west and south; area 302,250 sq. m.; population (1970) 8,233,034; capital Lourenço Marques. The territory was discovered by a fleet led by the Portuguese explorer, Vasco da Gama, in 1498; Portuguese colonists first went there in 1505. There are exports of sugar, maize, cotton, copra, sisal and cashew nuts; bauxite, berly and gold are mined. In 1962 Portugal agreed to allow U.N. observers to enter Angola and Mozambique to study the political and social situation. Since 1964 nationalist guerillas have opposed the government which spends 44 per cent of its annual budget in restraining them. In 1971 freedom of worship was extended to Portugal's overseas territories and a measure of self-government, which would include control of their own economy, was to be granted to them when their development justified it.

Mujibur Rahman, Sheikh. Bengali politician and first President of Bangladesh, *q.v.*; born in 1920 in Tongipara in the Faridpur district of East Bengal, into a family of middle-class landowners; the title of sheikh reflects his landowning status. After attending a mission school he studied law at the Calcutta Islamic College and at the University of Dacca. He went into student politics as a member of the All India Moslem Students' Federation, and later joined the Moslem League, *q.v.*, which he left to found the East Pakistan Students' League, an organization dedicated to the recognition of Bengali as an official language, and opposing the exclusive use of Urdu. In 1954 he was elected to the East Pakistan Provincial Assembly as an Awami League member, serving as Minister of Trade and Industry in the provincial administration from 1955 to 1958. He was arrested three times between 1958, when General Ayub Khan, *q.v.*, seized power, and 1966, on which occasion he was charged with conspiring with the government of India to bring about the secession of East Pakistan. After the popular uprising against President Ayub Khan's military regime, in which he was a *cause célèbre*, all charges against him were withdrawn in February 1969. Under his leadership the Awami League contested the elections of December 1970 on a programme of autonomy for East Pakistan; the party won all but two of the East Pakistan seats, and an overall majority in the National Assembly, which was not convened. After negotiations on the future Constitution of Pakistan had broken down he proclaimed the independence of the state of Bangladesh and was immediately arrested; in August 1971 he was convicted of treason. After Indian intervention had brought about the surrender of Pakistan troops in Bangladesh and the fall of President Yahya Khan, he was released from prison, returning to Dacca (renamed Mujib City) on 10 January 1972. Having been declared President of Bangladesh by the provisional government, he resigned the office to Abu Sayeed Chowdhury on 12 January in order to become Prime Minister. He has asserted his belief in democratic socialism, in parliamentary democracy, in religious toleration and in a neutralist foreign policy.

Multilateral Nuclear Force (M.L.F.). A proposal by the U.S.A. to create as the nuclear warhead of the North Atlantic Treaty Organization, *q.v.*, a force consisting of twenty-five surface vessels, each armed with Polaris missiles and manned by mixed crews from among the navies of N.A.T.O. member countries. It was designed to discourage France in particular from advancing its own programme of nuclear development, and to enable member countries to participate in the control of a European nuclear deterrent under the ultimate veto of the U.S.A. The plan was rejected outright by France but accepted by the German Federal Republic which signed an agreement with the U.S.A. in June 1964 to establish the M.L.F. by the end of the year. The U.K. modified the plan by proposing the creation of an Atlantic Nuclear Force, *q.v.*

Munich Agreement. The agreement between France, Germany, Italy, and the U.K., signed at Munich on 29 September 1938, and providing for immediate cession to Germany of certain Sudeten-German districts in Czechoslovakia, for plebiscites under international supervision to be taken in other districts, and for the frontiers to be settled by an International Commission.

After assuring Czechoslovakia in March 1938 that Germany had no designs upon Czech territory, Adolf Hitler had moved some ten divisions towards the frontier. The Czech government ordered partial mobilization on 20 May. France and the U.S.S.R. were pledged to defend the Czech frontiers against aggression but seemed unlikely to do so. The British Prime Minister, Neville Chamberlain, had stated that he would not guarantee Czechoslovakia, but that there might be circumstances under which the U.K. would intervene to defend the country. Early in August Lord Runciman was sent from London to see whether a compromise could be reached. Runciman proposed a solution which in his opinion embodied almost all the requirements of the Sudeten-German minority, and could, with some clarifications and extensions, have been made to cover them in their entirety. The Czech President, Eduard Beneš, accepted this solution, but on 7 September the Sudeten-Germans made a border incident the pretext for breaking off the talks. Negotiations were resumed but Hitler, in a speech on 12 September, incited the minority to acts of disorder. On 15 September Chamberlain went to Berchtesgaden to see Hitler and the French representative Edouard Daladier. The U.K. and France then recommended the Czechs to agree to cede all districts containing more than 50 per cent of Germans, without any plebiscite. On 23 September Hitler demanded larger concessions, asking Chamberlain at Godesberg for the immediate cession of a much greater zone, and a plebiscite in another area.

France and the U.K. mobilized and war seemed likely, when Hitler suggested a four-power conference at Munich, having been told by Chamberlain that he could get what he wanted without delay.

Chamberlain, Daladier, Hitler, and Mussolini met at Munich on 28 September. Hitler made insignificant modifications to his Godesberg demands, which were accepted by Chamberlain and Daladier. German troops crossed the border on 1 October. No representative of Czechoslovakia was present at Munich.

Muscat and Oman. A sultanate in eastern Arabia and the name by which the independent state of Oman, *q.v.*, was known before 1971.

Muskie, Edmund. U.S. Democratic Party politician; born 28 March 1914 in Rumford, Maine, the son of a tailor, Stephen Czarnecki, who had emigrated to the U.S.A. from Poland in 1903. He is a Roman Catholic. He was educated at Bates College, Maine, and Cornell Law School. After serving in the navy in the Second World War he resumed his law practice at Waterville, Maine, and went into politics in 1947 when he was elected to the State legislature. He became a member of the Democratic National Committee in 1952, and in 1954 was elected as Maine's first Democratic Governor for twenty years; he was re-elected in 1956. He entered the Senate in 1958 as the first elected Democrat in the history of the State. He was the Vice-Presidential nominee of Hubert Humphrey, *q.v.*, in the 1968 Presidential elections, which were won by the Republicans; and although he campaigned for the Democratic Presidential nomination in 1972 he refused to accept the invitation of the successful candidate, George McGovern, *q.v.*, to be his Vice-Presidential nominee.

Mutual Security Agency. A U.S. organization established by the Mutual Security Act of 1951 to furnish military, economic, and technical assistance in the interests of international peace. It helped friendly nations throughout the world and so was wider in scope than the Economic Co-operation Administration, *q.v.*, which it replaced with effect from 30 December 1951. The Foreign Operations Administration, *q.v.*, replaced the Agency on 1 August 1953.

N

N.A.A.C.P. National Association for the Advancement of Colored People, *q.v.*

Nagaland. An area of India near the Burmese border, it comprises areas which were once part of the state of Assam (the Naga Hills district) and part of the North-East Frontier Tract (the Tuensang Frontier division); area 6,366 sq. m.; population (1971 estimate) 520,000; headquarters Kohima. The Naga tribes demanded independence from India when the latter achieved independence in 1947, but the Indian government refused this, saying that its borders must be the same as those of British India. Efforts to subdue the Nagas, who claimed that they differed culturally, linguistically, and racially from the rest of India, proved unsuccessful; after the armed insurrection, which began in 1956, the Indian army could gain neither the complete control of the hills and forests, where the rebels operated, nor the loyalty of the other Nagas. The government made a partial concession to the Naga demands in 1961 by enacting the Nagaland (Transitional Provisions) Regulations, which on 1 December 1963 brought Nagaland into existence as a separate state. The rebels continued to demand complete independence, regarding themselves as being at war against Indian imperialism, and accepted help from the Chinese government in training guerillas. Many of these surrendered after the arrest in March 1969 of their leader, General Mowu Angami, and an anti-Chinese faction emerged among the rebels which expressed support for a peaceful settlement within the Indian Union.

Namibia. The former German colony and South African administered territory of South-West Africa, *q.v.* On 12 June 1968 the General Assembly of the United Nations voted a resolution proclaiming that, as from that date, the territory would be so renamed.

Nasser, Gamal Abdel. Egyptian political leader; born 15 January 1918 and educated at Cairo Military Academy. From 1942 onwards, while an officer in the Egyptian Army, he planned to overthrow the government with the assistance of his fellow officers. His aims were the introduction of social reforms, which he believed would never be carried out by the existing regime, and the withdrawal of British forces from the area of the Suez Canal, *q.v.* In 1948 he fought with the Egyptian forces which unsuccessfully invaded Israel, and said afterwards that the inefficiency of the Egyptian government was responsible for a shortage of munitions. In the same year he formed the secret Free Officers' Movement which chose as its leader the much respected General Mohammed Neguib. Nasser led the *coup d'état* of 23 July 1952 which caused King Farouk to abdicate, and in June 1953 became Deputy Prime Minister. He replaced Neguib as Prime Minister in April 1954 after accusing him of seeking absolute power; the young officers who had become the new rulers also considered that at such an early stage social reforms were more important than the return to parliamentary government which Neguib desired. Nasser became President of Egypt in June 1956 and of the United Arab Republic in February 1958. He was sworn in for a further term of six years as President on 25 March 1965, but died of a heart attack on 28 September 1970. He was succeeded by Anwar Sadat, *q.v.*

National Association for the Advancement of Colored People (N.A.A.C.P.). An organization founded in the U.S.A. in 1909 to secure and to enforce civil rights for negroes; it claims a membership of 400,000. It has played a leading part in the campaign against segregation, *q.v.*

National Labor Relations Act, 1935, also known as the Wagner Act. An Act passed by the U.S. Congress as part of President Franklin D. Roosevelt's New Deal, *q.v.* It declared the right of employees to form trade unions and to bargain collectively through their chosen representatives. Freedom of organization was granted under the Constitution, but many employers had refused to negotiate with unions and had discriminated against, or discharged, union members. The Act named certain 'unfair labor practices' which became punishable. Employers were forbidden: (1) to interfere with employees who organized and bargained collectively; (2) to interfere with or dominate any labour organization or to give financial or other support to it; (3) to encourage or discourage membership in any labour organization by discrimination in regard to hire or tenure; (4) to discharge or otherwise discriminate against an employee because he had filed charges or given testimony under the Act; (5) to refuse to bargain collectively with a chosen representative of the employees. The National Labor Relations Board was empowered to name the officially recognized unions, to conduct secret ballots to determine the exclusive representatives of employees, to issue orders requiring employers and employees to cease and desist from the specified unfair labour practices, and to petition the courts for the enforcement of its orders.

Nationalization. The acquisition by the state of any property, such as the steel industry, the railway system, the chemical industry or the land. Nationalization has been a common practice in the twentieth century even in countries with private-enterprise economies. Thus the French government has nationalized the Banque de France and holds 51 per cent of the shares in the national railway company, the Société Nationale des Chemins de Fer Français, and the Italian government monopolizes the production of salt and tobacco. Socialists and Communists tend to advocate nationalization as a general policy rather than as a remedy to be used in isolated cases. The constitution of the British Labour Party, *q.v.*, states that the aims of the Party are to be achieved 'upon the basis of common ownership of the means of production, distribution, and exchange', but this general approach has now been abandoned in practice; unsuccessful attempts have been made to amend this part of the constitution so that it would correspond with the actual policies of the Party.

N.A.T.O. North Atlantic Treaty Organization, *q.v.*

Nauru. A coral island in the central Pacific Ocean, 2,000 miles east of Australia; area 8½ sq. m.; population (1970) 6,664, of whom 3,407 are Nauruan, 883 Chinese, 560 European and the rest from other Pacific islands. It was formerly a trust territory of the United Nations and has been administered mainly by Australia since 1919. On 30 January 1968 it became an independent republic within the British Commonwealth, *q.v.*, of which it became a special member in November 1968. This new status gave Nauru the right to participate in all functional activities of the Commonwealth and eligibility for financial assistance but no representation at meetings of heads of governments. The island is a barren plateau except for a fertile coastal strip 200 yards deep, and deposits of phosphates estimated at 60 million tons. In 1964 the U.N. Trusteeship Council proposed that the population of Nauru should be resettled on Curtis Island, off the coast of Queensland, in anticipation of the exhaustion of stocks of phosphate within twenty-five years. The Nauruans refused to leave, and since 1966 soil has been shipped to the island to replace phosphate rock. A Legislative Assembly was elected in January 1968 which in turn elected a Council of State to govern the island until a Constitution was approved. The former Head Chief, Hammer de Roburt, a teacher, born in 1922 and educated in Australia, became Head of State, and was re-elected in January 1971.

Naxalites. Originally a group of pro-Chinese extremists who had resigned, or been expelled, from the Communist Party of India. They announced on 22 April 1969 (Lenin's birthday) the formation of a truly revolutionary Marxist-Leninist Communist Party which would reject parliamentary institutions and bring about the seizure of power by the peasants through a campaign of murder, confiscation and terror. The movement took its name from the Naxalbari revolt in 1967 in West Bengal, led by Kanu Sanyal, which had had similar objectives. Not all Indian Maoists, who have representation in the Lok Sabha as the pro-Peking Communist Party, support the Naxalites although they enjoy the approval of the Communist Party of China. From 1969 the Naxalites waged a campaign of terror in Andhra Pradesh, Assam, Bihar, West Bengal and six other states; this culminated in the launching of a cultural revolution on the Chinese model in Calcutta in April 1970, during which Naxalite students fired cinemas, raided universities and schools burning books and destroying pictures of Gandhi and Nehru, and murdered teachers, including the Vice-Chancellor of Jadavpur University. Justice was subverted because officials were too terrified to act. The Indian government imposed direct rule on those states in which law and order had broken down, and assumed special powers of detention which resulted in 6,000 Naxalites being put under arrest by February 1971 in West Bengal alone. In March 1972 the electorate indicated its approval of this policy by returning Congress majorities in 16 of the 21 states. In July 1972 the Naxalite leader, Charu Mazumdar, died after evading arrest for two years.

Nazis. Popular contraction of the name National-Socialists, the party led by Adolf Hitler. The term arose as a parallel to the word 'Sozi' (the first two syllables of 'Sozialisten'), with which the German Socialists had been labelled by their opponents in earlier times. National-Socialists were first styled Nazi-Sozi, but the second half of the term was later abandoned. Today groups in the German Federal Republic sympathetic to the National-Socialists' aims are called neo-Nazis.

Nehru, Jawaharlal. Prime Minister of India; born Allahabad, 14 November 1889. A high-caste Hindu of Kashmiri descent, he was educated in England at Harrow, Cambridge University, and the Inner Temple, where he qualified as a barrister in 1912. In 1920 he joined the nationalist, non-violence movement led by Gandhi and became a passionate advocate of Indian independence. Between 1920 and 1927 he was imprisoned eight times for his political activities. In 1929 he was General Secretary of the All-India Congress Committee and succeeded his father as President of Congress. In September 1946 he was appointed Vice-President of the Executive Council, or interim government, of India, set up by the Viceroy, Lord Mountbatten. Eleven months later he became the first Prime Minister, and Minister for Foreign Affairs, of the Dominion of India; from 1953 until April 1957 he was also Minister of Defence. In domestic affairs he made the problem of India's over-population his special concern; he was the first Hindu politician publicly to declare his approval of birth control. He died on 27 May 1964. On the death of his successor, Lal Bahadur Shastri, *q.v.*, in 1966, his daughter, Indira Gandhi, *q.v.*, became Prime Minister.

Nenni, Pietro. Italian Socialist leader; born 9 February 1891. He spent eleven years of his childhood in an orphanage. In 1911 he was imprisoned, with Benito Mussolini who later became dictator of Italy, for participating in Socialist riots against the Italo-Turkish war. His career in journalism, which began on the *Lucifero*, an Ancona newspaper, was interrupted by service in the Italian army from 1915 to 1918. After working on various other journals he became editor of *Avanti*, the official organ of the Italian Socialists, until its suppression by Mussolini in 1926 when he fled to France.

He was a political commissar of the Garibaldi brigade, which supported the government in the Spanish Civil War of 1936–9, and defeated a force of Italian Fascists sent to Spain by Mussolini to help the Spanish Fascist rebels under Franco. In February 1942, while in unoccupied France, he was arrested on the orders of Laval, the Vice-Premier of the Vichy government, and deported to Italy where he was imprisoned until 1943. He became Deputy Premier, and Deputy President of the Council of Ministers in 1945, Deputy Premier in the de Gasperi government until June 1946 and Foreign Minister from October 1946 to January 1947. In that month the right wing of the Socialist Party seceded, but Nenni continued to lead the left-wing Socialists. When the Italian Socialist Party (P.S.I.) joined the coalition government of Aldo Moro in November 1963, he was again appointed Deputy Premier, and when the P.S.I. in October 1966 merged with its former right wing, the Social Democratic Party, he was elected leader of the unified Socialist Party until July 1969 when it again divided. He contested the presidential election in December 1971 and was defeated on the twenty-third ballot by Giovanni Leone, *q.v.*, who received 518 votes to his 408.

Nepal. An independent kingdom in the Himalayas; area, including Mount Everest, 54,600 sq. m.; population (1971 estimate) 11,292,841, of whom 88 per cent are illiterate; capital Katmandu. The aborigines are of Mongolian type, with a considerable admixture of Hindu blood from India. There were once many hill clans and small principalities, one of which, Gurkha, became predominant in 1769 and has since given its name to men from all parts of Nepal. In 1846 the power of the King was usurped by the Rana family, who established for themselves the post of hereditary Prime Minister. The Kings became merely titular heads. The Rana Maharajas were in power until 1951, and took an annual revenue of £1,500,000 from Nepal, of which they kept 90 per cent for themselves, for investment in India, overseas, or in jewels. The other 10 per cent was spent largely on an army and on government information agents. The Ranas obtained the money from customs and from farming out the timber and rice resources to their relations.

In 1951 there was a revolt against the Ranas, and in November the Prime Minister, Maharaja Mohum Shamsher, handed over his post to Matrika Prasad Koirala. Subsequent governments were unstable in face of Rana opposition, and promised reforms were not introduced. Political frustrations produced 29 political parties and a civil disobedience campaign by the Nepali Congress Party, which demanded general elections, an independent judiciary, control of inflation, and a properly organized police force. In March 1955 the King dismissed the cabinet, which had been defeated in the Assembly, introduced direct rule, announced the introduction of income tax, and decided to tax the land holdings of the Ranas.

Amid the throng of competing politicians the most able and significant is probably Dr K. I. Singh, the left-wing former Nepali Congress leader, who led an abortive rising in Katmandu in January 1952, and subsequently escaped to Tibet and thence to Peking. He was repatriated in September 1955 and given a royal pardon. He has his own party, the National Democratic Front, often known as the 'China lobby', which provided a government for two months in 1957. He encountered opposition when he tried to abolish corruption in the Civil Service and when he opposed the acceptance of foreign aid. The King announced plans for the drafting of a Constitution and for the holding of elections, which took place in February 1959, when the Nepali Congress Party won 74 of the 109 seats. A government was formed in May 1959 by B. P. Koirala, a half-brother of M. P. Koirala, who was largely responsible for the fall of the Ranas in 1951. In December 1960 he was imprisoned by the King, who assumed full powers. The supporters of B. P. Koirala, and other dissident elements, were responsible for numerous acts of sabotage and guerilla raids in 1962 and 1963.

In December 1962 the King promulgated a new Constitution based on a four-tiered system of Panchayats or Councils. The national Panchayat has 109 indirectly elected members and some royal nominees. The King justified the system by saying that a parliamentary form of government was unsuitable in Nepal. This was eventually conceded by Dr Singh in 1968 and a reconciliation took place between the King and former politicians, who still command considerable support. An Advisory Committee of three was appointed in April 1969, and in 1972 a Council of Ministers was introduced when the Crown Prince, Birendra Bir Bikram Shah Deva, succeeded to the throne on the death of his father King Mahendra.

Nepal is poor; for years there were no industries but recently jute and sugar mills, paper and cement factories, hydro-electric plants, and chemical works have been established. There are few public utilities and the judicial system was only made uniform in 1956, while there was no taxation system until 1955. In all disputes between India and China, the two neighbouring states, Nepal is strictly neutral; a policy of non-alignment is considered essential to survival. However, the cordial relations established with China, which resulted in Chinese aid to construct a road from Katmandu to Lhasa, offended the Indian government which failed to renew a 10-year trade and transit agreement when it expired in October 1970.

Netherlands. Officially called the Kingdom of the Netherlands, an independent state on the North Sea and north of Belgium; area approximately 13,961 sq. m.; population (1970 estimate) 13,119,430; capital Amsterdam; seat of government The Hague. In 1815 the hereditary Stadtholder, or Governor, William of Orange-Nassau, was made King of a Netherlands which, by the Congress of Vienna, combined the northern United Provinces of the Netherlands, which had been under the domination of the French from 1795 to 1813, with those Belgian provinces which had been subject to Austria. This union was dissolved as a result of the Belgian revolution of 1830.

The Netherlands is a constitutional and hereditary monarchy under Queen Juliana of Orange-Nassau (born 1909; inaugurated as Queen in 1948). The legislature is the States-General comprising a First Chamber of 75 members, elected for six years by the Provincial Diets, and a Second Chamber of 150 members elected for four years by universal suffrage and on the basis of pure proportional representation, *q.v.* The Dutch system, by which the number of votes polled by each party is converted into a percentage of the total votes cast, and the 150 seats in the Second Chamber are divided among the parties according to the percentage polled by each, has made coalition government inevitable. Since 1948 the Catholic People's Party (until 1971 the largest political group) has insisted on coalition cabinets embracing as many parties as possible, a situation which became increasingly unworkable after 1954. The Catholics dislike government with the Labour Party (their most significant rival) in opposition because Catholic workers might be attracted to vote for the Labour

Party. This dilemma enabled the Labour Party to dominate the coalitions until 1959 when, for the first time since 1945, a government was formed without Labour members.

At the elections for the Second Chamber, held on 28 April 1971, and contested by 28 parties, the Labour Party won 39 seats (37 in 1967); the Catholic People's Party 35 (42); Liberals 16 (17); Anti-Revolutionaries (Calvinists) 13 (15); Christian Historicals (also Protestants) 10 (12); Communist Party 6 (5); Farmers' Party 1 (7); D-66 11 (7); Democratic Socialists 70 (DS-70), a breakaway group to the right of the Labour Party led by Dr William Drees, son of the post-war Labour Prime Minister, 8 (0); Radical Political Party 2 (0); others 9. The governing coalition of the Catholic People's Party, the Liberals, the Anti-Revolutionaries and the Christian Historicals, which had commanded 86 of the 150 seats in the Chamber, was reduced to 74 seats, and the Prime Minister, Piet de Jong, resigned. After prolonged negotiations a new government coalition was formed on 22 June 1971 comprising the same four parties with the addition of DS-70. Barend Biesheuvel, leader of the Anti-Revolutionary Party, became Prime Minister. His government, which as a right-of-centre coalition did not reflect the pronounced swing to the left and decline in support for the religious parties revealed in the 1971 elections, fell after one year in office; but as no alternative could be found fresh elections were called for 29 November 1972 with the following results: Labour Party 43 seats; Catholic People's Party 27; Liberals 22; Anti-Revolutionaries 14; Christian Historicals 7; Communists 7; D-66 6; Democratic Socialists 70 (DS-70) 6; Radical Party 7; others 11.

The Netherlands is dependent on foreign trade and its government has accordingly adopted policies of deflation and restraint at regular intervals to improve the balance of payments position. The Dutch, like the Belgians, have ensured an adequate level of industrial investment. They have been able to abandon most of their former discrimination against dollar imports, and their exports (including dairy products, horticultural produce such as bulbs and vegetables, and manufactures) are highly competitive in price with other countries. There has been a customs union with Belgium and Luxemburg, known as Benelux, q.v., since 29 October 1947, and the Netherlands has been a member of the European Economic Community, q.v., since 1 January 1958. The overseas territories of the Netherlands are the Netherlands West Indies, q.v., Netherlands Guiana (Surinam), and the Netherlands Antilles. Netherlands New Guinea, q.v. (West Irian), became part of Indonesia on 1 May 1963.

Netherlands New Guinea. The name by which West Irian, q.v., since

1 May 1963 part of Indonesia, was known while under Dutch sovereignty.

Netherlands West Indies. The overseas territories of the Netherlands, and formerly its colonies, in South America and the West Indies. They are of great economic importance to the Netherlands and comprise: (1) Netherlands Guiana (Surinam), in South America, bordered on the east by French Guiana, on the south by Brazil, on the west by Guyana, and on the north by the Atlantic Ocean. It has an area of 55,143 sq. m., and a population (1969 estimate) of 389,000. Surinam has some of the world's largest deposits of bauxite (the raw material from which aluminium is made), of which great quantities are exported to the U.S.A. (2) Netherlands Antilles, which are two groups of three islands each in the Caribbean Sea, 550 miles apart from each other. Their total area is 394 sq. m. and their population (1970) 220,000. They consist of the Netherlands Windward Islands (Curaçao, Aruba, Bonaire) and the Netherlands Leeward Islands (St Eustatius, Saba, and part of St Maarten, the other part belonging to France). The economy is based on the refining of oil imported from Venezuela to Curaçao (where over half the population live) and Aruba. The oil refineries, controlled by companies affiliated to Royal Dutch Shell and Standard Oil of New Jersey, are among the largest in the world.

On 15 December 1954 the Netherlands and the Netherlands West Indies were constituted as a single realm under the House of Orange, the three areas exercising full internal autonomy. In 1973 Dutch proposals to grant independence to the West Indies were strongly resisted in Surinam since they would entail forfeiture of the right of free entry to the Netherlands and could end the current migration of some 10,000 a year.

Neutrality. Non-participation in a war between other states. If a state wishes to be considered neutral and thus to have the rights enjoyed by a neutral, it must observe certain duties, and in particular must abstain from any interference with the war. It must neither favour nor hinder any belligerent, must prevent belligerents from making use of its territories, and must defend itself against any violation of its neutrality. No hostilities between belligerents may be undertaken or tolerated on neutral territory or in neutral waters. Public opinion, the press, and even the government of the neutral state may show sympathy with one belligerent, so long as these feelings do not find expression in actions violating impartiality.

Perpetual neutrality arises where a state, such as Switzerland, has been neutralized by a special treaty. Benevolent neutrality is a term used in some treaties which empowers a state to help a belligerent without actually going to war. Such help would usually be a violation of the modern duty of neutrality, but is consistent with the older, less precise, definition of neutrality. Partial neutrality exists where part of the territory of a state is neutralized, as are, for instance, the Åland Islands, *q.v.*

Neutrality, Treaty of. A treaty between states by which they agree that if any of them is attacked by a state not a party to the treaty, the others will remain neutral. Treaties of neutrality were concluded before the Second World War between Italy and Yugoslavia, 1933; Italy and the U.S.S.R., 1933; and between each of the Baltic states of Estonia, Lithuania, Latvia, and Finland, with the U.S.S.R., 1935.

New Deal. The policy inaugurated by Franklin Delano Roosevelt (born 1882, President of the U.S.A. from 1933 until his death in 1945) in 1933 to overcome the economic crisis which arose in 1929. Previous attempts to end depressions had employed orthodox deflationary means. The National Industry Recovery Act and the Agricultural Adjustment Act, parts of which were declared by the Supreme Court to be unconstitutional, gave the executive wide powers in industrial and agricultural matters. The government helped industry by a programme of public works planned by the Public Works Administration, and by providing credit at low interest. Legislation provided for extensive house-building supported by government subsidies. A Works Progress Administration provided jobs for the unemployed. The rights of workers to form trade unions were strengthened by the National Labor Relations Act, 1935, *q.v.* A social insurance scheme was introduced by the Social Security Act. The New Deal policies did not end unemployment, but helped to reduce the number of workless from 17 million to 7 million. The phrase can be compared with Great Society, *q.v.*, and New Frontier, *q.v.*

New Frontier. Epitomizes the forward-looking approach to economic, political and social problems said to have been adopted by Kennedy during his Presidency (1961–3). It can be compared with the New Deal, *q.v.*, and the Great Society, *q.v.*

New Guinea. A large island to the north of Australia which comprises the Indonesian territory of West Irian, *q.v.*, and Papua–New Guinea, *q.v.*, the combination of the Australian territory of Papua and the former German colony of New Guinea, which has been administered by Australia as a Trusteeship territory since 1945.

New Zealand. An independent state and member of the British Commonwealth; area of North and South Islands and a number of small islands, including the Island Territories, 103,939 sq. m.; population (1971) 2,862,631, of whom 2,051,363 live on North Island; capital

Wellington. It was first discovered by Tasman in 1642 and visited several times in the eighteenth century by Captain Cook; by the Treaty of Waitangi in 1840 the Maori chiefs accepted British sovereignty and the islands became a British colony. The Maoris later revolted against British rule but peace was established in 1870 when approximately half of the North Island was allotted to them. In 1907 New Zealand was given the status of a Dominion.

Executive authority is vested in the Governor-General, who must act on the advice of an Executive Council, appointed from a House of Representatives selected by popular vote for a three-year term. This period, in preference to four years, was confirmed by referendum on 23 September 1967. At the general election held in November 1972 the Labour Party, led by Norman Kirk, which had last been in power from 1957 to 1960, won 56 seats (39 in 1969); the National Party, led by John Marshall who had succeeded Keith Holyoake as Prime Minister in February 1971, secured 31 seats (45 in 1969).

The economy is largely agricultural and pastoral, with important exports of wool, butter, beef, cheese, hides and skins, dried and condensed milk, lamb and mutton. In 1971 35 per cent of all meat and dairy exports were to the U.K.; as a result of British accession to the European Economic Community these will be reduced by some 30 per cent by 1977. The U.S.A. and Japan are expanding export markets (27 per cent of all exports in 1970) and Australia, with whom New Zealand has a free trade agreement (N.A.F.T.A.), is an important trading partner. As a member of A.N.Z.U.S., *q.v.*, New Zealand now concentrates its defence efforts on the Far East and is reluctant to undertake Commonwealth commitments involving responsibility elsewhere. The policy of the Labour government is to transform S.E.A.T.O., *q.v.*, into a non-military association. Until 1 January 1962 New Zealand was responsible for the trusteeship territory of Western Samoa, which achieved full independence on that date.

Newfoundland. A Province of Canada; area (exclusive of its Dependency, Labrador, which has an area of 110,000 sq. m.) 46,185 sq. m.; population (1971 estimate) 524,000 including Labrador; capital St John's. Newfoundland is an island off the east coast of Canada and was England's first colony, having been occupied on behalf of Elizabeth I in 1583. It was constituted as a Dominion at the Imperial Conference of 1917, but encountered such grave financial difficulties that its Dominion status was suspended in 1933. A Royal Commission recommended that the island should be administered by a Commission of Government, comprising three members from Newfoundland and three from the U.K. A referendum in July 1948 decided by a narrow majority (78,408 to 71,464) in favour of confederation with Canada rather than a return to responsible government as it existed till 1933. Newfoundland accordingly became a Province of Canada on 1 April 1949. The Liberal Party, which had formed the provincial government since 1949, lost power in 1971 when the elections gave the Progressive Conservatives a majority of one. This proved unworkable and at fresh elections held on 24 March 1972 the result was: Liberals 9 (20 in 1971); Progressive Conservatives 33 (21); New Labrador Party 0 (1). Most of the population are engaged in fishing and its subsidiary industries; there is a large newsprint output, and there are several mines, which produce copper, asbestos, fluorspar, iron ore, lead limestone, and zinc.

Nicaragua. The largest and most sparsely populated Central American republic, bordering on the Atlantic and Pacific Oceans; area 54,143 sq. m.; population (1969) 1,841,759, mainly mestizo (of mixed Spanish and Indian descent); capital Managua. Sixty per cent of the population are illiterate. Nicaragua was ruled by Spain from the sixteenth century until it became independent in 1821. Under the Constitution of 1950 as amended the President, who may not serve two consecutive terms, is elected by popular vote every four years; Congress consists of a Senate (of 16 members and the ex-Presidents of the republic) and a Chamber of Deputies (of 42 members). Both houses of Congress are elected for four years. General Anastasio Somoza Garcia, dictator for fifteen years, was President from 1950 until his assassination in 1956, He was succeeded by his son, Colonel Luis Somoza, who retired at the end of his constitutional term, nominating Dr René Schick Gutierrez as the next Presidential candidate. Dr Schick was duly elected in February 1963 at the first elections ever held by secret ballot; his government introduced a more liberal policy, lifting restrictions on the press and on political discussion, and increasing economic stability through Nicaraguan participation in the Central American Common Market, q.v., and by attracting foreign investment. When he died in August 1966, Dr Lorenzo Guerrero assumed the Presidency until elections were held in February 1967. The new President was General Anastasio Somoza Debayle, son of the dictator and brother of the former President Luis Somoza. His election meant that the family, which holds extensive commercial and industrial interests (including the national airline and the Mamenic shipping line) had controlled Nicaragua for more than thirty years. The National Liberal Party (P.L.N.) which supports the Somozas and campaigns on a platform of secularism, won 28 seats in the Chamber of Deputies; the right-wing traditional Conservative Party, led by the Chamarro family, won 14 seats. On 30 August 1971 Congress voted to dissolve itself so that the Constitution could be reformed, and on 1 May 1972 President Somoza was succeeded by a triumvirate, consisting of one Conservative, Dr Fernando Agüero Rocha, and two Liberals, General Roberto Martínez Lacayo and Alfonso Lobo Cordero, which was to hold office until 31 December 1973 when it would surrender power to an elected President. It was anticipated that ex-President Somoza, who had assumed command of the army, would contest the proposed elections.

Agriculture is the principal source of national wealth and there are considerable exports of coffee, cotton, meat and sugar. Nicaragua has been in debt for many years; by an agreement between British creditors and the Nicaraguan government in 1911, renewed in 1917 and 1920, custom receipts and certain other revenues accrue to the Collector-General of Customs, who must be an American, and are applied to the payment of the external debt.

Foreign relations, especially with neighbouring Costa Rica, were formerly determined by the whim of the President. In 1948 José Figueres deposed President Teodoro Picado of Costa Rica who was an ally of the Somozas; Nicaragua retaliated by giving support in January 1955 to an invasion of Costa Rica (which had abolished its standing army) by Costa Rican exiles. At the request of the Organization of American States, q.v., the U.S.A. provided Costa Rica with aircraft to repel the invasion, and in January 1956 a treaty of friendship was signed between Nicaragua and Costa Rica. Membership of inter-American and Central American economic and political organizations has restrained Nicaragua from further unilateral action.

Niger. An independent republic; area 484,000 sq. m.; population (1970 estimate) 4,016,000, comprising Hausas, Djermas, Touareg, Peulh, Songhais, and 3,000 Europeans; capital Niamey. The Hausas (1,350,000) and the Djermas (600,000) form a distinct ethnic group, being black and living in the south, while the Touareg (330,000) and the Peulh (440,000) are pale-skinned. The population is predominantly Moslem. The country is land-locked, with Mali, Algeria and Libya to the west and north, Chad to the east, and Upper Volta, Dahomey, and Nigeria to the south. The French created the separate territory of Niger by decrees in 1922 and 1926 and it became one of the eight territories comprising French West Africa, q.v. It obtained self-government within the French Community, q.v., on 18 December 1958; and complete independence, after breaking with the Community in June 1960, on 3 August 1960.

At elections held in 1958 the Parti Progressiste Nigérien, the Niger section of the Rassemblement Démocratique Africain, led by Hamani-Diori, obtained control; the opposition party, the African Regroupment Party, which opposed any connection between Niger and the French Community, was dissolved and its leader, Djibo Bakary, exiled. A new Constitution, adopted in 1960, provides for a single chamber legislature of 50 members elected every five years by universal suffrage, and a President (Hamani Diori), appointed unanimously by the Assembly in November 1960, and re-elected by popular vote in October 1965 and October 1970.

The country is short of water and there are only two permanent waterways, the Niger (on which stands Niamey) in the extreme west, and the Kamadougou, which flows into Lake Chad, to the east. Beans, manioc and millet are produced, and there are exports of decorticated groundnuts, livestock, furs and gum arabic. Several companies are prospecting for petroleum, and uranium deposits have been discovered at Arlit in the north-west.

Nigeria. A West African republic and member of the British Commonwealth; area 356,699 sq. m.; population (1970 estimate) 66,174,000; capital Lagos. Until it achieved independence on 1 October 1960 it was the largest British colony; a republic was declared on 1 October 1963. Under the Constitution of 1963 Nigeria was a Federation of four Regions (Northern, Eastern, Mid-Western and Western) and the Federal capital of Lagos. By a decree of May 1967 the Federal government adopted proposals dividing the Northern Region into six states, and the Eastern Region into three states, thus creating, with the Mid-Western, Western and Lagos states, a Federation of twelve units.

In spite of the federal structure regional and tribal interests predominated. The Northern People's Congress, which was mainly a Hausa party, led by Alhaji Sir Abubakar Tafewa Balewa (Prime Minister of Nigeria from 1957 until his death in 1966), and the Nigerian National Democratic Party, led by Chief Akintola (from the Western Region), outnumbered the National Council of Nigerian Citizens, the party founded by Dr Nnamdi Azikiwe, *q.v.*, and led by Dr Michael Okpara, which was the ruling party in the Eastern and the Mid-Western Regions and reflected the interests of the Ibo tribe, and the Action Group of Obafemi Awolowo, *q.v.*, which had the support of five million Yoruba. In January 1966 civil government was brought to an end by the overthrow and assassination of two Regional Premiers and of the Federal Prime Minister, Tafewa Balewa. The army, under Major-General Johnson Aguiyi-Ironsi took control; in May 1966 the federal system was abolished and a unitary form of government introduced. However tribal persecution, particularly by the Hausa of those Ibo living outside the Eastern Region and away from the support of their own tribesmen, led to a breakdown in central authority, and to the assassination of Ironsi in July 1966. He was succeeded by the senior Northern officer to survive the January *coup*, Lt-General Yakubu Gowon, *q.v.*, who revived the Federation and appointed Military Governors to administer the Regions. A new Constitution, decreed in March 1967, vested all legislative and executive authority in a Supreme Military Council of which Gowon was the President. This was replaced in April 1972 by a Federal Executive Council with Gowon as Chairman.

During 1967 relations between the Federal government and the military government of the Eastern Region, under Colonel Odumegwu Ojukwu, deteriorated. The Ibo, who constituted two-thirds of the regional population (1963) of 12,400,000, became increasingly suspicious of a central authority dominated by Hausa. As a result of a dispute over the distribution of the oil revenues from the Region, which amounted to £2 million monthly, as between the Federal and Regional governments, the Eastern Region military government in April 1967 seized all Federal property, took over Federal institutions and collected its own taxes. In reply the Federal government proposed to split the Region into three states, thereby separating the Ibo people in the interior from the oil-producing coastal districts. Ojukwu then proclaimed the independence of the Eastern Region on 30 May 1967, and the State of Biafra came into existence. Ibo, and others, outside the Region were invited to accede. Fighting broke out between Federal and Biafran troops in July, and in August 1967 the Biafrans joined forces with mutinous soldiers in the Mid-Western Region, seizing the regional capital of Benin; they also advanced into the Western Region. By January 1968 Biafra had once more been contained within the boundaries of the Eastern Region, but the inevitable victory of the Federal army was delayed by the recognition accorded Biafra by Tanzania in April 1967, followed by Ivory Coast, and subsequently Zambia, which justified its actions on the grounds that the Federal government was being supplied with arms by the U.K. and the U.S.S.R., both being white, imperialist powers. France and Portugal, however, provided arms for Biafra and the rebellion was sustained, despite attempts at mediation by the Organization of African Unity, *q.v.*, until 12 January 1970 when General Ojukwu fled abroad and Colonel Philip Effiong surrendered to the Federal army.

There are valuable deposits of manganese ore, silver, and monazite, which contains the radio-active element thorium; mining rights are vested in the government. However agriculture is the mainstay of the economy, and palm oil and palm kernels, cocoa, cotton and groundnuts are exported in considerable quantity. Production of crude oil, the export of which tripled between 1963 and 1966, ceased during the war, but was re-established as the chief foreign exchange-earning commodity in 1971, in which year the government set up a National Oil Corporation, acquiring 35 per cent of the shares of S.A.F.R.A.P., a subsidiary of the French state-owned E.L.F.-E.R.A.P., and Nigeria joined the Organization of Petroleum Exporting Countries (O.P.E.C.), *q.v.* In July 1966 Nigeria became an associate member of the European Economic Community; the U.K. remains the most important trading partner.

Nixon, Richard Milhous. U.S. politician; born 9 January 1913 in California and educated at Duke University, North Carolina. He practised law from 1937 to 1942, when, after a short period as an attorney in the government service, he joined the U.S. navy, with which he served until 1946. He was then elected as a Republican member for Los Angeles in the House of Representatives. He was responsible for the citation for contempt of Congress of Gerhard Eisler, who had refused to testify before the House Committee on Un-American Activities. He became a Senator in 1950 and in 1952 was elected to the office of Vice-President. He was returned for a second term as Vice-President in 1956, and in 1960 was the unsuccessful Republican Presidential candidate in a close contest with John Kennedy, *q.v.* In November 1962 he was defeated by Governor Brown of California, a Democrat, in the contest for the governorship of that state. He was elected President in 1968, narrowly defeating the Democratic candidate, Hubert Humphrey, *q.v.*, in an election notable for the intervention of a third candidate, George Wallace, *q.v.* In 1972 he was returned for a second Presidential term with an overwhelming victory over his Democratic opponent, George McGovern, *q.v.*, winning 61 per cent of the popular vote and 49 of the 50 States.

Nkomo, Joshua. Rhodesian (or Zimbabwe) nationalist leader; born 1917 in Matopa; educated at Adam's College, Natal and the Jan Hofmeyer School of Social Work, Johannesburg. He worked as a welfare officer with the Rhodesia Railways at Bulawayo and then became organizing secretary of the Rhodesian African Railway Workers' Union from 1945–50. He was elected President of the African National Congress in 1957; when it was banned he was exiled to London from where he helped to organize, and was elected President of, the National Democratic Party in 1960. He then returned to Southern Rhodesia. When this Party in turn was banned he further organized, and was elected President of, the Zimbabwe African People's Union (Z.A.P.U.) in 1961. In 1962 Z.A.P.U. was declared an unlawful organization and in 1963 Nkomo was arrested and sentenced to six months' detention for obstructing the police. Although he has no acknowledged political authority and has spent many years as a political prisoner, he is the unquestioned leader of the African nationalists in Rhodesia (or Zimbabwe); his importance was recognized by the U.K. government in 1963 when he was invited to discussions in London on the future status of Southern Rhodesia, and in November 1968 and again in November 1971 when the Minister without Portfolio and the Foreign Secretary respectively visited him in detention to consult him on this issue.

Nkrumah, Kwame. Former President of Ghana; born 18 September 1909; educated at a Roman Catholic mission school and Achimota College. He became a schoolmaster in 1931 and later, with financial assistance from his uncle, a diamond prospector, studied sociology at the all-Negro University of Lincoln in Oxford, Pennsylvania, and became President of the African Students' Association of America and Canada. At the end of the Second World War he attended the London School of Economics and Political Science where he published a magazine *New African*, which was banned in the Gold Coast. In 1947 he became General Secretary of the United Gold Coast Convention, a popular nationalist party, which he left in 1949 to found the Convention People's Party. Nkrumah attacked the new Gold Coast Constitution, alleging that it impeded progress towards self-government, and was imprisoned for his political agitation. The Governor released him from jail in 1951, when his party won the Gold Coast General Election, and made him Prime Minister. He remained as Prime Minister when the Dominion of Ghana was established on 6 March 1957, and became President when Ghana became a republic, within the British Commonwealth, on 1 July 1960. While on a state visit to Peking, his regime was overthrown by an army *coup*, and he was deposed on 24 February 1966. He took refuge in Guinea, where President Sekou Touré, *q.v.*, declared him joint Head of State. He died in a Romanian sanatorium on 27 April 1971; in July 1971 his remains were flown to Ghana for burial in his birthplace at Nkroful.

Nobel Prizes. By the will of A. B. Nobel, a Swedish chemist and engineer who died in 1896, the bulk of the fortune which he amassed from the manufacture of explosives was left to establish five annual prizes. Four go to the persons who have done the most distinguished work in physics, chemistry, medicine or physiology, and literature. The fifth goes to the person who, or society which, has done outstanding work for peace. U.N.I.C.E.F., *q.v.*, was awarded the 1965 peace prize.

Non-Aggression Pact. An agreement between two states to abstain from the use of force against each other and to settle any differences by negotiation and arbitration.

Non-Proliferation Treaty. An agreement concluded on 1 July 1968 by the U.K., the U.S.A. and the U.S.S.R., and signed by sixty concurring states, to curb the spread of nuclear weapons. This was to be effected in three ways: (1) by forbidding nuclear-armed signatories to transfer to other states (including other nuclear powers) any kind of nuclear explosive device, whether or not it is deemed to be a 'weapon', or any control, direct or indirect, over such devices, or to encourage or assist a non-nuclear state to acquire any such device or such control. Non-nuclear signatories equally would undertake not to receive such devices or such controls, not to manufacture them, and not to seek or receive help in making them; (2) by the introduction of a comprehensive system of safeguards operated by an international inspectorate; (3) by offering additional safeguards to those non-nuclear signatories of the promise of immediate action by the U.N. Security Council should their security be endangered by a nuclear power which had not ratified the Treaty.

The Treaty compared favourably with the partial Test Ban Treaty, *q.v.*, of 1963, in that it committed every signatory to identifiable and verifiable action. The Treaty came into force on 5 March 1970 when the three main nuclear sponsors, the U.K., the U.S.A. and the U.S.S.R. together with 47 other states, including the German Federal Republic, had both signed and ratified it. A period of eighteen months had been allowed for non-nuclear signatories to negotiate inspection arrangements with the International Atomic Energy Authority to ensure that their nuclear industries were not secreting fissile material for military purposes. Several important non-nuclear states, to whom the Treaty was primarily addressed, had indicated that they would not ratify the Treaty until inspection arrangements had first been negotiated. This had been the attitude of the Commission of the European Atomic Energy Community (Euratom), which had advised its members to delay ratification until Euratom had completed negotiations on their behalf.

The weakness of the Treaty is that it does not include all the nuclear powers. France, which is prominent in the world uranium trade, refused to sign, and China, being at that time outside the U.N. organization, was excluded. Then the guarantees unilaterally offered by only three of the existing nuclear powers would apply only to those states which became party to the Treaty. The issue of commitment was particularly acute for those Asian states, for example, which have the capacity to develop a nuclear warhead but which have not yet done so; Japan and India, which fall into this category, having signed away, under the Treaty, their right to manufacture their own nuclear deterrent, would be all the more exposed to a nuclear attack from China, from which they would enjoy no guarantee. The invasion of Czechoslovakia in August 1968 by five of the nuclear-armed Warsaw Pact countries cast doubts on the validity of those guarantees offered by the U.S.S.R.

Nordic Council. Comprises representatives from Denmark, Finland, Norway, Sweden, and Iceland, who give advice to the governments of these five countries on measures to improve Scandinavian cooperation. It has urged the governments to take concerted action to establish the necessary conditions for a common market in certain goods, as a first step towards a customs union, but developments in this direction were arrested by the establishment in 1959 of the European Free Trade Association, *q.v.*, which included Denmark, Norway and Sweden, and the accession of Denmark to the European Economic Community, *q.v.*, in 1972. The Council is also concerned with minor measures of cooperation, such as the rule that Scandinavians no longer need passports when visiting other Scandinavian countries.

North Atlantic Treaty Organization. Set up by the North Atlantic Treaty, 4 April 1949, between the members of the Brussels Treaty Organization, *q.v.* (Belgium, France, Luxemburg, the Netherlands and the U.K.), and Canada, Denmark, Iceland, Italy, Norway, Portugal and the U.S.A. Whereas the Council of Europe, *q.v.*, and the Organization for European Economic Co-operation, *q.v.*, are European organizations, this Treaty links the two North American powers to a group of European states. Under Article Five the parties declare that they will regard an attack on one of them as an attack on all, and that, if an armed attack occurs, each will assist the country attacked by 'such action as it deems necessary'. This is less strict than the duty imposed on members of the Brussels Treaty Organization and the Western European Union, *q.v.*, to give each other 'all the military and other aid and assistance in their power'. The Treaty declares a determination by the parties 'to safeguard the freedom, common heritage and civilization of their peoples founded on the principles of democracy, individual liberty and the rule of law'. Since 1949 the following states have joined N.A.T.O.: the German Federal Republic, Greece and Turkey. In March 1966 France withdrew from the military side of N.A.T.O.; the headquarters of the North Atlantic Council (through which the Organization is administered), the Military Committee and the International Secretariat, together with the Supreme Headquarters Allied Powers, Europe (S.H.A.P.E.), were then transferred from France to Belgium.

The Treaty was originally inspired both by west European fear of the U.S.S.R. and by disappointment with the United Nations, in which the work of the Security Council, which is responsible for dealing with threats to peace and aggression, was being hindered by the Russian use of the veto. The Treaty was declared to be a regional arrangement of the type contemplated by the United Nations Charter. It was more significant than the Rio Treaty, *q.v.*, or the Brussels Treaty, because it was the first treaty in which the U.S.A. had ever undertaken European commitments in peacetime. The wording of Article Five ensures, however, that there is no automatic obligation to fight; the U.S. Congress, for example, would still be able to decide whether or not the U.S.A. should go to war.

North Borneo. The northern part of the island of Borneo, *q.v.*, comprising Brunei, *q.v.*, Sabah, *q.v.* (formerly British North Borneo) and Sarawak, *q.v.*

North Korea. The Democratic People's Republic of Korea, a state not recognized by the western powers, established after the partition of Korea, *q.v.*, in 1945; area 46,814 sq. m.; population (1939) 8,229,000, (1970 estimate) 13,900,000; capital Pyongyang. It was controlled by Japan from 1910 to 1945 and under Russian military occupation from August 1945 until December 1948. During this period a Communist-led provisional government was set up; from this evolved the Supreme National Assembly which adopted a Constitution modelled on that of the U.S.S.R., and on 12 September 1948 proclaimed a republic. The new state was immediately recognized by the U.S.S.R. and its satellites. It has since been in practice governed by the Politburo of the Korean Workers' Party, comprising 11 full and 4 candidate members, including the Prime Minister and Supreme Commander of the Armed Forces, Marshal Kim Il-sung. In December 1972 the National Assembly elected him as President.

Relations with South Korea, *q.v.*, deteriorated steadily in 1947 and 1948. U.S. attempts to reunify the country were thwarted by the U.S.S.R., and the matter was referred to the United Nations who, in 1947, voted for unification under one freely elected government and sent a commission to Korea to negotiate an agreement. Meanwhile an army of 200,000 was recruited in North Korea mainly from Korean repatriates who had taken refuge from the Japanese in Siberia and Manchuria and had been trained by the Chinese in guerilla warfare. In 1948, prior to the holding of South Korean elections to an assembly in which 100 vacant seats were to be reserved for representatives from the North, North Korea cut off the supply of electricity from their hydro-electric power plants, thereby causing an industrial standstill, and considerable temporary unemployment, in the South. There were innumerable incidents along the 38th parallel in 1948 and 1949 which culminated, on 25 June 1950, in the invasion of South Korea by the army of the North. The United Nations declared North Korea to be an aggressor and sent troops to the aid of the South; China recruited 200,000 volunteers who entered the fighting on the side of the North in November 1950 when the United Nations forces reached the Manchurian border. The war continued until 27 July 1953 when an armistice was signed by which the line of division between North and South Korea remained in the neighbourhood of the 38th parallel; although there has been no subsequent agreement on reunification, negotiations on the mutual reduction of forces were begun in 1972.

Although much of its generating and industrial plant was destroyed in the Korean War, North Korea has a valuable industrial potential, and this has been developed considerably since the end of the war. There are valuable deposits of coal and iron ore, and metallurgical, cotton-spinning, and hydro-electric power works were intensively developed by Japanese interests. Korea's major cement works, and the nitrogenous fertilizer works of the Chosun Chilso Company are all in the North. The U.S.S.R. is the main trading partner, but trade with Japan has increased steadily since 1969 when it represented nearly one-fifth of the total. A six-year plan aims at doubling production of coal, electricity, iron and steel by 1976.

North Viet-Nam. (Also known as the Democratic Republic of Viet-Nam.) The zone north of the 17th parallel allotted to the Viet-Minh, q.v., in July 1954 by the terms of the Geneva Agreements 1954, q.v., on the cessation of hostilities in Viet-Nam, q.v.; area 63,344 sq. m.; population (1960 census) 15,916,955, (1969 estimate) 21,340,000; seat of government Hanoi. According to the 1960 Constitution of the Democratic Republic of Viet-Nam the only source of legislative power is the National Assembly, elected every 4 years. An Assembly was elected in April 1964 but the administration is in the hands of the President of the Republic, Ton Duc Thang, who succeeded to the office in 1969 on the death of the founder President, Ho Chi Minh, *q.v.*, the Prime Minister (since 1955) Pham Van Dong, and the Deputy Premier and Commander of the Armed Forces, General Vo Nguyen Giap, who have governed through the Lien Viet (National Union Front) and the Dang Lao Dong or Workers' Party. The Geneva Agreements stipulated that North Viet-Nam was to be reunited with South Viet-Nam in July 1956, and that free elections were to be held then to determine the future government of Viet-Nam, but this part of the Agreements was not carried out. The chief products of North Viet-Nam are rice and coal. There is enough rice to feed the population in a good year. The coal mines are mostly around Hongai, east of Haiphong, and coal is exported to France and Japan. There are also rich phosphate deposits.

Northern Cameroons. *See* Cameroons, British.

Northern Frontier District (N.F.D.). The name of a former Kenyan province, of which part became the North-East Region of Kenya in 1963. The Region, with an area of 53,000 sq. m., has a population of 114,000 Somalis, who are Hamitic in origin, and 6,500 of other races. The N.F.D. was populated largely by Somalis. A commission set up by the Kenya constitutional conference (which met in London in 1962) reported that there were opposing elements in the District which disagreed strongly as to whether the area should secede and become incorporated in Somalia, which claims it; it stated that 87 per cent of the population of the N.F.D. wanted to secede and that 62 per cent were Somali or half Somali. The groups in favour of secession include the Northern Province People's Progressive Party; those opposing secession include the Northern Province United Association, which supports the Kenya African National Union (K.A.N.U.). In making its claim, Somalia relies on a provision in its own constitution, which states: 'The Somali Republic shall promote by legal and peaceful means a union of Somali territories.' Under pressure from the N.F.D. the British government amended its plan to create six Regions, thus dividing the N.F.D. between the Eastern and Coast Regions; instead the North-Eastern Region was created from the three districts of the N.F.D. where the population was predominantly Somali. These districts lay in that part of the N.F.D. which was to the east of the so-called Somali-Galla line. The three districts are: Garissa (area 23,000 sq. m., with a population of 34,000 Somalis and fewer than 3,000 of other races); Mandera (area 10,000 sq. m., with a population of 30,000 Somalis and 3,000 of other races); and Wajir (area 20,000 sq. m., with a population of 50,000 Somalis and fewer than 500 of other races). The situation is complicated by the presence in the

Isiolo District of the neighbouring Eastern Region (to the west) of 30,000 Boran; they are religiously and ethnically linked with the Somalis, and also wish to secede.

Northern Ireland. A part of the U.K., comprising the six Northern Irish counties of Antrim, Armagh, Down, Fermanagh, Londonderry, and Tyrone; area 5,462 sq. m.; population (1971) 1,525,000, of whom one-third are Roman Catholics; capital Belfast. It is often referred to as Ulster, *q.v.*, of which it forms a part. Under the Government of Ireland Act, 1920, as amended by the Irish Free State Act, 1922, Northern Ireland has a limited self-government exercised by a Parliament, comprising a Senate of 2 ex-officio and 24 elected members, and a House of Commons of 52 members elected for five years. The elected Senators are appointed by the House of Commons on a proportional representation basis. At elections held in February 1969 the results were: Unionists, the Northern Ireland Conservative Party, which opposes the unification of Ireland and wishes to remain within the British Commonwealth 36 (36 in 1965); Labour Party 2 (2); Nationalists (a Catholic party) 6 (9); Republican Labour 2 (2); Independents 3 (1). The last Prime Minister to hold office was Brian Faulkner. He had succeeded Major James Chichester-Clark in March 1971, and was suspended on 31 March 1972 when the U.K. government, by Act of Parliament, assumed direct rule over Northern Ireland for one year. William Whitelaw, *q.v.*, was then appointed Secretary of State for Northern Ireland. The situation arose out of the Unionist government's inability to control violence between the Protestant and Roman Catholic communities, despite the presence in Ulster since August 1969 of British army contingents. The legitimate grievances of Roman Catholics in certain areas (for example Londonderry), that under the electoral laws of Northern Ireland, which gave undue weight to ownership of property, they were unable to participate in local government even where they were in a majority, and the Special Powers Act by which the laws of the U.K. could be ignored to permit censorship, flogging, and imprisonment without trial, gave rise to a Civil Rights agitation in 1968. Despite the recognized need for immediate electoral reform the Unionist government failed to implement its promises and in August 1971 introduced internment of those suspected of membership of, or connivance in the activities of, the Irish Republican Army, *q.v.*, which had claimed responsibility for many of the bomb outrages and shootings occurring since 1969. A plebiscite on the border issue, held on 8 March 1973, which was boycotted by the Catholic population but in which 59 per cent of the electorate voted, resulted in a majority for Northern Ireland remaining within the U.K. (591,820), and only 6,463 in favour of unification with Eire.

Northern Rhodesia. Name by which Zambia, *q.v.*, was known from 1911, when the protectorate of Northern Rhodesia was created, until 24 October 1964 when it became a fully independent state within the British Commonwealth.

Northern Tier. The group of Near and Middle Eastern Powers, Turkey, Persia, and Pakistan, which, with the U.K., was originally associated in the Central Treaty Organization, *q.v.*

Norway. An independent state in Scandinavia; area 124,525 sq. m.; population (1970) 3,888,468; capital Oslo. It was united with Denmark from 1397 to 1814, and from 1814 until 1905 its throne was united with that of Sweden, when it broke away and chose as sovereign a Danish prince who became King Haakon VII. It is a constitutional and hereditary monarchy; legislative power is vested in the Storting (parliament), with 150 representatives elected every four years. The distribution of seats between the parties is based on a system of proportional representation. They choose one quarter of their number to form the Lagting (upper house), the other three quarters forming the Odelsting (lower chamber). Questions relating to laws are dealt with by each house separately; most other matters are discussed by both houses together. Executive power is vested in the King acting through the cabinet (Statsråd) comprising the Prime Minister and at least seven ministers.

The most powerful group in the Storting, since 1935, has been the Labour Party which at elections held on 7 and 8 September 1969 secured 74 seats (as compared with 68 seats in 1965). The Labour Party is divided from the other four main parties by its Socialist beliefs and its desire for a high degree of state direction and control over the economy. After the First World War the Labour Party had strong radical leanings, and until 1923 was a member of the Communist Third International, but later moderated its views and joined the Socialist Second International. The Party, led by Einar Gerhardsen, who was Prime Minister from 1945 to November 1951 and from January 1955 to August 1963, and since 1965 by Trygve Bratteli, brought Norway out of its traditional neutrality into full membership of the North Atlantic Treaty Organization. Other parties contesting the 1969 elections were: the Conservatives, who are reluctant to accept any extension of state controls, 29 seats (two fewer than in 1965); the Liberals, who are radical in outlook, 13 (18 in 1965); the Agrarian or Centre Party 20 (18); the Christian Popular Party 14 (13). Neither the Socialist People's Party (a left-wing breakaway from the Labour

Party which had won 2 seats in 1965) nor the Communist Party (no seats since 1957) was represented in the Storting.

Labour, which had been in power for 28 years, was defeated in August 1963 on a vote concerning the mine disaster which had occurred in the Spitzbergen Archipelago the previous November. The defeat was made possible by the Socialist People's Party which voted with the opposition. Gerhardsen resigned and the Conservative leader, John Lyng, formed a government which fell in September 1963; Gerhardsen then resumed office. He was succeeded after the 1965 elections by Per Borten, leader of the Centre Party, with Lyng as Minister of Foreign Affairs. Borten continued to lead a right-wing coalition government after the 1969 elections but resigned in March 1971 when it was revealed that he had disclosed confidential details of the negotiations concerning Norway's application to join the European Economic Community. He was succeeded by Trygve Bratteli who formed a minority Labour government and took responsibility for concluding the terms of entry to the E.E.C., against which a formidable propaganda campaign was then being waged. The terms eventually agreed were acceptable to Norwegian farming interests but did not satisfy the fishermen who had demanded permanent protection for their coastal fisheries irrespective of E.E.C. principles that all trade arrangements made by members should be subject to revision. A referendum held in September 1972 produced a majority of 53 per cent against entry, and Norway withdrew its application. Bratteli then resigned and Lars Korvaald, of the Christian Popular Party, formed a minority government of those opposed to E.E.C. membership and opened negotiations for a trade agreement.

Of the total area 73 per cent is unproductive and 23 per cent consists of forests, which are one of the chief natural sources of wealth. The principal exports are fish and its products, pulp and paper, iron ore and pyrites, and other minerals. The only coal deposits lie in the Spitsbergen Archipelago, q.v. Hydro-electric power production has doubled since 1945; the government plans to develop steel and aluminium industries and to expand the economy of north Norway. The country has the fourth largest merchant fleet in the world (more than 19 million gross registered tons in 1970). Apart from the immense number of rocky islands around its coast, Norway exercises sovereignty over the Spitsbergen Archipelago, 550 miles to the north of the northernmost part of Norway, Jan Mayen Island, 300 miles north of Iceland, Bouvet Island, an uninhabited island in the Southern Atlantic Ocean, Peter I Island in the Antarctic Ocean, and Queen Maud Land in the Antarctic Continent, q.v.

Nu, U. Burmese politician; born 25 May 1907 and educated at Rangoon University; he is a devout Buddhist and a Socialist. He was a school teacher before the Second World War and a member of the We Burmans nationalist society which demanded independence. The British government rejected his offer to help them to fight the Japanese in 1941, and imprisoned him; the Japanese released him and made him Foreign Minister of a Burmese government. After the war he was Vice-President of his party, the Anti-Fascist People's Freedom League, Speaker of the Constituent Assembly in 1947, and became Prime Minister when Burma became independent in January 1948. He was succeeded as Prime Minister by U Ba Swe in June 1956, when he decided to devote a year to reorganizing the Anti-Fascist People's Freedom League. He was Premier again from March 1957 to October 1958, resigning in favour of General Ne Win, became Premier once more in April 1960, and was again ousted by Ne Win in March 1962. Since 1969, when he formed the United National Liberation Front, he has directed a campaign of guerilla warfare against the Burmese army and government from neighbouring Thailand.

Nuclear Test Ban Treaty. *See* Test Ban Treaty.

Nuncio. From the Latin *nuntius*, herald, the title of the Papal envoy in foreign Catholic capitals. The Papal Nuncio is universally accepted as the doyen of the diplomatic corps.

Nyasaland. Name by which Malawi, *q.v.*, was known before it became a Dominion and member of the British Commonwealth on 6 July 1964.

Nyerere, Julius. Tanzanian politician; born 1922, one of 26 children of a chief, he is a Roman Catholic; educated at the University College of East Africa, Makerere, and Edinburgh University, where he studied history and economics, he was a teacher at a Catholic school near Dar-es-Salaam until 1955 when he decided to give all his time to political activity, and became the leader of the Tanganyika African National Union (T.A.N.U.) which was overwhelmingly successful at the 1958 and 1960 elections to the Legislative Council. He became Prime Minister on 1 May 1961 when full self-government was achieved, and held the office until 22 January 1962; he was elected President in November and took office on 9 December 1962. He was re-elected President in September 1965 and October 1970 for further five-year terms.

O

O.A.S. Organization of American States, *q.v.*

O.C.A.M. Organisation Commune Africaine et Malgache, *q.v.*

O.C.A.S. Organization of Central American States, *q.v.*

Occupied Arab Territories. Those areas of former Arab territory occupied by Israel since the Six Day War of June 1967. They are: Gaza and Sinai (population 372,400 and areas 140 sq. m. and 23,622 sq. m. respectively) which were taken from Egypt; Judea and Samarra (population 610,300 and area 2,270 sq. m.) known as the west bank which were taken from Jordan; and the Golan Heights, an area of 444 sq. m. overlooking Lake Tiberias which was taken from Syria. A U.N. Security Council resolution of 22 November 1967 demanded that Israel withdraw all troops to her former boundaries and that the political independence of every state in the area be guaranteed. Israel has refused to fulfil the first condition until the Arab countries accept the second and recognize the existence of Israel as a sovereign state. This would enable peace terms to be negotiated directly. The Palestine Liberation Organization, *q.v.*, which co-ordinates the activities of the Palestinian Arabs engaged in guerilla warfare against Israel, has received assistance from member states of the Arab League in its campaign to reconquer by force these lands which it has designated as the Occupied Arab Territories. Except for the old town of Jerusalem they have not been incorporated into Israel, but have been given the status of 'occupied areas' and administered separately.

Oder–Neisse Line. The boundary between Eastern Germany and Poland established after the Second World War; it is marked by the river Oder which flows into the Baltic Sea at Szczecin (formerly Stettin), and its tributary the Neisse which has its source in Czechoslovakia. The line was accepted by the U.K., the U.S.A., and the U.S.S.R. as part of the Potsdam Agreement, *q.v.*, of 1 August 1945. All German territory east of a line from the Baltic coast immediately west of Swinemünde, and thence along the Oder and the Western Neisse to the Czech frontier, was placed provisionally under the administration of Poland and withdrawn from the authority of the Allied Control Council in Berlin. This territory formed nearly a fifth of Germany's 1938 area, and contained about a quarter of its arable land and between one sixth and one seventh of its 1938 population. It included the best land for growing potatoes, sugar-beet and wheat, much of which used to feed Western Germany. Poland was awarded Stettin (as it then was) and a small area west of the town.

Although the three powers stated that the final delimitation of the western frontier should take place later, the Oder-Neisse Line was accepted as permanent by the Polish government, which expelled large numbers of Germans who later comprised nearly a quarter of the West German voters. An agreement describing the line as the permanent frontier was concluded between the German Democratic Republic and Poland on 6 July 1950; the Poles were, in addition, granted the whole of the thirty-mile long island of Usedom and some land in Mecklenburg. The German Federal Republic, the U.K., and the U.S.A. did not recognize this agreement. On 6 July 1955 the East German and Polish governments declared that the Oder-Neisse Line was the permanent frontier. The U.K. and the U.S.A. claimed that there was an understanding at Potsdam that the new frontier was conditional on the granting of free elections in Poland, and that final agreement could only be reached when a peace treaty was concluded with a government of a united Germany. After 1967 a new effort was made by the German Federal Republic to improve relations with eastern Europe, and in pursuit of this Ostpolitik, *q.v.*, a treaty was signed with Poland in November 1970. This stated that the Federal Republic accepted the Oder-Neisse Line as Poland's western frontier and affirmed the inviolability of existing borders. It did, however, avoid the word 'recognition', which would have been politically unacceptable to the West German electorate. The peace treaty, which was subject to ratification by the Federal Diet, came into force on 17 May 1972.

Odinga, Ajuma Oginga. Kenyan politician; born 1911 and educated at the Kikuyu Alliance High School and Makerere College. He founded the Luo Thrift and Trading Corporation and entered politics as a member of the Central Nyanza African District Council in 1947. He became a member of the Kenya Legislative Council in 1957 and Vice-President of the Kenya African National Union (K.A.N.U.) in 1960. He was made Minister for Home Affairs in 1963 and, in December 1964, Vice-President of the new republic of Kenya as well as Minister without Portfolio. He is a declared Communist, and owed his promotion in politics to the anti-European elements in K.A.N.U. President Kenyatta emphasized at the time that Odinga's appointment as Vice-President did not mean that he would automatically succeed to the Presidency. In April 1966 he resigned the Vice-Presidency and, with 19 members of the lower house and 9 members of the Senate, founded a new parliamentary opposition, the Kenya People's Union (K.P.U.). In the by-elections of 1966, at which those who had changed their party allegiance were constitutionally compelled to seek electoral approval, his principal support came from Luo areas, and in Kikuyu strongholds his candidates were defeated. The Luo tribe, of which he is a member, incurred the hostility of the Kikuyu, 80,000 of whom were in detention during the Mau Mau emergency, by accepting promotion to good jobs in the absence of Kikuyu competition. After the elections of 1970, from which K.P.U. candidates were banned, President Kenyatta introduced a tribal balance into his government, appointing several non-Kikuyu to ministerial office. When Odinga was released from a period of eighteen months' detention in March 1971, he re-joined K.A.N.U.

O.E.C.D. Organization for Economic Co-operation and Development, *q.v.*

O.E.E.C. Organization for European Economic Co-operation, *q.v.*

Ogaden. The name both of a tribe and of an area in eastern Ethiopia; a number of Somalis living there look to Somalia and wish to be granted the right to secede to that country. A comparable area in Kenya is the so-called Northern Frontier District, *q.v.* Somalia itself encourages the idea of a Greater Somalia and claims these areas.

Okinawa. Largest island of the Ryuku Islands, which lie 500 miles to the south-west of Japan, between the Japanese island of Kyushu and Formosa; the Peace Treaty which came into effect on 28 April 1952 gave the U.S.A. 'the right to exercise all and any powers of administration, legislation and jurisdiction', though it recognized that Japan had a residual sovereignty. The most northern group of the Islands, the Amami-Oshima group, was returned to Japan in 1953. The parts of the Islands which remained under U.S. control, comprising an area of 848 sq. m., a population of approximately 1,250,000, and the capital of the Islands, Naha in Okinawa, reverted to Japan by an agreement which came into effect on 15 May 1972. This agreement involved the retention by the U.S.A. of 88 of its 122 bases and facilities; an indemnity for all U.S. military acts during the occupation; the payment of compensation by the U.S. government to Japanese nationals whose lands were damaged prior to 1950; and the purchase by Japan of U.S. assets at a cost of $320,000,000 payable over five years. The existence of U.S. nuclear weapon bases on the Islands, which played an important part in U.S. military dispositions in the western Pacific, and which formerly provided employment for 50,000 Okinawans, had been a source of political friction in Japan for some years. The new agreement, while upholding the 1960 Treaty of Mutual Co-operation and Security between Japan and the U.S.A., prohibits the storing of nuclear weapons on the Islands without the consent of the Japanese government.

Oman. An independent state on the eastern corner of Arabia; area approximately 82,000 sq. m.; population 750,000, mostly Arab, but with a strong infusion of Negro blood. Oman is an area in the interior of the former Sultanate of Muscat and Oman, whereas Muscat (which includes the port of that name) is largely coastal. In July 1970 the Sultan, Sayyid Said bin Taimur, who had ruled since 1932 and who had been in retreat for the past four years, was overthrown in a palace *coup* by his son and heir, Qabus bin Said. A close relationship has been maintained with the U.K. for 150 years. In 1957 the former Imam of Oman, Ghalib bin Ali, who had for some time exercised a *de facto* control of the interior, led a revolt against the Sultan. Under the 1951 treaty of commerce and friendship signed by the Sultan and British representatives, British land and air forces helped to suppress the rising. Relations between the Iman and the Sultan are governed by the Treaty of Sib, *q.v.*, concluded in 1920. Since 1970 the new Sultan has attempted to settle all differences with the Imam in order to unify the country against the Dhofari rebels, a force of guerillas, supported by the Marxist Popular Front for the Liberation of Oman and the Arab Gulf, and supplied with arms by China across the South Yemen border, who have campaigned against the British presence since 1964.

Dates, fish, limes and pomegranates are exported; however, the possible existence of oil in the interior near Buraimi, *q.v.*, and the actual discovery of oil at Fahud, Natih and Yibal in 1963 by Petroleum Development (Oman) Ltd, a Shell subsidiary, and its export by pipeline to the Gulf terminal at Saeh el Maleh, have transformed the economy. In 1971 oil revenues exceeded £477,000,000. In November 1967 the Kuria Muria Islands, which lie between 20 and 40 miles off the coast, and which had been ceded to the British by the Sultan in 1854 so that a cable station could be built there, and subsequently ruled by the High Commissioner in Aden, were transferred to Muscat and Oman by the U.K. government after consultation with the inhabitants. In August 1971, together with Bahrain, *q.v.*, and Qatar, *q.v.*, Muscat and Oman, having adopted the new name of Oman, applied for membership of the United Nations and of the Arab League, *q.v.*

Ombudsman. An official who investigates complaints by private individuals against public bodies and officials, and who studies the ways in which officials apply the law to the public. There are ombudsmen in Denmark, Finland, New Zealand, Norway, Sweden, the U.K., since 1 April 1967, where he has the title of Parliamentary Commissioner for the Administration, *q.v.*, and France since 1 January 1973, where he is entitled Médiateur. A report published in 1961 by

'Justice', the British section of the International Commission of Jurists, said of the Swedish Ombudsman (the Justitieombudsman or the J.O.): 'In practice, the real sanction is the publicity which is given to the ombudsman's criticisms of the administration in his annual reports to Parliament but more especially in the daily press.'

One Glass of Water Doctrine. A belief, held by Communist revolutionaries during the early stages of the Russian and Chinese revolutions, that a good Communist should regard sexual desire as being no more important than a glass of water. This doctrine was revoked by Lenin when the revolution achieved success in Russia, but it is still the rule in China where it is known as Pei-shui-chu-i. Communist revolutionaries in the west are not believed to adhere to this doctrine.

O.P.E.C. Organization of Petroleum Exporting Countries, *q.v.*

Open Door Policy. The policy of trading with all nations or individuals on equal terms, and not giving monopolies or preferences to any individual country.

Organisation Commune Africaine et Malgache (O.C.A.M.). The successor to the African and Malagasy Union (Union Africaine et Malgache, or U.A.M.), it is an association of Cameroun, the Central African Republic, Chad, Dahomey, Gabon, Ivory Coast, the Malagasy Republic, Niger, Rwanda, Senegal, Togo, Upper Volta and Zaïre. Congo (Brazzaville), also an original member, withdrew in September 1972. The Organization exists to accelerate the political, social, economic, technical, and cultural development of member states within the framework of the Organization of African Unity (O.A.U.), *q.v.* The thirteen member states have set up a Development Bank, and have undertaken joint negotiations on economic matters with France and with the European Economic Community. A sugar agreement, which benefits in particular the sugar-producing states of Zaïre and Malagasy, came into force in 1966; similar agreements have been proposed for cotton and groundnuts. The members, except for Zaïre which joined the O.C.A.M. after its foundation, were at one stage known as the Brazzaville Group; the charter of the U.A.M. was signed at Tananarive, in the Malagasy Republic, on 12 September 1961. When the O.A.U. was established in May 1963, the U.A.M. ceased to be active, but in February 1965 it was revived as the O.C.A.M. It should not be confused with the Council for African and Malagasy Affairs, *q.v. See also* Entente, Council of the.

Organization for Economic Co-operation and Development (O.E.C.D.). Was established on 30 September 1961 by 20 nations (Austria, Belgium, Canada, Denmark, France, the German Federal Republic,

Greece, Iceland, Ireland, Italy, Luxemburg, the Netherlands, Norway, Portugal, Spain, Sweden, Switzerland, Turkey, the U.K., and the U.S.A.) to succeed the Organization for European Economic Co-operation, *q.v.* Its members are the 18 members of O.E.E.C.; Canada and U.S.A., which were associate members of O.E.E.C.; Japan, which joined in 1963, Finland which joined in 1968, and Australia. Its tasks are: (1) to encourage and coordinate the economic policies of member countries; (2) to contribute to the expansion of countries in a state of development, whether members or not; and (3) to facilitate the development of world trade and settle trade problems.

Organization for European Economic Co-operation (O.E.E.C.). Was set up in 1948 by 16 nations (Austria, Belgium, Denmark, France, Greece, Iceland, Ireland, Italy, Luxemburg, the Netherlands, Norway, Portugal, Sweden, Switzerland, Turkey, and the U.K.) in response to the Marshall Plan, *q.v.*, to coordinate the economies of countries receiving aid under the European Recovery Programme, *q.v.* The German Federal Republic and Spain joined O.E.E.C. as full members in 1955 and 1959 respectively; Yugoslavia was allowed to participate to a limited extent; Canada and the U.S.A. were associate members. O.E.E.C. was replaced on 30 September 1961 by the Organization for Economic Co-operation and Development, *q.v.*

Organization for Trade Co-operation. An international agency, which the parties to the General Agreement on Tariffs and Trade, *q.v.*, agreed in 1955 should be set up to administer the General Agreement. It was hoped that the International Trade Organization, *q.v.*, contemplated by the Havana Charter, *q.v.*, would do this work, but the I.T.O. was never set up because the U.S.A. failed to ratify the Charter.

Organization of African Unity. Established at Addis Ababa, Ethiopia, in May 1963, it aims, according to Article II (1) (a), 'to promote the unity and solidarity of the African and Malagasy States', and according to Article II (1) (d) 'to eradicate all forms of colonialism from Africa'. Its charter, which was signed in that month, was originally drafted for the Organization of Inter-African and Malagasy States, sometimes known as the Monrovia Powers, *q.v.* The signatories were: the 19 original Monrovia Powers who met in May 1961 (except Togo but with the addition of Zaïre); the 6 Casablanca Powers, *q.v.* (except Morocco, which did not then recognize or wish to negotiate with Mauritania); and Burundi, Libya, Rwanda, Sudan, Tanzania and Uganda. The following countries have since joined: Zambia, Mauritius, Malawi, Lesotho, Gambia, Equatorial Guinea, Swaziland, Kenya, as well as Togo and Morocco. The Organization has established a Co-ordinating Committee for Liberation Movements in Africa, with headquarters at Dar es Salaam, to provide financial and military aid in accordance with Article II (1) (d).

Organization of American States (O.A.S.). A regional agency set up by the Ninth International Conference of American States at Bogota, Columbia, in April and May 1948, to coordinate the work of all the various inter-American organizations. It is a successor to the International Bureau of the American Republics which was established by the First International Conference of American States in 1890. The 23 members (each with one vote) are: Argentina, Barbados, Bolivia, Brazil, Chile, Columbia, Costa Rica, the Dominican Republic, Ecuador, Guatemala, Haiti, Honduras, Jamaica, Mexico, Nicaragua, Panama, Paraguay, Peru, Salvador, Trinidad and Tobago, Uruguay, the U.S.A., and Venezuela. Canada is a permanent observer. Trinidad and Tobago, admitted 1967, became the first new member to join since the foundation of the organization, and the first Commonwealth member. Barbados joined in 1968, and Jamaica in 1969. Cuba was also a member until her expulsion on 31 January 1962, by 14 votes to 1 (Cuba), with 6 abstentions (Argentina, Bolivia, Brazil, Chile, Ecuador, and Mexico). Bolivia left the O.A.S. temporarily in 1962 and 1963, and withheld representation from the 1967 Conference, in protest at the failure of the O.A.S. to settle a dispute with Chile over the distribution of water supplies from the Lauca River and to consider the question of Bolivia's access to the sea.

The O.A.S. is a regional organization within the framework of the United Nations of the type permitted by the United Nations Charter and is a stronger version of the Pan American Union, *q.v.* The most important provisions of the Charter of the O.A.S. deal with the peaceful settlement of disputes between members and lay down the procedure for mediation, arbitration, and the reference of legal questions to the International Court of Justice. Such matters as the recognition of *de facto* governments and of territories acquired by force, the propagation of doctrines leading to aggression, and the civil rights of women, are also covered in the Charter.

The organs of the O.A.S. are: (1) the Inter-American Conference, meeting every five years, at which government representatives decide policy; (2) the Consultative Meeting of Ministers of Foreign Affairs, which considers urgent problems and takes decisions in matters covered by the Rio Treaty, *q.v.*, being helped by an Advisory Defence Committee; (3) the O.A.S. Council, comprising representatives of all members, to supervise the progress of O.A.S.; (4) the Pan American

Union, the central and permanent organ of the O.A.S.; (5) the Specialized Conferences, meeting to deal with special technical matters or to develop specific aspects of inter-American cooperation; (6) the Specialized Organizations, inter-governmental organizations established by multilateral agreements to discharge particular functions in their differing fields of action.

Organization of Arab Petroleum Exporting Countries. Founded in 1968 by Libya, Saudi Arabia and Kuwait to safeguard the specific interests of Arab producers of petroleum. Abu Dhabi, Algeria, Bahrain, Dubai and Qatar joined in 1970 and Egypt and Syria in December 1971. Iraq was refused admission when it made application to join in December 1970, but, with Syria, was given financial assistance to compensate for loss of oil revenues resulting from its nationalization in 1972 of the assets of Iraq Petroleum Company.

Organization of Central American States (O.C.A.S.). Set up in October 1951 by Costa Rica, Salvador, Guatemala, Honduras, and Nicaragua. Panama refused to join. Its aims are to promote economic, cultural, and social cooperation between its members. It encountered difficulties when Salvador proposed an anti-Communist resolution; this was opposed by Guatemala, which left the Organization from April 1953 until after the overthrow of the Arbenz regime. The first formal conference of the O.C.A.S. was held at Antigua, Guatemala, in August 1955. The conference passed a number of resolutions to promote economic, cultural, and social cooperation, agreed to set up a committee of jurists to study the codification of Central American legislation, and elected a Secretary-General. At San Salvador in November 1962 the members re-established the Organization and extended its activities to include political, educational, and defence matters. The new Charter became effective in 1965.

Organization of Inter-African and Malagasy States. Established by the Monrovia Powers, *q.v.*, it was expanded and became in 1963 the Organization of African Unity, *q.v.*

Organization of Petroleum Exporting Countries (O.P.E.C.). Constituted in January 1961 in Caracas by Iraq, Kuwait, Persia, Qatar, Saudi Arabia and Venezuela, and later joined by Indonesia, Libya, Abu Dhabi and Nigeria. The founder members resolved: (1) to demand that the oil companies should 'maintain their prices steady and free from all unnecessary fluctuations which affect the economic development of both producing and consuming countries'; (2) to ensure the stabilization of prices by regulating production; (3) to refuse preferential treatment in the form of increased exports or higher prices, from the oil companies should any one member suffer as a result of applying any unanimous decision of the Organization. O.P.E.C. members are responsible for approximately 45 per cent of the total world output of oil and 85 per cent of world exports outside the Soviet bloc.

During the 1960s O.P.E.C. negotiations with oil companies were largely concentrated on restricting excess capacity, but the situation changed radically in 1970 as a result of: (1) a sharp rise in demand; (2) the continued closure of the Suez Canal, *q.v.*, and the increased need for more and larger tankers for the Cape route which could not be met immediately; (3) the closure from May 1970 until January 1971 of the oil pipeline from Saudi Arabia to the Mediterranean; and (4) the consequent importance of Libyan supplies which enabled Libya to demand higher crude oil prices in September 1970, and in turn strengthened the position of the Gulf countries in their relations with the companies. At the O.P.E.C. Conference in Caracas in December 1970 it was decided to enforce a minimum tax level of 55 per cent on the net income of companies operating in member countries. On 14 February 1971 an agreement was concluded between 22 international oil companies and the six producing member countries of the Persian Gulf to this effect. This agreement, which established security of supply for five years and the termination of the 'leapfrogging' of prices which had occurred during 1970, would yield the Gulf states an estimated additional revenue of £500 million in 1971, rising to £1,200,000 in 1975. In October 1972 further agreement was reached on the participation of producing countries so that they would achieve majority shareholdings in concessions held by foreign oil companies.

Ostpolitik. The eastern policy developed in the German Federal Republic by Kurt Kiesinger, *q.v.*, in contrast to the Hallstein Doctrine, *q.v.*, which had prevailed while Konrad Adenauer was Chancellor. It was designed to normalize relations with Communist countries, other than the U.S.S.R., which had recognized the German Democratic Republic, *q.v.* Its pursuit by Kiesinger and then by Willy Brandt, *q.v.*, first as Foreign Minister in Kiesinger's government and then as Federal Chancellor, led to the conclusion of peace treaties with the U.S.S.R. and Poland in 1972, and the acceptance by the Federal Republic of the Oder-Neisse Line, *q.v.*, as the western frontier of Poland. It also resulted in a new agreement covering traffic, visits, posts and telecommunications between East and West Berlin, *q.v.*

O.T.C. Organization for Trade Co-operation, *q.v.*

Outer Mongolia. *See* Mongolian People's Republic.

Outer Seven. A term often used to describe the members of the European Free Trade Association, *q.v.*

Over-Full Employment. Defined by Lord Beveridge (1879–1963) in his *Full Employment in a Free Society* as a state of affairs in which, in the U.K., there was an unemployment rate of less than 3 per cent. A rate of 3 per cent would constitute Full Employment, *q.v.*

P

Pacific Security Pact. The tripartite security treaty concluded between Australia, New Zealand, and the U.S.A. on 1 September 1951 and more commonly known as A.N.Z.U.S., *q.v.*

P.A.F.M.E.C.S.A. Pan-African Freedom Movement for East, Central, and Southern Africa, *q.v.*

Pakhtunistan. Land of the Pakhtuns or Pathans; a name used by the Afghan government to describe a mountainous area in the Peshawar Division of Pakistan near the Afghan frontier; population approximately 2,500,000. In 1947 it was incorporated, with the consent of the inhabitants, most of whom are Moslem, into the Dominion of Pakistan, and administered by Pakistan political agents. In March 1955 Pakistan proposed to merge the states and tribal areas of West Pakistan into a single administrative unit, giving each region representation in the Provincial Assembly in proportion to its population. The Afghan Prime Minister denounced the move as an 'aggressive act', and insisted on the formation of the separate independent state of Pakhtunistan. Incidents occurred in Kabul, the Afghan capital, which resulted in the evacuation of Pakistan residents, the Afghan consulate in Peshawar was attacked and a state of emergency was declared in Afghanistan. The dispute really concerns the exact delimitation of the Afghan-Pakistani frontier. Pakistan is ready to fight to maintain the Durand Line, the boundary agreed by Afghanistan (reluctantly, as far as the Afghan ruler, Abdur Rahman, was concerned) and British India in 1892. The U.S.S.R. and India have declared their support for the Afghan claim.

Pakistan. An independent Asian republic comprising the following former territories of British India: Baluchistan, West Punjab, Sind, North-West Frontier, and thirteen princely states including Bahawalpur and Khaipur, all of which have a majority of Moslem inhabitants; area 310,403 sq. m.; population (1971 estimate) 55,774,000; capital Islamabad. Until November 1971 it also included East Bengal and the Sylhet district of Assam which, on 26 March 1971, had already declared the independent republic of Bangladesh, *q.v.* The need for a separate association of Moslem states within India became apparent to Moslem leaders when the Hindu-dominated Congress Party, *q.v.*, decided that in the struggle for Indian independence there was no room for minority religious organizations. In the 1935 Provincial elections, candidates of the Moslem League, *q.v.*, won a substantial minority of seats in the United Provinces Assembly; Congress Party refused to admit them into a coalition unless they dissolved their party organization. Moslem nationalists, led by Khaliquzzaman and Jinnah, left Congress Party, united under the slogan 'Islam is in danger', and, in response to the Viceroy's offer of Dominion status in 1940, rallied Moslem support for the idea of 'Pakistan'. They made it clear to the British government that there could be no peaceful withdrawal from India without partition.

In 1947 the right of self-determination was given to every Indian state and principality. As the Moslem population was concentrated in the north-west and in the extreme east, Pakistan comprised two areas separated by a thousand miles of Indian territory. When the U.K. relinquished its authority the boundaries between East and West Punjab had not been defined, administrative services were in a process of transfer, and the Pakistan government of East Bengal had its headquarters in a girls' school in Dacca. In the fighting which accompanied the trek of Moslems to Pakistan, and of Hindus to India, the Punjab was ravaged and more than half a million people killed. Only the personal intervention of Gandhi prevented a similar massacre in Bengal. The assets of British India were divided in the proportion of 17½ per cent to Pakistan and 82½ per cent to India. Disputes over the decisions by the states of Junagadh and Manavadar to accede to Pakistan (which were forestalled by Indian occupation), and by Kashmir, *q.v.*, to join India, although most of its people are Moslem, intensified hostility between India and Pakistan. The mutual defence assistance agreement with the U.S.A., signed on 19 May 1954, ostensibly to protect the Afghan frontier against Russian penetration, increased Indian hostility and further divided the militant western region from East Pakistan which resented the preoccupation of West Pakistan with Middle East affairs.

The country's first Constitution, which declared Pakistan an Islamic republic, was adopted on 23 March 1956; simultaneously the Assembly decided that Pakistan should remain within the British Commonwealth. From 1947 Pakistan had been administered by a parliamentary form of government operating through political parties, but this system ceased in 1958 when the Constitution was abrogated by President Iskander Mirza and martial law imposed by General (subsequently Field-Marshal) Mohammed Ayub Khan, *q.v.*, who succeeded to the Presidency on 28 October 1958. He was re-elected in January 1965 for a further five-year term, receiving approximately 64 per cent of the votes of 80,000 electors, or 'Basic Democrats', as against 35 per cent for Fatimah Jinnah (sister of Mohammed Ali Jinnah), the other presidential candidate. In November 1968 Air Marshal Asghar Khan, who had been highly critical of the repressive political regime of Ayub Khan, emerged from retirement to become the new focus of opposition. In the spring of 1969 Ayub Khan was forced to resign and he was succeeded on 24 March as President by General Yahya Khan, Commander of the Army. In December 1970 elections were held for a National Assembly which was to draw up a new Constitution. These were the first to be held on the basis of universal suffrage and the first in which women were allowed to vote. They resulted in an overwhelming victory for the Awami League, led by Sheikh Mujibur Rahman, *q.v.*, which supported the Bengali separatist movement, in East Pakistan, and a large majority for the Pakistan People's Party, led by the former Foreign Minister, Zulfiqar Ali Bhutto, *q.v.*, in the West. The Awami League secured 75 per cent of the votes and all but 2 of the 153 contested seats in East Bengal, and with 11 additional seats exercised an absolute majority in the new Assembly. The opening of the National Assembly was postponed indefinitely to allow the political leaders to frame a Constitution acceptable to both major parties. This proved impossible since the Awami League wanted autonomy for East Pakistan, with a separate external trade account and the right to levy its own taxes, whereas the Pakistan People's Party was committed to a unified Pakistan.

The civil war which followed the proclamation of the independent republic of Bangladesh and the arrest of Sheikh Mujib resulted in the occupation of East Bengal by the Pakistan Army, the flight of more than nine million refugees into India, and the subsequent invasion of Pakistan by India on 4 December 1971. The war was brought to an end by the unconditional surrender of the Pakistan Army in East Bengal on 16 December and the announcement of a cease-fire in West Pakistan the following day. Yahya Khan resigned on 20 December and was succeeded by Zulfiqar Ali Bhutto, who became the first civilian President of Pakistan. Although his attempt to keep Pakistan united by offering the Presidency to Sheikh Mujib was rejected, he refused to recognize the secession of East Bengal, and on the day that Bangladesh made application to join the British Commonwealth, 30 January 1972, Pakistan withdrew. By an agreement concluded with India at Simla in July 1972 Indian troops were withdrawn from over 5,000 sq. m. of Pakistan territory, but no decision was reached on the fate of 91,000 Pakistan prisoners of war and President Bhutto had to concede that the continuing dispute over Kashmir should be settled bilaterally and not by the U.N.

President Bhutto, who had appointed himself Prime Minister, introduced social reforms which included the abolition of the death penalty and of flogging, and an amnesty for political prisoners. To stop the flight of capital from Pakistan he confiscated the passports of the wealthy and abolished the privy purses and privileges of former rulers of some 70 princely states. He pursued a socialist policy of exercising government control over ten groups of basic industries, but reassured investors by leaving financial control in private hands. Pakistan faces huge budget deficits through over-extending the economy to achieve military parity with India, especially since the brief war over Kashmir in 1965. Economic stability cannot be achieved until more factories are built and agricultural production is improved. This is dependent on the success of irrigation schemes in the Punjab, but the Indus Waters Treaty, *q.v.*, with India in 1960, and the opening of the Mangla Dam, *q.v.*, have made these possible. The country has one of the longest irrigation systems in the world covering some 23 million acres. Economic, technical and agricultural assistance has been given by the U.S.A. Pakistan is a member of the Central Treaty Organization, *q.v.*, but left the South-East Asia Collective Defence Treaty, *q.v.*, in 1972. It has developed close relations with China whom it regarded, until the recent war, as its only dependable ally against India.

Palestine. An area of 10,429 sq. m. on the eastern Mediterranean Sea which was part of the Ottoman Empire until the end of the First World War. The state of Israel, *q.v.*, occupies most of Palestine. After 1918 Palestine was placed under British administration by a League of Nations Mandate which incorporated the Balfour Declaration, *q.v.*; the terms of the Mandate imposed on the U.K. the obligation to 'place the country under such political, administrative and economic conditions as will secure the establishment of the Jewish national home, while at the same time safeguarding the civil and religious rights of all the inhabitants of Palestine'. In accordance with this requirement Jews were admitted into Palestine, the population of which had in 1919 been almost entirely Arab, but only on limited annual quotas. Arab revolts in 1921 and 1929 were quelled by the British, but the Hope Simpson and the Passfield reports of 1930 recommended the suspension of Jewish immigration and a Legislative Council with an Arab majority. The plan was abandoned in the face of Zionist opposition. The persecution of Jews in Germany caused an increase in the flow of immigrants, both legal and illegal. In 1939 the British government declared that it was not a part of its policy that Palestine should become a Jewish state; it rejected the Arab claim for an Arab state, and said that the objective was an independent Palestinian state, 'the two peoples sharing authority in govern-

ment in such a way that the essential interests of each were secured'.
A Palestinian state was to be set up in ten years.

After the Second World War there was strong opposition among Palestinian Jews to continued British occupation. There was fierce fighting and the problem was referred by the U.K. to the United Nations in February 1947. The United Nations Special Committee on Palestine recommended partition; this recommendation was accepted by the United Nations General Assembly. On 14 May 1948 the British High Commissioner left Palestine and the state of Israel was proclaimed. Arab forces from Egypt, Iraq, Jordan, Lebanon, and Syria then attacked Israel, but hostilities ceased in January 1949. Although partition had been recommended, Israel occupied various areas allotted to the Arab state, increasing its share by 40 per cent; Jordan acquired parts of Palestine west of the river Jordan, and Egypt occupied the Gaza Strip, q.v., which had been allotted to the proposed Arab state. After the Arab-Israeli war of June 1967 Israel occupied the whole of Palestine, making withdrawal from the 'occupied areas' conditional on Arab recognition of its existence as a state. The Palestine Liberation Organization, q.v., then embarked on a campaign to establish an undivided Palestine by propaganda or by force; it does not accept that the Jews have any claim to any part of Palestine territory.

Palestine Liberation Organization. A body which claims to represent the 1,500,000 Arabs who are refugees from Palestine. It is financed by taxes levied on Palestinians in Arab countries, and its executive committee is elected by the 150 members of the Palestine National Council, meeting in Cairo, which includes representatives of the main Palestinian organizations, military and civil. The Chairman is Yassir Arafat, leader of Fatah, q.v., the largest guerilla movement. The executive committee comprises 3 more Fatah members, 2 from the Syrian-sponsored guerilla group el-Saiqa, one each from the Popular Front for the Liberation of Palestine, q.v., and the Popular Democratic Front and five others. It has denounced the plan proposed by King Hussein of Jordan, q.v., to create a federal Palestine state.

Pan-African Freedom Movement for East, Central and Southern Africa (P.A.F.M.E.C.S.A.). An association of governments, i.e. of Burundi, Zaïre, Ethiopia, Kenya, Malawi, Rwanda, Somalia, Tanzania, Uganda, Zambia, and African nationalist movements, i.e. of Angola, Mozambique, South Africa, Rhodesia, and South-West Africa. It aims to establish an economic association of independent African states in this area. It was founded in September 1958.

Pan-Africanist Congress. An African nationalist organization in South

Africa. Its founders had previously belonged to the African National Congress, *q.v.* but felt that more positive action was required; they broke away from the A.N.C. in 1958, founding the Pan-Africanist Congress in April 1959. Its immediate aim is the establishment of democracy in South Africa. Its activities have included campaigns to obtain equal treatment in shops for Africans and to disrupt the pass system by asking Africans to leave their passes at home and to surrender themselves to the police. Its national president, Robert Mangaliso Sobukwe, was imprisoned after the Sharpeville riots.

Pan American Union. An organization which arose out of the meeting on 14 April 1890, in Washington, D.C., of the First International Conference of American States. The Conference established the International Bureau of the American Republics, which later became the Pan American union and held annual conferences. The aim was to foster political and economic collaboration between the American states and a feeling of solidarity between North and South America. The work of the Union was often made difficult by the reticent attitude of the South American states, which feared the economic and political hegemony of the U.S.A. In spite of this, institutions were created to promote cultural and economic cooperation, and about 40 agreements relating to inter-American trade, traffic, migration, and other questions were concluded. At a conference at Panama on 3 October 1939, the 21 American republics established a 'neutrality zone' of 300 miles, and in some places of 600 miles, around the whole American continent except Canada. They did not prohibit absolutely all warlike acts in the zone, but provided for mutual consultation as to practical steps if hostilities should occur within it. The U.K. protested, claiming that the prohibition was incompatible with international law and that it created a sanctuary for German vessels.

After the Second World War the need for even greater Pan American integration became apparent, and in 1948 there was created the Organization of American States, *q.v.*, of which the Pan American Union is the central and permanent organ and general secretariat.

The Union has four administrative departments which deal with: (1) economic and social affairs; (2) international law; (3) cultural affairs; (4) administrative services. It also acts as adviser to the Council of the Organization of American States, and its organs, in the preparations for inter-American and Specialized Conferences; as a depository of instruments of ratification of inter-American agreements; and as a clearing-house for information on all the member countries.

Pan-Germanism. The belief that all German-speaking peoples should be brought together in one empire. Pan-Germanists have advocated particularly the absorption into Germany of the German-speaking provinces of Austria. Adolf Hitler, who was born in Austria, was brought up in an atmosphere of Austrian Pan-Germanism and realized some of its aims by his annexation in 1938 of Austria and the Sudeten territories of Czechoslovakia. In the west, strict Pan-Germanists would approve of the incorporation in Germany of Alsace-Lorraine, Luxemburg, and the German-speaking part of Switzerland, but claims of this sort have not been pressed since 1945. As for the territories to the east of Germany, many Germans still demand the return of the lands awarded to Poland under the Potsdam Agreement, *q.v.*, of 1945, and question the present frontier between the German Democratic Republic and Poland, which runs along the Oder-Neisse Line, *q.v.* Poland tried to forestall such demands by mass expulsions of Germans from these lands in 1945 and 1946.

Panama. An independent Central American state on the isthmus between the Caribbean Sea and the Pacific Ocean; area 28,576 sq. m.; population (1970) 1,428,082, not including the Panama Canal Zone, *q.v.*; capital Panama. It was formerly one of the nine departments of the Republic of Colombia but with U.S. encouragement a successful revolt was organized and it became independent on 3 November 1903. Fifteen days later Panama agreed that the U.S.A. should construct and maintain an inter-ocean canal and should hold in perpetuity the use, occupation and control of a Canal Zone (two strips five miles wide on each side of the Canal), in which it would exercise exclusive sovereign authority. The Canal was opened to traffic on 15 August 1914. In return the U.S.A. paid $10 million and an annual sum of $250,000 to begin in 1912.

The treaty was revised in 1936 (the annual payment being increased to $430,000), 1942, 1947 and 1955 when the annuity was increased to $1,930,000 and the Canal Company turned over to the republic of Panama railroad yards and other property valued at $25 million. The 1955 revision, which was negotiated for Panama by President José Antonio Remón, brought considerable benefits; it removed many discriminations against Panamanians employed in the Zone; it required Canal employees to make their purchases from local merchants instead of from tax-free commissaires in the Zone; it gave Panama the right to tax the incomes of some 17,000 workers who were not U.S. citizens, but were mainly descendants of British West Indians employed in the construction of the Canal, and who lived outside the Zone. President Remón was assassinated in January 1955

His Vice-President succeeded him but was later jailed for plotting the assassination. The Second Vice-President then completed the presidential term which expired in 1956, when Ernesto de la Guardia was elected President. From October 1960 to October 1964 the President was Roberto Chiari, leader of a coalition of four of the eight opposition parties (known as the National Union of Opposition), who had been President for a brief period in 1949. He was succeeded by Marco Aurelio Robles, who was determined to secure revision of the 1903 Panama Canal Zone agreement.

During 1964 disturbances in the Zone led to the severance of diplomatic relations with the U.S.A. and the intervention of the Organization of American States, *q.v.*, to which Panama belonged, which set up a peace committee. In September 1965 a new treaty was concluded between the U.S.A. and Panama, replacing that of 1903, which effectively recognized the sovereignty of the republic through the existing Canal Zone and in any future canal area; U.S. base rights were secured by a separate defence agreement. In March 1968 President Robles, whose four-year term of office was due to expire, was impeached by the National Assembly and dismissed from office on charges of violating the constitution by intervening on behalf of David Samudio, the Minister of Finance and the government candidate in the forthcoming presidential election. The first Vice-President Max Delvalle, was appointed in his place, but the National Guard refused to accept the impeachment and the Supreme Court, four out of whose nine judges were related to Robles, rejected its validity. The election was held according to the 1946 Constitution by which a President and two Vice-Presidents, who may not serve successive terms, are elected every four years by direct popular vote, with a single chamber legislature, the National Assembly, consisting of 53 elected members. Until the election results were officially made public on 30 May 1968 the republic was embarrassed by two Presidents. Dr Arnulfo Arias, the Panameñista candidate, who had twice previously been elected President and each time deposed within a year, was declared the new President; four months later he was again deposed by General Omar Torrijos, Commander of the National Guard, who established a two-man military junta with a civilian cabinet and appointed José Maria Pinilla to the Presidency. Following an unsuccessful attempt by the Chief of Staff of the National Guard to oust General Torrijos in December 1969, Pinilla and his Vice-President, Bolivar Urrutia, were removed, and Demetrios Lakas, an engineer and a former Director of Social Security, was appointed Chairman of a new provisional Government Council.

The land is extremely fertile, but only thirty per cent has been developed and very little is cultivated. About sixty per cent of the country's food is imported and there is a high level of unemployment. Bananas, which are grown by an associate of the United Fruit Company and shipped to the U.S.A., are the most important of the exports which also include fresh shrimps, cacao, coffee, refined petroleum and mahogany. One quarter of the total revenue is derived from the Canal Zone in lease fees and labour services; in addition there are shipping registration fees from the largely foreign-owned merchant fleet of six million gross tons.

Panama Canal Zone. An area of 647 sq. m. in the republic of Panama, *q.v.*, which comprises the Panama Canal, its water area within the three-mile limit at both the Atlantic and Pacific ends, and a strip of land on either side of the Canal. In 1971 the total civil and military population, of whom eighty per cent were U.S. citizens, was 50,000. It is governed by the Canal Zone Government and operated by the Panama Canal Company which were both set up on 1 July 1951. The Secretary of the U.S. Army holds all the shares of the Company. Income is derived almost entirely from tolls levied on vessels using the Canal, which amounted to $100,566,536 in 1971; expenses are barely covered, however, and the tolls have not been raised since 1914. The increasing size and number of ships using the Canal has made imperative the construction of a new canal (not necessarily in Panama). Agreement in principle was reached with the U.S. in March 1965 to build a new sea-level canal; it could be dug through Colombia (the Atrato-Truando route), along the Costa Rica-Nicaragua border (the Salinas Bay route) or through Panama itself (the San Blas route or the Sasardi-Morti route).

Pandit, Vijaya Lakshmi. Indian politician; born 18 August 1900 into a prosperous Brahman family and educated privately. Already a socialist, in 1928 she became a supporter of the non-violent non-cooperation movement led by Gandhi which opposed British rule in India. She was imprisoned in 1932, although she was a mother with three young daughters, for participating in the public observance of India Independence Day. She became a member of the Allahabad Municipal Board and later Chairman of the local Education Committee in 1935. She was the Minister of Local Self-Government and Public Health in the United Provinces Government, 1937–9, and as a member of the Congress Party was elected to the Legislative Assembly. In 1940 she was sentenced to four months' imprisonment for anti-war activities, and was detained under the Defence Regulations from August 1942 to June 1943. In 1946 she again became Minister of

Local Self-Government and Public Health; she led the Indian delegation to the United Nations in 1946-8; was Ambassador to the U.S.S.R. in 1947-9, to the U.S.A. in 1949-51, and President of the United Nations Assembly in the 1953-4 session. From 1954 to 1961 she was High Commissioner for India in London and Indian Ambassador to Ireland. She was Governor of Maharashtra from November 1962 but resigned this post to secure election, in December 1964, to the Indian parliament as the representative of Phulpur (in northern India, near Allahabad), which her brother, the late Jawaharlal Nehru, *q.v.*, also represented. She resigned from parliament on 8 July 1968 having voiced adverse criticism of the Congress leadership.

Papua-New Guinea. A territory in the South Pacific lying to the north of, and administered by, Australia. It consists of New Guinea Territory and Papua, both on the island of New Guinea, *q.v.*, New Britain and New Ireland (the Bismarck Archipelago), and Bougainville which was formerly part of the British Solomon Islands but was ceded by the British to German New Guinea in 1899 in return for trading concessions in Samoa and West Africa. New Guinea Territory, which comprises the north-east portion of New Guinea, Bougainville and the Bismarck Archipelago, was a German colony when Australia occupied it in 1914; it was entrusted by the League of Nations to Australia on 9 May 1921 to be administered as a mandated territory, and became a Trusteeship territory after the Second World War; area 92,160 sq. m.; population (1971) 1,772,740; administrative headquarters Port Moresby in Papua, but previously at Rabaul in New Britain. Papua, in the south of the island of New Guinea, was occupied by the Queensland government in 1883 and the Australian government assumed responsibility in 1906; area (including the Trobriand and other islands) 90,540 sq. m.; population (1971) 640,094; capital Port Moresby. Papua and New Guinea share an Administrator who acts through an Executive Council, in which elected members are in a majority and from which Ministers are appointed. There is a House of Assembly with 100 elected members; at elections held in February and March 1972 the Pangu Party, which demands immediate internal self-government, won 21 seats and the support of 13 other representatives, the United Political Society 40 seats, and the Popular People's Party 8 seats. Despite a U.N. recommendation in December 1968 that self-government should be introduced none of the three major parties wants independence of Australia. However, the Labour government of Australia has declared that delay will promote separatism, and the only hope of unifying the country is to grant self-government at once. The island of Bougainville, which has rich copper deposits, and the Tolai people of the Gazelle peninsula of New Britain, have already demanded separate autonomy and have asked for a referendum on the issue. The territory is not economically viable; Australia provides half the necessary revenue. The sole common language is pidgin English, and the House of Assembly recommended that, upon independence, the country should be renamed Niu Gini.

Paraguay. An independent South American state without access to the sea, situated between Argentina, Bolivia and Brazil; area 157,042 sq. m.; population (1970 estimate) 2,395,614, most of whom are Guarani Indians; languages Guarani and Spanish; capital Asuncíon. Paraguay was ruled by Spain from the sixteenth century until 1811, when independence was declared. During the nineteenth century a series of devastating wars were fought against Argentina, which tried to block the river route to the Atlantic, and against Brazil and Uruguay, who formed a triple alliance against Paraguay in 1864, closing the frontiers for many years. From 1870 there was continuous dispute with Bolivia over the area known as the Chaco, lying between the rivers Paraguay and Pilcomaya, which led to war in 1932; the boundary was decided by arbitration in 1938.

Agriculture is still primitive although the soil is productive and the climate suitable for many sub-tropical products, but less than 5 per cent of the cultivable land is farmed. Maize and manioc (an edible root, the source of tapioca) form the staple diet; wheat for the towns and live cattle are imported from Argentina, and there are exports of cotton, timber, coffee, meat products and quebracho extracts used in tanning. There is a constant drain of professional men and skilled workers to surrounding countries which offer higher wages and greater opportunities. As a member of the Latin American Free Trade Association, *q.v.*, Paraguay receives the concessions granted to the least developed of the member countries.

U.S. investment, in the form of technical assistance, road-building, development of agriculture, cattle-raising and forestry, improved health services and a better airport at Asuncíon, was attracted to Paraguay during the Second World War by the strategic need for a base on the borders of Argentina. The American presence encouraged the dictator, General Higinio Morinigo, as a concession to democracy, to declare an amnesty which allowed political exiles to return from abroad. On their return in 1948 civil war broke out, Morinigo was overthrown, and there followed years of disorder culminating in the seizure of power in 1954 by the commander-in-chief of the armed forces, General Alfredo Stroessner. To regularize his position Stroessner then had himself nominated as the presidential candidate of the right-wing National Republican Party (Colorados) which had official and army support. He was elected unopposed in July 1954, and re-elected in February 1958, 1963, 1968 and 1973 with large majorities. The continued success of the government, which had maintained economic and financial stability and had attracted substantial foreign aid to improve communications and begin a programme of land reform, encouraged Stroessner in 1967 to introduce a new Constitution, providing for an elected Senate and Chamber of Deputies. At elections held in May 1967 the seats were distributed as follows: in the Senate: Colorados 20; Liberals 9; Levi Liberals (a dissident Liberal group led by Dr Carlos Levi Ruffinelli), 1; in the Chamber of Deputies: Colorados 40; Liberals (moderate conservatives led by Dr Gustavo González) 16; Levi Liberals 3; Febrerista (led by Colonel Rafael Franco, to the left of the two major parties) 1. There is competition between Argentina, Brazil and the U.S.A. for predominance in Paraguay which is reflected in dissensions within the Colorado Party.

Parliament Acts, 1911 and 1949. Two British laws which define the powers of the House of Lords, *q.v.* All legislation needs the assent of both Houses of Parliament, as well as of the Queen, except in the circumstances described in the Acts. A Bill can be presented for royal assent without the agreement of the House of Lords if the House (1) fails in one month to pass a Bill which, having passed the House of Commons, *q.v.*, is sent up endorsed by the Speaker as a money Bill before the end of the session; or (2) refuses in two successive sessions to pass a public Bill (other than a money Bill) and if one year has elapsed between the date when it was read a second time in the House of Commons in the first session and a third time in the second session. A money Bill is one which only relates to the imposition, remission, repeal, and alteration of taxes, to charges on the Consolidated Fund, etc.; the power to shorten the period of delay by the House of Lords to six months in this way has only been used three times. The second part of the rule makes it impossible, in effect, for the House of Lords to delay a Bill for more than one year. The basic principle was established by the 1911 Act; the 1949 Act reduced the periods of delay to their present length. The 1911 Act exempted from its own provisions Bills to extend the life of Parliament; this is limited to five years, a period which cannot now be prolonged without the consent of both Houses.

Parliamentary Commissioner for the Administration. The British Ombudsman, *q.v.* The office was created on 1 April 1967, its status and its powers being conferred by Act of Parliament. The Commissioner may investigate complaints of personal injustice or maladministration by the Central government brought by individuals or companies 'lawfully resident' in the U.K. but can only act if the matter is raised by a member of the House of Commons. Certain areas of government, for instance state security and foreign relations, are outside the jurisdiction of the Commissioner. The first annual report of the Parliamentary Commissioner revealed evidence of maladministration in 19 out of the 188 cases in which investigations had been completed; a total of 1,069 cases had been referred during the year, but in 561 of these the Commissioner had no jurisdiction.

Pathanistan. Pakhtunistan, *q.v.*

Paul VI. Giovanni Battista Montini, 264th Pope; born 26 September 1897 at Concesio, a village near Brescia in northern Italy, the son of a lawyer and journalist who was also a member of the Italian parliament; ordained priest in 1920. He studied canon law at the Ecclesiastical Academy in Rome, and was for some months secretary to the Apostolic Nuncio in Warsaw, before returning to Rome. He became Substitute Secretary of State for Ordinary Affairs in 1937 and Pro-Secretary of State for Ordinary Affairs in 1952, dealing especially with internal church matters. In 1954 Pius XII made him Archbishop of Milan and in 1958 John XXIII made him a Cardinal. He was elected Pope in June 1963. He was responsible on 15 August 1967 for introducing a fundamental reform of the Roman Curia, the first for sixty years; the number of curial departments was reduced, major appointments which had formerly been for life were to be made for five years, and would terminate on the death of the Pope, and a Council for Public Affairs of the Church was created to act as a Foreign Ministry to the Vatican, *q.v.* In August 1968 he issued the encyclical *Humanae Vitae* in which he denounced all artificial forms of birth control.

Pentagon. A five-sided building in Virginia, U.S.A., on the outskirts of Washington, D.C., occupied by the Department of Defence.

Persia. An independent state; area 628,000 sq. m.; population (1972) 31,000,000; capital Teheran. Since 1949 foreigners have been permitted to call the country Persia, although the name had been previously altered to Iran. The despotic rule of the Qajar Shahs was modified in 1906 by the establishment of a National Assembly (Majlis) of 136 (now 268) members, elected for two (now four) years. Provision was also made for a Senate of 60 members, half elected and half nominated, but this was not constituted until 1950. The Shah retains the power to dissolve both chambers. In 1925 the reigning Shah of the Qajar dynasty was deposed by the National Assembly which elected Reza Khan Pahlevi, a Persian Cossack regiment officer as Shah. He abdicated in 1941, when British and Russian armies invaded Persia to expel the German agents whom he had admitted and encouraged, and was succeeded as Shah by his son Mohammed Reza Pahlevi (born 1919). In 1942 the U.K. and the U.S.S.R. guaranteed the independence of Persia which then declared war on Germany, Italy, and Japan. All allied forces were to be withdrawn after the end of the war, but Russian troops remained in Azerbaijan in north-west Persia, where an autonomous pro-Communist government was set up. The matter was referred to the United Nations and after direct negotiations between Persia and the U.S.S.R. the Russian troops withdrew.

The principal product is petroleum. In 1901 William Knox D'Arcy was given a 60-year monopoly of oil production in about five-sixths of Persia. The Shah was to receive 16 per cent of the profits. In 1909 D'Arcy founded the Anglo-Persian Oil Co., in which the U.K. bought substantial shares before the First World War in order to ensure adequate oil supplies for the Royal Navy. In 1933 the Company and the Persian government concluded a new agreement by which the concession was to run for 60 years from 31 December 1933, over about 100,000 sq. m. of Persia, and the Persian share of the royalties was increased. In 1951 the Majlis and Senate approved a Bill which nationalized the oil industry and took over the installations of the Oil Company, which had then become the Anglo-Iranian Oil Co. Oil exports and the Company's operations in Persia ceased. After internal disturbances, during which the Shah temporarily left the country and Dr Mussadiq, the leading supporter of nationalization, was arrested, the dispute between the government and the Company was settled in August 1954. The agreement provided for the operation of the installations by the National Iranian Oil Co. and an international consortium in which the interests are: British Petroleum Co. (formerly Anglo-Iranian) 40 per cent, Royal Dutch Shell 14 per cent, Gulf, Socony Mobil, Standard Oil of California, Standard Oil of New Jersey, and Texas Co. 7 per cent each, Compagnie Française des Pétroles 6 per cent, nine other U.S. companies 5 per cent. The joint operation was to continue until 1979, with a further 15 years' option. The Persian government receives 50 per cent of the earnings, with guaranteed increases in output.

Economic progress in Persia is being accelerated. The main exports are fresh and dried fruit, carpets, wool and hair, skins and leather, oil, and raw cotton. There is a growing textile industry and investment in mining; profit-sharing has been introduced in many factories. The Shah has promoted land redistribution: the first phase of the land reform, starting in January 1962, limited each landlord to one village, irrespective of size, the average village occupying about 400 hectares (988 acres); the second phase, starting in November 1964, reduced the limit to between 30 and 150 hectares (70 to 370 acres), but with a ceiling for mechanized farms of 500 hectares (1,235 acres). Two million acres have been redistributed but most of the wealth of Persia remains in the hands of a small number of people, and there has been widespread corruption in government. Conscripted Literacy, Health and Development Corps have since 1965 combatted rural illiteracy (60 per cent in 1970), disease and ignorance. Opium-smoking is no longer a major social problem; opium-growing was banned in 1955. Persia is a member of the Central Treaty Organization, *q.v.*, and participates in Regional Co-operation for Development, *q.v.*, with Pakistan and Turkey. In 1966 Persia acceded to the Colombo Plan, *q.v.*; at the same time an agreement was reached with the U.S.S.R. providing for the construction of a steel mill and machine tools plant in exchange for Persian natural gas. Diplomatic relations with Egypt, which had been broken off in 1960, were resumed in 1970.

Personality Cult. Encouragement of excessive adulation of individuals; a practice attributed by Khrushchev, *q.v.*, once First Secretary of the Communist Party of the U.S.S.R., to his predecessor, Marshal Joseph Stalin, *q.v.* At a secret session of the Party Congress on 25 February 1956, Khrushchev said that a cult of Stalin arose after Lenin's death, that Stalin had abused the prestige and popularity which he had gained by abolishing collective leadership inside the Party, and by using repressive measures against his opponents and against everyone who did not share his views. On 28 March 1956 *Pravda*, *q.v.*, stated: 'Stalin's disregard of the principle of collective leadership, and the frequent decisions taken by him personally, led to the distortion of party principles and party democracy, to the violation of revolutionary law, and to repression.'

Peru. An independent South American state on the Pacific Ocean; area 496,093 sq. m.; population (1970) 13,586,300, nearly half Indians; capital Lima. Spain ruled Peru from the sixteenth century until the revolutionary war of 1821–4. Under the Constitution of 1856, and amended in 1945 for the sixth time, the President is elected for six years by direct popular vote. Congress consists of a House of Representatives and a Senate, each House being elected by proportional representation every six years; there is a literacy qualification which effectively disfranchises most of the Indian population.

Peru comprises an almost rainless coastal plain, a vast tropical interior, and the Andean mountain ranges which divide them. Economic progress is beset by many difficulties; in the interior the Indians cling to primitive farming methods, while development of the mineral resources in the mountains requires considerable capital investment. All three regions face the problem of transport; there is only one trans-Andean highway. Agriculture, fishing and mining occupy more than 70 per cent of the inhabitants. The chief agricultural products are cotton, sugar, wool, hides and skins. Minerals produced include antimony, bismuth, copper, gold, lead, silver, vanadium (of which Peru is the world's largest producer), and zinc. Efforts are being made to develop the interior; these include the establishment of more railways, hydro-electric plants, smelting plants and refineries for minerals and five petro-chemical plants to be run by Petroperu. Roads and irrigation schemes, using the voluntary labour of the Indian population, have been undertaken by Cooperacion Popular, an organization launched in 1963 by President Belaúnde and aided financially by the Inter-American Development Bank and several west European countries. There is a substantial fishing industry, and Peru is the world's largest producer of fishmeal.

From 1945 to 1948 Peru was ruled by President J. L. Bustamante, who strove to hold the balance between the Alianza Popular Revolucionaria Americana (A.P.R.A.), the only Latin American movement with mass Indian support, and the conservative groups (sometimes called the Forty Families) who owned businesses in Lima. The Apristas had a majority in Congress but were unable to carry out the sweeping reforms which they had planned. In October 1948 General Manuel Odría overthrew Bustamante, becoming President in 1950 in an election in which he was the sole candidate and from which A.P.R.A. was banned. A small Socialist Party provided almost the only opposition in Congress. The leader of A.P.R.A., Victor Raúl Haya de la Torre, took refuge in the Colombian Embassy in Lima, where he spent several years before being permitted to leave Peru. He was allowed to return in March 1961.

In June 1956 Dr Manuel Prado y Ugarteche, a moderate conservative, who had been President from 1939 to 1945, was elected to succeed Odría, easily defeating the government's official candidate. Prado legalized A.P.R.A. and released many political prisoners. When the Presidential elections of 1962 proved inconclusive, no candidate receiving the necessary one-third of the votes, a military junta seized power. Further elections in June 1963 resulted in Fernando Belaúnde Terry, a wealthy architect and leader of the

Partido Acción Popular (A.P.), becoming President; his party, which was supported by the Christian Democrats (Partido Democratico Cristiano, or P.D.C.), is left wing, reformist and Catholic. In the Congressional elections of 1963 the A.P. and P.D.C. together won 52 seats in the lower house, and were allocated 19 seats in the Senate; A.P.R.A., still led by Haya de la Torre who had unsuccessfully contested the Presidency, gained the most seats, 57 and 15; Unión Nacional Odriísta, the right-wing party of the former dictator, 26 and 6; the Peruvian Democratic Movement and Independents shared the remaining five seats in both houses. The government coalition, frustrated by having no parliamentary majority, and continually defeated by the left and right combining against it, broke up in 1967. A severe currency devaluation in 1967 increased dissatisfaction with Belaúnde's policies, and when, in August 1968, a contract was signed between the government and the International Petroleum Company (Standard Oil of New Jersey) settling a dispute as to the ownership of petroleum deposits in La Brea and Pariñas, in the north, it was suspected that too many concessions had been made to I.P.C., particularly over the price which was to be paid for crude oil. On 3 October 1968 President Belaúnde was deposed by a military *coup* and exiled to Argentina. The junta, under General Juan Velasco, which assumed full powers, immediately repudiated the petroleum contracts, expropriated the oilfields, and occupied the installations. It also embarked on a programme of land reform. Since 1971, when the state petroleum concern, Petroperu, struck oil at Trompeteros on the Corrientes river, oil exploration contracts have been signed by 10 North American and 2 British oil companies. The contracts, which are for 35 years, establish that all oil found by foreign companies is Peruvian, and the property of Petroperu, which will refund the companies for their services on a 50–50 basis.

Philippines. Officially the Republic of the Philippines, it is an independent state in the western Pacific; total land area 114,830 sq. m., comprising 11 important islands, of which the largest are Luzon and Mindanao, and 7,089 others, mostly unnamed; population (1971 estimate) 37,959,000, mostly of Malay stock with a strong Chinese and Spanish admixture, and including 400,000 Chinese; capital Quezon City; administrative capital Manila, in Luzon. The islands were ceded by Spain to the U.S.A. for $20 million after the Spanish-American War of 1898. The Filipinos agitated for independence and the U.S.A. introduced various home-rule measures, including a 1934 Act of Congress which established a Philippine Commonwealth. The islands were occupied by Japan during the Second World War but after their liberation the independent Republic of the Philippines came into existence on 4 July 1946. Sovereignty is claimed over Sabah, *q.v.* (formerly known as British North Borneo).

Under the 1935 Constitution, amended in 1940 and 1946, a President and Vice-President are elected for 4 years; the legislature consists of a Senate of 24 members (elected for 6 years) and a House of Representatives of 104 members (elected for 4 years). In 1953 Ramon Magsaysay was elected President as the leader of the right-wing Naçionalista Party. The Naçionalistas were supported by business interests but also attracted a large popular following. A Naçionalista programme of social and economic reform weakened the Communist-led Hukbalahap movement, whose guerillas had challenged the authority of the central government since 1946. Magsaysay, who was regarded by the Liberals as a puppet of the U.S.A., was killed in an aircraft accident in March 1957. He was succeeded by his Vice-President, Carlos P. Garcia, also a Naçionalista, who was elected President in November 1957. Diosdado Macapagal, a Liberal with a reputation for incorruptibility, defeated Garcia at the next Presidential election and assumed office on 1 January 1962. He was in turn defeated in December 1965 by Ferdinand Marcos, Naçionalista leader and ex-Liberal, who was re-elected in November 1969. At elections for the House of Representatives held in November 1971 the Naçionalistas won 57 seats, the Liberals 42 and Independents 5.

The country is predominantly agricultural, with important exports of coconut oil, copra, manila hemp, sugar, gold, zinc, and silver. The U.S.-Philippine Trade Act of 1946 made trade between the two countries duty-free (except for rice, sugar, and tobacco) from 1946 to 1955 and gradually increased payments of duty thereafter (75 per cent from 1962 to 1964; 90 per cent from 1965 to 1973), rising to tariff duty on U.S. goods at the ordinary level by 1 January 1974.

The Japanese occupation of the Philippines from 1942 to 1945 caused war damage estimated in 1946 at $8,000 million; after years of negotiations the Japanese agreed to meet one-tenth of the claim in capital goods, services, investment funds, cash and development loans. The Philippines is a member of S.E.A.T.O., *q.v.*, of A.S.E.A.N., *q.v.*, and the Asian and Pacific Council, *q.v.*

Pindling, Lynden Oscar. Bahamas politician; born 22 March 1930 in Nassau, the son of a Jamaican immigrant who became a prosperous shopkeeper and horse-breeder; he was educated at the government high school and at London University where he studied law. After graduating in 1952 he returned to the Bahamas, *q.v.*, and practised as a barrister. He joined the wholly-negro Progressive Liberal Party (P.L.P.) shortly after its formation in 1953 and was elected its Parliamentary leader in 1956. When the P.L.P. won the same number of seats in the Assembly as the ruling United Bahamian Party at elections held in January 1967 he became Prime Minister and formed the first all-negro cabinet in the island's history. He continued in office after elections in 1968 and 1972 had produced convincing majorities for his policy of independence for the Bahamas and participation in the Caribbean Free Trade Association, *q.v.*

Podgorny, Nikolai Viktorovich. Russian politician; born 1903; educated at the Mikoyan Technological Institute at Kiev. He became a member of the Communist Party in 1930. From 1931 to 1939 he was chief engineer of the Ukraine sugar refineries and from 1939 to 1946 deputy commissar of the Ukrainian food industry. He graduated through the Communist Party of the Ukraine to become first secretary of its Central Committee in 1957 until 1963 when he was appointed secretary of the Communist Party of the Soviet Union. He was elected to the Presidium of the Supreme Soviet in 1955 and to the Presidium of the Central Committee in 1960. In November 1964, following Khrushchev's fall, he presented to the Central Committee the report which abolished separate party organizations for industry and agriculture, introduced by Khrushchev in 1962, and restored them to a territorial basis. In December 1965 he became Chairman of the Presidium of the Supreme Soviet.

Poland. An independent state in eastern Europe; area 120,733 sq. m.; population (1970 estimate) 32,670,000; capital Warsaw. After achieving considerable military successes between the fourteenth and sixteenth centuries Poland declined, and there were three partitions of the country in the eighteenth century (in 1772, 1793, and 1795) in which Austria, Prussia, and Russia shared. Though Napoleon created a small independent state, the Congress of Vienna, 1815, re-partitioned Poland except for the Republic of Krakow which was later seized by Austria.

Poland was declared independent in 1918, power being assumed by Josef Pilsudski who had recruited Poles to fight the Russians during the First World War; after 1926 government was by a semi-Fascist dictatorship, at first under Pilsudski and after his death in 1935 under officers loyal to his tradition. Nearly 40 per cent of the budget was spent on armaments owing to the fear of invasion by Germany or the U.S.S.R. Both powers invaded and partitioned Poland in 1939. During the Second World War the Germans murdered about 3,000,000 of the 3,500,000 Polish Jews. More than half of the population of Warsaw was killed and the capital was almost completely destroyed. By March 1945 the Russian army had liberated Poland. In June 1945 the Polish Provisional Government of National Unity was formed, comprising the anti-Communist government-in-exile in London under Mikolajczyk and the pro-Communist Polish Committee of National Liberation, which had been formed in Moscow and moved to Lublin. In January 1947 the government block won 382 out of the 444 seats in the Sejm (Parliament) but there was an atmosphere of police terror. Mikolajczyk fled to London in October 1947.

In 1948 and 1949 the Socialists and Communists merged into the United Workers' Party, and the Peasants' and the Polish Peasants' Parties into the United Peasants' Party. Under the 1952 Constitution supreme legislative power is vested in the Sejm, which is elected every four years. In practice supreme power is exercised by the Politburo of the United Workers' Party. At the elections held on 19 March 1972 a single list of National Unity Front candidates was offered to the electorate (of whom 97·94 per cent voted), the United Workers' Party (P.Z.P.R.) obtaining its customary 255 seats, the United Peasants' Party 117 seats, Democratic Party 39 and non-party deputies, including 12 Catholic representatives, 49. The Politburo is headed by Edward Gierek, who succeeded Wladyslaw Gomulka as First Secretary of the Central Committee of the United Workers' Party in December 1970. Gomulka, who had been in power since October 1956, resigned following strikes and rioting in the ports of Gdańsk, Szczecin and Gdynia in 1970 in protest against a steep rise in food prices. The Chairman of the Council of State is Professor Henryk Jablonski who was elected in March 1972 to succeed Jozef Cyrankewicz, the former Prime Minister, who had changed his post in December 1970. The Chairman of the Council of Ministers (the Council is elected by the Sejm) since 1970 has been Piotr Jaroszewicz.

There has been extensive industrialization and the key industries have all been nationalized but 86 per cent of agricultural land remains in private hands. Copper and sulphur deposits have been discovered and there are substantial exports of steel, coal, and lignite; only 20 per cent of the country's trade is with countries who are not members of Comecon.

By the agreement at Potsdam, *q.v.*, and Yalta, *q.v.*, Poland was in effect moved to the west. 70,000 sq. m. were yielded to the U.S.S.R., and in return Poland received 44,231 sq. m. of Germany, including Silesia, part of the Baltic coast, and most of East Prussia. About 8,500,000 Germans were expelled from these areas, a factor which delayed West German recognition of this frontier, the Oder-Neisse

Line, *q.v.*, as permanent. However, in December 1970, as a result of the success of Willy Brandt's Ostpolitik, *q.v.*, a peace treaty was signed between Poland and the German Federal Republic. Relations were normalized, agreement was reached on the release of ethnic Germans still remaining in Poland who wished to emigrate to Germany, the Oder-Neisse Line was recognized as constituting Poland's western frontier and its future inviolability was affirmed. In May 1972 the West German Parliament finally ratified the treaty.

Pompidou, Georges Jean Raymond. French politician; born 1911 at Montboudif in the Auvergne, the son of a teacher. He himself taught at Marseilles and in Paris. He took part in the resistance movement and from 1944–6 served on General de Gaulle's staff as an adviser on educational policy. He later held a number of technical and administrative posts, including that of deputy-director of the tourist industry, until 1954 when he joined the French House of Rothschild as its Director-General and became a director of the Compagnie Française des Recherches Pétrolières. When de Gaulle resumed power in 1958 he was appointed head of the cabinet and President of the Council of Ministers. He was a member of the Constitutional Council from 1959–62. In 1961 he was given the task of re-establishing contacts with the Algerian nationalists; he was largely responsible for the Évian negotiations by which peace was concluded. He succeeded Michel Debré, *q.v.*, as Prime Minister in April 1962, retaining most of the members of the former cabinet in his own administration, which was defeated on a censure motion in the Assembly in 1963. After the November 1963 general election, which the Gaullists won, he was re-appointed Prime Minister until 10 July 1968, when he was succeeded by Maurice Couve de Murville, *q.v.* He was elected President of France in June 1969, winning 58 per cent of the votes in a second ballot.

Popular Front. The collaboration of Communist, Socialist, and other political parties against Fascism, originally suggested by the Communist International in 1935. The French Popular Front government, under Léon Blum, was in office from 1936 to 1937 and for a short period in 1938. The Spanish government appointed in May 1936 by the President of Spain, who was the Popular Front leader, is normally described as a Popular Front government, but although it believed in radical social reforms it contained no Socialist or Communist members; it was eventually overthrown by Fascist rebels.

Popular Front for the Liberation of Palestine. A guerilla organization, founded in 1967, dedicated to the destruction of Israel and the creation of a revolutionary socialist Palestine Arab state. Its adherents have conducted a campaign of terror directed not only at Jews but designed to attract international attention to the plight of the Palestinian Arabs; this has included the multiple hijacking of aircraft and the massacre of non-Jewish passengers in transit at Lod airport in 1972, as well as raids on Israeli positions, and assassinations (for example that of the Jordanian Prime Minister in 1971). The movement was involved in the attempt to overthrow the Hashemite kingdom of Jordan in 1970. Its leader, re-elected for a further four-year term in 1970, is the Marxist George Habash.

Poqo. From the Xhosa word *Ukupoqa*. It means 'independent' or 'for ourselves alone'; it is said by the South African government to be an African nationalist organization active in South Africa; if it does exist as an entity separate from the Pan-Africanist Congress, *q.v.*, it does in any event oppose apartheid and the attempts of the government to move many Africans to tribal reserves, and appears to be prepared to pursue its aims by violence, as did Mau Mau in Kenya. Though its methods are not the same, its professed aims are similar to those of the Pan-Africanist Congress.

Portugal. An independent state in the western part of the Iberian peninsula; area 34,831 sq. m.; population (1970 estimate) 8,124,000; capital Lisbon. From the eleventh century it was a monarchy and became a great imperial power, sharing in the division of the New World with Spain in 1493. It ruled the greater part of South America, including Brazil, until the beginning of the nineteenth century. An armed revolt forced King Manuel II of Braganza-Coburg to flee to England and a republic was declared. Between 1910 and 1926 there were 24 revolutions and *coups d'état*, and no real progress was made towards a democratic form of government. The parliamentary regime was finally overthrown by a military *coup* in May 1926, but the Army officers who came to power had no solution for the country's economic difficulties. In 1928 the President, General Carmona, invited Dr Antonió de Oliviera Salazar, *q.v.*, to reform the economy as Minister of Finance. He was the virtual dictator of Portugal for the next forty years until illness incapacitated him, and he was released from his post as Prime Minister on the prerogative of the President. He was succeeded on 26 September 1968 by Dr Marcelo Caetano, *q.v.*

Under the 1933 Constitution, based on the Constitution of Fascist Italy, parliament consists of two houses, the National Assembly and the Corporative Chamber. The National Assembly has 130 members elected for four years by direct but limited suffrage, and exercises legislative and financial powers. At elections held in November 1953, November 1957, November 1961, November 1965 and November

1969, the National Union, the only authorized political party, which changed its name to National Popular Action (A.N.P.) in 1972, won all the seats. The Corporative Chamber consists of representatives of commercial, cultural, industrial and religious interests, and local authorities. All Bills introduced in the National Assembly must be submitted to the Corporative Chamber. So far the President has been elected for seven years by a direct but limited suffrage; Rear-Admiral Américo de Deus Rodrigues Tomás, the government candidate, took office as President on 9 August 1958, defeating General Humberto Delgado, whose supporters had demanded the restoration of fundamental democratic liberties. The substantial size of the minority vote received by Delgado (who was found murdered in Spain in 1965) was one of the factors which caused the government to amend the Constitution in 1961, so that thereafter the President was to be appointed indirectly, by an electoral college. Tomás was re-elected by this method in July 1965 and July 1972.

The remnants of Portugal's former overseas possessions constitute a large empire and are of considerable economic importance, providing in 1969 15 per cent of Portugal's imports, taking 25 per cent of its exports and yielding high dollar returns. The Azores (nine islands in the Atlantic) and the Madeiras (an island group 520 miles south-west of Lisbon) are part of Metropolitan Portugal. The Portuguese overseas territories, which ceased to have the status of colonies on 11 June 1951 and which, by a Constitutional amendment introduced in July 1972, are to be allowed some measure of autonomy as soon as their social and administrative development warrants it, are: in Africa, Angola (Portuguese West Africa), *q.v.*, sending coffee, diamonds, maize and sugar to Portugal; Portuguese Guinea, producing palm-oil, rice and seeds; Mozambique (Portuguese East Africa), *q.v.*, producing cotton, copra, maize, sizal and sugar; San Tomé and Principe Islands, producing cacao, coffee and copra; and Cape Verde Islands, producing coffee; in Asia, Macao in China, with a valuable transit trade; and Portuguese Timor, producing coffee and copra. Goa, *q.v.*, Damão and Diu, till then part of Portuguese India, were seized by India on 18 December 1961. Since 1961 the Portuguese government has been confronted with armed insurrection in Angola, since 1963 in Guinea and since 1964 in Mozambique. More than 40 per cent of the annual budget is spent on containing these nationalist guerila movements which are sustained by the Organization of African Unity, *q.v.*

Portugal's domestic resources are meagre, though there are important exports of cork and cork products (the largest in the world), pulpwood, olive oil, resin, wine and port, sardines, and wolfram and pyrites. The central feature of the economy, and therefore of Portugal's attitude to its empire, is the satisfactory trade balance achieved as a result of the contributions from the overseas territories; if these were suddenly to cease Portugal would be in serious economic difficulties. At home, the government has been slow to speed up industrial development, but there has been investment in the petro-chemical industries, in textile manufacturing, hydro-electric plants and railway electrification, and a considerable expansion of the tourist trade. There is an acute shortage of labour; more than half the labour force (1·6 out of 3·1 million) has migrated to other West European countries, has been conscripted into the army, or has left to work overseas.

Portuguese East Africa. Mozambique, *q.v.*

Portuguese West Africa. Angola, *q.v.*

Potsdam Agreement. Was concluded by the U.K., the U.S.A., and the U.S.S.R. at the Cecilienhof Palace at Potsdam, between 17 July and 1 August 1945. The three powers reaffirmed their policy towards Germany, outlined at the Yalta Conference, *q.v.*, in February 1945, and agreed that for the time being no central government should be established. The economy was to be decentralized to eliminate excessive economic concentration as exemplified by cartels, syndicates, trusts, and other monopolistic arrangements, but Germany was to be treated as a single economic unit, common policies being established in regard to its economic life. Production of metals, chemicals, machinery, and other items necessary to a war economy was to be restricted to Germany's approved post-war peacetime needs.

It was agreed that the city of Königsberg and the area adjacent to it should be transferred to the U.S.S.R., and that the Polish western frontier, about which no final decision had been made at the Yalta Conference, should be on the Oder-Neisse Line, *q.v.* The three powers agreed as to the transfer to Germany of many Germans remaining in Czechoslovakia, Hungary, and Poland. France, which had been promised an occupation zone in Germany when the three powers met at Yalta, was excluded from the Potsdam discussions.

Powell, John Enoch. British Conservative Party politician; born 16 June 1912 and educated at King Edward's, Birmingham and Trinity College, Cambridge, of which he was a Fellow from 1934 to 1938. He was Professor of Greek at the University of Sydney from 1937 to 1939, and in the Second World War became a Brigadier. He was elected to the House of Commons for South-West Wolverhampton in 1950, and was Parliamentary Secretary to the Ministry of Housing and Local Government from 1955 to 1957, when he was appointed Financial Secretary to the Treasury. In January 1958 he resigned with the Chancellor of the Exchequer, Peter Thorneycroft, in protest against public expenditure which he considered inflationary. He became Minister of Health in 1960, but declined to serve in the Douglas-Home cabinet formed in October 1963. He opposed the accession of the U.K. to the European Economic Community, on which issue he voted against the Conservative government legislation and he campaigned vigorously to limit the non-white population of the U.K. by ending Commonwealth immigration and by encouraging repatriation.

Pravda. A newspaper which is the official organ of the Central Committee of the Communist Party of the U.S.S.R. Its opinions on Communist policy are sometimes more authoritative than those expressed by *Izvestia*, *q.v.*, although there is rarely any difference in outlook between the two journals. The word *pravda* means truth; the newspaper was founded in 1912 with Joseph Stalin, *q.v.*, as editor and Vyacheslav Molotov, *q.v.*, as his secretary.

Privy Council. Originally an advisory Council to the British sovereign. As a body the Privy Council is not now asked to give advice. Orders in Council and Proclamations are approved by the Queen in the presence of three Privy Councillors (enough to constitute a quorum), after which it is announced that the Queen held a Privy Council. The matters considered, however, will have been previously recommended by the responsible departments of government. The Cabinet itself is in origin an informal committee of the Privy Council, and Cabinet Ministers (and some other Ministers) are Privy Councillors. Individuals retain the title of Privy Councillor even after resignation from the Cabinet. Sometimes the title of Privy Councillor (P.C.) is an honorary title bestowed for distinguished services to the state. Privy Councillors are addressed as 'Right Honourable'. There are various committees of the Privy Council, such as the Board of Trade, which seldom meet. An important committee which does meet is the Judicial Committee of the Privy Council, composed of Privy Councillors who are or have been in high judicial office (usually Law Lords and ex-judges). It hears appeals from parts of the British Commonwealth. It also hears ecclesiastical appeals from Church courts and any problems referred to it by the Crown.

Profumo Affair. John Dennis Profumo (born 30 January 1915) then the Secretary of State for War and Conservative Member of Parliament for Stratford-on-Avon, had an adulterous relationship in 1961 with a Christine Keeler. During part of that period she was also associating with Commander Yevgeny Ivanov, a Russian Assistant Naval Attaché, who was recalled to the U.S.S.R. in December 1962.

In the course of criminal proceedings arising out of an alleged shooting incident at Keeler's flat by a West Indian, and involving her failure to give evidence at the trial of the accused in March 1963, Profumo's association with her was discovered. The matter was raised in the House of Commons on 21 March by Colonel George Wigg, the Labour Member of Parliament for Dudley. On 22 March Profumo denied the allegations in a personal statement in the House of Commons which, by its own rules, was unable to discuss his statement; he threatened to issue writs for libel or slander against anyone who repeated the allegations, and after issuing one writ on 8 April recovered damages for libel from the English distributors of an Italian magazine, *Tempo Illustrato*. Some who were aware of the truth persisted in their inquiries, with the result that on 4 June, in a letter to the Prime Minister, Profumo admitted that he had lied; he then resigned from the government, the House of Commons, and the Privy Council.

Proletariat. From the Latin word *proles*, meaning offspring (alluding to the number of children of the poorer classes): the class of wage-earners with little or no property of their own who depend on the sale of their labour. Definitions of the limits of the proletarian class vary; at one time only manual workers were included, but a process of 'proletarianization' of the middle class is discernible in some countries, particularly where (as in the U.K.) many manual workers earn more than professional or white-collar workers.

Propaganda. Statements of policy or facts, usually of a political nature, the real purpose of which is different from their apparent purpose. In this sense propaganda existed before the twentieth century, but its importance has increased in an age when communication is easier and when it is more useful to influence ordinary people. The term is used to describe a statement which is believed to be insincere or untrue, and designed to impress the public rather than to reach the truth or to bring about a genuine understanding between opposing governments or parties. People do not usually admit that they are issuing propaganda, and the word is much misused. Propaganda by one's own government or political party is described as a policy statement or as part of its news service; genuine approaches and statements of policy by another government or party are frequently dismissed as mere propaganda.

Proportional Representation. An electoral system under which a legislature reflects the strength of the various political parties among the electorate at large. It has several forms, the simplest being one in which a country is divided into large constituencies each returning several members; those candidates are elected who obtain more than a certain fraction of the vote, and their surplus over that fraction is distributed among the other candidates according to the second and later choices indicated on the ballot-papers. Other candidates whose votes then reach the required quota are also elected. This is the method of the transferable vote. Under another method the votes given to a party in any constituency which are not sufficient for the election of a candidate are reserved for a second sorting, in which these remainder votes from various constituencies are added up. If the total is sufficient for the election of one or more candidates, these are taken from a national list of the party, and they become Members of Parliament without a constituency. Supporters of proportional representation say that it would satisfy the large numbers of citizens who might otherwise be unrepresented in Parliament, that the large parties would moderate their views, and that the system is inherently fair. Its opponents say that the electors do not want a Parliament which photographically represents each party and that the system makes for unstable coalition governments. The Labour Party advocated proportional representation until it became the second largest party in the U.K. in 1922, when the cause was taken up by the Liberal Party. It should not be confused with the Alternative Vote, *q.v.*

Protected State. A territory, with its own ruler, controlling its internal affairs but under the protection of another state which usually manages its foreign relations. A protected state is a special type of protectorate, *q.v.*, differing from most protectorates which generally contain groups of tribes with few acknowledged rulers, whereas a protected state resembles more closely a unified state. The powers of a protected state depend on its arrangement with its protector. Tonga, with its own sovereign, was an example of a British protected state before it achieved independence in 1970.

Protectorate. A territory, not formally annexed, over which the protecting state has power and jurisdiction but not full sovereignty. There are almost as many types of protectorate as there are protectorates and a detailed description of a protectorate is therefore impossible; in every case it is important to examine the way in which the protection began (by treaty, grant or usage, for example) and not simply to accept the title protectorate as a description of the particular territory. In the case of British protectorates the inhabitants are not citizens of the United Kingdom and Colonies and the territories are treated as foreign territories, but, although the inhabitants do not owe allegiance to the Crown, they owe an almost unlimited duty of obedience in return for its protection. A protecting state does not usually permit other states to enter into relations with the peoples of the protectorate. Botswana and Swaziland are examples of former British protectorates, all of which have now achieved independence. The term is often confused with the terms 'colony', *q.v.*, and 'protected state', *q.v.*: the latter may best be regarded as a special type of protectorate.

Provisional I.R.A. A group of Irish nationalists who seceded from the Official Irish Republican Army, *q.v.*, in December 1969 to form their own organization. They do not accept the traditional socialist policy of the I.R.A. but advocate the liberation and unification of Ireland by force. They were responsible for the intensification of terrorist activity in Belfast and Londonderry from 1970 and for the establishment of independent sectors within these cities (the 'no-go areas') during 1971 and 1972. By August 1971 the Provisional I.R.A., under Sean MacStiofan as Chief of Staff in Dublin, had become the dominant group. The introduction of internment by the Northern Ireland government in Ulster persuaded many Catholics to rally to them, but subsequent events, especially direct rule, encouraged Catholic support for a cease-fire, which MacStiofan describes as a defeat.

Puerto Rico. A group of islands in the West Indies belonging to the U.S.A.; area 3,423 sq. m.; population (1970) 2,713,147, three-quarters of whom are of Spanish descent; capital San Juan. It was ceded by Spain to the U.S.A. in 1898 as a result of the Spanish-American War; its name was changed from Porto Rico to Puerto Rico by an Act of the U.S. Congress in 1932. Although its foreign relations are in the hands of the U.S. State Department, the 1952 Constitution which established the Commonwealth of Puerto Rico gave it extensive powers of local self-government. Statehood has been offered to the legislature of Puerto Rico, and rejected in January 1954. A plebiscite held on 23 July 1967, in which 65·8 per cent of the electorate voted, confirmed that the majority (60·5 per cent) wished to retain the existing Commonwealth system; 38·9 per cent voted for statehood, and 0·1 per cent for complete independence. The standard of living is among the highest in Latin America. An increasing measure of investment from the U.S.A. has changed the economy from an agricultural to a mixed one, and has brought prosperity to the islands. The inhabitants are American citizens and liable for military service in the U.S.A., but they pay no federal taxes and exercise no federal vote.

Q

Qatar. An independent state in the Persian Gulf; area 4,000 sq. m.; population (1970 estimate) 112,000; capital Doha. From 1916 until 1 September 1971 when independence was declared it enjoyed a treaty relationship with the U.K. similar to that of the Trucial States, *q.v.* In 1968, when the British announced their proposed withdrawal of military forces from the Persian Gulf, Qatar joined the Federation of Arab Emirates, *q.v.*; but in 1971, together with Bahrain, *q.v.*, it decided to apply separately for U.N. membership and membership of the Arab League, *q.v.* On 22 February 1972 the Emir of Qatar and Head of State since 1960, Sheikh Ahmad bin Ali bin Abdullah al-Thani, was deposed by his cousin, Sheikh Khalifa bin Hamad al-Thani, the Crown Prince and former Prime Minister, in a bloodless *coup*. A programme of social and economic reform was promised, to include compulsory free education and the curbing of extravagance by the royal family which had previously drawn one quarter of the oil revenues. Oil production began in 1949, and the revenue derived from this is the principal source of income; it has been used to build water distillation and electricity plants as well as schools and hospitals. (As in Bahrain, Qatar residents are entitled to free medical treatment.) Concessions are held by Qatar Petroleum Co., the ownership of which is the same as that of the Iraq Petroleum Co., *q.v.*, by the Shell Co. of Qatar, a subsidiary of the Shell Group, which has access to the sea-bed deposits, and by the Continental Oil Co. of Qatar, which is a subsidiary of the Continental Oil Co. of the U.S.A. The Qatar National Petroleum Co., which was founded in 1972, intends to take over a majority of the Shell Co. and Q.P.C. shares, in accordance with the resolution of O.P.E.C., *q.v.*, calling on member countries to seek participation in oil-producing firms.

Quai d'Orsay. An embankment of the river Seine in Paris, where the French Foreign Office is situated.

Quemoy. An island which, with three smaller ones, is six miles from Amoy, on the mainland of China, but is occupied by Chinese forces loyal to the government of Taiwan, *q.v.*; area 70 sq. m.; population (1961) approximately 47,000 civilians and 60,000 troops; capital Quemoy City. It is surrounded on three sides by the mainland.

R

Rahman, Tunku Abdul. Prime Minister of Malaysia from its establishment on 16 September 1963 until February 1971. Born 8 February 1903, he was the seventh son of the sixth wife of the Sultan of Kedah and was educated at St Catharine's College, Cambridge; he returned to England in 1947 to complete his Bar examinations. He took over the leadership of the United Malays' National Organization (U.M.N.O.) in 1951. He became the first Chief Minister appointed under the 1955 Constitution after his Alliance Party won the elections, and became Prime Minister when Malaya became independent, on 31 August 1957. As President of the Alliance Party, he insisted on 'Malayanization' of the public services. In spite of his nationalist views he has taken pains to encourage foreign, and especially British, investment. He resigned in favour of his deputy, Tun Abdul Razak, when elections in 1969, and subsequent race riots, showed that the Alliance Party had failed to reassure the Malay population that their interests would be adequately protected against the Chinese minority.

Rann of Kutch. An area of some 7,000 sq. m. on the north-west border of India and the eastern border of West Pakistan. Sovereignty over the area was disputed for many years, with Pakistan claiming that part which lay to the north of the 24th parallel and which constituted nearly half of the total. The dispute was submitted to an International Tribunal which, on 19 February 1968, announced that it had awarded 3,200 sq. m. of the Rann to India, and 350 sq. m. to Pakistan. Both governments accepted the award as binding, but there was considerable opposition in India to the announcement because it was wrongly assumed that it entailed the cession of territory previously held by India to Pakistan. A campaign of *satyagraha*, *q.v.*, was launched in April 1968 in an unsuccessful attempt to persuade the Indian government to reject the Tribunal's award.

Rapacki Plan. A proposal for a central European zone free of nuclear weapons. It was contained in a memorandum delivered in Warsaw by the Polish government to representatives of nine states on 14 February 1958. The Plan took its name from the Polish Foreign Minister, Adam Rapacki, who proposed it to the U.N. General Assembly on 2 October 1957. The zone was to include Poland, Czechoslovakia, and Eastern and Western Germany. The memorandum stated: 'In this territory nuclear weapons would neither be manufactured nor stockpiled; the equipment and installations designed for their servicing would not be located there; the use of nuclear weapons against the territory of this zone would be

393

prohibited.' These obligations were to apply to the states in the zone, to France, the U.K., the U.S.A., and the U.S.S.R., and to the other states (which then included Belgium, Canada, Denmark, and the Netherlands) with forces in the zone.

The memorandum recommended control by aerial and ground inspection supervised by the member states of the Eastern European Mutual Assistance Treaty, *q.v.*, and the North Atlantic Treaty Organization, *q.v.* The Polish government expressed the hope that such a zone would lead to the reduction of conventional forces within the zone, and that the system would be a precedent for a broader agreement on disarmament, *q.v.*

The U.S.S.R. supported the Plan, while the U.K. and the U.S.A. objected to it, partly because it would favour the eastern powers, with their predominance in conventional weapons, and partly because it did not provide for German reunification.

Rapallo, Treaty of. A treaty of friendship signed in 1922 by Germany and the U.S.S.R., at Rapallo, near Genoa, where an international conference on economic questions and reparations was being held. The terms were unimportant but the Treaty was significant as it secured for the U.S.S.R. its first official recognition by a major power. It offended the other major powers, but was a direct result of their policy of treating Germany and the U.S.S.R. as inferior states.

Rapprochement. A diplomatic term meaning the re-establishment of good relations between states.

Rassemblement Démocratique Africain. French West African political party founded in October 1946 by Félix Houphouët-Boigny. It was affiliated to the French Communist Party until 1950, and to the Union Démocratique et Socialiste de la Résistance (U.D.S.R.) until 1958 when the U.D.S.R. declared its opposition to de Gaulle. The strongest French African political movement, it favoured close cooperation with France and was recruited mainly from Ivory Coast, Congo (Brazzaville), the former French Congo, and Upper Volta. At the party congress at Bamako in 1957 a minority, led by Modibo Kéita, of Mali, and Ahmed Sekou Touré, *q.v.*, of Guinea, forced Houphouët-Boigny, who advocated the direct link with France, to approve a policy of federalism among the French Community, *q.v.* Not wishing the Ivory Coast to be involved in the ephemeral Mali Federation, *q.v.*, he encouraged the formation of the Conseil de l'Entente (*see* Entente, Council of the).

Ratification. The formal adoption by a state of a treaty signed by its representatives. It is effected by an exchange of documents, embodying their formal adoption of the treaty, between the states concerned.

This gives an opportunity, particularly in democratic countries, for public opinion to express itself, although most representatives today are careful not to sign a treaty unless they are certain that it will be ratified. It is an essential process in countries in which the treaty-making power is, under the Constitution, vested in some organ which cannot itself carry on negotiations with other states; thus in the U.S.A. the treaty-making power is vested in the President, subject to the advice and consent of the Senate. In the U.K. treaties are ratified by the Sovereign. A discussion in the Houses of Parliament of the contents of a treaty has no effect on its binding force as between the U.K. and the other contracting states. However, no treaty concluded by the U.K., whether or not it has been ratified, can affect the private rights of British citizens until its provisions have been put into the form of a statute and passed by Parliament.

Minor matters of an international nature are frequently agreed by the government departments of various states. These are not considered to need ratification. Under the category of 'executive agreements', for example, arrangements are sometimes made by representatives of the U.S. State Department with representatives of other states, and these are not subject to the constitutional rules about treaties.

Reciprocal Trade Agreements Act. A U.S. law, first enacted in 1934, empowering the President to reduce import tariffs in return for concessions granted to U.S. exports. The U.S. Tariff Commission reports to the President if the reductions, proposed or actual, injure, or threaten to injure, domestic producers. If he rejects the advice of the Commission he must give his reasons for so doing to Congress. The President's power to modify existing tariff rates was considerably extended by the Trade Expansion Act, 1962 (*see* Kennedy Round).

Redistribution. A reorganization of electoral districts, involving their creation, abolition, merging, and alteration, to ensure that each representative speaks for approximately the same number of voters. The districts represented by the members of the U.S. House of Representatives, and the British House of Commons, are subject to redistribution. In the U.K. the House of Commons (Redistribution of Seats) Act, 1949, provides for four permanent Boundary Commissions (for England, Scotland, Wales, and Northern Ireland) which have to report to the government at intervals of not less than three nor more than seven years, so that revision of parliamentary boundaries can be made by Order in Council. Each House of Parliament must approve of such Orders in Council before they can take effect. Redistribution must be distinguished from gerrymandering, *q.v.*

Referendum. A reference of a particular political question to the electorate for a direct decision by popular vote. In some countries alterations to the constitution can be made only with the consent of the electorate obtained by a referendum. The Australian Constitution, for example, which is contained in the Schedule to the Commonwealth of Australia Act, 1900, can only be altered by a referendum. This device need not be confined to constitutional matters. In Switzerland a referendum must be held not only on constitutional amendments but on any law if 30,000 citizens so insist. The referendum is not normally used in the U.K.

Regional Cooperation for Development. An organization set up by Pakistan, Persia and Turkey in 1964, to strengthen mutual economic, technical and cultural cooperation. It supplements the arrangements made under the Central Treaty Organization, *q.v.*, to which the three countries are party, which are concerned principally with defence.

Republican Party. One of the two great political parties in the U.S.A.; the other is the Democratic Party, *q.v.* The name was once an alternative title for the Democratic Party until in 1828 the advocates of high tariffs, led by John Quincy Adams and Henry Clay, broke away and were called National Republicans or Whigs. The present Republican Party emerged in 1854 out of an alliance between the National Republicans and the northern Democrats, both of whom opposed slavery. It came to power when Abraham Lincoln became President in 1861 and ruled (except for the administrations of Cleveland, 1885–9, 1893–7, and of McKinley, 1897–1901), until 1912. At the close of the nineteenth century it believed in high tariffs, U.S. imperialism, and the strengthening of the federal administration. It comprised an alliance of the industrial east and the agricultural west, giving tariff protection to the east and free land to the farmers of the west. After the second Woodrow Wilson administration, the Republicans came to power again in 1920, prevented U.S. ratification of the Versailles Treaty, *q.v.*, and supplied three successive Presidents, Warren Gamaliel Harding, Calvin Coolidge, and Herbert Hoover. It was defeated in 1932, largely as a result of the world economic slump, and replaced by a Democratic majority in Congress. The party was once isolationist in outlook but is now committed to an active U.S. foreign policy, though it has placed more emphasis on the significance of Asia and less on that of Europe than has the Democratic Party. It is often regarded as the more right-wing of the two parties, though it has members who are more progressive in outlook than most members of the Democratic Party. The late Dwight D. Eisenhower, *q.v.*, was President from 1953 to 1961. His Vice-President, Richard Nixon, *q.v.*, became President in 1969 and was re-elected in 1972 for a second term. The party emblem is an elephant.

Reuther, Walter. A Vice-President of the American Federation of Labor and Congress of Industrial Organizations, *q.v.*, the combined trade-union organization formed in 1955, and in charge of its Industrial Union Department; born in 1908 in West Virginia, the grandson of a German immigrant and the son of a trade-union organizer. He left school at sixteen and became an apprentice machinist. He went to Detroit in 1927 where he worked for the Ford motor firm and at the same time attended a high school and Wayne University. He was dismissed after trying, against the firm's rules, to organize his fellow-workers, and spent his savings on a world tour during which he worked with other Americans for 16 months in a factory at Gorky in the U.S.S.R. However, he remained unsympathetic to American Communists whom he described as 'the colonial agents of a foreign power'. On his return to Detroit he improved the organization of the automobile workers in Michigan and ensured that their strikes were successful; he was attacked and beaten up by Ford's private police in 1937. In 1941 Ford at last agreed to negotiate with organized labour. Reuther became President of the Union of Automobile Workers in 1946 and of the Congress of Industrial Organizations in 1952.

Revisionism. A revised or modified form of Marxism, *q.v.* It differs from orthodox Marxist-Leninist doctrine in its assertion that the transition from capitalism to socialism need not be violent. It originated in Germany where its chief exponents, Edouard Bernstein and Karl Kautsky, argued that by allowing history to take its course, instead of initiating violent insurrection, a Marxist was demonstrating his fidelity to the Marxist contention that revolution was inevitable and that capitalism carried within itself the seed of its own decay. Lenin regarded Revisionism as 'a bourgeois corruption of the workers', and the theory has remained a heresy in the U.S.S.R.; in 1961 the Congress of Soviet Communist Parties reiterated Lenin's condemnation of Revisionism. The Russians have themselves been accused of Revisionism by the Communist Parties of China, Cuba and Albania.

Rhodesia. A self-governing state in central Africa, nominally under the jurisdiction of the British Crown, with Zambia (formerly Northern Rhodesia) to the north, Mozambique to the east, South Africa to the south, and Botswana to the west; area 150,820 sq. m.; population (1969 census) 5,090,000 Africans and 225,580 Europeans; capital

Salisbury The country, which was once controlled by the British South African Company, was granted limited powers of self-government by the U.K. in 1923; it was part of the Federation of Rhodesia and Nyasaland, *q.v.*, from 1953 to 1963.

The Constitution of 6 December 1961 introduced Africans into the legislature for the first time, 15 of the 65 seats being reserved for them. At elections held in December 1962 the Rhodesian Front, led by Winston Field, sympathizing with the policies of the South African government, won 35 seats. The opposition was then the United Federal Party (U.F.P.) led by Sir Edgar Whitehead who, as Prime Minister, had introduced the 1961 Constitution; it won 29 seats, returning 14 European, 14 African and 1 Coloured candidates, on a programme of repeal of the Land Tenure Act, which in 1931 divided the country into African and non-African areas. The main African parties, the African National Congress, the National Democratic Party and the Zimbabwe African People's Union (Z.A.P.U.), led by Joshua Nkomo, *q.v.*, had been banned in 1962. They instructed their followers to boycott the elections; the 14 African members of U.F.P. therefore represented only 2,500 African voters. Another African party, the Zimbabwe African National Union (Z.A.N.U.), founded in 1963 by former Z.A.P.U. members including the Rev. Ndabaningi Sithole, was also banned from political activity. The Rhodesian Front formed a government under the premiership of Winston Field; he resigned in April 1964 in favour of Ian Smith, *q.v.*

At elections in May 1965 the Rhodesian Front won all 50 European seats (including 22 which were unopposed) and did not contest the African seats. On 11 November 1965 the Rhodesian government made a unilateral declaration of independence (U.D.I.), *q.v.*; this was regarded as illegal by the U.K. which dismissed the government of Ian Smith by an Order in Council. It imposed restrictions on exports to Rhodesia, suspended all aid and Commonwealth preferential tariffs, and banned the import of Rhodesian tobacco, sugar and chrome. A resolution of the U.N. Security Council in April 1966 empowered the U.K. to employ any means to prevent the delivery of oil, destined for Rhodesia, to Beira in Mozambique. In December 1966 a further resolution of the Security Council called on all members of the U.N. to apply economic sanctions to the illegal regime; this was disregarded by South Africa, Portugal, West Germany, Japan and U.S.A., who were rebuked by the Commonwealth Sanctions Committee. Resort to sanctions followed the rejection by the Rhodesian cabinet of proposals for a constitutional settlement which had been agreed by the Prime Minister of the U.K. and Ian Smith aboard H.M.S. *Tiger*.

A second meeting in October 1968, aboard H.M.S. *Fearless*, between the two men produced further proposals for a settlement but no agreement, the U.K. refusing to recognize Rhodesian independence without first securing guarantees, entrenched in the Constitution, that rapid progress would be made towards African majority rule.

On 2 March 1970 the Smith government declared Rhodesia a republic and adopted a new Constitution. Elections held on 10 April 1971, but boycotted by most African voters, gave Smith an emphatic majority. In November 1971 the U.K. government (now led by Edward Heath, *q.v.*) made a new attempt to negotiate a settlement. The Smith government accepted proposals based on progress towards ending racial discrimination and unimpeded, if slow, extension of the franchise to all Africans; it also agreed to halt the eviction of Africans from areas delimited as European under the Land Tenure Act. A Commission under Lord Pearce toured Rhodesia to test African opinion and reported in May 1972 that the constitutional proposals were unacceptable to the majority. The U.K. then resumed sanctions. The Rhodesian regime is not recognized by any other government.

Rhodesia and Nyasaland. *See* Federation of Rhodesia and Nyasaland.

Rio de Oro. An area to the west of Morocco and on the Atlantic Ocean; it was a Spanish colony until on 14 January 1958 the Spanish government announced its amalgamation with Saguia el-Hamra (to the north, between Rio de Oro and Spanish Southern Morocco, *q.v.*) into the province of Spanish Sahara, *q.v.*

Rio Muni. An enclave on the mainland of West Africa between Cameroun and Gabon; area 10,000 sq. m.; population (1966) 200,000, mainly Bantu, of whom the majority are Fangs; capital Bata. It is one of the two provinces (the other is Fernando Póo, *q.v.*) which form Equatorial Guinea.

Rio Treaty. The Inter-American Treaty of Reciprocal Assistance, signed at Rio de Janeiro, Brazil, on 2 September 1947, by representatives of all the states of the western hemisphere except Canada, Ecuador, and Nicaragua. Under the Treaty every signatory has, when an aggression has been committed against any American state, the obligation to intervene. An armed attack against any one of the American states is considered to be an attack against all. The nature of the intervention required to bring the Treaty obligations into force is not clearly defined; nor, if a conference of American states is summoned, does a decision of such a conference (which must be passed by two-thirds of all the signatories) bind a state to use its armed forces without its consent. If U.S. forces, for example, are attacked in areas outside the security zone of the Americas (which stretches from the North Pole to the South Pole) the other American countries are not automatically involved.

Some Latin American states wished the Treaty to include 'economic aggression' as a type of aggression; others wanted the U.S.A. to make proposals similar to the Marshall Plan, *q.v.*, which had just been put to the European states. The Treaty, however, was eventually confined to military matters, the U.S.A. arguing that European needs were greater than those of Latin America and that the latter would benefit more from individual arrangements with each state. Detailed provisions for the peaceful settlement of disputes between American states were later agreed at the Conference of Bogota, 1948, which set up the Organization of American States, *q.v.* (*See* under this last heading a description of this first occasion on which an American republic received aid under the Rio Treaty to enable it to repel external aggression.)

Rippon, Geoffrey. British Conservative Party politician; born 28 May 1924; educated at King's College, Taunton and Brasenose College, Oxford. He was called to the Bar in 1948. He entered local politics as a member of the Surbiton Council in 1945, becoming Mayor of Surbiton in 1951 at the age of 26, and was a member of the London County Council from 1952 to 1961. In 1955 he was elected to the House of Commons as the member for Norwich South, and in 1959 he was appointed Parliamentary Secretary to the Ministry of Aviation, and in 1961 to the Ministry of Housing and Local Government. From 1962 to 1964 he was Minister of Public Building and Works, entering the Cabinet in October 1963. He lost his parliamentary seat at the 1964 election, but was returned for the constituency of Hexham in 1966. From 1964 to 1969 he was chairman of Cubitt Constructions Systems Ltd. He was also President of the British Section of the Council of European Municipalities and led the Conservative delegation to the Council of Europe and to Western European Union. In 1970 he was appointed Minister of Technology, but quickly succeeded Anthony Barber, *q.v.*, as Chancellor of the Duchy of Lancaster in which office he was responsible for negotiating the terms of British entry into the European Economic Community, *q.v.* In November 1972 he became Secretary of State for the Environment.

Romania (Rumania). An independent state on the Black Sea; area 91,600 sq. m.; population (1970) 20,252,541; capital Bucharest. It became independent as a result of the Treaty of Berlin, 1878, which united the Danubian principalities of Wallachia and Moldavia with part of southern Bessarabia and northern Dobrudja. In 1881 it became a kingdom under the family of Hohenzollern-Sigmaringen. After the

First World War Romania gained the rest of Bessarabia, *q.v.*, from the U.S.S.R., Transylvania and the Bukovina from the old Austro-Hungarian Empire, and southern Dobrudja from Bulgaria. Between 1919 and 1939 there was much social unrest, and at least six different dictatorships. Although there were rich resources of oil (of which one third was owned by British companies), grain and timber, large numbers of the agricultural population were ruined by the activities of money-lenders who encouraged over-production. Free elections were held, but governments frequently altered the electoral laws in their own favour. Strong links existed with Germany, Romania's principal customer, and there was considerable sympathy among the Romanian ruling classes for Nazi anti-semitic policies.

In 1940 the U.S.S.R. demanded the return of Bessarabia and northern Bukovina and these were given up; southern Dobrudja was returned to Bulgaria. In November 1946, after the Russian army reached Romania, a government was formed by the Communists, Liberals, Ploughmen's Front (a pro-Communist Peasant party), and Social Democrats, who were later absorbed by the Communists; it compelled King Michael to abdicate and proclaimed a 'People's Republic' on 30 December 1947. A Popular Democratic Front, which became the National Council of the Socialist Unity Front in 1965, comprising the Workers' (Communist) Party, the Ploughmen's Front, the National Popular Party, and the Hungarian Popular Union, won overwhelming majorities at elections held in 1952, 1961 and 1965 to the Grand National Assembly, which is elected for four years with one member for every 40,000 of the population. There is now complete Communist control. Russian troops were allowed to be stationed in Romania under the Romanian Peace Treaty, to maintain lines of communication between the U.S.S.R. and Austria; when the Russians left Austria these troops remained in Romania under the 1955 Eastern European Mutual Assistance Treaty (Warsaw Pact), *q.v.*, but by July 1958 they had withdrawn.

The economy, which was formerly based on agriculture, is now an industrial one and has the highest growth rate in Europe. Oil is the major product, though there are also resources of salt, coal, gold, iron, lignite, mica, copper, bauxite, chromium, manganese, silver and uranium. The petroleum industry produced 13,246,000 tons of crude oil in 1970 as compared with an annual pre-war output of 8,700,000 tons. Agricultural collectivization was completed by 1962; wine, timber and fruit are exported. Approximately 56 per cent of all external trade is with Comecon countries, but the proportion has been falling rapidly since 1960. Encouragement has been given to joint production schemes with west European firms, and to forging direct links between Romanian producers and foreign buyers. In 1967 visas were abolished to promote tourism and in November 1971 Romania joined G.A.T.T., *q.v.*

The leading figures in the Communist Party after the Second World War was Gheorghe Gheorghiu-Dej, First Secretary from 1945 to 1954 and from 1961 till his death in 1965, Prime Minister from 1952 to 1955, and President from 1961. His successor as First Secretary, in March 1965, was Nicolae Ceausescu. Ion Gheorghe Maurer became Prime Minister in March 1961; Chivu Stoica, a trade unionist who played an important part in the industrialization of Romania, and who was Prime Minister from 1955 to 1961, became President in March 1965. Romania refused to participate in August 1968 in the invasion of Czechoslovakia by the U.S.S.R. and four other Warsaw Pact countries.

Rome Treaties. Two agreements, signed in Rome on 25 March 1957 by the representatives of Belgium, France, the German Federal Republic, Italy, Luxemburg, and the Netherlands, and providing for the establishment of the European Atomic Energy Community, *q.v.*, and the European Economic Community, *q.v.*

Ruanda-Urundi. This was a trusteeship territory under Belgian administration until 1 July 1962, when its component parts became completely independent, as Burundi, *q.v.*, and Rwanda, *q.v.* The district is in east Africa, with Zaïre (the former Belgian Congo), Uganda, and Tanganyika to the west, north, and east respectively; area 20,916 sq. m.; population (1958) 4,689,065 natives, comprising the Hutu (83 per cent), Tutsi (15 per cent), and Batwa (2 per cent) tribes, 7,105 Europeans, and 2,320 Asians; capital Usumbura. The kingdoms of Ruanda (in the north) and Urundi (in the south) became part of German East Africa shortly before the First World War, but Belgian forces entered the area in 1917 and Belgium took over the administration, under a League of Nations mandate, in 1923; the area became a trusteeship territory after the Second World War, when the United Nations succeeded the League of Nations and, on 13 December 1946, the trusteeship agreement was approved by the United Nations General Assembly. The territory was united economically and administered with the Belgian Congo until the latter became independent in 1960. In September 1961 the Tutsi King of Ruanda, Kigeli V, was removed peacefully by means of a referendum supervised by the United Nations. Independence for both territories followed on 1 July 1962.

Rumania. *See* Romania.

Russia. The name often used to describe the Union of Soviet Socialist Republics, *q.v.*, but also used with reference to the Russian Soviet Federal Socialist Republic (R.S.F.S.R.), which is the largest of the fifteen constituent Republics.

Rwanda. An independent republic in the centre of Africa, bounded by Uganda to the north, Tanzania to the east, Burundi to the south, and Zaïre (formerly Belgian Congo) to the west; area 10,166 sq. m.; population (1969) 3,667,000 and largely Roman Catholic; they are mostly Hutu, or Bahutu (85 per cent and Bantu) and Tutsi or Batutsi (traditional rulers, cattle-owners, and Nilotic); capital Kigali.

As a kingdom, the country was formerly part of the trusteeship territory of Ruanda-Urundi, *q.v.* The Tutsi monarchy was, as the result of a referendum in September 1961, abolished on 2 October 1961 and Rwanda became an independent republic on 1 July 1962. Tribal strife between the Hutu and their former Tutsi overlords in 1963 caused large-scale emigration to neighbouring states. Grégoire Kayibanda, leader of the Bahutu-supported Parmehutu Party (who had become Prime Minister in January 1961), took office as President when independence was declared; he was re-elected in 1965 and 1969. There are few natural resources and agriculture and cattle-breeding are the main sources of income.

Ryuku Islands. A group 500 miles to the south-west of Japan, nominally belonging to Japan but controlled by the U.S.A. from 1945 to 1971. A substantial U.S. military presence remains in Okinawa, *q.v.*

S

Saarland. A highly industrialized area of 800 sq. m. on the river Saar; population (1970) 1,127,000; capital Saarbrücken. In language and habits the people are German; the territory became a *Land* of the German Federal Republic on 1 January 1957. The area is part of the Middle Kingdom between France and Germany which was set up in A.D. 843 when Charlemagne's domains were divided among his three grandsons. It was ruled by France in Napoleon's day, but in 1815 most of it, including Saarbrücken, was included in the new Prussian province of the Rhineland. After the First World War it was placed under the control of the League of Nations, which permitted it to be administered by France for a fifteen-year period. At the end of that time a plebiscite was to decide whether the inhabitants wished to belong to France or Germany. They decided in 1935 to be reincorporated in Germany.

In 1945 it was occupied by the French; the Constitution of 8 November 1947 provided for economic union with France, and made defence and foreign relations French responsibilities. On 23 October 1954 France and the German Federal Republic agreed (1) that the economic and customs union should be maintained, (2) that the Saar should continue to have internal autonomy, (3) that a High Commissioner appointed by the Western European Union, *q.v.*, should represent the Saar in matters of foreign affairs and defence, and (4) that a referendum should be held on this proposed arrangement. This plan did not contemplate the economic Europeanization of the Saar, which had been recommended by the Council of Europe's Committee on General Affairs. The Committee's solution stressed that the Saar is part of the coal and steel community which covers Belgium, Luxemburg, the Ruhr, and eastern France.

By the referendum held on 23 October 1955 a majority of more than two to one of the electorate rejected the Franco-German plan. By agreement in 1956 between France and the German Federal Republic, the Saar (1) became a German *Land* on 1 January 1957; (2) was economically integrated with the German Federal Republic by stages, by 5 July 1959; and (3) has a special economic status in order to maintain Franco-Saar commercial exchanges on a high level.

Sabah. One of the three constituent parts of the Federation of Malaysia, *q.v.*, it is in the northern part of the island of Borneo, *q.v.*; area 29,388 sq. m.; population (1970) 655,622; capital Jesselton. The territory once belonged to the Philippine Sultan of Sulu, and others, who ceded control in 1878 to British commercial interests. The Philippines have claimed the area, arguing that the transaction was a lease. As a British protected state the territory was administered by the British North Borneo Company under royal charter from 1881 to 1946, when it became a colony. On 16 September 1963 British North Borneo became known as the State of Sabah and became part of the Federation of Malaysia, which was established on that day. The main exports are timber, rubber and copra.

Sadat, Anwar. Egyptian political leader; born 1918 in a village in the Nile delta, the son of a hospital clerk, and educated at religious and secondary schools and at the Cairo Military Academy where he first met Gamal Abdel Nasser, *q.v.* As an active nationalist, and a bitter opponent of the British protectorate, he joined the Free Officers' Movement which deposed King Farouk in 1952. He became Minister of State after the revolution and later edited the newspapers *Al Jumhuriya* and, from 1955–6, *Al Tahrir*. From 1957 to 1961 he was General Secretary of the Egyptian National Union (the predecessor of the Arab Socialist Union) and, as a former General Secretary of the Islamic Congress, presided over the Afro-Asian Conference held in Cairo in 1958. He was Speaker of the National Assembly from 1961 to 1969, and a member of the Presidential Council from 1962 until 1964 when he was appointed Vice-President of the United Arab Republic, *q.v.*, until 1967. He was re-appointed Vice-President in December 1969 and, on the death of Nasser on 28 September 1970, became interim President as required under the Constitution. He succeeded to the Presidency by the unanimous choice of the National Assembly, which was endorsed on 16 October 1970 by a national referendum in which he received 90·4 per cent of the votes cast. He was formally sworn in as President of Egypt on 17 October for a six-year term. Like Nasser he is politically left of centre and uncompromising in his hostility to Israel; but, although acknowledging the value of the support of the U.S.S.R. for the Arab cause, he adheres to a policy of non-alignment, and in 1972 expelled the Russian military presence from Egypt.

Sahel-Bénin Union. An association set up in 1959 by the states of Dahomey, Ivory Coast, Niger, and Upper Volta, all of which were once part of French West Africa. It is now more often known by the name of its supreme organ, the Conseil de l'Entente (*see* Entente, Council of the).

Salazar, Dr António de Oliveira. Portuguese Prime Minister; born 28 April 1889 at Santa Comba, the son of a poor smallholder. He studied law and economics at the University of Coimbra, where he became

Professor of Economics in 1918. After the military *coup d'état* of 28 May 1926 he was appointed Minister of Finance but resigned after a few days. He was recalled in the same capacity in 1928, reorganized the Portuguese budget, was offered the Premiership in 1932 and held it for 36 years, becoming virtually dictator of Portugal. Salazar is probably the only European dictator who came to power not by struggle but by invitation. He set out to rebuild Portugal on the lines of what he termed the 'Estado Novo', the New State. He drafted a new Constitution, authoritarian and corporate; it was accepted by plebiscite in 1933. He then carried out a programme of reforms, including the improvement of living conditions, industrial development, public works, and education. After he came to power he organized the União Naçional (the only authorized political movement in Portugal), the Portuguese Legion, and the Youth Movement. His administration was Fascist in character, both in concept and in execution. On 16 September 1968, as a result of serious physical incapacity, he was released from the Premiership on the prerogative of the President. He died on 27 July 1970. He was succeeded by Dr Marcelo Caetano, *q.v.*

S.A.L.T. Strategic Arms Limitation Talks, *q.v.*

Salvador, *or* **El Salvador.** An independent Central American state on the Pacific Ocean; area 8,236 sq. m., mostly mountainous; population (1971) 3,774,000, mainly illiterate, Spanish-speaking and Roman Catholic; capital El Salvador. It was ruled by Spain from the sixteenth century to 1821 in which year it became part of the Federation of Central American States; it has been independent since 1839. Under a Constitution adopted in 1950 which introduced universal suffrage, the President is elected for six years and the Legislative Assembly for two. In October 1960 the President, Lt-Colonel José Maria Lemus, was deposed as the result of a bloodless *coup d'état*; he was exiled and replaced by an army junta, which was itself supplanted by another junta in January 1961. A member of the second junta, Lt-Colonel Julio Adalberto Rivera, was elected, unopposed, to the Presidency on 1 July 1962. He was succeeded by Colonel Fidel Sánchez Hernández, Minister of the Interior, who contested elections held on 5 March 1967 as the candidate of the governing Party of National Conciliation (P.C.N.). He was, in turn, succeeded by Colonel Arturo Armando Molina (P.C.N.) who won the presidential elections held on 20 February 1972. As he failed to gain an absolute majority over his Christian Democrat opponent, his election was subject to approval by Congress, in which the P.C.N. had gained 36 of the 53 seats in the congressional elections of March 1970. He took office on 1 July 1972.

Coffee accounts for more than 50 per cent of the value of Salvador's exports, which also include cane sugar, cotton, and sisal; nearly half are sold to the U.S.A. The country is so densely populated that there is continuous emigration to neighbouring states.

Samoa. *See* American Samoa *and* Western Samoa.

San Francisco Conference. A meeting of delegates from 50 nations held at San Francisco, California, U.S.A., from 25 April to 26 June 1945, which drafted the Charter of the United Nations, *q.v.*, and the Statute of the International Court of Justice, *q.v.*

San Marino. Officially the Most Serene Republic of San Marino. An independent state in Italy, in the hills near the Adriatic Sea; area 23·8 sq. m.; population (1971 estimate) 20,000; capital San Marino. It was founded in the fourth century and subsequently resisted all Papal claims; its present-day independence is guaranteed by a treaty, signed on 29 April 1963, with Italy, with whom there has been a customs union since 1862.

The state is ruled by a Congress of 10 members, two of whom are elected as regents for six months and are thereafter ineligible for office for three years. The legislature consists of a Great and General Council of 60 members elected for five years by universal suffrage, although women, who have had the vote since 1960, may not stand for election. Results in the election of September 1969 were: Christian Democrats 27 seats (29 in 1964); Democratic Socialists 11 (10); left-wing Socialists 7 (7); Communists 14 (14). Government until 1957 was by a coalition of Communists and left-wing Socialists, who had been in office since 1943. Defections from these two parties enabled the Christian Democrats to come to power in coalition with the Democratic Socialists.

San Marino produces ceramics, cereals, cheese, textiles, olive oil, wine and varnishes, and also rears cattle; carved stone and white and hydrated lime are exported. Further revenue is obtained from the licences granted to companies which register there to avoid foreign taxes, from the tourist trade, from picturesque postage stamps, and from an Italian government grant.

Saragat, Giuseppe. President of Italy; born 1898 in Turin. He took a degree in economics, entered journalism and in 1922 joined the Socialist Party. He lived abroad while Italy was ruled by Mussolini but returned in 1943 and resumed his political career, becoming Minister without Portfolio in the first Bononi Government in 1944. He was President of the Constituent Assembly in 1946 and the following year went to Paris as ambassador. But, dissatisfied with the close ties then existing between the Socialist Party under Nenni and the Communist Party under Togliatti, he broke away from Nenni and, in 1947, founded the Italian Social Democratic Party which he led until it was re-united with the Italian Socialist Party in October 1966, and which participated in a number of government coalitions. He was deputy-premier in the government of de Gasperi from 1947–9, and again in the Scelba administration from 1954–7. In 1963 he held the Ministry of Foreign Affairs in the Moro government. He was elected to succeed President Segni in December 1964, on the twenty-first ballot, and became Italy's fifth post-war President and its first Social Democratic head of state. His election was due to the determination of the secular coalition parties to avoid the continuing domination of Italian politics by the Christian Democrats, who had provided the two previous Presidents.

Sarawak. In north-west Borneo, *q.v.*, it is one of the three territories (the others are Malaya and Sabah) of the Federation of Malaysia, *q.v.*; area 48,250 sq. m.; population (1970) 977,013, including Sea Dayaks, Chinese, Malays, Land Dayaks, and Kayans; capital Kuching. For over one hundred years it was ruled by the Brooke family, known as the White Rajahs, after the Sultan of Brunei had granted governmental powers to Sir James Brooke in 1841. From 1888 onwards Sarawak was a British-protected state, but it was ceded to the U.K. by the Rajah on 1 July 1946.

In July 1963 the U.K., Malaya, and Singapore agreed that Malaya, Sabah (formerly British North Borneo), Singapore and Sarawak should merge to form Malaysia, an independent country within the British Commonwealth; the Federation, from which Singapore seceded in 1965, was inaugurated on 16 September 1963. Sarawak, which has many navigable rivers, produces rubber, timber, sago, oil, rice, pepper, gold and bauxite. Sporadic fighting occurred with Indonesian forces based in Kalimantan (the Indonesian part of Borneo) from 1963 to 1966, while the Indonesian government pursued a policy of confrontation, *q.v.*, against Malaysia.

Satyagraha. A Sanskrit expression meaning 'faithful obstinacy' used to describe non-violent resistance to authority in India. It was practised by followers of Mahatma Gandhi against police and soldiers before the end of British rule in India, and by opponents of Portuguese rule in Goa.

Saudi Arabia. An independent state occupying most of Arabia; area 927,000 sq. m.; population about six million; capitals Mecca and Riyadh. It comprises the Hejaz (an area of 112,500 sq. m. with a coastline of 800 miles on the Red Sea, and the towns of Jedda and Mecca), Nejd, which means 'plateau' (an area of 800,000 sq. m. to the east and south of the Hejaz), and Azir, on the Red Sea coast between the Hejaz and Yemen. These three areas were unified to form the Saudi Arabian Kingdom by Ibn Saud (1880–1953) whose family had once ruled Nejd but had been deposed. The U.K. recognized by treaty the complete independence of the Kingdom in 1932.

The major source of revenue was once the tax imposed upon the Moslem pilgrims to Mecca, the holy city, but the discovery in 1936 of oil at Dammam, in Nejd, transformed the economy. The main concession was granted under agreements in 1933 and 1939 to the Arabian American Oil Company (Aramco), which is controlled by the Standard Oil Co.s of California and New Jersey, the Texas Co., and the Socony Mobil Oil Co. Aramco, whose most important oilfields are at Abqaiq, Ain Dar, and Dammam, has had its head office at Dharhan since 1953, and is the only major oil company with headquarters in the Middle East. The oil reserves are among the highest in the world, and the revenues from them represent 85 per cent of the national income of Saudi Arabia. In 1970 the income tax rate on the company was increased to 55 per cent. Aramco was the first oil company in the Middle East to concede a fifty-fifty division of profit between company and government.

Apart from the oilfields the country is still undeveloped, although 35 per cent of government expenditure is allocated to development projects. A substantial amount is spent on subsidies for tribes in the interior and on the 325 Saudi Arabian princes of the realm. Aramco has set up an Arab Industrial Development Division to promote the growth of light industries. Both natives and foreigners enjoy the benefits of a free medical service. In May 1958 King Saud (who came to the throne on the death of his father, Ibn Saud, in 1953, being the eldest of his 33 sons) introduced the cabinet system temporarily until December 1960, when he relieved his brother, Prince Faisal, of the office of Prime Minister, and assumed the task himself. Faisal became Deputy Prime Minister in March 1962, presiding over the cabinet even when the King was present, and Prime Minister again in October 1962. He came to the throne on 2 November 1964 when the Council of Ministers and the Consultative Assembly deposed Saud.

Egyptian intervention in the Yemen Arab Republic, q.v., led King Saud to support the deposed Imam, and from 1962 until 1964 diplomatic relations between Saudi Arabia and Egypt were broken off. However in June 1967 Saudi Arabia gave military assistance to the Arab states at war with Israel, and in September 1967 established, with Kuwait and Libya, the Arab Economic Development Fund to compensate Jordan and Egypt for the economic losses incurred by the Israeli occupation of the west bank of the Jordan and the closure of the Suez Canal, *q.v.*, Saudi Arabia's contribution to the Fund is £50 million annually; this was withheld in 1970 when Syria, *q.v.*, refused to allow the repair of the oil pipeline (Tapline) from Saudi Arabia to Sidon, with the consequent decline in revenue from the export of crude oil.

Schleswig-Holstein. A province in the northern part of the German Federal Republic; area about 6,125 sq. m.; population (1969) 2,557,000; approximately 40,000 being of Danish extraction; capital Kiel. Schleswig and Holstein were taken from Denmark by Prussia in 1864. The Danes in North Schleswig asked to be returned to Denmark, and in 1920 a plebiscite was held (under the Versailles Treaty) which resulted in their demands being fulfilled. The Danes have since renamed the area South Jutland. South Jutland includes a racially conscious German minority of 9,700 which returns one member (of the Slesvig Party) to the Danish parliament.

In South Schleswig, which had since 1920 remained a part of the German province of Schleswig-Holstein, differences emerged after the Second World War. The Danish voters were deprived of all their four seats in the Landtag (provincial parliament) in 1954 by an electoral law which required a party to obtain 5 per cent of the aggregate vote before it was entitled to a seat. Under a Danish-German agreement in 1955 the Schleswig-Holstein government supported modification of the electoral law to give Danes in South Schleswig representation similar to that enjoyed by the Germans in North Schleswig. Both governments agreed to give equal status to minority schools. Danish extremists demanded administrative separation of South Schleswig from Holstein and eventual self-determination for South Schleswig.

Schroder, Gerhard. West German politician; born 11 September 1910 in Saarbrücken, the son of a Friesian railway official; educated at Berlin and Bonn Universities, and studied history and law; he also spent two terms at Edinburgh University, studying international law, and obtained a doctorate from Cologne University. Before the Second World War he was a junior lecturer at Bonn University and joined the Nazi Party, which he left in 1941 after marrying the partly Jewish daughter of a Berlin banker. He joined the Confessional Church (led by Dr Martin Niemoller) at the time. During the war he was a corporal in the army and served in Russia, where he was wounded. After the war he was first in local government service in North Rhine-Westphalia, then in the legal profession in Düsseldorf-Mettman and in business in the Ruhr iron and steel industry; he then entered the Bundestag as a Christian Democratic

Union member for Düsseldorf in 1949. He became Minister of the Interior in 1953, Foreign Minister in November 1961, and Minister of Defence from 1966 to 1969.

S.E.A.T.O. The organization of the South-East Asia Collective Defence Treaty, *q.v.*

Secession. Formal withdrawal from an organization, such as a party, church, or state. A secession from a state is often preceded by a revolt. The fourteen colonies seceded from Great Britain and became the U.S.A. in 1776, the former Spanish South American states seceded from Spain in 1810, Brazil from Portugal in 1822, Greece from Turkey in 1830, Cuba from Spain in 1898, and Panama from Colombia in 1903.

Security Council of the United Nations. Consists of 15 members (including China, France, the U.K., the U.S.A., and the U.S.S.R. as permanent members) and has the primary responsibility for the maintenance of international peace and security. The 10 non-permanent members are each elected for a two-year term. The members of the United Nations agree, under the United Nations Charter, to accept and carry out the decisions of the Council. On procedural matters its decisions are made by an affirmative vote of any nine members, but on substantive matters the nine must include the concurring votes of the five permanent members. This is the device known as the 'veto', *q.v.*, which the U.K., the U.S.A., and the U.S.S.R. accepted in the Yalta Agreement, *q.v.*, in February 1945. When measures for the peaceful settlement of a dispute are being discussed a party to the dispute must abstain from voting.

The Security Council determines the existence of any threat to the peace, breach of the peace, or act of aggression. It makes recommendations or decides to take enforcement measures to maintain or restore international peace and security. It may take enforcement measures by calling on members either to apply measures not involving the use of armed forces (*e.g.* interruption of economic relations and of means of communication) or to provide air, sea, or land forces to deal with the offending nation. Member states can defend themselves, either individually or acting together, until the Security Council takes action.

Various commissions and committees have been set up by the Security Council from time to time, such as the standing committee on the Admission of New Members, and the United Nations Truce Supervision Organization in Palestine.

Segregation. Setting apart; a term used with special reference to the political and social disabilities of Negroes in the U.S.A. The Four-

411

teenth Amendment to the U.S. Constitution, passed in 1868, provided that no state should make or enforce any law abridging the privileges or immunities of citizens, and that no state should deprive any person of life, liberty, or property without due process of law. In 1896 the Supreme Court, dealing with a Louisianan law relating to railway accommodation, held that it could not say that such a law, whether authorizing or even requiring the separation of the two races in public conveyances, was unreasonable. In decisions made in 1954 and 1955, however, the Supreme Court held that in the field of public education the doctrine of 'separate but equal' had no place. It approved of the judgement of a Kansas court in which it was stated: 'Segregation with the sanction of law has a tendency to retard the educational and mental development of Negro children and to deprive them of some of the benefits they would receive in a racially integrated school system.' The Supreme Court added that solutions to local problems should be worked out 'with all deliberate speed', but in 1963 it qualified this approach, saying that it was never contemplated that the concept of 'deliberate speed' should permit indefinite delay in the elimination of racial barriers in schools.

The steps taken to end segregation (known as 'desegregation') have been taken largely by governmental Executive Orders as opposed to legislation. Thus President Truman forbade discrimination in the armed forces (1948); President Eisenhower sent federal troops to protect negro children going to the Central High School at Little Rock, Arkansas (1957); and President Kennedy sent federal troops to ensure that negro undergraduates could attend the University of Mississippi (1962).

It is arguable how far the above-mentioned judgements and governmental measures were primarily responsible for the growth of desegregation. Other factors which have affected the situation include the growing purchasing power of the Negroes and their increased racial consciousness, which results partly from their awareness of the growing number of independent African nations. This growing confidence has been reflected in measures designed to end segregation, ranging from boycotting of segregated public transport and 'sit-ins' at segregated lunch counters, to Freedom Rides to test desegregation of inter-state bus terminals and marches to dramatize Negro voter registration. In these activities the organizing bodies have included the National Association for the Advancement of Colored People (N.A.A.C.P.), *q.v.*, the Southern Christian Leadership Conference, the Students' Non-Violent Co-ordinating Committee, and the Congress on Racial Equality (C.O.R.E.). *See also* Civil Rights.

Sekou Touré, Ahmed. President of Guinea; born 1922 at Faranah into a family of Moslem peasant farmers (his father was a Soussou and his mother a Malinké); he claims as his grandfather the legendary national figure of Almamy Samoury who defended Guinea against the French. He was educated at a primary school in Koranic and at the French Technical School in Conakry from which he was expelled in 1937 for leading a food strike. He became a clerk in the firm of Niger Français and in 1941 went into the Posts and Telecommunications Service of French Guinea. He was active in his trade union organization, the Union of Post, Telephone and Telecommunication Workers, and was soon appointed its General Secretary. He took part in the formation in 1946 of the Rassemblement Démocratique Africain (R.D.A.) and in 1948 was appointed General Secretary of the National Confederation of Communist Trade Unions (Union Territoriale de la C.G.T.). Four years later he created one of the most effective political organizations in West Africa, the Marxist Guinea Democratic Party, of which he was Secretary, and in 1956 he was acknowledged as a political trade-unionist of international standing by his appointment as President of the General Confederation of African Workers. In the same year he was elected Mayor of Conakry and he represented Guinea in the French National Assembly. In 1957 he became Vice-President of the Council of Government of Guinea and Prime Minister in the territorial assembly. When Guinea declared its independence of France by referendum in 1958 he was elected, unopposed, as first President of the republic of Guinea; he was re-elected in 1961, 1963 and 1968, when he received 99·9 per cent of the votes cast. He has pursued a consistently neutralist foreign policy, but remains a determined Pan-Africanist and supporter of the Organization of African Unity, *q.v.*

Senate. The upper house of a bicameral legislature. The most important Senate, which is the upper house of Congress, *q.v.*, is that of the U.S.A. It has 100 members (2 from each of the 50 States, irrespective of the size of their populations) elected by popular vote for six-year terms, one third standing for election every two years. A member must be at least 30 years of age, must have been a citizen of the U.S.A. for nine years, and must be a resident of the State which he represents. A vacancy is usually filled by a temporary appointment by the Governor of the State in question. The Vice-President of the U.S.A. is *ex officio* President of the Senate. Treaties made on behalf of the U.S.A. with other countries must be ratified by a two-thirds majority of the Senate.

Senegal. An independent republic; area 77,814 sq. m.; population

(1971) 4,154,000, comprising Ouolofs (approximately 720,000, mostly Moslems), Bambaras, Peulh, Toucouleurs, and some 80,000 refugees from Portuguese Guinea; capital Dakar, the former capital of French West Africa, *q.v.* The country is on the west coast of Africa, with Mauritania and Portuguese Guinea to the north and south respectively, and Mali to the east; it completely surrounds (except for a narrow strip of Gambian coast) Gambia. It became French in 1840, when it consisted of a number of sultanates and territories controlled by chiefs; it later became one of the eight territories comprising French West Africa, and it achieved self-government within the French Community, *q.v.*, on 25 November 1958. On 4 April 1959 it entered into a federal union with the Soudanese Republic, known as the Mali Federation, *q.v.*, which itself achieved complete independence, still within the Community, on 20 June 1960. Senegal seceded from the Federation on 20 August 1960.

Legislative powers are vested in an assembly of 60 members elected by universal suffrage. At the elections held on 22 March 1959 all the seats were won by the Senegalese Progressive Union (U.P.S.). The other main parties contesting the elections were the African Regroupment Party (led by Abdoulaye Ly) which was opposed to any participation by Senegal in the French Community, and the Senegalese Solidarity Party, led by Ibrahim Seydou N'Daw. In December 1962 Mamadou Dia (leader of the African Federalist Party), the Prime Minister, was arrested when he used illegal means to try to prevent the assembly from passing a vote of censure on him. The President of the Republic, Leopold Sédar Senghor, was then unanimously voted chief executive by the assembly. According to the 1963 Constitution executive power is exercised by the President of the Council, who is invested by an absolute majority of the Assembly. In May 1963 Dia was sentenced to detention for life.

The principal exports are groundnuts, groundnut oil, phosphates and oilcake, while millet, maize, and rice are cultivated. The economy is predominantly agricultural. Nearly all the foreign trade of Mali and Mauritania passes through the port of Dakar. Strained relations between Senegal and Guinea caused the dissolution in 1971 of the Organization of Riparian States which had been set up with Mali and Mauritania to develop the Senegal River valley and to build a dam at Joina, in Mali, to provide hydro-electricity and irrigation for all four states. In March 1972 Senegal, Mali and Mauritania formed a new Organization for the Development of the Senegal River.

Separation of Powers. The custom, common in democratic countries, of dividing the powers of government into three – legislative, executive, and judicial. It implies that none of these three powers is able to control or interfere with the others (*e.g.* that judges should be independent of the executive), or that the same individuals should not hold posts in more than one of the three branches (*e.g.* that civil servants should not sit in Parliament), or that one branch of government should not exercise the functions of another (*e.g.* that ministers should not be allowed to make laws). The principle was outlined in the eighteenth century by the French writer, Montesquieu, who stated that the stability of English government was due to the separation of powers. In its first sense, that the powers should not control each other, it was rigidly applied in the Constitution of the U.S.A., where executive power is vested in the President whose departmental heads are responsible to him and not to Congress. In the U.K., however, the executive gradually became directly responsible to the legislature; the judiciary is still independent of the executive, but it must obey the laws passed by the legislature, although there can be no interference by Parliament with its day-to-day activities.

Separatism. A belief that a particular group or area should be separated from the larger organization of which it forms a part. It is applied to political movements which advocate independence; for example, those in Quebec who wish to sever all ties with the rest of Canada are separatists.

Servan-Schreiber, Jean-Jacques. French Radical politician and journalist; born 13 February 1924 and educated at the École Polytechnique. He trained in the U.S. Air Force during the Second World War, joining the Free French forces of General de Gaulle, *q.v.*, as a fighter pilot in 1943. He was diplomatic editor of *Le Monde* from 1948 to 1951 and founded the radical newspaper, *L'Express*, in 1953. In 1957 he published *Lieutenant in Algeria* in which he exposed the tortures practised on the Algerian insurgents by French troops. He remained as Director of *L'Express* until 1969 when he entered national politics, becoming the Deputy for Nancy in 1970. He organized the Social-Radical Party, of which he was General Secretary from 1969 to 1971, from which political base he challenged the regional policies of the first Pompidou government by contesting the by-election in Bordeaux in September 1970, caused by the death of the substitute member, in which the Prime Minister, Jacques Chaban-Delmas, *q.v.*, defended his parliamentary seat. He failed in his aim of forcing the election to a second ballot, polling only 16·59 per cent of the votes, but demonstrated that the Radical centre parties, who supported him, were stronger electorally than the divided left. As a result of his intervention and pungent criticism of Socialist policy he was expelled from the Socialist parliamentary group; 11 of the 13 other Radical deputies announced their resignation with him, and sat as '*non-inscrits*'.

Shastri, Lal Bahadur. Indian politician; born 4 October 1904 into a poor Kayasth family near Benares; went to the special university provided for student supporters of Gandhi at Varanasi, where he studied philosophy and graduated with the degree of 'Shastri'. He entered politics in Allahabad, home of the Nehru family, and became president of the district Congress Committee. Between 1930 and 1942 he took part in all the civil disobedience campaigns organized by the Indian National Congress (*see* Congress Party), spending a total of nine years in prison. In 1937 he was elected to the United Provinces Legislative Assembly and he became a leading figure in state politics. He was chosen by Nehru to succeed him as General Secretary of the Indian National Congress. He was elected to the Council of States in 1952 and immediately took office as Minister of Transport and Railways, a post which he resigned in 1956 after accepting personal responsibility for a serious railway accident. The following year he took a seat in the Lok Sabha, was re-appointed Minister of Transport and of Communications, moved to the Ministry of Commerce and Industry in 1958, and in 1961 succeeded Pandit Pant (his former chief minister in the United Provinces, which became Uttar Pradesh in 1947) as Minister for Home Affairs. He was responsible for the introduction of the law against separatism and caste, religious and language discrimination. In the 1962 general election he was the chief organizer of the Congress Party campaign and he spent most of the following year, after his resignation from the cabinet under the Kamaraj Plan, revitalizing the Party and canvassing for personal support. When Nehru fell ill he was brought back into the government as Minister without Portfolio, and then as deputy premier. On the death of Nehru in May 1964 he survived a challenge from the right wing of Congress for the leadership and was sworn in as Prime Minister the following month. The food crisis of 1964–5, his refusal to commit India to the development of nuclear armaments, and especially his policy of cordiality towards Pakistan over Kashmir, *q.v.*, made him unpopular; he died on 11 January 1966, and was succeeded by Indira Gandhi, *q.v.*

Short, Edward Watson. British Labour Party politician; born 17 December 1912 and educated at Bede College, Durham. After serving in the Second World War as a Captain in the Durham Light Infantry he resumed an interrupted career in education, taking up an appointment as Headmaster of Princess Louise County Secondary School, Blyth, in 1947. He entered local politics, becoming leader of the

Labour Group on the Newcastle City Council in 1950, and the following year he was elected to the House of Commons as the member for Newcastle on Tyne. From 1955 to 1962 he was an Opposition Whip, becoming Deputy Chief Opposition Whip in 1962. He was appointed Parliamentary Secretary to the Treasury and Government Chief Whip in 1964, Postmaster-General in 1966 and Secretary of State at the Department of Education and Science in April 1968, which post he retained until the general election of June 1970. On the resignation of Roy Jenkins, *q.v.*, from the Deputy Leadership of the Parliamentary Labour Party, he was elected to replace him, defeating Michael Foot on the second ballot by 145 votes to 116.

Shriver, Robert Sargent. U.S. Democratic Party politician; born 9 November 1915 at Westminster, Maryland; a Roman Catholic, and educated at Canterbury School and Yale University where he graduated in law. In 1941 he was admitted to the New York Bar, but after serving as a Lieutenant-Commander in the U.S. Naval Reserve from 1940–45 he went into journalism, becoming an associate editor of *Newsweek* in 1945–6. In 1948 he was appointed Assistant General Manager of the Merchandise Mart of Chicago where, from 1955 to 1960, he was President of the Board of Education. He relinquished his business appointment in 1961 to become director of the Peace Corps, the organization founded by his brother-in-law, President John Kennedy, *q.v.*, through which American youth was enabled to assist underdeveloped countries. From 1964 to 1968 he acted as Special Assistant to the President as Director of the Office of Economic Opportunity. From 1968 to 1970 he was U.S. Ambassador to France. He was selected, as the seventh choice of George McGovern, *q.v.*, to run as the Democratic Vice-Presidential candidate in the elections of November 1972.

Siam. An independent state in south-east Asia known since 1949 as Thailand, *q.v.*

Sib, Treaty of. An agreement signed in 1920 by the Sultan of Muscat and Oman, *q.v.*, and a group of sheikhs from the interior of Oman. The Sultan had exercised authority over Oman for over 200 years and, as Imam, had also been a spiritual functionary. The latter office was in abeyance for over 100 years until, in 1913, the tribes in Oman elected an Imam. The Treaty, of which few details have been published, stated that the Sultan was not to interfere in the internal affairs of the Omanis. The Imam Ghalib bin Ali (in exile in Saudi Arabia since 1957) claimed that the Treaty recognized that Oman was an independent sovereign state, and issued Omani passports. He also alleged that the oil concession granted in 1937 by the Sultan to a subsidiary of the Iraq Petroleum Company, and purporting to give rights to the Company over Oman, was a breach of the Treaty, as the Imam and the Omanis were not consulted. In December 1955 the Sultan led an expedition against Nizwa, in central Oman, as a result of which the Imam and his supporters were temporarily dispersed. Another rising in Oman in July 1957 was suppressed with the aid of British forces.

Sierra Leone. An independent republic and member of the British Commonwealth, on the west coast of Africa, bounded by Guinea to the north-west, north and north-east, and Liberia to the south-east; area 27,925 sq. m.; population (1970 estimate) 2,500,000; capital Freetown.

In 1787 land was sold by African chiefs to English settlers to provide an asylum for the many destitute Negroes then in England. Later the colony, as it became, was used as a settlement for Africans from North America and the West Indies, and especially for those rescued from slave ships. The country became a fully independent state on 27 April 1961. The first Prime Minister was Sir Milton Margai, whose party, the Sierra Leone People's Party, and its allies, won the most seats (28 out of 62) at elections for the House of Representatives held in May 1962. The chief opposition party, the All-People's Congress, led by Siaka Stevens, won 20 seats. On his death in May 1964 Margai was succeeded by his brother, Dr Albert Margai. Further elections were held in March 1967, but before the results were announced a military junta, led by the Commander-in-Chief of the Army, Brigadier Andrew Juxon-Smith, seized power. The Constitution was suspended, the House of Representatives dissolved, the Governor-General placed under house-arrest and the political leaders imprisoned. On 18 April 1968 the junta was ousted by a group of non-commissioned officers; Margai and Stevens were immediately released. A Commission of Inquiry into allegations of corrupt practices at the 1967 elections ruled that the All-People's Congress had won the elections, gaining 32 out of 66 seats. Stevens returned from exile in Guinea on 26 April 1968 to form a civilian government. He survived an attempt by the Army Commander, Brigadier Bangura, who had restored him to power in 1968, to oust him in March 1971 by calling in troops from Guinea, with which country he had previously concluded a defence agreement. On 19 April 1971 the House of Assembly approved a new Constitution and Sierra Leone was declared a republic with Stevens as the first President.

Tropical crops, such as cocoa, coffee, ginger, groundnuts, kola nuts, piassava, palm-kernels and palm-oil, and rice are produced, but the principal export is diamonds. Since 1965 Sierra Leone has been party to a Free Trade Agreement with Guinea, Ivory Coast, and Liberia.

Sikkim. An Indian protectorate to the east of Nepal and to the south of Tibet; area 2,664 sq. m.; population (1970 estimate) 194,000; comprising Nepalese (about 75 per cent); Lepchas, the original inhabitants; and Bhutias or Bothias, originating from Bhutan and Tibet; capital Gangtok. The relationship with India is governed by a treaty concluded on 5 December 1950, by which India was given special responsibility for communications, defence, and foreign affairs. The protectorate produces corn, millet, cardamom, rice, potatoes, apples and oranges. The ruler (His Highness Maharaja Gyalsay Palden Thondup Namgyal, born 1923, succeeded in 1963) governs with the assistance of a State Council of which 14 out of the 20 members are elected. China has claimed that Sikkim, with Bhutan (to the east), and Ladakh (part of Kashmir) are part of Tibet and thus part of China; it does not recognize the treaty relationship with India.

Singapore. An independent republic and member of the British Commonwealth, it lies at the southern extremity of the Malayan peninsula; area, comprising Singapore Island and adjacent islets in the Indian Ocean, 225 sq. m.; population (1970) 2,074,500, of whom approximately 1,579,850 are Chinese, 311,400 Malayans and Indonesians, 145,200 Indians and Pakistanis. Singapore was liberated from Japanese rule by British forces in September 1945 and in April 1946 it reverted to its former colonial status. Internal self-government was granted in 1959, and from 1963 until 1965 Singapore was a member of the Federation of Malaysia, *q.v.* On its secession from the Federation on 9 August 1965 Singapore became an independent republic.

At elections held in September 1963, the People's Action Party (P.A.P.), led by Lee Kuan Yew, and with a non-Communist left-wing outlook and multi-racial support, won 37 of the 51 seats in the Legislative Assembly. The ultra left-wing Barisan Socialist Party won 13 seats, and the United People's Party won 1. During 1967 the United People's Party went into voluntary dissolution and eleven of the thirteen Barisan Socialists resigned their seats. All twelve by-elections were won by the P.A.P. At elections held in April 1968, the P.A.P. was unopposed in 51 of the (now) 58 constituencies, and gained all the contested seats. Lee Kuan Yew, who became Prime Minister in 1963, continued to lead the government.

Singapore lives by its entrepôt trade, handling rubber, tin and oil, which accounts for 25 per cent of employment and 16 per cent of the national income. The threatened closure by Indonesia and Malaysia of the Straits of Malacca, *q.v.*, as an international waterway would seriously jeopardize the economy of Singapore. Since the U.K. withdrew most of its military force in 1971 the former British naval dockyard is being developed as a base for ship repairs. Singapore is a member of A.S.E.A.N., *q.v.*

Slump. A fall in prices or demand, usually the result of some failure in spending. A boom may be converted into a slump when wages do not rise enough to enable consumers to spend on a scale that will satisfy the producers, or when business firms do not embark on sufficient new capital outlay.

Smith, Ian Douglas. Rhodesian politician and farmer; born 1919 and educated at Rhodes University, South Africa. He served in the Royal Air Force from 1941 to 1946. He was a member of the Southern Rhodesian Legislative Assembly from 1948 to 1953 and again from 1962; in the intervening years he sat in the Parliament of the Federation of Rhodesia and Nyasaland, *q.v.* During this period he supported the United Federal Party and acted as its Chief Whip; in 1962 he helped to found, and became Vice-President of, the Rhodesian Front. In December 1962 he was appointed deputy Prime Minister and Minister of the Treasury in the government of Winston Field, *q.v.*, whom he succeeded as Prime Minister in April 1964. He opposed majority rule in Rhodesia and gained an overwhelming victory in the Rhodesian general election held in May 1965. In November 1965 his government made a unilateral declaration of independence, *q.v.* His decision to declare a republic and introduce an apartheid-type constitution was endorsed by a referendum in June 1969.

Social Credit. A movement based on the theories of Major C. H. Douglas and William Aberhart, who believed that prosperity could be achieved through a reform of the monetary system. They ascribed social and economic evils to the insufficient supply of money and its control by banks. They proposed the 'A + B theorem', saying that prices are made up from: A, payments to individuals as wages, salaries, and dividends, and B, payments by producers (for raw materials, bank charges, etc.) to other firms and which are working capital. Only A payments create purchasing power, while B payments, being capital, cannot be consumed. As national income is equal to the total of A payments, and as prices are determined by A + B, purchasing power for the extra amount must be provided for the proportion of the product equal to B. This extra purchasing power has hitherto been supplied by money created by the banks by repayable loans. Thus a constant flow of money to the banks has been lost as purchasing power. This has led to the total of prices exceeding the total of incomes, or to what is called over-production.

They suggested that banks should place the new money which they create every day in the hands of the consumer. The retailer would sell the goods below cost, and his loss, plus a commission, would be credited to his bank account. Prices would be arranged so that the total wages, salaries, and dividends would be sufficient to buy all the goods. Another method of increasing purchasing power was the 'national dividend', payable to everyone according to national prosperity.

Orthodox critics say that the system would lead to inflation and that it neglects the need to create fresh capital and unduly stresses the interests of consumption. Socialist critics say that the system seeks the remedies for social evils in the sphere of circulation only, instead of tackling the problem of reorganizing capitalist production; Hugh Gaitskell criticized the obscurity and dogmatism of Douglas, calling him 'a religious rather than a scientific reformer'.

Socialism. A political and economic theory according to which the means of production, distribution, and exchange should be owned and controlled by the people, everyone should be given an equal opportunity to develop his talents, and the wealth of the community should be fairly distributed.

Solid South. An American political term referring to the fact that most of the southern States of the U.S.A. have for a very long time voted for the Democratic Party. The majority in this political grouping are loyal Democrats, but in recent years there has emerged a considerable number of dissident right-wing Democrats. Their recent support of the Republicans has arisen partly out of a hope that a Republican administration would have greater respect for States' rights, q.v., and in particular that the Federal government would intervene less to protect civil rights, q.v., and to insist on social welfare measures. Southerners are easily discouraged from supporting the Republican Party by any decline in farm prices, and look to a Democratic administration to provide the farmers with subsidies.

Somalia. An independent republic, also known as the Somali Republic, in north-east Africa on the Gulf of Aden and the Indian Ocean, with French Somaliland to the west, Kenya to the south, and Ethiopia inland; area 246,135 sq. m.; population (1971) 2,730,000, mostly Sunni Moslems; capital Mogadishu. The country, which became independent on 1 July 1960, was created by uniting the protectorate of British Somaliland, q.v., and the territory of Somalia; the latter had been ceded by the U.K. to Italy in 1925, occupied by the U.K. in

February 1941, and returned to Italy as a trusteeship territory under a trusteeship agreement concluded in December 1950. Many Somalis support a scheme for a Greater Somalia which would include French Somaliland (with its deep-water port of Djibouti) and parts of Kenya, including parts of the Northern Frontier District, *q.v.*, and Ethiopia, including Ogaden, *q.v.*, and the Haud. At the first elections ever held in Somalia, in February 1956, 43 out of the 60 elective seats were won by the Somali Youth League, a nationalist party which repudiates tribal and religious differences. At elections held in March 1964, June 1967 and March 1969 the S.Y.L. retained its majority and continued to form the government under the premiership of Ibrahim Egal; but in October 1969 President Shermarke was assassinated and General Mohammed Siyad seized power. The country receives subsidies and technical advice from Italy, the Federal Republic of Germany, Egypt, the U.S.S.R., and the U.S.A. There are disagreements with Kenya and Ethiopia as to the demarcation of the border; an agreement was concluded with Kenya in October 1967 to end the border fighting. Somalia is a poor country, and the main occupations are cattle-rearing, largely by a nomadic population, and agriculture.

Soudanese Republic. The name given to the French overseas territory of Soudan, in French West Africa, *q.v.*, when it achieved self-government within the French Community, *q.v.*, on 24 November 1958, until, on the collapse of the Mali Federation, *q.v.*, it declared, on 22 September 1960 that it would thenceforth be known as the Republic of Mali, *q.v.*

South Africa. A republic, and former member of the British Commonwealth; area 472,359 sq. m.; population (1970 estimate) 20,536,000, of whom 69 per cent are Bantu (Zulu, Basuto, Xhosa, Pondo and others), 19 per cent are whites, 9 per cent are coloured people (the Cape Malays and the descendants of slaves from the east and of the now nearly extinct Hottentots, with a strong infusion of Dutch blood), and 3 per cent are Asians; capital Pretoria. The Union of South Africa consists of the provinces of Cape of Good Hope, Natal, Transvaal and Orange Free State.

A settlement was established at the Cape of Good Hope by the Dutch East India Company in 1652, and in the eighteenth century the settlers began to encounter, and to defeat in war, the various Bantu tribes which were moving south from Central Africa. In 1914 the British Cape Colony was founded; resentment at British intrusion and at the amount of compensation offered when slavery was abolished in 1833 incited the Dutch-speaking settlers (the Boers or Afrikaners) to trek northwards into the interior and to set up the South African Republic or Transvaal, and the Orange Free State

Boer hatred of the British increased when in 1895 Cecil Rhodes (Prime Minister of the Cape Colony and Managing Director of the British South Africa Company which controlled Rhodesia) organized an unsuccessful invasion of Transvaal, later called the Jameson Raid, in order to assist British exploitation of the Rand goldfields in Transvaal. War broke out in 1899 and in 1902 the Boers had to surrender and become British subjects, but were promised self-government; this was granted and a constitution was enacted by the U.K. in 1909 when the South Africa Act was passed. The Union of South Africa came into existence in 1910.

The result of the South Africa Act and the Statute of Westminster of 1931 (*see* Westminster, Statute of) had been to give South Africa the independence of a sovereign state with full power to amend its constitution, but only in the manner laid down in the entrenched provisions, *q.v.*, of the 1909 Act. Legislative power was vested in the Queen, represented by a South African Governor-General, acting with a Senate of 86 members, some nominated and some elected, and a House of Assembly of 160 members elected for five years. There were 3 Native representatives in the House, elected by those whose names appeared on the Cape Native Voters' Roll, but these members and 4 similar members of the Senate were deprived of their seats in June 1960. At elections held on 22 April 1970, the National Party, a right-wing, semi-Fascist group believing in white supremacy and apartheid *q.v.*, allied to the Dutch Reformed Church, with republican views, and led by Balthazar Vorster, *q.v.*, won 117 seats (126 in 1966); the Herstigte Nasionale Party, or Verkramptes, a right-wing Nationalist splinter group, failed to win support from Vorster's Verligtes or 'enlightened' Nationalists; the United Party, which accepts the principle of racial segregation but not the civic disabilities imposed on Africans or the unparliamentary and dictatorial approach of the National Party, led by Sir de Villiers Graaf, won 47 seats (39 in 1966); the Progressive Party, which advocates a universal franchise based on educational and property qualifications, returned Helen Suzman as its sole representative. The South African Labour Party was unrepresented, having lost all its 5 seats in the 1958 elections. These figures include the 6 representatives of South-West Africa, *q.v.*; the 4 representatives of coloured voters who had previously sat in the Assembly were excluded under an Act passed in 1968. The Senate has 54 members, 43 elected and 11 nominated.

A referendum held among white voters on 5 October 1960 decided, by a majority of 52 per cent to 48 per cent, in favour of a republic. South Africa became a republic on 31 May 1961, and withdrew from the Commonwealth, several members of which had expressed their strong disapproval of the implementation of apartheid. In 1962 the Transkei became the first of the 9 Bantu homelands to qualify as a self-governing state within the Republic, and in November 1963 the first Transkei Parliament was elected. More than 50 per cent of the African population live in the homelands which constitute less than 15 per cent of the total area of South Africa.

Immigration in general, and British immigration in particular, have been opposed by the Nationalists, who believe in selecting citizens who will favour their party; this policy, combined with recent expansion in mining and manufacturing industry and a rigid application of the colour bar, has led to a serious shortage of skilled labour. Despite this, the country has successfully diversified its economy, exporting gold, uranium, diamonds, copper, maize, textiles, fresh fruit, wines and wool. In 1967 Malawi, which exports labour to South Africa, became the first black African state to recognize the Republic.

South Arabian Federation. An internally self-governing British territory in South Arabia which achieved independence as the People's Republic of Southern Yemen, *q.v.*, on 30 November 1967; population approximately 771,000; capital Al Ittihad. On 11 February 1959 six of the territories of the Eastern and Western Aden Protectorates (known as the Aden Protectorate, *q.v.*) formed a Federation of Arab Emirates of the South. In April 1962 the name was changed to South Arabian Federation, and by 1963 Aden State, *q.v.*, and all the territories of the former Protectorates (except for a small group which retained, collectively, the title of Eastern Aden Protectorate, *q.v.*) had joined. The neighbouring state of Yemen opposed the Federation, regarding its creation as a breach of a 1951 agreement by which the U.K. promised to maintain the *status quo* in disputed frontier areas. In 1964 the U.K. proposed the fusion of the states of South Arabia when independence was attained into a unitary state. In November 1967, the Eastern Aden Protectorate was merged with the Federation to form the People's Republic of Southern Yemen.

South Korea. The Republic of Korea, inaugurated on 15 August 1948 when U.S. military government came to an end, and officially recognized by the western powers but not by the U.S.S.R. and its satellites; area 38,452 sq. m.; population (1970) 31,460,000; capital Seoul. While the country was under U.S. military occupation, from August 1945 until August 1948, an attempt was made to establish some form of democratic government in which North Korea, *q.v.*, could participate as soon as the U.S.S.R. permitted the reunification of Korea, *q.v.* Accordingly, a general election was held on 10 May 1948, under the observation of a United Nations Commission, at which 90 per cent of the electorate voted for 203 members of a National Assembly; 100 more seats were reserved for the one-third of the population living north of the 38th parallel. A Constitution (the first in 4,000 years of Korea's history) was adopted and a republic declared; Dr Syngman Rhee was elected President.

When North Korea invaded South Korea on 25 June 1950 the South was totally unprepared for war. U.S. policy had been to restrain the belligerent President Rhee; in order to avoid the charge that it was building a military base on the Asian mainland it supplied only light arms, and no tanks, to deal with local unrest, threatened cessation of economic aid should there be any movement of South Korean troops north of the 38th parallel, and withdrew all its military forces, except for an advisory mission of 500, by June 1949. When the Security Council of the United Nations asked all member nations to render assistance to the Republic of Korea the U.S. provided the commanders of the United Nations army, most of the men and practically all the equipment. There were 142,000 U.S. casualties in the war; British casualties numbered 4,451. An armistice was concluded on 27 July 1953 by which a demilitarization zone between the two states was established roughly along the 38th parallel and a Neutral Nations Supervisory Commission was appointed to see that the armistice terms were observed and to arrange for the exchange of prisoners.

South Korea was devastated as a result of the war. Although the Sangdong mine has one of the world's largest deposits of tungsten, and there is an abundance of amorphous graphite, and deposits of coal, the state is insolvent and dependent on economic aid from the west. Further relief is in the hands of the United Nations Korean Reconstruction Agency (U.N.K.R.A.), financed by voluntary contributions from governments. Since 1962 some foreign investment (particularly Japanese) has been attracted by the abundance of cheap labour and high rate of interest.

At the elections held in May 1958, the President's party, the Liberals, retained power with a reduced majority. Although Rhee secured re-election as President in March 1960 the corruption and repressive measures of his government resulted in his enforced resignation in April 1960. At the elections held in July 1960 under the new Constitution of that year, the Democrats won 181 out of 233 seats in the National Assembly, and Chang Myun, a Roman Catholic, became Prime Minister. Chang was ousted by a military junta in

May 1961 and replaced by Lt-Gen. Chung Hee Park who took charge of the Supreme Council of National Reconstruction and dissolved the National Assembly. He was elected President in October 1963. At the elections held in November 1963 his Democratic Republic Party won over 100 of the 175 seats in the Assembly, gaining its support mainly from the rural areas. In 1967 and 1971 both President Park and his government were re-elected with increased majorities, despite the unpopularity of a Treaty of Normalization signed with Japan on 22 June 1965. In 1971 negotiations were opened with North Korea for a mutual reduction of military forces; in 1972 these were extended to a consideration of re-unification, and on 17 October 1972 martial law was declared by President Park and the Assembly dissolved to facilitate the 'peaceful re-unification of Korea'.

South Pacific Commission. Founded 6 February 1947 by Australia, France, Netherlands, New Zealand, U.K., U.S.A. and all the independent and non-independent territories in the South Pacific. Its purpose was to act as an aid-coordinating body particularly to those areas affected by the war with Japan 1941–5. Its headquarters are at Nouméa in New Caledonia. In 1962 the Netherlands, having no further interest in the area after the cession of West Irian, *q.v.*, to Indonesia, withdrew.

South Pacific Forum. Was first convened in August 1971 in Wellington by the leaders of the independent and self-governing island states of the South Pacific. These were: Fiji, Tonga, Western Samoa, Nauru and the Cook Islands. The Prime Minister of New Zealand and the Australian Minister of External Territories also took part. The purpose of the Forum was to coordinate trade, shipping, tourism and education in relation to the limited resources of the islands. It was accepted that close economic cooperation with Australia and New Zealand was essential.

South Tirol. The portion of Tirol south of the Brenner Pass, formerly part of the Austro-Hungarian Empire, which was acquired by Italy in 1919; it was known as Bozen but since its cession to Italy it has been called Alto Adige or Bolzano; population 341,500, of whom 220,000 are German-speaking South Tirolese, 110,000 Italian-speaking, and 9,500 Ludin-speaking inhabitants; the capital of the province is Bolzano. By the Gruber–de Gasperi agreement of 5 September 1946 between Austria and Italy the South Tirolese were to be given 'complete equality of rights with the Italian-speaking inhabitants, within the framework of special provisions to safeguard the ethnological character and the cultural and economic development of the German-speaking element'; the agreement also stated: 'the populations of the above-mentioned zones will be granted the exercise of autonomous legislative and executive regional power.' The agreement was later incorporated in the Paris Peace Treaty of 10 February 1947 (ratified on 15 September 1947) and made part of the Italian Constitution by statute on 26 February 1948.

By the same statute there was established the autonomous region of Trentino–Alto Adige, comprising the two provinces of these names. Trentino (of which the capital is Trento or Trent) has a population of approximately 444,000, all Italians; the autonomous region has a total population of 785,491 and an Italian majority, whereas the South Tirol or Alto Adige itself has a German-speaking majority. The Austrian government persisted in its demands for a greater degree of autonomy for the South Tirol and accused the Italian government of breaking the 1946 agreement; the Italian government denied the breach, arguing that the 1948 statute had provided adequate provincial independence. The minority interests of the German-speaking population were represented politically by the Catholic and conservative South Tirolese People's Party (S.V.P.) which had 4 seats in the Italian Chamber of Deputies. Latterly a separatist movement, led by Professor Gunther Andergassen, was founded which engaged in acts of terrorism to bring its case before an indifferent Italian parliament. In 1969 a settlement was drafted giving considerable autonomy to the region and making provision for German-speaking schools; this was approved by the Italian Senate in June 1971. The following month Austria and Italy signed an agreement to submit any disputes arising from the settlement to the International Court of Justice, *q.v.* Since it included the Gruber–de Gasperi treaty of 1946 this effectively extended the validity of Article 27 of the European Convention on the peaceful settlement of international conflicts to cover cases arising prior to the Convention coming into force in 1960.

South Viet-Nam. The zone south of the 17th parallel allotted to the government of Viet-Nam in July 1954 by the terms of the Geneva Agreements 1954, *q.v.*, on the cessation of hostilities in Viet-Nam, *q.v.*; area 66,281 sq. m.; population (1970) 19,300,000, of whom more than one million are Catholics; capital Saigon. The government in Saigon is recognized by the U.K. and the U.S.A. as the legal government of Viet-Nam. In January 1955 the U.S.A. accepted responsibility for helping the country to organize and train its armed forces. A republic was declared in October 1955 by the President, Ngo Dinh Diem, who replaced the former Head of State, Bao Dai, as a result of a popular referendum. Diem governed by ordinance through a Cabinet chosen largely from his own relations. His regime was criticized as totalitarian and corrupt, but he had great difficulty in establishing his authority owing to the existence of several terrorist organizations and private armies. These included the Hoa Hoa sect (Buddhists), the Cao Daists, who were mostly Catholic fanatics, and the Binh Xuyen, whose leader, General Van le Vien, controlled the Saigon police and many brothels. Diem, a Roman Catholic, launched a programme of social reform which closed Saigon's opium dens, and introduced financial measures designed to improve the country's trade position. Meanwhile the Viet Cong (Communist) forces of the National Liberation Front of the South, supported by North Viet-Nam, *q.v.*, achieved striking successes, bringing much of the land outside the cities under their control, and imposing taxes and collecting levies on rice production. Diem was murdered in November 1963 shortly after the U.S. had withdrawn its support from him, his repressive measures having aroused widespread resistance among the Buddhist majority. From January 1954 until February 1965 the government was led by a Buddhist, General Nguyen Khanh, first as Prime Minister and later as President. Before and after the *coup* in which he was overthrown there was a series of Premiers, and an ineffectual prosecution of the war against the Viet Cong, until the Council of the Armed Forces in June 1965 installed Air Vice-Marshal Nguyen Cao Ky as Prime Minister and General Nguyen Van Thieu as Head of State. Thieu was confirmed as President in elections held in 1967 and 1971. These men envisaged a military solution to the disturbed political situation; this attitude was endorsed by the so-called 'Hawks', *q.v.*, within the U.S. State Department who advised an escalation, *q.v.*, of the war and an intensification of the bombing of cities and supply routes in North Viet-Nam. By June 1968 there were 510,000 Americans in Viet-Nam, and 55,000 Australian, South Korean, and other forces.

Peace negotiations between North Viet-Nam and the U.S.A. were eventually opened in Paris on 13 May 1968, but made little progress until President Johnson announced a temporary halt to American bombing of the North in November, and the South Viet-Nam government was persuaded to attend, despite its refusal to negotiate directly with the National Liberation Front which it regarded as a rebellious organization. The escalation of the war in 1970, when it was extended to Cambodia, and in 1971 when South Viet-Nam invaded Laos, *q.v.*, in an attempt to cut the North's main supply route, the Ho Chi-Minh trail, interrupted the talks, but the delegations continued to meet after April 1971. In the spring of 1972 North Viet-Nam launched a massive ground offensive against the South, which was countered by renewed American bombing and the mining of the sea approaches to Haiphong.

A cease-fire agreement was eventually signed by North Viet-Nam, South Viet-Nam and the U.S.A. on 27 January 1973.

South-East Asia Collective Defence Treaty. Agreed by Australia, France, New Zealand, Pakistan, the Philippines, Thailand, the U.K., and the U.S.A. at Manila in the Philippines on 8 September 1954. The Treaty set up the South-East Asia Treaty Organization (S.E.A.T.O.) with headquarters at Bangkok and provided for a Council and Secretariat. The eight signatories agreed to take collective action in the event of either external aggression against any one of them or internal subversion. They also agreed to cooperate in economic matters, but the main emphasis has been on military and anti-Communist rather than on economic measures. The area involved has been so defined in the Treaty that an attack on Taiwan or Hong Kong would not bring the Treaty obligation into operation. Pakistan ceased to be a member in 1972.

South-West Africa. A territory controlled by South Africa and once a German colony; area 318,621 sq. m.; population (1970 estimate) 746,328, of whom 342,500 belong to the Ovambo tribe, and 90,000 are Europeans; capital Windhoek. It was a German possession from 1884 until the end of the First World War when it was entrusted by the League of Nations to South Africa to be administered as a mandated territory. No trusteeship agreement was concluded by South Africa with the United Nations after the Second World War, and the International Court of Justice therefore held in 1950 that the area was still under an international mandate and that South Africa was obliged to submit it to the supervision and control of the U.N. General Assembly and to render annual reports on it. It is the only area, previously under League of Nations mandate, which has neither become independent nor been placed under trusteeship. By the South-West Africa Affairs Amendment Act, 1949, the territory is represented by 6 members in the South African House of Assembly and by 4 members in the Senate. The territory has its own Legislative Assembly of 18 members elected for five years by the 29,000 white voters, of whom 70 per cent are Afrikaaners, 22 per cent are German-speaking, and 8 per cent English-speaking. In elections held in April 1970, the Nationalist Party, which has the same aims as its parent organization in South Africa, won all 18 seats.

Although the 1949 Act involved a close association between the territory and South Africa it stopped short of incorporation. The South African government has thus observed the Court's ruling which forbade incorporation, but has refused to submit reports on the area. When the chiefs of the Herero tribe, which had suffered expropriation of its reserves by white settlers, attempted to make their own report to the United Nations, they were prevented from leaving South-West Africa. Following the extension of the Bantu Self-Government Act, by which apartheid was to be implemented, to South-West Africa, Ethiopia and Liberia, as former members of the League of Nations, applied, in November 1960, to the International Court for a judgement that South Africa had violated the mandate. It was thus anticipated that a judicial pronouncement on the legality of apartheid would have to be made. On 18 July 1966 the Court rejected the plaintiffs' claims of contravention of the mandate on the technical grounds that they had established no legal rights or interests in the subject matter of their claim against South Africa. The issue was then revived at the United Nations which, by resolution passed on 12 June 1968, renamed South-West Africa Namibia, *q.v.*, and called for its immediate independence. In June 1971 the International Court ruled that South Africa's presence in the territory was illegal.

Southern Rhodesia. Legally a largely self-governing country which was part of the Federation of Rhodesia and Nyasaland, *q.v.*, from its establishment in 1953 until its dissolution in 1963. After Northern Rhodesia became independent (as Zambia), in 1964, Southern Rhodesia became known as Rhodesia, *q.v.* Its white government made a unilateral declaration of independence, *q.v.*, on 11 November 1965.

Southern Yemen (The People's Republic of). The name by which Yemen, *q.v.*, was known from its creation as an independent state in November 1967 until 1972.

Soviet. Russian word meaning 'council'. Workers' councils, under the name of Soviets, emerged first in the Russian Revolution of 1905. They reappeared as the organs of the 1917 Revolution, and later of the national administration. Until 1936 the lower Soviets chose the higher Soviets (district, regional, and state Soviets) by indirect election. Features of the original system were unity of legislative and executive power, and of local and state authorities. It was claimed that the system ensured the participation of the masses in the administration. In 1936 the Constitution was amended and the system of indirect election abandoned, though the name was retained. All Soviets of whatever degree are now elected directly by the people and the lower Soviets do not control the higher ones, such as the Supreme Soviet, *q.v.*

Soviet Union. Union of Soviet Socialist Republics, *q.v.*

Spain. An independent state in south-west Europe; area 196,700 sq. m.; population (1970) 33,462,000; capital Madrid. It was ruled by monarchs of the Aragon, Bourbon and Habsburg dynasties until 1931 when the dictatorship of General Primo de Rivera was over-thrown, a republic was proclaimed, and King Alfonso XIII went into exile. A provisional government of Republicans and Socialists was formed (despite strong opposition from the right-wing parties) which ruled Spain until elections were held on 16 February 1936, in which the left-wing parties secured a clear majority over the right and centre. Manuel Azaña, the leader of the Popular Front, was elected as President on 10 May 1936. The government formed by Azaña, which contained neither Socialists nor Communists, initiated a land reform (at that time 1 per cent of the population owned 51 per cent of the land) and other social reforms which aroused the opposition of conservative circles, and particularly of the large land-owners. A revolt, led by General Franco, q.v., and supported and financed by the officer class, the feudal aristocracy, the bulk of the politically minded Roman Catholics, and the monarchists, began on 18 July 1936 in Spanish Morocco and then spread throughout Spain. By August, Germany and Italy had intervened to help the Fascist rebels; later the U.S.S.R., and volunteer forces from several European countries (the International Brigade), assisted the Spanish government. After nearly three years of disorder and bitter civil war, in which more than one million died, fighting ended in March 1939 with the success of the rebels.

In 1942 Franco, who had assumed the Presidency, reinstituted the traditional legislative assembly of Spain, the Cortes. Under the Organic Law of 1967 it comprises 19 Ministers; 109 representatives of the sole political party, the Falangists, q.v.; 5 presidents of various state organizations; 100 family members, elected by heads of families and married women; 150 representatives of the national syndicates; 12 university rectors; 116 representatives of local administration; 28 members of professional, academic and scientific bodies; and 25 members directly appointed by the head of state. The 100 family members were appointed as a result of elections, the first to be held since the Civil War, in 1967. The powers of the Cortes are limited to discussing and proposing legislation, which must first be initiated or approved by the Council of Ministers; the head of state has the right of veto. Spain is technically a monarchy, but under the 1947 Succession Law Franco was given absolute authority to choose his successor, providing that he had reached the age of thirty when he attained the throne. In July 1969 he named Prince Juan Carlos de Bourbon (born 1938), grandson of Alfonso XIII, as future king and head of state, ignoring the claim of his father, the Count of Barcelona, who had known liberal views. In July 1972 he nominated the Vice-President, Admiral Luis Carrero Blanco, to succeed him after his death as Head of Government.

During the Second World War Spain was in continual and sympathetic contact with the German and Italian governments, but, though anxious to seize Gibraltar, *q.v.*, from the U.K., remained officially neutral. In 1946 the United Nations resolved that Ambassadors should be withdrawn from Spain; however, although refusing to admit Spain to membership of the U.N. until 1955, most of the major powers subsequently resumed diplomatic relations. The U.S.A. appreciated its strategic importance, and on 26 September 1953 concluded an agreement at Madrid for military and economic aid, over a period of ten years, renewable in 1963 and 1968, in exchange for the lease of air and naval bases. Since 1963 Spain has intensified her claim to sovereignty over Gibraltar, gaining support at the U.N. by according independence, in October 1968, to the two former Spanish provinces of Equatorial Guinea, *q.v.*

The country is mainly agricultural, and its main exports are vegetables, oranges and citrus fruits, and wines; minerals, such as coal, anthracite, iron ore and pyrites, potash and silver, are also exported. Tourism, which is expanding rapidly and is a valuable source of foreign exchange, the presence of foreign firms with advanced techniques of wage negotiations, and the temporary migration of Spanish workers to other west European countries have all contributed to social and industrial discontent. There is continual unrest among the workers' Commissions, the only form of trade union organization which is permitted. Separatism, *q.v.*, which has always been strong in Catalonia and Galicia, re-emerged in the Basque provinces between 1968 and 1970 with the active support of local priests, many of whom were imprisoned.

Spanish Guinea. *See* Equatorial Guinea.

Spanish Morocco. The name formerly given to the northern portion of Morocco, *q.v.*, about 50 miles wide, between the Rif Mountains and the Mediterranean, which from 1912 to 1956 was recognized as a Spanish sphere of influence; it had an area of about 11,236 sq. m. and a population of 1,082,000 including 1,000,000 Moslems; capital Tetuan. It included the free ports of Melilla and Ceuta, which became Spanish possessions in 1496 and 1581 respectively. The division of Morocco into French and Spanish spheres of influence took place under a Protectorate Treaty between France and the Sultan at Fez on 30 March 1912 and a Convention between France and Spain at Madrid on 27 November 1912. The Sultan's powers in

Spanish Morocco were delegated to a Khalifa, whose administration was controlled by a Spanish High Commissioner. The frontier with French Morocco, *q.v.*, was never properly defined and the Spaniards tended to push southwards. In 1934 they occupied Ifni, *q.v.*, and obtained treaty rights south of the river Draa, in the areas later known as Spanish Sahara, *q.v.*, and Spanish Southern Morocco, *q.v.*

Spain followed the example of France in April 1956 by recognizing the independent status of Morocco, and agreed that the Convention of Madrid no longer governed its relations with Morocco. The Spanish government handed over the administration of Spanish Morocco to the representatives of the Sultan, Sidi Mohammed ben Youssef. In January 1958 Spain reorganized Ifni and Spanish Sahara so that they became provinces and in June 1969 ceded Ifni to Morocco.

Spanish Sahara. A province of Spain to the west of Morocco and on the Atlantic Ocean; area 125,000 sq. m.; population (1970 estimate) 50,000. It comprises the two former colonies of Rio de Oro and Saguia el-Hamra, to the south of Spanish Southern Morocco, *q.v.* Its establishment as a province was announced on 14 January 1958, at the same time as Ifni, *q.v.*, ceded to Morocco in June 1969, was also made a province. It is administered by the Director-General of African Provinces in Madrid. There may be substantial oil reserves, especially in the northern coastal area near Cape Bojador, south of the capital, El Aaiun; in 1964 rich deposits of phosphate were found with proven reserves estimated at 1,700,000 million tons.

Spanish Southern Morocco. Also known as Tarfaya, this mostly desert area of nearly 10,000 sq. m. was administered as part of the protectorate of Spanish Morocco, *q.v.*, from 1912 until the emergence of Morocco as an independent state in 1956. It lies on the Atlantic Ocean between the parallel of 27°40′ North latitude and the river Draa. On 10 April 1958 it was returned by Spain to Morocco. To the north and south respectively are Ifni, *q.v.*, which Spain ceded to Morocco in June 1969, and the Spanish province of Spanish Sahara, *q.v.*

Special United Nations Fund for Economic Development (S.U.N.F.E.D.). A fund proposed by the Economic and Financial Committee of the United Nations General Assembly, and unanimously recommended by the Assembly in December 1954. The Committee said that from the fund long-term, low-interest loans, or outright grants, could be made to finance basic development works, such as roads or harbours, which offered too little return to qualify for a loan from the International Bank for Reconstruction and Development, *q.v.*

Specialized Agencies. Inter-governmental organizations with wide responsibilities in economic, social, cultural, educational, health, and other fields, whose work is coordinated by the Economic and Social Council, *q.v.*, of the United Nations.

Spheres of Influence. Certain countries, or parts of countries, in which another state, without annexation, desires to exert exclusive influence. For many years after 1907 Persia was divided into British and Russian spheres of influence. The U.S. government regards it as vital that no pro-Communist regime should come to power in Central or South America, which it regards as one of its spheres of influence. Eastern Europe, with the exceptions of Finland, Yugoslavia, Greece, and Turkey, can be regarded as a sphere of influence for the U.S.S.R.

Spitsbergen Archipelago. Also known as Svalbard, a commercially important group of Norwegian islands about 550 miles north of the northernmost part of Norway; total area about 24,295 sq. m.; population approximately 3,000. It comprises a main island, West Spitsbergen, North East Land, Edge Island, Barents Island, and some smaller islands. There were Dutch, British and Norwegian claims to sovereignty in the seventeenth century when there was much lucrative whale-hunting, but the hunting ended and the claims lapsed until the twentieth century when rich coalfields were discovered. Once more there were disputes, but on 19 February 1920 Norwegian sovereignty was recognized by the Treaty of Paris between Norway and other interested states, and the Archipelago was officially taken over by Norway on 14 August 1925. The Treaty provided that the economic exploitation of the Archipelago should be open equally to all the signatory powers. After 1930 only Norway and the U.S.S.R. (Russia having annexed a coalfield in 1912) carried on mining there; in 1941 British, Canadian, and Norwegian forces dismantled or destroyed most of the mining plant to prevent the Germans from benefiting from the mines in case they arrived in the Archipelago. By 1959 coal production was over 600,000 tons annually; there were three Russian camps and three Norwegian camps, one of which was not being operated. Though earnings are high there is a heavy turnover of labour. The islands are ice-blocked for most of the year and there is total darkness from October to February. The mines, however, are a valuable source of supply for north Norway, and the Norwegian government has tried to increase production and to reopen the closed mine. Neither Russian requests, which were rejected, to discuss the defence of the Archipelago, nor Norway's commitments under the North Atlantic Treaty have altered its non-military status, for the 1920 Treaty provided that no military bases or fortifications of any kind should be established.

Sri Lanka. An island in the Indian Ocean off the southern coast of India, which is an independent republic and member of the British Commonwealth; area 25,332 sq. m.; population (1971 census) 12,747,755, of whom two-thirds are Sinhalese and the rest mainly Tamils from south India; capital Colombo. Buddhism is the religion of the majority but there are nearly two million Hindus. As the former British colony of Ceylon it achieved 'fully responsible status' by the Ceylon Independence Act of 1947. The use by British forces of the naval base at Trincomalee and the air base at Katunayake was sanctioned by the Act, but these were yielded to Ceylon in 1957 when the British reestablished a war-time air base in the Maldives, *q.v.* The Constitution of 1972, by which Ceylon became a socialist republic under the new name of Sri Lanka, absolved Ceylon from any defence obligation to the U.K.

The introduction in 1956 of the Official Language Act, by which Sinhalese replaced English as the official tongue, provoked violent opposition from the Tamils, whose language had previously had parity with Sinhalese. Separatist tendencies of both the immigrant Tamils from India and the Ceylon Tamils, who are mostly Hindus and who constitute a minority group in the Sinhalese-speaking, Buddhist, population, were encouraged by the enforcement of the Act, which was strengthened in 1961. In 1966 Tamil was restored as the official language in the northern and eastern provinces.

The House of Representatives (the lower house of Parliament until 1972 when a unicameral National Assembly was introduced) has been dominated by two major political parties, the Sri Lanka Freedom Party (S.L.F.P.), a socialist organization founded in 1951 by Solomon Bandaranaike, who was assassinated in 1959 by a Buddhist monk, and led by his widow Sirimavo Bandaranaike, *q.v.*, and the conservative 'Siro Kotha', the United National Party (U.N.P.), led by Dudley Senanayake. The S.L.F.P., in coalition with the People's United Front, was in office from 1956 to March 1960, Wijayananda Dahanayake succeeding Bandaranaike as Prime Minister in 1959. At elections held in March 1960 the U.N.P. emerged as the largest single party, winning 50 out of the 151 seats, and Senanayake was appointed Prime Minister. Further elections in July 1960 gave the S.L.F.P. 70 seats and reduced the U.N.P. strength to 40; the S.L.F.P. leader, Sirimavo Bandaranaike, thereupon became Prime Minister. Her popularity waned over the language issue, which came to a head between 1961 and 1964, and over a dispute with the U.S. over compensation for nationalized American oil interests which led to the suspension of U.S. technical assistance. At elections held on 22 March 1965 the S.L.F.P.

representation fell to 41 seats and the U.N.P. won 66. Senanayake became Prime Minister of a coalition of six parties including the U.N.P., the Federal Party, which was supported by many Tamils, and the S.L.F.P. The elections held on 2 May 1970 produced a left-wing landslide which was generally ascribed to the rise in the cost of living brought about by a termination of the free rice ration and a large increase in the numbers of graduate unemployed. The results were: S.L.F.P. 91 seats (41 in 1965); Lanka Sama Samaj Party (Trotskyites) supporting the S.L.F.P. and led by Dr N. M. Perera, 19 (10); U.N.P. 17 (66); Federal Party 13 (14); Communist Party 6 (4); Tamil Congress 3 (3); others 2. Mrs Bandaranaike took office as Prime Minister at the head of a left-wing coalition government consisting of the S.L.F.P., the L.S.S.P. (Trotskyites), and the pro-Soviet Communist Party. She pledged the administration to 'realize the objectives of a socialist democracy' and announced that banks and import-export agencies would be nationalized. Progress has been impeded since 1970 by the continuous guerilla activity of the People's Liberation Front, an ultra left-wing alliance, formed by Ronan Wijeweera, which is committed to the overthrow of parliamentary democracy, and has been supported from North Korea. By the new Constitution introduced on 22 May 1972 Ceylon became the republic of Sri Lanka; the severence of the link with the British crown ended the world's oldest island monarchy, Ceylon having had an unbroken line of 197 kings and queens from King Vijaya in 543 B.C. to Sri Vikrama Rajasinha, King of Kandy, who surrendered to the British in 1815.

The economy of Ceylon depends on the export of rubber and tea, of which it is the world's largest producer. Two-thirds of the cultivated land is devoted to these cash crops, and nearly three-quarters of the rice (the staple diet) required to feed the island's fast increasing population (20·5 per cent between 1963 and 1971) has to be imported. A fall in the world price of tea reduced the value of Ceylon's exports by 12 per cent between 1965 and 1966. This dangerous dependence on world tea and rubber prices has led to a reduction in the rubber acreage in favour of rice-growing, extensive land reclamation and deforestation. Agreement was reached with the World Bank in 1970 to finance the building of the Mahaweli Gange hydro-electric and irrigation schemes.

Stakhanovite. A worker who exceeds his allotted quota of work. Alexei Stakhanov, a Russian miner, regularly exceeded his quota, or 'norm', and was held up as an example to be followed. Stakhanovites were given higher wages, rewards in kind, and social privileges. Penalties were imposed for the under-fulfilment of norms. The system was sometimes abused, for propaganda purposes, by the establishment of low norms which would be exceeded by a wide margin. Norms would sometimes be raised to disguise a reduction in wages. The U.S.S.R. is now less interested in individual record-breaking than in an all-round increase in production, and piece-rates have been found to be adequate incentives for skilled workers.

Stalin, Joseph Vissarionovich. Russian statesman and First Secretary of the Communist Party of the Soviet Union for thirty years; born 21 December 1879 at Gori, near Tiflis in Georgia, the son of a cobbler, Vissarion Djugashvili; educated at the Gori Ecclesiastical School and at the Tiflis Theological College from which he was expelled for political activity. He joined the Tiflis Marxist Social-Democratic Organization in 1898, working for the Party in Batum and Tiflis until his first arrest in 1902. Between 1902 and 1913 he escaped from prison five times; during one of his intervals of freedom, in 1905, he met Lenin at a Party conference at Tammerfors. He founded *Pravda, q.v.,* in 1912 and guided the Party press and political activities until he was re-arrested in 1913 and exiled to a region near the Arctic Circle for four years. He returned to Moscow in 1917 to edit *Pravda,* and to prepare, with Lenin, the successful Bolshevik October Revolution. In that year he was appointed Commissar of Nationalities, and from 1918 to 1920 he fought in the Civil War, becoming in 1920 a member of the War Council. In 1922 he was elected to succeed Lenin, whose illness had incapacitated him and who died in 1924, as First Secretary of the Communist Party. He launched a plan of socialist industrialization in 1925 designed to restore Russia's pre-war productive capacity, and in 1928 an impending shortage of food led him to implement a plan of intensive collectivization of agriculture, in which many peasant farmers (kulaks) were liquidated.

From the moment of Lenin's death every word that had been written by him became sacrosanct. Criticism of the most informal and transient kind of Party members such as Trotsky, Zinoviev and Kamenev provided Stalin with the excuse for their prosecution, and subsequent extinction. (Trotsky was exiled in 1929 and assassinated in Mexico in 1940.) The adoption of a new Constitution in November 1936, the Stalin Constitution, gave him the absolute authority he required, and by 1937 he had eliminated all potential opposition to his leadership (by a succession of trials in which the defendants were compelled to make public confession of their 'crimes', culminating in the trial in June 1937, of Marshal Tukhachevsky and other senior officers of the Red Army). He directed the Russian war effort against the Germans from 1941 to 1945, accepting the honour of Marshal of the Soviet Union in 1943. By his intervention at international conferences at Teheran, *q.v.*, in 1943, and at Yalta, *q.v.*, in 1945 he achieved a considerable extension of Russian influence and authority in Europe and at the United Nations. His later years were associated with the policy of Russian detachment from Western Europe (the iron curtain, *q.v.*) and internal purges. He was condemned post-humously inside the U.S.S.R. for abolishing collective leadership within the Party and for developing a personality cult, *q.v.* In 1967 his daughter by his second marriage, Svetlana Alliluyeva, left the U.S.S.R. and applied for U.S. citizenship. He died on 5 March 1953, and was succeeded as First Secretary of the Communist Party by Nikita Khrushchev, *q.v.*

Stanfield, Robert Lorne. Canadian Progressive Conservative Party politician; born 11 April 1914 and educated at Colchester Academy, Truro, Ashbury College, Ottawa, and at the universities of Dalhousie and Harvard. A barrister, he took silk in 1950 and was Governor of Dalhousie University from 1949 to 1956. He became the leader of the Progressive Conservative Party in Nova Scotia, and Premier and Minister of Education in the provincial government in 1956. In September 1967 he succeeded John Diefenbaker as leader of the national Party. He represented Colchester County, Nova Scotia, in the Federal Parliament.

State Department. The branch of the U.S. government responsible to the President for the conduct of foreign affairs. It is the oldest department, having been established (as the Department of Foreign Affairs) on 27 July 1789 by the fourth Act of Congress passed after the adoption of the Constitution. Its head is the Secretary of State.

States Rights. The doctrine that member States of the American Union retain sovereignty over their internal affairs, especially in regard to race relations. It rejects the clause in the American Constitution that makes the Constitution itself the supreme law of the land, the ultimate interpretation of which rests with the Supreme Court, *q.v.* The doctrine is preached in many Southern States. It was an essential part of the electoral platform of Governor George Wallace, *q.v.*, in his gubernatorial campaign in Alabama, and in his presidential campaign in 1968.

Statute of Westminster, 1931. *See* Westminster, Statute of.

Sterling Area. A group of countries which decided in 1931, when the U.K. went off the gold standard, to tie their currencies to sterling rather than to gold and to hold their currency reserves in the form of balances with the Bank of England. During and after the Second

World War the acute shortage of gold and dollars compelled sterling area members to impose exchange control; this means that, although there is freedom of exchange within the sterling area, the territories that earn a net surplus of dollars sell their excess dollars to the British Treasury for sterling, and those that spend more dollars than they earn can buy dollars for sterling from the British Treasury. The territories in the sterling area, described in the Exchange Control Act of 1947 as the 'scheduled territories', were: the U.K. and its colonies; all British Commonwealth countries with the exception of Canada; and Burma, Iceland, Ireland, Jordan and the seven independent Trucial States, *q.v.*

Straits of Malacca. A 600-mile-long waterway which separates the Malay peninsula from Sumatra. For more than 200 miles it is less than 24 miles wide, and at its narrowest point only 21 miles. It is a much frequented shipping route; in 1970 37,000 vessels passed through the Straits. On 16 November 1971 the governments of Indonesia and Malaysia announced their intention to implement a 12-mile territorial offshore limit which would effectively close the Straits of Malacca to all but ships of innocent passage. In March 1972 both countries made it clear that they claimed the right of prior consultation from foreign governments wishing to use the Straits for the passage of naval vessels, and that for reasons of safety and pollution control they would impose a ban on tankers of more than 200,000 deadweight tons. The claim aroused fierce opposition from the Japanese and U.S.S.R. governments, the former because Japanese oil tankers regularly pass through the Straits on their way from the Persian Gulf, the Russians for strategic reasons, because the Straits are the shortest direct passage from the Indian Ocean, in which the Russian Fleet operates, to the South China Sea. Singapore, whose economy, which is based on her entrepôt trade, would suffer if Malaysia were to impose tolls on shipping using the Straits, refused to sign the declaration, which was approved by the Chinese government. Japan announced that it would seek settlement of the legal status of the Straits at the third U.N. Conference on the Law of the Sea at Geneva in 1973.

Strategic Arms Limitation Talks (S.A.L.T.). A series of negotiations begun in November 1969 which resulted on 26 May 1972, during the state visit of President Nixon to Moscow, in the conclusion of a Treaty on the Limitation of Anti-Ballistic Missile Systems between the U.S.A. and the U.S.S.R. It was accompanied by an Interim Agreement on the Limitation of Offensive Arms. The Treaty stipulated the numbers of anti-ballistic missiles and ballistic missile launchers each country should have, and the areas in which they should be sited. The Agreement extended this to include the numbers of ballistic missile submarines and launchers on submarines that each side might deploy. The Treaty represented the first significant advance in reducing the world total of nuclear weapons, and although it did not refer to underground nuclear testing, which had continued despite the Test Ban Treaty, *q.v.*, of 1963, an Environmental Protection Agreement, signed simultaneously with the Treaty in Moscow, emphasized a mutual concern about air and water pollution.

Strategic Trusteeship Territory. Any territory among the Trusteeship Territories, *q.v.*, which is designated by the administering country as a 'strategic area'.

Strauss, Franz-Josef. West German politician; born in Munich 6 September 1915, the son of a butcher; educated at Munich Gymnasium and Munich University; he is a Catholic. He was a Lieutenant in the artillery during the Second World War, and was at Stalingrad. In 1945 he became a Councillor at the Bavarian Ministry of the Interior, and from 1946 to 1949 he was Landrat (County Commissioner) of Schongau, under the U.S. Military Government. He became a member of the Bundestag in August 1949, in which year he also became General Secretary of the Christian Social Union (of which he was a founder), the Bavarian counterpart of the Christian Democratic Union. He was then successively Minister for Special Tasks (i.e. Minister Without Portfolio) from 1953 to 1955 and Minister for Atomic Affairs from 1955 to 1956. He was Minister of Defence from October 1956 until he resigned in November 1962, and became Minister of Finance in 1966 in the coalition government of Dr Kurt Kiesinger, *q.v.* His opposition to the peace treaties with Poland and the U.S.S.R. was instrumental in determining the abstention of the C.D.U.–C.S.U. on their ratification in May 1972.

Subversive Activities Control Act, 1950. An Act passed by the U.S. Congress, it set up the Subversive Activities Control Board which can decide whether any organization is a 'Communist action organization', a 'Communist front organization', or a 'Communist-infiltrated organization'. If the Board so decides, the organization can be required to file with the Department of Justice a list of its members, the sources of its funds, and a detailed account of how the funds are spent; it must state in its propaganda that the Board has made a finding against it. Members of 'action' groups and officers of 'front' groups cannot apply for, or use, a U.S. passport, or seek any office or employment under the government. Offences are punishable with a fine of $10,000 and imprisonment for five years; a person commits a fresh offence every day that he breaks the law. The aim was to bring Communists and their supporters into the open rather than to declare their organization illegal. In November 1965 the Supreme Court held that the section ordering registration by members of the Communist Party was unconstitutional and contrary to the Fifth Amendment. (*See* Fifth Amendment Communist.)

Succession States. The independent states which, after the First World War, either were set up on, or obtained a share of, the territory of the former Austro-Hungarian Empire. They included Austria, Czechoslovakia, Hungary, Italy, Poland, Romania, and Yugoslavia. Succession to territory usually involves succession to the international rights and duties of the former sovereign. The peace treaties made express provision, for example, for the apportionment between the states concerned of the pre-war debts of the Austro-Hungarian Empire.

Sudan. An independent state, and the largest in Africa, to the south of Egypt, which was an Anglo-Egyptian condominium from 1899 to 1 January 1956; area 976,750 sq. m.; population (1971) 15,963,000, partly Arabs and partly Negroes; capital Khartoum. Its status as a condominium administered by a Governor-General on behalf of Egypt and the U.K. was confirmed in the Anglo-Egyptian Treaty of 1936, but on 12 February 1953 the two governments approved proposals for Sudanese self-government. Sudan became an independent republic on 1 January 1956.

A crucial factor in Sudanese politics is the difference in outlook between the Islamic Arab-speaking north and the non-Islamic and more primitive south, which fears northern dominance and has clear memories of rapacious northern slave traders. The National Unionist Party (N.U.P.), which won a majority at the elections held in 1953, was supported by orthodox (Khatmi) Moslems who voted for N.U.P. largely because their religious rivals, the heterodox Mahdists (the Ansar sect), voted for the opponents of N.U.P., the Umma Party. The N.U.P. later suffered from internal dissension, but its leader, Sayed Ismail el Azhari, who became Prime Minister in January 1954, eventually accepted the principle of complete independence rather than a close union with Egypt, while the Khatmia and the Mahdists reached a measure of agreement on the methods by which self-government could be achieved. El Azhari resigned in July 1956 in favour of the Secretary-General of Umma, Abdullah Khalil, who was better able to secure the support of both rival sects.

From November 1958 until the end of 1964 Sudan was under military rule. The leader of the army *coup*, General Ibrahim Abboud, became President of the Supreme Council (which exercised absolute powers) and Prime Minister. After a prolonged political crisis he was succeeded as President by el Azhari, and as Prime Minister by Mohammed Ahmed Mahgoub, *q.v.*, leader of that section of Umma which was not dominated by Mahdists, in June 1965. The new government was a coalition of Umma (which had won 85 of the 173 contested seats in the Assembly in recent elections) and the N.U.P. (56 seats). The Communists won 11 seats. In July 1966 Mahgoub was replaced as Prime Minister by Dr Sadiq el Mahdi, leader of the majority Umma faction. Continuing unrest in the south, and an abortive Communist *coup d'état* in December 1966 led to the proscription of the Party, and the introduction of a new Constitution. In May 1967 the N.U.P. withdrew from the government and Mahgoub was invited by the Assembly to form a new coalition. Elections held in April 1968 confirmed the popularity of the N.U.P. which, as the Democratic Union Party, in alliance with the People's Democratic Party, won 101 out of the 233 seats in the Assembly. On 25 May 1969 a left-wing junta, supported by the Army, overthrew the regime. The Constitutional Assembly was dissolved, and a National Revolutionary Council, with Colonel Jaafar al-Nimiery as chairman, was established with a declared policy of 'freedom and socialism'. In May 1971 Sudan became a one-party state and the Sudanese Socialist Union the sole political party. A short-lived Communist *coup* in July 1971, engineered by Lieutenant-Colonel Babikr al Nur and Major Hashem Atta, who seized power for three weeks, was savagely repressed. One quarter of the Army officers were purged and prominent civilians, especially those with Communist sympathies including Abdul Khalik Mahgoub and the former Minister for Southern Affairs, Joseph Garang, were executed. In September 1971 Nimiery, now promoted to General, was elected President of the Republic for an initial term of six years, the Revolutionary Command Council was dissolved and a new cabinet appointed with Nimiery as Prime Minister. The three southern provinces, which had fought a civil war for fifteen years, latterly under the South Sudan Liberation Movement, led by Major-General Joseph Lagu, against the dominant north, were offered autonomy. On 28 February 1972 an agreement was reached which brought the fighting to an end; regional autonomy was granted to South Sudan and English was accepted as the common language for the area, although Arabic was still to be accorded official status. Major-General Lagu warned the Khartoum government that South Sudan would not accept accession to the new Federation of Arab Republics, *q.v.*; the North Sudanese he claimed, were closer to their compatriots of the South than to the Arabs of the Middle East.

Agriculture occupies 87 per cent of the population and land for farming is leased from the government. The economic development of Sudan depends largely upon the proper use of the waters of the Nile valley, which has created the cotton fields which yield Sudan's most valuable export. Most of the cotton, which is long-staple, is produced by the Gezira Scheme, irrigated from the Blue Nile. Recent developments have included: a hydro-electric station at the Sennar Dam on the Blue Nile, and its extension, the Managil Scheme, to provide power for the Gezira Scheme and for factories in Khartoum; a dam at Khashm el Girba to irrigate about 500,000 acres mainly to resettle the population of the Wahdi Halfa area which was flooded by the reservoir of the High Dam, *q.v.*; and a dam at Roseires on the Blue Nile to provide power and irrigation for 3 million acres.

Suez Canal. The canal, 101 miles long, connecting the Mediterranean and Red Seas. It was opened for navigation in 1869; the Suez Canal Company, an Egyptian company which owned the Canal and was managed largely by Frenchmen, was granted a concession to levy fees (£95 million in 1966) on all ships passing through. The concession was due to expire on 17 November 1968 when the ownership of the Canal would have reverted to the Egyptian government. The British government owned 353,504 of the Company's 800,000 shares and one-third of the transit tonnage was British.

Under the Convention of Constantinople, signed in 1888, the Canal was exempted in perpetuity from blockade, and all vessels whether armed or not, must be allowed to pass through in peace and war. The Anglo-Egyptian Treaty of October 1954 provided for the withdrawal of British forces from the Suez Canal Zone, as originally suggested by the British Labour government in 1946.

On 26 July 1956 the Egyptian government nationalized the Company, stating that the resulting revenue would be used to build the High Dam, *q.v.* Suez Canal Company shareholders were to be paid the Paris Stock Exchange closing prices (as on 26 July) for their shares. During the subsequent conflict with France, Israel and the U.K., the Egyptian government blocked the Canal; by April 1957 the obstructions had been removed by a United Nations mission and by April 1958 the daily average of ships in transit was greater than before nationalization. On 13 July 1958 an agreement was signed by representatives of the former shareholders and of the Egyptian government, by which the latter agreed to pay approximately £28 million as compensation for nationalization. The basis of the compensation was, as originally suggested by Egypt, the value of the shares at the date of nationalization.

Following the outbreak of war with Israel the Canal was closed on 6 June 1967; President Nasser announced that it would remain closed while Israeli troops occupied the east bank. Egypt receives £75 million annually, as compensation for the loss of shipping dues, from the Arab Economic Development Fund which was set up in September 1967 by Kuwait, Libya and Saudi Arabia.

Suharto. Indonesian General and politician; born 20 February 1921 near Jogjakarta, the son of a farmer, he joined the Army of the Netherlands East Indies at the age of nineteen. After the departure of the Japanese from Java in 1945 he held a guerilla command in the war of independence against the Dutch. In 1949 he became a career officer in the Army of the Indonesian Republic. He was Deputy Chief of the Army in 1962 when he was appointed to lead the campaign to wrest West Irian from the Dutch. After the negotiated settlement which gave Indonesia control of that territory in 1963 he took command of the Strategic Reserve, a mobile fighting force, which rounded up the leaders of the abortive *coup* in 1965, in which General Ahmed Jani, Army Commander and Chief of Staff, was murdered. Suharto immediately succeeded him, and in March 1966 assumed executive powers, forcing Ahmed Sukarno, *q.v.*, in February 1967, to resign to him the Presidential authority. He was elected President of the Republic of Indonesia in March 1968 for a five-year term by the Provisional People's Consultative Congress, the sole remaining constitutional authority. A close associate of the former Army Commander, General Nasution, he has long shared his antipathy to corruption in government and to Communists.

Sukarno, Ahmed. Former president of the Republic of Indonesia; born 6 June 1901 in Java. After participating in an unsuccessful revolt against the Dutch in 1926 he fused the native parties of the Netherlands East Indies into one nationalist organization modelled on the Indian Congress Party, *q.v.* He was imprisoned three times by the Dutch and exiled to Sumatra in 1940. When the Japanese invaded the islands in 1942 he negotiated with them on the future status of Indonesia. They appointed him President of the Java Central Council, and when a Republic of Indonesia was proclaimed in 1945 he became its first President. After the Japanese surrender the Dutch accused him of collaboration; he had difficulty in maintaining his position against Sjahrir, the Socialist-Nationalist, but regained political supremacy in 1947 and supervised the transfer of sovereignty on 28 December 1949 from the Netherlands to the Republic of Indonesia. From 1963, when he embarked on a confrontation, *q.v.*, with Malaysia, he followed a pro-Chinese policy. After an abortive Communist *coup d'état* in 1965, in which he was implicated, he was obliged to yield his authority to General Suharto, *q.v.*, who succeeded him as President on 12 March 1967. He died on 20 June 1970.

S.U.N.F.E.D. Special United Nations Fund for Economic Development, *q.v.*

Supreme Court. The highest Court in the U.S.A., described in the Constitution as follows: 'The judicial power of the United States shall be vested in one Supreme Court, and in such inferior courts as the Congress may from time to time ordain and establish.' It hears appeals from lower courts in civil and criminal cases and is empowered to interpret all laws and treaties passed by Congress and to decide whether they are constitutionally valid. The Chief Justice is paid $62,500 and his eight Associate Justices $60,000 annually. The choice by the President of persons to become Supreme Court Justices must be approved by the Senate. Many cases decided by the Court have been of fundamental constitutional significance. In 1954, for example, it decided that racial segregation in schools violated the constitutional rule relating to the equality of U.S. citizens; there could be no such thing, it ruled, as separate but equal educational facilities.

Supreme Soviet, *or* Supreme Council. The legislature of the U.S.S.R., comprising the Council of the Union and the Council of Nationalities. These Councils have equal powers and are elected for a term of four years. The Council of the Union is elected on the basis of one deputy for every 300,000 of the population; the Council elected on 12 June 1966 had 767 members. The Council of Nationalities, elected on the same day, comprises 750 deputies elected by the 15 constituent Republics and by various autonomous Republics, autonomous regions, and national areas within the constituent Republics. Voting, which is on the basis of universal suffrage with the exception of the insane and those deprived of civil rights, is by secret ballot. The electors vote for or against a single list, and the important part of the election is the preliminary decision in each constituency as to who should be included on the list. The Communist Party is the only legal political party, but non-members may be entered on the list.

The Supreme Soviet usually meets twice a year for about a week. It delegates most of its power to its elected Presidium, which acts on its behalf between the sessions. The Chairman of the Presidium since December 1965 has been Nikolai Viktorovich Podgorny, *q.v.*; the post is equivalent to that of President. The Supreme Soviet also elects the Council of Ministers, which is the highest administrative and executive organ in the U.S.S.R.; its Chairman is Alexei N. Kosygin, *q.v.* The First Vice-Chairmen are Kirill Mazurov and Dmitri Polyansky.

Surinam. Netherlands Guiana, which is part of the Netherlands West Indies, *q.v.*

Suslov, Mikhail Andreyevich. Russian politician; born 1902 in Shakhovskoe, Saratov Province, now Ulyanovsk Oblast. From 1921–4 he studied at the Prechistenka Workers' Faculty in Moscow, graduating from the Moscow Institute of National Economy in 1928. He continued his studies at the Economics Institute for Red Professors, teaching meanwhile at Moscow University and at the Industrial Academy. In 1931 he was appointed to the Central Control Commission of the All-Union Communist Parties, and from 1933 to 1934 helped to direct the Party purges ordered by Joseph Stalin, *q.v.*, in the Urals and in Chernigov Oblast. In 1939 he became First Secretary of the Rostov Oblast and Stavropol Krai Party Committees and was promoted to the Auditing Commission of the All-Union C.P. office. During the German invasion of the U.S.S.R. he was a member of the Military Council of the North Caucasian Front, directing the Stavropol Krai headquarters of the partisan troops. At the end of 1944 he was put in charge of the mass deportations from Lithuania. From 1946, when he became head of the Party Agitation and Propaganda Department, he concentrated on national propaganda. He succeeded Zhdanov in 1948 as leader of the Cominform, *q.v.*, and was instrumental in denouncing President Tito of Yugoslavia, *q.v.*, for deviationism. He was chief editor of *Pravda* from 1949 to 1950, when he became a member of the Presidium of the Supreme Soviet. In 1954 he was promoted to be Chairman of the Foreign Affairs Commission of the Council of Ministers, and in July 1955 he was made a member of the Presidium of the Central Committee of the Communist Party.

Svalbard. Spitsbergen Archipelago, *q.v.*

Swaziland. An independent monarchy within the British Commonwealth, and the smallest of the three former High Commission Territories, *q.v.*; it is bounded to the north and west by Transvaal, to the south by Natal and to the east by Mozambique; area 6,704 sq. m.; population (1971 estimate) 447,000, of whom more than 90 per cent are Swazi; headquarters of the administration Mbabane. It became a British protectorate in 1903 under the administration of the government of Transvaal; in 1907 the High Commissioner for South Africa assumed responsibility for the territory so that it remained under British protection when Transvaal became a province of the

Union of South Africa in 1910. A Constitution of 1964 granted internal self-government, and on 25 April 1967 the status of the territory was changed from a protectorate to that of a protected state. The Paramount Chief, or Ngwenyama, Sobhuza II, was recognized as King and Head of State, and Britain was to retain control of external affairs, defence and finance until Swaziland attained full independence. This was achieved on 6 September 1968. Government is by the King and parliament which consists of a Senate of 6 members appointed by the King and 6 members elected by the House of Assembly which in turn comprises 24 members elected on the basis of universal adult suffrage in eight three-member constituencies. At elections held in May 1972 the Imbokodvo Nationalist Movement, the royalist party founded shortly before the first elections of 1964 by Sobhuza II, and led by Prince Makhosihi Dhlamini, great-grandson of Sobhuza I, who became the country's first Prime Minister, won 21 seats (all 24 in 1968). The main opposition party, the Nganwe National Liberation Congress, led by Dr Ambrose Zwane, which advocates single-member constituencies under which system it would have secured representation in the Assembly in 1968, won 3 seats; the United Swaziland Association, which is the organization of the white community, supports the King's party.

Citrus, cotton, tobacco, rice and sugar are exported, and there are substantial deposits of asbestos and iron; under the Constitution these are vested in the Ngwenyama, or King, to be held in trust for the Swazi nation. The migration of Swazi labour to South Africa is diminishing, but is still on a considerable scale.

Sweden. An independent state in Scandinavia; area 173,436 sq. m.; population (1971) 8,849,000; capital Stockholm. It was involved in many international struggles from the sixteenth to the eighteenth century, and once dominated Finland and much of Germany, extracting a large income from the north German coastal ports. In 1815 the last Germanic possession, Pomerania, was exchanged for Norway, which remained united to Sweden until 1905. The country has been neutral since 1814. Under the 1809 Constitution, amended in 1864, the throne is hereditary in the House of Bernadotte, the family of Marshal Bernadotte, one of Napoleon's Marshals, who became King in 1818. King Gustav Adolf (born 1882) ascended the throne in 1950. The Riksdag (parliament) was reconstituted in 1970, a unicameral Diet of 350 members, directly elected for three years by universal suffrage, replacing the former First and Second Chambers. Proportional representation has been retained, 28 constituencies throughout Sweden electing 310 members who have obtained 12 per cent of the votes cast in their constituencies; the remaining 40 seats are distributed among parties which receive four per cent of the national vote. There is a state subsidy to all parties securing one seat in the Diet.

At elections held on 20 September 1970 the results were: Social Democrats 163 seats (125 in the former Second Chamber of 233 members); Liberals 58 (34 in 1968); Conservatives 41 (32); Centre (Peasant) Party or Agrarians 71 (39); Communists 17 (3). The Social Democrat Party has been in office since 1932, except for three months in 1936, during which time it has introduced one of the world's most highly developed schemes of social insurance, encouraged the growth of cooperatives, and exercised state control over the railways, public utilities, air transport, many bus routes, and some industries (e.g. iron ore, wood-pulp, sugar, alcohol, oil-refining), but not those concerned with manufacturing. It is led by Olof Palme who succeeded Dr Tage Erlander, who had been Prime Minister since 1946, just prior to the 1970 elections. The Agrarians, or Centre Party, with whom the Social Democrats formed a coalition in 1936–9, as well as since 1951, find most of their support in the rural districts, and look to the Social Democrats to protect agriculture from foreign competition, but suspect that this alliance loses them votes to the Conservatives, particularly in southern Sweden. The Liberals, who were of far greater importance during the struggle for a universal franchise, believe in a 'social-liberalism' rather than Socialism, and advocate a reduction in housing subsidies and technical adjustments to the health services. The Conservatives, led by Yngve Holmberg, oppose government intervention in trade and industry; they find support among industrialists and landowners. The Communist Party was formed in 1919 by dissident Social Democrats; it attributed its electoral defeat in 1968 to the Russian invasion of Czechoslovakia. The four main parties oppose all foreign alliances, while the Communists would welcome closer relations with the U.S.S.R. All five parties have rejected Swedish adherence to N.A.T.O., *q.v.* Sweden is an enthusiastic participant of the United Nations, having provided its second General Secretary (Dag Hammarskjöld); in 1964 it placed a permanent force of 1,600 men at the disposal of the Organization.

Half of Swedish manufacturing and nearly all Swedish exports are accounted for by the engineering, iron, steel, ship-building, and timber industries. There are huge deposits of iron ore in Lapland, north of the Arctic Circle, and smaller deposits farther south; most of the ore is exported to the U.K. and to the German Federal Republic. Substantial quantities of low-grade uranium ore have also been discovered. Sweden produces over 90 per cent of its own food requirements, although less than ten per cent of the working population is engaged in farming. Most of Sweden's trade is with the German Federal Republic which, in 1952, replaced the U.K. as its largest supplier of goods.

Switzerland. A federal republic in Central Europe; area 15,950 sq. m.; population (1971) 6,428,000; capital Berne. The Swiss Constitution is one of the most democratic in the world. The historical division of the country into 22 cantons (16 were federated by 1513) each of which has its own parliament and government, has produced a high degree of regional autonomy within a federal state. There is frequent use of plebiscites; in the smaller cantons the citizens gather in the open air to vote on local issues; any group of 30,000 citizens, or the representatives of 8 cantons, may demand a referendum on a law already passed by the federal parliament. Women were admitted to the federal franchise by a referendum held in February 1971, but not all the cantons have yet approved female suffrage, and some give it on an optional basis. The Constitution, most of which dates from 1848, stresses the principle of equality between the various racial and religious groups in Switzerland regardless of their numerical strength. German is the dominant language in 19 of the cantons; however, French, Italian, and Romansch, the language spoken by most of the people in the canton of Graubünden (Grisons), are also recognized as the official national languages. Protestants number 53 per cent of the population and Catholics approximately 45 per cent but there is complete religious toleration and state education is undenominational. In accepting a proposal to abrogate certain articles of the Constitution which banned the Jesuit Order, the Head of the Swiss Department of Justice stated: 'the decisive principles of Switzerland's democratic order, freedom of religion and conscience, freedom of religious expression and the denominationally neutral character of public education are so firmly rooted in the Constitution that any attempt to alter them is [in 1955] certain to fail.'

The country is of great strategic importance. Through its railway system it controls communications between north and south Europe; it acts as a buffer state between France, Italy, and Germany; its mountain defences are almost impregnable. Since 1815 its neutrality has never been violated. The absence of war, together with low taxes and a well-ordered economy – the harnessing of hydro-electric power to provide cheap fuel, heavy investment in specialized industries, *e.g* locomotive construction and grinding machinery, and intensive dairy-farming and afforestation – have brought economic stability which has, in turn, attracted foreign currency. Banking, insurance, and tourism are the most profitable industries.

The Swiss Federal Assembly consists of two Houses; the National Council (Nationalrat) of 200 members who are elected by direct vote every four years; and the Council of States (Ständerat) of 44 members to which the cantons each send two representatives. The Federal Assembly elects the Federal Council (Bundesrat), or government, of seven members, all of whom must be from different cantons; and the Prime Minister, who also acts as Head of State, is elected annually from the members of the government. In practice the government is always a coalition. At elections to the National Council held on 31 October 1971, the Radical Democrats (a progressive bourgeois party inclined to centralism) won 49 seats (49 in 1967); the Social Democratic Party (Socialist) won 46 seats (51); the Christian Democratic Party (right-wing and formerly the Catholic Conservatives) 44 (45); Farmers', Traders' and Citizens' Party 21 (21); Independents 13 (16); Liberal Democrats 6 (6); Communists 5 (5); Republican Movement, led by Dr James Swarzenbach who had been elected to the Nationalrat in 1967 as a representative of the National Campaign against Foreign Domination of People and Homeland, a party which campaigned for a reduction in the number of foreign workers employed in Switzerland, 7 (1); National Campaign 4 (0); others 5. It was the first Federal election in which women were allowed to vote and to stand as candidates; eleven were elected.

Switzerland is not a member of the United Nations, but maintains a permanent observer at the U.N. headquarters in New York.

Syria. An independent state at the eastern end of the Mediterranean Sea; area 71,210 sq. m.; population (1970) 6,432,000, mainly Moslems; capital Damascus. It was part of the Ottoman Empire until 1920, when it became a mandated territory of the League of Nations; the British approved of the proclamation as King of Syria of Emir Faisal, son of King Hussein of the Hejaz and supporter of the allied cause in the First World War, but when the French objected he had to leave, and later took the throne of Iraq. France was entrusted with the mandate, but treated Syria as a colony until the French Popular Front government under Léon Blum agreed in 1936 to grant independence after a probationary period of three years. The French administration thus acquired a temporary popularity; however French officers in Syria organized rebellions to prove that there was local opposition to the agreement, and the right-wing in Paris prevented its ratification. Allied forces, who included the Free French, occupied the country in 1941 to forestall a German invasion, and independence was immediately proclaimed. In 1945 French forces tried to retain power by shelling Damascus; they were forced to leave under threat of bombardment by British troops.

From 1949 to 1954 Syria was controlled by an army dictatorship led by Brigadier Adib Shishekly. He was elected President in July 1953, and his party, the Arab Liberation Movement, obtained a clear parliamentary majority but was overthrown by an army revolt in February 1954. A former President, the nonagenarian Hashem Bey Atassi, was restored, and Shishekly went into exile; he was murdered in Brazil in 1964. Atassi retired in 1955 and Shukri el-Kuwatli, another former President who had lived in Egypt during the Shishekly regime, was elected President. At that time the Syrian political parties were: the Arab Socialist Baath, *q.v.*, led by Akram Hourani, which opposed the Baghdad Pact, *q.v.*, between Iraq, Persia, Pakistan and Turkey; the Parti Populaire Syrien (P.P.S.), a Fascist group which advocated the union of Syria and Iraq, but was dissolved in 1955; the pro-Egyptian National Party, whose leaders were Faris el-Khury and Sabry Assali; and the Independents, led by Dr Khaled el-Azem, a wealthy and influential landowner and former Prime Minister. In the 1955 elections none of the parties secured a majority in the Chamber of Deputies, and in 1956, after a succession of inconclusive coalitions, the three main groups found themselves looking to Egypt for leadership. This resulted in the creation of a United Arab Republic, *q.v.*, and after its establishment on 1 February 1958 political parties were dissolved and replaced (as in Egypt) by a National Union.

The next three years were marked by political and economic instability and acute tension between Syria and Egypt. In September 1961 a group of officers seized power and the link with Egypt was severed, Syria reverting to its earlier status as an independent sovereign state. A further *coup d'état* on 8 March 1963 led to the establishment of a Baathist National Council of the Revolution under the Presidency of Lt.-General Amin al Hafez. This government proved no more successful administratively than its predecessors, and in February 1966, the Army, in a violent *coup* instigated by Baathist extremists, deposed President Hafez, replacing him by Dr Noureddine al Atassi. He resigned in October 1970 following criticism of Syrian intervention on the side of the Palestine guerillas in the civil war in Jordan, *q.v.*, earlier that year. After a month of political intrigue General al-Assad, the Minister of Defence, who had established his supremacy over the Army in February 1969, seized power. As an Alaouite Moslem he was not eligible to succeed to the Presidency since the Syrian

Constitution required that the head of state be a member of the Sunni sect; nevertheless in February 1971 he was elected President for a seven-year term. A People's Council comprising 173 members, 87 of them Baathites, was summoned; it was the first legislative body in Syria to meet since 1966.

As a member of the Arab League, *q.v.*, Syria has never recognized the state of Israel. Border incidents from March 1962 onwards were a major contributing factor in the war which broke out in June 1967, as a result of which Israel invaded and occupied the Golan Heights. Syria has given encouragement to the Palestine Arab guerilla bands operating on both banks of the river Jordan. Since September 1970, when membership of the Federation of Arab Republics, *q.v.*, committed Syria to act in accord with Egypt and Libya against Israel, these have been placed under Army control.

Agriculture is the main occupation of 74 per cent of the population. The country is poor in proved mineral resources (only phosphates and rock salt having been found in quantity), but in the continual search for oil a field has been discovered at Karachuk in the northeast. The government receives revenue from the pipelines of the Trans-Arabian Pipeline Company, *q.v.*, originating in Saudi Arabia and terminating at Sidon in Lebanon, and until 1972, when the Company's assets were nationalized, from the Iraq Petroleum Company, *q.v.*, whose pipeline from Kirkuk terminates at Banias. Between December 1966 and March 1967 the Kirkuk pipeline was closed and reopened only after I.P.C. had agreed to higher royalties. When in May 1970 the Syrian section of Tapline was damaged the Syrian government refused to allow its repair – an act which was interpreted as an attempt to exert political pressure on the Saudi Arabian regime, whose oil exports were interrupted, and on the U.S. company to increase its transit dues. Saudi Arabia threatened to abandon the pipeline altogether and to end its subventions to the war economies of Egypt and Jordan unless they intervened. The pipeline was reopened in January 1971 after increased transit fees had been conceded by the company, but the consequent rise in the cost of piped oil at a time of world surplus resulted in the Gulf states shipping their oil round the Cape, with disastrous effects on production in Iraq, *q.v.*, and on Syrian government revenues. The textile industry at Aleppo and Damascus has been expanded, and a dam, larger than the Aswan dam, *q.v.*, is being constructed with Russian aid at Tabka on the Euphrates. There is a shortage of capital for improvements, and of the 30 per cent of invested capital which does come from abroad practically all is from the U.S.S.R. and East European countries.

T

Taft-Hartley Act, *or* Labor–Management Relations Act. It became law
on 23 June 1947. By altering the law as established by the Norris–La
Guardia Act, 1932 (which outlawed injunctions against strikers
except where the government was a party to the dispute) and the
National Labor Relations Act, 1935, *q.v.*, it constituted an important departure from the labour policies of the New Deal, *q.v.*
The Act (1) empowered the President, in the case of an actual or
threatened strike which he considered prejudicial to public safety
or welfare, to appoint a board of inquiry, and, after hearing its
report, to direct the Attorney-General to petition a Federal District
Court for an injunction restraining the strike for a 'cooling-off'
period of 75–80 days, during which employees would vote secretly
on their employers' proposals; if no agreement was reached the
strike could be resumed; (2) extended the list of unfair labour practices; (3) prohibited 'closed shop' agreements, under which membership of the appropriate union is made a condition of employment;
(4) prohibited employers and employees from terminating or modify-
ing a contract unless they gave 60 days' notice to the other party
and offered to negotiate a new contract; (5) prohibited union expendi-
tures in connection with federal elections.

Taiwan (Formosa). A large island approximately a hundred miles off
the south-eastern coast of China; area 13,890 sq. m.; population (1972)
12,040,000; capital Taipei. It was part of the old Chinese Empire for
many years until it was ceded to Japan in 1895. In the Cairo Declaration, *q.v.*, the U.K. and the U.S.A. promised that Formosa, as Taiwan
was then known, and all other territories taken by Japan from China
(such as Manchuria, *q.v.*, and the Pescadores) should be restored to
China. In 1945 China, then led by Chiang Kai-shek, *q.v.*, was allowed
to occupy the island. By the end of 1949 the Chinese Communists had
become so powerful that Chiang's forces, which included most of the
scanty Chinese navy, occupied only Taiwan, Hainan and some parts of
western China. At one time the U.S. State Department decided to give
no further support to Chiang, condemning his government as inefficient and corrupt. Both the U.S. and British governments regarded
Taiwan as still forming part of Japan until a Japanese peace treaty was
signed, and in 1950 (at the outset of the war in Korea) President Truman ordered the U.S. navy to protect Taiwan from the Chinese Communists; but in the Japanese peace treaty of 1951 the issue of Taiwan
was not dealt with. The Chinese government stated repeatedly that
Taiwan should be brought into the Chinese People's Republic, but

the U.S.A. offered the protection of the Seventh Fleet to the island and the nearby Pescadores, and in 1954 signed a Mutual Security Pact with Taiwan, recognizing only the government of Chiang Kai-shek whose troops also occupied Matsu, *q.v.*, and Quemoy, *q.v.*, and who agreed not to invade the mainland without U.S. consent.

The Taiwan government, as the Republic of China, represented China at the United Nations, and as a permanent member of the Security Council, *q.v.*, until 1971 when the U.S.A., which had used the veto, *q.v.*, to obstruct resolutions of the General Assembly to admit the People's Republic to membership, changed its policy. It was defeated, however, in its attempt to admit the Chinese People's Republic without simultaneously depriving Taiwan of representation, and on 25 October 1971 the Taiwan representatives were expelled from the U.N. In Moscow in March 1972 President Nixon agreed that the U.S. would progressively withdraw its forces and military installations from Taiwan.

Tammany Hall. An important U.S. political organization, officially the New York County Democratic Party Committee. It began as a club, the Society of Tammany, in 1789, but since about 1825 the club has been the official organization of the Democratic Party in one of the counties (Manhattan) of the State of New York. In the nineteenth century the Society was often corrupt, but made itself responsible for the welfare of European immigrants, receiving their votes in return. There are four other counties in New York City: The Bronx, Queen's, King's (Brooklyn), and Richmond (Staten Island). Each county has a similar Democratic Party Committee but Tammany Hall is the most powerful and usually controls the votes of the New York State representatives when the Democratic Party Presidential candidate is chosen.

Tanaka, Kakuei. Japanese politician; born 4 May 1918 in Nishiyama, a village in the Niigata Prefecture, the only son among seven children whose father failed successively as a horse trader, a carpenter and dairy farmer. His formal schooling ended at 15 when he went to Tokyo to work in a construction company and attended engineering courses at night. He passed the entrance examination to the Naval Academy, but enlisted in the army at the age of 18 and fought against the Russians on the Manchurian border. After being invalided out of the army in 1940 he set up in business as a building contractor in Tokyo, successfully negotiating contracts for the construction of factories in Korea and Manchuria. In 1947 he was elected to the House of Representatives as the Liberal member for Niigata constituency. He held office briefly as Parliamentary Vice-Minister for Justice, in which post he was accused, but later acquitted, of accepting bribes, and as Minister of Posts, but until he became Finance Minister from 1962 until 1965 in the Ikeda administration he concentrated on expanding his business interests to include railway and road transport companies. He was appointed Secretary-General of the Liberal-Democratic Party in 1966, resigning in 1971 prior to a cabinet reshuffle in which he became Minister of International Trade and Industry. On 5 July 1972 he was elected to succeed Eisaku Sato as leader of the ruling Liberal-Democratic Party; on the following day he was acclaimed as Prime Minister by the Japanese Diet. He has declared his intention to achieve more harmonious trading relationships with Europe and the U.S.A., and to reconcile Japan and China.

Tanganyika. Part of the United Republic of Tanzania, *q.v.*, it is in east Africa, on the Indian Ocean, bounded by Kenya to the north and Mozambique to the south; area 362,699 sq. m.; population (1965 estimate) 9,855,000 Africans (in 127 tribes), 22,000 Europeans, 123,000 Asians, Arabs and others. The area was a German colony from 1884 to 1918; it was administered by the U.K. under a League of Nations Mandate until 1946 and under United Nations Trusteeship until 1961. In September 1960 elections were held to return 71 members, 50 representing ordinary constituencies, the Asian and European communities having 11 and 10 reserved seats respectively. The Tanganyika African National Union (T.A.N.U.) led by Julius Nyerere, *q.v.*, won 70 seats; on 1 May 1961 internal self-government was granted and Nyerere became Prime Minister. On 9 December 1961 Tanganyika became a fully independent state. Nyerere was sworn in as President on 9 December 1962, on which day Tanganyika became a republic, still within the British Commonwealth. On 25 April 1964 Tanganyika united with Zanzibar, *q.v.*, to form the United Republic of Tanganyika and Zanzibar or, as it became known later that year, Tanzania.

Tangier. A city in Morocco, *q.v.*, which was an integral part of Spanish Morocco, *q.v.*, from 1912 to 1923. By the Tangier Conventions of 18 December 1923 and 8 July 1925, Tangier and some land surrounding it (with a total area of 225 square miles) became a neutralized and demilitarized International Zone, under a committee of control on which were represented Belgium, France, Italy, the Netherlands, Portugal, Spain, Sweden, the U.K., and the U.S.A. A Legislative Assembly with a European majority represented the Tangerines and the foreign communities; it was presided over by a Mendoub, representing the Sultan of Morocco who in theory remained sovereign after 1912. Spanish forces re-occupied the Zone on 14 June 1940, when German and Italian armies were conquering Europe, but had to withdraw in October 1945, when the Zone was again internationalized. When Morocco achieved independence in March 1956, the committee of control agreed that the Zone should again become part of Morocco proper. On 29 October 1956 a declaration was signed by Morocco and the members of the committee of control, terminating the international status of the area. On 19 April 1960 the Zone was incorporated financially and economically in Morocco; on 1 January 1962 it became a free port.

Tanzania. The United Republic of Tanzania, on and off the east coast of Africa, comprises the former independent states of Tanganyika, *q.v.*, and Zanzibar, *q.v.* The two countries, which had become fully independent within the British Commonwealth in 1961 and 1963 respectively, united on 25 April 1964 to form the United Republic of Tanganyika and Zanzibar, or, as it became known later that year, Tanzania. The total area (of Tanganyika and the two main islands of Pemba and Zanzibar) is 363,708 sq. m.; population (1971 estimate) 14,100,000, including more than 100,000 Asians, Arabs and others, and 15,000 Europeans; capital Dar es Salaam. Under the agreement by which the union took place the President of Tanganyika, Julius Nyerere, *q.v.*, became President, and the President of the People's Republic of Zanzibar and Pemba, Sheikh Abeid Amani Karume (succeeded in 1972 by Aboud Jumbe), became First Vice-President, of Tanzania; Rashidi Mfaume Kawawa, formerly Vice-President of Tanganyika with virtually the same functions as Prime Minister, became Second Vice-President. At elections held in October 1965 and November 1970 for the Assembly, in which, under the 1964 Constitution, there are no reserved seats for Asians or Europeans, Nyerere's party, the Tanzania African National Union (T.A.N.U.) returned all the members. Electors had a choice in each constituency of one of two T.A.N.U. candidates.

Tanganyika is the world's principal exporter of sisal and produces approximately half of the world's supply; cotton, coffee, beans and oilseeds are also produced, and diamonds, gold, lead and mica exported. Industrial development is concerned with the processing of raw materials for either export or local consumption. Zanzibar is the world's leading exporter of cloves and also produces coconuts, oranges, chillis and copra. On 15 December 1965, in protest at the failure of the U.K. government to put down the rebellion in Rhodesia, Tanzania broke off diplomatic relations with the U.K., the first

Commonwealth country ever to do so; these were resumed in July 1968. Throughout 1971 there was intensive border fighting between Tanzania and Uganda following the overthrow by General Amin of the regime of President Obote, who took refuge in Dar es Salaam. Since this was imperilling the continued existence of the East African Economic Community, *q.v.*, President Kenyatta intervened to reconcile the parties, and by 1972 the guerilla warfare had subsided.

Tapline. Trans-Arabian Pipeline Company, *q.v.*

Tashkent Agreement. A truce between India and Pakistan, brought about largely by Russian mediation, which was signed by President Ayub Khan, *q.v.*, and Lal Bahadur Shastri, *q.v.*, Prime Minister of India, in January 1966. It terminated the war which had broken out on the Kashmir border between India and Pakistan in August 1965, although it did not solve the issue of Kashmir, *q.v.*, which remained on the agenda of the U.N. Security Council.

Teheran Conference. A meeting between President Franklin D. Roosevelt of the U.S.A., Winston Churchill, Prime Minister of the U.K., and Marshal Stalin of the U.S.S.R., at Teheran in Persia between 28 November and 1 December 1943. The joint statement issued after the meeting said that plans for the destruction of the German forces had been concerted and that agreement had been reached as to the scope and timing of the operations to be undertaken against Germany from the east, west, and south.

Tennessee Valley Authority. A federal agency established in the U.S.A. in 1933 by Act of Congress. It is concerned primarily with the generation, sale, and transmission of electric power, with flood control, with the development and production of fertilizers, with re-afforestation and the prevention of erosion, and with the maintenance of navigation. It operates in an area of some 41,000 sq. m., embracing parts of the States of Alabama, Georgia, Kentucky, Mississippi, North Carolina, Tennessee, and Virginia, which are all in the valley of the Tennessee river. The Authority has built 21 dams. Its activities have for many years been strongly opposed by business interests, which believe that projects of this sort should be developed by private enterprise, and which resent the refusal of the T.V.A. to make profits as large as those which private enterprise would make. The T.V.A. was financed at the outset by the U.S. Treasury, and has been able to make regular repayments of the sums lent to it.

Terms of Trade. The relationship between the demand for a country's exports and the cost of its imports. If the demand for its exports increases, or the cost of its imports decreases, or if both these things happen, then a country's terms of trade are said to have improved;

if the converse happens, the terms of trade are said to have worsened. A favourable movement in the terms of trade, which may only be temporary, will improve a country's balance-of-payments position, but may conceal a decline in its real power as a seller of exports. In the case of a manufacturing country, such as the U.K., a typical example of an unfavourable movement of the terms of trade would be an increase in the cost of primary products which was not accompanied by a corresponding increase in the price of manufactured goods.

Terrorist. One who resorts to violence and terror to advance his political aims, which frequently include the overthrow of the established order. The word is often used by the supporters of a particular regime to describe and to vilify any of its opponents who resort to acts of violence. The opponents of a regime, however, would wish to be called partisans, nationalists or resistance workers rather than terrorists.

Test Ban Treaty. An agreement between the U.K., the U.S.A. and the U.S.S.R., concluded in Moscow in July 1963, by which each party to the treaty undertook 'to prohibit, to prevent, and not to carry out any nuclear weapon test explosion, or any other nuclear explosion, at any place under its jurisdiction or control: (a) In the atmosphere; beyond its limits, including outer space; or under water, including territorial waters or high seas; or (b) In any other environment if such explosion causes radioactive debris to be present outside the territorial limits of the state under whose jurisdiction or control such explosion is conducted.' The parties further agreed to refrain 'from causing, encouraging, or in any way participating in the carrying out of any nuclear weapon test explosion, or any other nuclear explosion, anywhere which would take place in any of the environments described'. In the preamble to the treaty the parties declared that their ultimate intention was to conclude a further agreement by which all nuclear explosions, including underground explosions, would be banned permanently; the provisions of this treaty were, therefore, not intended to prejudice the conclusion of any subsequent agreement.

The treaty was open to all states for signature. By August 1965 nearly 100 states, including the German Federal Republic, had signed; France and China did not do so, and continued to carry out nuclear tests in the atmosphere. The other three nuclear powers observed the agreement but continued underground tests. The treaty was weakened still further by a clause permitting any signatory to withdraw at three months' notice if it decided that its interests had been jeopardized by some unspecified nuclear development on the part of an unfriendly power.

Thailand (formerly Siam). An independent state in south-east Asia bordered by Laos and Cambodia in the east, by Malaysia in the south, and separated from Burma by a 200-mile stretch of the river Salween; area 198,247 sq. m.; capital Bangkok; population (1970) 37,768,000 of whom 4 per cent are Moslem and 1 per cent Chinese; Buddhism is the principal religion. By the Conventions of 1896 and 1904 the U.K. and France agreed to regard the country as a neutral zone between their Burmese and Indo-Chinese possessions, and although it became involved in frontier disputes with Cambodia and, more recently, with Laos, Thailand has not since been invaded. As the ally of Japan in the Second World War it was ceded in 1945 the two Shan states and the four Malay states, which were all returned to the U.K. in 1946.

The assassination, in 1946, of King Ananda Mahidol was followed by the accession to the throne of his brother, the present King, Bhumibol Adulyadej (born 1927) and the return to power, and the appointment as Prime Minister, of the former dictator Field-Marshal Pibul Songgram. In practice the country was governed by Songgram (until a bloodless *coup d'état* in September 1957, led by Field-Marshal Sarit Thanarat) with a council of Ministers all of whom held commands in the armed services. After the general election on 15 December 1957 the balance of power remained with the 123 nominated members of the assembly who supported the military junta which had overthrown Songgram. Despite constitutional provision for a new Constituent Assembly Thanarat continued to act as Prime Minister and to rule corruptly (his successors said that he had appropriated approximately £7 million from state funds) and by decree until his death in 1963. He was succeeded as Prime Minister on 9 December 1963 by Field-Marshal Thanom Kittikachorn who introduced a new Constitution in 1968 under which elections were held in February 1969. The threat to security posed by the crossing of the Thai border by Viet-Minh forces in 1970 and the intensification of the war in neighbouring Laos led to the re-establishment of military rule in November 1971.

The chief product and export is rice. The rise in the world price of rice has made it increasingly difficult to sell, and Thailand relies on foreign loans, especially from the U.S.A., for all internal investment and development. Japan is interested in the possibility of constructing an oil pipeline across the Kra isthmus from the Indian Ocean to the Gulf of Siam. Thailand is a member of the South-East Asia Collective Defence Treaty, *q.v.*, and the Colombo Plan; in 1961 it joined with Malaya and the Philippines to form the Association of South-East Asia, and in August 1967, with Indonesia and Singapore in addition, to create the Association of South-East Asian Nations (A.S.E.A.N.), *q.v.*

Thant, U. Secretary-General of the United Nations; the son of a land-owner and rice miller, he was born on 22 January 1909 at Pantanaw in the Irrawaddy Delta region of Burma; educated at the National High School, Pantanaw, and University College, Rangoon. In 1928 he became senior master at his old school, where U Nu (then known as Thakin Nu), who later became Prime Minister of Burma, was the headmaster. He succeeded U Nu as headmaster in 1931, and held that post (apart from wartime interruptions) until 1947. In 1942 he was appointed as secretary of the Burmese government's Educational Re-organization Committee. He then became Press Director for the government in 1947, Director of Broadcasting in 1948, and Secretary to the Ministry of Information from 1949 to 1957. During that period he also represented Burma at the United Nations, in 1952, and was Secretary for Projects in the Office of the Prime Minister (U Nu) in 1953. From 1957 to 1961 he was the permanent Burmese representative to the United Nations General Assembly. He was Vice-President of the General Assembly in 1959 and Chairman of the United Nations Congo Conciliation Commission in 1961. The Secretary-General, Dag Hammarskjöld, was killed in an air accident in the Congo on 18 September 1961, and in November 1961 U Thant was elected in his place. He retired on 31 December 1971 after serving for two five-year terms. The General Assembly elected the Austrian representative to the U.N., Dr Kurt Waldheim, *q.v.*, to succeed him.

Third Reich. The Nazi regime in Germany from 1933 until 1945. The term was coined by Möller van den Bruck, a nationalist German writer, in his book, *Das Dritte Reich*, published in 1924. Nazis said that the First Reich was the Holy Roman Empire (962–1806) and that the Second Reich was the German Empire, established by Bismarck in 1871, which came to an end when Kaiser Wilhelm II abdicated in 1918. The Nazi leader Adolf Hitler hoped that the Third Reich would survive for a thousand years.

Thorpe, John Jeremy. British Liberal Party politician; born 29 April 1929, the son and grandson of Conservative Members of Parliament; educated in the U.S.A. at Rectory School, Conn., and in England at Eton and Trinity College, Oxford, where he took a law degree. He became a barrister in 1954 and a member of the Devon sessions, entering the House of Commons in 1959 as the member for North Devon. In 1962 he was appointed to the National Advisory Committee of the British Broadcasting Corporation and from 1962 to 1967 he was Treasurer of the United Nations' Parliamentary Group. He became the honorary Treasurer of the Liberal Party in 1965, and was elected leader of the Parliamentary Liberal Party in 1967 in succession to Joseph Grimond.

Tibet. An autonomous western region of China, north of the Himalaya mountains; area 470,000 sq. m.; population about 1,300,000, of whom one-fifth are Lamas (Buddhists monks); capital Lhasa. The area is governed ultimately by China, but the nominal ruler is the fourteenth Dalai Lama. When a Dalai Lama dies an infant born at the moment of his death is sought and brought up as the successor as he is deemed to be a reincarnation of the dead man. A successful military power in the ninth century, Tibet was overrun by the Chinese Manchu Empire in the eighteenth century, but the latter's authority was not exerted until the end of the nineteenth century. Following the overthrow of the Manchu dynasty in 1911, the Chinese garrisons were driven out in 1912. Between 1931 and 1933 China began once more to assert her power, in 1950 reoccupied eastern Tibet, and later reoccupied Lhasa. A rival deity, the Panchen Lama, was supported by China in opposition to the Dalai Lama, but the Dalai Lama then appeared to support the regime, and both deities attended the meeting of the National People's Congress of China in 1954. In March 1959 there was an unsuccessful armed uprising against the Chinese, and the Dalai Lama fled to India. In December 1964 both the Dalai and Panchen Lama were removed from their posts; restrictions were placed on monasteries and the recruitment of novices halted. On 9 September 1965 Tibet became an autonomous region of China, which has since introduced some industry to Lhasa and started irrigation projects.

Tito, Marshal. President of Yugoslavia; born Josip Broz, the son of a peasant, near Zagreb, Croatia, 25 May 1892. He left school at 12 and worked as a farm labourer, dishwasher, and mechanic until he joined the Austro-Hungarian army, rising to the rank of regimental sergeant-major. In 1915 he was captured on the Russian front and sent to various prison camps. He was freed during the Russian Revolution, fought for three years with the revolutionaries and then returned to Yugoslavia. Eventually he became a full-time political organizer; from 1927 to 1928 he was the district secretary of a metal-workers' union and was active in the illegal Yugoslav Communist Party. He then spent over six years in jail, as a political undesirable, and on his release in 1936 left the country and helped to recruit Yugoslavs for the International Brigade in the Spanish Civil War. After the invasion of Yugoslavia by Germany in 1941 he organized the National Liberation Front of partisan forces and proved to the western powers that his army was the only effective anti-German movement in Yugoslavia; the troops of General Draja Mihailović, who were supported by the Royal Yugoslav government in London, fought no major battle after the autumn of 1941. Although the leadership was largely Communist, the majority of Tito's partisans had other, or no, political affiliations. He was acclaimed as the national leader.

He became Marshal of Yugoslavia and President of the National Liberation Committee in November 1943, when he demanded that the allies should cease to recognize the exiled Yugoslav government. From 1945 until 1953 he was Prime Minister and Minister of National Defence. He carried through a policy of extensive nationalization of industry and living accommodation, and of investment in hydroelectric schemes and railroad construction. However, land reform was restricted to the breaking-up of large holdings and redistribution of plots in excess of $4\frac{1}{2}$ acres. Tito has resisted all persuasion by the U.S.S.R. to force through collectivization of agriculture against the wishes of the peasant small-holders who represent eleven-twelfths of the population and on whom he relies for political support.

In 1953 he was elected President of the Republic, Chairman of the Federal Executive Council, and Supreme Commander of the Armed Forces. He claims that Yugoslavia represents in Europe the same independent, neutral, Socialist position that India holds in Asia.

Togo. An independent West African state which consists of a narrow strip of land between Ghana and Dahomey; area 21,000 sq. m.; population (1970) 1,955,000, the Ewe being the dominant tribe; capital Lomé. Under the name of Togoland, *q.v.*, the country was part of a German colony from 1894 to 1914, and administered by France until independence was achieved on 27 April 1960. The Prime Minister appointed at independence was Sylvanus Olympio, leader of the Committee for Togolese Unity, who in April 1961 became President; a graduate of the London School of Economics and a former employee of the United Africa Company, he was assassinated in January 1963. He was succeeded by Nicolas Grunitzky, his brother-in-law and a former Prime Minister, and leader of the opposition Democratic Union of the Togolese Peoples. In May 1963 elections were held by which Grunitzky became President and a new National Assembly of 56 members was returned. The new Assembly contained representatives of Grunitzky's party, of Olympio's party, and of the latter's youth section, Juvento, which took its name from the initial letters of Justice, Union, Vigilance, Égalité,

Nationalisme, Ténacité and Optimisme. On 13 January, the fourth anniversary of the death of Olympio, Grunitzky was overthrown by an Army *coup*. He was succeeded as President on 14 April 1967 by the Army Commander-in-Chief, Lt-Colonel Étienne Eyadema (born 1937) who was reputed to have been his brother-in-law's assassin. The country exports cocoa, cotton, coffee and teak, and there are substantial deposits of bauxite and phosphate. In March 1965 Togo joined the Conseil de l'Entente (*see* Entente, Council of the).

Togoland. Name of an area in West Africa which was a German colony from 1894 to 1914, was divided between France and the U.K. on the outbreak of the First World War and placed under League of Nations Mandates after the war, and became a trusteeship territory in 1946; the British portion became, under the name of the Volta Region, a Region of Ghana, *q.v.*, upon the establishment of that Dominion on 6 March 1957, and the French portion became an independent state on 27 April 1960, as the republic of Togo, *q.v.* The trusteeship territory comprised 34,934 sq. m., of which France administered approximately two-thirds. The decisions that British Togoland should enter Ghana, and that French Togoland should become independent, were taken by plebiscites in May 1956 and October 1956 respectively.

Tonga (Friendly Islands). An independent monarchy and member of the British Commonwealth comprising a group of islands in the South West Pacific, the largest of which is Tongatapu, lying 400 m. east of Fiji; area 270 sq. m.; population (1971) 123,000, of whom 77 per cent are Wesleyan Methodists; administrative capital Nuku'alofa. Tonga came under British protection in 1900. It was given self-government in 1959 and achieved independence on 4 June 1970. The King, Taufa' ahau Tupon IV, who succeeded his mother, Queen Salote, on 5 July 1967, presides over a Privy Council, the highest organ of government, and a Legislative Assembly of 7 members, elected by those islanders who qualify as literate, and 7 nobles appointed from among their own number. Every male Tongan, on reaching the age of sixteen, is allocated $8\frac{1}{4}$ acres of land for cultivation at an annual rent of 8 shillings. The islands are economically viable and export copra and bananas. Oil was discovered in 1969 through seepage into water wells and exploration has been started by an international consortium of 6 companies.

Tory. A word often used to describe a supporter of the British Conservative Party. In the seventeenth century the 'Tories' were the robbers who roamed Ireland in plundering bands after the Irish rebellion. The name was applied derisively after 1680 to those who approved of the succession of a Catholic heir to Charles II, by people who wanted to suggest that they were a set of 'Popish thieves'. Most Tories favoured the Stuart cause after 1689, but later became supporters of the established monarchy. After 1832 they called themselves Conservatives.

Totalitarian. A term denoting a single-party, dictatorial system of government, based on the 'totality of the state', as opposed to the liberal conception which allots to the state only certain functions, reserving others to the free decision of the individual. The totalitarian state extends its influence over the whole of life, private as well as public, and exacts full submission of the individual to its demands. The term has been used to describe the Nazi and Fascist governments which were headed by Hitler and Mussolini respectively in Germany and Italy. Examination has shown that although individuals and groups were subjected to treatment and laws which they could not oppose and which were often cruel and illiberal, there was not the complete centralization of power and authority that would exist in a truly totalitarian state. The term is widely used, however, to describe political systems which aim at, even if they do not achieve, the 'totality of the state'. In this wider sense it may be correctly applied to the U.S.S.R., China, Nazi Germany, and Fascist Italy.

Trade Disputes and Trade Union Act. A British law enacted in 1927 after the General Strike and wholly repealed in 1946 by the Labour government of 1945–51. It declared sympathetic strikes to be unlawful, if conducted on a scale calculated to coerce the government, and, by the 'contracting-in' clause, made it illegal to require any member of a trade union to make a contribution to the political fund of a trade union unless he had declared in writing his willingness to do so.

Trade Unions. Associations of workers for the common representation of their interests. They try to secure higher pay, better working conditions, shorter working hours, and other advantages for their members. On these matters they aim to conclude with the employers collective agreements which will apply to non-members as well, although sometimes it is part of their policy to prevent employers from employing non-members. If negotiations fail they sometimes withdraw their labour. Trade unions were frequently suppressed and persecuted in the first half of the nineteenth century, but achieved general recognition in Europe by the end of the century. In the U.S.A. the National Labor Relations Act, 1935, *q.v.*, legally recognized the rights of workers to organize trade unions. There are national trade union organizations in most countries; since the Second World War there have been attempts to create a genuinely international trade union movement, in the course of which the World Federation of Trade Unions, *q.v.*, and the International Confederation of Free Trade Unions, *q.v.*, have been established.

Trades Union Congress. An association of approximately 142 British trade unions with a membership (1970–71) of 10,002,204, founded in 1868 when the Manchester and Salford Trades Council took the initiative in calling the first Congress. The primary function of the T.U.C. is to bring union representatives together each year to consider matters of common concern to their members. Its elected General Council keeps in touch with government departments and takes an interest in all legislation affecting organized labour. The affiliated unions, however, remain autonomous, the T.U.C. having no control over their actions in wage negotiations.

Trans Alaska Pipeline. A pipeline 48 inches in diameter which is to run 800 miles from the Alaskan North Slope oil fields in Prudhoe Bay to the ice-free port of Valdez in south Alaska. When completed, the pipeline, which is to be built by a consortium of oil firms comprising Standard Oil of New Jersey, Standard Oil of Ohio and British Petroleum, Atlantic Richfield, Mobil, Phillips, Union and Amerada Hess, is expected to be able to carry 2 million barrels of oil daily, and would make the U.S.A. independent of supplies from the Middle East. An environmental lobby has opposed the construction of the pipeline, and the delay occasioned by the public hearings of objections in Anchorage in 1971 has doubled the original cost. The objectors have received support from the Canadian government which would prefer the pipeline to run through the Mackenzie River valley, thereby stimulating the economy of northern Canada.

Trans-Arabian Pipeline Company (Tapline). The operator of a pipeline which carries oil from Saudi Arabia through Jordan and Syria and to the Lebanese port and terminal of Saida (Sidon) on the Mediterranean Sea. Tapline is associated with the Arabian American Oil Company (Aramco), which has concessions in Saudi Arabia. Transit dues are payable to the governments concerned, who conduct periodic negotiations with Tapline as to the formulae for payment.

Transport House. An office block in Smith Square, Westminster, London, used as a headquarters by the Labour Party. The building is owned by the Transport and General Workers' Union.

Transylvania. The mountainous western region of Romania. It was part of the Turkish Empire until 1699 when it was ceded, with Hungary, to Austria after the Turks had been defeated in battle. The majority of its inhabitants are Ruman peasants and not of Magyar stock; they welcomed the transfer of Transylvania to Romania after the First World War when the Austro-Hungarian Empire collapsed. The territory was formally awarded to Romania by the Treaty of Trianon in 1920. In the Second World War Germany rewarded the Hungarians for their help by returning Transylvania to them, but the region was restored to Romania under the Paris Peace Treaty of 10 February 1947.

Treaty. A formal agreement between two or more states. Other terms, such as convention, pact, act, and declaration, are sometimes used, but the binding force of such arrangements is the same as that of a treaty. The Final Act of the Congress of Vienna, 1815, the Declaration of Paris, 1856, the Geneva Conventions on the Protection of Civilians in Wartime and on the Treatment of Prisoners of War, 1949, and the Balkan Pact, 1954, were all treaties which bound their signatories. A treaty differs from a contract between two individuals because it is valid even where the parties have not freely entered into it; duress does not invalidate consent as it does in the ordinary law of contract. A treaty is really a type of international legislation, which binds those concerned irrespective of their wishes; treaties which prescribe general rules of conduct for a number of states are often called law-making treaties. The two stages in the making of a treaty are usually its signature by plenipotentiaries on behalf of the contracting states, and its later ratification by or on behalf of the heads of the states. Ratification is not essential in all cases, and is frequently omitted in minor agreements.

Trieste. An important port and legally a Free Territory from 1947 to 1954; area 285 sq. m. The port was a product of the railway age. In the 1840s it was developed by the German Baron Bruck from a Slovenian fishing village into the main port of the Austro-Hungarian Empire. Resident Italian merchants secured control of its commerce, thereby providing an ethnic justification for Italy's claim to sovereignty. France and the U.K. recognized this claim in 1915 in order to bring Italy into the European war against Germany; despite American protests that the port belonged to the new Yugoslavia, which embraced Slovenia, the Treaty of Rapallo, in 1920, confirmed Italy in possession of Trieste.

Under the terms of the Paris Peace Treaty of 10 February 1947, Italy gave up Trieste and the Istrian peninsula and these were constituted a Free Territory. This was divided, temporarily, into two zones: Zone A (which included the city of Trieste) was administered jointly by a U.K. and U.S.A. Military Government, and Zone B (south of Trieste) was placed under Yugoslav Military Government. In 1948 the western powers proposed to restore the entire territory to Italy, but changed their policy when Yugoslavia left the Cominform, *q.v.* Ill-feeling which resulted in riots was provoked between the two countries. Military Government in both zones was terminated by a Memorandum of Understanding which was signed by the U.S.A., the U.K., Italy, and Yugoslavia on 5 October 1954. Yugoslavia agreed only after strong pressure had been exerted by the U.S.A. The administration of Zone A (population 297,000, of whom 90 per cent are Italian) was handed over to Italy, which undertook to maintain Trieste as a free port, *q.v.*, and to rent to Yugoslavia docks and wharves; Yugoslavia retained Zone B (population approximately 70,000, of whom 55 per cent are Slovene) to which a 200-yard strip of territory from Zone A was added. Since 1946 Yugoslavia has concentrated on expanding Rijeka (formerly Fiume) as the main port for itself and for the Austrian and Hungarian hinterland, with such success that by 1959 Rijeka was dealing with more cargo than Trieste.

Trinidad and Tobago. An independent state and member of the British Commonwealth, comprising two islands off the coast of Venezuela; area 1,864 sq. m. and 116 sq. m.; total population (1970 estimate) 1,206,000; capital Port of Spain. At the 1960 census 47 per cent of the population was of African, and 36 per cent of East Indian, origin. Trinidad, which was discovered by Columbus in 1498, was once Spanish; it was occupied by English forces in 1797 and ceded by Spain to England under the Treaty of Amiens in 1802. Tobago was ceded to England in 1814. For many years it was administered with the Windward Islands to the north, but it was united with Trinidad in 1889. The islands belonged to the West Indies Federation, *q.v.*, from its establishment in January 1958 to its dissolution in May 1962; they were given complete independence on 31 August 1962.

The bicameral legislature consists of a Senate of 24 members nominated by the Governor-General, 13 of whom are appointed on the recommendation of the Prime Minister, and a House of Representatives of 36 members elected directly by universal suffrage. At elections held on 24 May 1971 the People's National Movement, led by Dr Eric Williams, a democratic Socialist party with policies similar to the People's National Party of Jamaica, *q.v.*, won all 36 seats. The Democratic Labour Party, led by an East Indian lawyer, Vernon Jamada, which has a large Indian following and won 12 seats in 1966, boycotted the election, objecting to the use of voting machines and demanding a return to the ballot box.

Trinidad is the Commonwealth's third largest producer of oil, and supplies a considerable proportion of the world's natural asphalt. As well as oil-refining the major industries include the manufacture of sugar, molasses and rum, fruit juices and cotton textiles, but there is substantial unemployment (20 per cent of the work-force in 1971) and urgent need for social reform. Most of the economy is foreign-owned. In 1970 militant Black Power demonstrations against the government were followed by an Army mutiny which threatened the stability of the regime. In 1967 Trinidad and Tobago joined the Organization of American States, *q.v.* (the first Commonwealth country to do so), and in 1968 became a member of the Caribbean Free Trade Area, *q.v.*

Tripartite Declaration of 1950. A guarantee of the *status quo* in Palestine. France, the U.K., and the U.S.A. bound themselves in May 1950 'should they find that any of these states [Israel or the Arab states] was proposing to violate frontiers or armistice lines . . . immediately to take action, both within and outside the United Nations, to prevent such violations'.

Trotskyite. A Communist who supports the view advanced by Leon Trotsky (a leading Russian revolutionary who, in 1924, was ousted by Stalin in the struggle for power and was later exiled) that excessive Russian nationalism is incompatible with true international Communism. Stalin believed in concentrating on the economic development of the U.S.S.R. to an extent which, in Trotsky's opinion, was bound to produce a bureaucracy with a predominantly national outlook.

Trucial Coast. A coastal strip (once known as the Pirate Coast) on the Persian Gulf and the Gulf of Oman, in which are the seven Trucial States, *q.v.*, of the United Arab Emirates, *q.v.*

Trucial States. Seven member states of the United Arab Emirates *q.v.*, on the Trucial Coast of the Persian Gulf. They are: Abu Dhabi, *q.v.*, Ajman, Dubai, *q.v.*, Fujairah, Ras al Khaimah, Sharjah and Kalba, and Umm al Qaiwan; total area about 32,300 sq. m.; estimated population 130,000, of whom approximately 10 per cent are nomads. They were formerly under British protection and their relationship with the U.K. was governed by a Treaty of 1820 under which they agreed to abstain from plunder and piracy, a Treaty of Perpetual Peace in 1853, and the Exclusive Agreement of 1892 by which the British government controlled their external affairs. The decision of the British government in January 1968 to withdraw all military forces from the Persian Gulf by 1971 signified the termination of this relationship, and in March 1968 the Trucial States, together with Bahrain, *q.v.*, and Qatar, *q.v.*, formed a Federation of Arab Emirates, *q.v.* When Bahrain and Qatar sceded from the Federation and declared their own independence the remaining states of the Federation, with the exception of Ras al Khaimah, decided to establish a United Arab Emirates which achieved independence on 2 December 1971, and to which Ras al Khaimah acceded later the same month.

Persia, which had yielded its claim to sovereignty over Bahrain following a U.N. referendum in 1970, gave notice that it would contest the sovereignty of three islands in the Gulf – Greater and Lesser Tumbs, belonging to Ras al Khaimah, and Abu Musa which was controlled by Sharjah. The British government was unable to adjudicate in the matter since the origin of the claim went back to a date prior to their protection. On 29 November 1971 an agreement was concluded between Persia and Sharjah over Abu Musa, by which the revenues accruing from Buttes Gas and Oil Co., a U.S. oil company which held the island concession, were to be shared equally. Persia was to grant £1,500,000 in aid every year until Sharjah's annual revenue from oil exceeded £3,000,000. On 30 November 1971, the day preceding British withdrawal from the Gulf, Persian military forces occupied Greater and Lesser Tumbs. Ras al Khaimah eventually accepted the occupation as permanent and Persia made no objection to its accession to the United Arab Emirates on 23 December. Iraq, Libya and South Yemen, however, expressed particular displeasure at this assertion of Persian 'imperialist' domination of the Trucial Coast.

Trudeau, Pierre Elliott. Canadian Liberal politician; born in Montreal 18 October 1919, the eldest son of a wealthy businessman. On his father's death in 1935 he was left a millionaire. He was educated at the Jesuit College of Jean-de-Brébeuf and at the University of Montreal where he graduated in law. In 1943 he was called to the Quebec Bar, but subsequently took a master's degree in political economy at Harvard University and studied at the Sorbonne and the London School of Economics. He joined the Cabinet Secretariat in Ottawa in 1949 as an economic and constitutional adviser but left Ottawa in 1951 to practise law in Montreal. He became active in Quebec politics in 1951, campaigning for the separation of Church and State through *Cité Libre*, a magazine he helped to found in opposition to the policies of the Union Nationale government of Maurice Duplessis, and in 1956 organizing the 'Rassemblement', a union of left-wing forces against the provincial government. In 1961 he was appointed Associate Professor of Law at Montreal University. He joined the Canadian Liberal Party in 1965, and entered Parliament the same year as the member for the Montreal constituency of Mount Royal. In 1966 he was made Parliamentary Assistant to the Prime Minister, Lester Pearson, and in 1967 was promoted to the Cabinet as Minister of Justice and Attorney General. He has constantly opposed Quebec separatism in both provincial and federal politics. On the resignation of Lester Pearson as federal leader of the Liberal Party, Trudeau was elected to succeed him, and when Pearson also resigned as Prime Minister on 20 April 1968 he immediately assumed office. At elections held on 25 June 1968 the Liberal Party won an overwhelming victory, confirming him as Prime Minister. He remained in office, leading a minority government, after elections held in October 1972 in which the Liberal Party won only 109 of the 264 seats.

Truman, Harry Swinomish. President of the U.S.A. from 1945 to 1952; born at Lamar, Missouri, 8 May 1884. He worked on the *Kansas City Star* in 1901, as a timekeeper for a railroad contractor in 1902, with the National Bank of Commerce and the Union National Bank in Kansas City from 1903 to 1905, and then returned to the family farm. He served in the U.S. army in France in the First World War. From 1922 to 1924 he was a judge at the Jackson County Court, and studied at the Kansas City School of Law; he was the presiding judge from 1926 to 1934 when he was elected as a Democrat to the U.S. Senate. He was re-elected in 1940 and was elected Vice-President of the U.S.A. on 7 November 1944, taking office on 20 January 1945. On the death of President Franklin Delano Roosevelt on 12 April 1945 Truman became President; he was responsible for deciding that atomic bombs should be dropped on Hiroshima and Nagasaki. At the end of his term he stood for election as President on 2 November 1948 and was successful. During his first term he formulated the Truman Doctrine, *q.v.* He died on 26 December 1972.

Truman Doctrine. A policy expounded by President Harry S. Truman on 12 March 1947 when he said that the U.S.A. ought 'to support free peoples who are resisting attempted subjugation by armed minorities or outside pressure. If we falter,' he said, 'we may endanger the peace of the world and we shall surely endanger the welfare of our own nation.' The occasion of this statement was his speech to Congress asking for the appropriation of $400 million worth of aid to Greece and to Turkey as an emergency measure. Shortly afterwards, on 5 June 1947, the Marshall Plan, *q.v.*, was put forward.

Trusteeship Territories. Areas placed under the international trusteeship system, by which the administration of certain non-self-governing territories is supervised by the United Nations. The remaining Trusteeship Territories are: New Guinea Territory, in New Guinea, *q.v.*, administered by Australia, and the Trust Territory of the Pacific Islands, administered by the U.S.A. Nauru, *q.v.*, which was formerly administered by Australia, became independent on 30 January 1968.

Each Territory is the subject of a Trusteeship Agreement between the United Nations and the administering country. The country must agree to encourage respect for human rights and fundamental freedoms within the Territory, and to prepare its people for self-government and independence; it must submit annual reports to the United Nations, which sends out visiting missions to inspect the conditions in the territories. The Trusteeship Council, one of the six main organs of the United Nations, helps the General Assembly to supervise the Trust Territories. The Council is composed of: (1) member countries administering Trust Territories; (2) permanent members of the Security Council which are not administering Trust Territories; and (3) as many other members (elected for three-year terms by the General Assembly) as may be necessary to secure equality in numbers between administering and non-administering members.

Until a Trusteeship Territory becomes independent or self-governing the administering country has full rights of legislation and administration under the Trusteeship Agreement. In the Agreement all or part of a Territory may be designated by the administering country as 'strategic', in which case the Security Council supervises the Territory with the help of the Trusteeship Council. This device was not used in the case of the mandated territories, which were the equivalent of Trusteeship Territories when the League of Nations was in existence. The Trust Territory of the Pacific Islands (which comprises a number of islands, formerly German possessions, which were administered by Japan as a mandatory power between the two world wars) has been designated as a strategic area by the U.S.A., which can by its Agreement close certain areas for strategic reasons. Under this power the U.S.A. has closed the areas around Bikini and Eniwetok atolls, in the Marshall Islands, for nuclear fission experiments.

Tshombe, Moïse-Kapenda. African politician; born 10 November 1919 at Musumba in the Katanga Province of the Belgian Congo; educated at an American Methodist mission school. His father was a prosperous businessman who owned a hotel, plantations near Musumba, and shops in and near Elisabethville. When his father died in 1951 he succeeded him in the business, but although he became President of the African Chamber of Commerce in Elisabethville, his business career did not flourish. From 1951 to 1954 he was a member of the Katanga Advisory Provincial Council. In 1956 he was elected President of the Confederation of Mutual Associations of the Lunda Empire (the Lunda inhabit Kasai, Katanga, and part of Angola); from this there emerged, in 1959, the Conakat (Confédération des Associations du Katanga) Party, of which he became President, and which was supported by the Union Minière du Haut-Katanga. The Party won a majority in the Katanga provincial elections in May 1960 (the Balubakat Cartel was the minority party) and Tshombe became Prime Minister. The Republic of Congo (Kinshasa) came into existence on 1 July and Tshombe announced the secession of Katanga, *q.v.*, on 11 July 1960. He lost control of the province to United Nations forces in December 1962, and went into exile in June 1963. He returned to Léopoldville in the summer of 1964, and was Prime Minister of Congo (Kinshasa), with a coalition government from July 1964 to October 1965, when he was deposed by General Mobutu. In March 1967 a Kinshasa court sentenced him to death *in absentia*. He was arrested and imprisoned by the Algerian government in June 1967 when a British aircraft, in which he was travelling, was diverted to Algiers. He died in June 1969.

T.U.C. Trades Union Congress, *q.v.*

Tunisia. An independent state on the North African coast lying between Algeria and Libya and extending southwards to the Sahara; area 63,379 sq. m.; population (1971) 5,147,000 of whom the majority is under twenty; capital Tunis. It was occupied by France in 1881 because the French authorities considered that an independent Tunisia threatened the security of their rule in neighbouring Algeria, *q.v.* Although the French appropriated half of the cultivable land, thereby driving many peasants into migrant, seasonal, agricultural work (which now absorbs more than one-third of the population) and causing severe unemployment, the country has a substantial middle class, a land-holding peasantry, few nomads, and the only real trade-union organization in the Moslem world. The largest unions are the General Union of Tunisian Agriculturalists (U.G.A.T.) and the U.G.T.T. which organizes the labourers and is affiliated to the International Confederation of Free Trade Unions, *q.v.* These have lent support to the Néo-Destour (known since October 1964 as the Parti Socialiste Destourien), the moderate nationalist party of Habib Bourguiba, *q.v.*, who, with Tahar Ben Ammar, successfully negotiated an agreement with the French, signed in Paris on 3 June 1955, which was a prelude to independence. The first all-Tunisian cabinet since 1881 was formed on 17 September 1955 and consisted of six members of the Néo-Destour, five independents, including the Prime Minister Tahar Ben Ammar, and one Socialist. The Vieux-Destour, which maintained an uncooperative attitude to the French, and the Communist Party were excluded.

Civil unrest forced the French government to accelerate the transfer of power to the Tunisians, and on 20 March 1956 Tunisia became an independent sovereign state. The treaty concluded in 1881 was abrogated, as were all such provisions of the protocol of 3 June 1955 as might be inconsistent with the new status of Tunisia. At the first general elections, held on 25 March 1956, the National Front (comprising the Néo-Destour, the U.G.T.T., and other organizations) won all 98 seats in the Constituent Assembly. Tahar Ben Ammar resigned and Habib Bourguiba formed a government consisting largely of Néo-Destour members. On 25 July 1957 the Constituent Assembly abolished the monarchy and Habib Bourguiba became President as well as Prime Minister. Under the 1959 Constitution he was re-elected by popular vote in November 1959, November 1964 and November 1969. At the 1959 elections the National Front again returned all the members of the Assembly, and in 1964 and 1969 the Parti Socialiste Destourien was the only party to present candidates for election, winning all 101 seats.

That most of Tunisia's trade is with France has not prevented the country from pursuing an independent foreign policy. This has included the giving of assistance to the Algerian rebels before Algeria achieved independence in 1962, the adherence of Tunisia to the Arab League, *q.v.*, and the confiscation in May 1964 of land belonging to French settlers. In 1964 Bourguiba aroused antagonism in the Arab world by advocating a compromise with Israel, and by refusing to follow other Arab states in breaking off diplomatic relations with the German Federal Republic because of its recognition of Israel. There are exports of wheat, oranges, citrus fruits, dates, olive oil, iron and lead ore and phosphates, of which Tunisia is the world's fourth largest producer. Oil was discovered in 1964 and is being exploited with the aid of Italian capital.

Tupamaros. A revolutionary urban guerilla movement in Uruguay, which takes its name from Tupac Amaru, a Peruvian Indian leader who led a revolt against the Spaniards in the sixteenth century and was beheaded in Cuzco in 1571. It was founded in 1963 among the sugar workers of northern Uruguay, largely by Raul Sendic, a former law student and dedicated Marxist, but by 1968 was organized from Montevideo. The aims of the Tupamaros are imprecise; they are left-wing and well organized but without a defined ideology; they claim to have imitated the Algerian *wilayas* (the territorial divisions created by the Algerian insurgents in their war of independence against the French), and take pride in attacking local oligarchies without directly confronting the armed forces or the police. Their activities have in-

cluded: the raiding of the files of important organizations and submission of any irregularities for police prosecution; the arson of the
General Motors assembly plant in Montevideo because it made police
cars which 'oppressed the workers'; and the kidnapping of prominent
politicians, bankers and diplomats in order to secure the release of
political prisoners. In February 1971 they captured the British
Ambassador, Geoffrey Jackson, whom they released seven months
later; they have also murdered a Uruguyan banker and a U.S. adviser
to the Uruguayan police force, Dan Mitrione, on the grounds that he
was responsible for the introduction of torture against suspect
Tupamaros. In the presidential elections held in November 1971 the
Tupamaros endorsed the Wide Front alliance of left-wing groups
whose candidate was General Liber Seregni, as a 'last chance' for
the democratic electoral system.

Turkey. An independent state partly in Asia Minor, and partly in
eastern Europe; area 294,502 sq. m.; population (1971) 36,910,000,
of whom 99 per cent are Moslems; capital Ankara. The Ottoman
Empire, which once extended from Morocco along the North African
coast to Cairo, included eastern Europe as far as the Adriatic Sea, and
had its eastern boundaries on the Caspian Sea, collapsed after the
First World War. A Turkish Republic was set up in 1923 under the
Presidency of Kemal Atatürk (1881-1938). Atatürk assumed dictatorial powers, separated Church and State, banned polygamy, the
veil and the fez, ordered Turks to wear European clothes, abolished
titles, abandoned Arabic in favour of a Latin script, suppressed
Communism, took the first census, developed industries, and generally
westernized Turkey.

The Republican People's Party, founded by Atatürk, with a policy
of nationalism, laicism, and étatisme (state control of the economy),
was virtually the only political party for many years, but after some
encouragement from the government the Democratic Party was
created. It first came to power in 1950; in the elections of October
1957, under Adnan Menderes, it won 48 per cent of the votes cast
as opposed to the 41 per cent for the Republican People's Party. On
27 May 1960 there was a *coup d'état* led by General Cemal Gürsel,
Commander-in-Chief of the Turkish land forces, who abrogated the
Constitution of 1924 and ruled by a Committee of National Union.
Celal Bayer, President of the Republic since 1950 (who was condemned to death, reprieved in 1961 and released in 1964), and
Menderes (who was condemned to death and hanged in 1961) were
arrested and in September 1960 the Democratic Party was dissolved.
The leaders of the revolt believed that the Menderes regime had

betrayed the tradition of Atatürk and placed too much emphasis on conservatism and the Moslem religion.

At elections held in October 1961, under the new Constitution of that year, the Republican People's Party, led by Ismet Inönü, won 173 seats in the Grand National Assembly; the Justice Party which, to some extent, carried on the tradition of the outlawed Democratic Party won 158 seats. On 26 October Gürsel was elected President for a seven-year term by the necessary two-thirds majority of both the Senate and the Grand National Assembly. In November 1961 Inönü formed a coalition with the Justice Party until December 1963 when he joined with the independents in a minority government. He resigned in February 1965 after his government had been defeated in the Assembly; this was said to be the first time in Turkish parliamentary history that a government had been brought down by an adverse vote. He was succeeded by Zuyat Hayri Ürgüplü, an independent allied to the Justice Party who committed his government to immediate social reform. However, the elections held in October 1965 gave a decisive majority to the Justice Party (240 out of the 450 seats) and its leader, Süleyman Demirel, became Prime Minister. In 1970 a split occurred in the Justice Party, the expelled members founding a new Democratic Party to press for speedier reforms; the government was defeated in the Assembly and extremist violence broke out, involving the kidnapping of U.S. servicemen. The Air Force Commander demanded social reform, and especially agrarian reform, higher pay for the armed services and a more equitable tax system, as a 'matter of urgency', and under military pressure for a 'strong and credible government' Demirel resigned in March 1971. President Sunay (elected 1968 to succeed Gürsel) appointed an R.P.P. lawyer, Dr Nihat Erim, to lead a coalition government which would implement the reforms promised in the 1961 Constitution. At elections held in November 1971 the Justice Party suffered an electoral reverse, winning only 222 (257 in October 1969) seats; the splinter Democratic Party won 41 seats, and the R.P.P., whose right-wing had seceded rather than participate in the Erim government, won 140 seats (144 in 1969). Following further outbreaks of anarchic violence, the murder of three foreign radar technicians by members of the Turkish Liberation Movement, and the unwillingness of the major parties to grant exceptional powers to the government to deal with the crisis, Erim resigned in April 1972. Ferit Melen, of the National Reliance Party, then formed a government pledged to restore order and reform.

Eighty per cent of the population work on the land, where there has been extensive mechanization of agriculture; there are considerable exports of grain, tobacco, cotton, and dried fruit. The output of Turkish metals (iron, chrome, copper, and manganese), which find a ready market for hard currency, has also been greatly expanded. Nearly 700,000 Turks are employed as 'guest workers' in Germany, the Netherlands and Switzerland. The increase in productivity, the liberal distribution by the government of agricultural credits and subsidies, and the devotion to defence of sums equal to half of the budget, have combined with the rise in world prices to produce inflation and budget deficits. The extraction of taxes, especially from the landowners and farmers, is made difficult by the fact that all the political parties are closely associated with strong feudal interests.

In the Second World War Turkey, whose active support of the allied powers would probably have involved occupation by Germany and liberation by the U.S.S.R., chose to remain neutral. Its present commitments are to Yugoslavia and Greece (under the Balkan Pact, *q.v.*), to Pakistan, Persia, and the U.K. (Central Treaty Organization, *q.v.*), and, as a member of N.A.T.O., to the North Atlantic Treaty powers. There is a long-standing fear of the U.S.S.R.; in 1945 the Russians denounced their Treaty of Neutrality, Non-Aggression, and International Co-operation which had been signed in 1925. The Dardanelles, *q.v.*, which are part of the straits connecting the Mediterranean with the Black Sea, are of strategic significance.

T.V.A. Tennessee Valley Authority, *q.v.*

U

U.A.M. Union Africaine et Malgache, *or* African and Malagasy Union, *q.v.*

U.A.R. United Arab Republic, *q.v.*

U.A.S. United Arab States, *q.v.*

U.D.I. Unilateral Declaration of Independence, *q.v.*

U Nu. *See* Nu, U.

U Thant. *See* Thant, U.

Ubangi-Shari. A territory of French Equatorial Africa, *q.v.*, which on 1 December 1958 achieved self-government within the French Community as the Central African Republic, *q.v.*

Uganda. A republic and member of the British Commonwealth, in East Africa, bounded by Congo (Brazzaville), Sudan, Kenya, Tanzania and Rwanda; area 93,981 sq. m.; population (1970 estimate) 9,500,000, including 88,000 Asians and 9,000 Europeans; capital Kampala. The territory came under British influence in 1890 and was made a protectorate in 1894; it achieved internal self-government on 1 March 1962. Uganda then comprised the Region of Buganda, *q.v.*, and the Eastern, Western (including the district of Bunyoro), and Northern Regions, Buganda and three of the four districts of the Western Region (Ankole, Bunyoro and Toro) having native monarchs and a special relationship with the central government. At elections held in April 1962 the Uganda People's Congress (U.P.C.), led by Dr Milton Obote, won 37 seats; the mainly Catholic Democratic Party, led by Benedicto Kiwanuka (until then the Prime Minister), won 24 seats; the Kabaka Yekka (K.Y.), a Buganda party supporting 'the Kabaka alone', secured the 21 Buganda seats. Obote became Prime Minister of a coalition of the U.P.C. and K.Y. Uganda achieved complete independence on 9 October 1962. One year later a republic was declared and the Kabaka of Buganda was elected President.

In February 1966 the Prime Minister, Dr Obote, announced his own appointment to the Presidency on 15 April. He replaced the 1962 Constitution by one which made the country a unitary state and which abolished the four Regions. This was rejected by the Buganda Lukiko (Assembly), but after a military assault on the Kabaka's palace in May 1967, the authority of the central government was restored in Buganda, and the Kabaka fled to the U.K. In September 1967 a new republican Constitution was introduced giving the President wide powers. The former hereditary kingdoms were abolished and the country was divided into eighteen administrative districts. In January 1971 President Obote was ousted by General Idi Amin, a northerner, but supported by the Baganda. Obote took refuge in Tanzania, whose government refused to recognize Amin until the mediation of President Kenyatta reduced border tension in which troops from both sides had been involved in heavy fighting. In January 1972 President Amin announced his intention to expel from Uganda those members of the Asian community who had not accepted Ugandan citizenship and had retained their U.K. passports; between August and November some 40,000, of whom 27,200 were admitted to the U.K., were forcibly expelled. These were followed by British nationals. Asians remaining in Uganda were deported from the urban areas to the villages and instructed to integrate with the African community.

Uganda is mainly agricultural and production is almost entirely in African hands. The principal crops, which provide 75 per cent of the value of the exports, are cotton and coffee. There has been considerable investment in hydro-electric plants and the Owen Falls scheme generates power for export to Kenya. Uganda is a member of the East African Economic Community, *q.v.*, with Kenya and Tanzania.

U.K. United Kingdom of Great Britain and Northern Ireland, *q.v.*

Ukraine, formerly known as South Russia. One of the 15 constituent Republics of the U.S.S.R.; area 232,046 sq. m.; population (1970) 47,400,000; capital Kiev. It is inhabited by Slavs speaking a language different from but akin to Russian: it is situated in the south-western part of the European area of the U.S.S.R. Tsarist Russia regarded the Ukrainians as a branch of the Russian people, calling them 'Little Russians', as compared with the 'Great Russians' of North Russia, and forcing the Russian language upon Ukrainian officials and teachers. After the Russian Revolution of 1917 the Ukraine was occupied by German and Austrian armies and then became a theatre of civil war until December 1919 when the Ukrainian Soviet Socialist Republic was formed. It joined with the other Soviet Socialist Republics in Russia in July 1923 to form the U.S.S.R. From 1920 until 1939 Western Ukraine, an area of some 34,400 sq. m. with six million Ukrainian inhabitants, was ruled by Poland, which had rejected the Curzon Line, *q.v.*, a line proposed by the U.K. and largely following the ethnical border between Poles and Ukrainians. This territory was reincorporated in the Ukraine on 1 November 1939, after the U.S.S.R. and Germany had partitioned Poland. Ukraine also acquired Northern Bukovina and parts of Bessarabia, *q.v.*, from Romania in 1940, and Ruthenia (Sub-Carpathian Russia) from Hungary in 1945. These areas all contained substantial numbers of Ukrainians. The Ukrainian Soviet Socialist Republic is, like Byelorussia, *q.v.*, a member of the United Nations Organization.

Ulbricht, Walter. Communist politician in the German Democratic Republic; born 30 June 1893 in Leipzig. He became an active trade unionist in 1910, while employed as a woodworker; he joined the Socialist Party in 1912 and left it in 1919 to join the Communist Party. After five years as a member of the German parliament (Reichstag) he fled from Germany to the U.S.S.R. to escape from the Nazis. In 1946 he was elected to the Central Secretariat of the Communist-controlled Socialist Unity Party (S.E.D.), and in 1949 became Deputy Premier of the German Democratic Republic. He was appointed Secretary-General of the S.E.D. in 1950, and subsequently First Secretary. In September 1960 he became Chairman of the Council of State which was formed to replace the office of President. On 3 May 1971 he resigned as First Secretary of the Party in favour of Erich Honecker.

Ulster. A province of Ireland before the Government of Ireland Act of 1920. It comprised 9 counties: Antrim, Armagh, Down, Fermanagh, Londonderry, Tyrone, Cavan, Donegal, and Monaghan. Under the 1920 Act the first 6 of these counties, described collectively as Northern Ireland, *q.v.*, elected a Parliament on 24 May 1921. The southern Irish ignored the Act and in 1922 the Irish Free State Act created a Dominion called the Irish Free State, from which the 6 counties expressed their desire to be excluded.

U.N.E.S.C.O. United Nations Educational, Scientific, and Cultural Organization, *q.v.*

U.N.H.C.R. United Nations High Commissioner for Refugees, *q.v.*

U.N.I.C.E.F. United Nations International Children's Emergency Fund, *q.v.*

Unilateral Declaration of Independence (U.D.I.). A declaration by a state which is in subordinate relation to another state, or is part of a federation, *q.v.*, of its own autonomy. Since it does not have the consent of the governing authority the action is illegal. The expression was first used by the Rhodesian government of Ian Smith, *q.v.* He purported to declare Rhodesia independent of the U.K. on 11 November 1965, an announcement which was immediately rejected by the U.K. government which reaffirmed, by the Southern Rhodesia Act, 1965, its jurisdiction and responsibility for the territory.

Union Africaine et Malgache (U.A.M.). *See* African and Malagasy Union.

Union Movement. A minor political party of the U.K.; it was formed in 1948 by Sir Oswald Mosley, a former Member of Parliament and Cabinet Minister in the 1929 Labour government. Its precursor was the British Union of Fascists (B.U.F.), created as the New Party by

Mosley in 1931, and renamed in 1932, after he had been to Italy to study Mussolini's 'modern movements' (*see* Fascism). The B.U.F. fought a number of by-elections in 1939 and 1940 before it was banned by the British government on 30 May 1940. The Union Movement, which has made the prohibition of immigration into the U.K. its main platform, put up three candidates at the 1966 General Election; they gained on average only 3·7 per cent of the vote.

Union of Soviet Socialist Republics (U.S.S.R.). Area 8,650,000 sq. m.; population (1970) 241,748,000; capital Moscow. It comprises 15 constituent Republics, of which the largest (covering 77 per cent of the total area) and most important is the Russian Soviet Federal Socialist Republic (R.S.F.S.R.), which occupies most of the European part, and most of the northern sector of the Asiatic part, of the U.S.S.R. The Emperor Nicholas II, Tsar of Russia, was forced to abdicate as a result of the revolution which broke out in Russia in March 1917, and the R.S.F.S.R. was set up after the Communists seized power in November 1917. The U.S.S.R. was formally established in 1923, and the constituent Republics were then the R.S.F.S.R., Byelorussia, *q.v.*, the Ukraine, *q.v.*, and the Transcaucasian Soviet Socialist Republic. These were joined by Uzbekistan and Turkmenistan in 1925, and by Tadjikistan in 1929. In 1936 the Transcaucasian S.S.R. was split up into the three Republics of Armenia, Azerbaijan, and Georgia; Kazakhstan and Kirghizia were proclaimed as Republics. In 1940 Estonia, *q.v.*, Latvia, *q.v.*, Lithuania, *q.v.*, and Moldavia were added; the Karelo-Finnish S.S.R., set up in that year, was merged with the R.S.F.S.R. in 1956.

The 1936 Constitution states: 'The economic foundation of the U.S.S.R. consists of the Socialist economic system and the Socialist ownership of the tools and means of production, firmly established as a result of the liquidation of the capitalist economic system... The economic life of the U.S.S.R. is determined and directed by a state plan of national economy in the interests of increasing the public wealth, of steadily raising the material and cultural standard of the working people, and of strengthening the independence of the U.S.S.R. and its capacity for defence. Work in the U.S.S.R. is a duty and a matter of honour for every able-bodied citizen, on the principle: "He who does not work shall not eat." '.

Legislative authority is vested in the Supreme Soviet, *q.v.*, which acts between sessions through its Presidium, and is responsible for electing the Council of Ministers, the highest administrative and executive organ. Most of the real power in the U.S.S.R. is exercised by the Presidium of the Central Committee of the Communist Party, of which the First Secretary is Leonid Brezhnev, *q.v.* The Communist Party pervades every representative body and all other Russian organizations. Its members are a small minority, varying in size, but usually about 4 per cent of the population.

After the 1917 Revolution British, Japanese, Polish, and other forces attacked Russia in an attempt to overthrow the new Communist government, but their efforts proved unsuccessful, and by 1920 the civil war had come to an end. For many years relations between the U.S.S.R. and the western powers were marked by hostility and mistrust. In 1939 the U.K. abandoned its policy of appeasement of Nazi Germany and tried to conclude a treaty with the U.S.S.R., but instead a Russo-German pact was signed on 23 August 1939. Germany's invasion of Poland on 1 September 1939 was followed by a declaration of war on Germany by France and the U.K. on 3 September; on 17 September Russian forces entered Poland from the east by arrangement with Germany and the country was partitioned. On 23 June 1941 Germany, helped by Finland, Hungary, and Romania, invaded the U.S.S.R., which thus entered the Second World War in alliance with the U.K. Since 1945, and particularly since 1947, when the Marshall Plan, *q.v.*, and the Truman Doctrine, *q.v.*, were put forward by the U.S.A., relations between the U.S.S.R. and the western powers have been strained. The western powers have been concerned about: (1) Russian domination of the countries of eastern Europe (Poland, the German Democratic Republic, Hungary, Bulgaria, Romania, and Czechoslovakia) which have pro-Russian governments; (2) Russian influence over countries in the Middle and Far East which the western powers have previously regarded as subjects for western colonial or economic expansion or as western military strongholds; and (3) the possibility that the U.S.S.R. may launch an aggressive war. From 1963 ideological differences between the Communist Parties of China and the U.S.S.R. have considerably reduced the threat of joint Communist expansion in Asia.

Since 1917 the U.S.S.R., then primarily an agricultural country, has become one of the world's foremost industrial producers. The economy has been developed by a series of plans including the six Five-Year Plans of 1928–32, 1933–7, 1938–42 (interrupted in 1941), 1946–50, 1951–5, and 1956–60, the Seven-Year Plan for 1959–65 and the Twenty-Year Plan for 1961–80. In 1960 the volume of production of coal, petroleum, electricity, pig iron, and crude steel was in each case more than double that of 1940. Production of coal, steel, and electricity exceeded the combined amount produced by the U.K. and the German Federal Republic. There were also remarkable increases in agricultural production. Under the Seven-Year Plan industrial output was to increase by 80 per cent and agricultural output by 70 per cent; under the Twenty-Year Plan the proposed increases included: electric power, ninefold; steel, fourfold; cement and oil, fivefold; and grain, double.

Uniscan. An agreement concluded in 1950 by Denmark, Norway, Sweden, and the U.K. to develop closer economic cooperation. It envisaged the mutual exchange of privileges, such as the raising of tourist allowances, permission for Scandinavian countries to repatriate sterling capital and to borrow in the London market, and concessions as to royalty payments.

United Arab Emirates. A union of the seven Trucial States, *q.v.*, of the Persian Gulf, which came into existence on 2 December 1971. It comprises seven of the former members of the Federation of Arab Emirates, *q.v.*, which dissolved when Bahrain, *q.v.*, and Qatar, *q.v.*, declared their independence in August 1971; these are: Abu Dhabi, *q.v.*, Ajman, Dubai, *q.v.*, Fujairah, Sharjah and Kalba, and Umm al Qaiwan. Ras al Khaimah, whose islands of Greater and Lesser Tumbs had been forcibly occupied by Persian forces on 30 November, joined the union three weeks later after it had become clear that neither the U.K. nor the Arab League would intervene. Sheikh Zaid bin Sultan al-Nahayan, the ruler of Abu Dhabi, became the first President of the union, and the ruler of Dubai, Sheikh Rashid bin Said al-Naktum, the first Vice-President. The U.K. government, which had terminated on 1 December 1971 its special treaty relationship with the six emirates at that time in membership of the union, concluded a new Treaty of Friendship on the declaration of independence by which the Trucial Oman Scouts were to become the nucleus of the union's defence forces.

United Arab Republic (U.A.R.). Name by which Egypt, *q.v.*, was known from February 1958 until August 1971.

United Arab States. A federation established on 8 March 1958 by the United Arab Republic, *q.v.*, and Yemen, *q.v.* Article One of the charter signed by President Nasser and the Crown Prince Al Badr of Yemen said that the federation was to include 'the United Arab Republic, the Kingdom of Yemen, and those Arab states which will agree to join this union'. The charter provided for unified defence and foreign policies, for a supreme council consisting of the heads of the two states and any others which joined, and for a federal council comprising equal numbers of representatives from each state. The permanent seat of the federal council was to be the Yemeni port of Hodeida. On 26 December 1961 (three months after Syria had seceded from the U.A.R.)

Egypt severed its link with Yemen, of whose Imam it disapproved, by ending the U.A.S.

United Kingdom of Great Britain and Northern Ireland. Area 93,053 sq. m.; population (1971 census) 55,521,534. The U.K. consists of the Kingdoms of England and Scotland, the Principality of Wales, Northern Ireland and the dependencies of the Channel Islands, *q.v.*, and the Isle of Man, *q.v.* Except for Northern Ireland, *q.v.*, the constituent parts of the U.K. are not autonomous, although Scotland has a separate legal system and the Crown dependencies enjoy some measure of fiscal control. The rules of the British Constitution are to be found not in any single document but in a large number of parliamentary enactments, judicial decisions, and generally accepted conventions. The most important enactments are Magna Carta (1215), the Act of Union with Wales (1536), the Petition of Right (1628), the Habeas Corpus Act (1679), the Bill of Rights (1689), the Act of Settlement (1701), the Union with Scotland Act (1707), the Union with Ireland Act (1800), partly repealed in 1921, and the Parliament Acts, 1911 and 1949, *q.v.*

Supreme legislative power is vested in the Queen, acting with the advice and consent of the House of Lords, *q.v.*, and the House of Commons, *q.v.*, and legislative proposals (Bills) do not become laws (Acts of Parliament) until they have received the royal assent. The Queen has in theory a right to veto Bills by refusing her assent, but the veto is never used. Although the legislature is bicameral, the power of the House of Lords to prevent or impede legislation has been strictly limited by the Parliament Acts. In her executive capacity the Queen acts only on the advice of her Ministers, except in certain minor matters, such as the granting of personal honours. Her Ministers are in turn collectively responsible to the House of Commons, which by an adverse vote on a serious matter could force the Prime Minister to advise the Queen to dissolve Parliament, when a General Election would ensue. A number of senior Ministers (18 out of 51 in 1972) are members of the Cabinet, an inner group which decides government policy.

The U.K. has one of the most comprehensive schemes of social welfare in the world. The National Insurance Act, 1946, provides for unemployment, sickness, maternity and widows' benefits, guardians' allowances, retirement pensions, and death grants. The National Insurance (Industrial Injuries) Act, 1946, provides a system of insurance against personal injury by accident arising out of, and in the course of, employment and against certain diseases due to the nature of the employment. The Old Age Pensions Act, 1936, provides for the payment of non-contributory old age pensions, and the National Assistance Act, 1948, provides for grants of financial assistance to all persons without resources or whose resources (including national insurance benefits) need to be supplemented. The National Health Service Act, 1946, established a health service free to all in the U.K. This service extends to foreigners, to whom political asylum is almost invariably granted, although stringent legislation was introduced in 1971 to restrict the numbers of Commonwealth and foreign immigrants entering the country. Under the Education Act, 1944, full-time schooling is compulsory for all children from the age of five to sixteen, and free in publicly maintained primary and secondary schools.

The most valuable physical exports of the U.K. include electric and non-electric machinery, road vehicles and aircraft, chemicals, cotton yarns and woven fabrics, and iron and steel. The chief buyers of British goods are Australia, South Africa, the U.S.A., Canada, New Zealand, India, France, Italy, the Netherlands, Sweden, Denmark, and the German Federal Republic.

The foreign policy of the U.K. is conditioned by its desire to cooperate with the United Nations, its firm friendship with the U.S.A., its alliance with France concluded in 1904 and reaffirmed in 1946 by Ernest Bevin and Léon Blum, and its membership of the North Atlantic Treaty Organization, *q.v.*, the Central Treaty Organization, *q.v.*, and the South-East Asia Collective Defence Treaty, *q.v.* Although a member of the European Free Trade Area, *q.v.*, the U.K. twice made application to join the European Economic Community, *q.v.*, in 1961 and again in 1967, and on 22 January 1972, after prolonged negotiation concerning Commonwealth sugar and dairy imports and fishery protection, signed the Treaty of Accession.

United Nations. An international organization which came into existence on 24 October 1945 as a result of decisions made at international conferences during the Second World War, and as a successor to the League of Nations, *q.v.* At the Moscow Conference on 1 November 1943 the representatives of China, the U.K., the U.S.A., and the U.S.S.R. declared that they recognized 'the necessity of establishing at the earliest practicable date a general international organization, based on the principle of the sovereign equality of all peace-loving states, and open to membership by all such states, large or small, for the maintenance of international peace and security'. The Dumbarton Oaks Conference, *q.v.*, which ended on 7 October 1944, made proposals for the structure of the world organization, and delegates of 50 nations met at San Francisco between 25 April and 26 June 1945 to draft the United Nations Charter and the Statute of the International Court of Justice, *q.v.* Membership of the United Nations is open to all peace-loving states which accept and, in the judgement of the organization, are able and willing to carry out the obligations of the Charter. New members are admitted by a two-thirds vote of the General Assembly, *q.v.*, upon the recommendation of the Security Council, *q.v.* There have been disputes as to the admission of new members and several states are still excluded. North Korea, South Korea, North Viet-Nam and South Viet-Nam, for example, have been unsuccessful in their applications. Some non-members have been admitted to certain specialized agencies.

The Secretariat consists of a Secretary-General and such staff as the United Nations may require. The Secretary-General is the chief administrative officer of the United Nations and is appointed for five years by the General Assembly on the recommendation of the Security Council. Dr Kurt Waldheim, *q.v.*, was appointed to succeed U Thant, *q.v.*, as Secretary-General in 1971. He submits an annual report to the General Assembly on the work of the United Nations. The permanent headquarters of the United Nations is in New York City on land provided partly from money given by John D. Rockefeller, Jr, and partly by the City of New York.

The United Nations has six principal organs: the General Assembly, *q.v.*, The Security Council, *q.v.*, the Economic and Social Council, *q.v.*, the Trusteeship Council, the International Court of Justice, *q.v.*, and the Secretariat. In all these organs, other than the International Court of Justice, the official languages are Chinese, English, French, Russian and Spanish, and the working languages are English and French. In the General Assembly, Spanish is also a working language. The official languages of the International Court are English and French.

The aims of the United Nations are declared in the United Nations Charter to be 'to save succeeding generations from the scourge of war ... to reaffirm faith in fundamental human rights, in the dignity and worth of the human person, in the equal rights of men and women and of nations large and small, and to establish conditions under which justice and respect for the obligations arising from treaties and other sources of international law can be maintained, and to employ international machinery for the promotion of the economic and social advancement of all peoples'. The activities of the United Nations are discussed under the title of the appropriate organ, *e.g.*, General Assembly, or under the titles of the areas in question, *e.g.*, Cyprus, Kashmir, Korea. One of the most important functions of the United Nations is its quasi-diplomatic task of assessing world opinion, and urging its decisions on the governments concerned.

United Nations Educational, Scientific, and Cultural Organization (U.N.E.S.C.O.). Came into existence on 4 November 1946 with the object, according to its Constitution, of contributing 'to peace and security by promoting collaboration among the nations through education, science, and culture in order to further universal respect for justice, for the rule of law, and for the human rights and fundamental freedoms which are affirmed . . . by the Charter of the United Nations'. Its three bodies are: a General Conference, comprising one representative from each member state, which meets every two years to approve the programme and budget; an Executive Board of 24 members which meets at least twice a year and is responsible for the execution of the programme adopted by the Conference; a Secretariat under a Director-General and with headquarters in Paris. U.N.E.S.C.O. is one of the specialized agencies, *q.v.*, of the United Nations.

The activities of U.N.E.S.C.O. fall under the following eight broad headings: (1) Education: eliminating illiteracy and encouraging fundamental education, raising educational standards, promoting through education greater respect for human rights, making available information on educational techniques. (2) Natural Sciences: creating greater collaboration between scientists and encouraging the popularization of science. (3) Social Sciences: encouraging the study of the psychological and social problems involved in the development of mutual understanding, such as racial prejudice and religious differences. (4) Cultural Activities: developing cultural exchanges between member states and giving people access to works of art, literature, and philosophy. (5) Exchange of Persons: providing information as to the opportunities for work and study abroad, and providing travelling fellowships. (6) Mass Communication: keeping the public informed about the work of U.N.E.S.C.O. and significant events in the fields of education, science, and culture, and campaigning to help people to obtain easier access to knowledge. (7) Rehabilitation: assessing and making provision for the educational needs of schools, libraries, and scientific institutions in war-devastated areas and underdeveloped countries. (8) Technical Assistance: providing expert advice in the fields of fundamental education, teacher training, technical and general education, scientific research, and scientific advisory services. Member states are advised in such matters as their literacy campaigns, school building programmes, surveying of mineral resources, teacher training, and development of electrical engineering.

United Nations High Commissioner for Refugees (U.N.H.C.R.). Appointed on 1 January 1951, he has two main tasks: (1) to provide international protection for refugees, and (2) to promote activities designed to establish refugees economically, socially, and legally, either in countries where they are living or in new communities. The work of the Commissioner and his Office (which is in Geneva) covers all refugees, except those who have been given full rights of citizenship by their country of asylum or for whom other arrangements have been made, as in the case of the Palestine refugees. The small administrative expenses of the Office are financed by the United Nations, but the members of the United Nations decided in 1950 that the size of the remaining refugee problem did not warrant the expenditure of official international funds, and the work itself therefore has to depend on voluntary contributions, from governmental and non-governmental sources. In 1954 the office was awarded the Nobel Peace Prize.

United Nations International Children's Emergency Fund. Was established by the United Nations General Assembly on 11 December 1946; it functions under the supervision of the Economic and Social Council, *q.v.* It was originally responsible for helping child health and welfare programmes in countries devastated during the Second World War, but has since extended its interests to the children of the underdeveloped countries. The Fund, which has its headquarters in New York, is dependent on voluntary contributions from members of the United Nations and from the public. One example of its work is the assistance that it has given, by supplying emergency supplies of milk, to the mothers and children of the Arab refugee population in Jordan. In 1965 the Fund was awarded the Nobel Peace Prize.

United Nations Relief and Rehabilitation Administration (U.N.R.R.A.). The first large agency to help people in Europe and the Far East who became refugees as a result of the Second World War, and to attempt to reconstruct the industry and agriculture of nations whose economies had been damaged by the war. It was established on 9 November 1943 and ceased its activities on 31 March 1949. It spent $2,500 million, of which the U.S.A. contributed nearly three quarters, on food, clothing, agricultural and industrial rehabilitation material, and medical supplies. It prevented starvation in Albania, Czechoslovakia, Greece, Italy, Poland, and Yugoslavia.

Much of the work of U.N.R.R.A. was taken over by other international organizations, its health work by the Interim Commission of the World Health Organization, *q.v.*, its child welfare work by the United Nations International Children's Emergency Fund, *q.v.*, its agriculture work by the Food and Agriculture Organization, *q.v.*, and its work on behalf of refugees and displaced persons, by the Preparatory Commission of the International Refugee Organization, *q.v.* The activities of U.N.R.R.A. as a guarantor of large-scale financial aid were taken over by the U.S.A. in the spring of 1947, when Congress appropriated $400 million as emergency aid to Greece and Turkey, and in June 1947 when the Marshall Plan, *q.v.*, was put forward.

United Nations Relief and Works Agency (U.N.R.W.A.). Has been responsible for the resettlement of the Arab refugees from Palestine since December 1949. In 1971 it was estimated that out of a total of 1,468,000 refugees, 560,000 were still living in camps in Jordan, Lebanon, Syria and the Gaza Strip, *q.v.* Since 1967 Canada, the German Federal Republic, Sweden, the U.K. and the U.S.A. have provided 80 per cent of the Agency's income.

United States of America. Continental area 3,548,974 sq. m.; area including the states of Alaska and Hawaii and the outlying territories of Guam, Panama Canal Zone, *q.v.*, Puerto Rico, *q.v.*, Samoa, Virgin Islands, etc., 3,553,898 sq. m.; population of continental U.S.A. (1971) 206,481,000 (it has doubled since 1918); capital Washington, in the federal District of Columbia, *q.v.* There are 50 States of which 13 were the original members after the Constitution was drafted in 1787. The Constitution is federal in character, a substantial part of the administration being carried on by the States. The legislative power is vested in Congress, consisting of the Senate, *q.v.*, and the House of Representatives, *q.v.* The two political parties are the Democratic Party, *q.v.*, and the Republican Party, *q.v.* After the elections on 15 November 1972 the state of the parties was: Senate, 57 Democrats and 43 Republicans; House of Representatives, 244 Democrats and 191 Republicans.

Executive power is exercised by the President who is elected for a four-year term by indirect election. The Constitution provides that each State shall appoint a number of electors equal to the combined number of its senators and representatives in Congress; the framers of the Constitution thought that an inter-State convention, known as the Electoral College, of all these electors should choose a President. The electors are appointed directly by the people, who in effect choose either the Democratic group or the Republican group in each State. These groups do not decide independently who should be President, for the College never meets; the successful Presidential candidate is the one whose party has a majority among the electors. Since 1937 the President's term of office has begun on 20 January, two months after his election, which takes place in November every leap year. No President can serve more than two terms. The President has a right of veto over any measure presented by Congress for his approval, but the veto can be overridden by a two-thirds vote of Congress. He chooses his own Cabinet Ministers, who are responsible only to him.

Judicial power is vested in the Supreme Court, *q.v.*, which interprets the Constitution. The doctrine of the 'separation of powers', *q.v.*, is thus part of the U.S. Constitution, and the legislature has not the sovereign authority that it has in the U.K.

There is an elected Governor, a group of executive officials, a judicial system and a bicameral legislature in each State (except Nebraska, which has had a unicameral legislature since 1937). A State legislature is empowered to deal with all matters not reserved to Congress by the Constitution nor prohibited by the State Constitution. It can, for example, enact its own rules as to the right to vote, the criminal law, marriage and divorce, labour, and education. In some States one must pay a tax (poll-tax) to qualify for the suffrage. The State Governors are chosen by direct vote, and their terms of office vary from two years to four years.

The most valuable exports of the U.S.A. include motor vehicles, grains, electrical machinery, petroleum and its products, metals and manufactures from iron and steel mills, textile fibres and manufactures, and construction and mining machinery. Its chief customers are Australia, Canada, Japan, Mexico, the U.K., Venezuela, the German Federal Republic, France, Brazil, Netherlands, Belgium and Luxemburg, India, and Italy. Its chief imports include coffee, non-ferrous ores and metals, non-metallic minerals, petroleum, wood and paper, cane sugar, and crude rubber. It imports mostly from Canada, Brazil, the U.K., Venezuela, Mexico, the German Federal Republic, Hong Kong, Japan, France, Belgium and Luxemburg, and Italy. The U.S.A. produces approximately one third of the goods and services and one half of the factory products of the world. Under the Reciprocal Trade Agreements Act, *q.v.*, the U.S.A. pursues a policy of reducing trade barriers, but this policy is qualified by rules which give protection to many U.S. industries which fear foreign competition.

Since the attack by Japan on Pearl Harbour in the Hawaiian Islands on 7 December 1941, the U.S.A. has abandoned its pre-war isolationism and has intervened directly in Asian and European affairs. The Monroe Doctrine, *q.v.*, still forms an integral part of U.S.

foreign policy, but both Democratic and Republican Parties have accepted the need for positive commitments, and approve of U.S. membership of the North Atlantic Treaty Organization, *q.v.*, the South-East Asia Collective Defence Treaty, *q.v.*, and the United Nations, *q.v.* The country was one of the original members of the United Nations, although it had refused to join the League of Nations set up by the Versailles Treaty, *q.v.*, after the First World War. The U.S.A. regards itself as the leader of a world-wide struggle against the advance of Communism, and has sought, by military and economic aid to threatened countries, to prevent China and the U.S.S.R. from extending their influence. It has financed the post-war recovery of much of the world.

U.N.R.R.A. United Nations Relief and Rehabilitation Administration, *q.v.*

U.N.R.W.A. United Nations Relief and Works Agency, *q.v.*

Untouchables. The lowest group in the Hindu caste system. There are over 55 million Untouchables in India who have hitherto been treated as a lesser race by high-caste Hindus and have suffered such disabilities as being refused admission to shops and restaurants, and access to public wells and bathing *ghats*. Under the Indian Constitution of 1950 untouchability was abolished and its practice forbidden. However, cases are continually being reported, although in 1955 the Indian Parliament passed a Bill making discrimination against Untouchables a legal offence punishable by six months' imprisonment and a fine of £37 10s. The Indian government has been embarrassed in its campaign to improve the status of Asians in South Africa by the practice of caste discrimination at home.

Upper Volta. An independent West African republic; area 106,011 sq. m.; population (1971 estimate) 5,346,000, mainly of the Mossi tribe; capital Ouagadougou. It is landlocked, being surrounded by the republics of Mali and Niger to the north and those of Ivory Coast, Ghana, Togo and Dahomey to the south. The main port of access is Abidjan, capital of the Ivory Coast, with which Ouagadougou is linked by railway. The French established the separate colony of Upper Volta in 1919 out of the colony of Upper Senegal and Niger, which they had created in 1904. It was divided between adjacent colonies in 1932 but re-established in 1947 as one of the eight territories comprising French West Africa, *q.v.*; self-government was achieved within the French Community, *q.v.*, in December 1958, and complete independence, after seceding from the Community, on 5 August 1960.

The Constitution of 1960 provided for the quinquennial election of a President and a National Assembly. Maurice Yaméogo was President until January 1966 when the army seized power, the Constitution was suspended and Lt-Colonel Sangoulé Lamizana became chief of state. At elections held in December 1970, under a new Constitution of May of that year by which President (now General) Lamizana was confirmed in office for four years, the Union Démocratique Voltaïque (the Upper Volta section of the Rassemblement Démocratique Africain, *q.v.*) won 37 of the 57 seats in the National Assembly. Gérard Kango Ouedraogo, the leader of the U.D.V., was appointed the country's first Prime Minister.

The economy is agricultural; millet, maize, rice and yams are produced and there are meagre exports (mostly to France, Ghana and Ivory Coast) of livestock, gold, beans and karité nuts. There are deposits of copper, chromium, diamonds and manganese, but their extraction has only recently begun.

Uruguay. The smallest South American state, situated between Argentina and Brazil and on the Atlantic Ocean; area 72,172 sq. m.; population (1970 estimate) 2,945,000, mostly white and predominantly of Spanish and Italian descent; capital Montevideo. Uruguay was ruled by the Portuguese during the seventeenth century, and from 1726 to 1814 by Spain, as part of the Spanish Viceroyalty of the River Plate. After several wars it was declared an independent state in 1828, and a Republic was inaugurated in 1830.

From 1880 to 1958 the Batlle family led the governing party, the Colorados ('reds' or liberals). Since 1900 there has been a number of constitutional innovations designed to protect Uruguay from the emergence of a dictatorship. Under the 1951 Constitution the presidency was abolished and all executive power was vested in a bipartisan National Council of Government (of nine men), modelled on the Swiss Federal Council. Parliament consists of the Senate, with 30 members elected for four years, and the Chamber of Representatives, with 99 members, elected on a district basis for four years. There is universal adult franchise for the literate. The Senate seats are divided between the two political parties obtaining the highest number of votes, providing that they poll an absolute majority; if they do not, there is proportional representation. The divisions within the parties have led *El Debate*, a Montevideo newspaper, to describe the system as one of 'institutionalized anarchy'.

At the elections held in November 1958 the National Party, or Blancos, led by Luis Alberto de Herrera, defeated the Colorados who thus lost power for the first time for 94 years. Although the Colorados had nationalized industries and conferred many social benefits on

Uruguay, a system of intricate exchange rates, equivalent to export duties, had damaged the export trade in wool and beef; this encouraged the farm labourers, as well as the landowners and the middle class, to give support to the Blancos, nominally the party of the rich and of the Church. The National Party retained power by a narrow margin at the elections held in November 1962, but at the elections of November 1966 the Colorados recovered their majority and re-introduced the presidency. On 1 March 1967 the Colorado candidate, General Oscar Gestido, was elected President for a five-year term, defeating Jorge Batlle, the son of a former President. The Vice-President, Jorge Pacheco Areco, succeeded to the Presidency on the death of Gestido on 6 December 1967, but did not obtain sufficient support in a referendum to enable him to stand for a second term At elections held in November 1971 the Colorado candidate, Juan Maria Bordaberry, was elected President despite the inability of his predecessor to repress the Tupamaros, *q.v.*, whose guerilla activities had damaged the country's economy by frightening away tourists from neighbouring Argentina. The elections were contested by a Wide Front coalition of left-wing parties and, after a recount, the results were: in the Senate Colorados 14 seats (16 in 1966), Blancos 12 (13), Wide Front 5 (1 Communist in 1966); in the Chamber of Deputies Colorados 41 (50), Blancos 40 (41), Wide Front 18 (5 Communists and 3 Christian Democrats in 1966). The government was therefore in a minority in Parliament, and President Bordaberry's cabinet, although not a coalition, included two Blancos and one Socialist.

Uruguay, which until recently has been the most stable South American democracy, has a high standard of living, no personal income tax, an advanced system of old age pensions, maternity and child-welfare centres, accident insurance and education. Its wealth is obtained from its pastures, which support enormous herds of sheep and cattle. However, modernization is urgently needed, especially in industry, and since 1965 there have been several devaluations of the peso, and much labour unrest. In 1972 the foreign debt equalled more than three years' export earnings.

Urundi. The name by which the southern part of the Belgian trusteeship territory of Ruanda-Urundi, *q.v.*, was known, until it became, on 1 July 1962, the independent sovereign state of Burundi, *q.v.*

U.S.A. United States of America, *q.v.*

U.S.S.R. Union of Soviet Socialist Republics, *q.v.*

V

Vatican City State. This is the smallest independent sovereign state in the world (0·16 sq. m.); population approximately 1,000. After the incorporation of the former Papal States of Central Italy into the Italian Kingdom in 1870, the sovereignty of the Pope was limited to the palaces of the Vatican. The Popes refused to acknowledge Italy's action, and as a sign of protest no Pope left the Vatican after his election. This continued until 1929 when the Lateran Treaties were concluded between the Vatican and Italy, owing to the Italian Fascist dictator Mussolini's desire to settle the 'Roman question'. The Pope's sovereignty over only the Vatican palaces, the Lateran palace in Rome, and the Papal villa at Castel Gandolfo was confirmed, and the Vatican, thenceforward known as Vatican City, assumed external signs of sovereignty such as a coinage, police, radio station, and a postal system of its own. A large sum was paid to the Vatican as compensation for its territorial claims. In Italy the Vatican owns the controlling interest in numerous industries and has holdings in banks, shipping and insurance companies, chemical, textile, mining, and hydro-electric industries.

The Vatican is governed by the 264th Pope, Paul VI, *q.v.*, elected on 21 June 1963 to succeed John XXIII (1881–1963). Full legislative, executive, and judicial power is vested in the Pope. Nuncios are posted in many capitals and Apostolic Delegates in others. As the centre of the Roman Catholic Church, it commands the spiritual allegiance of more than 530 million Roman Catholics, and is a political power of great importance. Its policy is to promote Catholicism all over the world. Catholic parties usually belong to the moderate right; before the Second World War they occasionally supported the extreme right, and Catholic Bishops blessed both the Italian legions which invaded Ethiopia and the Franco rebels in the Spanish Civil War. The Catholic Church opposed Nazism when Hitler attacked the Church in Germany and confiscated its properties. During the Second World War many priests supported left-wing underground movements in France and Italy. Roman Catholic political parties today are strongly opposed to Communism.

Velasco Ibarra, José María. Ecuador politician, born 1893 in Quito, he took his law degree at the University of Quito and later studied at the Sorbonne. He became an academic lawyer of international repute and taught at universities in Argentina, Chile, Colombia and Venezuela. He was first elected President of Ecuador in 1934, but was overthrown the following year. In 1939 he returned from exile to run again for the Presidency, but was defeated and exiled to Chile after trying to obtain power unconstitutionally. He offered himself as a Presidential candidate in 1944, returning from exile when he was elected by a large margin; he held office for three years before being overthrown and exiled yet again. He was elected President for the third time in 1952, on this occasion serving the full four-year term of office and going into voluntary exile at its conclusion. Elected for a fourth presidential term in 1960 he was overthrown by a military *coup* the following year, and lived in Argentina until 1968 when he returned to Ecuador to contest the presidential elections. In June 1968 he was elected for a fifth presidential term but was unable to implement the liberal programme which he had promised, and in June 1970 installed a dictatorial regime. In March 1971 an attempt by the army to oust him was foiled by General Rodriguez Lara, who was then appointed Commander in Chief of the Army. On 16 February 1972, having refused to suspend elections planned to take place before the expiry of his term of office in August 1972, he was deposed by General Rodriguez and deported to Panama.

He does not represent any of the political parties; he has committed himself in the past to land reform and to public investment in housing and roads, and he enjoys wide popular support.

Venezuela. An independent republic on the north-west coast of South America, it is a federation of 20 states, a federal district and 2 federal territories; area 352,051 sq. m.; population (1971 estimate) 10,778,051, Spanish-speaking; capital Caracas. Venezuela was ruled by Spain from the sixteenth century until the revolt, led by Simon Bolivar, a native of Caracas, who defeated the Spanish forces in battle in 1813 and 1821. Venezuela became part of the Federal Republic of Colombia in 1822, and achieved complete independence in 1830.

Petroleum, discovered in 1922, accounts for ninety per cent of the total value of the exports of Venezuela, which is one of the world's largest oil producers. The government receives 70 per cent of the gross profits from petroleum by agreement with the Mene Grande (a subsidiary of Gulf Oil), Royal Dutch Shell, Creole (an affiliate of Standard Oil of New Jersey) and Texas Oil Companies, whose installations are to be nationalized, under the Oil Reversion Bill of 1971, when their concessions expire in 1983. Most of the crude oil is refined in the neighbouring Netherlands West Indies, *q.v.*, but an increasing percentage is being refined inside Venezuela. In December 1970 the income tax on oil was raised from 52 to 60 per cent. No new oil concessions were granted after 1958 until November 1970 when Occidental Petroleum Corporation and Royal Dutch Shell were given 20-year service contracts to drill in southern Lake Maracaibo. Diversification of the economy has included the development of rich iron ore deposits by subsidiaries of the United States Steel Corporation and Bethlehem Steel Company, the construction of the Guri dam, due to be completed in the 1990s when it will be one of the largest in the world, exploration for natural gas, and investment in the cement and meat-processing industries and in agriculture. There are exports of coffee, cocoa and gold.

Marcos Pêrez Jiménez seized power in 1948 from a government led by the left-wing anti-Communist party, Acción Democratica en el Gobierno (A.D.). He remained in control until January 1958 when he was overthrown by a military junta under Rear-Admiral Wolfgang Larrazábal Ugueto who, in December 1958, with the support of the left-wing Democratic Republican Union (U.R.D.), stood for election in the second free presidential elections ever held in Venezuela (the first were in 1947), but was defeated by Rómulo Betancourt, *q.v.*, leader of A.D. His government was threatened by left-wing riots in 1960 and by a right-wing attempt, organized from the Dominican Republic, to assassinate him. However, Betancourt became the first President to complete his term of office when Raúl Leoni (also A.D.) was elected to succeed him in December 1963. He defeated Dr Rafael Caldera, leader of the Social Christian Party (C.O.P.E.I.) who was successful in the presidential elections of December 1968, winning with 29 per cent of the votes cast a narrow victory over the A.D. candidate. Under the 1961 Constitution legislative power is exercised by a Congress consisting of a Senate and a Chamber of Deputies, elected by universal suffrage, and executive power lies with a President, directly elected for five years, who may not serve two consecutive terms. At elections held in December 1968 to elect 188 Deputies, A.D. had the largest representation (66 as opposed to 65 in 1963); C.O.P.E.I., which had been in coalition with A.D. from 1969 to 1964, won 50 seats (40 in 1963); People's Electoral Movement 26 seats; National Civic Crusade 20; U.R.D. 14; others 12.

President Caldera, in March 1969, legalized the Communist Party (which had been banned since 1962) as part of his policy of ending guerilla warfare by offering the left the possibility of legitimate political activity. All political outlaws were offered an amnesty, which was rejected by the Fuerzas Armadas de Liberación, led by Douglas Bravo, and the left-wing guerilla menace continued to undermine open politics. The former dictator, Marcos Jiménez, and the former President, Betancourt, announced in May 1972 their intention to contest the 1973 presidential election.

Versailles Treaty. Concluded on 28 June 1919 between the victorious powers of the First World War and Germany. The first part of the Treaty concerned the structure of the League of Nations, *q.v.* As a result of the second part of the Treaty, Germany ceded Alsace-Lorraine to France; Eupen-Malmédy to Belgium; part of Upper Silesia (after a plebiscite), Posen, and West Prussia to Poland; the port of Memel and its hinterland to Lithuania; Hulchin to Czechoslovakia; and part of Schleswig (after a plebiscite) to Denmark. Germany had to renounce its sovereignty over Danzig, *q.v.*; abstain from union with Austria except with the unanimous consent of the League Council; disarm; abolish conscription; maintain an army of not more than 100,000 men and a navy of six battleships with a corresponding number of cruisers and destroyers; possess no submarines, no military aircraft, no heavy guns; and build no fortifications. The Rhineland was to be occupied by the victorious powers for 15 years and the Saar (now Saarland, *q.v.*) was to be internationalized; German rivers were to be internationalized and the German colonies were shared out among the victors and administered under League mandates. Germany was obliged to 'accept the responsibility of Germany and her allies for causing all the loss and damage to which the Allied and Associated Governments and their nationals have been subjected as a consequence of the war imposed upon them by the aggression of Germany and her allies' and had to pay reparations, fixed in 1921 at £6,600 million. Most of the territorial concessions were the subjects of disputes between the First and Second World Wars; in particular Upper Silesia, Posen, West Prussia, Memel and its hinterland, the Saar territory, and the Rhineland had all been reacquired by Germany by the end of 1939. All the military prohibitions were disobeyed by the Nazis who came to power in 1933, while the sum due as reparations was gradually reduced, and entirely abrogated in 1932.

Verwoerd, Hendrik Frensch. South African Nationalist Party politician; born 8 September 1901 in the Netherlands, taken to South Africa as a child when his Dutch father emigrated there; educated at Stellenbosch University, studying psychology, and later at the Universities of Hamburg, Leipzig, and Berlin. At Berlin he was a lecturer in applied psychology and later head of the sociology department. After his return to South Africa and to Stellenbosch University he was one of the six members of the staff who protested against the admission into South Africa of German Jewish refugees. In 1937 he became editor of the Johannesburg Nationalist newspaper, the *Transvaaler*. When (as editor) he brought an action against the Johannesburg *Star* for criticizing his treatment of war news, the judge dismissed his action and held that Verwoerd had knowingly given moral support to the enemy, i.e. to Germany. Shortly after his election to the Senate he was, in 1950, appointed Minister of Native Affairs, in which office he was able to put into practice his uncompromising belief in the principles of apartheid, *q.v.* He was elected as leader of the Nationalist Party, and so automatically to the vacant Premiership, on 2 September 1958, in succession to Johannes Gerhardus Strijdom, who died in August 1958. On 9 April 1960 an attempt was made to kill him, but he recovered from the serious gunshot wounds which he received. He was assassinated on 6 September 1966 by Dmitri Tsafendas, a Portuguese East African of Greek extraction, who was found to be mentally deranged.

Veto. The right to reject. The word is commonly used to describe the right of any of the five permanent members of the United Nations Security Council, *q.v.*, to prevent the Council from making a decision on non-procedural matters. The right is given by the Charter which states: 'Decisions of the Security Council on procedural matters shall be made by an affirmative vote of seven members. Decisions of the Security Council on all other matters shall be made by an affirmative vote of seven members (amended to nine in 1965) including the concurring votes of the permanent members.' This was agreed at the Yalta Conference, *q.v.*, in 1945 between the U.K., the U.S.A., and the U.S.S.R., and was a modification of the Russian view that the Security Council should take no action without the unanimous consent of the major powers. One exception was allowed; a party to a dispute should not vote when it was a matter of seeking a solution by peaceful means. When peaceful means of settling a dispute fail, every member of the Security Council can vote, even though it is a party to the dispute, and the majority required to take action to stop aggression must in theory include all the permanent members (China, France, the U.K., the U.S.A., the U.S.S.R.). In practice, a permanent member's abstention from voting on a substantive question is not regarded as a Veto, although a strict reading of the Charter would suggest that it should be regarded as a Veto.

The United Nations Charter declares: 'The organization is based on the principle of the sovereign equality of all its members'; but the allocation of permanent seats has given to five powers a privileged position, from which they could only be removed by an amendment of the Charter; this would itself require the concurrence of the

Security Council and of the power or powers which it was sought to remove.

Vichy France. The central and southern parts of France which were not occupied by the Germans after the defeat of France in 1940, and which were ruled by a French administration from Vichy. The government was led by Marshal Pétain, to whom the National Assembly (by 569 to 80 votes) gave absolute powers when it brought the Third Republic to an end on 10 July 1940.

Viet-Minh. A political organization in North Viet-Nam, *q.v.*, founded by Ho Chi-Minh, *q.v.*; it was created in 1941 to resist the Japanese in Indo-China. It was transformed in 1951 into the Lien Viet Front (known also as the Fatherland Front). The organization works closely with the Dang Lao Dong or Workers' Party and the country's efficient, politically-educated army which decisively defeated the French at Dien Bien Phu in 1954. Its authority north of the 17th parallel was recognized by the Geneva Agreements, 1954, *q.v.*

Viet-Nam. A French consolidation of the three ancient provinces of Annam (the central part), Tonkin (the northern part) and Cochin-China (the southern part); area 129,607 sq. m.; population (1950) about 30,000,000, most of whom are Taoists or Buddhists, but including nearly 2,000,000 Roman Catholics; capital Hanoi. The French occupied Cochin-China in 1858 and established a colony; Annam became a protectorate in 1874 and Tonkin in 1892. The mineral resources of the area – zinc, tin, iron, and coal – the rubber, and the two 'rice-bowls' of the Red river and Mekong river deltas, attracted French capital. In 1940 the country was occupied by the Japanese and used as a base for the invasion of Malaya. Resistance groups were active in Annam and Tonkin, and in August 1945 a Republic of Viet-Nam (an old Chinese name meaning 'Farther South') was declared, the Emperor of Annam, Bao Dai, overthrown, and a government formed, comprising various nationalist, anti-Japanese, and Communist revolutionary parties, of which the Viet-Minh, *q.v.*, was the most important. The French negotiated with this government, through its leader, Ho Chi-Minh, *q.v.*, for an Indo-Chinese federation of Laos, *q.v.*, Cambodia, *q.v.*, and Viet-Nam. Their proposals were rejected because Cochin-China was excluded; apart from its economic value it belonged to the Union of the Three Ky, or Annamite peoples, and was considered to be an integral part of Viet-Nam. In December 1946 Viet-Minh forces attacked Hanoi; hostilities continued until 1954.

The successes of the Viet-Minh forced the French to conciliate nationalist opinion in the areas they still controlled. In 1949 Cochin-

China was incorporated in Viet-Nam, Bao Dai was installed as head of state, and a union of the three Associate States of Indo-China was created which gave Cambodia, Laos, and Viet-Nam a measure of self-government. The defeat of the French at Dien Bien Phu in 1954 brought the war to an end. An armistice was agreed at Geneva in July 1954 between the French government and the Viet-Minh leader, General Vo Nguyen Giap, which the Viet-Nam foreign minister refused to sign, by which Viet-Nam was temporarily divided along the 17th parallel into two zones of North Viet-Nam, *q.v.*, and South Viet-Nam, *q.v.* It was also agreed that partition should end in July 1956 when free elections for a government of reunified Viet-Nam would be held. The partition did not end, nor were the elections held, in July 1956. The Geneva Agreements, 1954, *q.v.*, completed the transfer of sovereignty from France to Cambodia, Laos, and Viet-Nam.

Vorster, Balthazar Johannes. South African Nationalist Party politician; born 13 December 1915 at Jamestown, Cape Province; educated at Sterkstroom High School and Stellenbosch University, where he graduated in arts and law in 1938. During the Second World War he joined the Ossewabrandwag, a pro-German, extreme Afrikaner nationalist, organization in which he rose to the rank of 'General' and became active in its militant wing, the Stormjaers. He was arrested in 1942 and kept in detention for seventeen months. He first entered the South African House of Assembly in 1953 as the member for Nigel, and in 1958 was made Deputy Minister of Education, Arts, Science, Social Welfare and Pensions. He became Minister of Justice in 1961, and in 1966 Minister of Police and Prisons as well. He was responsible for the Act of 1963 which provided for the indefinite detention of political offenders, and contained the '90 day' clause by which they were automatically released after 90 days' imprisonment but became subject to immediate re-arrest; he also introduced the Criminal Procedure Amendment Act of 1965 which permitted the detention of witnesses for up to six months. He was unanimously elected leader of the Nationalist Party on 13 September 1966 in succession to Hendrik Frensch Verwoerd, *q.v.*, who had been assassinated. He then took office as Prime Minister, retaining personal responsibility for Police and National Security.

W

Wagner Act. *See* National Labor Relations Act, 1935.

Waldheim, Kurt. Secretary-General of the United Nations; the son of a teacher, he was born in 1918 in the village of St Andrea-Woerden in Lower Austria; educated at the University of Vienna and at the Vienna Consular Academy. He entered the Austrian Foreign Service in 1945 as a career diplomat. After serving as First Secretary at the Paris Embassy from 1948 to 1951 he headed the Personnel Division of the Foreign Office in Vienna until 1955 when he was appointed observer to the United Nations. He was then sent to Canada as a Minister Plenipotentiary and from 1958 to 1960 as Ambassador, returning to Vienna to become Director-General of the Political Affairs Department at the Foreign Ministry. In 1964 he was appointed Austrian representative at the U.N. with ambassadorial rank; he had been a member of the Austrian delegation to all U.N. sessions since 1955 when Austria was admitted to full membership. In January 1968 he became Foreign Minister in the People's Party government of Dr Josef Klaus, holding office until the Party's defeat in the general election of March 1970. He then resumed his post as representative at the U.N., relinquishing it temporarily to contest the Austrian presidential election of April 1971 as the candidate of the People's Party. After his defeat by the incumbent President he returned to the U.N. where he was elected on 22 December 1971 to succeed U Thant, *q.v.*, as Secretary-General for a five-year term from 1 January 1972.

Wall Street. The site of the New York Stock Exchange. The term is used as a synonym for U.S. banking and financial interests.

Wallace, George Corley. U.S. lawyer and politician; born 25 August 1919 near Clio, Barbour County, Alabama. He graduated in law from the University of Alabama and went into legal practice. As an Alabama State judge he fought a losing campaign against the Supreme Court's interpretation of the Constitution on the legality of segregation, *q.v.*; he was the first judge to issue an injunction against the removal of segregation signs from railway stations. He entered the State Legislature as a Democrat and protagonist of States' Rights, *q.v.*, becoming Governor of Alabama in 1963. His term of office was remarkable for his efforts to prevent the desegregation of the University of Alabama, in defiance of a Federal injunction, and his dispersal of the march from Selma to Montgomery in 1965, led by Dr Martin Luther King, *q.v.*, of demonstrators supporting the movement for civil rights, *q.v.* He failed to get approved a constitutional amendment to allow him to succeed himself as Governor in

1967, but had his wife Lurleen (who died in May 1968), elected in his stead. He was re-elected Governor of Alabama in November 1970, defeating Albert Brewer who had succeeded his wife in office. He contested the Presidential election in 1968 as the candidate of the American Independence Party, dedicated to the defence of States' Rights, and uncompromisingly hostile to the advancement of the American Negro, to Communists, and to the Federal administration. On 8 February 1968 he declared, 'The so-called civil rights laws are really an attack on the property-rights of this country and I would try to have them changed in Congress.' In the election he carried the five southern States of Alabama, Arkansas, Georgia, Louisiana and Mississippi, and won 14 per cent of the popular vote. On 15 May 1972, while contesting the Democratic Party Primary elections for the Presidency in Maryland, he was shot and critically wounded by Arthur Bremer of Milwaukee.

Walloons. Predominantly French-speaking inhabitants of southern Belgium, with whom may be contrasted the predominantly Flemish-speaking and Germanic Flemings, *q.v.*, of northern Belgium. They tend to be anti-clerical, liberal, and anti-royalist, and to live in the heavily industrialized areas. In the Belgian population of over nine million the Flemings, who are increasing more rapidly, now outnumber the Walloons by more than a million. There is a continual dispute as to languages, and as to their use in schools and in the public services, the Flemings often priding themselves on being bi-lingual (in Flemish and French) whereas most of the Walloons are unilingual.

War Crimes. Those acts of an enemy soldier or civilian which may be punished when the offenders are captured. They consist of breaches of the laws or customs of war. An act may be a war crime even though committed on superior orders; this was a basic principle of the Charters of the International and Far Eastern Military Tribunals set up in 1945, although it was conceded that the fact that a person had acted on the order of a superior could be considered in mitigation of punishment if the Tribunal decided that justice so required. In practice the war crimes tribunals mitigated the punishment where the defendant would have suffered a dire penalty for disobedience, but did not reduce it in the case of senior officers who faced no such penalty and should have refused to carry out their orders.

During the Second World War there were large numbers of war crimes, of which the vast majority was committed by Germany and its allies. On 8 August 1945 France, the U.K., the U.S.A., and the U.S.S.R. concluded an Agreement for the Prosecution and

Punishment of the Major War Criminals of the European Axis. The Agreement provided for the creation of an International Military Tribunal to try those accused of war crimes. Article Six of the Charter annexed to the Agreement stated that the crimes coming within the jurisdiction of the Tribunal were: '(a) Crimes against Peace: namely, the planning, preparation, inititation, or waging of a war of aggression, or a war of violation of international treaties, agreements, or assurances, or participation in a common plan or conspiracy for the accomplishment of any of the foregoing; (b) War Crimes: namely, violations of the laws or customs of war. Such violations shall include, but not be limited to, murder, ill-treatment or deportation to slave labour, or for any other purpose, of civilian population of, or in, occupied territory, murder or ill-treatment of prisoners of war or persons on the seas, killing of hostages, plunder of public or private property, wanton destruction of cities, towns, or villages, or devastation not justified by military necessity; (c) Crimes against Humanity: namely, murder, extermination, enslavement, deportation, and other inhumane acts committed against any civilian population, before or during the war, or persecutions on political, racial, or religious grounds in execution of, or in connection with, any crime within the jurisdiction of the Tribunal whether or not in violation of the domestic law of the country where perpetrated.' A similar International Military Tribunal was set up in the Far East, and the governments of the various allied states established tribunals in countries where war crimes had been committed.

An objection made on behalf of the defendants at the International Military Tribunal held at Nuremberg, Germany, was that the victorious states did not define the jurisdiction of the Tribunal so that it could deal with war crimes committed by their own subjects, although there was no doubt that some such offences, however few in comparison with those of the enemy, had taken place.

Warsaw Pact. The Eastern European Mutual Assistance Treaty, *q.v.*, signed at Warsaw in May 1955.

Weimar Republic. A description given to the Republic established in Germany, *q.v.*, after the First World War and the abdication of the Emperor Wilhelm II. Its Constitution, which was characterized by centralizing and socialistic tendencies, was adopted in July 1919 by a National Assembly which met at Weimar. Its Presidents were Friedrich Ebert (1919–25) and Field-Marshal Paul von Hindenburg (1925–34); the Republic virtually came to an end in 1933 with the appointment of Adolf Hitler as Chancellor or Prime Minister and the institution of the Third Reich, *q.v.*

West Indies Associated States. A group of Caribbean islands, the former Windward and Leeward Islands, with the exception of Montserrat. They comprise Antigua, Dominica, Grenada, St Lucia, and St Kitts –Nevis–Anguilla and St Vincent. In 1967 each of these former British colonies, except St Vincent which made application in 1969, concluded an agreement with the U.K. establishing its Associate Status, *q.v.* This gave the island full internal self-government while it still recognized the British sovereign, represented by a Governor, as head of state. A decision to end the Status requires a two-thirds majority in the lower house of parliament and a two-thirds majority in a referendum, unless the Association is terminated for the purpose of joining a federation, union or association with an independent Commonwealth country in the Caribbean.

The Association derives from the former West Indies Federation, *q.v.*, and the subsequent withdrawal of Barbados, *q.v.*, which achieved independence on 30 November 1966, from a proposed new federal arrangement incorporating the Little Seven, *q.v.* St Vincent and Montserrat rejected Associate Status, Montserrat explicitly preferring to remain a British colony. St Vincent eventually accepted Associate Status in October 1969. Anguilla (area 35 sq. m. and population 6,000), the smallest island of St Kitts–Nevis–Anguilla, also refused to associate with the U.K., and declared itself a republic. This was not condoned by St Kitts–Nevis (population 52,000), which asked the U.K. for military assistance to put down the rebellion. The constitutional crisis was resolved in July 1971 by legislation in the U.K. parliament which gave the British government power to make provision for the future governance of the island and to appoint a Commissioner to conduct its administration.

West Indies Federation. An association of British colonies in the West Indies which existed as a federation from 3 January 1958 until its dissolution by a British Order in Council with effect from 31 May 1962; land area approximately 8,030 sq. m.; population was then about 3,152,500, over 70 per cent being of African Negro origin; the seat of government was Trinidad. Proposals for its establishment were made in 1947 when the association was known as the Caribbean Federation, *q.v.* It comprised Barbados, *q.v.*, Jamaica, *q.v.*, Trinidad and Tobago, *q.v.*, the Leeward Islands (except the Virgin Islands which decided not to join), and the Windward Islands. Negotiations for the inclusion of British Guiana, *q.v.*, in South America, and British Honduras, *q.v.*, in Central America, were unsuccessful.

Under the 1958 Constitution the Governor-General had to act

on the advice of the Council of State (the Cabinet) except in matters concerning defence, the financial stability of the Federation, and foreign affairs. In respect of these three matters the Crown could legislate by Order in Council, and the Governor-General could, with the approval of the British Colonial Secretary, act against the advice of the Council of State. The Federation was therefore not an independent sovereign state.

Legislative powers were vested in a Senate appointed on a territorial basis by the Governor-General, and a House of Representatives elected, on a population basis, by adult suffrage. At the first elections held in March 1958 the results were: Federal Labour Party (led by Norman Manley, *q.v.*, of Jamaica, Eric Williams, leader of the Trinidad People's National Movement, and Sir Grantley Adams, leader of the Barbados Labour Party) 25; Democratic Labour Party (led by Sir Alexander Bustamante, *q.v.*, of Jamaica, and Albert Gomes of Trinidad) 19; Barbados Independent Party, 1. Sir Grantley Adams became Prime Minister of the Federation.

In September 1961 Jamaica decided by referendum to leave the Federation, and in April 1962 the anti-Federation Jamaica Labour Party defeated Manley's People's National Party at the Jamaica General Election. The U.K. then dissolved the Federation. Jamaica became an independent member of the British Commonwealth on 6 August, and was followed by Trinidad and Tobago on 31 August 1962. Discussions then took place as to whether it was feasible to establish an Eastern Caribbean Federation (*see* Little Seven), comprising Barbados, the Leeward Islands (Anguilla, Antigua, Barbuda, Dominica, Montserrat, Nevis, and St Kitts) and the Windward Islands (Grenada, St Lucia, and St Vincent). But when Barbados decided upon independence, achieved on 30 November 1966, the remaining islands were offered Associate Status, *q.v.*, within the Commonwealth; those that accepted then formed the West Indies Associated States, *q.v.*

West Irian (Irian Barat). The western half of New Guinea, *q.v.*, it has been a province of Indonesia since 1 May 1963; area 160,000 sq. m.; population about 700,000, mostly Papuans, a different ethnic group from the inhabitants of the other Indonesian islands to the west; capital Kota Baru (known till 1 May 1963 as Hollandia).

The area was not included in the transfer of sovereignty to Indonesia of Dutch Asian possessions on 27 December 1949, and it was agreed that its future should be decided by negotiation within a year from that date, but no agreement was reached, and discussions broke down in 1951. The Political Committee of the United Nations

General Assembly encouraged the Dutch and the Indonesians to resume discussions. In November 1954 the Netherlands government accused Indonesia of violating Netherlands territory by sending an armed landing party to Netherlands New Guinea. Moderate Dutch politicians advocated a temporary condominium, until such time as the inhabitants could decide their future. Others favoured an international conference which could be attended by the Netherlands, Indonesia and the S.E.A.T.O. countries, as a result of which Dutch New Guinea might be placed under United Nations trusteeship. At the Afro-Asian Conference, *q.v.*, in April 1955, the Afro-Asian nations supported the Indonesian claim. Indonesia asked for a complete transfer of sovereignty, and after the United Nations took over formal administration of the territory on an interim basis in October 1962, it was handed over to Indonesia. In August 1969, by a process of collective consultation, known as the exercise of the 'Act of Free Choice', and arranged by a U.N. supervisor, it was decided that West Irian should remain permanently under Indonesia.

Western European Union. Created on 5 May 1955, it is essentially an expanded version of the Brussels Treaty Organization, *q.v.*, which came to an end on that day. Its members are the Brussels Treaty powers (Belgium, France, Luxemburg, the Netherlands, and the U.K.), Italy, and the German Federal Republic, which became sovereign on the same day. There is a council of the seven Foreign Ministers, an Assembly consisting of the representatives of the seven members of the W.E.U. in the Consultative Assembly of the Council of Europe, *q.v.*, an Armaments Control Agency, various committees, and a secretariat. Its Standing Armaments Committee works in conjunction with the North Atlantic Treaty Organization, *q.v.*

Western Germany is the part of Germany which, under the Berlin Declaration of June 1945 and under the Potsdam Agreement, *q.v.*, of August 1945, became the Occupation Zones of France, the U.K., and the U.S.A. at the end of the Second World War. In December 1946 the U.K. and the U.S.A. agreed to an economic fusion of their Zones (which became known as Bizonia); this union, which came into effect on 1 January 1947, was later joined by the French Zone. These economic moves were largely the results of disputes with the U.S.S.R., particularly over the Russian demand for reparations. Under the Marshall Plan, *q.v.*, announced in June 1947, Western Germany received economic aid from the U.S.A. After the currency reform of June 1948 industrial production, which had made only a slow recovery after the heavy wartime bombing, increased rapidly from approximately 40 per cent to over 70 per cent of the 1936 level by the end of 1948. A Constituent Assembly, elected by the *Länder* of the three Zones, met in Bonn on 1 September 1948 to draft a Constitution (known as the Basic Law) for Western Germany. The Law became effective on 23 May 1949 upon receiving the approval of a two-thirds majority of the parliaments of the *Länder*, and on that date the German Federal Republic, *q.v.*, came into existence.

Western Samoa. An independent state and member of the British Commonwealth, comprising the islands of Savai'i (area 703 sq. m.) and Upolu (area 430 sq. m., including nearby islands) in the Pacific Ocean, north-east of the Fiji Islands; population (1971) 199,000; capital Apia, on Upolu.

Until the First World War the islands were owned by Germany, which then lost them to New Zealand. They came under a League of Nations mandate in 1920 and became a trusteeship territory after the Second World War. New Zealand gradually transferred power to locally elected bodies and granted full internal self-government in 1959. The country became completely independent, and the first sovereign Polynesian state, on 1 January 1962.

There are exports of bananas, cocoa, and copra from these islands, which are formed mainly of volcanic rock. The country lies between longitudes 171 degrees and 173 degrees west. Under a Tripartite Treaty of 7 November 1899 Germany and the U.K. agreed that islands to the west of the meridian of 171 degrees west longitude (which included Western Samoa) should be assigned to Germany; those of the Samoan Group to the east of the meridian were renounced by Germany and the U.K. in favour of the U.S.A. The latter thus became American Samoa, *q.v.*, an unincorporated territory of the U.S.A.

Westminster, Statute of. An Act of Parliament of the U.K., passed in 1931, defining the legislative powers of the Dominions of the British Commonwealth, *q.v.*, and giving statutory effect to resolutions passed by the Imperial Conferences held in 1926 and 1930. No Act of Parliament of the U.K. passed after the Statute of Westminster was to extend to a Dominion as part of the law of that Dominion, unless the Dominion requested, and consented to, the Act. Each Dominion was given full power to make laws which applied beyond its boundaries, and to repeal or amend Acts of Parliament of the U.K. in so far as they formed part of the law of that Dominion, and no Dominion law was to be void on the ground of its repugnancy to the law of the U.K. Nothing in the Statute was to give any new power to alter the Constitutions of Australia and New Zealand. The relationship between the central government and the provinces of Canada was to remain unchanged and as stated in the British North America Acts, 1867 to 1930. As a result of the Imperial Conferences and of the Statute of Westminster most of the Dominions then in existence passed constitutional measures which emphasized their independent sovereign status within the British Commonwealth.

W.E.U. Western European Union, *q.v.*

W.F.T.U. World Federation of Trade Unions, *q.v.*

Whig. A member of the English political group which, from 1680 onwards, wished to limit the power of the monarch and to give more power to Parliament. The original Whigs were the rebels who held out in the Scottish lowlands after the failure of their insurrection of 1679, and who opposed any attempt to bring Scotland into ecclesiastical uniformity with England. In 1680 those English politicians who wanted to exclude from the throne any Roman Catholic monarch were derisively called Whigs. The Whig nobles dominated the anti-Tory forces until the appointment of Gladstone as Prime Minister in 1868. From that date it is correct to describe these forces as Liberals rather than Whigs. The name is still used to describe the political parties in Liberia, *q.v.*

White Army. The Russian anti-revolutionary army in the civil war of 1917–21, so called in contrast to the Red Army of the Communists and in allusion to the royalist forces of the Vendée which attempted an insurrection against the republicans during the French Revolution, and which had as their badge a white lily, the emblem of the French monarchy.

White House. The official residence of the U.S. President in Washington, the capital of the U.S.A. Building began in 1792, but President Washington died before the house was ready for occupation. The first President to live in it was John Adams, who took up residence there in 1800. The building was partly destroyed in the course of a war with the British in 1814. Its grey walls were painted white to cover the smoke marks, and thereafter it was known as the White House.

White Russia. One of the 15 constituent Republics of the U.S.S.R. and otherwise known as Byelorussia, *q.v.*

Whitehall. A street in London in and near which a number of important government ministries (including the Foreign Office, Home Office, Ministry of Health, War Office, Treasury, and Admiralty) are situated.

Whitelaw, William Stephen Ian. British Conservative Party politician; born 28 June 1918 in Edinburgh, and educated at Winchester College and Trinity College, Cambridge. A farmer and landowner, he became a regular officer in the Scots Guards, resigning his commission in 1947. He entered the House of Commons in 1955 as the member for Penrith and the Border, becoming Parliamentary Private Secretary to the President of the Board of Trade from 1956 to 1957, and to the Chancellor of the Exchequer from 1957 to 1958. He was appointed an Assistant Government Whip from January 1959 until 1961, and Parliamentary Secretary to the Ministry of Labour from July 1962 until 1964 when he became Opposition Chief Whip, which office he retained until the general election of June 1970. He then became Lord President of the Council and Leader of the House of Commons until March 1972 when he was appointed Secretary of State for Northern Ireland, *q.v.*

Whitlam, Edward Gough. Australian politician and Labour Party leader; born 11 July 1916, educated at Grammar schools in Sydney and Canberra and at the University of Sydney where he studied law. He served in the Royal Australian Air Force from 1941 to 1945 when he returned to legal practice as a barrister. He entered the House of Representatives in 1952, becoming deputy leader of the Australian Labour Party in the Federal Parliament in 1960. In 1966 he succeeded to the leadership on the retirement of Arthur Calwell, and was re-elected in 1968, defeating Dr James Cairns, the candidate of the Victorian, and left-wing, faction of the Labour Party by 38 votes to 32. In November 1970 his re-election was unanimous. When the Labour Party won a majority of seats in the elections of November 1972 he became Prime Minister.

W.H.O. World Health Organization, *q.v.*

Williams, Shirley. British Labour Party politician; born 27 July 1930; educated at Summit School, Minnesota and St Paul's School, London, and at Somerville College, Oxford and Columbia University. She is a Roman Catholic. She went into journalism, working on the *Daily Mirror* from 1952 to 1953 and on the *Financial Times* from 1954 to 1958. She was General Secretary of the Fabian Society from 1960 until 1964 when she was elected to the House of Commons as the member for Hitchin, and immediately appointed Parliamentary Private Secretary to the Minister of Health. In 1966 she became Parliamentary Secretary to the Ministry of Labour, in 1967 Minister of State at the Department of Education and Science, and from 1969 to 1970 she was Minister of State at the Home Office. As an advocate of British accession to the European Economic Community she voted against the Labour Party whip on 28 October 1971 and in favour of the government's decision to join the Community. In 1970 she was made the Opposition spokesman on the Front Bench for Health and Social Security and subsequently for Home Affairs.

Wilson, James Harold. British Labour Party politician; born 11 March 1916 and educated at Jesus College, Oxford. He became a Lecturer in Economics at New College in 1937 and a Fellow of University College in 1938. During the Second World War he held a number of Civil Service posts as an economic adviser. He was elected to the House of Commons as the Member for Ormskirk in 1945 and was Parliamentary Secretary to the Ministry of Works, 1945–7, Secretary for Overseas Trade in 1947 and President of the Board of Trade from 1947 to 1951. Since 1950 he has represented the Lancashire division of Huyton in the House of Commons. He succeeded Hugh Gaitskell (1906–63) as leader of the Parliamentary Labour Party in February 1963, having obtained 144 votes in a final ballot against George Brown, who obtained 103 votes. He was Prime Minister from October 1964 until the Labour Party's electoral defeat in June 1970.

World Bank. The International Bank for Reconstruction and Development, *q.v.*

World Federation of Trade Unions. An international organization established in the autumn of 1945 by labour organizations from 54 countries, including the Congress of Industrial Organizations, *q.v.*, the Trades Union Congress, *q.v.*, and the Russian trade unions. The American Federation of Labor, *q.v.*, declined to participate in the formation of the W.F.T.U. on the ground that the Russian unions did not constitute a free and democratic trade union movement. In January 1949 the C.I.O., the T.U.C., and several other national groups withdrew from the W.F.T.U., which still has 48 members affiliated to it, representing 137,938,000 workers. Later that year there was formed the International Confederation of Free Trade Unions, *q.v.*

World Health Organization (W.H.O.). Came into being on 7 April 1948 as a result of proposals made at the San Francisco Conference, April–June 1945, and the International Health Conference at New York (convened by the United Nations Economic and Social Council), June–July 1946. The New York Conference set up an Interim Commission of W.H.O., pending ratification of the W.H.O. Constitution by members of the United Nations. When a cholera epidemic broke out in Egypt in September 1947 the Interim Commission appealed to all countries, and considerable quantities of vaccines and medical equipment flowed in from all parts of the world. W.H.O. organized the distribution and use of the materials and the epidemic was mastered in six weeks.

The legislative organ of W.H.O. is the World Health Assembly, meeting yearly and comprising representatives of all member states. It determines policy and votes on the budget. The Executive Board, representing 24 member states, meets twice yearly to give effect to the decisions of the Assembly. Current work is entrusted to the Secretariat under the Director-General. The permanent headquarters are at Geneva. W.H.O. is one of the specialized agencies of the United Nations.

W.H.O. has two main groups of activities: (1) Advisory services which help countries to develop their health administration. Public health teams explain how to combat such maladies as malaria, tuberculosis, the venereal diseases, plague, typhus, cholera, and diphtheria, and how to improve maternal and infant hygiene, sanitation, and nutrition. Training is given so that countries will eventually have sufficient skilled personnel to apply modern techniques. (2) Central technical services such as the administration of health conventions, biological standardization, establishment of an international pharmacopoeia, and publication of health statistics. It has an annual expenditure of about $38 million.

Y

Yalta Conference. A meeting between President Franklin D. Roosevelt of the U.S.A., Winston Churchill, Prime Minister of the U.K., and Marshal Stalin of the U.S.S.R., at Yalta, a Crimean health resort, between 4 and 11 February 1945. Final plans for the defeat of Germany were agreed; the German surrender was to be unconditional and each of the three powers was to occupy a separate Zone of Germany, coordination being ensured through a Control Commission consisting of the supreme commanders of the occupation forces, with headquarters in Berlin. France was to be invited to take a Zone and to participate as the fourth member of the Commission.

The three powers said that Germany should never again be able to disturb world peace; that German armed forces would be disbanded; that German military equipment would be removed or destroyed; that all war criminals would be brought to justice and swift punishment; that all German industry that could be used for military production would be eliminated or controlled; that reparation would be exacted in kind for the destruction wrought by the Germans; and that all Nazi and militarist influences would be removed from the life of the German people. The U.S.A. abandoned its previous proposal, known as the Morgenthau Plan, that Germany should have a pastoralized economy, stripped of all heavy industry.

It was decided to establish an international organization to maintain peace and security. Its foundations had been laid at the Dumbarton Oaks Conference, *q.v.*; a preliminary conference of the United Nations (the San Francisco Conference, *q.v.*) was arranged for April 1945 to prepare a United Nations Charter, and to discuss voting procedure, on which there had been no agreement at Dumbarton Oaks. The three statesmen agreed on a formula suggested by Roosevelt that (1) each member of the Security Council should have one vote; (2) decisions of the Security Council on procedural matters should be made by an affirmative vote of seven members; (3) decisions of the Security Council on all other matters should be made by an affirmative vote of seven members, including the concurring votes of the permanent members (amended to nine, 1965), provided that a party to a dispute abstains. The words 'including the concurring votes of the permanent members' permitted the device known as the Veto, *q.v.*; or Yalta formula. It was agreed that the U.S.S.R. should have three seats in the United Nations, in respect of the Russian Soviet Federal Socialist Republic, the Ukranian Soviet Socialist Republic, and the Byelorussian Soviet Socialist Republic; the U.S.S.R. abandoned its request, made at Dumbarton Oaks, that each of its constituent Republics (there were then 16) should have a seat.

The three powers reaffirmed the principles of the Atlantic Charter, *q.v.*, and said that they would help any liberated or former Axis satellite state in Europe to carry out emergency measures for the relief of distress, and to form interim governments broadly representative of all democratic elements and pledged to the earliest possible establishment through free elections of governments responsive to the will of the people. The U.K. and the U.S.A. discontinued their support of the Polish government in exile in London but insisted that Poland should hold free elections; the eastern frontier of Poland was to follow the Curzon Line, *q.v.*, and Poland was to receive substantial accessions of territory in the north and west.

Yemen (formerly known as Southern Yemen). The People's Democratic Republic of. An independent republic in south-west Arabia, to the south of Saudi Arabia with the Yemen Arab Republic to the north-west and Oman to the east; area 117,075 sq. m.; population 1,500,000, mostly Arab; capital Madinet al-Shaab (the former Al Ittihad). It comprises the port of Aden, a large desert hinterland and the islands of Kamaran and Perim at the southern end of the Red Sea. It was created from the former British colony of Aden State, *q.v.*, the various small states of the Aden Protectorate, *q.v.*, which, together with the three members of the Eastern Aden Protectorate, *q.v.*, formed the South Arabian Federation, *q.v.*

In 1964 the U.K. promised the Federation, which was internally self-governing, independence by 1968. The authority of the Federal Government, which consisted of many of the local rulers and four Adenis, was challenged by three nationalist groups: the National Liberation Front (N.L.F.), a proscribed organization; Front for the Liberation of South Yemen (F.L.O.S.Y.), *q.v.*, which was backed by the Egyptian government and which recruited an army in the Yemen Arab Republic; and the South Arabian League. Civil war broke out, and by 1967 nationalist groups controlled several states; British forces were used to restore order in Aden. The U.K. eventually reached agreement with the N.L.F., which had been pressing for immediate independence, by which the other two nationalist parties were suppressed, British forces were withdrawn, although the civil disturbances continued, and independence was declared on 30 November 1967. Qahtan Mohammed as-Shaabi became first President of the People's Republic of Southern Yemen. On 22 June 1969 he was deposed by the left-wing of the N.L.F., led by Mohammed Ali Haithem, who became Prime Minister and member of the Presidential Council until August 1971. On 30 November 1970 a new Constitution provided for the transfer of legislative authority from the N.L.F. to a People's Supreme Council of 101 members, and the country was renamed the People's Democratic Republic of Yemen. Negotiations were opened in 1972 with the Yemen Arab Republic to unite the two states.

Apart from exports of cotton there is only subsistence agriculture and fishing to sustain the economy, which in the past depended heavily on British Forces' expenditure and on the revenues from the free port of Aden. The closure of the Suez canal in 1967 and the decline in the tourist trade, caused by the recent political troubles, have impoverished the country and compelled it to negotiate for foreign aid. In 1970 it gave support to the Dhofari rebels in Oman, q.v.

Yemen Arab Republic (formerly Yemen). An independent state in Arabia (the 'Arabia Felix' of the ancients), at the southern end of the Red Sea; area 75,000 sq. m.; population (1970) 5,728,000; capitals Ta'iz (the residence of the Imam) and San'a. The Imam Ahmed, head of the Zeidi sect of the Shiah Moslems, who are predominant in the north, succeeded to the throne on 14 March 1948. He defeated the forces which had seized power on the death of his own father and which were opposed to the feudal rule of the Imams, who for many years have monopolized all government posts and most of the commercial life of the country. In April 1955 the Imam put down another revolt led by two of his brothers, one of whom, Abdullah, was Foreign Minister. He had his brothers executed, but then abandoned the traditional policy of isolating Yemen from the outside world, and in April 1956 concluded a tripartite military alliance with Egypt (which had already agreed to supply aircraft, tanks and guns), and with Saudi Arabia. The 1927 Treaty of Friendship with the U.S.S.R., which expired in 1954, was renewed the following year, and economic relations between the two countries strengthened. From 9 March 1958 to 26 December 1961 Yemen was a member of a federal union with the United Arab Republic, q.v., known as the United Arab States, q.v., which was dissolved by President Nasser on the latter date.

The present Imam, Saif al Islam Muhammad Al-Badr (born 1920) succeeded to the throne on his father's death in September 1962. In the same month there was an army insurrection, supported by Egypt; soon afterwards the country was divided into the areas (in the north) controlled by the deposed Imam and those (including the capitals) controlled by the new regime, led by General Abdullah al Sallal who became its President. Although he belonged to the Zeidi sect of the Shiah Moslems his republican supporters were from the one-half of the population who belong to the Shafai sect of the Sunni Moslems, and who live mainly in the south and along the coast. Sallal was over-thrown in November 1967 by General Hassan al-Amri who became Head of State and, in September 1968, Military Governor-General of the Yemen. Despite the withdrawal, by agreement with Saudi Arabia, *q.v.*, of most of the 70,000 Egyptian troops who were present in the country before the Middle East War of 1967, fierce fighting continued, the Republican government retaining the active support of Egypt, and the royalists depending on arms from Saudi Arabia. In May 1970 a peace agreement was negotiated between the royalists and the Republicans, largely at the instigation of Saudi Arabia, by which the Imam was permanently exiled and four royalists were taken into the government.

The boundaries of the Yemen Arab Republic and Saudi Arabia are fixed by the Treaty of Taif, 1934; the boundaries with Yemen, *q.v.*, have not been completed delimited, and agreements between the Republic and the U.K. (which came into force in 1934 and 1951) provide for a joint commission to undertake this task. The Yemen Republic claims that the establishment by the U.K. firstly of the South Arabian Federation, and then the People's Republic of Southern Yemen, amount to a breach of the 1934 agreement. It frequently referred to the Federation as 'occupied South Yemen', and since the People's Republic was declared on 30 November 1967, has co-operated with the anti-government Front for the Liberation of Occupied South Yemen (F.L.O.S.Y.), *q.v.* During 1972 it entered into negotiations with the Yemen government about possible unification of the two states. The Yemen Arab Republic, which lies in the most fertile part of Arabia, exports coffee, raisins, grain and hides. Be-tween 1959 and 1967 it received $42 million in U.S. aid; this was rejected in April 1967 by the Republican government and withdrawn. An oil concession, granted to a U.S. company, the Yemen Develop-ment Corporation of Washington, in 1955 was terminated. Economic assistance is now received from China and the U.S.S.R.

Yugoslavia. Officially known as the Socialist Federal Republic of Yugo-slavia, it is a federation comprising Serbia, Croatia, Slovenia, Crna Gora (Montenegro), Bosnia and Herzegovina, Macedonia, and the two autonomous provinces of Vojvodina and Kosovo; area 98,725 sq. m.; population (1971) 20,924,000, of whom 42 per cent are Serbs, 22 per cent are Croats and 8 per cent are Slovenes; capital Belgrade. Yugoslavia achieved nationhood in 1918; Serbia and Bosnia were removed from Turkish influence and Slovenia and Croatia were separated from Austria-Hungary and a Kingdom of Slovenes, Croats and Serbs was established under the rule of a Serbian king, Alexander Karageorgević. Unity was imperilled by religious quarrels (the Slovenes and Croats were mainly Roman Catholic, the Serbs Serbian-Orthodox, Bosnia had a large proportion of Moslem converts, and the Macedonians belonged to the Greek Orthodox Church), and the indifference of a Serbian king to the interests of his other subjects. As a result of uproar in the Constituent Assembly in 1928, during which the Croat peasant leader, Stepan Radić, was shot dead, King Alexander abrogated the Constitution and assumed dictatorial powers. After his assassination in 1934 his brother, Prince Paul, acting as regent for the King Peter, continued to rule with the support of the army and the ruling caste.

When the Germans invaded they met resistance from two partisan organizations: the Chetniks, led by General Mihailović, who operated in Serbia, and the National Liberation Front, led by Marshal Josip Broz Tito, *q.v.*, which recruited followers in Bosnia, Croatia, Montenegro, and Slovenia. When it was discovered that Mihailović had cooperated with the Germans the Serbian partisans joined Tito. His forces, in 1945, numbered 800,000 – the largest and most effective resistance movement in Europe – and had immobilized forty Axis divisions. On the liberation of Belgrade in 1944 a People's Republic was proclaimed and King Peter deposed. In elections held the following year 90 per cent of those who voted supported the new regime and Tito was made President.

Under the Constitution of April 1963, authority is vested in the Federal Assembly of 670 members which elects the President and comprises five chambers; these are the federal, economic, educational and cultural, social and health, and political and administrative chambers, each with 120 members. In 1969 a Chamber of Nationalities, with 140 deputies delegated to represent republican and provincial interests, replaced the federal chamber which has exclusive responsibility for defence, foreign affairs, and other fundamental policy matters. A directly elected socio-political chamber was substituted for the former political and administrative chamber which, like the other three institutions, was indirectly elected. No senior government official, including the President and Prime Minister, may hold office for more than four years. An exception has been made in the case of President Tito, who has been elected for life. In 1971 the Constitution was amended to allow a collective presidency to succeed him. This is to consist of 22 members, 3 from each republic and 2 from each province, which will exercise all the powers of a Head of State. The Constitution separates Church and State, gives equal rights to women, and provides for maximum private land holdings of 10 hectares (24·7 acres).

Between 1918 and 1941 the Karageorgević family dominated the national economy; it controlled most of the industry, opposed land reform, discouraged national investment, and allowed the economic assets of the country to pass into foreign ownership. In 1941, 98 per cent of the copper, lead, timber and cement industries were foreign-owned. A decree of 1945 which confiscated, without compensation, the property of enemy nationals, war criminals and collaborators, brought into state ownership nearly 80 per cent of the country's industry without affecting Yugoslav property. Since 1971 working organizations have been permitted to invest abroad, and the rights of foreign investors in the state have been guaranteed.

Immediately after the Second World War Tito antagonized the western powers by his aggressively independent Communist policy. He threatened to refuse to sign the Italian Peace Treaty (*see* Trieste), he assisted Communist troops in Greece and he shot down U.S. planes in flight from Vienna to Trieste. But although he concluded military and economic agreements with the east European bloc and with the U.S.S.R., he refused to accept direction from Moscow, and purged the Yugoslav Communist Party of its pro-Russian elements. He carried out land redistribution but would not forcibly collectivize agriculture, and by encouraging investment in peasant smallholdings he prevented the alliance of industrial workers and poorer peasants against the rich peasants (or kulaks) which occurred in the U.S.S.R., claiming that the peasants were 'the most stable foundation of the Yugoslav state'. For this 'fundamental error in Marxist-Leninist theory' he was expelled from the Cominform, *q.v.*, in January 1948. A rapprochement then took place with the western powers as a result of which Yugoslavia obtained credit from the Export-Import Bank, and loans from the International Monetary Fund and the World Bank. In the first ten years of the Federation more than 40 per cent of the national income was invested in heavy industry; recently greater emphasis has been placed on the development of secondary industries and consumer products. The tourist industry has been encouraged as a valuable source of foreign exchange, and nearly 600,000 Yugoslavs are employed as migrant workers in west European countries. Yugoslavia was the first east European state to have a trade agreement with the European Economic Community, *q.v.*

Yugoslavia is a party to the Balkan Pact, *q.v.*, with Greece and

Turkey. Although normal relations with the U.S.S.R. were resumed in May 1955, Yugoslavia remained the only Communist country in Europe (except Albania) not committed to a military alliance with Russia, and denounced the invasion of Czechoslovakia, by the U.S.S.R. and four of its Warsaw Pact associates, in August 1968.

Z

Zaïre. An independent African state (formerly Belgian Congo, *q.v.*); area 905,582 sq. m.; population (1970 census) 21,637,876, including Hamites, Pygmies and Negroes (Bantu, Nilotics and Sudanese); capital Kinshasa (until 1966 known as Léopoldville). There are 150 major tribes speaking 38 different languages.

The territory became the Congo Free State in 1885 when Leopold II, King of the Belgians, was recognized as its personal sovereign head by the great powers at the Conference of Berlin. It was officially annexed by Belgium in 1907 and ruled as a colony until it became independent on 30 June 1960. Belgian administration was paternalist; African participation in politics was forbidden and the professions were restricted to Europeans. After the Second World War and the intensification of industrialization (especially in mining) from which many Africans acquired technical skill, it was found increasingly difficult to arrest the political development of the country. In 1959 serious riots occurred in Léopoldville and elsewhere and the Belgian government was forced to agree, in January 1960, to complete independence for the Congo.

After attaining independence the country was plunged into civil war. The first President was Joseph Kasavubu of Léopoldville, leader of the Abako Party which represented 800,000 Bakongo tribesmen of south-west Congo. The Prime Minister was Patrice Lumumba, a member of the Batatele tribe from Stanleyville in the Eastern Province, leader of the Congolese National Movement (M.N.C.), which was the largest of the 60 political groupings. Separatist tendencies became evident among the Baluba of Kasai Province (where Albert Kalonji created, in August 1960, the 'Autonomous Mining State of South Kasai'), the Mongo of Equator Province, the Bakongo of Léopoldville Province and in Eastern Province, where, at Stanleyville, Lumumba's Vice-Premier and political heir, Antoine Gizenga, claimed that the true Congolese government resided. The most serious was the purported secession, on 11 July 1960, of the rich mining province of Katanga, *q.v.*, led by the Conakat Party under Moïse Tshombe, *q.v.*, and helped by Belgian interests. In view of the danger of intervention by the major powers the United Nations landed an emergency force. President Kasavubu dismissed Lumumba in September 1960; he was seized by Katangese troops in January 1961 and later found dead.

Fighting continued until 1963 by which time the efforts of the U.N. had virtually ended the secessionist attempts, and Katanga was reabsorbed into the Congo. The U.N. mission withdrew and Tshombe returned to Léopoldville in 1964 replacing as Premier Cyrille Adoula who had held the office since 1961; elections held in 1965 confirmed Tshombe in office, giving a majority to his new party, the Congolese National Convention (Conaco), which received particular support in Kasai, north and south Katanga, Kivu, and in the Léopoldville area where the Abako Party declared in its favour. The results were challenged by the chief opposition party, the Lumumba Congolese National Movement, and outbreaks of violence recurred in Stanleyville and Kivu. In October 1965 Tshombe was forced to resign and to flee the country; the following month General Joseph Desirée Mobutu deposed President Kasavubu and replaced Tshombe's successor, Evariste Kimbe, by Colonel Leonard Mulamba. In October 1966 Mobutu ousted Mulamba and founded a political party, the Mouvement Populaire de la Révolution (M.P.R.), dedicated to national unity, to the ending of tribalism and to implacable opposition to African socialism. The country was reorganized into 21 provinces (later reduced to 8) instead of the former 6, each new province providing a member of the cabinet. Under a new Constitution, endorsed by referendum in June 1967, the President was granted full powers. A single chamber legislature was to be elected by universal suffrage but consisting of representatives of only two political parties, one of which was to be the M.P.R. At elections held in November 1970 President Mobutu was returned with 100 per cent of the votes cast, and the M.P.R. won all 420 seats in the chamber.

Further insurrections occurred in the eastern states during 1967. The white mercenaries who led these rebellions were repatriated in 1968 by the Organization for African Unity, *q.v.*, which obtained an agreement from the home countries that the mercenaries would never be allowed to return to Africa. A political amnesty was declared in August 1968 following which Pierre Mulele, who had led the rebellion in 1963, returned from exile in Congo (Brazzaville). His immediate execution brought a severance of diplomatic relations between the Congo Republics. On 27 October 1971 President Mobutu, as part of his detribalization programme and in an attempt to end confusion with the neighbouring People's Republic of Congo (Brazzaville), Africanized the name of the country. Zaïre was chosen because it was the name by which the Congo river was known in the fifteenth century. In January 1972 a Nationality Law required all officials to take authentic African names, and the President became Sese Seko (vice Joseph Desirée) Mobutu.

The country has substantial mineral resources including copper, diamonds, gold, silver, tin, manganese, uranium, radium, zinc, and cobalt, of which it is the world's largest supplier. Oil was discovered in 1968 in Central Congo Province and in 1972 work began on the Inga Dam, on the lower reaches of the Zaïre river, which, when completed, will be the largest hydro-electric power project in Africa. There are also exports of coffee, palm oil, cotton and rubber. The economy suffered a setback from the prolonged disturbances, and the nationalization of European industries and mines (including, in December 1966, the Union Minière at Katanga) resulted in the withdrawal of many of the technical experts needed to exploit the country's mineral wealth. Zaïre was in an economic union with Chad and the Central African Republic from April to December 1968 when the C.A.R. rejoined the French-orientated Union of Central African Republics.

Zambia. An independent republic and member of the British Commonwealth, known until 1964 as Northern Rhodesia, it is in central Africa, with Zaïre and Tanzania to the north, Malawi and Mozambique to the east, Rhodesia to the south, and Angola to the west; area 288,130 sq. m.; population (1971) 4,608,000, including 50,000 Europeans most of whom work in the copper mines; capital Lusaka.

Until 1911 the country was administered by the U.K. as the provinces of North-Eastern Rhodesia and North-Western Rhodesia; these were then merged and the protectorate of Northern Rhodesia was created, its legislative council being given an unofficial majority in 1945. It became part of the Federation of Rhodesia and Nyasaland, *q.v.*, in 1953. Negotiations began in December 1960 to draft a new Constitution. Among those concerned were the British government; the United Federal Party (the ruling party in Northern Rhodesia which supported the Federal government of Sir Roy Welensky); the representatives of the African nationalists, who included Kenneth Kaunda, *q.v.*, of the United National Independence Party (U.N.I.P.), and Harry Nkumbula of the African National Congress (A.N.C.) which has the allegiance of the Tonga, the second largest Zambian tribe; the right-wing Dominion Party; and the Liberal Party led by Sir John Moffat. Under the new and complex Constitution which came into force on 11 September 1962 the first African-dominated government was formed; in December 1962 Kaunda was appointed Minister of Local Government and Social Welfare, and Nkumbula Minister of African Education.

After the dissolution of the Federation of Rhodesia and Nyasaland on 31 December 1963 the country was given a new Constitution which came into force on 3 January 1964. At elections held on 21 January

1964 the results were: U.N.I.P. 55 seats; A.N.C. 10 seats; National Progress Party (Europeans) 10 seats. The N.P.P. disbanded in 1966, but 8 of their 10 former representatives continued to sit in Parliament as Independents. The number of seats was increased from 75 to 105 before the elections of 19 December 1968, but the 10 seats reserved for Europeans were abolished and European, Asian and Coloured voters lost the franchise unless they became Zambian citizens. In 1969 retail trade in suburban areas was restricted to African ownership. Kaunda was appointed Prime Minister after the 1964 elections, and President when an independent republic was declared on 24 October 1964. Elections held in December 1968 confirmed both the predominance of the U.N.I.P. (81 seats) and the persistent strength of the A.N.C. opposition (23 seats). Legislation was introduced in 1972 by which Zambia was to become a one-party state.

The unilateral declaration of independence, q.v., by Rhodesia in November 1965, and the subsequent application of economic sanctions, while initially creating enormous difficulties for a land-locked Zambia, has stimulated industrial investment and lessened Zambian dependence on South African and Rhodesian markets. Coalfields have been opened, industrial production more than doubled in the three years 1965–8, an oil pipeline from Ndola to Dar es Salaam was completed in August 1967 and the construction of a railway to Tanzania was begun in 1970 with Chinese aid. A power station on the north bank of the Zambesi river, a dam at Kafue and a highway across the Zambesi at Kazungula, q.v., are likely projects for future investment. Much of the finance is available from the profits of the Zambian copper belt, which is the world's fourth largest source of copper and is responsible for 90 per cent of the gross national product, making Zambia one of the richest countries in Africa. The copper, which is extracted by two non-African companies, Anglo-American, in whose shares the state acquired a controlling interest in 1969, and Roan Selection Trust, is exported by rail through Portuguese Mozambique to the east or Portuguese Angola to the west; hence the proposed rail link to the Indian Ocean through Tanzania. Maize, tobacco, millet, Kaffir corn and Rhodesian redwood timber are also produced. Opposition to President Kaunda reflects tribal discontent; Barotseland, q.v., in western Zambia, has demanded autonomy, and has given support to the United Party (banned in 1968 after disturbances at Chililabombwe in the copper belt), the party of the Lozi, traditional rivals of the major northern Bemba tribe. There are 19,000 members of the Lumpa sect, who rejected central authority, in exile in Zaïre.

Zanzibar. Part of the United Republic of Tanzania, q.v., it was formerly a Sultanate and British protectorate off the coast of Tanganyika, comprising the islands of Zanzibar and Pemba, and several much smaller islands; area of the two main islands 1,020 sq. m.; population (1967 census) 354,360; capital Zanzibar. There is a strong Arab influence, originating in the seventeenth century when Omani Arabs helped the inhabitants to expel the Portuguese. The Sultanate became independent of Oman in 1856, and at that time it included a substantial part of the east African coast. Much of this was ceded to Germany and Italy outright in 1890, 1904, and 1924, but there remained a coastal strip, administered as part of Kenya, for which the Sultan received £10,000 annually. Zanzibar and Pemba came under British protection in 1890.

A measure of self-government was introduced in 1961, and was extended in June 1963. Zanzibar became fully independent within the British Commonwealth on 9 December 1963. On 12 January 1964 the Sultan (H. H. Seyyid Jamshid bin Abdulla, great-grandson of the first Sultan, who founded the local clove industry), who had succeeded his father in 1963, was overthrown and exiled by a revolt of Afro-Shirazi (African-orientated and looking to Tanganyika for assistance) politicians, who established the People's Republic of Zanzibar and Pemba, with their leader, Sheikh Abeid Amani Karume, as President. After his assassination in April 1972 he was succeeded by Aboud Jumbe. On 25 April 1964 Zanzibar united with Tanganyika to form the United Republic of Tanganyika and Zanzibar or, as it became known later that year, Tanzania.

Zimbabwe. African name for Rhodesia, *q.v.* The African political parties in that country include the Zimbabwe African People's Union (Z.A.P.U.) and the Zimbabwe African National Union (Z.A.N.U.).

Zionism. A belief in the need to establish an autonomous Jewish community in Palestine, *q.v.* Many movements have tried to satisfy the desire of the Jewish people to return to the Holy Land. Modern Zionism was conceived by Theodor Herzl (1860–1904), a Hungarian-born journalist, working in Vienna, who, though an assimilated Jew, believed as a result of his own experience and particularly the lessons of the Dreyfus case that there was no security for the Jewish people unless they had a state of their own. His ideas were opposed by assimilated Jews who felt themselves secure in the countries in which they lived, but today Zionism is supported by the vast majority of the Jewish community. Although the original object of Zionism has been attained in the creation of the state of Israel, *q.v.*, it is still an active international force engaged in protecting the welfare, and extending the influence, of Israel.

MORE ABOUT PENGUINS
AND PELICANS

Penguinews, which appears every month, contains details of all the new books issued by Penguins as they are published. From time to time it is supplemented by *Penguins in Print*, which is a complete list of all titles available. (There are some five thousand of these.)

A specimen copy of *Penguinews* will be sent to you free on request. For a year's issues (including the complete lists) please send 50p if you live in the British Isles, or 75p if you live elsewhere. Just write to Dept EP, Penguin Books Ltd, Harmondsworth, Middlesex, enclosing a cheque or postal order, and your name will be added to the mailing list.

In the U.S.A.: For a complete list of books available from Penguin in the United States write to Dept CS, Penguin Books Inc., 7110 Ambassador Road, Baltimore, Maryland 21207.

In Canada: For a complete list of books available from Penguin in Canada write to Penguin Books Canada Ltd, 41 Steelcase Road West, Markham, Ontario.

SOME PENGUIN REFERENCE BOOKS

'Penguin reference books are becoming indispensable; they are easy to travel with and, if they wear out, cheap to replace' – Cyril Connolly in the *Sunday Times*.

A DICTIONARY OF GEOGRAPHY

W. G. Moore

Because geography is largely a synthetic subject the items in this dictionary are derived from many sciences. The student will find in this revised and enlarged edition all the terms so frequently employed and seldom defined in geographical works.

A DICTIONARY OF MODERN HISTORY 1789–1945

A. W. Palmer

This book is intended as a reference-companion to personalities, events, and ideas. The prime emphasis is on British affairs and on political topics although the Dictionary aims to represent trends in the history of all the major regions of the world. There are entries on economic, social, religious and scientific developments, but not on the Arts.

SOME PENGUIN REFERENCE BOOKS

A DICTIONARY OF ART AND ARTISTS

Peter and Linda Murray

This dictionary covers the last seven centuries and contains short and critical biographies of nearly 1,000 painters, sculptors and engravers as well as definitions of artistic movements, terms applied to periods and ideas, and technical expressions and processes. The art of eastern and primitive peoples is not covered.

THE PENGUIN DICTIONARY OF ARCHITECTURE

John Fleming Hugh Honour Nikolaus Pevsner

Every facet of architectural design and the art of building is covered. The entries are supplemented by more than a hundred clear and detailed architectural drawings set into the text they illustrate.

A NEW DICTIONARY OF MUSIC

Arthur Jacobs

A basic reference book for all who are interested in music, containing entries for composers (with biographies and details of compositions); musical works well known by their titles; orchestras, performers and conductors of importance today; musical instruments; and technical terms.

SOME PENGUIN REFERENCE BOOKS

A DICTIONARY OF SCIENCE

E. B. Uvarov   D. R. Chapman   Alan Isaacs

New material has been added to make this third edition more valuable to both student and layman, who can find in it reliable definitions and clear explanations of the numerous scientific and technical terms that are increasingly an important part of daily life.

A DICTIONARY OF COMPUTERS

Anthony Chandor with John Graham and Robin Williamson

This is a glossary of some 3,000 words, phrases and acronyms used in connection with computers. It has been designed to assist both technical readers and those non-specialists whose work is affected by a computer.

A DICTIONARY OF PSYCHOLOGY

James Drever

'It is commended with confidence as a document relevant not merely to the experimental psychology of former days, but to recent developments in psychometrics, social psychology, psychopathology, and industrial psychology – *Higher Education Journal*.

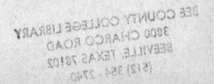

THE PENGUIN ENGLISH DICTIONARY

REVISED EDITION

This Dictionary for today is:

Modern

Unrivalled as a catalogue of English words as they are now used in print and speech. Includes hundreds of post-war words and senses, in addition to the established vocabulary. Lists variant meanings in order of present-day frequency.

Simple

Definition given in the most direct form possible, showing acquired overtones and the degree of acceptance of words. Only roman, italic, and bold types used, with two kinds of bracket and only one space-saving symbol. Introduces a new and immediately understandable system for pronunciation.

New

Specially commissioned for publication in Penguins. Written and prepared by a team led by the late Professor G. N. Garmonsway, Professor of English in the University of London (King's College). The result of seven years' work.

Comprehensive

More than 45,000 main entries, from the most colloquial words to the most formal. The finest storehouse of modern English available at any price.